W9-AFW-547

Mysterious Canada

Strange Sights, Extraordinary Events, and Peculiar Places

John Robert Colombo

DOUBLEDAY CANADA LIMITED, TORONTO

Copyright © 1988 by John Robert Colombo
All rights reserved
Reprinted 1989
Design: Don Fernley

Canadian Cataloguing in Publication Data
Colombo, John Robert,
Mysterious Canada

Bibliography: p.
Includes index.
ISBN 0-385-25150-5

1. Curiosities and wonders – Canada.
2. Canada – Miscellanea.   I. Title.
FC176.C64 1988   001.9′3′0971
C88-094114-6   F1029.9.C64   1988

Published in Canada by
   Doubleday Canada Limited
   105 Bond Street
   Toronto, Ontario
   M5B 1Y3

Printed and bound in Canada

CONTENTS

Preface *v*

Acknowledgements *xi*

Newfoundland *1*

Nova Scotia *17*

New Brunswick *47*

Prince Edward Island *65*

Quebec *73*

Ontario *119*

Manitoba *277*

Saskatchewan *299*

Alberta *311*

British Columbia *337*

Yukon Territory *385*

Northwest Territories *389*

Bibliography *420*

Index *425*

There is another world, but it is in this one.
Paul Eluard

PREFACE

There are more questions in this book than there are answers.

Do ghosts exist? Are there UFOs? Is there any evidence for the existence of ESP or Psi? Does astrology work? Is it possible to predict the future? Is reincarnation a fact, a fiction, or a little of both? What is the evidence for life after death? Does the sasquatch roam the interior of British Columbia? Has any treasure ever been found on Oak Island?

These are only a few of the questions that will be asked by anyone drawn to read a book called *Mysterious Canada*. I have been searching for the answers to such questions long before I reached the age of reason. Some years ago I decided to see what evidence there is for the existence of "the mysterious" in this country.

Mysterious Canada, a book about the major and minor mysteries of Canada, is the result of my quest. Books have been published devoted to British mysteries, American mysteries, and French mysteries. There are specialized books on the mysteries of the land, the sea, and the air; on the spirits of the theatre and the spectres of warfare; and on such great global mysteries as the notion of "ancient astronauts," the Nazca Lines, and the Pyramids of Egypt. Occasionally one comes across a reference or two to Canada in the pages of these books. So I thought it was high time that there was an entire book devoted to Canadian mysteries. We should know more about the mysteries that surround us.

Now we can know. In *Mysterious Canada* there are more than five hundred mysteries. They are presented geographically in the form of a gazetteer. About three hundred and sixty-five locations — cities, towns, villages, communities, settlements, reserves, rivers, regions — are arranged alphabetically within province or territory, and the provinces and territories are ranged from east to west to north. Thus the book begins in Newfoundland and ends at the North Pole.

It is true that some of the mysteries do not lend themselves to regional considerations; after all, a UFO is an unidentified flying object whether it hovers over Lake Ontario or the Eve River Rest Area on Vancouver Island. But the majority of the mysteries which I have discussed seem to be rooted in place as they are

in time. A book with a dozen chapter-length essays, each devoted to a single kind of anomalous phenomenon, would necessarily be polemical and debatable. After all, what is so mysterious about the disappearance of Ambrose Small? Was the cause of the Great Amherst Mystery an incendiary, a ghost, or a poltergeist? Such questions deserve to be asked, but with the majority of mysteries so little known, my efforts have been directed to making all of them better known, not explaining away those that never seem to go away.

Anyone who looks long and hard enough will no doubt find rational explanations for the mysteries in this book. There is no need to resort to a supernatural explanation to account for any one of them. At the same time I am aware of the fact that many of the mysteries are motifs of folklore which are widespread in distribution. They are so tangled in history and lore that it would be fruitless to do more than record their presence and suggest their nature and appeal. Yet there is always the possibility — the hope, the fear — that the genuinely inexplicable is operative.

The existence of psychic gifts or Psi factors has yet to be established to the satisfaction of the scientific community. If such factors are indeed operative, they operate spontaneously, sporadically, and subjectively. There is as yet no body of indisputable evidence which may be cited to demonstrate the operation in controlled circumstances of extrasensory perception, clairvoyance, precognition, psychokinesis, etc. Even a practice as old, tried, and true as "water-witching" has failed in test conditions. The so-called "shyness factor" has been invoked to account for the fact that in scientific tests nothing over and above chance expectations is observed when the protocols and the controls are overseen by eagle-eyed magicians who are familiar with all the paths of deception. It is instructive to recall at this juncture the Scots' judicial practice as described by one authority: "Beside the verdicts of 'guilty' and 'not guilty,' a Scots jury may return a verdict of 'not proven,' which has legally the same effect as not guilty in releasing the accused from further proceedings on the particular charge, but inflicts on him the stigma of moral guilt."

There are various systems to classify the occult and

the unknown. The one which follows has the single virtue that it was evolved for this book.

1. *Native Traditions*. Myths, legends, traditions, customs, rituals, and beliefs, associated with native North Americans, that is, the Inuit and Indian population. This category specifically includes rock art, unnatural or unknown creatures, superbeings, superstitions of locale, medicine wheels, and shamanism.

2. *Prehistoric America*. Sites, artifacts, and lore associated with contact prior to the Cabot landfall of 1497. There is discussion of the evidence for Chinese, Phoenician, Irish-Gaelic, Norse, Basque, and other voyages of exploration and colonization. Attention has been paid to the epigraphic evidence of petroglyphs in Early America.

3. *Lost Worlds*. Traditions associated with lost colonies, communities, cities, and entire civilizations. Some instances of lost worlds in the past are Avalon, Isles of the Blessed, Norumbega, Saguenay, Valley of Mystery, and Tropical Valley.

4. *Sacred and Profane Places*. Sites and localities believed consecrated or cursed by human or non-human agency. Included are shrines and shunned sites, churches, haunted woods, haunted houses, "devil" names, and the lore and legends of the North Pole.

5. *Treasure Troves*. Locales rumoured to be repositories of treasures — lost, misplaced, buried, hidden — spiritual or material. Also dealt with are lost ore-bodies and mines, especially those that are cursed or haunted, as almost all are said to be.

6. *Wild Creatures*. Lower order of natural or unnatural creation; cryptozoology; creatures marine, terrestrial, aerial, extra-terrestrial; dinosaurs and mammoths. Descriptions are given of the sasquatch, Ogopogo, Windigo, Thunderbird, land monsters, sea serpents, merfolk, wild men, humanoids, and hominids.

7. *Spirits and Spectres*. Higher order of natural or unnatural creation; ethereal entities, insubstantial or spiritual, who or which resemble angels, ghosts, ghouls, forerunners, wraiths, spectres, etc. Special consideration has been given to hallucinations, *folie à deux*, crisis apparitions, visions, spiritualism, mediumism, poltergeists, and so on.

8. *Wild Talents*. Charles Fort's term for "gifts beyond the normal" granted to individuals. They may be prodigies or prophets or "fire-starters," witches, seers, mediums, clairvoyants, telepaths, psychokinetics, "human magnets," or victims of spontaneous human combustion.

9. *Extraordinary Experiences*. Personal and subjective accounts of impersonal or objective experiences or events. Discussed are the Philip Phenomenon, psychical research, parapsychology, faith healing, miraculous cures, psychic surgery, intuitive archaeology, sightings of supernormal or paranormal "fireships," forerunners, out-of-body accounts, and near-death experiences.

10. *Anomalies and Phenomenologies*. Real or apparent irregularities and peculiarities. The range includes dinosaur fossils and hoodoos, the Beardmore Relics and the "moonscape" of Sudbury, "falls" and "wildfires," instances of simultaneity, riddles and enigmas, inventions, mirages, and quasi-mystical experiences.

11. *Alien Encounters*. Visions or visitations, extending from sightings of fireballs and phantom lights to alien craft, including flying saucers and UFOs, alien contactee and abduction scenarios. This category also embraces scientific radiotelescopy and the search for extra-terrestrial intelligence (SETI).

12. *Belief Systems*. The country's contribution to world religions, cults, sects, superstitions — especially native and ethnic and French Canadian — notably those at odds with orthodox practices connected with secular or rational Christianity. Mention is made of the British-Israel connection. Ten Lost Tribes, wicca or witchcraft, astrology, reincarnation, past-life regression, esotericism, occultism, spiritualism, Theosophy, mysticism, New Thought, New Age, *ad infinitum*.

I am not about to offer a definition of a "mystery" other than to say that for the purposes of this book a "mystery" is an occurrence — an event or an experience — that seemingly resists a natural explanation and begs for a supernatural one. A natural explanation is one that is rooted in reason, especially in the cause-and-effect relationship; a supernatural explanation is rooted in some other system of belief and is held to be essentially acausal.

Most people are interested in the mysterious, the occult, the inexplicable, the paranormal, the supernatural — call it what you will. But not all. It is common to divide people into two groups in regard to their acceptance or non-acceptance of such matters: the psychics and sceptics. The former are sometimes called "sheep," the latter "goats." Many factors may account for the fact that some people are predisposed to be believers in the supernatural and that other people are predisposed to be doubters. It has little to do with intelligence or intuition, will or imagination, training or sensitivity. In the majority of people it is probably a matter of balance. There is a tiny psychic and a tiny sceptic inside each one of us. These twin figures argue a lot and one of them argues more persuasively or more percussively than the other. At least that has been my experience. And as Robertson Davies once noted, "Canada needs ghosts, as a dietary supplement, a vitamin taken to stave off that most dreadful of modern ailments, the Rational Rickets."

For as long as I can remember I have been fascinated by the mysterious. I have a "taste" for it which is both emotional and intellectual. Long before I was introduced to Canadiana, I read widely in the literature of the occult and the paranormal. Around 1967, when I began to collect quotations and references to what could be called "mainstream" Canadiana, I also kept a weather-eye open for what could be called "fringe" Canadiana. I found a surprising amount of it in books by Frank Edwards, Vincent Gaddis, Donald Keyhoe, Colin Wilson, Brad Steiger, and Louis Pauwels. There was less of it in the books written by the system-builders: Erich von Däniken, Barry Fell, Immanuel Velikovsky, H.P. Blavatsky, and Rudolf Steiner. Even fewer Canadian references appeared among the serious speculations of Geoffrey Ashe, Paul Brunton, Juddi Krishnamurti, P.D. Ouspensky, George I. Gurdjieff, and René Guénon. Most of the miraculous material turned up when I travelled not the roads but the byroads of Canadiana — the narratives of David Thompson, the publications of Richard Maurice Bucke, etc. In astrological terms, I determined the conjunction of Canada and the occult. This book is the result.

Mainstream Canadiana is hardly public knowledge, even in Canada, so it is not surprising that fringe Canadiana is so little known. Deciding to dramatize this neglected or discarded knowledge or lore, I now see myself as a connoisseur of the curious, as the marshaller of these mysteries. I draw attention to them. I present them. Perhaps I am a folklorist after

all. My principle aim has been to demonstrate that Canada, in common with other countries, has its share of mysterious occurrences. As for my own attitude to the subject of the supernatural, it resembles the North Magnetic Pole which "wanders." The North Pole may be steadfast, but the North Magnetic Pole has a discernible drift observable from decade to decade. But each day the focus of its field flies about. One day I am sympathetic sceptic; the next day I am a sceptical sympathizer. Who knows where I now stand? Emotional and intellectual needs are met through the exploration of these mysteries, at least on the printed page; there are also intellectual and emotional imperatives that I be critical of them. As the poet Earle Birney noted, "It's by our lack of ghosts we're haunted." The lack is a void that needs to be filled, but with what? Ectoplasm? Folklore? Scientific-sounding hypotheses? Let me side with another poet, Louis Dudek, who argued thus: "There is enlightenment in questions, but only barbarism in belief."

People always ask, "Do you believe in ghosts?" as if ghosts were a category of belief rather than a category of experience. Whenever that question is asked, I always recall the response of Madame du Deffand who, when asked if she believed in ghosts, admitted: "No, but I am afraid of them." Equally ambivalent is the reaction of Samuel Taylor Coleridge who said, "No, I have seen too many of them to believe in them."

Mysterious Canada may be the most comprehensive book about this subject but it is not the first. It is preceded by two notable books that were written by former Englishmen. R.S. Lambert was a psychical researcher in London long before he settled in Toronto. He is the author of the first general book on the subject, Exploring the Supernatural in Canada (1954), which has remained in print to this day. It is a well-written book which sheds a fair amount of light on "the weird in Canadian folklore" to quote the subtitle. A.R.G. Owen is a geneticist from Cambridge, a parapsychologist, and the principle founder of the New Horizons Research Foundation in Toronto. He is the author of Psychic Mysteries of Canada (1970), which is a study of the phenomena of the past and particularly of the present in the light of modern research. These are not the only authors and titles in the field, but the only national ones. What remains to be prepared is a comprehensive bibliography of the field, thematically arranged, plus a scholarly treatment of selected aspects of the subject.

Many areas of Canada go unrepresented or at least under-represented in this commodious tome. With some exceptions I have paid little attention to organized religious practices. Various sects and cults in the country, as well as the belief-systems of its organized church bodies, could well have been included. It was a late nineteenth century English writer A.W. Kinglake who argued that all church buildings should bear the following inscription: IMPORTANT IF TRUE. Not enough attention has been paid to folklore—especially of the urban variety. A thick book could be devoted to the lore of even the smallest province. My feeling is that such lore, far from being fanciful, is factual in a psychological sense and dramatizes the felt interaction between the people and the land. Moving from folklore to Fortean phenomena, the format of the gazetteer does not lend itself to recording such evanescent phenomena collected by Charles Fort as "falls"—strange things descending from the heavens. Also shortchanged are "devil names." Thousands of geographical features in the country bear names with negative connotations. Forteans noted that they seem to attract negative phenomena and give rise to "lexilinks." Lake monsters, too, are too numerous to cover fully. Canada has more lakes than any other country in the world; 7.5% of its surface is covered with water. Practically every lake has its lake monster. The reports are there, if not the monsters. Canada, the second-largest country in the world, has the world's second-largest expanse of sky. As J. Allen Hynek pointed out, on a *per capita* basis more reports of sightings of UFOs originate in Canada than in any other country. Canadians are also prolific in the field of invention. There was not enough time or space to survey activity in this field, a field in which it would be necessary to separate the wheat of innovative invention from the chaff of crackpot devices. Finally, the book could not do justice to the narrative accounts of the extraordinary experiences of ordinary Canadians. Who knows how many Canadians have experienced the power of the extraordinary: instances of simultaneity, telepathic impressions, precognitive dreams or visions, and so on? Such narrative accounts, being subjective and circumstantial as well as lengthy, could

not easily be worked into a book of this sort. These are some of the subjects and categories to be explored in future books. As Noël Coward observed about Los Angeles, "There is something delightfully real about what is phony here."

Let the author share with the reader a few insights that were attendant upon the researching and writing of this book.

1. Behind every mystery lurks a mystery-monger. There is usually someone behind the scenes who has a vested interest or a hidden agenda. This is particularly true of events in the past which today are taken at face value. The Great Amherst Mystery is a good instance of a mystery wherein the sole informant, the actor and author Walter Hubbell, was also the sole beneficiary of any benefits resulting from the poltergeist activity.

2. Human motivation is mysteriously complex. Ralph Nader and Mother Teresa may be pure of heart, but psychics, parapsychologists, and debunkers with fixed agendas usually have mixed motives. On both sides of the line there are people who are dumb, deluded, deceived, dishonest — and dedicated. There are serious searchers on the trail of truth among both those who accept and those who reject. There are charlatans who "fudge" the results in both communities. Both believer and the sceptic alike need to assess human motivation at the level of deepest conviction, strongest hopes, and worst fears.

3. One argument for the existence of a phenomenon like UFOs is the old saw: "Where there's smoke there's fire." Yet a dozen zeros in a row are no more impressive or meaningful than a single zero, unless that zero is preceded by a digit of some value. When I encounter that line of reasoning I find myself countering it with the thought that the phenomenon may resemble TV news. Television news, according to the contemporary saw, is all "smoke and mirrors." Then I am reminded of the remark that has been attributed to John F. Kennedy: "Where there's smoke there's generally a smoke-making device."

4. The supernatural is experienced, not understood. Most people have experienced the "inexplicable" once or twice in their lives; some people experience it routinely. Yet what is in question is not the experience itself but its explication or explanation. The study of the experience is properly the province

of the psychologist or the psychiatrist; the study of the explication lies within the competence of the psychologist although there is no one more familiar with the forms of such cases as the parapsychologist. Most mysteries are not experienced first hand at all, but through word-of-mouth or through the medium of the printed page. Indeed, there is no way to study ghosts or UFOs; one studies reports of sightings of ghosts or UFOs. It is here that humanists have sizeable contributions to make. Folklorists are familiar with the principles of the transmission of oral lore, its distribution and distortion; ethnologists understand the dynamics of group communications; philosophers ask questions about the real, the factual, the actual, the possible, and the veridical; psychologists appreciate the principle of confabulation, the process of interweaving the real and the unreal; literary scholars routinely distinguish between the devices of description and dramatization; literary theorists of the school known as deconstruction regularly detect the voices of contradiction; journalists may expand upon the conventions inherent in the news story, the interview, and the feature article. As a collector and compiler, my own experience has been that oral or printed accounts or descriptions of the miraculous are routinely lacking or deficient in one respect or another. But at the same time is there an account or description of anything that is complete and faultless?

5. Distance may diminish news but it magnifies mysteries. One thousand people will have to starve in Manila to be as newsworthy as one person who does the same in Montreal. It is easier for a swami to levitate in Lhasa for the simple reason that no fellow or affiliate of the Committee for the Scientific Investigation of Claims of the Paranormal is within driving distance of the Tibetan capital. Consequently the physical properties of Moncton's Magnetic Hill seem more astonishing to Andrew Tomas in London and Jacques Bergier in Paris than they do to Stuart Trueman, the discoverer of New Brunswick's optical illusion. The North Pole, being inaccessible to virtually everyone who writes about it in an imaginative way, is the domain of incredible mysteries.

6. This does not mean that there are no mysteries. There are always mysteries. We are immersed in them. They are eternal and immortal. "No dragon ever dies." It is impossible to prove a negative.

Besides, there is a place for mysteries. They add a note of piquancy to life, a *soupçon* of the supernatural to the realism of everyday life. But how "real" is everyday life? In the words of the philosopher, John Stanbough, "The Real is not the rational." Even when a mystery is decapitated it continues to captivate. It persists in meeting deep-seated human needs, not all of them complex. One need is the desire to hear a good story. The debunking operation performed by the researcher Dwight Whalen on the mysterious return of Charles Coughlan to his birthplace in Prince Edward Island is a good instance of how a mystery is disproved, yet survives intact. Such lore is the marrow of our bone. It enriches everyday life which daily becomes more mechanized and hence more mindless, more computerized and hence more heartless. These stories add a note of drama to lives increasingly undramatic.

7. There are mysteries yet to explore in Canada and around the world. I know I would like to do more than retell a number of these tales. The UFO encounter of Stephen Michalak at Falcon Lake, Manitoba, is one that requires more work. The origins of the legends surrounding the Valley of Mystery in the Nahanni River valley have more to tell us about human expectation than we often recognize. A lot of good would be done by comparing the Grey Ladies seen on the Atlantic shores with the sasquatches seen in the interior of the Pacific provinces. The Medicine Wheels which lie across the prairies roll across the mind.

An interesting observation about the nature of belief, disbelief, and non-belief was made by Northrop Frye in a passage from his *The Critical Path: An Essay on the Social Context of Literary Criticism* (1971). Professor Frye wrote:

> For any uncommitted reader of the Gospels, the question "could it really have happened just like that?" is bound to occur with great frequency. But at a certain point the question begins to turn into the form: "If I had been there, is that what I should have seen and experienced?" At this point the doubts become overwhelming, because most of these doubts are of one's own capacity for spiritual experience. Sir Thomas Browne's "I thank God that I never saw Christ or his

disciples'' begins to sound like a very shrewd remark. If I had been out on the hills of Bethlehem on the night of the birth of Christ, with the angels singing to the shepherds, I think that I should not have heard any angels singing. The reasons why I think so is that I do not hear them now, and there is no reason to suppose that they have stopped.

My favourite mystery was not included in the book. Since it is a mini-essay about the country as a whole, it has no real place anywhere in its pages. I suppose it could have been worked in as an entry on Ottawa, as the capital city represents the entire country. But instead I saved it for the Preface. Here it is:

Canada is *four* billion years old. The country occupies some *four* million square miles of the Earth's surface. Its landforms have been established for the last *forty* thousand years. For almost *fourteen* thousand years it has served as the habitat of human beings. It has known *four* centuries of Western history, originally as a colony, latterly as a dominion.

Anyone who adds together the *four* digits of the year 1867 (the year the Act of Confederation took effect) will find that the sum is twenty-two and that the sum of these two digits is *four*. The country has *four* well-defined regions: Eastern, Central, Western, Northern. Traditionally and historically the land has been populated by *four* distinct groups of people: The Aborigines, the French, the British, and the Americans. A collective decision was made by the *Canadien* and Canadian people to decline the invitation of the Continental Congress to become a ''*Fourteenth* Colony'' of the United States.

So Canada is a *four-square* country!

ACKNOWLEDGEMENTS

I received considerable assistance with this book, as with previous books, from Philip Singer and Michael Richardson, who are librarians with the North York Library system, where much research was conducted with the help of the staff at the Central, Bathurst Heights, and Locke libraries. Research was also carried out at the Metropolitan Toronto Reference Library and the John P. Robarts Research Library of the University of Toronto. Work was undertaken, as well, at the CBC Reference Library and the Academy of Medicine Library and at two other specialized libraries: the Spaced Out Library, part of the Toronto Public Library system, and the IAO Research Centre Library of Divine Sciences and Healing Arts, Toronto, which is privately owned and operated. Lorna Toolis of SOL and Robin Armstrong of IAO were especially helpful.

The book could not have acquired its present shape without the assistance of researcher and writer Dwight Whalen of Niagara Falls, Ontario. With open arms he offered me the use of his extensive collection of vertical-file material of a Fortean nature. He also turned over to me his extensive collection of newspaper clippings, especially Canadian Press (CP) stories and stories which originated in the Niagara region. Should the reader come to the conclusion that the Niagara Peninsula is the most haunted part of the country, the person to blame is Dwight Whalen. As a matter of fact, Niagara-on-the-Lake *is* the most haunted community in the land; it has more ghosts relative to population than any other community in Canada.

I must also single out the generosity of Mr. X, an investigator and researcher who lives in the vicinity of Kingston, Ontario. When I call him Mr. X, I am not hiding his real identity; many years ago he legally changed his name to X. I called him X when we began to correspond; now that I know him a little better I call him x. He is as Fortean a person as one is likely to meet. His data base of anomalous phenomena is second to none in the country. His generosity was such that he went to considerable trouble to answer my queries and share with me his data.

I am indebted to a quartet of independent researchers for their information and their positive attitude. Loren Coleman of Portland, Maine, whose *Mysterious*

America (1983) was a stimulus to me, offered more assistance than I could absorb. John Magor, publisher of CUFOR books at Duncan, British Columbia, was conscientious, cheerful, and generous, especially with photographs. W. Ritchie Benedict, a contributor to Fortean-type publications, helpfully offered information on the lore of Calgary, Alberta. Another Calgarian, Ted Davy, was most encouraging, unstinting, and tactful.

I am pleased to acknowledge the assistance of research trainees through the Futures Program of the Ministry of Skills Development in the Government of Ontario. The researchers-in-training were David Sidders and Farbod Riahi. Janet Bord of the Fortean Picture Library, Corwen, Wales, was especially helpful.

I am indebted to the following tourism boards — federal, provincial, territorial — for responding to my request for information: Government of Canada (Regional Industrial Expansion, Donna Allen); Nova Scotia (Stan Fitzner); New Brunswick (Debbie Gibson); Manitoba (R.W. Yuel); Saskatchewan (Gerard Makuch); Alberta (Shellcy Johnson); Yukon Territory; Northwest Territories (Frona Scott). There is no mystery why I am not thanking the other provincial tourism bodies — Nfld., P.E.I., Que., Ont., B.C. — for they did not deign to reply to my request for information.

In addition to the men and women whose assistance has been acknowledged, I wish to draw attention to the specific contributions of the following thoughtful people: Susan M. Adams, University of Virginia, Charlottesville, Virginia; Alexandre L. Amprimoz, Brock University, St. Catharines, Ont.; Larry E. Arnold, Parascience International, Harrisburg, Penn.; Geoffrey Ashe, Glastonbury, Somerset; Richard E. Bennett, University of Manitoba Libraries, Winnipeg, Man.; Ingrid Birker, Redpath Museum, Montreal, Que.; Kamala Bhatia, Mohawk College, Hamilton, Ont.; Jacques Boisvert, Magog, Que.; Joel Bonn, Concordia University, Montreal, Que.; R.W. Bradford, National Museum of Science and Technology, Ottawa, Ont.; Michael Bradley, Toronto, Ont.; Victoria Branden, Waterdown, Ont.; Arthur Bray, Ottawa, Ont.; Brien Brothman, National Archives of Canada, Ottawa, Ont.; Susan E. Brubaker, Atlantic Mutual Companies, New York, N.Y.; Alice M. Buse, Philosophical Research Society, Los Angeles, Calif.; Ed Butts, Mississauga, Ont.; Philippa Campsie, Toronto, Ont.; W. Glen Curnoe, London Public Libraries, London, Ont.; Ian Currie, Toronto, Ont.; P.J. Currie, Tyrrell Museum of Palaeontology, Drumheller, Alta.; Rene Dahinden, Richmond, B.C.; Hugh A. Dempsey, Glenbow Museum, Calgary, Alta.; Donna Dunlop, Toronto, Ont.; Gene Duplantier, Willowdale, Ont.; Don Evans, Orillia, Ont.; Jon Fear, Kitchener, Ont.; Paul A. Feldman, National Research Council, Ottawa, Ont.; R.G. Forbis, University of Calgary, Calgary, Alta.; Stanton T. Friedman, Fredericton, N.B.; Mary Margaret Fuller, *Fate* Magazine, Highland Park, Ill.; Frank Germann, Athol Murray College, Wilcox, Sask.; Howard Gerwing, University of Victoria, Victoria, B.C.; Henry and Zita Gordon, Ontario Skeptics, Toronto, Ont.; William Gough, Toronto, Ont.; B.R. Grad, McGill University, Montreal, Que.; Cyril Greenland, McMaster University, Hamilton, Ont.; David Haisell, Streetsville, Ont.; George D. Hathaway, Hathaway Consulting Services, Toronto, Ont.; Anthony R. Hawke, Downsview, Ont.; Helen S. Hogg, David Dunlap Observatory, Richmond Hill, Ont.; Christopher Holmes, Rainbow Centre, Toronto, Ont.; Jessica Hunt, Toronto, Ont.; Dorothy Izatt, Richmond, B.C.; Michel Pierre Janisse, University of Manitoba, Winnipeg, Man.; Alex Johnston, Historical Society of Alberta, Lethbridge, Alta.; M.T. Kelly, Toronto, Ont.; Barbara Kilvert, Canadian Cancer Society, Toronto; K. Corey Keeble, Royal Ontario Museum, Toronto, Ont.; Richard T. Lambert, Emsdale, Ont.; Robert E. Lee, Ottawa, Ont.; Odette Legendre, Montreal, Que.; Jon Lomberg, Toronto, Ont.; Sheila Lowe, University of Lethbridge, Lethbridge, Alta.; Robert McGee, Archaelogical Survey of Canada, Ottawa, Ont.; Roy MacGregor, Ottawa, Ont.; Alberto Manguel, Toronto, Ont.; Ted Mann, York University, Toronto, Ont.; Joan Melvin, Deep River, Ont.; Anna Mitchell-Hedges, Kitchener, Ont.; Gil Murray, McMaster University, Hamilton, Ont.; Mark McNeil, *The Hamilton Spectator*, Hamilton, Ont.; A.S. Narayana, Mississauga, Ont.; Mary Alice Neal, Richmond Hill, Ont.; George and Iris M. Owen, New Horizons, Toronto, Ont.; Michael A. Persinger, Laurentian University, Sudbury, Ont.; Gerald Pratley, Ontario Film Theatre, Don Mills, Ont.; James Randi, Plantation, Florida; Alan Rayburn, Geographic Names, Ottawa, Ont.; Jessica Riddell, Ottawa, Ont.; Mrs. M. Robertson, New Brunswick Museum, Saint John, N.B.; John F. Roy, Ridgetown, Ont.; Chris Rutkowski, Winnipeg, Man.; Howard Ryshpan, Montreal, Que.; Eric Ruff, Yarmouth County, N.B.; Dale A. Russell, National Museum of Natural Sciences, Ottawa, Ont.; Heath Rieder, Agincourt, Ont.; Anna Sandor, Toronto, Ont.; David Schatzky, CBC, Toronto, Ont.; Denise Schon, Toronto, Ont.; Ivan Semeniuk, Ontario Science Centre, Don Mills, Ont.; Allen Spraggett, Richmond Hill, Ont.; John Steckley, Thornhill, Ont.; J.C.M. Shute, Guelph, Ont.; Robin Skelton, Victoria, B.C.; Guy Spittal, Iroqrafts, Ohsweken, Ont.; Robert W. Stephens, Hay River, N.W.T.; Philip H.R. Stepney, Provincial Museum of Alberta, Edmonton, Alta.; Ethel Stewart, Ottawa, Ont.; Ann Tompkins, The Guild Shop, Toronto, Ont.; Jonni Turner, CBC, Charlottetown, P.E.I.; Jerry Tutungian, *Leisure Ways*, Toronto, Ont.; Devendra P. Varma, Dalhousie University, Halifax, N.S.; Joan M. Vastokas, Trent University, Peterborough, Ont.; Hugh Washburn, Panorama City, Calif.; Susan Watson, National Museum of Science and Technology, Ottawa, Ont.

Dwight Whalen would like to thank the following staff members of the Niagara Falls, Ont., Public Library: Elizabeth Allen, Kathy Barker, Betty Beam, Claire Beckermann, Sheena Crow, Connie Dick, Mary Joselin, Beverley Rodman, Inge Saczkowski, Dorothy Van Slyke, and Millie Willson; and Donald Loker, Local History Specialist of the Niagara Falls, N.Y., Public Library. As well, he would like to acknowledge the assistance of Joseph W. Zarzynski, Henri A. and Adèle Lacroix, Père Prud'Homme, and Mark Chorvinsky, editor and publisher of *Strange Magazine*.

I am pleased that the enthusiasm for the work-in-progress was shown by members of the Editorial Department of Doubleday Canada Limited, especially the editor Frances Hill.

Once again I must record my principal indebtedness. It is to Ruth Colombo, my wonderful (and at times mysterious) wife!

For personal reasons this book is dedicated to the memory of Alex Watt (1890–1961), a man of power.

NEWFOUNDLAND

Admiral's Cove/
"Nephew of the Almighty"

The notorious Richard Brothers was born at Admiral's Cove, an outport on the east coast of Newfoundland's Avalon Peninsula, on Christmas Day in 1757. Brothers was the religious prophet who laid the theoretical basis for the identification of the British people with the descendants of the Ten Lost Tribes of Israel. He styled himself "Richard Brothers, Nephew of the Almighty, Cousin of the Lord Jesus, Rightful King of England, Prince of the Hebrews, Lion of the Tribe of Judah, anointed to lead them to the Land of Canaan."

In 1794–95, Brothers wrote and published the two volumes of his master work, *A Revealed Knowledge of the Prophecies and Times*, in which he informed the world that the Millennium would commence on 17 November 1795 and that the "Nephew of the Almighty" would lead the Ten Lost Tribes back to Jerusalem. *The Times* called him the "great prophet of Paddington Street." But Brothers overstepped himself in March 1795 when in an address he ordered George III to hand over the Crown and acknowledge Brothers as the world leader. The prophet was arrested on suspicion of treason and subsequently committed to a lunatic asylum.

His ideas were initially derided but by the time of his death in Great Britain in 1824 they had begun to bear fruit. They influenced independent thinkers like the poet William Blake, and they led to the establish-ment of the British-Israel World Federation, an organization founded in England in 1919 to foster the work of identifying the British people with the people of Ancient Israel.

The notion that the descendants of the Ten Lost Tribes were not lost to history but trod "England's green and pleasant land" may have flattered the vanity of the inhabitants of the British Isles, but the idea failed to win Brothers a following at home. "The only place where Brothers made absolutely no impression on the Anglo-Saxon Israelites was in Newfoundland," explained writer Harold Horwood in *Newfoundland* (1969). "At Admiral's Cove, where the Brothers family still lives, you had better not mention the name of Richard. They regard him as a dark stain on the escutcheon."

L'Anse aux Meadows/
First Authentic Norse Site

The first authentic Norse site found in North America is located at L'Anse aux Meadows on the northern tip of the Great Northern Peninsula. It is generally believed that the site was lost for a thousand years until 1960, the year it was discovered and described by the Norwegian explorer Helge Ingstad. But the liveyeres, the local residents, knew of the presence of the ruins and remains of some ancient settlement, but no one questioned or even listened to them. There is no question that Ingstad deserves credit as the founder of L'Anse aux Meadows, but local traditions should be granted greater respect.

The site was excavated by the Norwegians and by Parks Canada. Three building complexes were uncovered with evidence of ironworking and carpentry. Radiocarbon tests have dated a period of short occupancy between A.D. 990 and 1050. Were the occupants led by Leif the Lucky, the Viking from Greenland, the first known European to set foot on the North American continent? Is L'Anse aux Meadows the site of the long-sought "land of vines," the Vinland, Vineland, or Wineland of the Old Norse sagas? Ingstad not only identified L'Anse aux Meadows with Vinland, he identified other locales in the Norse Tales: Helluland ("flagstone land") with Cape Dyer, Baffin Island, N.W.T., and Markland ("forest land") with Cape Porcupine, Labrador.

The author Wayland Drew visited the ruins and meditated on them in *The Sea Within: The Gulf of St. Lawrence* (1984), where he pondered the fate of the Norse colonists.

> The Norse likely inhabited L'Anse aux Meadows for no more than twenty years before emboldened skraelings, loosening ties with the mother colonies, and attrition by disease and accident forced the survivors to return to Greenland. Then again, perhaps they did not leave at all. Perhaps they were finally overwhelmed by raiders slipping down the surrounding slopes in the dusk. Perhaps they left their bones at L'Anse aux Meadows to be scattered by tides and animals. Or perhaps they came to an accommodation with the skraelings at last, joining in their hunting when the spring knorrs from Greenland failed to come, mingling with them in other bays and shelters far from L'Anse aux Meadows. Perhaps the legacy of those lost colonists rests in the genes of blue-eyed Eskimos.

Avalon Peninsula/
Ancient Colonies and Empires

Allow the Avalon Peninsula its secret identity. It may lie in the Atlantic Ocean, but it also lies in the ocean of the world's imagination. This body of land has long represented the location in the New World of ancient colonies and empires founded by the sea-faring monks and captains of the Old.

If the landfalls of history are represented by the Newfoundland community of Bonavista, the entire Avalon Peninsula may stand for the landfalls of prehistory. These landfalls were made by the explorers and discoverers who lack sections of their own in the textbook histories of the world, but who from time to time are fleetingly mentioned in introductory passages reserved for fanciful, apocryphal, or legendary navigations. This is their permanent realm. So what then is the Avalon Peninsula, the name of which implies a legendary connection with the Arthurian past of Albion or Britain?

Númenor is the name of the "Land of the Star" in the fiction of J.R.R. Tolkien. In the dim and distant past it was an island set in the seas between Middle-earth and Valinor, the Land of the Gods. The inhabitants of this island realm were an ambitious and sacrilegious people. Their island kingdom sank beneath the waves of the Atlantic Ocean. There were some survivors who went on to become the founders of Middle-earth. They spoke Quenya, the oldest of the Elva languages. Like doomed Númenor, it is now lost. It is known that in Quenya the word Númenor meant "Heart-of-the-West" — a phrase that brings to mind the occult writer Dionne Fortune's description of Glastonbury as "The Avalon of the Heart."

When Tolkien wrote about Númenor he was telling tales. He may have been writing fiction and not fact, but in doing so he was drawing on Irish and Celtic legend and myth and introducing modern readers to an ancient Nordic centre of cultural concentration. Númenor was called "the Atlantis of the north, the Celtic Atlantis" by Louis Pauwels and Jacques Bergier in *The Eternal Man* (1973) translated by Michael Heron. Today the site of Númenor is occupied by the Avalon Peninsula, the name of which implies a legendary connection with the Arthurian past of Albion or Britain.

The ancient Celtic captains and sea kings are more ancient and more numerous, it seems, than the

Vikings. Chronicles of the past describe the migration of men and women from an old world to a new in search of a terrestrial paradise. The names of many of these captains and kings have come down to us. Among those whose deeds have been described in saga and song are the following: Bailie an Sedil, Barinte, Brendan the Navigator, Brecan, Brightleith, Connla, Cormac the Navigator, Corra, Cuchulainn, Foin Barr, Labhraidh, Laegaire MacCrinmthain, MacErca, Maeldune, Malo, Madoc, Osin, Tagd. They and their brethren sought Murias, the western city of mystery, in Tir-nan-Og, the terrestrial paradise.

Chief among the Celtic captains and kings were Corra and Madoc. Corra, or O'Corra, was one of the earliest of the Irish sea-faring captains. It is said he visited twenty-three places, beginning with the Avalon Peninsula and including "the Place of the Ice Bridge" and "the Isle of the Seal Rookery." The Welsh nobleman, Prince Madoc ab Owen Gwynnedd, is credited with completing two transatlantic crossings, the first in 1170. This voyage was one of exploration; the second was for the purpose of colonization. The colony which he established in the temperate wilds must have had a name. Perhaps the name was noted by Robin Palmer in *A Dictionary of Mythical Places* (1975):

> Aztec legend claim that their people originated on an island known as Aztlan. . . . The name Aztlan has also been used in a poem by Robert Southey. It tells about a Welsh hero, Prince Madoc, the youngest son of Owen Gwynned who lived in the twelfth century. Despite his royal rank, Madoc was a brave sailor and fisherman. One day, distressed by a war between his father and his brothers, he set sail into the unknown Atlantic and founded a settlement far off in the west. All this is part of Welsh tradition.

There is some confirmation of this Aztec tradition, for as R.C. Padden explained concerning the founding of the Aztec kingdom in eleventh-century Mexico in *The Hummingbird and the Hawk: Conquest and Sovereignty in the Valley of Mexico, 1503–1541*:

Moving from place to place, the Aztecs wander aimlessly; but ever so gradually they drift to the south, possibly because the living seems to grow easier, the face of nature less grimly fixed. Legend tells us that they call themselves Aztec after their mythical ancestral home of Aztlán. Later, as they wandered, they called themselves Mexica in honour of the great tribal leader named Mecitli.

The author explained that Aztlán is "White Place" or "Land of the White Heron" and that its location has "been postulated everywhere from Michoacán to Puget Sound, although never upon physical evidence.

A final leap of the imagination is to Arthur's Avalon. Where did King Arthur go when he "went west"? Was he really buried in the Abbey at Glastonbury? Is it true that the monks there discovered his tomb? Or is this a twelfth-century fraud — an attempt to increase piety and the Abbey's prestige? Surely Arthur lies where his tomb will not be disturbed, for he is asleep all these centuries awaiting the cry for his return.

Alfred Lord Tennyson thought in geographical terms when he wrote "The Passing of Arthur" in *Idylls of the King* (1873). The poet-laureate described the aged and dying king boarding a "dusky barge" and setting sail into the western sunset. From the bounds of his destination could be heard a great cry as if "from beyond the limit of the world." Tennyson felt strongly about "that true North," his epithetical reference to the Dominion of Canada which at the time was newly minted and full of hope for all the values of "a vaster Britain." In his imagination the West and the North were linked, as in the phrase "the North West." It is pleasant to imagine King Arthur asleep in "that true North" where his presence holds at bay "The darkness of that battle in the West,/ Where all of high and holy dies away."

Bay du Nord/ The Land of the Stone Cross

An account of a visit by land and sea to the land of the Stone Cross appeared in *Early Canadian Life*, July

1980. The account was titled "The Search for the Cross Between Us" and was written by Dawn French who in August 1972 was a resident of Pushthrough, an outport which lies about thirty miles west of Bay du Nord on the island's rugged south coast.

From liveyeres she learned about the existence of the Stone Cross and its healing properties, traditions which went back to the days of the Micmac Indians. She found the site inland from Bay du Nord, over the towering cliffs of Devil's Dancing Table. On this barren ground, edged by spruce-clad hills, appeared the outline of a somewhat diamond-shaped open cross, ringed by white boulders and stones. It measured about thirty feet from north to south. It seemed to be guarded by heaps of boulders, statue-like sentinels, from one of which, it was said, would be visible the image of a man upon the cross. There were two basins, one for holy water, which was dry; another for offerings, which had coins, some of which dated back to 1865. "Micmac and liveyeres say that each rock has the power to heal, and can be removed as long as another is put back in its place."

Dawn French concluded the account of her and her family's visit with more questions than answers:

> I climbed atop one of the statues and took a picture of the cross, and then we gathered together around it. Looking down at it once more before we left, we wondered many things: How old was it? Who was the last to see it before us? What illnesses had been cured? How many had been truly healed; and how had they climbed to the top? So many questions. So few answered. So many bordering on disbelief. . . . Yes, our disbelief was still there. But so was the cross. After all these years it had survived, despite wind, weather and time.
>
> We saw the cross still lay between us, our differences remained. But we saw something else up there that day: the vision of a strong people who believed in themselves — and more.

Catalina/
The Mystery of the *Resolven*

"It is Newfoundland's most famous mystery of the sea, and, though barely known outside local circles today, it was ranked with the world's most bewildering nautical conundrums at the time that it occurred," wrote Michael Harrington in *Sea Stories from Newfoundland* (1958).

He was referring to the mystery ship the *Resolven*, a brigantine of 143 tons under full sail, which the gunboat the H.M.S. *Mallard* encountered on 29 August 1883 about fifty miles east of Catalina, a port on the east coast. The *Resolven* was drifting and showed no signs of life. When boarded it was found to be slightly damaged but still seaworthy. The lifeboats were missing, but the logbook lay open in the captain's cabin and a small fire was still burning in the galley-stove. A search was made for survivors but none were ever found.

The mystery brig was towed to Catalina, where it was established that it had left Harbour Grace thirty-six hours earlier *en route* to Snug Harbour. Originally built in Prince Edward Island, it was registered at Aberystwyth, Wales. Marine investigators hazarded a guess that Captain John James was a good skipper but unfamiliar with icebergs so he instructed his passengers and crew to abandon the vessel when an iceberg was seen to approach.

The fate of the *Resolven* recalled that of the Nova Scotia-built *Mary Celeste* which a decade earlier was found abandoned on the high sea. As Harrington noted, "This bizarre event happened within fifty miles off the coast of Newfoundland, yet not a trace of one of the fourteen men was ever found. We can guess all we like, we can put two and two together, we can reconstruct the incident, but as for the answer, we can explain nothing."

Estotiland/
Lost Island

Not much is known of the mysterious lost island of Estotiland off the northern coast of Labrador. Alberto Manguel and Gianni Guadalpui in *The Dictionary of Imaginary Places* (2nd ed., 1987) describe it as "an island smaller than Iceland in the north Atlantic, crossed by four rivers and with a mountain in its centre." They go on to say, "The people of Estotiland possess every single art in the world, except that of using a mariner's compass."

The purely imaginary island was created by Nicolò and Antonio Zeno, the two Venetian brothers who are reputed to have sailed from Italy to the North Atlantic about 1380 where they visited Estotiland and reached Nova Scotia. Their account was published by the Zeno family in Venice in 1558. The map-maker Mercator accepted the authenticity of the account, and Sir Martin Frobisher took with him on his Arctic voyage of 1576 a fascimile of Zeno's map with its imaginary locales, including Estotiland.

Flatrock/
The Flatrock Fires

A phenomenon familiar to connoisseurs of the curious is the frightening one of mysterious fires which break out unexpectedly for no known reason. Many such cases are reported. The one that follows is based on a Canadian Press news report published in the Niagara Falls *Evening Review*, 11 December 1954.

The RCMP was asked to investigate the outbreak of mysterious fires in the home of Mike Parsons at Flatrock, north of Carbonear, on Conception Bay. Officers failed to determine the reason for the rash of flames and so informed the Attorney-General.

Over a two-week period the five members of the family were alarmed when the following incidents occurred at intervals of two or three days. A dictionary burst into flames for no apparent reason. A sack of sugar ignited of its own accord. A box of religious literature, stowed in an upstairs bureau, turned into a bonfire. A blaze appeared under the eaves of the house. The floorboards in one room of the house flared up. Finally a doll was consumed in flames.

While the mysterious fires were small and easily extinguished, the family members were understandably frightened and afraid to go to sleep at night. The Attorney-General had no comment to make on the RCMP's investigation of the Flatrock Fires.

Gander/
Gander UFO Case

"A circular, bright orange-red disk" was observed by the pilot, co-pilot, and navigator aboard a U.S. Navy R5D four-engine transport cruising ten thousand feet over the North Atlantic en route from Iceland to Newfoundland. It was about 1:00 a.m., GMT, 10 February 1951. The weather was clear except for a few nearly transparent clouds below the aircraft. The "disk" was observed for several minutes and then it appeared to zoom toward the plane, suddenly reverse its course, and head back over the horizon where it disappeared. The airplane commander communicated with Air Traffic Control at Gander and asked Gander to notify the U.S. military at Argentia of the sighting of a UFO. Upon landing the crew members made their reports and these found their way into the U.S. Air Force's official Project Blue Book.

The strange sighting was recalled in 1970 when the National Investigations Committee on Aerial Phenomena (NICAP), the largest private organization devoted to investigating UFO sightings, published an interview with the pilot based on his recollections more than a decade after the encounter. As he recalled, "It appeared to be from 200 to 300 feet in diameter, translucent or metallic, shaped like a saucer, a purple-red fiery ring around the perimeter and a frosted white glow around the entire object."

The Gander Case was drawn to the attention of the "Sherlock Holmes of UFOlogy," Philip J. Klass, who examined the Project Blue Book records, made an independent analysis, and reported his findings in *UFOs Explained* (1974). By establishing the exact position of the moon below the horizon, the presence of stratus clouds with ice crystals on the horizon, and the degree of below-the-horizon coverage due to refraction in the atmosphere, he concluded that what the pilots had seen and described was a lunar reflection, a "Sub-Moon."

"In my numerous years as a UFO investigator I have encountered many cases that proved to be mis-identifications of unfamiliar objects, and occasionally of familiar objects seen under unusual conditions," Klass wrote. "But until my analysis of the Gander case, I would have had difficulty believing that so many experienced pilots and others in a flight crew could mistake the moon for a giant UFO that seemed to be zooming toward them on a collision course."

"One contributing factor in the Gander case," he continued, "may have been the fact that there had been a considerable number of UFO reports in the press during the several months preceding this incident, and in 1951 the possibility of alien spaceships was still a conceivable hypothesis."

Goose Bay/
The Traverspine Gorillas

Two creatures that plagued Traverspine, a community at the west end of Lake Melville, near Goose Bay, Labrador, are worthy of attention. They were called "the Traverspine Gorillas" by Eliot Merrick in his book *True North* (1933). Their story is well told by Bruce Wright, director of the Northeastern Wildlife Station at the University of New Brunswick, in his book *Wildlife Sketches Near and Far* (1962):

> About 1913 the little settlement of Traverspine at the head of Lake Melville was visited in winter by two strange animals that drove the dogs to a frenzy and badly frightened the people. They left deep tracks about twelve inches long indicating great weight and they rooted up rotten logs with great strength and they tore them apart as if searching for grubs.
>
> They sometimes stood erect on their hind legs (at which time they looked like great hairy men seven feet tall, and no doubt from this description Merrick got his title of the Traverspine

Gorillas). But they also ran on all fours. They cleaned up some seal bones "too big for the dogs," and what is too big for a husky is really big, and many dogs followed them and did not return when they came around the settlement at night. This was a serious loss as dogs were the people's sole means of transportation.

> These two strange animals, which the inhabitants called the man and the woman because one was larger than the other, stayed about the settlement despite attempts to trap them or drive them away. One day Mrs. Michelin was alone in her house with her young daughter playing in the edge of the bush behind. Suddenly the child rushed in crying, "It's following me, Mummy, it's following me!"
>
> Mrs. Michelin reached for a shotgun loaded with buckshot which she always had near when her husband was away, and stepped out the back door.
>
> "All I could see was the moving bush and the shape of a great animal standing seven feet tall in the alders. It seemed to have a sort of white ruff across the top of its head, I could not make out the rest. I fired into the bushes and I heard the shot hit. I went back into the house and bolted the door. It never came back and there was blood where it had stood when the men from the sawmill came back."
>
> The sawmill closed down and the men turned out in force to look, but they never found it. Similar animals have been reported since; their tracks have been found at intervals, the last being about 1940.
>
> I asked Mrs. Michelin point blank if this could have been a bear. "It was no bear, Mr. Wright. I have killed twelve bears on my husband's trap-line and I know their tracks well. I saw enough of this thing to be sure of that. I fired a shotgun at it and I heard the shot hit."

John Green, in *Sasquatch: The Apes Among Us* (1978), who quotes both Eliot Merrick's account and Bruce Wright's, concludes: "I have never known what to make of this story. It seems to me to have the ring of truth, in both versions, but they are not quite the same and neither of them fits either the sasquatch or any known animal.''

Goose Bay/
UFO Accounts

"Goose Bay Air Force Base in Central Newfoundland and has been a veritable 'hot spot' of UFO activity,'' claimed Yurko Bondarchuk in *UFO: Sightings, Landings and Abductions* (1979). "Over the years, dozens of incidents were witnessed by a number of Canadian and U.S. Military pilots.''

Bondarchuk discussed in his book several incidents in some detail. The first incident, dated 15 December 1952, is an account of how the pilot of a USAF T-33 jet trainer and of an F-94B interceptor spotted "a brilliant red and white object, seemingly motionless in the sky,'' at an altitude of fifteen thousand feet. According to Donald E. Keyhoe in *The Flying Saucer Conspiracy* (1955), the fighter's radar readings corresponded with those of ground radar. Nonetheless, the pilots went on a fruitless half-hour chase that literally went in circles. The U.S. Air Force's explanation is that the pilots saw the planet Venus.

Eighteen minutes of UFO activity began at 9:05 p.m. local time on 29 June 1954. They took place some nineteen thousand feet over the wastes of southwestern Labrador, about a hundred miles northeast of Sept-Iles, Quebec. Four hours earlier the BOAC Stratocruiser had left New York en route to London. Then the encounter occurred witnessed by twenty people including seven crew members. When the plane refuelled at Goose Bay, Captain James Howard and the crew were questioned by U.S. Air Force Intelligence. The Captain called what he had seen "a solid thing,'' manoeuverable and controlled intelligently. "It must have been some weird form of spaceship from another world!'' he added.

Upon landing in London, Captain Howard described the "thing'' using an apt image: "It was something like an inverted pear suspended in the sky.'' In fact, in addition to the large "inverted pear,'' there were six smaller "things'' moving among themselves and in formation. They maintained a course parallel to the plane at a distance of about five miles. Then the pear-shaped craft altered its appearance. "It turned into what looked like a flying arrow — an enormous delta-winged plane turning in to close with us!'' In time it altered its shape again, and the smaller "things'' merged into the big "thing,'' which then shot away in a tremendous burst of speed.

Captain Howard's account of the "inspections'' was detailed and responsible. It was included by Richard H. Hall in *The UFO Evidence* (1964).

Another incident occurred on 4 September 1968 and involved two USAF pilots, flying in the vicinity of Goose Bay Air Force Base, who spotted an unidentified spherical craft headed in a southerly direction. They watched it go through manoeuvres of its own for five minutes. They filed an official report to the Herzberg Institute of Astrophysics, Planetary Sciences Section, National Research Council, Non-Meteoritic Sightings File, which makes interesting reading:

> Approximately round, silver metallic in colour, no sound and no vapour trail. Appeared to be one-half the size of a jet in flight between thirty-three and forty-one thousand feet. Speed was approximately the same as a jet. Object crossed high-flying jet track behind jet (ours). Stopped. Did two 360 degree turns. Continued for one to two minutes and stopped again. Object disappeared from view at approximately 30 degrees above the horizon and was one-half size in relation to first observation. All local facilities checked. Results negative.

"This report is typical of most classified military documents and the data is, to say the least, fragmentary,'' Bondarchuk noted.

Grand Banks/
"A Very Lion to Our Seeming"

A remarkable description of a strange creature of the sea appears in the account of Sir Humphrey Gilbert's voyage of discovery of 1583. In this account the creature bears some resemblance to a lion. It was seen by Gilbert aboard his vessel, the *Squirrel*, and by the captains of the four other vessels under his command, the principal one being the *Golden Hind*. The locale of the sighting was the Grand Banks near Cape Race.

> So upon Saturday in the afternoon, the 31 of August, we changed our course, and returned back for *England*. At which very instant, even in widing about, there passed along between us and towards the land which we now forsook a very lion to our seeming, in shape, hair, and colour, not swimming after the manner of a beast by moving of his feet, but rather sliding upon the water with his whole body, excepting the legs, in sight, neither yet diving under, and again rising above the water, as the manner is of whales, dolphins, tunnies, porpoises, and all other fish: but confidently showing himself above water without hiding: notwithstanding, we presented ourselves in open view and gesture to amaze him, as all creatures will be commonly at a sudden gaze and sight of men. Thus he passed along turning his head to and fro, yawing and gaping wide, with ugly demonstration of long teeth, and glaring eyes; and to bid us a farewell, coming right against the *Hind*, he sent forth a horrible voice, roaring or bellowing as doth a lion.

Perhaps the strange creature took a dislike to the appearance of Gilbert and made a reappearance. Whether or not it did, nine days later the *Squirrel* encountered rough weather and icebergs and sank without a trace. As it was sinking the crew aboard the *Golden Hind* could discern Gilbert sitting towards the stern with a book in his hands, repeatedly calling out, "We are as near to heaven by sea as by land!"

The description originally appeared in *The Principall Navigations, Voiages and Discoveries of the English Nation* in 1589 by Richard Hakluyt. The text in modern spelling comes from *Select Narratives from the Principal Navigations of Hakluyt* (1909) edited by Edward John Payne.

Grand Banks/ The Triangle and the *Titanic*

The Grand Banks of Newfoundland extend over the low continental shelf into the Atlantic Ocean and form a triangle, a shape which has long served as a symbol of the Trinity. Charles Berliz added a demonic twist by giving the three-sided enclosed figure a sinister character. He did so in his bestselling book *The Bermuda Triangle* (1974) in which he popularized the notion that a loosely defined area of the Atlantic Ocean is "deadly" — the graveyard of ships and planes.

Rudyard Kipling was among the first to realize that the shape of the Grand Banks was roughly triangular. In his novel *Captains Courageous* (1897) he described the Grand Banks as "a triangle two hundred and fifty miles on each side — a waste of wallowing sea, cloaked with dank fog, vexed with gales, harried with drifting ice, scored by the tracks of reckless livers, and dotted with the sails of the fishing-fleet." The notion that it was "the devil's playground" never entered his mind.

Over the centuries the Grand Banks have known considerable sea traffic and overseen tragedies too numerous to compute. Indeed, one of the greatest peacetime marine disasters of all time took place in these foggy and turbulent waters. The sinking of the White Star liner *Titanic* occurred 350 nautical miles southwest of Newfoundland on the evening of 14 April 1912. If ever a vessel represented the *hubris* of humanity it was the *Titanic*. The existence and even the name of the ocean-going vessel seemed to defy nature. It was the biggest ship that had ever been constructed. Technologically it was a marine triumph on a par with its aerospace cousins — the *Concorde* and the *Challenger*. Yet on its maiden voyage the *Titanic* duelled with an iceberg and lost. Not until 1987 were salvage operations commenced in earnest — live, on television, and carried by satellite.

Grand Banks/
"Sea Giraffe"

An unusual sea serpent that looked like a "sea giraffe" was spotted by Second Officer G. Batchelor and Quartermaster Ayres of the Allan Line steamer *Corinthian* on the Grand Banks in the early morning of 30 August 1913.

The "sea giraffe" had "great blue eyes" which were not those of a fierce sea serpent, but orbs that evoked a feeling of tenderness in the Second Officer, who decided not to shoot the animal with his rifle. First thinking it to be an overturned boat, the second officer of the *Corinthian* steered within sixty metres before a curious head rose six metres up out of the water. For a minute the creature churned water and gazed over the *Corinthian* and then drove off. A piercing wail "altogether out of proportion to its size" was heard and compared to the cry of a baby. The sighting is described by Bernard Heuvelmans in his book *In the Wake of the Sea Serpents* (1968) translated from the French by Richard Garnett.

Grates Cove/
Curious Inscriptions

Grates Cove is a settlement located on the northernmost tip of the Avalon Peninsula, where Trinity Bay and Conception Bay join the Atlantic Ocean.

About two centuries ago curious inscriptions were discovered on a boulder near the outport community of Grates Cove. The inscriptions attracted the attention of W.A. Cormack, who was the first white person to trek across Newfoundland on foot. When he did so in 1822, he made a point of visiting the remote fishing village in order to examine the markings. He noted they were man-made, they were in Latin characters, and they could be the names of the earliest explorers of the region. Harold Horwood visited the site in the postwar period, and described what he saw and thought in *Newfoundland* (1969):

> Grates Cove has a well-known rock with some old carvings on it on a cliff face well above high

water. Some of those who formerly examined it, including a curator of the Newfoundland Museum, professed to be able to read the names, "IO CABOTO," "SANCIUS," and "SAINMALIA" quite plainly. It was, of course, attributed to the first Cabot voyage, "Io Caboto" being the Italian form of John Cabot, who had gone to England from Venice. For my own part, I am unable to read anything on the rock. It certainly had some kind of inscription at one time, but I doubt that anything can be deduced from it today.

For the record, John Cabot's landfall on the east coast was made on 24 June 1497.

Heart's Content/
The Great Eastern

A new era in communications was born on 27 July 1866 when Heart's Content was linked with Valentia, Ireland, by the first successfully laid transatlantic cable. Thereafter messages between the British Isles and North America would be exchanged instantaneously by a combination of undersea cable and telegraph transmission. The undersea cable was laid by the *Great Eastern*, a passenger vessel which was specially equipped to unreel the all-important cable along the Atlantic seabed — all-important, that is, until Marconi's wireless experiments at St. John's Signal Hill in 1901.

If there ever was a jinxed ship, it was the *Great Eastern*. It was five times larger than the next-largest ship afloat. Its length was 692 feet, and it could accommodate 4,000 passengers. In fact, it was the largest ship afloat until the launching of the *Lusitania*. It was named on 31 January 1858, and was "the most ambitious project of the great nineteenth-century engineer Brunel. At nineteen thousand tons, it was the world's largest ship. Misfortunes began when a riveter and his boy apprentice disappeared during its construction," wrote Colin Wilson in *Mysteries: An Investigation into the Occult, the Paranormal and the Supernatural* (1978). "In June 1859, as it was about to be launched, Brunel realized that the splash might drown spectators and ordered a halt; the ship became stuck in the runway and took three months to free. When it was finally launched, Brunel collapsed on the deck with a stroke and died a week later.'' Wilson continued:

> From then on, the career of the *Great Eastern* was one long disaster. A funnel exploded when someone accidentally closed a safety valve; five firemen died; another was crushed in the paddle wheel. In port for repairs, the ship was damaged in a storm. The captain was drowned in a boat with a young boy. In America, another sailor was crushed in the wheel, and a man fell overboard and drowned. A two-day excursion was a non-stop catastrophe, climaxed when the ship drifted a hundred miles out to sea; many passengers got off at the first opportunity and went home by train. Now the ship had acquired such a bad reputation that she seldom carried enough passengers to pay the wages of the crew (over 400). And the disasters continued — wrecked paddle wheels, wrecked funnels, storm damage. When the ship was hired to lay the trans-Atlantic cable, she lost it halfway across and had to return empty-handed. A mere fifteeen years after its launching it was left to rust in Milford Haven. And when it was finally broken up for scrap in 1889, the skeletons of the missing riveter and his boy apprentice were found trapped in the double hull.

There is no question that the *Great Eastern* was a white elephant. But was it a hoodoo or jinxed vessel? Were the skeletons of the riveter and his apprentice found between the hulls when the vessel fell into the hands of the wreckers along the Mersey at New Ferry, Liverpool, England? It seems the story first appeared in print in *The Great Iron Ship* (1953), in which the author James Dugan described the work of the shipwreckers:

> One day they were breaching a compartment in the inner shell of the port side, when a shriek went up that stopped all work and ran widely through the port and country. One who hurried to New Ferry to see it was David Duff. He wrote me: ''They found a skeleton inside the ship's shell and the tank tops. It was the skeleton of the basher who was missing. Also the frame of the bash boy was found with him. . . . ''

Dugan's account is based on the hearsay reminiscence of a sailor sixty years after the event in question. But as Lionel T.C. Rolt, the biographer of the engineer Brunel, wrote in *Isambard Kingdom Brunel* (1957):

> In the first place, as any shipbuilder will confirm, the possibility of a riveter and his mate becoming trapped in this way is so remote as to be almost inconceivable, and in the second it is on record that twice, once at the time of floating off and again in July 1859 during the fitting out, Brunel gave orders for the space between the two hulls to be scrupulously cleaned out. When we recall the tonnage of water ballast that was pumped in and out of her the reason for these orders will be obvious.

Rolt concluded that the tale originated with ''a gang of those stalwart Merseyside shipbreakers 'telling the tale' to some credulous journalist. Anyone who has ever worked among such men will know how they delight and excel in just this kind of leg-pulling.''

Labrador/ ''The Land God Gave to Cain''

The most haunting image ever applied to Canada was the earliest and the most arresting. It is a sobering thought that, unprejudiced by the opinions of others, the otherwise unimaginative explorer Jacques Cartier turned to the Old Testament to capture in a few words the appearance and effect on him of the bleak northern shore of today's Labrador.

Sailing the Gulf of St. Lawrence during the summer of 1534, the French navigator was shaken by the wilderness that he saw. As he wrote in his ''Première Relation'': ''In fine I am rather inclined to believe that this is the land God gave to Cain.'' More than four centuries later the historian Samuel Eliot Morison retraced Cartier's voyage, but by plane rather than by ship and wrote: "The desolation is the same today: granite hills smoothed by a glacier, stunted spruce in the valleys and the only green, and all extending northwards as far as the eye can see."

The desolation of Labrador is said to be the haunt of the Phantom Trapper or the Damned Trapper. Following several accounts there was once a trapper who led a wicked life. Despite his vile acts, which included peddling poisoned alcohol and attacking local women, he never repented his crimes and sins and died a natural death. But in death he found no rest, for to atone for his sins he was cursed to drive through the snow throughout eternity a matched team of fourteen pure white huskies. The vision of the Phantom Trapper making his ghostly rounds is said to be a harrowing one. Yet Newfoundlanders rejoice in the sight of him and his team, for he helps to guide lost travellers and trappers through blizzards to safety. This cursed, Cain-like creature was last spotted on his life-saving rounds in 1959.

Northwest River/
A Case of Hexing

The following case of hexing occurred at the Hospital at Northwest River, a local improvement district northeast of Goose Bay in Labrador. The account comes from *Arthur C. Clarke's World of Strange Powers* (1984) by John Fairley and Simon Welfare.

> In 1965 three doctors from Labrador in Canada wrote to *The British Medical Journal* about a case of a mother of five children who had suddenly died after an apparently successful minor operation. She was one week short of her 43rd birthday. Only afterwards did the doctors discover that, 38 years previously, when she was five years old, a fortune teller had informed her she would die before the age of 43.
>
> The woman had come through the operation, for an incontinence problem, at the Northwest River Hospital in Labrador, perfectly normally: she regained consciousness and seemed fine. Then suddenly, an hour later, she collapsed with all the symptoms of shock, including low blood pressure. Oxygen, cortisone, the full array of indicated treatment, had no effect and she died the next day at five in the morning. On the morning of the operation she had told a nurse she was sure she was going to die. Unknowing, the doctors went ahead with the operation. At the post-mortem they found bleeding round the adrenal glands and elsewhere, but nothing to indicate why a perfectly healthy woman had succumbed, as she had prophesied. Only then did it emerge that she had told her sister, who knew of the prophecy, that she did not expect to emerge from the anaesthetic, and that for years she had told her daughter that she would die by the age of 43.

Peckford Island/
The *Brendan* Landfall

St. Brendan, the Irish abbot and navigator, flourished between 484 and 579. Some three centuries later an unknown scribe set down the narrative of his wonderful voyages. The narrative is a concoction: the distillation of the North Atlantic experience with the bouquet of the Celtic imagination.

Yet these fabulous voyages inspired Tim Severn, a modern-day adventurer, to attempt the Atlantic crossing from Ireland to Newfoundland to prove it a medieval possibility. He constructed a traditional, coracle-like vessel of leather, and christened it the *Brendan*. In it he braved the North Atlantic; with it he made his landfall on Peckford Island.

The bleak island on which he landed on 26 June 1977 lies off the east coast of Newfoundland, southeast of Fogo Island. It has no known associations with the semi-legendary St. Brendan. Yet it is conceivable that St. Brendan, in search of the Earthly Paradise, found Newfoundland; certainly Tim Severin, in recreating one of a number of possible medieval voyages of the North Atlantic, reached Peckford Island.

As the researcher Geoffrey Ashe noted in *Land to the West: St. Brendan's Voyage to America* (1962), the ancient accounts describe St. Brendan in search of "the land promised to the saints" and "the land on the far side" making a landfall on what he and his fellow voyagers mistakenly believed to be an island. Here they dined and celebrated mass. Midway through the service the island moved and was ascertained to be the broad back of a whale! They hurriedly make for their coracles. On the Piri Re'is Map there is a tiny drawing of St. Brendan lunching on the back of a whale and entertaining an angelic-looking siren. It is tempting to imagine St. Brendan dining on Peckford Island, if not on the back of a humpback whale.

Portugal Cove/
Battle with a Sea Serpent

An exciting battle with a sea serpent, as vivid as anything that takes place underwater in Jules Verne's novel *Twenty Thousand Leagues Under the Sea*, may have occurred off Portugal Cove in Conception Bay. The date of the epic encounter between two local men and one local monster is generally given as 26 October 1873.

According to the earliest reports recorded by the Rev. Moses Harvey, two fishermen, Theophile Piccot and Daniel Squires, saw something floating on the water's surface. Striking it with a boat-hook, the mass came alive, revealing itself to be a huge squid with glaring eyes and a beak "as large as a six-gallon keg." Two arms shot out from the water as the monster seized the boat and appeared ready to drag it under.

Despite his terror, one of them grabbed a small axe and chopped through the two arms till they were severed. The monster retreated and blackened the water with clouds of ink. The men hauled the arms into their boat and made for shore in haste. The arms were proof of their brush with a true kraken. One arm became food for the dogs; the other was measured and found to be 19 feet in length. If there was another 10 feet of the arm left on the giant, and its body was at least another 10 feet in length, then its entire length would have been nearly 40 feet.

The remaining arm was brought to St. John's, examined by the Rev. Harvey and Alexander Murray of the Geological Commission of Canada, and preserved in an alcohol solution. Later versions of this story not only give the date as 27 October 1873, instead of the 26th, as first recorded, but also introduce Piccot's ten-year-old son as the wielder of the axe and the one whose presence of mind saved all their lives.

Moses Harvey's accounts may be found in the Montreal *Gazette* of 26 November 1873 and in the *Maritime Monthly*, March 1874. He also mentions the event in *Newfoundland* (1883), co-authored with Joseph Hatton.

St. John's/
"A Maremaid"

The earliest and most celebrated single description of a strange creature in the annals of Canadian history and literature is the account of "a maremaid" which was recorded by Captain Richard Whitbourne. Although the account is close to four centuries old, its peculiar charm helps it to withstand the ravages of time.

The creature, whether mermaid or not, was seen in St. John's harbour by Whitbourne, his navigator William Hawkeridge, and crew members of their ship and other ships in the harbour in the summer of 1610. The mermaid was spotted under favourable viewing conditions. Their ship was at rest, and they watched in wonder as the creature attempted to board their vessel.

Whitbourne went on to become governor of Vaughan's colony and his descriptions of Newfoundland life are prized today for their historical interest. Here is what he said he and others saw:

> I espied verily swiftly to come swimming towards me, looking cheerfully, as it had beene a woman, by the Face, Eyes, Nose, Mouth, Chin, Eares, Necke and Forehead: It seemed to be so beautifull and in those parts so well proportioned, having round about upon the head,

all blew strakes, resembling haire, downe to the Necke. . . . I beheld the shoulders and backe downe to the middle, to be as square, white and smooth as the backe of a man, and from the middle to the hinder part, pointing in proportion like a board hooked Arrow. . . . The same came shortly after unto a Boate, wherein one William Hawkridge, then my seruant, was . . . and the same Creature did put both his hands upon the side of the Boate, and did strive to come in to him and others then in the said Boate. . . . Whether it were a Maremaid or no, I know not; I leave it for others to judge.

The celebrated description from the voyage to Newfoundland of 1610 appeared in Whitbourne's treatise *A Discourse and Discovery of New-found-land* (1620). The account was preserved by Samuel Purchas and Richard Haklyut.

St. John's/
The *Charles Haskell*

An accident occurred when the *Charles Haskell*, a Boston fishing schooner, was being outfitted for cod fishing. It was said that during the outfitting a workman slipped on the companionway and broke his neck. The maiden voyage of the fishing vessel was also marred when the captain refused to take it out and at the last minute a substitute had to be found.

But the incident that marked the *Charles Haskell* and turned it into one of the best-known hoodoo vessels occurred off Georges Bank. Accounts differ, but it seems that on 7 March 1866 there was a sudden storm at sea. The captain observed the rapid approach of another fishing vessel, the *Andrew Jackson* of Salem, Massachusetts. He gave orders to cut the anchor, with the result that the *Haskell*, cut loose, rammed the *Andrew Jackson*. The latter ship sank and all hands were lost. The *Haskell* sustained some damage but recorded no loss of life. It limped back to St. John's harbour.

The following spring it was taken back to the Georges Bank area and after six days out something

inexplicable occurred. Two men on the midnight watch were alarmed when they observed the bobbing of human heads in the sea around the *Haskell*. Men in oilskins, streaming with water, silently slipped over the rails. They spoke not a word. They had no eyes, merely empty sockets. The two horrified men called for the captain and he too observed the ghostly crew. Twenty-six phantom sailors took up positions along the rail and went through the motions of baiting and sinking. With the approach of dawn, they silently slipped over the rails and returned to the depths of the sea.

The same thing happened the next night. At dusk the spectral sailors appeared and fished until dawn. But when they slipped over the rails, they did not return to the sea. Instead, when they left the vessel, they walked across the waves in a grim, mute procession in the direction of Salem. The *Haskell* returned to St. John's, and word got around that the ship was a hoodoo. No sailor would agree to set foot on the vessel. Consequently it was tied to the wharf and abandoned by its owners. It was finally towed out to sea and burnt to the waterline.

St. Lunaire-Griquet/
The Ogham Stone

Possible proof of the Celtic occupation of the east coast of Canada lies in the yet-to-be deciphered inscription on the so-called Ogham Stone. This mysterious stone is a large boulder imbedded in the side of a cliff halfway up the steep slope of a wild and deserted cove on the northern tip of Newfoundland. The locale is close to St. Lunaire-Griquet, which is somewhat south of L'Anse aux Meadows where Viking ruins have been reconstructed.

Any Celtic exploration and occupation of the east coast would have occurred five centuries prior to the establishment of the Norse settlement, which took place about A.D. 1000. Ogham is the name given an ancient script that was employed by the ancient Druids. With its long lines and smattering of dots, it looks quite unlike any Indian petroglyphs or Norse runic characters. Ogham went out of use when Ireland

The markings on the Ogham Stone may or may not offer evidence that wayfaring Irish monks visited Eastern Canada a thousand years before Cabot made his landfall in 1497. In 1974, Robert McGhee of the Archaeological Survey of Canada was led to the rock which lies southwest of L'Anse aux Meadows on the northern tip of Newfoundland. McGhee has speculated on the origin of the markings. "I doubt very much that the inscription is Irish," he concluded in 1988, "but have no idea what it could be." [Robert McGhee]

was converted to Christianity in the fifth century. The odd markings on the boulder at St. Lunaire-Griquet may be the handiwork of man; may be Ogham or some other script; or may be the work of natural forces like erosion or glaciation.

The boulder was brought to national attention in the early 1970s when two archaeologists, James Tuck and Robert McGhee, were directed to the site by a local fisherman, Lloyd Decker, who had acted as a caretaker at L'Anse aux Meadows in 1960. Lichen covered the surface of the boulder. "If it was a hoax," wrote Noel Moore in *Maclean's*, April 1975, "it was perpetrated in the late 1700s or later by someone in a remote part of the island with a working knowledge of a script that hadn't been used since the fifth century.

By coincidence, when McGhee made his find he was carrying a copy of Robert Graves' *The White Goddess* (1947), and the similarities between the carvings on the rock and the Ogham code reproduced in Graves' book about Druids leaped out at him."

As Moore pointed out, the Druids hold an anomalous position in world history. Little is known of their philosophy and practices, but global cultural influence has been attributed to this Celtic sect. "Clement of Alexandria, who had access to the great library of Alexandria before the Romans burned it, wrote that, far from being barbarians, it was the Druids who taught geometry, philosophy and civilization to the Greeks. Pythagoras claimed that the Druids of Gaul were the wisest men in the world."

It has been noted that straight tracks or lines, sometimes called ley lines, connect sacred sites throughout Britain and Western Europe. There may well be transatlantic ley lines, for as Moore observed:

> If you take a globe, with the meridians clearly marked, and place a line halfway between the 51st and 52nd degrees of north latitude it will pass through all the ancient places of Druidic mythology. The line will pass south of the Dingle Peninsula in Ireland, where Brendan started his journey; it will pass through Stonehenge, Avebury and a half a dozen other famous sites. If you continue that line across the Atlantic, it will pass somewhere between l'Anse aux Meadows and the Ogham Stone.

Trinity Bay/
The Monster Devil Fish

A fascinatingly detailed account of the beaching of a giant cuttle-fish appeared on 27 October 1877 in the *Canadian Illustrated News*. It is unsigned.

THE MONSTER DEVIL FISH

The latest edition to the remarkable collection in the New York Aquarium is by far the most curious of all specimens. It is a monster cuttle-fish, made familiar to the public by Victor Hugo as the devil-fish. The present one is the largest that has ever been seen, and, while to the student it is a choice object of examination, to the uneducated public it is a most horrible-looking creature. On the 22nd September a heavy equinoctial gale swept the shores of St. John's, Newfoundland, and this wanderer was driven ashore in an exhausted condition at Catalina, on the northern shore of Trinity Bay. The tail had got fast on a rock as it was swimming backward, and it was rendered powerless. In its desperate efforts to escape, the ten arms darted about in all directions, lashing the water into foam, the thirty-foot tentacles in particular making lively play as it shot them out and endeavoured to get a "purchase" with their powerful suckers, so as to drag itself into deep water. It was only when it became exhausted and the tide receded that the fishermen ventured to approach it. It died soon after the ebb of the tide, which left it high and dry on the beach. Two fishermen took possession of the "treasure trove," and the whole settlement gathered to gaze in astonishment at the monster. The two men loaded their little craft with the body of the gigantic cuttle, and arrived with it at St. John's on the 26th ult., in a perfectly fresh condition. As soon as the news spread an eager desire to view the monster was awakened, and the fishermen were advised to exhibit it before the public. The Government granted the use of the drill-shed for the purpose, and on the floor, supported by boards, the creature was laid out in all its gigantic proportions. The lucky fishermen reaped a golden harvest and found the big squid by far the best catch they had ever made. The scene was very curious. There lay the cuttle with its ten arms stretched out, two of them 30 feet in length, having rows of powerful suckers an inch in diameter at their broadened extremities. The other arms, eight in number, were entirely covered with suckers on the under side, and were 11 feet in length. The body is 10 feet in length and nearly 7 feet in circumference, and terminates in a caudal fin 2 feet 9 inches across. When taken from the water the color of the squid was a dusky red, but that has disappeared, and the body and arms are now perfectly white. There is the usual horny beak, the parrot-like mandibles of which project from a membraneous bag in the centre of the mass which contitutes the head, and from which the ten arms radiate. Certainly the idea of being clutched in those terrible arms, from which there could be no escape when once they had closed, and then torn and rent by the formidable beak, is enough to send a shuddering thrill through the stoutest heart. Posterior to the head were a pair of huge staring eyes, the sockets being eight inches in diameter. Their expression, when the creature was alive on the beach, is said by the fishermen to have been particularly ferocious.

15

The Giant Squid or Monster Devil Fish was the largest squid reported to that time. Such finds were called Krakens, after the mysterious creatures of the deep. Creatures of such size and shape have a menacing appearance, to say the least, and they must have given fishermen and sailors pause. It is small wonder that such living creatures have been associated with the legendary monsters of the deep from the ancient past.

"Capture of a Monster Devil-Fish, at Catalina, Trinity Bay." So reads the caption of this engraving, which astonished readers of the 27 October 1877 issue of the Canadian Illustrated News. *The giant cuttle-fish, driven ashore during a storm, caught its tail on a rock and was unable to return to the sea. Two fishermen took possession of the beached fish and exhibited it. Each of the eight arms was said to be eleven feet in length. Its final home was the New York Aquarium.* [Metropolitan Toronto Library]

NOVA SCOTIA

Acadia/
Greek and Egyptian Parallels

The east coast of North America was explored in 1524 by Giovanni da Verrazzano. He was a Florentine and the most highly educated of the early explorers, so it is reasonable to assume that when he gave the name *Acadie* or *Acadia* to the lands he claimed, he wished to equate them with the Arcadia of Ancient Greece, the rustic and pastoral land of myth and legend. Verrazzano's region grew to comprise the southeastern portion of Quebec, eastern Maine, and all of New Brunswick, Nova Scotia, and Prince Edward Island. Another reasonable assumption is that Verrazzano was familiar with the local Micmac word, *quoddy* or *cady*, which means "land" or "territory." The fortuitous francized pun identifies the Micmacs of the Maritime Acadia with the Arcadian inhabitants of the Greek Arcadia.

The Greek Arcadia, isolated in the Peloponnesus, was a region of shepherds and huntsmen who worshipped nature deities long after the more advanced Greeks had established city states. The Athenians saw the Arcadians as preserving man's customs in an uncorrupt state from the earliest days of the world. However, in a later period the Arcadians were seen as a primitive and ignorant people. The stone-age Micmacs may have brought to Verrazzano's mind the iron-age Arcadians.

The prehistorian and epigrapher Barry Fell suggested there are also parallels between the Micmacs and the Ancient Egyptians. Some two thousand years ago, he contended in *America B.C.: Ancient Settlers in the New World* (1976), the Egyptians sailed to America and back, perhaps on a regular basis. They introduced to the natives of the New World one of their most prized possessions, knowledge of their system of hieroglyphic writing. Fell went as far as to make a more provocative suggestion by asking the following leading question: "Are the Micmac and related Algonquians the descendants of ancient settlers from Egypt?" He concluded that there is no proof to support this possibility. But he went on to note a wealth of circumstantial evidence for a theory of cultural diffusion — parallels between Old World and New World cultural traditions; epigraphy (principally inscriptions on rocks), and language (loan words, glyphs) — all of which suggested that the Micmacs owe an unacknowledged debt to the Ancient Egyptians for their traditions and language.

Lake Ainslie/
Eels for Real?

Many sightings of a serpent-like monster have been reported from Lake Ainslie, a large body of water near the west coast of Cape Breton Island. Stuart Trueman mentions these in *Tall Tales and True: Tales from Down East* (1979):

> "We must find a valid physical explanation for the very convincing reports that have come from

17

places like Lake Ainslie and Lake Utopia," said Dr. Carl Medcof, a retired research scientist formerly with the St. Andrews, New Brunswick, Fisheries Biological Station. "Such reports should not be lightly dismissed. If we laugh at the people who report the sightings, we are the fools, not they."

It was Medcof's intriguing suggestion that the serpent-like monsters were really balled-up eels — hundreds of them in one conglomeration, like worms dumped out of an angler's tin can. Medcof himself observed these. "He has seen big clumps of eels such as those reported from time to time in Cape Breton's Lake Ainslie," Trueman noted.

Eel-balls are seen in deep water in late summer. They can measure six feet in diameter, and they bob up and down in the water in a slow rolling motion. It would not be difficult to mistake them for sea serpents.

Amherst/
The Great Amherst Mystery

Today there stands a Canadian Tire Store at the corner of Princess Street and Church Street in downtown Amherst. One would think there would be a plaque to mark the Cox Family Cottage which stood at 6 Princess Street. After all, in 1878–79 it was the site of the Great Amherst Mystery, one of the world's most widely reported hauntings. At one time all that anyone in Canada or elsewhere in the English-speaking world knew about Amherst was that it was the "home" of the Great Amherst Mystery.

American actor and author Walter Hubbell lived for six weeks in the Cox Family Cottage at 6 Princess Street and penned a graphic account of the events that took place there. His paper-bound booklet, sixty pages in length, went through innumerable printings. It was one of the most widely read, real-life accounts of a poltergeist-like experience ever published.

A sense of the contents of Hubbell's book may be gleaned from a glance at its wordy title page, for its full title runs as follows: *THE HAUNTED HOUSE: A*

Here is how the town of Amherst appeared—the calm before the storm—in this engraving based on a sketch by the artist A.J. Hill. The engraving appeared in the Canadian Illustrated News *on 9 December 1876. The Cox Family lived here in a little cottage. In 1878-79, the cottage housed the most notorious poltergeist in the history of the hauntings of the nineteenth century in Canada and the United States. [Public Archives of Nova Scotia]*

True Ghost Story. Being an account of the Mysterious Manifestations that have taken place in the presence of ESTHER COX, the young Girl who is possessed by Devils, and has become known throughout the entire Dominion as THE GREAT AMHERST MYSTERY, by WALTER HUBBELL. The Author Lived in the House and Witnessed the Wonderful Manifestations (1879).

Walter Hubbell presents himself to the reader as an honest man, one who came to scoff but remained to accept. He explains his interest in what he calls the "manifestations" by informing the reader that he followed the newspaper accounts of the astonishing state of affairs in Amherst since their inception in September 1878. He says he resolved to visit the Nova Scotian town to see for himself and be prepared to expose fraud, if necessary. The truth is much more interesting, for he had a secret agenda. He wanted to combine spiritualism and showmanship.

Hubbell, completing a theatrical tour with an engagement in Newfoundland, made his way to Amherst, arriving on 11 June 1879. By this time the manifestations were more than ten months old and had but another two months to run. He claims he interviewed all the members of the Cox family and various members of the community, gradually coming to the conclusion that the manifestations were genuine and that Esther Cox was possessed. Indeed, the young woman was possessed of more than one spirit. When he was not busy with other matters, he wrote his booklet, which is best known under its reprint title, *The Great Amherst Mystery*.

An extended close-knit family of eight people was living in the Cox Family Cottage, a two-story, yellow-painted wooden house, in September 1878. The cottage was owned by Daniel Teed, a shoemaker, and his hard-working wife Olive. They had two children, Willie, five, and George, seventeen months. In addition, two brothers lived in the cottage, John Teed, Daniel's brother, and William Cox, Olive's brother. Finally, two of Olive's sisters lived there, Jane and Esther. Jane, twenty-two, was described as both lady-like and beautiful; Esther, eighteen, was short and stout. The sisters shared an upstairs bedroom.

Esther Cox, the centre of all the poltergeist-like happenings, was born in Upper Stewiacke, New Brunswick, on 28 March 1860. She was underweight at birth, at nine months weighing only five pounds. Her mother died when she was three weeks old, her father married again and moved to Maine, so Esther was raised by a kindly grandmother. "Esther's early years having been spent with her grandmother, she very naturally became grave and old-fashioned, without knowing how or why," explained Hubbell.

The two young women retired early the night of 4 September 1878, and Jane fell fast asleep, but Esther did not sleep well. Perhaps she was still bothered by an event that had taken place one week earlier, memories of which deeply disturbed her. That evening she accepted the invitation of a handsome young shoemaker named Bob McNeal to ride in his buggy through the woods. Suddenly McNeal dropped the reins and leaped from the buggy. He drew a large revolver and pointing it at Esther ordered her to get out or he would kill her. She refused and told him to stop acting like a crazy man. With that he became enraged and uttered several terrible oaths. Aiming the revolver at her heart, he was about to fire when there was the sound of wheels in the distance. He immediately jumped into the buggy, seized the reins, and drove at breakneck speed back to Amherst. Esther cried herself to sleep that night.

One week later she was still crying herself to sleep. Her sister was worried. "Esther," said Jane, "do you know I think you are losing your mind, and that if you keep on this way you will get so crazy that we will have to put you in the Insane Asylum." But Esther complained of mice in the bed, and then both girls heard a rustling sound.

> So they both arose, and on hearing a rustling in a green paste-board box, filled with patch-work, which was under the bed, they placed it out in the middle of the room and were much amazed to see the box jump up in the air about a foot and then fall over on its side. The girls could not believe their own eyes; so Jane placed the box in its old position in the middle of the room, and both watched it intently, when to their amazement the same thing occurred again. The girls were now really frightened, and screamed as loudly as they could for Dan, who put on some clothing and came into their room to ascertain what was the matter. They told him what had just taken place, but he only laughed, and after pushing the box under the bed, and remarking that they must be insane or perhaps had been dreaming, he went back to bed.

The next evening Esther leapt with a sudden bound into the centre of the room screaming, "I'm dying, I'm dying!"

> Jane thought her sister only had the nightmare, but when she lit the lamp, she was considerably alarmed by her sister's appearance. There stood Esther in the centre of the room, her short hair almost standing on end, her face as red as blood, and her eyes really looked as if they were about to start from their sockets, her hands were grasping the back of a chair so tightly that her nails sank into the soft wood.

19

Jane summoned help and the whole family crowded into the little bedroom. They declared that Esther was insane and assisted her back into bed. She felt feverish yet her features looked as pale as death. Then something truly surprising happened: "While the family stood looking at her, wondering what would relieve her, for her entire body had swollen to an enormous size and she was screaming with pain and grinding her teeth as if in a fit, a loud report like thunder was heard in the room." More terrible sounds were heard directly under the bed. "They were so loud that the whole room shook, and Esther who a moment before had been swollen to such an enormous size, immediately assumed her natural appearance, and sank into a state of calm repose. As soon as they found that it was sleep and not death that had taken possession of her, they all left the room except Jane, who went back to bed beside her sister, but could not sleep a wink for the balance of the night."

Four nights later the bedclothes suddenly flew through the air in the direction of a low-burning lamp. Esther's body swelled, retorts were heard, the body subsided, and Esther fell into a deep sleep. The next day the family physician, Dr. Caritte, was consulted. He dismissed the events as "nonsense" but promised to examine Esther that evening. He arrived and no sooner had he diagnosed Esther's condition as "nervous excitement" than he and the rest of the family observed the pillow under his patient's head moving backward and forward of its own accord. He heard the same sounds as were reported the previous evenings, and he watched in amazement the flight of bedclothes across the room. Then everyone heard a peculiar noise.

. . . the sound as of some person writing on the wall with a sharp instrument was heard. All looked at the wall whence the sound of writing came, when to their great astonishment there was seen written, near the head of the bed, in large characters, these words: "Esther Cox, you are mine to kill." Everybody could see the writing plainly, and yet only a moment before nothing was to be seen but the blank wall.

Thereafter the doctor called daily. Poltergeist-like happenings were reported day and night as emanating from different rooms of the house. Esther did not have to be in the room in question, but no manifestations took place when she was outside the house. In the cellar, potatoes were pitched through the air. Pounding sounds could be heard from the roof of the cottage, as if someone with a hammer were trying to break through the shingles. Esther finally unburdened her mind of the incident with Bob McNeal. The doctor felt that this accounted for his patient's agitated state. Then loud reports were heard and Jane suggested that "whatever agency makes these noises" could hear and understand them. They asked the "agency" how many were present in the room. It knocked five times on the floor, the correct answer.

Esther was taken ill with diphtheria and confined to bed for two weeks in December during which time the manifestations ceased. Upon her recovery she stayed with a married sister, Mrs. John Snowden, in Sackville, New Brunswick. No sooner did she return to the homestead than she heard a voice saying that the house would be set on fire that very night. As if to dramatize the danger, eight or ten lighted matches materialized on the ceiling and fell to the floor and had to be extinguished by those present. As long as Esther remained in the cottage, there were bursts of flame, some large, some small. Often they broke out simultaneously in different parts of the cottage.

It was decided that Esther should leave the cottage. She was taken in by friendly farmers, Mr. and Mrs. John White, and she had spent two weeks on their farm in January 1879 when their utensils and implements began to appear and disappear.

There is something still more remarkable, however, about the following manifestation: Some person tried the experiment of placing three or four large iron spikes on Esther's lap while she was seated in the Dining Saloon. To the astonishment of everybody, the spikes were not removed by the ghost, but instead, became too hot to be handled with comfort, a second afterwards were thrown by the ghost to the far end of the saloon, a distance of twenty feet.

In late March, Esther was the guest of Captain James Beck in Saint John, New Brunswick, who arranged a sort of *séance* at which the spirit was queried through the use of knocks, one for yes, three for no. It emerged that Esther was possessed of a host of contending spirits of dead persons.

After three weeks with Captain Beck she was the guest of Mr. and Mrs. Van Amburgh and remained with them at their residence outside Amherst for eight weeks of calm. Then she returned to Amherst where the occupants of the household were joined by Walter Hubbell, who arrived on 21 June 1879.

No sooner had Hubbell entered the "haunted house" and set down his umbrella than it took off under its own power and passed through the air a distance of fifteen feet. Then a carving knife flew at him, clattering harmlessly to the floor. These were only the first of hundreds of objects to take flight over the days and weeks to follow. Other objects disappeared from one place to appear later in another.

Hubbell devoted almost a full day to extracting pins that suddenly sprouted from Esther's arms. At other times she would drift into "a mesmeric sleep, during which she talked about people invisible to all present; among others, her dead mother." Then there was a *séance* that offered a round of introductions:

> During the afternoon, while in the parlour, the author made the acquaintance of all the ghosts, — Bob Nickle, the chief ghost; Maggie Fisher, another ghost almost as bad as Bob; Peter Cox, a quiet old fellow of very little use as a ghost, because he never tries to break chairs, etc.; Mary Fisher, (who says she is Maggie's sister) Jane Nickle and Eliza McNeal.

Hubbell's booklet is notable for both its inclusions and its exclusions. Hubbell reconstructed the events of the first ten months, events that he himself did not witness. Then there is the problem of dates. He said he arrived in Amherst to meet Esther Cox for the first time on 21 June 1879. Yet a news report published in the Moncton *Despatch* three days earlier placed him in the province in the company of Esther Cox and the neighbour John White.

What were they doing together? Hubbell was certainly not there to expose her manifestations as fraud; in fact, he was there to promote them. He was combining his two interests in spiritualism and his sense of showmanship by mounting a theatrical entertainment based on the Great Amherst Mystery, starring himself, the popular tragedian, and Esther Cox, the new-found medium. The première of the Hubbell-Cox show was held in Moncton, New Brunswick, at Ruddick's Hall, on Friday, 13 June. There was a repeat performance Saturday evening.

On Wednesday, 18 June, they left by train for Chatham, New Brunswick, where Hubbell's concluding remarks were interrupted by an old man in the audience rising, shaking his cane, and shouting, "Young man, beware!" Hubbell continued his speech, Esther took a fast bow, the curtain was quickly brought down, and Hubbell, Esther, and John White braved the mob that had gathered outside the hall to reach the safety of their hotel. They cancelled their second night's program and returned to Amherst on 20 June 1879. It is true he set foot in the Cox Family Cottage the following day, but for the second time.

Hubbell's contribution to the Great Amherst Mystery did not end with the publication of his booklet later that year. Over the subsequent years he must have brooded about the incidents that took place in 1878–79. Thirty years later, in June 1908, he paid a return visit to Amherst, found the Cox Family Cottage still standing, and boarded there again. He sought out members of the family and the community and interviewed them. Sixteen of them supplied him with a testimonial vouching for the veracity of every word in his booklet.

Later, Esther secured a position on the farm of Arthur Davison, Clerk of the County Court. When his barn burned down he had her arrested and charged with arson. The judge and jury found her guilty, sentencing her to four months in prison, but she was released after serving only one month. Davison is on record as saying that in her presence he and his wife watched things fly about "but we got so used to it we put up with all those things as it was hard at the time to get help. . . . "

The record becomes unclear at this point. One source suggested that Esther was exorcised by a Micmac medicine man and that the exorcism was completely successful. Another source, noting that the disturbances around Esther were cyclic and came to a climax every twenty-eight days, observed that they died out completely when she married. She married a Mr. Adams in Springdale, Nova Scotia, and after his death a man named Shanahan. She had a son by each marriage. For many years she lived in Brockton, Massachusetts, where she was interviewed by the renowned psychical researcher Hereward Carrington. She died at the age of fifty-two in Brockton on 8 November 1912 and is buried there.

Thus ended the Hubbell-Cox presentation called the Great Amherst Mystery, which R.S. Lambert in *Exploring the Supernatural in Canada* (1955) called "a classic case of poltergeist haunting, rarely equalled in any part of the world."

The German philosopher Hegel suggested that history repeats itself, the first time as tragedy, the second time as farce. It certainly occurred tragically with the haunting of the Cox Family Cottage in Nova Scotia in the late nineteenth-century; it was certainly replayed farcically in early twentieth-century England as the haunting of Borley Rectory.

Borley Rectory was a squat, unattractive brick residence erected in 1863 near Sudbury, Essex. The spectre of a nun and a phantom coach were reputed to haunt the Rectory. But it was not until the 1930s that the simple haunted house became the seat of a series of poltergeist-like disturbances. These were investigated and publicized by Harry Price, the journalist and "ghosthunter," who "boomed" the occurrences in newspaper articles and in the two books he devoted to Borley called *The Most Haunted House in England* (1940) and *The End of Borley Rectory* (1945). Although the residence was destroyed by fire in 1939, for many years thereafter it was known as "the most haunted house in England."

Borley's notoriety was at its height during the years that it was occupied by the Rev. Lionel Algernon Foyster and his wife Marianne. Their period of incumbency, corresponding to the years from 1930 to 1935,

attracted the attention of the historian of psychical research Trevor H. Hall; it also prompted Iris M. Owen and Paulene Mitchell to examine the effects reported during these years in "The Alleged Haunting of Borley Rectory," *Journal* of the Society for Psychical Research, Sept. 1979.

Owen and Mitchell, building on Hall's work, established for a fact that the effects reported by Price and others as occurring at Borley Rectory in the 1930s were a replay of those reported at Amherst in the 1870s. The two hauntings continents apart were linked by Lionel and Marianne Forster, both of whom were born in England. Lionel accepted a Church of England rectorship at Sackville, N.B., and was thereafter joined by Marianne who was twenty-one years his junior. They were married in Sackville in 1922. It was at this time that Lionel read Hubbell's book on the Great Amherst Mystery; he was later to find some use for it. The couple resided briefly in Saint John before returning to England and taking up residency at Borley Rectory.

Lionel's health was poor, they had no savings, so he was worried about Marianne's prospects. He encouraged her to marry, bigamously, a travelling salesman from Ipswich, which she did. He also wrote a number of fictional accounts of life at Borley Rectory, capitalizing on its local reputation as a haunted house. He simply transported across the Atlantic the effects that were reported from the Cox Family Cottage and said that they had occurred at Borley. Lionel made no attempt to hide his gentle deception; indeed, he named one of his fictional characters Teed, after the shoemaker and *pater familias* in Amherst. Harry Price—true to the traditions of Fleet Street journalism of the day—simply reported Lionel's fiction as observed fact. He gave it national—and international—exposure.

Thus what had worked for Hubbell at Amherst worked even better for Price at Borley. What impressed the historian Hall was that Amherst and Borley had in common "the almost precisely similar pattern of the 'phenomena'." Hall quoted Lionel's admission that he had never seen any of the apparitions that were said to be so plentiful at Borley at the time of his incumbency. Marianne, although she disliked

Price, was not averse to reporting an effect or two of her own for good measure—and for future prosperity perhaps. But Price was the only person to prosper from the Borley revelations.

What happened to Marianne? There is no record that she divorced the salesman from Ipswich, but following Lionel's death she had an affair with an American G.I. stationed in England. During his absence in Europe she faked a pregnancy and secretly adopted an infant. A bigamous marriage resulted. At the war's end, with child, she emigrated to the United States—a war bride.

Some years later there was an amicable divorce. In the late 1970s, Marianne herself was in her late seventies and living in the vicinity of Philadelphia. When interviewed by Pauline Mitchell, Marianne cagily suggested that all the events at Borley Rectory had been staged.

Annapolis Royal/
The Grey Lady

The Grey Lady is reputed to haunt Stony Beach, on the Annapolis River, not far from the Habitation at Annapolis Royal. Many years ago a small vessel sailed up the Annapolis Basin. Aboard it was a lady dressed in grey and a deep-sea fisherman from these parts who would run ships to foreign ports. When the vessel sailed down again, the lady was not to be seen. It was believed that the fisherman, who was married with a family living in the region, brought this lady back with him from a foreign port. He knew not what to do with her, so he took her ashore at Stony Beach and murdered her.

It is this lady who appears, wearing a short skirt on some occasions, a long gown on others, a shawl, and a bonnet, all coloured grey. As she moves her feet do not seem to touch the ground. She pauses as if she wishes to unburden herself of the tragedy that befell her, but she disappears before a word is said.

Annapolis Royal/
The Deadly Duel

Today there is a branch of the Royal Bank of Canada in Annapolis Royal, which stands on the site of an

inn that was in operation in the 1830s. Helen Creighton tells an intriguing story about that inn in *Bluenose Ghosts* (1957).

A young officer staying at the inn arrived late for a rendezvous with a young woman. Pale and trembling, he apologized, explaining, "I spent the night at the inn and, after I had been asleep for a while, I woke up and heard somebody fumbling at my door. The door was bolted on the inside, so I knew nobody could get in. But they did get in, not only one man but two. I noticed particularly how they were dressed. They both wore top boots turned down, long military coats, and tricorn hats with plumes. They appeared to be very gallant gentlemen. Then without a word to me, or any sign that they were aware of my presence, they took off their coats, drew their swords, and had a duel right there in my room. I was in such a state of terror that I couldn't speak, and I could do nothing but watch in a horrid fascination. The duel went on until one man ran the other through with his sword, and then wiped the bloody blade on the counterpane. Then, as though that were not enough, he picked the body up and threw it out the window."

Today nobody remembers whether the young woman believed the young officer. But when the Royal Bank was built, the body of a man was found dressed as described by the young officer. The body was dressed in a uniform that was either French or English of the seventeenth or eighteenth century. Officers of both countries at various times were garrisoned in the vicinity.

Antigonish/
"Mountain Rory"

The following tale was told at Antigonish Harbour.

There lived at the rear of a farm at Antigonish Harbour an old man who was remarkable for Second Sight. He was popularly known as "Mountain Rory." One morning the owner of the farm came into the house and said: "Mountain Rory had a strange story for me this morning. He told me that when he was coming over the mountain early today he saw a great many men working out there, some digging, some building a railway, and so on. Whoever lives to see it, there will be some kind of works set up out at the rear of this farm yet.'' This year (1928) the prediction is being verified. A company has bought up that land, with its fine gypsum deposits, and are at this writing building a railway out to the Harbour.

The tale was recorded by Mary L. Fraser in *Folklore of Nova Scotia* (1932, 1975).

Antigonish/
"The Little Man Who Wasn't There"

A newspaper story of a haunted house in Antigonish inspired what must be the most widely known verse about a Canadian ghost. The ghost has vanished long ago, the house has probably been torn down, and now no one recalls any of the particulars, but the verse is imperishable. The quatrain is called ''Antigonish'' and it was written by the American educator and versifier Hughes Mearns. It goes like this:

> As I was going up the stair
>   I met a man who wasn't there!
> He wasn't there again today!
>   I wish, I *wish* he'd stay away!

Mearns composed the quatrain in 1899 after reading a series of stories carried in the press about a house in the Nova Scotia village of Antigonish that was reported to be haunted by the ghost of a man who was always somewhere else when the reporters called. A talented versifier, not content with writing one imperishable classic, he burlesqued ''Antigonish'' on a number of occasions but never rose to his former height of inspired nonsense. His parodies were collected by Franklin P. Adams in *Innocent Merriment: An Anthology of Light Verse* (1942).

Barrachois/
The Phantom Train

They still speak of the Phantom Train on Cape Breton Island. Its tracks ran beside St. Andrews Channel. The tradition was recorded by Mary L. Fraser, a Roman Catholic sister, in *The Folklore of Nova Scotia* (1932).

Some years ago, people who live on a certain hill at Barrachois, Cape Breton, used to watch a phantom train glide noiselessly around the headlands of the Bras d'Or, and come to a stop at a gate leading to one of the houses. One who saw it herself told me how at seven o'clock every evening for a whole month every family on the hill would go out of doors to see it. Every coach was lighted, but no people could be seen. At the hour of its approach, some people sometimes went down to the track to get a better look at it, but were disappointed at its not coming at all, although the watchers on the hill saw it as usual. At the end of the month, a man was killed by a train just at the gate to which the phantom train used to come. Nobody saw it afterwards.

Bay of Fundy/
Ulysses

Ulysses is the Roman name for Odysseus, the seafaring hero of *The Odyssey*, the epic poem attributed to the blind bard Homer. Did Ulysses include the Maritimes in his celebrated Odyssey of the Ancient World? At least one author has raised the possibility, as unlikely as it may seem. Henriette Mertz, an American lawyer and student of ''unsolved mysteries,'' wrote *The Wine Dark Sea* (1964) in which she placed Ulysses in the Bay of Fundy, the body of water that lies between Nova Scotia and New Brunswick.

Henriette Mertz identified Scylla and Charybdis, monsters from the poem, not with the Straits of Messina but with two islands in the Bay of Fundy. In her study of the voyage in question, Ulysses passed between Chignecto Bay and the Whirlpool at the head of the Bay of Fundy. He almost perished in the Whirlpool, but was dashed ashore on Hopewell Rock, Chignecto Bay, high tides being an everyday occurrence in the Bay of Fundy.

Big Indian Lake/
The Man in a Sou'wester

A man in a sou'wester is said to haunt Big Indian Lake. He is seen walking along across the dam of Big Indian Lake, a small body of water located north of St. Margarets Bay on the south coast. Groups of fishermen as well as solitary fishermen have reported seeing him. Locally he is believed to be the ghost of a man who drowned in the lake.

Bras d'Or/
The Ghost of Kelly's Mountain

The beautiful Bras d'Or region of Cape Breton Island has lakes that resemble the misty lochs of Scotland, so it is not surprising this region of Nova Scotia has more than its share of legends and traditions.

"Are you familiar with Kelly's Mountain, which rises over the Bras d'Or Lakes on Cape Breton Island?" asked the writer Ed Butts. "Legend (and a popular folk song by Charlie McKinnon) has it that in pioneer times an Irishman named Kelly lived on the mountain, and spent most of his time brewing Irish booze. He was distrustful of strangers, especially those who came looking for a drink. After he died, his ghost stayed around to haunt the mountain.

"When the Trans-Canada Highway was built across Cape Breton, a section of it went over Kelly's Mountrain. On the descent from the summit to the Bras d'Or Bridge, there are a couple of steep, treacherous curves. According to local lore, this piece of road has been the scene of several bad car accidents. People say that the Ghost of Kelly's Mountain, angry at the trespassers, has caused the problems."

Brier Island/
The Fate of Joshua Slocum

Joshua Slocum, the sea captain who became the first person to sail alone around the world, was born in 1843 in the village of Westport, the main community on Brier Island off the end of Digby Neck at the entrance to the Bay of Fundy. Although he never saw the need to learn to swim, he became a master mariner and one of the world's greatest sea-farers. He accomplished the first solo circumnavigation of the Seven Seas in 1895–98 in the *Spray*, a converted oyster boat only thirty-six feet long.

A strange incident occurred during the solo voyage. In July 1895 the mariner ran into squally weather between the Azores and Gibraltar. At the same time he was afflicted with severe stomach cramps and had to abandon the wheel and go below to rest. He slept and upon returning to the deck he was astonished to see at the helm a tall, foreign-looking sailor! "Senor," the figure said, "I have come to do you no harm." It smiled and added, "I am one of Columbus' crew, the pilot of the *Pinta*, come to aid you. Lie quiet, senor captain, and I will guide your ship tonight." The next day Slocum found that the *Spray* was exactly on course, despite the fact that there was no one at the helm — except the foreign-looking phantom! In his memoirs Slocum wrote, "Columbus himself could not have held her more exactly on her course. I felt grateful to the old pilot . . . I had been in the presence of a friend and a seaman of vast experience."

Slocum was sixty-six and in excellent health when he outfitted the *Spray* for another long, solo voyage. The outfitting was done at the yard at Bristol, Rhode Island. Asked where he was heading, he replied, "Some far away places." Then, on 14 November 1909, he set sail from Martha's Vineyard and was seen no more. No one ever saw Slocum or the *Spray* again.

According to Bill Wisner in *Vanished — Without a Trace!* (1977). "The question is still asked: What really happened to the *Spray*?" Was there a mishap at sea, sickness, suicide . . . ? He concluded his account with a rhetorical flourish: "Somewhere between Bristol and Grand Cayman these inseparable companions, veterans of amazing adventures all over the world, vanished forever, becoming still another secret in Davy Jones' Locker.''

Slocum, the master mariner, disappeared in the Atlantic Ocean in the ''region of mysteries'' which Charles Berlitz was later to dub ''the Bermuda Triangle.''

Caledonia/
The Macdonald Poltergeist

Poltergeist-like activities were reported from the farm of Alexander Macdonald at Caledonia, southwest of Antigonish. The incendiary pranks of the ''fire-spook,'' as it was called, commenced on 6 January 1922 and continued for some months. Family members—including fifteen-year-old Mary Ellen Macdonald — and neighbours were frightened when fires broke out unexpectedly. The flames were small and easily extinguished but were not the only malific manifestations. Windows were broken and mysterious tapping sounds were heard.

The house quickly acquired the reputation of being haunted and was shunned by the local population. But its notoriety attracted psychic investigators, including Walter F. Prince, principal research officer of the American Society for Physical Research, who travelled from Boston to learn what he could about the poltergeist.

''It remained as much a problem as ever until 'Peachy' Carroll, retired detective of Pictou, took charge,'' noted the Canadian Press reporter in a discussion of the case published in the Niagara Falls *Evening Review*, 14 January 1935. ''As a result of his investigation it was proved the teenage Ellen was the cause of all the mysterious fire, window breaking and odd noises.''

Cape Blomidon/
Glooscap Country

North of the village of Blomidon, on the shore of Minas Basin, lies Cape Blomidon, a rocky region said to be the home and haunt of Glooscap, the culture hero of the Micmacs. It is a picturesque region well-suited to stories of the legendary and the lost.

Glooscap, the friend and teacher of the Algonkian-speaking Indians of the Maritimes, was the most human of heroes, ''the man who might have been a god.'' In the tales told about him, collected by Cyrus Macmillan and S.T. Rand, he appears as both a giant and a giant among men. Evil acts associated are really caused by his twin brother, a malefactor named Maslum.

The prehistorian Frederick Pohl peered behind the visage of Glooscap and discerned the features of Henry Sinclair, Prince of Orkney and ruler of the Shetland Islands. There are suggestions that around the year 1398 Sinclair voyaged to the New World and wintered among the Micmacs. If this is so, Glooscap may well be the dim memory of an amazing man from Scotland. Glooscap's stature and strength and his amazing deeds may be legend-overlaid memories of the appearance and the acts performed by the indomitable explorer and colonist.

The spirit of Glooscap continues to haunt this picturesque region of the province. ''It is an old belief that anyone who takes amethyst away from Blomidon Mountain is bound to return there.'' This bit of lore was quoted by Helen Creighton in *Bluenose Magic* (1968). The folklorist noted that in the region amethyst is known as the ''eye of Glooscap'' and that ''it always brought ill-luck to those who found it and by some means of sorcery always made its way back to the brow of the mountain.''

Cape John/
The Fire-Ship

The Fire-Ship of Northumberland Strait was seen twice in three days by residents of Cape John on the north shore. The one sighting occurred at dusk, the other at night. In both instances the three-masted vessel was visible for about an hour. The numerous observers could plainly see fire streaking from its rigging and hull. Despite the choppy waters the vessel itself showed no signs of motion. According to the report from Cape John, published in the Niagara Falls *Evening Review*, 5 December 1953:

> There is a difference of opinion as to the identity of the ship. Some people say it is the phantom of a pleasure ship that was destroyed by fire during a drinking bout many years ago. Others will tell you that it is a Scottish immigrant ship that set sail for Nova Scotia in the 18th century and became lost at sea. And, of course, some people say it's an optical illusion. Or that it's caused by gases breaking through the water from the submarine coal fields.

Cape Sable Island/ Creature of the Sea

An immense and frightful creature of the sea was sighted by veteran fishermen on three occasions over a period of five days in July 1976. The sightings took place around ebbtide in the vicinity of Pollock's Shoal, off Cape Sable Island, which is the southernmost point of Nova Scotia. The reports were the basis of an unusually perceptive and sympathetic account written by Ralph Surette and published as "Canadian Notebook" in *Weekend Magazine*, 30 October 1976.

On 5 July, Eisner Penny spotted what initially looked like a whale but proved to be "bigger than anything I have ever seen at sea." He came within two hundred feet of it and estimated its length to be seventy or eighty feet. "It had a massive peaked head — with a longish mouth like an alligator — which bobbed up and down from ten to fourteen feet above the water as it swam. He said he observed it for half an hour until he lost it in the distance."

Two days later, Keith Ross and his twenty-four-year-old son Rodney reported seeing the same creature:

> By that time, the two men said, its head was eight to ten feet out of the water — higher than the boat's cabin — and it had its mouth open. Rodney Ross gaped into that mouth and dove into the cabin in terror. The two men said they saw two tusks about two and a half feet long

and about three inches thick at the base, as well as rows of smaller teeth between. On top of its head, they said, it had a brown mass of flesh like the cab of a car extending to the back of its neck. It had protruding eye sockets the size of saucers. They also saw its tail, a fish tail which they said was vertical like that of a shark rather than horizontal like that of a whale.

Then they lost it in the fog.

Two days after that, in the same fishing ground, Edgar Nickerson and his fifteen-year-old son Robert were amazed and terrified when they beheld a creature's head emerging not twenty feet from the cabin of their boat.

> Nickerson turned on his depth sounder which normally scares off whales. The creature wasn't scared. Its head kept coming and rearing up "right over my cabin, not five feet away." His son jumped in a panic to the walkboard on the other side of the cabin.
>
> Nickerson turned on his motor full blast and roared off — while still at anchor! The anchor line ripped off the railing to which it was attached. Nickerson says he never looked back to see if the creature was following him. "I never want to see that again," he says. "It was a horrible looking thing, I tell you. If there's a devil, that was it."

Digby Neck/ The Mystery of Jerome

Digby Neck is the peninsula that extends from the northwestern part of the province into the Bay of Fundy. Digby Neck's tiny community of Sandy Cove on St. Marys Bay was witness to the so-called Mystery of Jerome. Helen Creighton describes the mystery in *Bluenose Ghosts* (1975).

> Many years ago Martin Albright looked out from his house at Sandy Cove and he saw on the beach what seemed to be a large otter. When it did not move he walked down to the beach. As

he drew near it, he was amazed to see that this was a man. Upon closer examination he was horrified to find that he was helpless, for both legs had been amputated and he had been left upon the beach with a bottle of water and some bread within his reach. Mr. Albright spoke to him, but the stranger made no reply, nor did he ever speak in all the years he lived in Nova Scotia. All anybody could ever get out of him were the words that might have been "Colombo" and "Jerome" and he became known by the latter name. The amputation was half way between the knees and the thighs, and had been very well done for those days.

Jerome was carried to Albright's house where he lived for some years. He was a large man and Central European in appearance. He was well bred but moody. He never spoke and the only clue to his past was that he became agitated at the rattling of chains. He lived for many years and died at the almshouse at Marshall-town in the care of the Roman Catholic Sisters of Clare. Why did Jerome appear one morning on the shore of Sandy Cove? Who amputated both his legs? Why did he fear the rattle of chains? For what reason did he refuse to speak? No one knows the answers to these and many other questions.

Fourchu/
The Mikado Forerunner

No fishermen would spend the night in a small fishing shack at Winging Point near Fourchu, on the southern coast of Cape Breton Island. It was avoided because no one could fall asleep in it on account of the sounds. The sounds that were heard were the shrieks of men in agony. No one could explain them.

Then, in the spring of 1924, a trawler named Mikado foundered a few hundred yards from the shack. The people at Winging Point looked out helplessly while the sailors shrieked in agony as they drowned. But as soon as the weather permitted, they brought the bodies of the sailors to hand. The fishing shack, which had been empty for five years, was

opened up and pressed into service. The bodies were stored on the floor of the shack until suitable arrangements for burial could be made. It was then that those who had heard the shrieks from the Mikado remembered the shrieks heard in the fishing shack and wondered whether the sounds were a forerunner of this event.

Glace Bay/
The MacDonald Wildfire

Wildfire is a rarely reported condition which comes and goes of its own accord. For no known physical or understood psychological reason, innumerable small fires suddenly break out. The series of fires is no sooner extinguished than a new rash of flames appears. Wildfire is sometimes associated with a poltergeist; sometimes not. It is quite often associated with adolescent girls.

One of the most dramatic instances of inexplicable combustion is the MacDonald Wildfire. Vincent H. Gaddis reported on this case in Mysterious Fires and Lights (1967). On the afternoon of 16 April 1963, there was a fire on the second floor of the Douglas MacDonald home in Glace Bay. Damage was heavy and faulty electrical wiring was suspected. The current was cut off and the family—Mr. and Mrs. MacDonald and their three adopted daughters, Sheilah and Marie, both twenty-five, and Betty, twenty-one — moved into temporary quarters.

Mrs. MacDonald was cleaning up the mess when an insurance adjustor called. They smelled smoke and found a new fire on the second floor but it was easily extinguished. The adjustor left and other members of the family arrived to help clean up. A few hours later another fire broke out on the same floor. It spread so rapidly that the fire department was summoned to extinguish it. The blaze caused additional damage to the house and destroyed new furniture that had been brought in to replace furniture lost in the first fire.

Faulty electrical wiring was not the cause of any of the subsequent fires since the current was still switched off. The MacDonalds decided to have the house rewired and lodged elsewhere while the work was in progress. On May 16, one month after the original fire, Mrs. MacDonald and daughter Betty stopped by to see how the work was progressing. No sooner had they entered the house than they smelled smoke. They called the fire department and the firemen found papers in the first-floor bathroom ablaze. They extinguished the blaze and left. Half an hour later they were back, extinguishing a fire in a bedroom closet.

> After it was extinguished, the irritated and perplexed fire-fighters tried unsuccessfully to find a cause. The two fires had occurred over ten feet apart on either side of a wall. There was no trace of fire, or even heat, between the two places within the flooring or along the basement ceiling. There was no sign of fire inside or outside the wall. It was obvious that both fires had originated where they were found, yet there were no materials at either place that could cause spontaneous combustion.

Finding nothing suspicious or dangerous, they left. Two hours later they were back, putting out a blaze inside a wall cupboard. Again they left and again half an hour later had to return. "The fire, a small one this time, was on the back porch, and was quickly extinguished. The fire chief called the police chief. An officer was assigned to remain at the house." He took up his post when a wallboard broke out in flames and had to be extinguished.

"This was the final outbreak," Gaddis explained. "Investigators reached no conclusions. Insurance failed to cover all of the loss. Weeks later the family moved back into the house and as far as I know is still there."

Halifax/
The Colonel's Ghost

The Colonel's Ghost is said to appear in the vicinity of the Prince's Lodge. The story of the Colonel and his Ghost was a favourite of the broadcaster and author William Coates Borrett. He recounted it at some length in *Historic Halifax: Tales Told Under the Old Town Clock* (1948).

The story begins at the Prince's Lodge, a Halifax landmark which overlooks Bedford Basin, now reconstructed. The original domed music room was built in 1794 at the request of Prince Edward, Duke of Kent. In July of the following year, the Duke and his consort Madame de St. Laurent hosted a brilliant reception for three hundred officers and their guests and the Prince's Lodge never looked more spectacular.

At that reception a certain Colonel and a certain naval Officer, having drunk their fill of brandy, exchanged words. They agreed to meet at 2:00 a.m. that morning at the cove south of the Round House with swords and seconds. Contrary to army and navy regulations, they engaged in a duel. Both were wounded but the Colonel died of his wounds. He was buried without military honours, and to this day the Colonel's Ghost is said to appear in the vicinity of the Prince's Lodge. The haunt is near the Round House where the duel was held.

Halifax/
The Robie Street Palace

The wooden residence at 1714 Robie Street, known locally as the Robie Street Palace, has a long history of being haunted. It was built in the 1840s as a residence for William Caldwell, the first elected mayor of Halifax, and now serves as architectural offices.

A wide, columed verandah surrounds the residence. Many years ago an old man living in the house looked out the window and spied witches dancing on the verandah. Their dance came to a halt when they realized they were being observed. They conjured the window black, the colour it remains to this day. In another story, a resident shot through the window at a boy who was stealing apples in the yard, then hanged himself in remorse when the child died.

From the 1870s on there have been reports of poltergeist-like occurrences: cold drafts, objects flying through the air, nocturnal groans and creaks. According to *Early Canadian Life*, September 1979:

The house is now owned by architect Aza Avramovitch. He takes pride in its long and mysterious heritage. He too has experienced ghostly phenomena. One day, he and a group of employees at an afternoon coffee break were interrupted by the securely latched door mysteriously opening of its own accord, three times in succession. . . . In all his years as its present owner, he has avoided spending a night there.

Yet the blackened window may be explained architecturally if not supernaturally. Barry Conn Hughes wrote in "Houses That Go Bump in the Night," *Canadian Magazine*, 31 October 1970: "Architect Aza Avramovitch . . . explains that the designer of the house wanted an unbroken series of large windows all around the house but sliding doors on that side made a window undesirable. So a fake wooden one was installed for balance."

Halifax/
All Saints Cathedral

The following story about the Cathedral Church of All Saints, which was erected in 1907–10 to mark the two hundredth anniversary of the first Anglican service in Nova Scotia, was told by Helen Creighton in *Bluenose Ghosts* (1957).

Some years ago Dean Llwyd of All Saints Cathedral in Halifax passed away and he was mourned greatly by all who knew him. Two weeks after his death one of his fellow clergymen was attending the Sunday evening service when he saw the Dean go into the pulpit and look over the congregation as he always did. He thought his affection for his old friend and his sense of loss in the place where he had seen him so often had caused him to imagine this, so he made no mention of it. Some time later, however, one of the ladies of the congregation told him she had experienced a strange thing, and described exactly what he had seen. They checked the time and the service, and they were the same.

Halifax/
The House at Hurd and Water

Helen Creighton tells of a house haunted by "a sort of wraith-like presence" in Halifax in *Bluenose Magic* (1968).

There was once a dark red house at the corner of Hurd and Water Streets in Halifax where a woman was supposed to have been murdered by her husband. This was a high four-storey house without an attic, and a Halifax resident, Mary Williams, lived there as a child. She said that one evening she and her brothers and sisters were playing outside their house and were a bit later than usual in going in, so that when their mother called, they had to go through a darkened hall. For a moment they thought their mother had come downstairs with a lamp to guide them because they distinctly saw a kerosene lamp with a reflector being carried through the hall. They soon saw that it was not their mother but a sort of wraith-like presence that passed in front of them and glided along the hall until it disappeared in the dark towards the rear of the house.

Nobody ever stayed in this house for long because this lady with the lamp wandered so often about the halls. In Mary's family she seemed to be especially fond of the baby, and of the three children who slept in the same room, two at least saw the baby being tucked in. Mary herself often felt her presence in the room. It would happen after the bedroom window would close with a slow deliberate motion, and the imprint of fingers could be seen on the bed covers for a few moments afterwards.

Halifax Harbour/
Henneberry House

At the time when fishermen still lived on Devil's Island in Halifax Harbour, they talked a lot about the haunted house occupied by the Henneberry family.

The house would glow inside and out with six unnatural blue flames, yet nothing was ever burnt.

When Henry Henneberry drowned at sea, the moment of his passing was conveyed to his wife in the house. She heard his characteristic footfall and saw on the floor marks left from his rubber boots. Unaccountable noises were heard, odours were overpowering, knocks sounded on doors when no one else was around. Children saw a man in oilskins stalking across the rooms and right through the walls of the house.

Henneberry House was finally torn down by the islanders board by board. Those who made use of the old boards in their own houses soon regretted the act for their walls began to make strange sounds.

Helen Creighton saw the house before it was demolished, as she noted in *Bluenose Ghosts* (1957):

> I can recall the fear in the voices of both men and women as they walked by and then talked about it. I am sure there were many more experiences than I might have had first hand if I had realized then the importance of every slightest detail connected with the haunting of a house. In those days it looked to me like a bleak, unpainted, and unfriendly frame dwelling, and I was glad to leave it to the wind and the weather and any family unfortunate enough to have to live there. The house is gone now and so are the people; there is no one left but the lightkeeper and his family.

Inverness/
The Shean

Inverness, a community on the west coast of Cape Breton Island, was founded on land formerly known to the Scots settlers of the district as the Shean, a word derived from *Sithean*, Gaelic for "the house of the fairies." Celtic tradition held that here there once was "a small hill, shaped something like a large hay stack, where the old people used to see the 'little people' in thousands. People in general would not walk about in that place at night; but when they did so, as soon as they approached the hill the little visitors vanished."

The fairy lore comes from Mary L. Fraser's *Folklore of Nova Scotia* (1932).

Liverpool/
"Fifteen Ships"

The earliest account of unidentified flying objects being seen in North America, exclusive of any account that may be derived from native sources, is believed to be the entry in the diary kept by Simeon Perkins (1735–1812), the Loyalist merchant and judge. He lived in Liverpool, the town on the province's southeast coast, and his gracious home, Perkins House, is preserved as a museum.

The Champlain Society in Toronto issued *The Diary of Simeon Perkins* in three volumes in 1948–61. The third volume, edited by C.B. Fergusson, includes the following entry for Wednesday, 12 October 1796:

> A Strange Story is going that Fleet of Ships have been Seen in the Air in Some part of the Bay of Fundy. Mr. Darrow is lately from there by Land. I enquired of him. He Says they were Said to be Seen at New Minas, at one Mr. Ratchford's, by a Girl, about Sunrise, & that the Girl being frightened, Called out, & two men that were in the House went out & Saw the Same Sight, being 15 Ships and a Man forward of them with his hand Stretched out. The Ships made to the Eastward. They were So Near that the people Saw their Sides & ports. The Story did not obtain universal Credit, but Some people believed it. My Own Opinion is that it was only in Imagination, as the Cloud at Sunrise might Make Some Such appearance, which being Improved by Imagination, might be all they Saw. Exceeding pleasant day & Evening.

New Minas is a community near Minas Basin near the northwest shore. Each age is inclined to depict unidentified flying objects in the imagery of the day, so it is not surprising that in the days of sail there should be a description of an aerial flotilla of fifteen ships following a navigator.

Mahone Bay/
The Teazer Light

From Borgals Point on Mahone Bay there are reports of sightings of the so-called Teazer Light. This is the spectacle of a sailing ship in flames. It is usually observed on foggy nights, within three days of a full moon, and prior to a storm. It appears a mile or two offshore, but it may also be seen at closer range from the decks of ships, which the apparition threatens to ram. It has never caused any destruction but when it puts in an appearance it strikes terror in the hearts of mariners.

On 26 June 1813, a privateer's vessel called *Young Teazer* was trapped by British warships in Mahone Bay. The British would have captured the vessel had it not been for one of the pirates who set his vessel on fire, preferring death on its deck to death on the yard-arm. Since then the Teazer Light has made innumerable appearances in Mahone Bay, one of the last on record being in 1935.

Merigomish/
"A Marine Monster"

The naturalist Sir Charles Lyell devoted an entire chapter to sea serpents in his book *A Second Visit to the United States of North America* (1850). One he mentions was seen by the fishermen of Merigomish on Northumberland Strait.

In August 1845, two men had seen "a marine monster, about 100 feet long" struggling in shallow water near the shore. The monster was easily seen for half an hour before it made its way back into the deep water. Its head was raised occasionally and resembled that of a seal. Its back had a number of protuberances, upon which the witnesses differed as to whether they were true humps or folds of the body, and was black in colour. No paddles for locomotion were seen, but it did not bend itself around side to side rapidly in its struggles. Lyell wrote that the fishermen were terrified of this monster all summer long, but it seems the monster did not attract the attention of the newspaper editors of the day, only that of the visiting naturalist.

Mount Uniacke/
Uniacke House

Mount Uniacke is a small community located about half way between Halifax and Windsor. Here the provincial government has restored Uniacke House, the colonial mansion once occupied by Richard John Uniacke, Attorney General of Nova Scotia in 1797–1808. The eight-bedroom, two-storey white wooden house built in 1813–15 is reputed to be haunted. "A former member of the family is supposed to have been seen on numerous occasions sitting in a chair in the beautiful garden that overlooks the lake," Helen Creighton, the folklorist, laconically noted in *Bluenose Ghosts* (1957).

Northumberland Strait/
Sea and Shore

Between the east coast of New Brunswick and the west coast of Prince Edward Island lies Northumberland Strait. Helen Creighton in *Bluenose Ghosts* (1957) writes about "the phantom ship that appears in the Northumberland Strait before a northeast wind. It starts as a ball of flame and develops before the onlookers' eyes into a three-masted ship. She has been seen as early as 1780 and is observed on the same night over a large area. Three years ago at the time of the harvest moon she was seen near Pictou Lodge."

The ghostly figure of a young woman in a flowing white gown is reportedly seen on Pictou Island in Northumberland Strait. She has made appearances at odd times since the late nineteenth century. The apparition appears to stand on the beach, arms outstretched before her, hair streaming even when there is no wind. Oblivious of any or all observers, she gazes longingly or beseechingly across the waters of Northumberland Strait. The vision sometimes appears in conjunction with that of the Phantom Ship.

Oak Island/
The Money Pit

Conventional wisdom holds that there are 365 islands in Nova Scotia's Mahone Bay and that one of them,

Oak Island, is the repository of untold wealth in the form of buried teasure. The real number of islands in the Bay is a matter of debate — three hundred is a good round number — but the truth behind the rumour of the island's buried treasure is not so easily determined.

The island, which is covered with a stand of red oak trees, is very small—only one mile long and half a mile wide—but for its small size it has a long history of attracting treasure-seekers. Yet after close to two centuries of exploration and excavation, after fifteen

Oak Island's Money Pit appears in this photograph taken in 1955 during Charles Green's extensive excavations. As the British author Rupert Furneaux observed, "More money has been poured into it than is likely to be taken from it." [Hawkshead Services]

separate expeditions mounted between 1795 and 1987, after the accidental deaths of six treasure-seekers, no one is yet in a position to answer the pertinent question: Is there buried treasure on Oak Island?

Without question Oak Island is Canada's best-known mystery. It has inspired more books and articles than any other mystery — with the exception of the mystery of the *Mary Celeste*. Over the years the latter mystery may have generated more interest, but while it continues to puzzle aficionados of mysteries of the sea, in the last half-century no new information has come to light; every decade or so a major news story emerges from Oak Island. Tales of treasure appeal to people of all ages; the abandonment of what has been called *the* Mystery Ship is a matter of conjecture more suitable for adults than for children. Also, it is unlikely anyone will ever determine the cause or causes of the ship's abandonment on the high seas, whereas it is conceivable that someday someone will determine if there is buried treasure on Oak Island.

Tradition holds that the island is haunted, and that its mysteries will not be exposed until there have been seven deaths. From the earliest days of digging on the island until 1965, two deaths were reported. Then, in 1965, four men perished in a shaft, overcome by carbon monoxide poisoning from a leaky gas pump. That tragedy brought the tally abruptly to six deaths.

There are no historical records that single out this island or any other island in Mahone Bay as the burial place for booty or treasure. No evidence exists that Norsemen were ever in the vicinity. It is unlikely that the great pirate captains of the past—such gentlemen of the Atlantic Main as William Kidd, Henry Morgan, and Blackbeard—ever set foot on the island. Nor is it reasonable to theorize that fugitive Incas, fleeing the wrath and avarice of the Spanish *conquistadores*, deposited their gold here in 1795. More feasible is the theory that a group of Spanish or British officers secreted their payroll in a shaft, pending a cessation of war in the region. To such speculation must be added the reports, made over the centuries, of the appearance of strange fires and lights on and over the island.

One day in 1795, three youths, John Smith,

Anthony Vaughn, and David McGinnis, rowed from the mainland to Oak Island for a day of exploration. An oak tree with a sawed-off limb projecting over a large circular depression in the ground caught their attention. The following day they returned with picks and shovels, and their digging revealed a circular shaft about thirteen feet wide. Their discovery became their obsession. They discovered a platform of logs at the ten-foot level, and again at the twenty and thirty-foot levels. Continuing with heavy equipment over the years to come, they came upon a log platform every ten feet to a depth of eighty feet. At ninety feet a round flat stone was unearthed bearing markings they could not decipher. At ninety-eight feet, confident the treasure was near, they stopped digging for the weekend. On their return the following Monday, they were dismayed to find more than half the pit filled with sea-water. They found nothing at the 110-foot level and, with reluctance, they abandoned the dig and the island.

Subsequent expeditions might well have done the same. Over the years men have tackled the Money Pit. They have dug innumerable shafts and tunnels; erected a coffer dam across Smith's Cove to prevent flooding; allegedly recovered two chests at the 154-foot depth in 1897; attained the depth of 170 feet in 1935, and 180 feet two years later; encountered a second tunnel in 1942; caused the causeway to the mainland to be erected in 1963.

In 1971, Triton Alliance Ltd., a Montreal-based consortium, reached a water-filled cavity at the 212-foot level. According to news reports of the day, a submarine television camera, lowered into the cavity, sent back images of three chests and a severed hand. Divers were lowered into the cavity but arrived too late, for in the meantime it had been eroded by sea-water.

According to Rupert Furneaux, the British author of *The Money Pit Mystery: The Costliest Treasure Hunt Ever* (1972), the following items are the only treasures that have been recovered: three links from a chain; a scrap of parchment with two letters (*V* and *I*) written with a quill pen; and a flat stone inscribed with symbols which, when deciphered, apparently read "ten

feet below two million pounds are buried." The flat stone, seemingly substantial, was never photographed and its whereabouts since 1935 is unknown.

Oak Island is not Crown land, as many believe, but privately owned by David Tobias, the Montrealer who is the major backer of the Triton syndicate. He was quoted by Ralph Surette of *Maclean's* on 10 August 1987 as saying that in the near future Triton would make a public share offering to undertake the "deepest and most expensive archaeological dig ever made in North America." It remains to be seen whether there are remains of treasure on the island in Mahone Bay.

Oak Island is by no means the country's sole location of mysterious treasure. Fortunes have been made and lost, and presumably buried and found, in Canada for centuries. There is even a guide to such caches. Rosemarie D. Perrin's *Explorers Ltd.: Guide to Lost Treasure in the United States and Canada* (1977) lists many burial sites and lodes.

In the East, the treasures that lie in wait are mainly identified with pirates and sunken vessels; in the West, there are fabled mines and mother lodes to find. Specifically, Alberta has the Lost Lemon Mine. British Columbia boasts the Polson Mine, Fairview Gold Mine, Bulldog Kelly Treasure, Leechtown Tunnel Treasure, Lost Foster Mine, Indian Point Treasure, and Vancouver Island Gold Mine. Nova Scotia claims the H.M.S. *Tillbury*, Le Chameau, Granby, Oak Island Treasure, H.M.S. *Barbadoes*, and L'Americaine. In Ontario waiting to be found are Atlantic, Kent, Young Zion, Northerner, *Griffon*, Glendora, and Le Blanc Henri. Indeed, for treasure-seekers there are innumerable "treasure trails."

Parrsboro/
The Maiden's Cave

There is a cave in the hills at Black Point, outside Parrsboro, that is known as the Maiden's Cave. "If the wind is just right, you will be startled to hear the forlorn cries of a frightened girl echoing from the mouth of the cave . . . at the mouth of the cave you will near no sound. But as you step away for only a few feet, you will hear again, faintly but clearly, the wailing cry of a girl in distress.''

Roland H. Sherwood recalled the tale of the Maiden's Cove in *Legends, Oddities, and Facts from the Maritime Provinces* (1984). The story goes that a beautiful young maiden was sealed into the cave when she refused to accept the advances of a pirate captain named Deno who captured her father's ship, forced her father to walk the plank to his death, and then made advances on her. She died of starvation in the cave rather than live with her father's murderer.

Pleasant Harbour/
The Phantom Ship

Pleasant Harbour is a small fishing community near Tangier on the south coast of the province. As Helen Creighton noted in *Bluenose Ghosts* (1957):

> At Tangier they told of a phantom ship that used to sail in the shoal at Pleasant Harbour. She had often been heard before on clearing moonlight nights coming in and dropping her anchor, but she had never been approached. One calm evening she was seen so clearly, and with her sails apparently filled with wind, that some of the braver fishermen went out to meet her. When they arrived they reported all hands on deck and they said the men were drinking and talking in a foreign language. As they watched, she went right up to the shore and disappeared in the woods, and they concluded her appearance had something to do with treasure buried there. From that time she was never seen again.

Sable Island/
The Ghost of Dr. Copeland's Wife

One of the most popular of Maritime legends concerns the Ghost of Dr. Copeland's Wife. The legend's setting is Sable Island, a bleak rocky island in the Atlantic a hundred miles east of Nova Scotia. The island is surrounded by shallows and hidden sandbars which are obscured by fog. More than four hundred ships have been wrecked on them, earning for the small island the description the Graveyard of the Atlantic.

In 1802, it seems, the wife of a Dr. Copeland (both their first names have been lost) was sailing on the *Princess Amelia* when it ran against the rocks. Mrs. Copeland made it to the island but when the wreckers and salvagers arrived they murdered her and chopped off the third finger of her left hand to steal her wedding ring which could not otherwise be removed. Since then at intervals of fifty years the ghostly figure of a middle-aged woman dressed in white is seen to drift up and down the shifting sands of the beach, presumably in search of her finger and its ring, if not for revenge.

St. Croix River/
Lost Colony of Norumbega

There are place names that continue to intrigue historians and scholars long after they have lost the interest of cartographers. One of these lingering names is Norumbega which is "no longer on the map." The phrase is that of the student of cartography Robert H. Ramsay, but even the phrase is not strictly accurate, for Norumbega continues to identify a small community in Northern Ontario, although the name has disappeared entirely from the maps of the Maritimes.

The word Norumbega was originally used in reference to a river and is said to derive from the Abnaki word for "at the clay inlet." It might refer to the Penobscot River or the Narragansett River, both in Maine, New Brunswick's St. Croix River, or some other river known to early explorers or even earlier colonists. Then again the *Nor* of Norumbega may identify the Norsemen, deriving from a hypothetical colony known as Nova Norvega. For more than three centuries it has referred to a river, a region, a settlement, a city, a colony, or an empire. Whether native or early European, Norumbega was invariably civilized, prosperous, advanced, and remote enough to be mysterious.

Norumbega appeared on Verrazzano's map of

1524; on Mercator's map of 1569, it identified a fortified capital city in the region of the Bay of Fundy. Pierre Crignon described the region in *Discourse of a Great French Sea Captain of Dieppe* (1545) in almost fanciful terms: "The land overflows with every kind of fruit; there grow the wholesome orange and the almond, and many sorts of sweet-smelling trees. The country is called by its people Norumbega." It was while searching for Norumbega that Sir Humphrey Gilbert discovered Newfoundland in 1569. Samuel de Champlain, on his voyages of 1604–07, plied the coastline as far south as Cape Cod to locate the elusive river and region, writing in 1632 about one inlet in the account of his voyage:

> I believe that this is the river which several pilots and historians call Norumbega, and which most of them have described as large and spacious with a number of islands in it. . . . They describe also the existence of a large town thickly peopled with skilled and clever Indians who use cotton thread. I am convinced that the majority of those who mention it have not seen it, and speak of it because they have heard people talk of it who knew no more about it than themselves.

The same note was sounded with the stops pulled by Marc Lescarbot, sharp-eyed lawyer and Champlain's one-time companion and colonist, who would have nothing to do with "the wonders described by some." He dismissed out of hand the legendary land of "a River, whereof many have written fables one after another."

The dismissal meets the human need to tidy up, as noted by the American poetaster J.W. Whittier in his verse "Norumbega" which ends: "He needs the earthly city not / Who hath the heavenly found." Yet the revival or reinstatement of Norumbega meets an equally human need, specifically the one to act as a repository of references to early transatlantic voyages and lost colonies, references like the romantic one associated with Prince Henry Sinclair of Rosslyn, Earl of Orkney and of Caithness in Northern Scotland.

The expedition of Prince Henry Sinclair (or St. Clair) to the New World is said to have taken place in 1395. The account of his voyage of colonization is something of an old sailor's tale: that is its charm and its conviction. The details are derived from a letter written by the Venetian seaman Nicolò Zeno who, with his brother Antonio, served the Prince on the voyage of 1395. Nicolò wrote the narrative to members of his family in Italy; it was claimed that the very letter was found in the family home some two centuries later by Zeno's great-great-great grandson, who published it in 1558 as an exciting account by an adventurous ancestor. The full story of Sinclair's voyage, which is semi-legendary, and the Zeno Letter, which most historians regard as a fraud, appear in *Prince Henry Sinclair: His Expeditions to the New World in 1398* (1974) by the prehistorian Frederick J. Pohl.

Seaforth/ The Grey Lady

The rector of the Anglican Church at Seaforth, a community on the south shore, east of Halifax, was Dr. Joseph Norwood, who repeatedly saw the Grey Lady. Once in 1939, on the landing of the Rectory, he spoke to her. He made the sign of the cross and said, "In the name of the Father and the Son and the Holy Ghost, speak." She replied, "Why haven't you spoken before?" From her words he realized that one must address a ghost before it feels free to speak. She explained that a great wrong had been done her in life, and she asked him to deliver a message to a certain address on Morris Street in Halifax. He went to the address and there met a woman who turned out to have a deceased sister. The woman had a photograph album, and Dr. Norwood was able to point out a photograph of the deceased sister, the Grey Lady. He delivered the message from beyond the grave, and thereafter was never again troubled by the apparition of the Grey Lady.

Shag Harbour/ UFO Crash?

Shag Harbour is a small fishing community on the province's southern tip. The community was briefly the focus of national and even international attention in 1967 when an unidentified flying object was seen to streak through the sky and crash into the waters of the harbour.

Arthur Bray described the incident in *The UFO Connection* (1979):

> A large unidentified, lighted object over sixty feet in diameter descended from the sky in front of RCMP witnesses, settled onto the sea, then slowly sank beneath the waves. Navy divers failed to find a trace of it on the bottom. Did it or did it not exist? If so, what was it?

This incident occurred on the night of October 4th, 1967, off the coast of Shag Harbour, Nova Scotia. A number of boats, including a Coast Guard vessel with RCMP officers aboard, rushed to the scene of the landing. Observers aboard the vessels reported a thick yellow foam on the surface at the apparent point of impact.

The Royal Canadian Navy sent a team of seven divers to search the sea bottom but gave up after four days, having found nothing. Civil and military authorities confirmed no aircraft was missing.

Does finding nothing there prove there was nothing there to start with? We have RCMP officers as witnesses to the fact that a large, lighted flying object landed on the sea and sank. This incident clearly shows that UFOs are elusive, not illusions.

Shelburne/
Carthaginian Epigraphy

Did the Carthaginians trade with the Micmacs in ancient times? An inscription found near Shelburne suggested as much — at least to Barry Fell, Professor Emeritus of Zoology at Harvard University and in 1981 President of the American Epigraphic Society in San Diego, California.

In 1975, a lighthouse-keeper on McNutts Island, a body of land in the Atlantic due south of Shelburne, came upon a brush-covered rock with markings that appeared to be an inscription in the alphabet of some long-forgotten language. Six years later, George Young, an amateur archaeologist and author from Queensland, Nova Scotia, sent a photograph of the inscription to Fell, who studied the markings and determined that they derived from the characters of a Micmac hieroglyphic system which had been adapted from an ancient script of Cypriot origin used in North Africa. He even translated the inscription to mean: "Inscribed as a memorial to [or by] Chief Kese."

Young felt that the inscription was proof that by A.D. 410 Carthaginians were crossing the Atlantic and trading with the Micmacs, introducing them to a system of hieroglyphics based on their own, the theme of a 1980 booklet written by Young called *Ancient Peoples and Modern Ghosts.*

Scholars felt otherwise, wondering about the wisdom of the *ad hoc* translating of Micmac inscriptions without any knowledge of the Micmac language. One even punned that he wished "to bury Fell." This controversial reading of the Carthaginian epigraphy —if indeed the markings constitute an inscription— was noted by Michael Clugston in *Maclean's*, 2 November 1981.

South East Passage/
Ghost House

The house which Helen Creighton in *Bluenose Ghosts* (1957) calls the Ghost House was erected on a high point of land at South East Passage on the south shore overlooking the approach to Halifax. It is a large frame house, two storeys high, with a high-pitched roof, set well back of the road with the woods behind it. It was built in 1910 from wreckage, apparently, washed ashore from shipwrecks.

It was certainly in a dilapidated state in the early 1950s when she visited the family that owned and occupied the house. The railings on the verandahs on either side were broken, and it was badly in need of a coat of paint. In the dead of night both parents and children would hear someone walking about downstairs. At other times some members of the family but not all of them at once could hear a phantom team of horses galloping over the roadway. Heavy objects would fall to the floor with a bang. One evening the bedcovers in the master bedroom levitated a foot or so above the bed, to the horror of the occupants. There was no rhyme or reason to the disturbances. No one was ever harmed. The house did not burn down, which is surprising, as this is the fate of many haunted houses. So it is presumably still standing where it was—one hundred feet from the main road, with an open field in front of it and a coniferous forest behind it—the Ghost House of South East Passage.

Spencers Island/
The *Mary Celeste*

The most famous mystery ship of all time was constructed at the shipyard of Joshua Dewis in the tiny community of Spencers Island. Although the shipyard is long gone, its location is marked by a plaque. A master shipwright, Dewis specialized in twin-masted brigantines. On 10 June 1861, at the nearby port of Parrsboro, he registered the twin-masted, 99.3-foot-long brigantine, calling it the *Amazon*.

Its maiden voyage was fatal for its captain and a forewarning of its fate. A few hours out of port, the ship had to turn back. Captain Robert McClellan

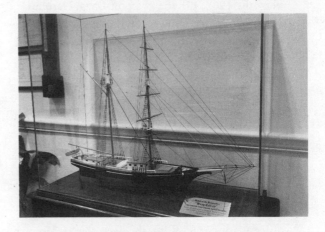

The fame and fate of the Mary Celeste *are recalled in the* Mary Celeste *Room of the Atlantic Mutual Companies. The Room is part of the firm's Executive Offices at 45 Wall Street in New York City. The Room is a faithful reconstruction of an insurance adjustor's office of the latter half of the nineteenth century and keeps alive the memory of the* Mary Celeste, *the most famous "mystery ship" of all time, which was found unaccountably abandoned in mid-Atlantic on 10 June 1861. The Atlantic Mutual Companies, as successors of one of the ship's five original underwriters, commissioned the reconstruction, which includes a scale model of the vessel and an impressive oil painting by Gordon Johnson. The artist depicted the crew of the* Dei Gratia *at the dramatic moment of sighting the derelict vessel.*
[Atlantic Mutual Companies]

sickened, was taken back to Spencers Island, and died of pneumonia before a doctor could be summoned from Parrsboro. Subsequent voyages back and forth across the Atlantic under Captain John Parker proved to be uneventful, so much so that Parker commissioned a waterfront artist in the French port of Marseilles to paint a likeness of the *Amazon*. The painting now hangs in the museum at Fort Beausejour, near Amherst, Nova Scotia.

The period of good luck ended on 9 November 1867 when the *Amazon* went aground a few miles from Glace Bay. It was acquired under shady circumstances in auction by American shipmaster Richard W. Haines who changed its name to *Mary Celeste* to avoid paying import taxes. Sailors, a superstitious lot, are adverse to the renaming of vessels, tending to regard any renamed ship a "hoodoo." Later that year it was sold for debt to James H. Winchester, a former Nova Scotia sea captain, who pressed it into service between U.S. ports and the West Indies. It was refitted in New York in 1872 and a Yankee shipmaster Benjamin S. Briggs became part owner and was placed in command.

The new captain, his wife Sarah, their newborn baby Sophy, and the crew of seven, plus a cat, boarded the *Mary Celeste* at Pier 50 in New York's East River. The cargo was 1701 barrels of industrial alcohol in oak casks. They set sail 7 November 1872 for Genoa. Sailing past Staten Island they nodded to the captain of the *Dei Gratia*, another brigantine built in Nova Scotia which was commanded by Captain David Morehouse, a native of Digby, Nova Scotia. As it turned out, the *Dei Gratia* was also bound for Genoa, but was to leave eight days later.

At 1:00 p.m., December 4, the *Mary Celeste* was spotted "evidently in distress" by a seaman aboard the *Dei Gratia*. Captain Morehouse noted the disorderly state of the sails, some of which were furled, some hanging loose, two in tatters. The lifeboats were gone. Nobody was at the wheel; nobody was on deck. Two hours later three seamen boarded the derelict. "They found themselves in the silent presence of a mystery that was to tantalize the minds of landsmen and seamen ever after," wrote Thomas H. Raddall in

Footsteps on Old Floors: True Tales of Mystery (1968).

It was an eerie experience standing on the deck of an abandoned vessel pitching aimlessly on the high sea. The doors and hatches were open or loose. The cargo was intact. There was some slight damage and some signs of a hasty departure in the captain's cabin. The chronometer and sextant were missing and the bedding in the berth was unmade. There were regular entries in the ship's logbook up to 24 November, and the "working log" showed the following inscription: "Monday, 25th. At 5 o'clock made the island of St. Mary's bearing E.S.E. At 8, Eastern point bore S.S.W. 6 miles distant." The *Mary Celeste* had drifted eight hundred miles in ten days.

Three seamen boarded the derelict and made the necessary repairs. The ships sailed in company the six hundred miles to Gibraltar, arriving on Friday the 13th. The *Mary Celeste* was taken into custody and hearings were begun on 18 December. The prosecutor decided there was evidence of foul play and insinuated that someone had bribed the sailors of the *Mary Celeste* to murder their officers and abandon the ship and cargo intact off the Azores where it would be discovered and claimed by salvagers, perhaps by the captain of the *Dei Gratia*. None of this could be proved, but it was not until 10 March 1873 that the *Mary Celeste* was released, refitted, and able to sail with a new crew to Genoa to deliver its cargo.

Why would the captain and crew abandon their vessel on the high sea? It was Captain Morehouse's theory that the cargo was leaking and fumes of the escaping alcohol in the warm atmosphere of the Azores caused the men to panic and abandon ship. An untimely wind then blew the ship away from the lifeboat and the gale-force wind sank the lifeboat. Thomas H. Raddall, whose knowledge of marine practice is extensive, found this the most likely explanation, noting that when the barrels were unloaded in Genoa, nine of 1701 barrels of the cargo had evaporated.

The subsequent history of the mystery ship was as checkered as its past history. It was offered for sale in Boston but there were no buyers. It was eventually sold at a loss in New York in 1873. The new owners found it an unlucky ship, operating it at a loss for five years until they were able to dispose of it to a Boston firm which kept it for four years. Then under Captain Gilman C. Parker it was loaded with a mixed cargo for Haiti in the West Indies. It left Boston on 15 December 1884. The cargo was more "mixed" than it should have been for Captain Parker was working an insurance-claim scheme that called for deliberately wrecking the ship and claiming the insurance. The captain and the crew then made their way to the port of Miragoane. But an insurance investigator determined what had happened and Captain Parker was indicted for barratry and conspiracy. The jury could reach no decision and Parker went free though he never got another command at sea and eventually died a pauper. As Randall noted:

> Of all the captains of the *Mary Celeste*, from first to last, only John Nutting Parker seemed immune to the hoodoo that went with her. All the others suffered hardship, disappointment, disgrace or death — three of them actually died while in command. One lies in a lost grave in what is called "The Marsh Field" near the shore of Economy, N.S. Another lies on Saint Helena, that lone speck in the South Atlantic where Napoleon Bonaparte came in the very year that the builder of the *Mary Celeste* was born. The bones of Ben Briggs lie somewhere on the sea floor near the Azores, in the legendary sunken land of Atlantis.

With that the "hoodoo" or "jinxed" ship disappeared from history. Yet the mystery of the *Mary Celeste* lingers to perplex and intrigue. It is without question the world's most famous mystery ship. The reason for its abandonment and the ultimate fate of its captain and crew are matters that have only been conjectured, never explained. Innumerable articles and entire books have been devoted to explicating the mystery. Even Hollywood was excited by it, casting Bela Lugosi as a mad seaman in *The Mystery of the Marie Celeste* released in 1928.

One of the few memorials to a marine mystery is the Mary Celeste Room located in the home office of the Atlantic Mutual Companies at 45 Wall Street in New York. Atlantic was founded in 1842 and is the sole surviving insurance company that underwrote a portion of the insurance on the *Mary Celeste*'s ill-fated journey. The room, a small museum, is the reconstruction of a typical underwriter's office of the late nineteenth century. Among the memorabilia is Gordon A. Johnson's oil painting of the sighting of the mystery ship, commissioned by Atlantic in 1965, and a thirty-five-inch scale model of what Vincent Gaddis has called "the most famous of all mystery ships."

Strait of Canso/ The Merman

The Strait of Canso separates the mainland of Nova Scotia from Cape Breton Island. In 1656, it was the site of a sighting of a merman, according to Nicolas Denys, a merchant from La Rochelle and the author in 1672 of *The Description and Natural History of the Coasts of North America (Acadia)* (1908) edited by William F. Ganong.

Denys told of how, while fishing for cod in the afternoon, Captain Pierre Rouleau and the crews of three ships noticed a peculiar commotion farther out to sea. The men in fishing boats returned to their ship to fetch a telescope. Through it they saw more clearly what was causing the disturbance. It was a monster with the appearance of a human being: a merman. Captain Rouleau, who was in command of the ship farthest out from shore, ordered his men to remain quiet. He descended into one of the three boats with men and ropes. They rowed out past the monster so as to approach it unseen and unheard from behind. They managed to throw a rope over the head of the merman, but before the loop could be drawn tight, the creature shot down underwater. The boats converged, the men hoping again to rope the merman when it reappeared. When next seen, the creature had moved farther out to sea, where it appeared to be brushing the wet hair from its eyes with its webbed hands. The fishermen tried to approach it again, but the merman dove under and disappeared altogether.

Sydney/
The Wynyard Apparition

The Wynyard Apparition is one of the most notable reports in the long history of accounts of apparitions, spectres, ghosts, and phantasms. This classic report raises the following question: Is it possible for the dying or the dead to appear to their relatives or loved ones despite the distance and the circumstances?

The sole source for the account of the Wynyard Apparition is a single text but a solid one: Volume I of *Life and Letters of the Right Honourable Robert Lowe, Viscount Sherbrooke, G.D.B., D.C.L., Etc., With a Memoir of Sir John Coape Sherbrooke, G.C.B., Sometime Governor-General of Canada* (1893) written by A. Patchett Martin. The incident took place in Sydney, Cape Breton Island, at approximately 4:00 p.m. on 15 October 1785, in the quarters of Lieutenant George Wynyard. (Whether the officers occupied quarters in the British garrison or were billetted in town remains unclear in Martin's account.)

Lieutenant (later General) Wynyard was conversing with Captain John C. Sherbrooke, later Lieutenant-Governor of Nova Scotia and later still Governor General of Canada (1816–18) when . . . but let Martin tell the story:

> One evening Captain Sherbrooke and Lieutenant (afterwards General) George Wynyard, were seated in the latter's room, which had two doors, the one opening into an outer passage, the other into the bedroom. These were the only means of ingress or egress; so that anyone passing into the bedroom must have remained there, unless he returned through the sitting-room. The story goes that Sherbrooke suddenly perceived, standing by the passage door, a tall youth of about twenty, pale and wan, to whom he called his companion's attention. "I have heard," said Sherbrooke, "of a man being pale as death, but I never saw a living face assume the appearance of a corpse, except Wynyard's at that moment." While they were gazing, the figure, which had turned upon Wynyard a glance of sorrowful affection, glided into the bedroom. Wynyard, seizing his friend's arm, said in a whisper: "Great Heavens! my brother!" "Your brother?" replied Sherbrooke. "What do you mean? There must be some deception; let us follow." They darted into the adjoining room, only to find it empty. Another young officer, Ralph Gore, coming in at this moment, proceeded to join in the search. It was he who suggested that a note should be taken

Sir John Cope Sherbrooke served as Governor-in-Chief of Canada in 1816-18. As a young Captain stationed at Sydney, N.S., he witnessed and later recorded one of the most famous "crisis apparitions" of all time. On 15 October 1785, he and his friend Lieutenant (later General) George Wynyard beheld a spectral figure, which Wynyard recognized as that of his brother who was in England. They later learned that the brother on that day was on his deathbed. The engraving of Sherbrooke (signed W. Nicholls) appeared in Sherbrooke's Life and Letters *published in 1893. [PAC 6056]*

of the day and hour of the apparition. The mail brought no letter from England for Wynyard, but there was one for Sherbrooke, which he hastily opened, and then beckoned Wynyard away. When he returned alone to the mess-room he said in a low voice to the man next to him: "Wynyard's brother is dead!" The first line in the letter had run: "Dear John, — Break to your friend Wynyard the death of his favour-ite brother." He had died at the very moment when the apparition appeared in his brother's room.

It may be added Lieutenant Wynyard's brother was named John Otway Wynyard, according to Raymond Lamont Brown in *A Casebook of Military Mystery* (1974). There are no particulars about the cause of the young man's death.

Corroboration of the story of the Wynyard Appar-ition was added by Edgar A. Collard in "The Gov-ernor Who had Seen a Ghost" in *Canadian Yesterdays* (1955):

> Evidently the story was being discussed after dinner in Quebec, as it was in England. Sir John Harvey was much interested in trying to find out if it could possibly be true. At that time Sir John was deputy adjutant-general of the forces in Canada. It was he who defeated the Ameri-cans at the battle of Stoney Creek in 1813, and in later life he was successively Lieutenant-Governor of New Brunswick, Governor of Newfoundland, and Lieutenant-Governor of Nova Scotia.
>
> It so happened that in the Quebec garrison at that time was Col. Ralph Gore, one of the offi-cers of the 33rd Regiment who had been in Cape Breton at the time when Capt. Sherbrooke and Lieut. Wynyard were stationed there. Sir John Harvey, for the interest of himself and the other officers, drew up a list of queries and submitted them to Col. Gore. As the last survivor of that Cape Breton garrison, Col. Gore gave explicit answers.
>
> He had been in Cape Breton, he said, when

the incident occurred. More than this, he was one of the first persons to enter the room after the supposed ghost had been seen. He had heard what had happened, and had assisted in the search. In examining the bedroom into which the ghost had disappeared, he noted not only that there was no way anyone could have left without being seen, but that the windows had been puttied as a protection from the cold, and could not have been opened.

> Furthermore, Col. Gore said he had, the next day, suggested to Capt. Sherbrooke that he should make a memorandum setting down what had happened. This Sherbrooke had done.
>
> He also testified that he could remember the day when the letter had arrived from England bringing the news young Wynyard had died at the very hour they had seen his ghost.

Tatamagouche/
Leading Psychical Researcher

A stone marker near Tatamagouche, west of Pictou, identifies the birthplace of the scientist Simon New-comb (1835–1909). Newcomb attained pre-eminence as an astronomer and as a psychical researcher, serving as the first president of both the Astronomical and Astrophysical Society of America and the American Society for Psychical Research, assuming the latter position in 1885. A profoundly curious sceptic, New-comb came to the conclusion in 1909 that decades devoted to psychical research had been interesting but inconclusive. He added, "We live in a world where in every country there are millions of people subject to illusions too numerous to be even classified."

"The Cross"/
Michael Bradley the Rehistorian

"The Cross" is the name given an actual community situated almost midway between Mahone Bay on the province's east coast and the Bay of Fundy on its west coast. The community is so identified on old maps, according to the author Michael Bradley, in his book *Holy Grail across the Atlantic* (1988). Bradley has declined to name the community in question, other than to mention the presence, on farmland in the region, of large-scale ruins.

These ruins may be the legacy of Norse colonists in pre-Columbian times or the work of the Micmacs. They may be rubble-work. Then again they may be the handiwork of an illustrious group of colonists whose names are recorded in history. Do the ruins at "The Cross" figure in the secret history of Canada? It is a safe bet that they will become the object of some controversy when the contents of Bradley's book are digested, for the book takes the quest for the Holy Grail, so long a part of Mediterranean and European history and legend, onto Canadian soil.

Michael Bradley is Canada's leading rehistorian— someone who writes speculatively yet scholarly about the past to prove a single thesis. (It is only fair to add that he sees himself as much a revisionist historian as he does a rehistorian.) He was born in 1944 in Talledgega, Alabama, of mixed Cherokee and Louisiana Acadian stock. His legal name is Michel de Sackville but he adopted the more "American" name of Michael Bradley. He emigrated to Canada in 1959, studied at Dalhousie University, and then led a somewhat nomadic existence, working in journalism, authorship, advocacy, and advertising. Odd and arcane subjects, like Ponik the lake monster and the Knights-Templar, catch his eye. With a vigorous prose style and a lively way of speculating on original and published materials, he has written topical books with provocative theses. These books include:

- *The Cronos Complex I* (Toronto: Nelson, Foster & Scott, 1973).
- *The Iceman Inheritance* (Toronto: Dorset Publishing, 1978).
- *Imprint* (Toronto: Dorset Publishing, 1978).
- *The Mantouche Factor* (Toronto: Dorest Publishing, 1979).
- *Crisis of Clarity* (Toronto: Summerhill Press Ltd., 1985).
- *Dawn Voyage* (Toronto: Summerhill Press Ltd., 1987).

- *Holy Grail Across the Atlantic* (Toronto: Hounslow Press, 1988).

Truro/
The Crying Hyde House

An old house in Truro, once owned by a stage coach operator named Hiram Hyde, was noted for the weird crying sounds that could be heard in rooms on the east side of the house on stormy nights. Hyde sold the house to the lumberman Thomas McMullen who cut down an old apple tree in the belief that its branches rubbing against the house wall produced the sounds. This proved to be a false assumption. When the house was moved to a new location on Part Street, the old foundations yielded a surprise, the skeleton of an infant. The bones were appropriately buried, but the disturbance accompanied the house to its new location and could still be heard on stormy nights.

Some years later fire broke out and the east side of the house had to be repaired. Let Roland H. Sherwood continue the story in *Maritime Mysteries: Haunting Tales from Atlantic Canada* (1976):

> In one of the large chimneys in the fireplace was found a harp that had been built into the chimney. When the harp had been installed by the original owners it was designed to give sweet music when the wind was in the right direction in the chimney. But over the years the strings became broken, so that the wind, playing among the broken strings, produced the sounds as if a baby were crying.
>
> With the removal of the harp and its broken strings, all the unusual sounds ceased.

Windsor/
Haliburton House

Rumoured to be haunted is Haliburton House, the fifteen-room mansion built in 1834–35 at Windsor. It is haunted by the restless spirit of the mansion's original owner and builder, Thomas Chandler Haliburton, judge and author of *The Clockmaker* and other humorous stories about the Yankee peddlar Sam Slick. The grounds are said to be haunted by an unnamed kilted soldier. The provincial government has restored Haliburton House as a museum.

Apparently many years ago "a number of the Black Watch regiment were marching through Windsor to Annapolis and they went through this property. As they were passing the pond one of the men dropped his watch. He reached over to get it, lost his balance and fell in. He was never seen again. The man was a piper, so the place became known as Piper's Pond." So wrote Helen Creighton in *Bluenose Ghosts* (1957). Local children were told that if they ran around the pond twenty times a soldier would come up on a horse's back. They often ran nineteen times, but they always lost their courage on the twentieth. The pond has since been drained.

At least two former residents of Haliburton House have claimed that the place was haunted by Judge Haliburton. On a number of occasions his ghost was seen to emerge from a secret panel in the wall of the reception hall. The spirit would wander around the hall for some time before passing back through the panel.

Wolfville/
The Prophet's Room

The Women's Residence, a gracious classical building erected in 1879, is the oldest of the twenty-six major buildings on the campus of Acadia University in Wolfville. One of its suites, called the Prophet's Room, is put at the disposal of visiting lecturers. It is felt by members of the academic community to be haunted.

This was certainly the feeling of Alexandre L. Amprimoz, the poet and professor of Romance languages and literature at Brock University, St. Catharines. He stayed in the Prophet's Room and described his experience in a letter to the author dated 26 February 1987:

In September of 1984, during a lecture tour of the Maritimes, I was given the Prophet's Room

where I stayed three nights. I had not been told that the building was haunted by the ghost of a young woman who had hanged herself there several years ago.

The first night I suddenly awoke and saw that the windows were opened and a light wind moved the curtains. I saw a young blonde woman combing her hair at the dresser. She was semi-transparent. I closed my eyes and hid under the sheets. I could hear noises, pacing, but a few minutes later all returned to silence.

Today members of the faculty do not recall why this particular room is known as the Prophet's Room. Perhaps it should be called the Spirit's Room.

Yarmouth/
The Yarmouth Stone

The most intriguing display in the Yarmouth County Museum and Historical Research Library, at Yarmouth, is the four-hundred-pound boulder known as the Yarmouth Stone. The stone was found in 1812 by a physician named Richard Fletcher in a cove at the head of Yarmouth Harbour and is intriguing to scholars because of the inscription which appears on its single planed surface.

So far the inscriptions have defied the efforts of translators and interpreters. Over the years those who have examined the stone have pronounced its markings to be: Mycenian images; Japanese glyphs; Micmac pictographs; Norse ruines; Basque characters; the natural product of erosion. The inscriptions—should they be inscriptions—are from time to time cited as proof of the pre-Columbian discovery of America.

Frederick J. Pohl discussed the Yarmouth stone in *Atlantic Crossings before Columbus* (1961). The prehistorian was able to determine that the twenty-one inches of inscription consisted of fourteen separate characters, but then he ran up against a stone wall, so to speak. "The question for us is, of what alphabet is it?" In frustration he suggested either that the carver was ignorant or illiterate or that the carver was a runemaster intent to baffle posterity.

Barry Fell, the principal proponent of the theory of prehistoric contacts between the Old World and the New, discussed the stone in his influential book *America B.C.: Ancient Settlers in the New World* (1976), where he decided that the inscription was Basque in origin. In later years he favoured a Norse source.

Given the fact that the Yarmouth Stone's inscription remains as mysterious today as it was when it was discovered in 1812, there might be some truth to Pohl's suggestion. If there was a ''runemaster,'' he has succeeded in baffling posterity.

The rune-like markings of the Yarmouth Stone are highlighted for visitors to the Yarmouth County Museum and Historical Research Library. The 400-pound boulder was discovered in 1812 in a cove at the head of Yarmouth Harbour. The markings have been variously "identified" as characters written in Mycenian, Japanese, Micmac, Norse, and Basque. They may also be the end-product of time and tide. [Nova Scotia Department Government Services]

NEW BRUNSWICK

Beaubear's Island/
The Headless Nun

Beaubear's Island is a small body of land in the Mir-amichi River. It was named after Charles des Champs de Boishebert, who established French Fort Cove here and assisted the Acadians at the time of the Expulsion. There are rumours of forgotten treasure and of a cannon that tradition held could be fired only in defence of French Fort Cove. In the 1890s it was discovered mired in the mud by a group that included young Max Aitken, the future Lord Beaverbrook. It was stored for some years in the Aitken's Newcastle barn, then transferred to the University of New Brunswick in Fredericton, when Beaverbrook became its Chancellor. Repaired for a ceremonial salute, it was loaded and fired. It exploded into pieces.

The Headless Nun haunts the old bridge across the upper end of the cove. She carries her head in her hand, and she offers whomever she meets a thousand guineas to take her head back to France. "Why a French lady should offer guineas, which are English coins, I cannot think," commented Louise Manny, the folklorist. The story goes that the nun was grabbed by a deranged trapper who sliced off her head with one swipe of his razor-sharp knife. He ran off with her head and buried it in the woods. The nun's body was found, but no trace of her head or of the murderer. The body was sent back to France to be buried in a cathedral.

Chaleur Bay/
The Gougou

Chaleur Bay, or Baie des Chaleurs, is the largest bay in the Gulf of St. Lawrence. It lies between New Brunswick's North Coast and Quebec's Gaspé Peninsula. Its rough weather demands a lot from those who sail its choppy waters, from time to time reporting the fascinating apparitions of fire-ships and phantom ships and other mysteries of the sea. Yet before the mariners saw their first fire-ship on its waters, there was the Gougou.

The Gougou? The very name, with its babyish syllables, sounds silly. Yet the name, according to Silas T. Rand, in his English-Micmac dictionary of 1888, is related to the Micmac word for "earthquake." But the Gougou, according to Samuel de Champlain, referred to a frightful sea monster. The French explorer described it in detail in *Des Sauvages* (1603). Here is the passage in translation as it appears in Volume I of *The Works of Samuel de Champlain* (1922–26), edited by H.P. Biggar.

There is another strange thing worthy of narration, which many savages have assured me was true; this is, that near Chaleur bay, towards the south, lies an island where makes his abode a dreadful monster, which the savages call *Gougou*. They told me it had the form of a woman, but most hideous, and of such size that according to them the tops of the masts of our vessel would not reach his waist, so big do they represent him; and they say that he has often devoured and still devours many savages; these he puts, when he can catch them, into a great pocket, and afterwards eats them; and those who had escaped the danger of this ill-omened beast said that his pocket was so large that he could have put our vessel into it.

The monster, which the savages call the Gougou, makes horrible noises in that island, and when they speak of him it is with unutterably strange terror, and many have assured me that they have seen him. Even the above-mentioned Sieur Prevert from St. Malo told me that, while going in search of mines, as we have mentioned in the preceding chapter, he passed so near the haunt of this frightful beast, that he and all those on board his vessel heard strange hissings from the noise it made, and that the savages he had with him told him it was the same creature, and were so afraid that they hid themselves wherever they could, for fear it should come to carry them off. And what makes me believe what they say, is the fact that all the savages in general fear it, and tell such strange stories of it that, if I were to record all they say, it would be considered untrue.

Samuel de Champlain, a practical man, declared his belief in the existence of the Gougou. Marc Lescarbot, the educated man, whose contact with the New World was wintering at Port Royal, Acadia, in 1606–07, would have none of it. In his *Histoire de la Nouvelle-France* (1609), translated by W.L. Grant as *The History of New France* (1907), the one-time colonist, lawyer, and versifier took two swipes at Champlain's credulity:

But indeed, and to speak frankly, what gave credence to the idea of the Gougou was the story of Monsieur Prevert, who one day told Monsieur de Poutrincourt a fable wrought of the same stuff, declaring that he had seen a savage playing at lacrosse with a devil, and that he had clearly seen the crosse which the devil used, but as for the Old Gentleman himself, he remained invisible. . . .

And as to the Gougou, I leave its credibility to the reader, for though a few savages speak of it, and hold it in dread, it is in the same way that some feeble-minded folk at home dread the Phantom Monk of Paris. For the truth is that those tribes who live at constant war, and are never out of it . . . one must not wonder that from time to time they have panic terrors and imaginations, like those of hypochondriacs, thinking, like them, that they see and hear things which are not. . . .

In the Twentieth century it is commonplace to divide mankind into two groups in regard to belief-systems: the believers and the sceptics. The believers are sometimes called the sheep, the sceptics the goats. Among the sheep is Champlain, among the goats Lescarlot. But for the French explorer's sheepish reference to the Gougou, there would not have been the French lawyer's sharp rebuttal, and the losers would have been students of the Micmac belief-system and world legends. To make the long winter nights at Port Royal pass faster, Champlain established the Order of Good Cheer. Should the Committee for the Scientific Investigation of Claims of the Paranormal (CSICOP) establish a name a national chapter for Canadian sceptics, CSICOP should call it the Order of Lescarbot.

Deer Island/ Hopper's Headstone

Deer Island lies between Passamaquoddy Bay and the Bay of Fundy, north of Campobello Island.

There is a tradition of a restless spirit on this island of fishermen and resort owners. The restless spirit is that of John Hopper, a strong-willed farmer who suffered bouts of depression. After two suicide attempts, he succeeded in drowning himself in a pond on his property. In life he had made it known that he wished in death no gravemarker. Despite his known wishes, the neighbours who buried his body near the pond in the pasture behind his farmhouse, erected a headstone over his burial place. The headstone bore the simple inscription: "John Hopper / 5 May 1850."

The Mystery of Hopper's Headstone has it that the headstone will not stand of its own accord. It is always toppled. If someone sets it right, in three days' time it will be found knocked over again. Once someone cemented it in place but three days later it was found to be cracked in two. Hopper's spirit is indeed a restless and busy one!

Dungarvon River/
The Dungarvon Whooper

The Dungarvon River runs through central New Brunswick which is a well-storied region. One Sunday in winter in the late 1860s, at a logging camp along the Dungarvon River, an Irish-born logger known as Young Ryan invited the camp's cook to accompany him on a hunting trip in the woods. The cook agreed but made the mistake of wearing his moneybelt. When the two hunters were all alone in the woods, the temptation of easy money overcame the greedy logger. He shot the cook to death, removed the moneybelt, dug a hole in the deep snow, and buried his companion's body. He concocted a tale to account for the disappearance of the cook on his way back to camp.

No one ever found the grave of the cook and nobody recalls the fate of Young Ryan and the moneybelt. But everyone in the Mirachimi area has heard of the Dungarvon Whooper. It seems that to this day the cook's spirit protests the murder and the improper burial in the deep snow. Travellers in the area claim that at sundown they can hear horrible, eerie screams. This wailing or whooping will last ten minutes or so and then subside into silence. In the early 1900s a parish priest from nearby Renous performed the rite of exorcism, but reports of screams persist.

The Dungarvon region of the Miramichi enjoyed railway service for four decades. The service ended in 1936 but not before the train was given the name The Dungarvon Whooper. As Stuart Trueman noted in *Ghosts, Pirates and Treasure Trove* (1975), "It was the first train in the world named in honour of a ghost." The Dungarvon Whooper is celebrated in story and song and has been called "the storied Miramichi country's greatest ghost story."

Fredericton/
Christ Church Ghost

The pride of Fredericton, the capital of New Brunswick, is Christ Church Cathedral, which was built in 1845–52. It is one of the finest examples of decorated Gothic architecture in North America. It bears the distinction of being the first new cathedral erected on new foundations on British soil since the Norman Conquest of 1066. It was established largely through the efforts of the Rt. Rev. John Medley, first bishop of Fredericton. His memorial tomb in marble lies at the end of the north aisle.

By tradition the Cathedral is haunted not by the ghost of Bishop Medley but by the spirit of his wife. It is said that her ghostly form may be seen making its way from the old Dr. Crockett home on Queen Street, gliding along Church Street, and entering the west door of the Cathedral. There the restless spirit surveys the Cathedral, as if in wonderment, and then disappears. Reports of the apparition go back for almost a century.

Fredericton/
Black Peter

The Glasier Mansion at Lincoln, ten miles from Fredericton, is a grand home with two-and-a-half storeys and twenty-one rooms. The main part of the house is over 200 years old, the so-called old wing only 125 years old. The house is owned by Barry and Colleen Thompson. Barry Thompson is the Dean of Students at the University of New Brunswick in Fredericton.

When the Thompson family moved in they began to realize that they were not alone in the house. There was too much noise! The sounds were unnatural and the Thompsons came to the conclusion that the hubub was being caused by spirits — three spirits, to be precise: a friendly ghost, a poltergeist, and another undefined presence. Only that would account for the warm, friendly feeling exuded by the house; the creaking and cracking noises that suggested that the house was being torn apart; the footsteps of Black Peter, the undefined presence.

Mrs. Thompson learned that John Glasier, the original owner of the house, had a faithful servant named Black Peter who lived in a little house on the property but who died in the old wing, nursed by the master of the house. A recent visitor who heard about Black Peter in the dining room, impulsively yelled out, "Come on, Peter!" Suddenly he looked shocked. "Someone just touched me on the shoulder!" he exclaimed. On occasion Black Peter puts in an appearance—"a little old white man, with a fringe of white hair all around and a little pot belly, dressed in a strange old-fashioned nautical uniform of coarse material," in Stuart Trueman's description in *Ghosts, Pirates and Treasure Trove* (1975).

Fredericton/
The Coleman Frog

Visitors to the York-Sunbury Historical Society Museum in Fredericton may view the renowned and

Many are the tales told about the Coleman Frog. Apparently in the 1880s it subsisted on June bugs, Scotch whisky, and locally churned buttermilk. Whether frog of nature or fraud of man, the immense freak is now a prized exhibit at the York-Sunbury Historical Society Museum in Fredericton, N.B. [Tourism/Tourisme New Bruswick]

possibly remarkable Coleman Frog. Whatever they may be seeing, it rests in a hermetically sealed glass case. Is the monstrous bullfrog a genuine freak of nature or an outrageous fraud? The adage "only time will tell" does not apply in this instance. An impartial examination of the contents of the sealed display case would settle the issue once and for all, but the officers of the York-Sunbury Historical Society Museum are not going to authorize *that*.

The story goes that more than a century ago Fred B. Coleman, the proprietor of the Fredericton hostelry called Barker House, would regale guests and tourists with tales of the monstrous bullfrog which made its "happy hopping ground" in Killarney Lake where Coleman operated a summer resort hotel. Guests would coax the frog out of the lake with June bugs and even Scotch whisky, but Coleman attributed its remarkable growth to its consumption of huge portions of locally churned buttermilk. It was described as having a length of five feet four inches, and a weight of forty-two pounds.

In 1885, poachers exploded dynamite in the lake to kill fish. In the process they killed the giant amphibian. Coleman had its body stuffed and displayed in the lobby of the Barker House. It was donated to the museum by the Coleman family in 1959.

"While most Frederictonians prefer to accept it as genuine, there are skeptics who say it is a *papier-mâché* imitation made long ago to advertise a patented cough medicine called Frog-in-the-Throat. They say that it sat in the window of a Fredericton drugstore until Fred Coleman bought it, hid it away until others had forgotten it, then produced it as a tourist attraction." So wrote Mary McKinney in "Canadianecdote" in *Maclean's*. The Coleman Frog gained international fame when it was drawn and described by Robert L. Ripley in his well-known feature "Believe It or Not!"

Fredericton/
The Boyce Mansion

The old Boyce mansion is one of Fredericton's best-known haunted houses, according to a Canadian Press story published in the *Toronto Star*, 2 November 1985. The three-storey residence, located on the bank of the St. John River, "could have been the inspiration for the creepy mansion of Alfred Hitchcock's classic horror film *Psycho*."

The mansion, for many years the property of the University of New Brunswick, serves as a student residence. It is said to be haunted by a gentle, maternal ghost who is known to approach male students when they are asleep. She will run her spectral fingers through his hair, and if he awakes, she will calm him, "It's all right, dear, it's all right."

It seems the ghost once appeared to a former don of the residence who addressed it "in the name of the Father, the Son, and the Holy Ghost" to explain her presence and to justify her actions. The spectral figure answered that she was searching for a letter. This gave rise to the story that the ghost was that of a distraught mother whose sick son died in another city soon after sending her a letter which begged her to come to his bedside. Apparently she never received the letter. Her tragic spirit remained in the house, awaiting the arrival of the letter.

Fredericton/
Belmont House

Belmont House, a rambling mansion with seven bedrooms and a cavernous cellar, overlooks the beautiful St. John River outside Fredericton. It is alleged to be haunted.

The house was built in 1820 by Jonathan Bliss, New Brunswick's first Chief Justice, and it served as the boyhood home of Robert Wilmot, a future Father of Confederation. There were rumours about the house which circulated over the years. One rumour had it that hidden in the immense cellar was the entranceway to a secret tunnel used by fugitive slaves escaping from the United States into the Maritimes.

From 1972 to 1984, Belmont House was rented by Jackie Webster, a matronly grandmother, who felt the presence of someone or something in its rooms. She heard the slamming of doors, footsteps in the next room, and the sounds of someone hurriedly mounting the stairs. She arranged for a *séance* to be held in the house and two weeks later the disturbances increased.

She and her visitors reported feeling a great uneasiness, especially at night. They heard the scratching of rats immensely magnified, followed by a cacophony of thumps, rattles and bangs, not from just one room of the house but throughout the entire house. Then the room in which she was in would turn terribly cold.

After Jackie Webster moved out, the house was divided into apartments, according to the Canadian Press report carried by the St. Catharines *Standard*, 6 November 1986. There are no further reports of poltergeist activity in Belmont House.

Fredericton/
Stanton T. Friedman

As unlikely as it may seem, Fredericton is the home of the nuclear physicist, lecturer, and UFOlogist Stanton T. Friedman. His background interests are science and technology; his foreground interests are all aspects of the UFO experience. He is in demand throughout North America as a writer, lecturer, speaker, and guest on radio and television programs.

Born in Elizabeth, New Jersey, in 1934, he studied Physics and graduated from the University of Chicago with a B.S. in 1955 and an M.S. in 1956. He worked for several major companies in the space and nuclear fields in Ohio, Indiana, Pennsylvania, and most recently in California. In a lecture delivered in 1979, he noted:

> Prior to becoming the only space scientist in North America *known* (who knows who is working under security?) to be devoting full-time to UFOs, I spent fourteen years working as a nuclear physicist on classified government-sponsored research and development programs involving nuclear airplanes, nuclear rockets, nuclear power plants for space applications. Almost all the relevant data was classified and

did not appear in the conventional "scientific" journals. It was a good way to find out about advanced technology and about security and about how the intelligence community operates since I even spent two years working as a project engineer on a classified intelligence study effort under the aegis of the very same organization (Foreign Technology Division of the Air Force) which sponsored Project Blue Book.

> There is no doubt in my mind after twenty-one years of study and investigation that the evidence is overwhelming that planet Earth is being visited by intelligently controlled vehicles whose origin is extraterrestrial. There are no acceptable arguments against flying saucer reality, only people who either haven't studied the relevant data or have a strong will not to believe that Earth is at the bottom of the heap sociologically and technologically in our local galactic neighbourhood.

Friedman became a landed immigrant in August 1980. In a letter written on 26 May 1987, he gave some reasons for the move:

> My wife is a Canadian citizen who grew up in New Brunswick and several of her eight siblings and her aging parents had settled in Fredericton, thus providing lots of family for us and my three children. There was no family in California. Nothing mysterious about the move here.

> Fredericton is an excellent place to raise a family, two major industries—government and the university—safe, peaceful, lots of community spirit, and non-stop jet service to Montreal, Toronto, etc.

> I am something of a big fish in a small pond because of my professional background in advanced technology (leading to lots of consulting work) and my background in radio and TV. I did a weekly radio science commentary for the CBC here for six years, and have been involved in starting three technical companies.

> I am something of an expert on the radon problem, radiation processing, etc. I have now

lectured at well over 500 colleges and to dozens of professional groups in eight provinces (missing P.E.I. and Nfld.) and forty-nine states — all but Alaska. I belong to a diversity of professional groups and have participated in more than a dozen scientific conferences on UFOs.

This is a publicity photograph of Stanton T. Friedman, the "flying saucer physicist," who moved from California to Canada in 1980 and makes his home at Fredericton, N.B. He travels widely and lectures on the subject "Flying Saucers are Real." It was Friedman who coined the phrase "Cosmic Watergate" to refer to his belief that national governments are engaged in a massive "cover-up" of UFO information. Lately he has been preoccupied with the release of documents which purportedly show that the U.S. government has in its possession debris from a UFO that crashed near Roswell, New Mexico.
[Stanton T. Friedman]

Gagetown/
The Female Phantom of Gagetown

The Female Phantom of Gagetown is said to inhabit the Jenkins House in the village of Gagetown on the Saint John River. The two-and-a-half-storey residence with its four chimneys was built in 1810 in a pastoral setting by its original owner, the Honourable Hugh Johnson. A number of tragic events occurred within its walls before it was acquired by its present occupant, the well-known weaver and tartan designer Patricia Jenkins.

On more than one occasion, according to Stuart Trueman, writing in *Tall Tales and True Tales from Down East* (1979), Jenkins has felt a "presence" in one of the upstairs bedrooms and in the main rooms of the house. The "presence" seems to move from room to room. Visitors to the house feel it, not to mention the Jenkins cat which swivels its head as if watching the slow progress of what has been called the Female Phantom of Gagetown.

The house has known some tragedies. Hugh Johnson's eldest daughter married an Englishman and died here in childbirth. One of the sons and his fiancée drowned in the river before they could be wed. Another of his sons, also engaged to be married, broke off the engagement at the last moment because he had fallen in love with his fiancée's younger sister. Some time after their wedding, the older sister was invited to move into the mansion with the married couple. "She accepted, then she found she couldn't stand seeing her sister in her former sweetheart's arms. She hanged herself in the closet of an upstairs bedroom."

Well before Jenkins acquired the house, but well after these tragic occurrences, twelve-year-old Peggy Lucas was an overnight guest in the house. She was sound asleep in one of the upstairs bedrooms when she woke with a start. "I awakened just as a lady in white walked slowly from the direction of the closet right past my bed, toward the window. Her hair was down around her shoulders. I saw her plainly." The terrified young girl cried out but there was no answer. Then the lady in white vanished before her eyes.

Grand Manan Island/
Island Mysteries

Grand Manan, the largest of the islands at the entrance to the Bay of Fundy, is renowned for its beauty and is called the "Bermuda of the Maritimes." Although it is small in area, being only fifty-five square miles, legends and mysteries told about it abound. Here are a few.

The west coast of the island is rocky and uncharacteristically bleak and desolate. It is maintained that pirates' treasure lies buried some two miles north of Dark Harbour. Buccaneers are said to have captured a shipwrecked couple — Edmond Chatfield and Desilda St. Clair from Maine — who accidentally observed them burying their cache. They hanged Edmond from the limb of a tree before the eyes of the hysterical Desilda. Set free, she took to the woods. Once there she lured each pirate in turn into the woods, where she murdered him in exquisite revenge. It is said that Edmond's headless ghost walks the shoreline, while the spirit of Desilda, wild of countenance, flies by, wailing, "Edmond! Edmond! Edmond!"

Ghost Hollow lies south of Dark Harbour. Here on foggy nights may be seen the apparition of the Little Man. He wears a flat-topped hat and is the despair of motorists. He will dart out of the woods and race alongside a speeding automobile. Then he will overtake the vehicle and, to the horror of the driver, throw himself in front of the vehicle. The motorist will slam on the brakes and bring the car to an abrupt halt. There will be no impact, no collision. When the motorist looks around, there will be no Little Man.

Little Dark Harbour is haunted by the Rowing Man. Collectors of dulse, the edible purple seaweed found on the shores, report that on some moonlit nights, generally on 19 November and again on 25 November for no known reason, they can hear the sound of rowing and see the apparition of a man in a dory. The Rowing Man appears for a minute or two, slowly rowing by. Then he and the dory vanish.

Indian Beach is reputed to be haunted by the Flaming Indian Squaw. This is a Passamaquoddy woman named Lemushahindu. She stands at the water's edge, engulfed in flames. Those who have seen her have reported hearing a gurgling sound. She makes an appearance about once every seven years.

The most memorable and most photographed site on Grand Manan Island is the Hole-in-the-Wall. Over the millennia tidal action eroded an oval aperture in a thick ridge of rock protruding from one of the island's steep cliffs. This spectacular natural formation gives rise to speculation, as such openings have been traditionally seen as entrances to other worlds.

Grand Falls/
Malabeam

Grand Falls is a town on the Saint John River adjacent to the State of Maine. According to legend, the disturbingly plaintive cries of Malabeam may be heard above the roar of the seventy-four-foot-high cataract at Grand Falls. Malabeam, a brave and loyal Maliseet woman, was captured by the Mohawks who were invading traditional Maliseet territory. She feigned friendship with the invaders and agreed to guide their invasion party over the tricky waterways to the Maliseet encampment. What she did instead was lead the armada of one hundred Mohawk warriors in their rafted canoes over the brink of the cataract. They perished and so did she for she was in the lead canoe, and her cries may be heard to this day.

Hampton/
The Mysterious Stranger

Kings County Historical Society Museum, in the village of Hampton, has a series of display cabinets filled with artifacts concerned with local history. In one of the cabinets may be seen the handcuffs, the iron key, and the leg shackles once worn by Henry More Smith, "the mysterious stranger." To quote Stuart Trueman in *Tall Tales and True Tales from Down East* (1979), Smith was "the most mysterious man who enlivened the long history of this part of Canada."

Smith was elusive and inventive if not mysterious.

Legion are the legends that have grown up around him, but basically he was a petty thief and a confidence man. No shackles or jail cells could hold him long. He used a number of aliases, among them Henry Moon, and he was wont to imply a connection between his surname and the lunar body. Trueman described him as he appeared to his contemporaries: "In actuality he was an early-day Houdini, a super-confidence man, magician, mystic, will-o'-the-wisp, bilingual fraud, preacher and religious hypocrite, prophet, mind-reader, fire-maker, master tailor, puppeteer, mesmerist, contortionist, natural-born engineer—and, of course, a very likeable horse-thief."

At one point in his career of crime and mystification, Smith was apprehended trying to steal a horse, which was a capital offence. He was held in close custody in the new jail at Kingston, New Brunswick. In May 1815, he was tried, found guilty, and sentenced to death. The account of how he idled away the time in his cell is typical of the stories told about the man. From bedding-straw and scraps of clothing, held together with his own blood, he fashioned a series of miniature figures which made music and danced of their own accord as he sang or whistled. He read teacups, made mysterious pronouncements, proclaimed his innocence, and even predicted that he would be pardoned. Indeed, he was pardoned, and at the precise hour he said he would be, the reason being there was an outside chance that he had not stolen the horse that he was convicted of stealing.

Smith headed for Upper Canada and then the American South, where he committed a series of petty and pesky crimes. Thereafter he disappeared from history. Most of what is known about Smith comes from the biography *The Mysterious Stranger* (1817) written by Walter Bates, Loyalist and "Sometime High Sheriff of the County of Kings." Bates, Smith's jailer, believed that the prisoner performed acts "unequalled in the history of man." A modern appreciation of "the mysterious stranger" is Barbara Grantmyre's *Lunar Rogue* (1963). Today he is a folk hero in Kingston, and there is a caged Henry More Smith that is part of the historical float in the parade during the annual Kingston Loyalist Days celebration.

Hartland/
The Blazing Barn

Hartland, a town on the Saint John River in western New Brunswick, is the home of the world's longest covered bridge. The region is also the home of the Blazing Barn, which may be found two miles south of Hartland on a small island in the Saint John River.

"Time and time again a barn was seen afire from afar—but when volunteer firefighters rushed to the scene there was no sign of flames or smoke or even smouldering embers," explained Stuart Trueman in *Ghosts, Pirates and Treasure Trove* (1975). "It continually amazed people to go by on the river bank at night and see the barn ablaze in the distance, then go by the next morning and see it still standing intact. Some ascribed the phenomenon to the restless spirits of men slain in an early clash of English against French and their Indian allies. Whatever the reason, Indians of bygone generations refused even to go near the island."

Moncton/
The Magnetic Hill

The principal tourist attraction of New Brunswick is the Magnetic Hill, north of Moncton. Far from being a "magnetized mountain," it is an optical illusion of the first order. Here the countryside is so tilted that what appears to be an upgrade is really a downgrade. A car driven to the bottom of the hill will appear to coast back up to the top of the hill when the brakes are released.

The attraction, known locally since the 1920s, was first brought to national attention in 1933 when Stuart Trueman and other journalists began to write about it. There are other Magnetic Hills, but Moncton's is the best known on the continent. At least four others may be found in Canada. There are two in Ontario—one at a hill outside Dacre, southwest of Renfrew; another in Burlington, near Hamilton. Two more are in Quebec: one is part of a commercial attraction in the Eastern Townships; another is in Montreal where the illusion is sustained at one point

55

The world's best-known Magnetic Hill is located outside Moncton, N.B., and is shown here in a 1970s photograph. Drivers of automobiles are led by an optical illusion into thinking that their vehicles are coasting uphill when they are really coasting downhill. Some authors of occult books have made some surprising statements about this Magnetic Hill. Andrew Tomas explained that its effect is akin to "anti-gravitation." Jacques Bergier noted that it is so powerful that "an entire Indian village totally vanished not far from here." [Metropolitan Toronto Library]

on the Chemin de la Côte-des-Neiges. The effect was reported in the vicinity of Collingwood but declined or disappeared with the resurfacing of the roads.

Magnetic Hills have attracted an undue amount of attention from European researchers who find them inexplicable. For instance, the Hungarian-born writer Andrew Tomas has this to say about them in *We Are Not the First: Riddles of Ancient Science* (1971):

> Anomalies in the moon's gravity and its gravitational belts, discovered by Apollo 8, caused the craft to be diverted from its course and altitude by these belts or mascons. On our planet gravitational anomalies are not uncommon. One of the most spectacular examples is Magnetic Hill near Moncton, New Brunswick, Canada, where

cars travel uphill without power. Gravity reserves its rule at the bottom of the hill and as drivers switch off ignition and release brakes, their cars are pulled up to the top of the hill by an invisible force. It is generally thought that a pocket of magnetic iron, deep underground, is responsible for this gravity phenomenon. But a magnet or lodestone supposedly attracts metal only.

However, the magnet of Magnetic Hill affects not only metallic objects such as cars but others as well — a wooden stick or a rubber ball, for example. Under certain conditions even water can flow upwards in some spots!

It also affects people and many witnesses testify to its unusual influence.

"There is something here in the ground. You feel it in your bones. It makes you shivery. It almost makes you dizzy," writes one tourist.

Another says: "When I was walking and turned around, it gave me a spin. I felt it in my forehead."

"You'd think there was a giant hand pulling you back," describes another person the sensations on Magnetic Hill.

There is a vast difference between electromagnetism and gravity. The phenomenon on Magnetic Hill may help to solve the mystery of anti-gravitation.

Andrew Tomas is not alone in his musings. The French writer Jacques Bergier has decided that Moncton's optical illusion is one of Earth's anomalies, the site of a "secret door", a magic passageway to a strange hidden world, created by the presence of a "negative mascon." (Scientists are familiar with the ordinary *mascon*, which is a concentration of mass out of the ordinary with gravitational properties of its own; but they have yet to encounter, as apparently have Tomas and Bergier, a "negative mascon" with "negative gravity.") Bergier waxes eloquent about the Moncton attraction in his book *Secret Doors of the Earth* (1975), translated by Nicole Taghert:

Another very good example of a site of a secret door is Magnetic Hill, near Moncton, New Brunswick, Canada. Gravitation here is literally inverted. A car can roll up to the top of a hill without having its motor started. The magnetic field is equally upset, but the gravitational effects are the most astounding. A rubber ball will roll back uphill. A wooden cane, which is not usually susceptible to electric or magnetic forces, rises in the air. If a water dropper is used, the water will climb back inside.

Although a magnetic field affects no physiological sensations, witnesses here experience vertigo, feel pains in their foreheads, and sometimes have the impression of being pulled backwards by powerful hands. There have been a number of disappearances in this vicinity, and an entire Indian village totally vanished not far from here.

Unfortunately Bergier gives no particulars about the "entire Indian village." But he does express some discontent: "We can only surmise that the area has been modified, all the while regretting that official science is not studying this kind of problem in more depth."

Richibucto/
The Barque *Amity*

Most readers with a mania for mysteries will be familiar with the Amityville Horror, the said-to-be haunted house on Long Island, New York. Few readers, except some in or from the Maritimes, will know anything at all about the mystery of the barque *Amity*.

Sometime in the 1860s, the *Amity*, heavily loaded with timber for the Atlantic crossing to Liverpool, England, left Richibucto on the east coast and ran aground on a sandbar and would not be moved. It remained there over the winter with a watchman on board. He complained he heard footsteps, as if someone were walking in the hold. With the spring came new workmen who independently reported hearing footsteps. Searches turned up nothing, although it seemed the stacks of timber were shifting in the hold.

Finally the *Amity* was refloated and moved to Rexton, New Brunswick, where the vessel was unloaded and the damage to the hull was repaired. The vessel was reloaded with another cargo of lumber and once more set sail for Liverpool. There, when emptied of its cargo, workmen found the decomposed body of a seaman. The body could not be identified. It had been decomposing for over three months.

"How did it escape detection during the many searches carried out in the hold? Where was that body when the original lumber cargo was discharged?" Roland H. Sherwood asked these and other questions in *Maritime Mysteries: Haunting Tales from Atlantic Canada* (1976), adding: "Down through the long years the name of the New Brunswick barque *Amity* has always been linked with this unexplained mystery of the sea."

Richibucto/
The Flying Spectre

There are a number of lonely stretches on the highway which runs between Richibucto and Rexton. The highway passes through woods and at points over-looks the Richibucto River. The Flying Spectre is said to haunt one of these lonely stretches.

The Flying Spectre is a white-robed woman, with streaming blonde hair and her hands held out as if in supplication, who suddenly steps out of the woods onto the side of the road and races alongside the speeding vehicle, as if appealing to its driver to stop and assist her. In the nineteenth century she tried to halt stage-coaches. In the early twentieth century it is automobiles, though some years have passed since she last appeared to a motorist. The story goes that the woman is seeking justice or revenge. It seems she was attacked and decapitated for no reason by a de-ranged man armed with a long knife at Dan Irwin's Inn at Richibucto a century or so ago.

Rothesay/
"A Molecular Dance"

The distinguished poet P.K. Page has never forgotten the appearance of a ghost and the message it had for her. In June 1987 the vision was as vivid to her as the evening it was experienced, despite the passage of forty-seven years.

During the early years of the Second World War, Page was in her mid-twenties and living in a house that was neither old nor new in the town of Rothesay, northeast of Saint John. She was alone in her room one evening, grieving the loss of a close friend.

> I had loved her dearly, and hers was my first death. During our years of friendship, we had talked about many things, including the possi-bility of life after death. I suggested that it might be possible; she took the other view. But neither of us had strong opinions on the matter. After all, we didn't *know*.
>
> Then before me in the room I saw a curious, molecular dance. I stared at it and it began to look like a Morse Code printed on the air. Then it densed, and became the very real shape of my friend. She looked radiant and extraordinar-ily beautiful.
>
> "So I was right after all," I said, overjoyed.
>
> "Yes," she replied. "That's why I came back — to tell you."
>
> "Then, what is it like? Tell me — what is dying like?"
>
> "Every death is personal. My death is of no use to you. But there is nothing to grieve about." And *I* believed her.
>
> That is all we said. We smiled at each other, placed our fingers on each other's arms, the beginning of an embrace. I could feel her flesh with my fingertips. Then I felt it disintegrate, like uncooked rice. I pulled back and again I saw a molecular dance, a swarm of midges in the air, and then nothing.
>
> The interesting thing is that since that eve-ning I never have grieved for her. I have missed her, of course, and still do, but since that evening I know there is nothing to grieve about.

Sackville/
The Woman in Black

Sackville in eastern New Brunswick is the home of Mount Allison University. There is a century-old, two-storey dwelling in Sackville that was once haunted by a Woman in Black. For four years it was rented by the Macfarlane family. John Macfarlane was a member of the Physics Department of Mount Alli-son University. The family consisted of Mr. and Mrs. Macfarlane and their three sons. The youngest, Andrew, then aged four years six months, slept in his own room. In the morning he would talk about the kind woman who came into his room at bedtime and said, "It's time to go to sleep now." The family discounted this as the product of Andrew's imagina-tion, but that was not the end of it. Mrs. Macfarlane would catch the unexpected scent of lavender coming from the master bedroom when it was unoccupied. Family members reported catching glimpses of a woman emerging from Andrew's bedroom doorway and gliding across the hall and down the stairs. The Woman in Black wore an old-fashioned long black gown and held before her a lamp dating from the 1890s.

Then they learned something of the history of the house. Apparently Andrew's bedroom was the same bedroom occupied decades earlier by a boy who died in his tenth year after a lingering malady and after being attended by his devoted mother. Eventually the Macfarlane family moved out and the house is now occupied by descendants of the original builders who have never seen the Woman in Black.

Saint John/ "Steer North-West!"

Robert Bruce, a sailor of Scottish background, was the pilot aboard a merchant vessel sailing between Liverpool, Nova Scotia, and Saint John, New Brunswick. He was plotting the course and, not altogether satisfied with the results, called out to the captain, whom he believed to be in the next cabin, "What do you think about it, sir?" There was no reply so he entered the cabin and found there a complete stranger sitting in the captain's chair and writing on the slate on his desk. He left in a hurry and raced onto the deck where he encountered the captain. Both men hurried below only to find the cabin empty. But written on the slate were the words: "Steer north-west."

A search for the stowaway was conducted in vain. Each member of the crew was asked to write those words on the slate in his own handwriting, but the handwriting did not match. The captain decided to follow instructions and steer north-west. At the worst it would mean the loss of a few hours of sailing time. Before long a ship in distress was sighted. It was a wreck, completely ice-bound, originally bound for Quebec. But for the message on the slate the two vessels would not have met and the passengers aboard the wreck would have died.

When the shipwrecked company came aboard, Bruce spotted among them the stranger he had seen sitting in the captain's chair and writing on the slate.

The stranger stared back in amazement. The captain asked the stranger to write the words "Steer north-west" on the back of the slate. It was the same handwriting as on the other side. The captain of the wrecked vessel explained that the stranger, his passenger, had fallen into a deep sleep about midday. When he awoke, he said, "We shall be saved today." The stranger explained that he had dreamt that he was actually on board the ship that would rescue them. When the ship finally came into sight later that day, the captain had no trouble recognizing it from the description. The stranger recognized everyone on board the vessel that rescued them.

This tale of the high seas was originally reported by R. Dale Owen, former U.S. envoy to Naples, in *Footfalls on the Boundary of Another World* (1860).

Saint John/ The *Countess of Dufferin*

Helen Creighton in *Bluenose Magic* (1968) tells the story of the rescue on the high sea of the *Countess of Dufferin*. The Quebec-built vessel was loaded at Saint John with lumber and on Christmas day in the 1880s it sailed for Londonderry, Ireland. A few days of fine weather gave way to days of foul weather followed by a hurricane which blew the vessel off course. The mast was destroyed and to keep the vessel afloat the cargo had to be jettisoned. The remaining food supply was swept overboard. The captain informed the crew that although they would not drown they would starve to death. They were so far off their usual course that there was nothing left for them to do but pray.

As if in answer to their private prayers, help came from the *Arlington*, a vessel built in Yarmouth, Nova Scotia, on its way from Liverpool, England, to New York. The crew had enjoyed a week of fine weather when Captain Davis made a surprise appearance on deck. He shouted to the wheelman to change course.

"Captain Davis," the second mate asked, "What's the matter?"

"Didn't you hear the hail of distress?" replied the Captain.

The mate assured him that no sounds of distress had been heard. "You were dreaming," the mate suggested.

"I was not dreaming; I was wide awake," insisted the captain, adding, "The strange part of it is that whoever called for help also gave the course we should take. It was 52 north by 21 west."

That was three days' sail from their position, and the crew showed reluctance to go so far off course. But Captain Davis gave the wheelman the change of course. They sailed into turbulent waters and three days later came upon the luckless *Countless of Dufferin*.

"Will you stand by and take us off?" yelled the captain.

"Certainly we'll stand by and take you off; that's what we came for," replied Captain Davis.

As Helen Creighton concluded,

When daybreak came the seas were still high but the rescue was effected. The last one to step over the *Arlington*'s rail from the stricken ship was, of course, the captain and at that precise moment the sun came out and they were able to take their position. Officers and crew looked at Captain Davis with a new respect, for they were exactly 52 north by 21 west, the very spot where the voice had directed him.

Saint John/
The Codfish Man

There is the tradition in West Saint John of the Codfish Man, whose appearance was described by Stuart Trueman in *Tall Tales and True Tales from Down East* (1979):

And April 18 is the magic date for the Codfish Man. If you happen to be strolling around West Saint John that evening, fishermen say, you may see a man clad in oilskins and sou'wester trudging up from the wharves carrying a giant codfish over his shoulder — a cod so huge it hangs down his back and forces him to walk slightly bent forward like the label picture of an old well-known brand of cod liver oil emulsion.

"You can almost catch up to him," recalls a believer, "but then he vanishes and reappears thirty feet past you. Later you may meet him walking back to the harbour — without the fish."

The Codfish Man is believed to be the spectre of Daniel Keymore, a fisherman in the days of sail. An unexpected gale hit the Bay of Fundy on 18 April, capsizing his boat. He drowned, to the sorrow of his wife and young children who lived in a small house in West Saint John. Every year on the anniversary of his death a giant cod was deposited on the doorstep of his house, to the astonishment of his widow. The gifts from the seas continued to be made until her remarriage some years later.

St. Martins/
The Union Premonition

St. Martins is a fishing village on the south coast and overlooks the Bay of Fundy. Stuart Trueman calls it a "village of sea captains" and the province's "most prolific source of ghost tales."

St. Martins Bay is the setting of the so-called Union Premonition. The following account of the mysterious premonition concerns a sailor named Jack Dyre — an ominous name for a sailor or for anyone else for that matter — and is based on the account as told by Joyce Banaszak in "The Ship Cried a Warning" in *Fate*, July 1982.

It was shortly before ten o'clock on a Sunday night in 1889. Jack Dyre made a final tour of inspection of the sailing ship *Union* which was anchored in St. Martins Bay. It was a newly built vessel and was soon to make its maiden voyage to Nova Scotia. Dyre was alone in his duties for he had volunteered to serve as watchman while the captain and three other crewmen went ashore to visit their families.

Nothing was amiss so Dyre turned in and fell fast asleep. He was awakened with a start to hear a voice calling out his name, warning him to leave the *Union*. He got up and walked around the ship for the source of the voice. He found no one, decided he was dreaming, and climbed back into his bunk. He had hardly fallen back to sleep when he was again awakened by the same voice crying out the same warning. Again he walked around the ship and again found nothing out of the ordinary.

When he was awakened for the third time, he admitted defeat. Packing his belongings, he retreated to the breakwater where on Monday morning the others found him haggard and nervous. The captain tried to convince him to forget about the strange warnings, but Dyre refused. The captain had to sign on a new man as a replacement. At noon the *Union* dropped away from the breakwater and drifted northward with the tide. There was no wind and soon the ship was becalmed in the bay with about forty other ships. All of a sudden, on that windless mid-afternoon, the *Union* rolled violently and capsized!

As Joyce Banaszak concluded, "Local fishermen in a small boat managed to rescue the captain and one crewman—but three of the sailors, including the man hired to replace Dyre, drowned."

Shediac/
The Graveyard Treasure

The first white settler of Shediac, a village overlooking Northumberland Strait, was an Englishman named William Hannington, whose body lies in the graveyard of the Church-of-Saint-Martin-in-the-Wood. His monument is an imposing affair, consisting of a slab of stone supported by four pillars with a memorial inscription beneath. The inscription was obscured for centuries.

When the graveyard was spruced up in 1964, workmen removing the moss from Hannington's inscription were surprised when the cement fell away to reveal a twelve-inch square cubicle with a secret drawer within which was found "a single sheet of paper, neatly folded and well preserved. Upon the paper was a message in a bold hand." The message read: "To the place of disembarkment, by the will of God, treasure will be found."

At first the workmen kept the message a secret, knowing that "the place of disembarkment" was a small island in Shediac Bay where the first settlers had landed. But the secret was soon common knowledge and the island was overrun with prospectors and treasure-hunters. No treasure was ever found. As Roland H. Sherwood concluded in *Maritime Mysteries: Haunting Tales from Atlantic Canada* (1976): "The mystery of the treasure at Shediac Island remains as unsolved as the mystery of the note and the secret drawer in the tombstone of William Hannington, first English settler at Shediac in New Brunswick."

Lake Utopia/
The Lake Utopia Monster

Lake Utopia, which lies in the southern part of the province, was depicted in an article in the *Canadian Illustrated News*, 30 November 1872, as "the Queen of New Brunswick lakes." The author, who signed the article E.J.R., evoked its picturesque location and its "majestic silence." He also drew attention to the origin of the unusual place name, employing the earlier spelling of Eutopia. The author was impressed by the small size of the lake—nine miles in length and three miles in width in some places—and by its romantic air:

> As a *tout ensemble*, no matter from where you view it, Lake Eutopia is charmingly romantic— alas! that there should be any drawback to such a beautiful piece of creation.
>
> When night throws its dark mantle over land and lake and river, the red man cautiously paddles shorewards, he trusts not its witchery of beauty. He believes that fathoms down lurks a monster that may, without warning, suddenly appear and make a meal of Mic-Mac, paddles and canoe. Nor is this superstition confined to the aborigine. The dwellers by the lake nearly without exception firmly believe that a huge fish or serpent has a home in "Eutopia," for have they

The Lake Utopia Monster is the terror of anglers and canoeists — at least in this illustration from the Canadian Illustrated News *on 30 November 1872. The engraving, signed B. Kroup, illustrates an unsigned article about the small lake which is found in southern New Brunswick. The author of the article stated that the illustration is a "faithful representation of the Lake Monster" as described by a local "medicine man." [The New Brunswick Museum]*

not seen it, basking sometimes full length of 100 feet or thereabouts, like a huge pine log on the surface of the waters? And does it not occasionally, when in a sportive mood, raise "Ned" generally at the bottom, sending up old logs, spruce edgings, and ancient deposits of various kinds and sorts, causing the water to boil and foam, as if a geyser had suddenly broke loose?

The article went on to describe how "not long since" a joint stock company was formed in nearby St. George "with a capital of $200, for the purpose of procuring nets and apparatus for the capture of the monsters." On that occasion the Lake Utopia Monster proved to be elusive, but on another occasion showed itself in full fury:

> The chief Medicine Man of the Mic-Macs swears that a fearful creature with head as large as a puncheon followed him and a brother Indian in their canoe some distance soon after the ice was cut this spring, snapping its bloody jaws in a

most horrible manner. The sketch is a faithful representation of the Lake Monster as described by the Medicine Man.

Over the years there have been numerous sightings of the Lake Utopia Monster.

Woodstock/
The Death Chuckle

South of Woodstock, a town on the Saint John River, is the Lower Woodstock Indian Reserve. The Maliseets who live there still talk of the Death Chuckle. It is maintained that when the chuckle is heard — not a merry gleeful sound but a gutteral croaking sound — someone on the Reserve will die in three or four days time.

Apparently in the middle of the nineteenth century a Maliseet moose-hunting guide named Noel Lolar died. Because he was not a practising Christian, he was refused burial in consecrated ground, so his family interred him in the cellar of their cabin. This resting place was not to his spirit's liking and the Death Chuckle began to be heard on the Reserve. It was not until the 1930s, when the cabin was levelled and the cellar was excavated and Noel Lolar's remains were reburied, this time in consecrated ground, that the Death Chuckle became but a grim memory.

Woodstock/
Fire-Starter

Charles Fort was the world's leading collector of anomalous phenomena, so it is only appropriate that following his death in 1932 the material he collected and prized has come to be known as "fortiana." Inexplicable occurrences are commonplace, Fort felt, and always have been. They have only to be collected, categorized, and publicized to show that science is scientific only to the degree that it ignores the anomalous—what he called "damned facts."

It was Fort who brought to the attention of the readers of his book *Wild Talents* (1932) the fact that there was a "fire-starter" at Woodstock. The following item is reproduced from the 8 August 1887 issue of the *New York World*:

> *Fire Plays Ghostly Tricks*
> A Family Terrified by Articles in the House
> Bursting into Flames
> (Special to the *World*)

Woodstock, N.B. August 7 — The people of this town are greatly excited over the strange and inexplicable scenes which for the past twenty-four hours have been enacted in a little two-story frame house on Victoria Street, occupied by Reginald O. Hoyt, a picture-frame dealer. His family, consisting of his wife, five children and two nieces, are in a state of mental fear and anxiety, and will probably vacate the house to-night. Since 11 o'clock yesterday morning no less than forty fires have broken out in various parts of the house, and bedding, furniture, window-shades, clothing and various household articles have been partially destroyed. Only untiring vigilance has prevented the house and its contents from burning to the ground, and this would have caused the destruction of other buildings in the vicinity.

Three fires can be traced to no human agency and even the most sceptical are staggered. Without premonition and with no lamps lighted or stoves in use, various articles would burst into flames. Now it would be a curtain high up out of reach, then a bed quilt in another room would begin to smoke and smoulder, and as if to still further nonpluss the theorists, a carpet-covered lounge was found to be all afire underneath, among the jute stretched above the springs. A basket of clothes on the shed burst into flames and the basket itself was partially consumed. A child's dress hanging on a hook, a feather bed, a straw mattress were ignited and would have been consumed but for water poured on them. The villagers here believe the house haunted.

PRINCE EDWARD ISLAND

Bay Fortune/
The Legends of Abel's Cape

Abel's Cape in Fortune Bay bears the name not of a biblical character but of Edward Abel who lived hereabouts and died violently of a wound inflicted by a bayonet on the lower part of the body. Since his death on 28 August 1819, it is maintained, his ghost may be seen and heard from time to time on the shore of the Cape, bent over groaning as if in agony.

Abel's violent death seems appropriate for a parcel of land that has long been held to be the burial place of pirates' gold. Tradition has it that Captain Kidd, the best known and most feared of the pirate captains, secretly buried his treasure-trove in an ancient place of burial near the cape. The long-lost site is protected by guardian ghosts and phantom dogs.

The Legend of Abel's Cape is another matter. It has nothing to do with pirate's treasure or violent death, yet it has leapt to the status of an archetype. As the archetypical form of two later legends about once-living people, it supplied the imaginative under-pinnings for the tall tales concerning the Fantastic Return of Charles Flockton and Charles Coughlan Comes Home. It seems Abel's Cape attracts tales the way it once attracted American theatrical folk, serving in the tens and twenties of this century as a Broadway summer colony. The most dramatic of the tales is the following one.

It seems there was once a Mr. Haskell who had a low old home on the Cape. His only relative was a

During his lifetime no one would have called Irish-American classical actor Charles Coughlan a "theatrical legend." Yet following his death—which occurred in 1899 in Galveston, Texas—he achieved "near-legendary status" through an odd turn of events: the so-called Mystery of Coughlan's Coffin. It is said that the Gulf Stream floated his coffin from Galveston, along the Atlantic seaboard, and deposited it at Bay Fortune, P.E.I., on land where he had once lived.
[Metropolitan Toronto Library]

daughter, his sole confidant. Here is how the tale is recalled. "He wishes to have his last resting place out on or near the point of the Cape just back from the highly rocky bank that juts out on Fortune Bay, where the water washed the stones and bank during each high tide," in the words of an Islander quoted by Sterling Ramsay in *Folklore: Prince Edward Island* (1973). But he died while on a trip with his daughter to San Francisco. Contrary to his wishes, she had him buried in California. "A short time later there occurred a terrible earthquake that released the casket and set it free on the water where it floated until it came to Fortune Bay. There it was reburied where the old man had wished."

Bay Fortune/
The Mystery of Coughlan's Coffin

If a "mystery" may be said to have an "author" then the author of the Mystery of Coughlan's Coffin is the cartoonist and columnist Robert L. Ripley, the creator of the internationally syndicated newspaper feature "Believe It or Not!" Ripley wrote and illustrated the following item for his feature which appeared in the daily press on 15 September 1927:

> Charles Coughlan Comes Home! He died in 1899 and was buried in Galveston. When the tragic flood came his coffin was washed out to sea — and the Gulf Stream carried him around Florida and up the coast to Prince Edward Island — 2,000 miles distant — where he lived.

Thus did the Mystery of Coughlan's Coffin pass into history.

Ripley's extraordinary tale of the floating, homecoming coffin is a fascinating amalgam of fact and fiction. First the factual basis.

Charles Francis Coughlan (1841–1899) was born to Irish parents in Paris, France. He achieved success on the London and New York stage, joining the convivial colony of Broadway theatre personalities who summered at Bay Fortune. Coughlan was touring with *Hamlet* when he died in Galveston, Texas,

on 27 November 1899. His body was interred in a cemetery vault. Floodwaters from the violent hurricane that hit Galveston on 8 September 1900 engulfed the cemetery and swept a great number of coffins into the Gulf of Mexico, including Coughlan's.

So much for the factual basis; now the fictional basis of the yarn. The Gulf Stream carried the rough wooden box containing the casket with Coughlan's remains into the Atlantic Ocean, and from there into the Gulf of St. Lawrence, and from there into Northumberland Strait, where it was finally deposited on the shore near Bay Fortune. This occurred sometime in October 1908. It was found by fishermen who dragged it onto the beach. When they read the legend on the lid of the coffin, "Charles Coughlan (1841–1899)," they recognized the name of an Islander and quietly reburied the coffin in the village church cemetery. Thus the return of the native son.

One of Ripley's readers was the actor's daughter, Mrs. Gertrude Coughlan Pitou, who had long lived in ignorance of her father's burial place. As the result of her query to Ripley, it is known that the cartoonist based this item for his column on the tales told in the published memoirs of fellow thespians, Sir Johnston Forbes-Robertson and Lillie Langtry. But as reporter Neil A. Matheson showed in "Coughlan's Body Story Is Colorful 'Nonsense,'" in the Charlottetown *Guardian*, 20 June, 1965; as Dwight Whalen explained in "Charles Coughlan Never Came Home" in *Fate*, March 1979; and as Melvin Harris proved in *Investigating the Unexplained* (1986), "The whole story is a fantasy. The fate of Coughlan's coffin is unknown to this very day."

The basis of the tale told by the thespians in their memoirs seems to be the "homecoming" not of Charles Coughlan but of Charles Flockton, a fellow actor and sometime summer resident of Bay Fortune. Following Flockton's death in Los Angeles in 1904, David Belasco and Mrs. Leslie Carter carried out Flockton's wishes and arranged for his ashes to be placed in the base of the sundial erected in his memory on property he owned at Abel's Cape. The land is now owned by Belinda Dingwell and the sundial still stands, bearing the following inscription:

To a Faithful Friend and Loyal Servant
The Creeping Shadows Mark Another Hour
of Absence
From Mrs. Leslie Carter and David Belasco

It was one small step from one Charles to another Charles; and one giant leap from ashes to coffin. But the steps were taken and a memorable mystery was created. The yarn was repeated by broadcaster and author Frank Edwards in *Strange World* (1964), by writer Vincent H. Gaddis in *Invisible Horizons* (1965), by researcher Alan Vaughan in *Incredible Coincidences* (1979), and by a pack of researchers plainly intrigued by this instance of an incredible and appropriate coincidence which proved to their satisfaction "you can go home again."

Charlottetown/
The *Fairie Queene*

Without cause or reason the bell of St. James Church tolled a total of eight times early Friday morning, 7 October 1859.

After five tolls, two men who lived in the vicinity went to investigate. They were startled when the bell tolled for the sixth time and the church doors were suddenly flung open and inside stood three women dressed in white. Just as suddenly the bell tolled for the seventh time and the doors swung shut. They tried the doors only to find them locked. Peering through a small window, they could see a lone woman in white ascend the stairs to the belfry. By this time the minister and sexton had arrived to learn the cause of the disturbance. They unlocked the doors and together the four men entered and found not a living soul in the body of the church. But as they made their way up the stairs to the belfry, they heard the bell toll for the eighth and last time. They found no one in the belfry and the bell-rope was securely tied. Everyone was puzzled.

That evening they were equally puzzled when the *Fairie Queene* failed to arrive at the Charlottetown wharf. The passenger steamer regularly plied the Northumberland Strait between Nova Scotia and Prince Edward Island. They learned that it had left Pictou and they knew that it was fine sailing weather. But the vessel never arrived at Charlottetown, a run of no more than half a day. It was some days before they learned that the vessel had sunk with the loss of eight passengers, five men and three women. Had the bell of St. James Church foretold the disaster? Was its tolling a coincidence? Is it all a legend? "That mystery remains unsolved to this day," noted Roland H. Sherwood in *Maritime Mysteries: Haunting Tales from Atlantic Canada* (1976).

East River/
The Spirits of the Binnstead Estate

Binnstead Estate was the name of a large farm set on some two hundred acres at East River not far from Charlottetown. Its location was quite isolated in 1856, when the so-called Spirits of the Binnstead Estate first made their presence known.

It seems that the grounds of the estate were originally cleared about 1840 by a rich Englishman who erected a house and lived there until he sold it to a man named Piggott whose tastes and habits recalled his name. He employed as servants two sisters, daughters of the Newburys, local labourers. Each sister gave birth to a boy. Then one sister and one child disappeared. Shortly thereafter Piggott sold the estate to an English gentleman named Fellows and left the area. The sister returned to the Newbury home, presented the baby which was then under two years of age to her parents, and left for the United States. She told her parents only that the boy was her sister's, her own being dead.

In 1856–59, the estate was occupied by Mr. and Mrs. Jas. E. Harris of Charlottetown who noted unusual occurrences. Throughout the house at irregular intervals there were rumbling noises and the house seemed to vibrate. Then there were shrieks, sobs, moans, and half-uttered words. These seemed to emanate from a tree which stood a little distance from the dining-room window. Finally there was the apparition which took the form of a bright light that illuminated the main bedroom. By the fireplace stood the

67

figure of a woman wearing a check shawl. Her left arm held a young baby and her right hand stirred the ashes in the fireplace. The figure turned to reveal the features of a young woman with an anxious, pleading look. The spectral figure appeared many times to many people, including Harry Newbury, the sister's son, employed as a servant.

It seems the poet-laureate Alfred Lord Tennyson, hearing the tale of the Spirits of Binnstead Estate from Wilfred Ward, a Conservative Member of the British House of Commons, urged that the particulars be committed to paper. Ward originally heard it from his daughter, a Mrs. Pennce of Sainte-Anne-de-Beaupré, Quebec. She wrote it down and sent it to the British Society for Psychical Research, when she was living at Weston Manor, Freshwater, Isle of Wight, close to Tennyson's estate. These details appear in Sterling Ramsay's *Folklore: Prince Edward Island* (1973).

Fort la Joie/
The Acadian Apparition

The Expulsion of the Acadians in 1758 was not limited to the French farmers of New Brunswick but extended to those of Prince Edward Island as well. Tradition holds that one evening at dusk, before news of the expulsion arrived, the Island's Acadians foregathered in the little Eglise Saint-Jean at Fort la Joie. While they were reciting their prayers, and in the midst of an "Ora pro nobis," Colonel Lord Rollo burst into the building with a detachment of soldiers and dispersed the congregation, ordering the worshippers to aration for their deportation from the Island.

"Even to this day, it is said, strange lights are seen passing to and fro in that vicinity. As the evening star appears, the outlines of a church are said to become visible — it is the little Church of St. John," wrote Sterling Ramsay in *Folklore: Prince Edward Island* (1973). The apparition is accompanied by the rustle of the winds, the roar of the waves, and the words of supplicating voices reciting "Ora pro nobis." The pastor and his flock return to complete their orisons, so rudely interrupted by the English.

Gulf of St. Lawrence/
Crippen's Curse

Could a curse be the cause of 1012 people drowning in the Gulf of St. Lawrence? Henry Kendall believed that it could be the cause and was.

Henry Kendall was in a position to know, for he was the Captain of the S.S. *Montrose*. The ocean liner was *en route* from Liverpool to Montreal via Antwerp and Quebec City. The ocean voyage was uneventful and the ship was crossing the Gulf of St. Lawrence when something unexpected happened. Captain Kendall received a wireless message which informed him that one of his passengers was suspected of murder and that he was to detain him until a police inspector could be boarded. The inspector was brought on board on 31 July 1910, and in the presence of Captain Kendall the surprised suspect was arrested.

The suspect was a Dr. Hawley Crippen, a fashionable Harley Street physician, who had poisoned and dismembered his wife. Fleeing England with his mistress in hand, he hoped to go into hiding in the United States. But the couple had not counted on news of the savage murder reaching America as soon as it did. Wireless messages were still something of a novelty; in fact, the arrest of Crippen marked the first such use of the invention. Crippen was not amused to be detained under arrest. Apprising himself of Captain Kendall's role in the affair, he cursed him: "You will suffer. . . . "

Captain Kendall did not think much of the wife-murderer's so-called curse, especially after Crippen was tried, found guilty, and hanged. No doubt the curse was in the back of his mind when, four years later, as Captain of a Norwegian collier named the *Storstad*, he guided the vessel to the point in the Gulf where Crippen had cursed him. In the wee hours of the morning of 29 May 1914, something unexpected happened. There was a tremendous crash. The *Storstad* had rammed the Canadian Pacific's *Empress of Ireland*, a luxury liner outbound from Quebec. The disaster occurred during a period of calm, clear weather. Yet a small patch of fog had developed. As the upbound *Storstad* approached the liner, a few kilometres east of

Pointe au Père, fog swirled out off the north shore and engulfed both vessels. The loss of life made it the greatest marine disaster in the history of the Gulf; 1012 persons drowned. One of the few survivors was Captain Henry Kendall, the man cursed by Crippen. He certainly suffered.

Wayland Drew drew attention to the curse in *The Sea Within: The Gulf of St. Lawrence*, adding the following postscript: "Forty-seven unidentified victims of the disaster lie in a little cemetery between Pointe au Père and Rimouski, maintained to this day by the CPR. One hundred and eighty-eight were borne in crude pine coffins up-river to Quebec aboard the revenue cutter *Lady Grey*, a 'fairy-white funeral ship.' Bells tolled along the river as she passed."

Lot Seven Shore/ The Phantom Ship

The Phantom Ship of Northumberland Strait has been reportedly seen by residents all along the Island's South Shore. Edward D. Ives, a folklorist at the University of Maine, found reports especially prevalent

The Spectral Ship and the Phantom Ship, two different types of mystery vessels, are depicted in these two late nineteenth century engravings. The Spectral Ship (also called the Fire Ship) appears to glow in its own light. At dusk and at night it seems to be enveloped in flames, yet it speeds on its way as if to its doom. The Phantom Ship, in contrast, is a ghostly vessel. Oblivious of the elements, it appears to scud across the horizon on some errand of its own. Reports of sightings of both types of mystery vessels in Maritime waters have been widespread, at least until recent times. [Metropolitan Toronto Library]

among the residents of the area known as the Lot Seven Shore, corresponding to Cape Wolfe, Glengarry, Burton, and Campbellton. Sterling Ramsay wrote in *Folklore: Prince Edward Island*:

> One such report is that of a resident of Glengarry who said that one night as he and his wife were preparing for bed, she pointed out the window and asked him whose light that was over there. He was puzzled, because there were no houses in the direction she was pointing, just the waters of the Strait, so he went over to look. What he saw was a full-rigged ship in flames sailing northward up the Strait at an impossible speed. The two of them watched it for about an hour before it disappeared from view.

The Phantom Ship seems to be a harbinger of bad weather. According to some, it is seen only in the calm before the storm; according to others, it is seen only at the height of a storm at sea.

Point Prim/
Legends

Point Prim lies on the southern coast of the island and extends into Northumberland Strait not far from Orwell Bay. The following legend is reprinted from the Cataract *Journal*, Niagara Falls, N.Y., 30 November 1903, where it is reprinted from *Donahoe's Magazine*.

> There is a delightful legend among the people of Point Prim to the effect that when the English attacked the French fort at that place a chain ball from one of the attacking vessels cut the steeple from the old church located on the very point. In falling it toppled over the promontory and carried the bell which it contained into the sea. Dwellers along the point affirm that from time to time the sound of that bell comes over the waters at eventide and that its phantom tone is ever a warning of a fierce storm or some imminent danger to those who make their living by the spoils of the ocean.

There are knowing references among the residents of Point Prim to "the oldest inhabitant" of the region.

> Many individuals have reported seeing the melancholy figure of an old hunchback man making his way along the shoreline, carrying over his shoulder a deeply hollowed hand-made shovel quite unlike any they had ever seen before. He is described as having an oblong-shaped livid scar midway between his ear and his nose giving him a queer, unearthly look.

So wrote Sterling Ramsay in *Folklore: Prince Edward Island* (1973), who added that traditionally the mysterious hunchback is the ghost of a disgruntled Acadian settler exiled in 1758. He managed to bury his treasured belongings near an old pine tree near the shoreline before he was put aboard the *Violet*. The transport vessel sank and all the Acadians drowned, including the hunchback. But "even in death he came back to find and guard his treasure."

Tignish/
Blimphey's Return

The ghostly figure of a fisherman was at one time said to haunt the stretch of road from St. Felix to Tignish, the resort and fishing community near the northern tip of the province. The figure was named Blimphey and the fishermen who encountered the figure described it as extremely unfriendly. It is possible the ghost's century or so of unrest has come to an end, for in recent years there have been no sightings of Blimphey.

The ghost is said to be that of a morose Irish settler named Blimphey who committed suicide and was buried in a shallow grave on the bank of MacLeod's pond. The bank caved in and the burial area was exposed but no human remains were found. Consequently, it is said, Blimphey returned and walked the stretch of road he knew in life to find his earthly remains.

Wellington/
The Phantom Train

The Phantom Train of Wellington was first seen crossing the railway bridge outside the village of Wellington, west of Summerside, one evening in December 1885.

The apparition was seen and heard by about forty villagers at Mill House who had gathered to celebrate a wedding but remained to grieve the death of a drowned youngster. There was no midnight train from Summerside or anywhere else, so the mourners were surprised when a train whistle shattered the night air and the beams of its headlight illuminated the front of Mill House. They saw a railroad engine pulling three cars stop at the station, passengers board the cars, and the train pull away from the station — and disappear.

Islanders and visitors have reported seeing the Phantom Train of Wellington at odd times but generally during December evenings. The tradition is reported by Sterling Ramsay in *Folklore: Prince Edward Island* (1973).

QUEBEC

French-Canadian habitants *and* artisans *expressed preferences for motifs of the fantastic variety. The* Winged Dragon *inspired one unknown craftsman in nineteenth-century rural Quebec to cut from a sheet of tin this splended weather-vane figure. [Royal Ontario Museum]*

Acton-Vale/
Poltergeist Activity

Poltergeist activity was reported in the home of the Saint-Onges family of Acton-Vale, a town situated east of Montreal and south of Drummondville. The events took place over a number of hours one day in January 1969.

Something unseen snatched the rosary from the hand of the six-year-old girl Guylaine who was attempting to dress for school. The family watched in horror as a series of supernatural events followed. As Sheila Hervey reported in *Some Canadian Ghosts* (1973), a religious painting flew the length of the room, leapt to a dresser, then enacted a weird rhythmical dance. Beds were stripped of their linen, mattresses were tossed about. An array of rosaries, ashtrays and vases filled the air around Guylaine.

Three local priests were summoned. Abbé Claude Léveilleé, Abbé Normand Bernier, and Abbé Wilfrid Bérard sprinkled holy water and tried to exorcise the spirit. "The thing had no intention of being removed so easily. A table and two religious statues were broken in the upsurge of mindless violence." Then, as unexpectedly as chaos had broken out, peace reigned. A week later the three priests issued a statement which included the following remark, "We believe that the message that God wanted to transmit to Acton-Vale was transmitted. The supernatural exists, even if our scientific spirit leads us to doubt it, and we are invited to better observe our faith and to pray more and more for sinners." No further supernatural events were reported.

Iles des Allumette/
UFO Sighting

A farmer witnessed the landing of a strange-looking craft on his farm near the village of Chapeau on les Iles des Allumette in the Ottawa River west of Ottawa. The UFO sighting took place on 11 May 1969. As Yurko Bondarchuk reported in *UFO: Sightings, Landings and Abductions* (1979), farmer Leo-Paul Chaput was awakened by the barking of his dog about 2:00 a.m. He noticed a brilliant light shining through one of the windows. "Looking out, he was astonished to see a dome-like object on the ground, not more than five hundred feet away from his farmhouse. The craft was approximately thirty feet in width, and vaguely resembled the military helmets worn by the French army during World War I." The craft seemed to vanish, as a soft hum receded into the night. The next morning Chaput explored the landing area.

> He discovered a large circular imprint in the ground that had not been there on the previous day. The deep doughnut-shaped marking of dehydrated soil and vegetation was thirty-two feet in diameter and three feet wide. Inside the circle, the vegetation had not been damaged but there were three circular depressions which looked as if they had been arranged in a perfect triangular pattern, fifteen feet in width. These imprints, presumably caused by some form of landing apparatus, measured about eight inches in diameter and three inches deep. Their depth clearly suggested an object of considerable weight.

Elsewhere Chaput found two more doughnut-like markings. The traditional explanation of the formation of such rings is a form of fungi known as fairy-grass, but such rings do not leave symmetrical depressions in the soil.

Ile d'Anticosti/
Graveyard of the Gulf

The shores of Ile d'Anticosti have seen so many wreckages that it was dubbed the "Graveyard of the Gulf." It is said that in the eighteenth and nineteenth centuries some four hundred ships were lost off its coasts. The large island—in area it is one-third larger than Prince Edward Island—lies at the mouth of the Gulf of St. Lawrence. It was once owned by Henri Menier, the millionaire French chocolate manufacturer. This immense villa, Chateau Menier, lies in ruins. It was demolished in the fire set by an arsonist in 1953.

The story of one wreck is sketched by Wayland Drew in *The Sea Within: The Gulf of St. Lawrence* (1984):

> Because of the profusion of wrecks on Anticosti, the government in 1810 established emergency supply posts at Fox Bay and Ellis Bay, and at the mouth of the Jupiter River. Signposts gave guidance along the shore and, later, cabins were built. These shelters, however, did not save the passengers and crew of the *Granicus*, a timber ship driven by storms onto Anticosti not far from Fox Bay in 1828. Exactly what happened to the survivors will never be known, since the written records have all vanished — except for one: an affidavit sworn the following spring by one Basile Giasson, a schooner captain who took shelter early that May in Fox Bay. Inside the cabins, Giasson and his crew found the butchered, hung, cooked, and salted remains of perhaps twenty people, in various stages of putrefaction. They also found a large, well fed man, comfortably slung in his hammock: dead.

Réservoir Baskatong/
UFO Sightings

UFOs have been reported on at least two occasions by hunters in the wilderness area called Réservoir Baskatong, 110 miles north of Ottawa.

74

Two Montrealers, Richard Huot, left, and Jacques Lavoie, are shown holding photographs of a UFO they took while on a camping trip. One of the men managed to take several photographs of the oval-shaped object as it skimmed across the dark surface of a lake before it disappeared. The sighting took place on 11 March 1978 in a wooded area northwest of Montreal. [Montreal Star/ Canapress]

Jacques Jacobson and three other witnesses saw "a bright sphere much larger than the moon" hovering above a hill two or three miles away from them over Lac Baskatong at 9:00 p.m., 6 November 1957. The UFO was visible for about fifteen minutes. During its appearance their regular radio reception was blacked out, and so was their shortwave reception, except for a single wavelength which brought in a very strong signal in a rapidly modulated code. The incident is recounted by Aimé Michel in *Flying Saucers and the Straight-line Mystery* (1958).

Richard Huot and Jacques Lavoie were vacationing at the camp at the southwest tip of the area when they too saw and succeeded in photographing a strange sight. At 6:30 p.m., 11 March 1978, they noted what at first appeared to be a "falling star" approaching from the northwest. But the object in the sky continued its descent until it appeared to be a "brilliant object floating above the frozen lake." They took four photographs of the UFO before it shifted its position and then lifted off. Yurko Bondarchuk discusses the sighting in *UFO: Sightings, Landings and Abductions* (1979) and gives this description of the photographed UFO: "The luminous craft — symmetrical in shape—resembles a bell flattened on top."

Beauport/
Witchcraft in New France

The earliest record of the practice of witchcraft in New France is contained in a letter of September 1661 written from Quebec City by Marie de l'Incarnation.

The Royal Edict of 1682 put an end to criminal prosecutions for the practice in France and its colonies. According to Marie-Aimée Cliche in "Abracadabra!" in *Horizon Canada*, No. 80, 1986, roughly 140 people were accused of witchcraft in the British colonies in 1638–97, about fifteen of whom were executed. In the witchcraft trials in Massachusetts in 1692–93, several people were hanged for the practice of the "black arts." In all of New France there was one execution for witchcraft, and the case concerned a miller named Daniel Vuil who wanted the hand in marriage of a young serving girl named Barbe Halay. Both lived in Beauport, a community northeast of Quebec City.

The letter concerning this case was translated and the details appeared in R.S. Lambert's *Exploring the Supernatural: The Weird in Canadian Folklore* (1955).

> Furthermore, it has been discovered that there are sorcerers and magicians in this country. This has been made clear by the case of a miller who emigrated from France at the same time as Monseigneur the Bishop, and was caused by His Reverence to abjure his heresy — for he was a Huguenot. This man wanted to wed a girl who had taken passage, along with her father and mother, in the same ship as himself. But as he

was a person of bad character, they refused to listen to his suit.

After this refusal, the miller sought to attain his object by having recourse to the practices of Satan. He caused demons, or "esprits follets," to appear in the girl's house, accompanied by apparitions that caused her great pain and terror. The cause of these phenomena was not at first understood, until an apparition of the magician himself put it into the heads of the good folk to conclude that there must have been "maleficium" on the part of the wretched suitor; for he appeared by day and night, sometimes alone, sometimes in the company of two or three others, whom the girl named, although she had never seen them before.

Monseigneur the Bishop now sent some of the Fathers to the house, and himself paid a visit there for the purpose of exorcising the demons by the prayers of the Church. However, nothing was accomplished by this, and the noises continued louder than ever. Phantoms were seen, a tambourine and a flute were heard playing, stones were detached from the walls and thrown about, flying hither and thither — and all the same the magician and his companions were found to be troubling the girl. Their intent was to cause her to marry the wretch, who wanted to possess her, but to corrupt her first.

Bishop Laval himself journeyed from Quebec City to Beauport to drive out the evil one. The exorcists failed, so the girl was taken from Beauport and committed to the care of the sisters of the Hôtel-Dieu in Quebec City. She exclaimed that Vuil appeared before her in the company of witches and was intent upon her virtue. Each evening the nuns would sew her into a sack, releasing her the next morning. In the meantime Vuil renounced his Catholicism and re-embraced his Protestant Huguenot faith. He was tried for witchcraft and pronounced guilty by Bishop Laval. Jailed in February 1661, he was executed for witchcraft in October 1662. There is no further report of the fate of Barbe Halay.

Lac Beauport/
The Legacy of Nikola Tesla

It is only proper to begin the incredible story of the legacy of Nikola Tesla with some plain facts about this remarkable man.

There are memorials to Nikola Tesla (1856–1943), the Serbo-American inventor, on both banks of the Niagara River. A memorial "Tesla Tree" was planted in Queen Victoria Park on the Ontario side. On the New York state side an immense and imposing statue on Goat Island, between the American and Horseshoe Falls, acknowledges the man's theoretical and practical contributions towards "harnessing" the hydroelectric power potential of the Falls. His specific contribution was to introduce alternating current in opposition to Thomas A. Edison's direct current.

Perhaps because he was bested by Tesla on the Niagara project, Edison referred to the reclusive inventor as "the poet of science." The description fits, for Tesla possessed not only a genius for invention but also a grandiose sense of himself and of the greatness and mystery of his electrical experimentation. According to Margaret Cheney's biography *Tesla: Man Out of Time* (1981), the inventor worked on such projects as "terrestrial night light" (a plan to incandescently ignite the gasses of the planet's upper atmosphere and thus illuminate the Earth at night); a device to detect electrical radio waves beamed to Earth from outer space; a weapon to create and direct disintegrator rays or beams; and (in a proposal to the Canadian Power Commission) "efforts to transmit hydroelectric power wirelessly and inexpensively through the Earth." It could be argued that Tesla was not only "the poet of science" but also its original "mad scientist."

The facts are fantastic enough without the superfantastic legacy of Nikola Tesla. "Nikola Tesla was not an earth man," according to Margaret Storm, writing in *Return of the Dove* (1959). "The space people have stated that a male child was born on board a space ship which was on a flight from Venus to Earth in July, 1856. The little boy was called Nikola." It is not surprising that his inventions were so unworldly, given his alien ancestry. Storm explained: "Tesla was an Adept, an Initiate, a Venusian." Then she identified the source of this revelation: "The space people released this information in 1947 to Arthur H. Matthews of Quebec, an electrical engineer who from boyhood was closely associated with Tesla."

Arthur H. Matthews, E.E., B.Sc., told his own story in a photocopied mimeographed manuscript of 134 pages complete with illustrations called *The Wall of Light: Nikola Tesla and the Venusian Space Ship, the X-12* (1973). It seems Matthews's father was an electrical engineer employed by Lord Kelvin in England. Tesla was briefly associated with Kelvin and met the father and the son. He took a fancy to young Arthur, so much so that by 1938, when Tesla was nearing the end of his life, he entrusted young Arthur with his legacy. Arthur was by then an electrical engineer with a laboratory of his own on an old, hundred-acre farm outside Lac Beauport, northeast of Quebec City. The legacy consisted of full knowledge of the great range of Tesla's inventions (apparently there are more than twelve hundred of them, not the eighty-five patents listed in the public records) and, more specifically, the plans for two inventions known only to Matthews.

These inventions are remarkable indeed. The first is known as "the Tesla anti-war machine." Details are hard to come by, but Tesla himself experimented with the device in 1917–20 at three locales in Quebec: outside Tadoussac, in the Lac Saint-Jean region, and at Lac Beauport. The machine was designed to project a "standing beam" or "wall of light" to insulate entire countries from any form of explosive attack.

Matthews called the second remarkable invention "the Tesla interplanetary communications set," although he sometimes more simply refers to it as "the Tesla Scope." By following Tesla's plans, Matthews was able to construct and operate the device in 1941. Tesla's plans called for a transmitter and receiver of incredible power; Matthews's model could only send and receive signals to destinations in space that were between five thousand and thirty thousand miles from the planet's surface. The Tesla Scope was the device that permitted Matthews to communicate with the Venusians.

The Venusians were interested in the use Matthews was making of Tesla's communication equipment, so they landed their space ship, the X-12, on his isolated farm. Their ship was an immense flying saucer seven hundred feet in diameter, three hundred feet in height, with a central "tube" or dome with a diameter of fifty feet. The X-12 visited for the first time in the spring of 1941. Thereafter it visited every other year until the spring of 1961 when it made its last landing.

Matthews was understandably apprehensive about the appearance of the Venusians, and was really relieved to discover they were in most ways indistinguishable from Earthlings. The first two he met were tall, handsome, and blue-eyed. "You may call us Frank and Frances, for we stand for Truth," they told him. When Matthews got to know them a little better, Frank boasted that he was more than 800 years old, and Frances was 250 years his junior. They invited him aboard the X-12 and took him for a trip. He went on later journeys, visiting their home planet Venus and even Mars, the plains of which reminded him of "our beautiful Eastern Townships."

There is no real conclusion to *The Wall of Light*, but it does attest to his personal philosophy of life. "I am probably the last living person who knew and loved Tesla," Matthews noted. He went on to declare his belief in God and his faith in Christ. He expressed pride in his Christian Science principles and his membership in the Laymen's Movement for a Christian World. But the one lesson that Matthews learned and wanted his readers to understand is the one he repeated every so often. "If you would understand Tesla," he noted, "you must first attune your mind to God."

Lac Champlain/ The American Champ

Lake Champlain is a lean, loch-like lake which drains into the St. Lawrence via the Richelieu River. For most of its length it serves as the border between the states of New York and Vermont. Only its northernmost tip extends into Quebec.

Lake Champlain was named after Samuel de Champlain who first explored its shores in July 1609. Indians reported that a "horned serpent" lived in its depths. It is frequently said that the French explorer saw the creature and described it as "serpent-like, about twenty feet long and as thick as a barrel, with a head that resembled that of a horse." In the 1870s, P.T. Barnum offered the sum of $50,000 for the capture or carcass of "the Champlain Sea Serpent." The showman wanted to exhibit it in his museum in New York. Between Champlain's description of 1609 and 1987, there have been approximately 300 recorded sightings. Over the years the lake monster acquired the nickname Champ.

Some two hundred people attended a seminar at Shelburne, Vermont, devoted to the subject "Does Champ Exist?" It was held on 29 August 1981 and was organized by Joseph W. Zarzynski, the founder of the Lake Champlain Phenomena Investigation and the author of *Champ: Beyond the Legend* (1984). In 1982, Zarzynski acted as the catalyst for the introduction and subsequent passage of a resolution in the Vermont House of Representatives and the New York State Senate which sought to protect the lake monster "from any willful act resulting in death, injury or harassment."

The creature is the subject of an extensive literature — being an American rather than a Canadian lake monster — and it has even been photographed. Sandra Mansi of New Haven, Connecticut, snapped a colour photograph of Champ in 1977. "It looked around, but never swam," she recalled. "It was really quite majestic, but I was terrified." Her husband and children saw it too and were also terrified.

The following Canadian sighting occurred in Missisquoi Bay and was described by the Swanton *Courier* on 31 July 1880.

Recently Dr. Brigham and Ashley Shelters of Bedford, P.Q., saw the sea serpent in the waters of Missisquoi Bay. They furnished the following description: "The strange monster appeared to be of great length, portions of its body fully 20 feet in length appeared above the surface of the water. Its head, which [was] described as being as large as a flour barrel, is of irregular shape,

its eyes, being of greenish tinge, looked hideous and disgusting in the extreme. The strange creature, when first seen, was quite near the shore, and when alarmed made for the deep waters of the lake, causing a great commotion in the usually quiet waters. The noise it made in moving sounded like the paddle wheels of a steam yacht.

Les Ecureuils/
Les Ecureuils Iron Mass

This incident involves two pieces of metal found near the shore of the St. Lawrence River, near the town of Les Ecureuils, about twenty miles upriver from Quebec City. "Although there is no direct link between this metal and UFOs, circumstantial evidence indicates this possibility, and the metal is very much part of the UFO literature," according to the entry written by Arthur Bray in *The Encyclopedia of UFOs* (1980) edited by Ronald D. Story.

The two pieces of metal were found on shale flats with no sign of impact craters in June 1960. The smaller of the two, which weighed about eight hundred pounds, was carted away and sold as scrap. The larger piece, known as Les Ecureuils Iron Mass, weighs about three thousand pounds. Shaped somewhat like an oblong inverted mushroom, it measures approximately seventy inches by fifty-four inches by twenty-four inches at the centre. At the top centre of the object are the remains of two "pipes" of obvious fabrication. The main material is so hard it defies cutting by hacksaw.

The metal was removed and analyzed by the Canadian Armament Research and Development Establishment (CARDE), which reported that it was foundry slag. The report added: "A small electronic potting can was imbedded near one of the outer edges. By scratching away the potting plastic, it is possible to identify an electronic component which appeared to be a transistor." In 1971, the Mines Branch of the Canadian Department of Energy, Mines and Resources examined the metal, finding that the mass consisted of two major components, carbon steel (magnetic) and manganese steel (nonmagnetic), and concluding that it was most probably produced in a foundry by dumping excess metal from ladles into a hollow in sand, a process known as "pigging."

Members of the Ottawa Flying Saucer Club retrieved it in 1961 and brought it to the capital, where it rested for a number of years on the lawn of the residence of Wilbert B. Smith, who headed the UFO study called Project Magnet. Then it was moved a few miles out of town to the residence of another club member where it presumably still rests.

"In summary," concluded Bray, "no proof exists concerning the origin of this metallic mass, and it remains a mystery."

Rivière Gatineau/ La Chasse-Galerie

The legend of la Chasse-Galerie, first recorded in 1891, tells of events that occurred in an isolated lumber camp in the woods of north-central Quebec not far from the bank of the Gatineau River. It is reprinted by Edith Fowke in *Folktales of French Canada* (1981).

One night a young lumberman, pining for his sweetheart in faraway Lavaltrie, admits his loneliness to his companions. They inform him that they may travel to Lavaltrie and return in only a few hours. This would leave them plenty of time to dance with

People everywhere and at all times have dreamed of magical flight. The aerial vision of the habitant *in Quebec in the early nineteenth century was expressed in terms of* la Chasse-Galerie, *the "flying canoe." The Devil would permit a lovesick* voyageur *to make a flying visit to see his* blonde, *the cost being that of forfeiting his immortal soul. Such visions may recall the reality of UFOs; then again they may not! This illustration by Henri Julien comes from* La Chasse-Galerie: Légendes Canadiennes *(1900).*

their sweethearts who live there too. All they have to do is board *la Chasse-Galerie*, the flying canoe. They take the incredulous young man to see the long bark canoe and Baptiste explains that before the six of them pile into the canoe they must promise the Devil to forfeit their souls should they pronounce the name of "your master and ours, the good God" or as much as touch a cross during the journey. They so swear and pile in and Baptiste cries out, "*Acabris! Acabras! Acabram!*" and they are off.

Soon they are flying over Montreal Mountain and on to Lavaltrie where they land and hide their canoe and surprise their sweethearts at the dance. They have a great time and in good time they return to their canoe. But it seems Baptiste has drunk too much at the dance, and on the way back he almost crashes into Montreal Mountain. He comes close to pronouncing the name of "your master and ours, the good God." But he avoids doing so by the skin of his teeth, and they return to the lumber camp after their night of dancing. Once more they are safe, at least until their next flight aboard *la Chasse-Galerie*.

Rivière Gatineau/ Poltergeists

The valley of the Gatineau River is a region rich in legend and tradition, so it should come as no surprise that it resembles the Ottawa Valley in that it has more than its share of haunted farmhouses and poltergeists — "noisy ghosts."

The accounts which follow come from Gunda Lambton's article "Folklore in the Gatineau" included in *Up the Gatineau!* which is a 1984 publication of the Historical Society of the Gatineau.

> Two houses in the Fieldville and Brennan's Hill area displayed similar Poltergeist symptoms which may also have been caused by a high emotional charge from, usually, teen-age children, often but not always, girls. In the Fieldville farmhouse people would see a strong and very strange light, rather like others that have been described when waking up in a haunted house.

Passing the Bennan's Hill farm at night, Jim Kelly, going to night-shift at the Paugan dam, would see a similar light. Others heard a dog bark, a piano play in the middle of the night; yet others told of a piano that refused to be moved out of the house. Poltergeists are different from regular ghosts in that they are confined to a certain time when this charge is produced in ways of which we know little, but which we could compare to the "tent-shaking" of Indian medicine men. Father MacGregor, the Farrellton priest for twenty years after 1937, exorcised the Poltergeist in the farmhouse between Farrellton and Brennan's Hill, but such houses do not always react to exorcising. However, in the 1970s, two friends of mine, one after the other, have lived there without hearing or seeing anything supernatural. The two families whose houses were temporarily haunted during the second quarter of this century were Irish Catholics, and the Otter Lake house where a ghostly lady gently pulls at one's bedclothes also belonged to an Irishman, Robert Farrell, the nineteenth century manager of the Gilmour farm on Farm Lake, where his wife is said to have met an unnatural death. There are also stories of haunting at the George Derby farm which is near the confluence of the Picanoc and the Gatineau, close to Gracefield. This family is English and Anglican, and they lived on an old supply farm for lumber camps which before that time may have been an Indian camping place, even a burial ground. Arrowheads have been found there. The haunting may go back to an event that happened a very long time ago. Sometimes all that is remembered of a house is that it was haunted, like that of the Goods in Wakefield, in the valley of the Lapêche river. The Goods, who were Anglicans, had come from Ireland around 1870, according to the census.

One of the most fascinating haunted places belongs to our president, Mr. [R.A.J.] Phillips, though it is hard to tell whether the haunting or Poltergeist is due to the area or to the house where most of it takes place. The farm is a former Foley farm, also an Irish name; but the log-house in question is a log-house moved from Carp where it once belonged to a Montgomery family. The area where it was moved to had been greatly changed through the construction of the dam on the Gainteau. When there were still rapids an Indian girl is said to have drowned there.

Many of us, at the time of a picnic of this Society at the Phillips' place, were intrigued by Mr. Phillips' stories of the odd behaviour of a large picture of Queen Victoria, which at times could be seen literally bouncing on the wall, before it fell down and broke. As soon as this picture was covered by a poster of an ordinary landscape, it ceased acting up. In another house the Phillips' had been disturbed by footsteps just before dawn; their mother, when living there, also complained of "someone walking around." The tenant of the log-house, waking up at night, might find his room brilliantly lit, in the way I described other Poltergeist lights. At one time, the cat refused to enter the building, its hair standing on end — just as the horse had balked meeting a ghost on the Borough Road. While all this sounds like a Poltergeist, the recent appearance of a shadowy figure with long dark hair shows that ghosts may continue, rather than recede in time, depending on their grievances being solved; something hard for us to know unless we know the history of the place.

Grenville/
Eozoon Canadense

Grenville may be the name of a village along the Ottawa River, but to earth scientists the word refers to a geological region — or province — of the landmass of Canada. The Grenville Region lies in a southeastern direction between the Canadian Shield and the north shore of the St. Lawrence River.

For almost half a century it was argued that the limestone of the Grenville Region held fossil evidence of the earliest form of life on Earth. In the 1850s, naturalists found structures of two minerals of contrasting physical and chemical properties in these ancient rocks. Sir William Logan, first director of the Geological Survey of Canada, discovered some "bulbous lumps" in the gneiss of the Precambrian Shield and reported them as "stromatocerium-like forms" in his *Geology of Canada* published in 1863. He then turned to Sir J.W. Dawson, Canada's sole accomplished microscopist, for an examination. In an address to the Natural History Society of Montreal, delivered on 18 May 1864, Dawson named the tiny formations *Eozoon canadense*, "the dawn animal of Canada," and declared Eozoon to be a "foraminiferan" more complex in nature and many times greater in size than any hitherto found.

The controversy over the nature of Eozoon — was it the fossil of an organic lifeform or merely a lump of inorganic mineral? — coincided with the period dominated by the discussion of Charles Darwin's theory of evolution. When Dawson became aware of the dramatic possibilities Eozoon offered in combatting the evolutionary theory, he was determined to exploit them to the fullest.

Sir William Logan remained on the sidelines of the controversy. He died in 1875, three years before *Eozoon canadense* was stricken from the list of fossil organisms and Dawson reluctantly admitted that he was in error when he included it as a lifeform. Sir J.W. Dawson, until his death in 1899, considered the analysis of Eozoon to be among his many significant scientific achievements. He unswervingly maintained his interpretation of these structures as "formaniferans," the oldest fossils on Earth. He never did learn that he had uncovered not the remains of the earliest-known unicellular animal but rhythmically banded structures of two minerals. It was not until 1913 that *Eozoon canadense* was shown to be formed by the contact of Grenville limestone with igneous obstrusives.

Thus died the notion that preserved in the Grenville Region of the Canadian Shield for millions of years was evidence of the earliest form of life on Earth — "the dawn animal of Canada."

Is this the portrait of a Norseman? The high cheekbones and the imposing headband are the distinguishing features of the carved sandstone head which was found in 1976 by a group of hunters on the shore of Lac Guérard, Que. The head measures nine-and-a-half inches in height and four inches in width. After examining the head the dissident archaeologist Thomas E. Lee suggested it was Norse in both workmanship and facial features. The pen-and-ink sketch was executed by M. Harris. [Dwight Whalen]

Lac Guérard/
Portrait in Stone

An unusual carving, a portrait in stone, was discovered in 1976 by a group of hunters on a sandy beach on the shore of Lac Guérard. When it was found it was covered with moss. Lac Guérard flows through the isolated interior of Northern Quebec northeast of Schefferville.

The portrait in stone, cut from local sandstone, preserves the facial features of a strange-looking person. The face, lacking in symmetry, has high cheekbones and appears to be wearing an imposing headband. The subject is neither Inuit nor Indian; nor is the style of the carving. It weighs somewhat more than two pounds. It measures nine-and-a-half inches long and four inches wide. In May 1979 the unusual work was acquired by the Séminaire de Sherbrooke, Sherbrooke.

The carving is pure Norse, according to a Canadian Press story carried by the St. Catharines *Standard*, 4 July 1979. This was the view of the dissident archaeologist Thomas E. Lee who was interviewed by John Heney in Ottawa. Among Lee's discoveries are ruins in the Ungava district of Northern Quebec which may very well be Norse. Lee, who examined the carving, felt it was Norse in workmanship and Norse in facial features. So in his view it was carved by a Norseman and depicted a Norseman at some point in the prehistory of the region.

Iles Harrington/
Ile des Démons

There is no present-day map to identify the Ile des Démons, but on seventeenth-century maps it appears as a desolate island off the coast of Quebec or Newfoundland between the Strait of Belle Isle and the mouth of the Rivière Saint-Paul. Jacques Cartier regarded it as haunted by demons or imps. Wayland Drew, writing in *A Sea Within: The Gulf of St. Lawrence* (1984), narrowed it down to one of the Iles Harrington. These islands are suitably gloomy:

Unless one has been born to this place, or has grown to love the dark moods of the sea, the Harringtons are one of the most desolate places on earth. Even today, despite the little community nestled in their securest harbour, to be marooned on the Harringtons at certain seasons would mean death. Yet here, in 1542, on one of the group then called Ile des Démons, two women and a man were abandoned by their comrades.

Ile des Démons, wherever it may be found, is a romantically doomed locale, being associated with the 1541 voyage of Jean-François de La Rocque de Roberval. A hard-hearted Calvinist, Roberval was appointed ''lieutenant-governor of the country of Canada'' by the French king François as soon as he turned Catholic. He set off to New France in the spring of 1541 accompanied by his niece, Marguerite de La Roque. Marguerite was beautiful but indiscreet and openly consorted with a young man from Picardy, her lover, aboard his ship.

Roberval was shocked by her conduct and set her down on an uninhabited island in the St. Lawrence called the Ile des Démons. The only companion Marguerite had was her servant-girl, Damienne, a native of Normandy, although Roberval did leave her with some provisions and firearms. The young man from Picardy, learning of Marguerite's fate, abandoned ship and swam to the island to join her.

Their lot was a tragic one. Marguerite gave birth to a child which died. Then the young man died, followed by the servant-girl. Marguerite survived for three years until she was rescued by fishermen and returned to her native Périgord in France.

There are two sources for this tale of doomed love, according to the entry on Marguerite de La Roque in Volume I of the *Dictionary of Canadian Biography*, and these are a narrative account by the Queen of Navarre and an historical account by André Thevet. The Queen of Navarre said that she based the story she told in the *Heptameron* on what she heard from Roberval himself, whereas Thevet maintained his version came from Marguerite's own lips.

Hudson/ The Haunting of Willow Place Inn

Hudson is a town on the south shore of the Lac des Deux Montagnes. Overlooking the lake is the Willow Place Inn, which is reputed to be the haunt of the ghost of Maud.

The Willow Place Inn was built as a private residence in 1820. At the time of the Rebellion of 1837, it was the home of François-Xavier Desjardines, who met secretly with the Patriotes and assisted them. Their plans for the uprising at Saint-Eustache, which occurred on 14 December 1837, were overheard by Maud, the servant girl. As she had made known that her sympathies lay with the militia and not with the Patriotes, she was murdered and her body was clandestinely buried beneath the mud floor in the basement of the residence. It is Maud's ghost that is said to haunt the building.

Today the former residence is run as a country inn, an attractive building of Victorian and Georgian design. The owners report that there are poltergeist-like disturbances which seem to commence ''when the wind begins to blow across the Lac des Deux Montagnes and there is snow in the air.'' Traditionally the haunting starts on Halloween Night and extends throughout the month of November. Then it inexplicably lets up until the following October 31. Employees have found rocks piled up outside the door of Room 8. Mushrooms grown in the basement, above the place where Maud is said to lie buried, are found beheaded. The basement door slams shut of its own accord. Chairs are knocked over. Pretty songs are heard being sung when no one is singing, and there are those who discern in the air the perfumed presence of Maud.

According to Sonya Ward, writing in the Montreal *Gazette*, 31 October 1978, the story as it concerns Maud may not be just another ghost story. It seems that a Scots serving girl was employed at the time of the Rebellion. The girl's name is recalled as Mary Kirbride, and her sympathies were with the local militia and not with the Patriotes.

Island-Brook/
The Walling-in of Peggy Green

Travellers on the Old Mexico Road in the vicinity of Island-Brook, east of Cookshire in the Eastern Townships, will pass the Irish Cemetery. There they will see that one of the low mounds of the cemetery has been walled-in. Local inhabitants identify the walled-in area with the burial-place of Peggy Green.

In the Eastern Townships, especially around Island-Brook, they point out Peggy Green's burial-place in the Irish Cemetery on Old Mexico Road. The Roman Catholic Irish farmer's wife was reputed to be a witch. She died in the 1880s but her spirit could still be felt, so the farmers in the district walled in her burial-place. Thereafter the disturbances ceased. The wall of rocks remains to this day. [Howard Ryshpan]

In the 1880s farmers found that entire herds of their cows were yielding no cream. They laid a trap, caught a large white rabbit, and notched its ears before setting it free. Shortly thereafter an old Roman Catholic Irish farmer's wife named Peggy Green died. It was noted that her ears were notched in the manner of the rabbit's. She was buried in the Irish cemetery but the curse did not lift. The cows still did not give cream. So the farmers walled-in her burial-place to "contain" her ghost. The stones did the job and the cows began to produce normally.

The u-shaped, walled-in area may be seen to this day. Old-timers shun the cemetery by night. But then it is commonly believed by the old-timers of the area that if on the night of a full moon you take the bones of a black chicken to the crossroads you will see the devil!

Kahnawake/
Kateri Tekakwitha

The Kahnawake or Caughnawaga Indian Reserve is located on the St. Lawrence River opposite Lachine. The word means "a rapid" in Iroquois. The land was set aside for the use of the Christian Iroquois in 1676. The pagan Iroquois settled on the Six Nations Reserve near Brantford.

Kahnawake is associated with Kateri Tekakwitha (1656–1680), the native woman who is known for her purity as the Lily of the Mohawks. She was born and raised near Auriesville in New York State, where the Roman Catholic shrine honours her memory and preserves mementoes of her earthly existence. She lived a life of sanctity at Kahnawake, even taking a vow of chastity. She suffered ill health and died the next year. Her relics are preserved in the Mission Church of St. François-Xavier. There is a native tradition that when she died her body remained incorrupt for many days. Miraculous cures are reported from Kahnawake.

A statue of Kateri Tekakwitha was raised "in faithful memory of our faithful Indians" by the Roman Catholic missionaries at the Mission of San Francisco de Assis (Mission Dolores), San Francisco, California.

She became the first North American Indian candidate for sainthood when she was beatified by Pope John Paul II on 22 June 1980.

The possible sainthood of Tekakwitha brings to mind the status of other men and women of exemplar sanctity. The first Canadian to be declared a saint was St. André Grasset de Saint-Sauveur (1758–1792). Born in present-day Quebec, St. André Grasset was martyred not in any part of Canada but during an uprising in Paris, France.

The first North Americans to be canonized by the Roman Catholic Church were the Jesuit Martyrs. These are the eight Jesuit missionaries who were martyred in Huronia and elsewhere in the 1640s. Their names are: Jean de Brébeuf, Noël Chabanel, Antoine Daniel, Charles Garnier, René Goupil, Isaac Jogues, Jean de La Lande, and Gabriel Lalemant. Their lives and works are recalled at the Martyrs Shrine, Midland, Ontario. Their canonization took place in 1930, and their collective feast day is 18 October. Subsequently canonized in 1982 was the Quebec nun Marguerite Bourgeoys.

Beatification is a step toward canonization. What follows is a list of Canadian men and women who have been beatified. Presumably their causes are being examined and considered for sainthood: Brother André (1982), Bishop Laval (1980), Marie de l'Incarnation (1980), Mère Marie-Rose (1982), Kateri Tekakwitha (1980), Mère Marie-Léonie (1984), and Mère d'Youville (1982).

Kamouraska/
"A Ware-Wolfe"

The following news item is about "a Ware-Wolfe," or werewolf, or *loup-garou*. It appeared in the 10 December 1764 issue of the *Quebec Gazette*:

INTELLIGENCE EXTRAORDINARY.

Kamouraska, Dec. 2. We learn that a *Ware-Wolfe*, which has roamed through this Province for several Years, and done great Destruction in the District of Quebec, has received several considerable Attacks in the Month of October last,

by different Animals, which they had armed and incensed against this Monstre; and especially, the 3d of November following, he received such a furious Blow, from a small lean Beast, that it was thought they were entirely delivered from this fatal Animal, as it some Time after retired into its Hole, to the great Satisfaction of the Public. But they have just learn'd, as the most surest Misfortune, that this Beast is not entirely destroyed, but begins again to show itself, more furious than ever, and makes terrible Hovock wherever it goes. — *Beware then of the Wiles of this malicious Beast, and take good Care of falling into its Claws.*

Lauzon/
The Vengeance of La Corriveau

In Quebec the nickname "La Corriveau" has long been applied to a murderess or a witch. Its use among French Canadians goes back to the time of the Ancien Régime in New France.

La Corriveau is the name history has bestowed upon Marie-Josephte Corriveau (1733–1763), the Quebec woman who was convicted of murdering her second husband with an axe. She was hanged near the Plains of Abraham on 18 April 1763. The authorities had her decomposed body placed in an iron cage and exposed at the crossroads in Lauzon, across the river from Quebec City at Pointe-Lévy. Her remains, including the iron cage, were secretly buried about 25 May. When Corriveau's iron cage was rediscovered almost century later, it attracted considerable attention. For a time it was exhibited by P.T. Barnum in his celebrated museum in New York. It is now on permanent display in the Chateau Ramezay in Old Montreal.

According to the historian John A. Dickson, exposing the body of a hanged person in a cage was "an unusual punishment unknown during the French regime and reserved in England for persons found guilty of particularly heinous crimes. This treatment fired the popular imagination and gave rise to many legends and myths."

85

The folklorist Luc Lacourcière contributed three articles on the woman and her influence to *Cahiers de Dix*: "Le Triple Destin de Marie-Josephte Corriveau" (No. 33, 1968), "Le Destin Posthume de La Corriveau" (No. 34, 1969), and "Présence de La Corriveau" (No. 38, 1973).

The infamous witch La Corriveau murdered her husband with an axe. The other atrocities she committed are too numerous and horrible to relate. On 18 April 1763 she was hanged and her body was displayed in an iron cage at Pointe-Lévy, Que. The sculptor Alfred Laliberté, who had a special feel for Quebec's religious and historical subjects, cast her statue in bronze. La Corriveau is in the collection of the Musée du Québec. [Collection Musée du Québec/Photographer Patrick Altman/Permission Mme Odette Legendre]

In the folk traditions of Quebec, the murderess was transformed into a wicked witch. So La Corriveau's spirit, imprisoned in its iron cage until the Day of Judgment, is said to sweep unaided through the dark midnight skies on such special nights as the Witches' Sabbath (30 April), Walpurgisnacht (1 May), Hallowe'en (31 October), and All Souls' Day (2 November). It raises no end of havoc. She is the Baba Yaga of New France.

An unlikely epilogue to the life and legend of La Corriveau was contributed by Val Cleary, the author of *Ghost Stories of Canada* (1985). In his book one of the stories, "The Curse of La Corriveau," adds much to what is known about the woman and the witch. It seems one of her distant descendants, Romeo Dionne, a used car salesman in Toronto, inherited from his father a rusty old iron cage. The father lived in Burlington, Ontario, and died by accident when the heavy cage he kept in storage toppled over on top of him. Years later the son died in a freak accident while driving through a thunderstorm on the 401. He was driving a pickup truck which he had borrowed to transport a load of scrap metal from Burlington to Toronto. The load slammed into his back, killing him instantly. As Cleary wrote, "I think of La Corriveau and that ghastly cage. Is it still lying rusting in some scrap yard, waiting to claim another in its long succession of victims? Or has the rusted iron been swept up into a smelter to take on some other form? Has Corriveau's vengeance been brought to an end? Or will it go on and on, forever?"

Lac Memphrémagog/ Memphré

Memphré is the name of the creature—long-necked, dark-coloured, snake-like—which is said to make its habitat in the deep waters of Lac Memphrémagog, a Scottish loch-like lake in Quebec's Eastern Townships. The southernmost tip of the lake extends into the neighbouring State of Vermont. The lake monster was reportedly seen by 137 people on seventy-one occasions between 1816 and 1987. It has never been known to bring harm to anyone.

It seems Memphré is seen as more friendly than monstrous, largely due to the efforts of Jacques Boisvert, an insurance broker and resident of the city of Magog, which lies on the shore of the lake. Boisvert is also a local historian and an accomplished scuba diver. In 1983 he became co-founder of the International Dracontology Society, an organization which is recognized by the International Society of Cryptozoology.

The society of which Boisvert is president is committed to promoting the recognition of Memphré as "the friendly creature of Lake Memphrémagog." The neologism *dracontology* in its name refers to the study of serpent- or dragon-like creatures, regardless of whether these creatures are real, legendary, or imaginary. The dracontologists were responsible for the official recognition of Memphré by organizing an international news conference and by acting as a repository for reported sightings. They also issued t-shirts bearing the message J'AIME MEMPHRE and for an unusual resolution of the Legislative Assembly of the State of Vermont. The Assembly resolved on 17 March 1987 to recognize "the possible existence of the animal commonly known as Memphré," which it characterized as "an unidentified aquatic animal or animals described as long-necked, serpentine, or snake-like." The resolution observed that "the presence of these animals in Lake Memphrémagog would constitute the only known instance of such animals holding dual citizenship."

The society was also responsible for the signing of an unusual International Agreement by the mayors of the City of Magog, Quebec, and the City of Newport, Vermont. The mayors agreed that Memphré should be a "protected species" and should be studied by the "scientific community."

Boisvert is aware of many parallels between Lac Memphrémagog and Loch Ness in Northern Scotland. Both the lake and the loch are about the same size — some twenty-five miles long, one mile wide, and exceedingly deep. Both lie at a diagonal — northeast to southwest — and both run south to north. As well, both have Benedictine monasteries on their shores — at Saint-Benoît-du-Lac and at Fort

Augustus — and the two monasteries are similar in appearance. Finally, both have oft-sighted lake monsters, Memphré and Nessie.

Boisvert founded the International Dracontology Society with a fellow dracontologist, Barbara Malloy of Newport, Vermont, who once spotted Memphré.

Jacques Boisvert, co-founder of the International Dracontology Society, has found innumerable points of similarity between Scotland's storied Loch Ness and Quebec's Lac Memphrémagog, as well as parallels between the sightings of the Loch Ness Monster and Memphré. Boisvert, an insurance broker by vocation and an underwater diver by avocation, is shown here in 1987 in his Magog farmhouse surrounded by part of his collection of over 10,000 objects retrieved from the mysterious depths of Lac Memphrémagog. [La Société d'histoire du lac Memphrémagog]

Here is a third-person newspaper account of her sighting:

> Barbara Malloy and three other witnesses in a car at the top of the hill overlooking Lake Memphrémagog, near Horseneck Island, saw the creature. It was 5:00 p.m. on August 12, 1983. The lake was calm, and she and the others had stopped to take a look at the scenery. In the water, about two kilometres away, they saw a creature swimming extremely fast. In its wake it left waves "like a speed boat would make." According to Mrs. Malloy, the creature was dark brown and had a head like a horse's, with a long neck. She estimated its size to be "longer than a house." On viewing the creature, she said she became very excited and said, "Let me out of the car. It can't be a jet skiier." She and the others watched for one or two minutes until the animal swam out to the middle of the lake and disappeared.

Although Boisvert is an accomplished scuba diver who has descended some 2600 times into depths of Lac Memphrémagog — despite quadruple heart by-pass surgery — he has yet to be granted a sighting of Memphré.

Métis-sur-Mer/
Emmy the Psychic Cat

A monument was raised to the dead who are buried in the cemetery outside Métis-sur-Mer, a village northeast of Rimouski, on the South Shore of the St. Lawrence River. The monument recalls a marine disaster and the story associated with it.

On 28 May 1914, the Canadian Pacific passenger ship the *Empress of Ireland* cast off from Quebec City bound for England. The following day, moving through dense fog, it was rammed by the Norwegian freighter *Storstad* in the St. Lawrence River off Rimouski. The passenger ship sank in fourteen minutes; 1014 passengers and crew were drowned; 465 survived. The bodies of the drowned were gathered in the village of Ste-Luc and buried near Métis-sur-Mer.

There is much supernatural lore about animals which are widely held to be psychic. Dogs growl at ghosts and ghouls, cats make common cause with witches, rats desert sinking ships. The story goes that the *Empress of Ireland* had a cat. The ship's cat was named Emmy. While the passenger ship was loading on the wharf at Quebec City, Emmy left the ship and refused to reboard. In effect she jumped ship, even abandoning her litter of kittens in the process. The ship sailed on its fated voyage without her. No one knows the subsequent fate of Emmy, but the "psychic cat" was not one of the victims of the worst marine disaster in Canadian history.

Montreal/
Piety at Ville-Marie

The branches of the modern metropolis of Montreal lead back along the trunk of time to roots of a religious nature — the founding of the tiny missionary colony of Ville-Marie in 1642. The French officer Paul de Chomedey de Maisonneuve was directed by the Société de Notre-Dame de Montréal to establish a mission among the Iroquois. He did so, planting the colony at the foot of the tallest mountain on the largest of the islands in the St. Lawrence River. He became the first governor of the island of Montreal.

The founding was accomplished with appropriate religious ceremony and sacrament, according to an account of the Jesuit Superior Father Vimont, quoted Marie-Claire Daveluy in the entry on Maisonneuve in Volume I of the *Dictionary of Canadian Biography*:

> On the seventeenth of May of the present year, 1642, Monsieur the Governor placed the sieur de Maison-neufve in possession of the Island, in the name of the Gentlemen of Mont-real, in order to commence the first buildings thereon. Reverend Father Vimont had the *Veni Creator* chanted, said Holy Mass, and exposed the Blessed Sacrament, to obtain from Heaven a

happy beginning for the undertaking. Immediately afterwards, the men were set to work, and a redout was made of strong palisades for protection against enemies.

The following spring the safety of the colonists was threatened. It looked as if the waters of the St. Lawrence would flood the fledgling colony. Maisonneuve rose to the occasion. After consulting with Fathers Poncet and Du Peron, he made a promise. If the waters, which were already rising against the gate of the fort, subsided without serious damage, he would carry a cross on his shoulders to the top of Mount Royal and plant the cross at its peak. He put the promise in writing and had his words proclaimed. The proclamation was fastened to a cross which was planted on the bank of the raging river.

Father Vimont recorded what happened. "The waters, having stopped a little while at the threshold of the gate, without swelling further, subsided by degrees, put the inhabitants out of danger, and set the Captain [M. de Maisonneuve] to the fulfillment of his promise." Thus was the colony saved.

It was quite a mountain to climb, although in the 1880s Oscar Wilde would dismiss it as "a hill." Mount Royal, an extinct volcano, rises 764 feet above sea level. Today, atop the mountain, there stands a giant illuminated cross, a reminder of Maisonneuve's promise.

Montreal/
The Talking Head

From the days of Ville-Marie comes the strange story of the Talking Head.

Jean de Saint-Père (1618–1675) was a colonist who moved from France to New France to contribute to the conversion of the Indians. He was a responsible and pious man, and served as the first clerk of the court and the first notary in the colony of Ville-Marie. Sieur de Maisonneuve thought so much of him that when he signed Saint-Père's marriage contract, he included a generous grant of land "to reward him for his good and faithful services."

Saint-Père came to a tragic end on 25 October 1657. While he was busy building a house he received a group of Iroquois. Apparently without warning they turned on him, killing him and cutting off his head. They did so, in the account quoted by André Vachon in the entry on Saint-Père in Volume I of the *Dictionary of Canadian Biography*, "in order to have his fine growth of hair."

As they were fleeing with their trophy, Saint-Père's decapitated head began to speak. It spoke in very good Iroquois, a language Saint-Père had never learned during his life. It reproached the Indians for their faithlessness: "You kill us, you inflict endless cruelties on us, you want to annihilate the French, you will not succeed, they will one day be your masters and you will obey them."

Once it started speaking, the Talking Head would not stop reprimanding the Iroquois. Noted Vachon, paraphrasing contemporary accounts, notably those of Dollier de Casson and Marguerite Bourgeoys: "It was useless for the Iroquois to put the head some distance away, to cover it or to bury it, the avenging voice continued to make itself heard. They finally got rid of the skull, but since they retained the hair the Iroquois could not help but hear the voice of Saint-Père coming from the place where they kept the scalp."

The Talking Head became a tradition among the Oneida Indians of the Iroquois Confederacy.

Montreal/
The Phenomenon of 1819

A "dark day" is a not uncommon phenomenon. According to meteorologists, when a dark day occurs, daylight is replaced by utter darkness. The sky grows dark with heavy clouds, and midday turns into midnight. The many descriptions of the effect stress its freakish appearance as well as the fear and terror it strikes into the hearts of those who witness it. There are many causes of dark days, some of them simple, some complex; some of them mundane, some mysterious.

Montreal was the centre of the dark day that is known to history as the Phenomenon of 1819. An unusual dark day, it was accompanied by untypical electrical and luminous characteristics that were noted in the account below, written more than seventy years after the event, and to this day continue to evoke professional interest.

The follow account "The Phenomenon of 1819" appeared in the 21 May 1881 issue of the *Scientific American*. It is reprinted from *The Unexplained: A Sourcebook of Strange Phenomena* (1976) by William R. Corliss.

On the morning of Sunday, November 8, 1819, the sun rose upon a cloudy sky, which assumed, as the light grew upon it, a strange greenish tint, varying in places to an inky blackness. After a short time the whole sky became terribly dark, dense black clouds filling the atmosphere, and there followed a heavy shower of rain, which appeared to be something of the nature of soapsuds, and was found to have deposited after settling a substance in all its qualities resembling soot. Late in the afternoon the sky cleared to its natural aspect, and the next day was fine and frosty. On the morning of Tuesday, the 10th, heavy clouds again covered the sky, and changed rapidly from a deep green to a pitchy black, and the sun, when occasionally seen through them, was sometimes of a dark brown or an unearthly yellow color, and again bright orange, and even blood red. The clouds constantly deepened in color and density, and later on a heavy vapor seemed to descend to the earth, and the day became almost as dark as night, the gloom increasing and diminishing most fitfully. At noon lights had to be burned in the courthouse, the banks, and public offices of the city. Everybody was more or less alarmed, and many were the conjectures as to the cause of the remarkable occurrence. The more sensible thought that immense woods or prairies were on fire some-

where to the west; others said that a great volcano must have broken out in the Province; still others asserted that our mountain was an extinct crater about to resume operations and to make of the city a second Pompeii; the superstitious quoted an old Indian prophecy that one day the Island of Montreal was to be destroyed by an earthquake, and some even cried that the world was about to come to an end.

About the middle of the afternoon a great body of clouds seemed to rush suddenly over the city, and the darkness became that of night. A pause and hush for a moment or two succeeded, and then one of the most glaring flashes of lightning ever beheld flamed over the country, accompanied by a clap of thunder which seemed to shake the city to its foundations. Another pause followed, and then came a light shower of rain of the same soapy and sooty nature as that of two days before. After that it appeared to grow brighter, but an hour later it was as dark as ever. Another rush of clouds came, and another vivid flash of lightning, which was seen to strike the spire of the old French parish church and to play curiously about the large iron cross at its summit before descending to the ground. A moment later came the climax of the day. Every bell in the city suddenly rang out the alarm of fire, and the affrighted citizens rushed out from their houses into the streets and made their way in the gloom toward the church, until Place d'Armes was crowded with people, their nerves all unstrung by the awful events of the day, gazing at, but scarcely daring to approach the strange sight before them. The sky above and around was as black as ink, but right in one spot in mid-air above them was the summit of the spire, with the lightning playing about it shining like a sun. Directly the great iron cross, together with the ball at its foot, fell to the ground with a crash, and was shivered to pieces. But the darkest hour comes just before the dawn. The glow above gradually subsided and died out, the people grew less fearful and returned to their homes, the real night came on, and when next morning dawned everything was bright and clear, and the world was as natural as before. The phenomenon was noticed in a greater or less degree from Quebec to Kingston, and far into the States, but Montreal seemed its center. It has never yet been explained.

Montreal/
Dr. Brunelle's Ghostly Visitor

The following news story appeared in the Winnipeg *Free Press* on 26 January 1898. The date of the "crisis apparition" which appeared to Dr. Brunelle is Sunday, 28 December 1897.

A Strange Experience
of a Montreal Physician Last Month

Dr. Brunelle is Visited by the Spirit
of Dr. Garceau Who Had Just Died

Montreal, Jan. 25.—Dr. Brunelle, a prominent French Canadian physician living at 698 Sherbrooke street had a strange experience the last Sunday in December. He was sitting in his office reading a book, when he heard some one knock on his door. Thinking it was his son he did not look up, but merely asked what was wanted. He received no reply except another knock on the door. Looking up he was amazed to see standing before him his old friend Dr. Treffle Garceau, of Boston. Brunelle asked, "How did you get into the house," for he did not hear the bell ring, and then rose to shake hands, but the visitor seemed to fade from his sight. Brunelle looked everywhere, but could find no trace of his old friend, and gave a loud exclamation of surprise. Madame Brunette entered and inquired what was the matter, but he answered evasively and asked to be left alone. He was still thinking over the mystery half an hour later when he received a telephone message stating that Garceau had just died in Boston. Brunelle was astounded, but was loathe to make the matter

public and told only a few intimate friends. The story, however, spread abroad, and created quite a sensation, especially among the spiritualists, who are very numerous in Montreal. When questioned Brunelle admitted the story and said his explanation, which appeared to be most natural, that it was some kind of supernatural intervention. He did not formerly believe in apparitions but cannot refuse to believe that Providence is able to act in that way and to employ those means to make him believe in that kind of phenomena. Dr. Garceau, who studied medicine here, practiced over thirty years in Boston and paid particular attention to the religious community and the poor. He was a brother-in-law of L.O. David, the city clerk, and a great friend of Louis Frechette, the well-known writer.

Montreal/
The Eyes of Christ

SAY EYES MOVE IN HOLY PICTURE was the headline of a news story in the Buffalo *Daily Courier*, Monday, 10 February 1902. The eyes in question in the holy picture were those of Jesus Christ.

According to the news story, there was movement in the eyes of the Saviour's portrait which hung in the parlour of the cottage occupied by the stonelayer Joseph Pelletier and his family on Lalonde Avenue in Montreal. On Tuesday, 4 February 1902, about 9:00 a.m., Mrs. Pelletier saw the eyes move and summoned her three children into the room, and the four continued to pray all day long.

Pelletier, at night, found them with their fast unbroken. Fascinated, as were the others, the father's complete belief was such that his work for the next few days was forgotten. Four relatives were called in and the nine persons became absolutely prostrated for want of food and sleep.

On Friday it was decided to tell the neighbours and send for a priest. Crowds began to gather around the house and this morning the chief of police was appealed to send a posse of men to keep order.

According to the news report, the miracle was observed by "hundreds of people" because "a large section of Montreal" was "thoroughly mystified."

Montreal/
St. Joseph's Oratory and Brother André

Montrealers may be excused for feeling that St. Joseph's Oratory is misnamed. An oratory is defined as a small chapel or a simple place of prayer. This immense structure on Mount Royal, domed and designed in the Renaissance style, is instead a basilica. Although the Oratory may be dedicated to St. Joseph, its prime mover in 1924 was Brother André. So it is popularly referred to as Brother André's Basilica.

The Oratory occupies the site of the little wooden chapel built to honour St. Joseph in 1904 by Brother André, who was born Alfred Bessette (1845–1937) and joined the Congregration of the Holy Cross as a lay brother. He was functionally illiterate but gained a reputation for piety and preached salvation through suffering. He endured poor health all his life yet acquired the reputation of a faith healer. Tens of thousands of people claimed they were cured not by Brother André but through his intervention on their behalf with his patron saint.

St. Joseph's Oratory and Brother André's humble living quarters on the slope of Mount Royal attract millions of tourists and thousands of pilgrims each year. Some of the pilgrims mount the steps leading to the shrine on their knees. The number of canes and crutches, left as votives, has dwindled in the last decade or two. It is uncertain whether this is to be ascribed to the decline in miraculous cures or the attitude of the Roman Catholic hierarchy.

In a grotesque act, Brother André's preserved heart, displayed in the Oratory, was stolen in March 1973. It was recovered from the basement of a Montreal house in December 1974. Called "the miracle-worker of Montreal" and "the man who tried to walk in the footsteps of a saint," Brother André was beatified in 1982. Thus one day he may be St. André, and the Oratory he worked so hard to build may be St. André's Oratory.

In his book *The Faith Healers* (1987), the Toronto-born magician and debunker James Randi described living in Montreal in the 1940s and visiting St. Joseph's Oratory where he would "watch the long lines of faithful supplicants painfully 'walking' up the long flight of stone steps on their knees to earn their confidently expected rewards. Inside the shrine, rows upon rows of crutches, canes, braces, and orthopedic devices covered the walls. Testimonials to the miracles wrought in the name of Brother André were posted everywhere, and the air was saturated with the sweet odor of burning candles." He went on to say:

Off to one side was the inevitable souvenir shop, where one event took place that convinced me, at age 12, of the fakery practiced there. I was squatting at a sales counter reading one of the comic books that told the story of Brother André's life. I was out of sight of the young man who approached—on the other side of the counter—and began refilling the many bins of medals, crucifixes, beads, rings, and buttons that were for sale to the faithful. There were two adjacent bins of crucifixes, one labeled "Blessed at the Oratory," and the other "Blessed at Rome." The hand of the clerk appeared above me and poured half a paper bag of crucifixes into the first, then emptied the rest of them into the second. Seeing he had gone to the far side of the counter, I stood up and looked at those bins. I discovered that though the holy items were not differentiated as represented—coming as they did from the same bag—they were at least both the same price. It started me thinking.

But it was my father who gave me the biggest jolt concerning the oratory's souvenir business. At that same counter, I'd seen a row of two-inch squares of cloth stapled to gold-colored cards. These were being sold as pieces cut from the very cassock worn by Brother André on his deathbed. My dad told me that he'd been employed by the tailor shop of Morgan's Department Store in downtown Montreal when I was a boy, and that on one occasion his manager had sent him and his close friend James Hamilton, who was my godfather, to St. Joseph's Oratory to deliver a bolt of heavy wool cloth.

His boss had instructed them to stay there after delivering the goods and do some "cutting" for the priests. They were given two large pairs of pinking shears to take along with them. To my father's amazement, the two found themselves assigned to marking the wool fabric into two-inch squares with tailor's chalk and then cutting it up for sale in the souvenir shop!

Montreal/
Sir Arthur and the Poltergeist

Sir Arthur Conan Doyle delivered his final lecture on Spiritualism in Montreal. On his 1922 lecture tour he and his wife travelled from New York to San Francisco and from Vancouver to Montreal. In one hundred days he spoke no less than forty times about spirit return and spirit communication. He recorded the details in *Our Second American Adventure* (1923).

"I had not expected large audiences at Montreal, as the heat was great, and as the community is largely Roman Catholic, and of the opinion that the psychic phenomena which occur within its own ranks are saintly, while those experienced by others are diabolical," he wrote. "However, the two lectures were splendidly attended, and the second was quite full. It was my last appearance in this series, and so it was rather a solemn moment for our little party. I took the occasion to thank with all my heart the Canadian and American Press and public for the splendid way in which they had treated me."

Sir Arthur's attention was caught by the report of a poltergeist which appeared in the Montreal papers.

A singular case of *poltergeist* haunting came under my notice whilst at Montreal. It had occurred to a couple, the man an experienced journalist, the wife a rather nervous lady of middle age. They lived alone, their only child having gone out into the world. These people were haunted by a very active and mischievous but at the same time harmless spirit or spirits. The box of bricks which had been their child's toy was dragged out and fantastic buildings erected, which were put up again as soon as dismantled. When one of these buildings was photographed, a queer little mannikin figure came out in the photograph behind the bricks, and beside it what looks like a female head. There seemed to be two haunters, for presently direct writing began to appear upon pieces of paper scattered over the house. I examined these and found distinctly two scripts, one of a grown-up person and the other of a child, which corresponded with the photograph. A picture of a house was also drawn, an extraordinary high, thin erection of twelve stories, with "the Middlesex House" written underneath. It was very well drawn. Occasionally the pranks were of a less harmless nature. The electric lights were switched off at untoward moments, and the pictures were stripped from the walls. Twice the husband was assaulted by pillows until his incredulity had been buffeted out of him. Prayer seemed of no avail. Unhappily it seldom is in such cases. I have notes of one where a large fur hearthrug was the centre of the disturbance. A priest was brought in to exorcise the force, and whilst he was in the midst of his exorcism the rug sprang at him and enveloped his head and shoulders, so that he ran terrified from the house. One is dealing with a mischievous and rather malicious child, and reason together with kindness is the only weapon. In this particular case at Montreal the couple were finally compelled to abandon the house. The haunting seemed to be local, for it did not follow them.

Montreal/
The Death of Houdini

There are a number of mysteries surrounding the life and especially the death of the great magician Harry

93

Houdini (1874–1926). At first sight it seems appropriate that the element of mystery should adhere to the magician's life. After all, on stage, he produces what appear to be miraculous effects. And if, like Houdini, he is also an escape artist, his deeds are described to be "death-defying." The modern-day magician is a showman who is skilled in directing and misdirecting his audience's attention. He deals not with reality but with the perception of reality, highlighting its paradoxical or illusory appearance. The practice of the magician has nothing to do with the practice of magic, or the Black Arts. In fact, the Amazing Randi goes as far as to eschew the term "magician" entirely, favouring the word "conjurer."

Houdini boasted that he could duplicate through manipulative means any of the feats of the spiritualists. He spent much of his later years exposing the fraudulent practices of the better-known spirit mediums, including the Canadian-born Mina Crandon of Boston, Massachusetts. Houdini's boast and his exposés irritated Sir Arthur Conan Doyle who in his later years was a great proponent of the cause of spiritualism. Doyle tried to "explain" Houdini's effects by claiming that the magician was unconsciously employing psychic means to attain his entertaining ends. Houdini argued that there was nothing at all mysterious about the practice of magic, for he was dealing in effects, not realities. But he would never reveal to Doyle how he performed his tricks.

There is no question that Houdini aroused anger in spiritualist circles. Rumours abounded that his life was in danger. It is said that shortly before his death Houdini boasted to the editor Fulton Oursler: "I have news for you. I am a marked man, marked for death. My detective system reports that they are predicting my death in spirit circles all over the country." The prediction was noted by Vincent H. Gaddis in "Mystery of Houdini's Death" included in *Strange Fate* (1965) compiled by the editors of *Fate*, introduced by Frank Edwards.

Houdini was at the height of his fame in 1927 and performing at the Princess Theatre in Montreal. The theatre is now a movie theatre Le Parisien 5. He addressed a group of students on the McGill campus and one student made some sketches which interested the magician. He generously invited a group of students to visit him in his dressing room backstage. Thus before his performance on Friday, 22 October, he entertained a handful of students. One of them was a university boxing star whose name is recalled as J. Gordon Whitehead — yet McGill has no record of a student by that name. Whitehead expressed interest in the magician's ability to receive blows to the abdomen without wincing. Houdini explained that it was a matter of tensing the muscles to receive the blow and offered an impromptu demonstration. But before he had time to prepare, Whitehead delivered a hard blow to Houdini's abdomen.

That blow effectively killed Houdini. The magician made light of it at the time. Although in pain, he was able to perform his act that evening at the Princess. In great pain, he travelled that night to Detroit where he took the matinee at the Garrick Theatre in stride. But he staggered through the evening performance, which proved to be his last, and he was rushed to the Detroit hospital. He died later that evening of peritonitus caused by a ruptured appendix. His wife Beatrice was with him.

Even the day of Houdini's death is symbolic. The magician died on the thirty-first of October — Halloween Night. Some time before he died, he entrusted his wife with a secret message, a code word, should spiritualists subsequently claim to be in contact with his departed spirit. The events surrounding the secret message, bizarre in themselves, are recounted in the entry on the Houdini Magical Hall of Fame in Niagara Falls, Ontario.

As for J. Gordon Whitehead, what became of him? Was he a *bona-fide* McGill student? Was he a boxing star? Was he a dupe of the spiritualists? Having made his brief appearance on the stage of magical and spiritualistic history, he seems to have vanished.

Montreal/
Prophecy and Prediction

Prophecy and prediction are separated by a thin line. A prophecy is always about to come true; a prediction either comes to pass or not. As it happens, Montreal is the locus of both a major prophecy and a major prediction. Both the prophet and the predictor are well-known figures.

The prophet is the famous French seer Michel de Nostre-Dame (1503–1566), better known as Nostradamus, who wrote obscure quatrains or four-line verses about future events, publishing them in a widely reprinted collection called *Centuries* (1555). Verse VII, 32, has been dubbed the "Canadian prophecy" because of its apparent reference to Mount Royal. The verse runs as follows:

> Du Mont Royal naistre d'une casane,
> Qui duc, & comptre viendra tyranniser,
> Dresser copie de la marche Millane,
> Favence, Florence d'or & gens espusier.

What is the meaning of this quatrain? Henry C. Roberts in *The Complete Prophecies of Nostradamus* (1947) has translated and interpreted the four lines to mean that "A Canadian leader, of lowly birth, shall be raised to great power and eventually assume command over men of the nobility." The meaning of *that* message is anyone's guess, although with the arrival of Pierre Elliott Trudeau onto the national political scene in 1968, many commentators identified "Mont Royal" with Montreal and "une casane" with the new, Montreal-born Prime Minister. Twenty years later, it seems that another of Nostradamus's prophecies has yet to be fulfilled.

The predictor is the Jewish poet A.M. Klein (1909–1972). He was a resident of the house at 4857 Hutchison, near St. Joseph Boulevard, when in the early 1940s, depressed by the events in Europe, he penned the following four lines:

> They are upon us, the prophets, minor and major!
> Madame Yolanda rubs the foggy crystal.
> She peers, she ponders, the future does engage her;
> She sees the *Fuehrer* purged by Nazi pistol.

The lines come from the verse "Psalm XXV" which appeared in his volume called *Poems* published in New York in 1944. Whatever his aim and objective in writing these lines, Klein predicted not only the dramatic death of the Nazi *fuehrer* or leader Adolf Hitler, which occurred in 1945 after the collapse of his Third Reich, but also the means by which he took his own life ("by Nazi pistol").

Montreal/
The Sinister Sound of MKULTRA

There is a somewhat sinister sound to the seven letters of the alphabet that compose MKULTRA. Is it an acronym? Is it an abbreviation? While it is tempting to suggest that M stands for *mind* and K for *control* and ULTRA for *ultra* in the sense of *advanced*, all that is known is that MKULTRA was the code name adopted by the U.S. Central Intelligence Agency (CIA) for its interest in the mind-control or brainwashing experiments conducted at the Allan Memorial Institute of Psychiatry, a highly respected medical institution associated with the Royal Victoria Hospital and McGill University.

There is nothing mysterious about the experiments in themselves, but they were clandestinely conceived, secretly subsidized, questionably conducted, indirectly reported, and routinely denied. While all this took place decades ago, the effects of the experiments are still being felt—directly in the form of the unwitting victims' pain and suffering, indirectly in the hidden costs of the continued concealment. These are mysteries in themselves: the refusal of the CIA to publicly admit liability and make proper amends; the failure of the Department of External Affairs to divulge its part in the affair and to press the cause and claims of the Canadian victims. Then there is the damage that has been done to the prestige of the psychiatric community which for many years closed its eyes to what was happening.

Reports that the Soviets and the Chinese were conducting thought-control or brainwashing experiments alarmed Washington in the early 1950s. Officials were concerned that the Communists might win the war of ideologies by imposing their propaganda on unwitting minds through some new form of indoctrination. The CIA, not to be left behind, began to subsidize its own experiments on American campuses. It is said that the Agency spent a total of $25 million to fund 150 projects of classified research in this area. Canadian involvement commenced with a secret meeting held at the Ritz-Carlton Hotel in Montreal on 1 June 1951. The meeting was attended by Dr. O.M. Solandt of the Defence Research Board, the Sir Henry Tizard of the British Defence Research Board, two CIA representatives. The participants discussed the implications of the work that was already underway — the classified research of Donald O. Hebb of the Department of Psychiatry at McGill University. The Defence Research Board was subsidizing Dr. Hebb's Isolation Experiments (about which more later). It is probable that the main item on the agenda was MKULTRA.

Whatever the outcome of the meeting, Cornell University's Society for the Investigation of Human Ecology, Inc., a CIA front organization, made funds available to the Allan Memorial Institute of Psychiatry for its American director Dr. Ewen Cameron to conduct clandestine research in what has been called mind-control or brainwashing but which might also be called de-patterning or de-programming. The research required the use of adult men and women, and the less they knew about it the better. In fact, they knew nothing about it. More than fifty patients admitted to the Royal Victoria Hospital for emotional and physiological disorders were referred to his clinic at the Allan Memorial Institute. There they were subjected to non-standard, controversial treatment.

As Don Gillmor noted in his study *I Swear by Apollo: Dr. Ewen Cameron and the CIA-Brainwashing Experiments* (1987), Cameron had strange notions of what constituted appropriate medical treatment.

The results of Dr. Hebb's Isolation Experiments were not widely publicized — indeed, his report was classified and its circulation was restricted by the Defence Research Board—but they held more-than-passing interest to Aldous Huxley. The famous author and student of mysticism, a resident of California, was following the work of Hebb at McGill and of John Lilly with watertanks in the United States.

What interested Huxley was not the notion of indoctrination but the idea of the artificial induction of altered states of consciousness. "Where is Hebb's work on the effects of restricted environment published?" he asked Dr. Humphry Osmond in a letter dated 7 Nov. 1954. Osmond was a medical researcher then living in Saskatoon, Sask. He had introduced Huxley to LSD and coined the word "psychedelic." Osmond's reply is not on record, but Hebb's report was not issued on a restricted basis until Oct. 1955. It was titled "Effects of Radical Isolation upon Intellectual Function and the Manipulation of Attitudes."

Huxley related his interest in Hebb's work to his intense concern for mystical experience in a later letter to Osmond written on 20 May 1957. "What men like Hebb and Lilly are doing in the laboratory was done by the Christian hermits in the Thebaid and elsewhere, and by Hindu and Tibetan hermits in the remote fastnesses of the Himalayas." The quotations from Huxley's letters come from his book *Moksha: Writings on Psychedelics and the Visionary Experience 1931–1963* (1983) edited by Michael Horowitz and Cynthia Palmer. One wonders if Hebb was aware of Huxley's interest in his experimental work in perceptual isolation and of how the author saw it shedding light on the mystic's perennial quest for the state of spiritual ecstasy.

Hebb's work was continued by his associate John P. Zubek at the University of Manitoba in Winnipeg. Dr. Cameron tested his theories and techniques, perhaps as much for his research purposes as for his patients' well-being. They became his victims, his guinea pigs. It is said that he treated fifty-three patients between 1953 and 1963, although some reports extend the period of research both backward and forward in time from 1949 to 1973. Although Dr. Cameron died in 1967, under circumstances suggestive of suicide, it was not until 1977 that John Marks of the *New York Times* obtained evidence of his research through the U.S. Freedom of Information Act. That resulted in nine of his former patients preferring charges against the CIA which met with stonewalling by both the American agency and the Department of External Affairs. It is said that other victims — a dozen of them — have pressed charges against the Royal Victoria Hospital and the estate of Dr. Cameron. There is talk of the nine taking their grievance to the World Court at The Hague.

Dr. Cameron treated his patients or subjected his subjects to a range of techniques which include the following: inducing sleep through the use of drugs over extended periods of time (not days, but weeks); employing hallucinogenic substances (including LSD); applying electro-shock therapy; using the repetition of recorded messages in sleep to effect changes in attitude and behaviour (a method now known as ''psychic driving''). These techniques are as contentious in the 1980s as they were controversial in the 1950s.

The Isolation Experiments of 1951–54 were conducted by Dr. Donald O. Hebb on students at McGill who volunteered and were paid for their participation, not on mentally and emotionally disturbed people who had no idea they were being subjected to non-traditional treatment. Sixty-three students were employed at $20 a day and then by the hour to remain in environments of sensory deprivation or perceptual isolation — in darkened rooms — and to report on their experiences and attitudes. Periods of time spent in deprived environments varied from under one hour to six days. Hallucinations and altered states of consciousness were regularly reported. Following such exposure there was some evidence of increased suggestibility. The research grant was said to amount to $40,000. Dr. Hebb died in 1985.

Montreal/
The Grad Experiments

The so-called Grad Experiments were a series of experiments designed to determine whether or not the health and growth of animals and plants could be affected by someone who claimed to possess such psychic abilities as ''the power of healing'' and ''a green thumb.'' The experiments were conducted between 1957 and 1964 under laboratory conditions by Dr. Bernard Grad of the Department of Psychiatry at McGill University. Grad, whose special interest is

biology, employed the services of Oskar Estebany, a former Hungarian Army colonel who had left Hungary in 1956. He had worked as a riding master at a military college and felt he could demonstrate his psychic gifts.

The experiments were undertaken in the basement and in the tower of the Allan Memorial Institute of Psychiatry, McGill University, Montreal. From 1963 onwards, the experiments were conducted in the laboratories of the newly constructed Research and Training Building which sits next to the old mansion and which now is exclusively devoted to patient care.

In effect the experiments measured Estebany's psychic abilities in controlled circumstances. Results of the Grad Experiments were reported in such publications as the *Journal of the American Society for Psychical Research* and the *International Journal of Parapsychology*. They suggested that the presence of an independent beneficial force had been demonstrated.

Estebany claimed to possess the power of ''the laying on of hands.'' At no time was he permitted to touch the animal or plant subjects. In one animal experiment, forty-eight mice with skin wounds were divided into three groups, Estebany ''treated'' one group and the others were kept as controls. Treatment consisted of Estebany holding the mice, which were confined to a cage, between his hands for fifteen minutes twice a day. Differentiated rates of recovery which favoured the healing of the group so treated were noted after eleven days. In another experiment with plants, accelerated germination and growth rates were observed over fourteen days between barley seeds and plants ''treated'' by Estebany and those which received no special consideration.

In another series of experiments Dr. Grad worked in 1969–70 with the psychic Dr. Jan Merta of Montreal. Biographical details on Merta are scarce. He was born in 1944 at Stare Mesto, Moravia, and attended the University of Prague. About 1968 he attended McGill University, majoring in psychology, eventually acquiring a doctorate. From an early age he believed himself to possess psychic powers. Dr. Grad studied his abilities in a laboratory setting. His power over plants was noted by Peter Tompkins and Christopher Biro in their enthusiastic book *The Secret Life of Plants* (1973).

Merta's single publication seems to be *Exploring the Human Aura* (1975), which appeared as written by Nicholas M. Regush and Jan Merta. The book is subtitled "A New Way of Viewing — and Investigating — Psychic Phenomena." Regush is an American-born academic and writer, a Montreal resident, sometime teacher of sociology at Dawson College, and an occasional columnist for the Montreal *Gazette*. He is the author of a number of books, notably *PSI — The Other World Catalog: The Comprehensive Guide to the Dimensions of Psychic Phenomena* (1974) and *The New Consciousness Catalog* (1979), both written with June Regush.

A person who speaks with awe of the powers of Dr. Jan Merta is Dr. Bernard Grad, the biologist with the Department of Psychiatry at McGill University who conducted experiments with the Hungarian healer Oskar Estebany. In a private communication dated 2 September 1987, Dr. Grad wrote:

> Dr. Jan Merta worked under me for some years beginning in 1969 or 1970 and during that time set up a device involving a feather whose movements he could apparently influence psychokinetically. I have also seen him put out lighted cigarettes on the palm of his hands, and seen a film where he touched a white hot glowing rod without burning himself. He has apparently chewed and swallowed an electric light bulb in front of a live audience. However, he is no longer publicly active in parapsychology but has become a well-known authority in deep-sea diving, with several inventions and awards to his credit in this subject and holding a high-level position in this field in Ottawa. He is quite an extraordinary man who has succeeded against great odds.

Montreal/
"Angel Hair"

"Angel Hair" is a filament-like substance associated with the sightings of UFOs. The substance, which recalls the webs of spiders, floats or falls from the sky. A gossamer shower of "Angel Hair" landed in a marine area, as the following account shows. The report was made on the deck of the M.V. *Roxburgh Castle*, moored at Montreal on 10 October 1962. It was included by William R. Corliss in *Handbook of Unusual Natural Phenomena* (1986):

> At 2000 GMT, while the *Roxburgh Castle* was moored to her berth (Section 24) in Montreal, I was walking around outside my accommodation and noticed fine white filaments of unknown kind hanging around stanchions and topping lift wires of derricks.
>
> Calling the attention of the Chief Officer, I pulled one of these strands from a stanchion and found it to be quite tough and resilient. I stretched it, but it would not break easily (as, for instance, a cobweb would have done), and after keeping it in my hand for 3 or 4 minutes it disappeared completely; in other words, it just vanished into nothing.
>
> Looking up, we could see small cocoons of the material floating down from the sky, but as far as we could ascertain there was nothing either above or at street level to account for this extraordinary occurrence.
>
> Unfortunately I could not manage to preserve samples of the filaments as the disappearance took place so quickly (*Marine Observer*, 33: 187–88, 1963).

Montreal/
Dr. Ian Stevenson and Past Lives

"You only live once" is *not* the maxim of Dr. Ian Stevenson, who is the best-known, Canadian-born psychical researcher of all time.

Dr. Stevenson has successfully combined two levels of activities: instruction in medical science and research into the subject of reincarnation. He was born in Montreal on 31 October 1918. He is a graduate of the medical school at McGill University and both a physician and a psychiatrist. From 1957 he has been associated with the school of Medicine at the University of Virginia, Charlottesville, Virginia.

As well as being a member of the requisite professional associations, he holds membership in the American Society for Psychical Research and the Parapsychological Association. In 1967, he established in the School of Medicine a Division of Parapsychology. It was renamed the Division of Personality Studies in 1987. It is a small research unit which offers no courses or credits.

Since 1961, Dr. Stevenson has tracked down reports of "cases suggestive of reincarnation" wherever they may occur. As Frank Touby wrote in "Born Again," *Today*, 4 October 1980:

> To collect his cases, Stevenson has travelled to the Indian subcontinent, Sri Lanka, the Middle East, southwest Asia and Indochina. Those cultures have belief systems that include reincarnation, so it's less likely that a parent will dismiss out of hand a child's claims to have lived before. The same is true of Inuit and many Canadian Indians, including the Tlingits and the Haida of the Queen Charlotte Islands. Stevenson says children's recall of past lives is more significant than that of adults who profess recall, because children are close to the alleged past lives and less likely to have researched or experienced events they claim to remember.

When he was asked by Touby why he was interested in reincarnation, Dr. Stevenson was non-committal. All he would say was, "I've always been curious about it." Yet his study of ideas and experiences associated with non-Western cultures sheds light on the unexamined assumptions and presumptions of Western cultures. An instance of this is the scientific paper on "Gender Dysphoria" which makes the suggestion that "gender identity confusion" may derive from influences of a previous life as a member of the opposite sex. As he told Touby:

> The attitudes we have toward children and ourselves as parents are a strong factor in human

thinking. In the West, the child is the exclusive product of his parents, built by them from conception on.

> In the cultures that believe in reincarnation, the child had a *history* before he came into the family. And he's regarded as being in the family situation as a consequence of a long, antecedent existence. There's a definite therapeutic value in such a viewpoint. The child is granted respect as an individual, and that could greatly decrease parental guilt.

The most influential of Stevenson's books is *Twenty Cases Suggestive of Reincarnation*, which was originally issued as Volume 26 of the *Proceedings of the American Society for Psychical Research* in 1966. The second edition, revised and enlarged, was issued by the University Press of Virginia, Charlottesville, Virginia, in 1974. It established a high watermark for the collection, presentation, and analysis of the evidence in such cases, raising them from the lower depths of anecdote to the Plimpsoll level of scientific statement. Dr. Stevenson's work displays intellectual rigour, yet individual analyses have been faulted, notably in his study in the realm of xenoglossy — the apparent ability of rare individuals to speak in languages otherwise unknown to them.

Other books written by Stevenson and issued by the University Press of Virginia include the following:

• *Telepathic Impressions: A Review and Report of Thirty-five New Cases* (1970)
• *Xenoglossy: A Review and Report of a Case* (1974)
• *Cases of the Reincarnation Type* (four volumes, 1975)
• *Unlearned Language: New Studies in Xenoglossy* (1984)
• *Children Who Remember Previous Lives: A Question of Reincarnation* (1987)

Dr. Stevenson's maxim — should he wish one — could well come from Voltaire: "After all, it is no more surprising to be born twice than it is to be born once."

Montreal/
The October Crisis and the Psychic

The October Crisis commenced with the kidnapping of James (Jasper) Cross from his Montreal home on 5 October 1970. Cross was held hostage by a group of terrorists until 3 December when he was released in exchange for safe passage to Cuba for the kidnappers. The terrorists were collectively known as the Front de Libération du Québec (FLQ), a clandestine organization pledged to facilitate the independence of the State of Quebec. To this day no one has explained why the FLQ singled out Cross, a British trade representative. Perhaps his last name was of symbolic significance. Maybe it was enough that he was *un anglo*.

On 10 October, while the government was negotiating with one cell of the FLQ for Cross's release, another cell kidnapped the Quebec Minister of Labour, Pierre Laporte. The government invoked the War Measures Act and the FLQ responded on 17 October by murdering Laporte. No explanation was needed for the savagery shown this hostage. Laporte was a successful cabinet minister and a noted federalist.

Irene Hughes has no direct connection with the October Crisis, only a psychic one. She is an American, a former model, and a clairvoyant whom Brad Steiger has called "the Queen of Psychic Chicago" in his book *Psychic City: Chicago—Doorway to Another Dimension* (1976). On 14 October, when Cross and Laporte were both in captivity, she was phoned at her Chicago home and interviewed live on the air. The interview was conducted by Robert Cummings, host of the radio program *Afterthought* which originates from CJCI in Prince George, British Columbia.

Cummings told Mrs. Hughes about the October Crisis and asked her, as a clairvoyant, to share her impressions with his listeners. She predicted that no physical harm would come to Cross but that there would be physical harm to Laporte. She went on to say that it would probably be two or three months before the guilty parties would be arrested. She pinpointed one date as being of genuine importance. "I feel some very striking and unusual news may come on the sixth of November."

Mrs. Hughes was right about Cross and Laporte and was right about the length of the crisis. Cross was detained for two months, and Laporte's murderers were captured three months after the crisis broke out. As for the date she pinpointed, on 6 November the police in Montreal West apprehended Bernard Lortie who confessed to his part in the Laporte abduction.

Robert Cummings telephoned Mrs. Hughes again on 18 October. She stressed that Cross was still alive and would not share Laporte's tragic fate. "I feel that he is alive but that he may be ill and very weak." She suggested that he was in bed and on intravenous feeding. She sensed that he was being held captive about five miles northwest of Montreal. "It seems that the place he is in is about three stories high. I feel that it is red brick, a kind of old place, and it actually could be an apartment building." She said, "It is my impression that some major changes are coming about in your police force . . . to create a different type of protection, but I don't know what this is." These details, as reported, were close to the mark. Cross was quite ill though never intravenously fed. His place of captivity, the three-story brick duplex northwest of Montreal at 18945 rue des Récollets, matched her description closely. The "different type of protection" was not the War Measures Act, which was invoked on 16 October; perhaps it was the legislation which on 2 November replaced the Act.

Cummings taped four more interviews with Mrs. Hughes on 18–21 October. At the request of "the authorities" these were not immediately broadcast. Transcripts and duplicate tapes were made available to them. Radio clearance was granted on 28 October, and a two-part radio program was aired on CJCI on 6 November.

"My mind almost boggles when I consider the remarkable accuracy and detail of Irene's many psychic evaluations concerning this case," Cummings told Steiger. "Undoubtedly, this endeavour represents an impressive documentation of ESP at work in a 'now' manner in modern history."

Montreal/
The Physicians vs. Ian Bortz

Ian Bortz, a psychic healer in Montreal, was accused by the Professional Corporation of Physicians of Quebec of practising medicine in Quebec without a licence. When the case was heard the courtroom was packed. Judgement was rendered 1 June 1987 by the Hon. Mr. Justice Jacques Lessard of the Court of Sessions of the Peace who found the defendant guilty of violating the Medical Act. The charge is currently (November 1987) under appeal.

The defence was most unusual. Defence counsel readily admitted that the accused was not a licensed medical doctor, and it readily agreed that a cassette recording of the medical consultation held on 21 November 1984 which was made by Bortz and given to his client could be admitted in evidence.

The client, Louis Lemieux, was identified as a former policeman. When he went to see Bortz, he was met by a secretary who seated him in an armchair opposite another chair in which Bortz would sit. The secretary left and an assistant appeared and had him sign a document in which Lemieux agreed that he was going to undergo a type of experiment and that Bortz was not giving medical advice. Bortz entered and stretched out in his armchair. At this point the assistant counted backwards from one hundred, apparently to induce a hypnotic state in Bortz. Lemieux then put a series of precise questions to Bortz, including a number relating to his health.

The entire interview was taped and when it was over a copy of the cassette was given to Lemieux, apparently as a matter of course. Bortz diagnosed Lemieux's health problems as arising from the improper alignment of certain cervical vertebrae and recommended that he consult a chiropractor named Gilles Gervais. He gave other diagnoses as well.

Mr. Justice Lessard wrote, "If one had to stop here, all the essential elements of the offence committed having been virtually established, the verdict of guilt on the part of the accused would follow ineluctably, and the case would thenceforth be disposed of.

"However, we point out immediately that during the preliminary argument the lawyer for the accused, emphasizing the fact that his client had the right to a full and complete defence, intended to raise as a defence the existence of a parapsychological phenomenon relating to an occult science."

Bortz argued that he was not conscious of the questions put to him by Lemieux and that the answers given by him were not at all his. The defence counsel argued, "Being in a state of hypnotic trance and acting as a medium, his body only served as an intermediary between his visitor and beings from another world whom he defined as being 'speakers,' whence his denial of all responsibility as to the offence with which he has been accused." The accused had studied "mind awareness" and read numerous books on parapsychology, learning the ability to master such techniques as inducing a self-hypnotic trance state.

Expert witnesses attested to the accuracy of Bortz's diagnoses and to the altered voice that offered them. Among the witnesses were a neurologist, a chiropractor, a theologian, a psychologist identifying herself as a parapsychologist, and some patients who expressed an interest in the healing techniques of Edgar Cayce.

The Judge ruled: "It is not among the prerogatives of the Court to give judicial approval to the existence of such a science [i.e., the phenomenon of mediumship], with the result that the Court cannot uphold such a defence, based on theories of a scientific nature, whatever value one may give them." The Judge concluded, "The Court cannot arrive at conclusions other than that the accused was delictually liable for the act of which he was accused."

Montreal/
The Montreal Canadiens

The Montreal Forum is the home of the Montreal Canadiens, arguably the country's finest professional hockey team. Hockey fans, like sports fans and personalities everywhere, have their share of superstitions. These range from the numerology of sweater numbers — "retiring" various numbers like "Number Four, Bobby Orr" — to sequences of "wins."

When hockey's hallowed Montreal Canadiens were on the verge of winning yet another Stanley Cup in 1986, several sports writers were quick to point out that they had won the trophy in 1946, 1956, 1966, and 1976. And, by golly, they did win it again in 1986. One writer phrased it this way: "Is this an omen?" At the risk of seeming to be skeptical, I'd call it merely a coincidence.

The observation was made by Henry Gordon in *ExtraSensory Deception: ESP, Psychics, Shirley MacLaine, Ghosts, UFOs . . .* (1987). Gordon is a magician and a Fellow of the Committee for the Scientific Investigation of Claims of the Paranormal (CSICOP). In 1987 he helped establish the Ontario Skeptics.

It will be interesting to see if the Montreal Canadiens again win the Stanley Cup in 1996. If they do it may well be a coincidence, it could be an instance of what Carl Gustav Jung called "simultaneity," but it will likely be because the team is in top form — aided and abetted by the sense that a win is expected of them.

Ile d'Orléans/
Island of Sorcerers

Ile d'Orléans is the largest island in the St. Lawrence River after the island of Montreal. It is twenty miles long and five miles wide and was originally named Ile de Bacchus by Jacques Cartier in 1535 who was struck by its growth of vines. The following year he renamed it in honour of the Duc d'Orléans. The first church was erected in 1669.

The original settlers were farmers who were quite insular and independent and expressed the *ésprit de clocher*, the sense that one's world properly extends as far as the sound of one's parish bells and not one league more. The bridge to the mainland was built only in 1935. The Quebec government declared the island to be an historic *arrondissement* in 1970.

The spirit of the legendary figure of Jean-Pierre Lavallée broods over the island. The child of Indian and French parents, Lavallée grew up on the island, imbibed its ways, and became recognized as a sorcerer. It seems he was particularly adept at weather prediction and casting spells. In fact, he is credited with saving the island from the British. The British Admiral, Sir Hoveden Walker, led his fleet of eight warships up the St. Lawrence in an attack on Quebec City on 24 August 1711. Lavallée cast a powerful spell and a dense fog descended. Some of Hoveden's ships drifted onto the rocks around the island and capsized; the surviving ships withdrew. Quebec City and the Ile d'Orléans were saved.

Were—or are—the islanders gifted in weather lore and second sight? They were, as far as local tradition was concerned. As the Jesuit missionary Pierre-François-Xavier de Charlevoix wrote on 22 September 1720 from his *Journal of a Voyage to North-America* (1766) as translated by an unknown hand:

> I found this Country fine, the Soil good, and the Inhabitants pretty well at their Ease. They have the Character of being given to Witchcraft; and when they are consulted, the say, upon future Events, and concerning what passes in distant places. For Instance: If the Ships of *France* do not arrive as soon as usual, they are consulted to hear News of them, and it is said they have sometimes answered pretty true; *that is to say*, having guessed right once or twice, and having out of Diversion made People believe that they spoke from a certain Knowledge, People fancied they had consulted the Devil.

From time to time there are reports of "mystery lights" which appear to play over the Ile d'Orléans. In the past the bright lights were said to be the souls of fishermen mending their nets in the sky. In the twentieth century they are seen as UFOs.

Lac Pohénégamook/
Ponik, la Bête du Lac

Ponik, the Beast of the Lake, is said to inhabit Lac Pohénégamook which is a small lake fed by the Rivière

Ponik is the name of the monster said to inhabit Lac Pohénégamook, a small and cold lake near the Quebec-Maine border. This pen-and-ink drawing of Ponik was executed by an eye-witness to the creature, the Abbé Léopold Plante. While fishing near the church at Saint-Eleuthère in 1957, the Abbé spotted la bête du lac. *Ponik's serpentine body is said to extend thirty-five feet. [Bangor Daily News]*

Saint-François and found within a mile or two of the Quebec-Maine border. The Indian name is said to mean "mocking lake," a reference to the echoes heard over the body of water which is surrounded by hills. Native tradition holds that the name could mean "sleeping man," a reference to the lake's outline when viewed from the hilltops.

There are native traditions of a serpent-like inhabitant of the lake. A lumberjack named Louis Berube is the first white man credited with sighting "a huge fish" in 1874. Since then there have been almost a thousand sightings. The consensus seems to be that the lake is inhabited by a "beast" named Ponik with a serpentine body thirty-five feet long. It has two or three humps, flippers, a barrel-thick neck, and a horse-like head with a huge mouth. It appears for a few seconds, leaving in its wake a v-shape wave.

The legend was promoted by the Abbé Léopold Plante who saw the "beast" in 1957. He was fishing near the church at Saint-Eleuthère when he spotted it about a thousand feet from shore. He recalled the sighting in an interview with Claude Adams published in the Montreal *Star*, 13 September 1976:

> I was down on the beach and I met one of my confreres. I asked if he wanted to stay for supper, and he said sure, so I threw my line in to catch a trout. The lake was as calm as a mirror, you could see a toothpick floating.
>
> All of a sudden, about a thousand feet from shore, I saw this big black thing floating. It was like two pieces, with a depression in the middle. Then as I was pulling my line in, it went swoosh under the water and it was gone.

Although there were a great many sightings before the Abbé's, there were a great many more immediately thereafter. The opinion was expressed by the author Michael Bradley and others that the creature of the deep had been profoundly disturbed by the introduction of low-frequency vibrations—the operation of motorboats on the lake in 1956 and the blasting by highway crews opening a new road to the region.

Marine biologists examined the lake in 1958 to determine why it produced so few fish. The Abbé insisted that the scientists make an attempt to capture Ponik, so they strung up a net, caught nothing, and filed a negative report. The Abbé's efforts were not wasted, however, for what followed was an official one-man investigation by Dr. Vadim Vladikov, director of the Quebec Department of Game and Fisheries

Laboratory, who arrived in October 1958 and spent three weeks studying the waters with the expressed intent of trying to "harpoon" Ponik.

Although the respected scientist never set eyes on the beast, he came to the conclusion that the lake was the habitat of "some living thing of great size." It could be a giant, saltwater sturgeon, perhaps twenty feet in length, which had been artificially introduced. He recommended that it could be and should be captured before it died a natural death, if only to put an end to rumour and speculation. The government department refused to release the funds for a full-scale expedition, so he appealed to *Le Soleil* for the funds to acquire a large net with which to entangle the beast, but the Quebec City newspaper declined to participate in the fundraising of the necessary $3000. With that ended all official and quasi-official investigations of Ponik.

The sightings continued. "As many as one-third of the people who live near the lake have seen mysterious shapes or water movements or even the creature itself," noted Stephen P. Morin in an article published in the Providence Rhode Island *Journal-Bulletin*, 18 November 1979. Scuba divers and others equipped with solar devices reported mixed results throughout the late 1970s and early 1980s. Down there might be swimming an oversized sturgeon or a giant plesiosaur, a prehistoric serpent extinct for 50 million years; then again there might not.

Lac Pohénégamook is an unusually cold and rather small lake, measuring only seven miles by one mile. It is not particularly deep, the official depth being 135 feet. There are legends that it is bottomless or, as the Abbé liked to maintain, that it attains a depth of 1001 feet. Tales are told of mysterious underground river which runs all the way from Lac Pohénégamook and under the St. Lawrence River to the subterranean waters in the region of Chicoutimi!

Ponik became the mascot of Saint-Eleuthère in 1974 when the resort and fishing community celebrated its centennial. Elzear Sirois, a retired fisherman who lives at nearby Estcourt, has constructed large-size wooden replicas of Ponik, the Beast of the Lake, and these are on display on his grounds.

Quebec City/
Marie de l'Incarnation

Marie de l'Incarnation is likely the most remarkable woman ever associated with this country. Marie Guyart (1599–1672) was born in Tours, France, and from her earliest years seemed concerned with both material and mystical matters. As a child she saw the Lord in a dream, and heard him ask her: "Do you want to be mine?" She immediately replied, "Yes." However, she did not enter a convent but married and bore a son.

Not long after she was widowed she experienced what she called her "conversation," which occurred on 24 March 1620. She was twenty years old. She felt herself immersed in the blood of the Son of God. The experience left her with "a clearness more certain than any certitude." In later years she described it as "an inner paradise." These details come from the entry on Marie de l'Incarnation by Marie-Emmanuel Chabot in Volume I of *The Dictionary of Canadian Biography*.

She entered the Ursuline order at Tours, taking her vows in 1633 and the name in religion of Marie de l'Incarnation. She dreamt of a vast country full of mountains, valleys, and heavy fogs. She had another dream or vision in which the Lord spoke to her and said, "It was Canada that I showed you; you must go there to build a house for Jesus and Mary." In 1639 she set sail for Quebec.

Marie de l'Incarnation regarded her actions as guided by God, so certain was she of her apostolic vocation. It gave her strength to establish the Ursuline order in New France, to establish a convent school to educate young French and Indian girls, to master the Algonkian language and compile word lists, to write some 13,000 letters, a couple of hundred of which have survived. From the time of her death in Quebec in 1672, she was venerated as a saint. Bishop Laval wrote that "she was dead to herself . . . and Jesus Christ possessed her so completely." Her correspondence is surprisingly rich in matters spiritual and secular. Joyce Marshall translated and edited *Word from New France: The Selected Letters of Marie de l'Incarnation* (1967).

Marie de l'Incarnation had a strange experience which she confided to her son in a letter written on 20 August 1663. "My very dear son," she wrote, continuing:

> I have waited to give you an account separately of the earthquake this year in our New France, which was so prodigious, so violent, and so terrifying that I have no words strong enough to describe it and even fear lest what I shall say be deemed incredible and fabulous.
>
> On the 3rd day of February of this year 1663 a woman Savage, but a very good and very excellent Christian, wakened in her cabin while all the others slept, heard a distinct and articulated voice that said to her, "In two days, very astonishing and marvellous things will come to pass." And the next day, while she was in the forest with her sister, cutting her daily provision of wood, she distinctly heard the same voice, which said, "Tomorrow, between five and six o'clock in the evening, the earth will be shaken and will tremble in an astonishing way."
>
> She reported what she had heard to the others in her cabin, who received it with indifference as being a dream or the work of her imagination. The weather was meanwhile quite calm that day, and even more so the day following.
>
> On the fifth day, the feast of St. Agatha, Virgin and Martyr, at about half past five in the evening, a person of proven virtue [Mother Marie-Catherine de Saint-Augustin], who has frequent communication with God, saw that he was extremely provoked against the sins committed in this country and felt at the same time disposed to ask him to deal with these sinners as they deserved. While she was offering her prayers for this to divine Majesty, and also for souls in mortal sin, that his justice be not without mercy, also beseeching the martyrs of Japan, whose feast was being held that day, to consent to make application for this as would be most suitable to God's glory, she had a presentiment — or rather an infallible conviction — that God was ready to punish the country for the sins committed here, especially the contempt for the ordinances of the Church.
>
> She heard the voices of these demons saying, "Now many people are frightened. There will be many conversions, we know, but that will last but a little time. We will find ways to get the world back for ourselves. Meanwhile let us continue to shake it and do our best to turn everything over."
>
> The weather was very calm and serene and the vision still had not passed when a sound of terrifying rumbling was heard in the distance, as if a great many carriages were speeding wildly over the cobblestones. This noise had scarcely caught the attention than there was heard under the earth on the earth and from all sides what seemed a horrifying confusion of waves and billows. There was a sound like hail on the roofs, in the granaries, and in the rooms. It seemed as if the marble of which the foundation of this country is almost entirely composed and our houses are built were about to open and break into pieces to gulf us down.
>
> Thick dust flew from all sides. Doors opened of themselves. Others, which were open, closed. The bells of all our churches and the chimes of our clocks pealed quite alone, and steeples and houses shook like trees in the wind — all this in a horrible confusion of overturning furniture, falling stones, parting floors, and splitting walls. Amidst all this the domestic animals were heard howling. Some ran out of their houses; others ran in. In a word, we were all so frightened we believed it was the eve of Judgement, since all the portents were to be seen.
>
> I close this account of the 20th of the same month, not knowing where all this commotion will end, for the earthquakes still continue. But the wondrous thing is that amidst so great and universal a wreckage, no-one has perished or even been injured. This is a quite visible sign of God's protection of his people, which gives us just cause to believe that he is angry with us only to save us. And we hope he will take his

glory from our fears, by conversion of so many souls that had slept in their sins and could not waken from their sleep by the movements of interior grace alone.

In this manner did Marie de l'Incarnation record the prediction that an earthquake would rock Quebec —a prediction made by "a woman savage, but a very excellent Christian."

Relics of Marie de l'Incarnation are to be found in Madame de la Peltrie's House which is now a museum associated with the historic Ursuline Convent. The original building, erected in 1644, was demolished and rebuilt in 1836 using materials from the old. Immured in a gap in the chapel's wall—a gap caused by the explosion of a British shell — is the body of General Montcalm. Separately displayed is the General's skull, which was severed from the body. On the altar there is also a votive lamp which was lit in 1717 and has shone continuously ever since.

Much of the piety and pietism characteristic of French Canada has its origin in people like Marie de l'Incarnation. The visionary experiences described in her letters are without parallel in the literature of New France and that of the New World. To conclude, here is her account of an encounter with God:

> No, my love, You are not fire, You are not water, You are not what we say. You are what You are in Your glorious eternity. You are: That is Your essence and Your name. You are divine life, living life, unifying life. You are all bliss. You are infinitely adorable, ineffable, incomprehensible unity. In a word You are Love and my Love.

Quebec City/
The Great Treasure of the Citadel

There is a tradition that in the summer of 1759, as General James Wolfe was massing his forces for his attack on Quebec City, the Marquis de Montcalm, as commander of the French forces, was ordering all families of nobility and wealth to bring their valuables, jewels, and personal fortunes to the Citadel of Quebec for safekeeping. According to John P. Shriver in "Lost Treasure of the Citadel of Quebec," *Canadian Treasure*, Vol. 3, No. 1, 1975, the valuables were sewn into leather sacks, labelled with their owners' names, placed in coffers and boxes, and entrusted to four officers who, sworn to secrecy, transported the bulky fortune up the St. Lawrence River by night. No trace of the fortune was ever found. Or was it?

Quebec fell, Montcalm died, families of wealthy nobility returned to France, and the traditions of New France died hard. What about the treasure of the *Ancien Régime*? One hundred and fifty years later, in 1909, a farmer who was repairing an old fireplace removed a hearthstone only to find a small iron chest with a silver key. The chest contained an old parchment which bore the seal of Montcalm. Unable to read the script, the farmer took it to the village priest who translated it for him. It read: "At a little bay, on the River St. Charles, 10 feet up the east bank, you will find buried in plaster, burnt wood, gold and silver, jewels, ingots of silver and a sheep's skull. Beneath is the secret of the great Treasure of the Citadel of Quebec."

The farmer hastened to follow the directions and after much digging he uncovered another iron chest. This one contained a chart and another set of instructions which, translated, read: "Across the River St. Charles, to the wood, near the bay, and peninsula, 20 feet, north northwest by north, toward a clump of fir trees, 50 deep, set in plaster, our Treasure of the Citadel of Quebec." The farmer again hastened to follow the directions, but this time, unable to distinguish one clump of fir trees from another, he found nothing despite repeated digging.

"The treasure is still hidden," wrote Shriver, "A few years later the property was taken over by the Holy Mother Church and no further searching was allowed."

Quebec City/
The Plains of Abraham

Did Major-General Wolfe foresee his own death?

The dying of Wolfe on the Plains of Abraham after taking the Citadel of Quebec from the French is one of the most memorable moments in the history of England and of North America.

There are traditions connected with the life of General James Wolfe, who led the British against the French at Quebec and died on 13 September 1759 on the Plains of Abraham. There is even a tradition associated with the painting of The Death of Wolfe, *which was finished in London in 1770 by the fashionable historical artist Benjamin West. Lord Nelson admired the work and took comfort in West's promise to paint him in a like manner should the occasion warrant. Nelson promised that it would with the next battle. Nelson made good his promise or prophecy and so did West. [National Gallery of Canada/8007/Gift of the Duke of Westminster, 1918]*

Wolfe died on 12 September 1759. Eighteen hours earlier he might have entertained intimations of his own mortality. At the time he was pacing the deck of his vessel in the St. Lawrence River above Quebec preparatory to initiating the amphibious landing at Wolfe's Cove and the assault on the cliffs. He was in a melancholy mood. It is said that he turned to his fellow officers and recited Thomas Gray's "Elegy, Written in a Country Churchyard," which includes these lines:

The boast of heraldry; the pomp of power,
    And all the beauty, all the wealth e'er gave,

Await alike th' inevitable hour:
    The paths of glory lead but to the grave.

Tradition holds that he lingered over the fourth line, adding the ominous note: "Gentlemen, I would rather have written those lines than take Quebec tomorrow."

The authority for this famous statement derives from the testimony of John Robison who was in the boat with Wolfe at the time. Robison later taught natural philosophy at Edinburgh University and related the remark to a student who committed it to memory and was the first person to commit it to

This is the celebrated Golden Dog inscription which may be seen today above the peristyle of the Upper Town Post Office, Quebec City. The inscription is a verse which reads, in translation: "I am a dog that gnaws his bone/I crouch and gnaw it all alone/The time will come which is not yet/When I'll bite him by whom I'm bit." [Direction Général du Tourisme-Québec]

paper in 1804, almost half a century after the remark was said to be made.

"Did this really happen?" asked the historian C.P. Stacey in *Quebec, 1759.* "The answer seems to be that the tale has more foundation than most of the Quebec legends, but that the incident did not take place as the boats moved down the river in the early morning of the 13th. Wolfe had issued orders enjoining strict silence. There are cases on record of generals who disobeyed their own orders when it suited them — but hardly in circumstances like these."

Rigaud/
The Virgin and the Devil

Each year thousands of pilgrims journey to pray at the Shrine of Our Lady of Lourdes, and thousands of tourists travel to see the Devil's Garden. The sacred and the secular attractions, so symbolically twinned,

are located on Rigaud Mountain which overlooks the town of Rigaud near the Ottawa River west of Montreal.

The Devil's Garden is the older of the two attractions, as it was formed at the same time as the Laurentian Mountains some fifty million years ago. It consists of a field of stones and rounded rocks which are of interest to geologists who describe the field as a glacial deposit. The field of stones has its own legend. It seems Baptiste Laronde, a *habitant* of Rigaud Mountain, was anxious to finish ploughing his field to plant his crop of potatoes. He was warned by his pastor Père Mollette not to plough on Sunday, as this was the Lord's Day. Baptiste disobeyed and took it upon himself to suffer the consequences. As he ploughed, he began to sink into the field, deeper and deeper, until he finally disappeared beneath it. His crop was transformed into a field of stones, each rock the size of a potato. It is said that on Sundays, at dawn, one may see faint whisps of smoke rising from the rocks and hear faint sounds, like the crackling of fire.

The Shrine of Our Lady of Lourdes, located on the

The Curé of the Shrine of Our Lady of Lourdes, left, and the researcher, Dwight Whalen, stand at the edge of the Devil's Garden, a field of stones outside Rigaud, Que. Legend has it a habitant failed to observe the Sabbath and his crop of potatoes was turned into a field of stones. Stones from the field were used to build the way-stations for the Stations of the Cross near the Shrine. [Hawkshead Services]

side of the mountain opposite the Devil's Garden, has been called the Canadian Lourdes. The dogma of the Immaculate Conception was proclaimed in Rome in 1854, and four years later Bernadette Soubirous, a young peasant girl of Lourdes in rural France, reported seeing apparitions of the Virgin Mary and reported hearing the words, "I am the Immaculate Conception." Sixteen years later, at Rigaud, the Canadian Lourdes was founded to foster Marian devotion in North America.

The Canadian Lourdes dates back to 4 October 1874. Brother Ludger Pauzé, a cleric from France who was teaching at Bourget College in Rigaud, placed a statue of the Virgin on a high rock and built a niche around it. Public devotion was encouraged, but Brother Ludger died two years later, so he did not live to see the monument created by his own faith and love of Mary. In 1886, a grotto was constructed and the first pilgrimage from outside the parish was organized. The following year a chapel was constructed. In 1890, the first trainload of pilgrims from Montreal arrived. It is interesting to note that when the Stations of the Cross were built, they were made of rocks taken from the nearby Devil's Garden.

The present chapel dates from 1954 and the present statue of the Virgin was crowned by Archbishop Léger in 1958. A sound-and-light show was displayed on the mountain for the first time in 1974. Over the years there have been innumerable reports of miraculous cures and blessings flowing from the Shrine.

Rimouski/
UFO Sightings

The sky above the Rimouski region was the setting of UFO activity reported in the 23 July 1971 issue of *Le Devoir*. The newspaper account was published in translation by Yurko Bondarchuk in *UFO: Sightings, Landings and Abductions* (1979):

> Several round unidentified objects, continuously pulsating, were observed in the sky from various locations in the Rimouski area, causing some consternation with the local population.
>
> The phenomenon, sighted Tuesday night,

July 20, 1971, at Rimouski, St. Odile, Sacré Coeur and Bic, was described by many witnesses as rotating, fire-red in colour with green and blue rays flashing around. The most acceptable hypothesis is that the objects could have been artificial satellites of earthly origin, seen under special conditions, but this has been rejected by the Chairman of the Physics Department at the Centre d'Etudes Universitaires de Rimouski. Michel Campagnat stated that such satellites cross the sky in an arc in ten minutes and cannot in any way be geostationary, as in the case of the sighted objects.

Three days later, at 8:26 p.m., 23 July 1971, much of Quebec was struck by a massive power blackout. Bondarchuk noted the seeming coincidence.

Rivière Saguenay/
The Kingdom of Saguenay

The fabulous Kingdom of Saguenay was the goal of Jacques Cartier on his second voyage of 1535. Cartier's two native guides, Domagaya and Taigonagny, assured him that he could sail up the Saguenay River to reach the Kingdom of Saguenay, a region of untold mineral wealth. They maintained that "there are immense quantities of gold, rubies and other things . . . the men there are white as in France and go clothed in woollens." Once there he would find "marvels too long to relate." Cartier never abandoned hope that he would one day find this fabled kingdom at the head of the Saguenay River. It was the object of his third and last voyage of 1541.

Cartier was not alone in believing in the existence of this kingdom of wealth and wonder. Jean Alfonse, the master mariner and pilot for Roberval's expedition of 1542, who later cruised in search of the Northwest Passage to Cathay, becoming the first Frenchman to reach Baffin Bay, claimed not only that the kingdom existed but also that its inhabitants were tall men and women who wore sables, spoke in a Latin-like language, and worshipped the sun.

Further details about the fabulous kingdom and its equally fabulous capital city of Sagana were offered by one Lagarto in his letter to John III, King of Portugal, 22 January 1539, reproduced by H.P. Biggar in *A Collection of Documents Relating to Jacques Cartier and The Sieur de Roberval* (1930): "And beyond the falls the King of France says the Indian King told him there is a large city called Sagana, where there are many mines of gold and silver in great abundance, and men who dress and wear shoes like we do; and that there is abundance of clove, nutmeg and pepper."

There is always the sceptic. Marc Lescarbot, the French lawyer who wintered at Port Royal in 1606-7, had no doubts about the existence of the Kingdom of Saguenay and its capital city of Sagana. He knew it was all nonsense, and he knew the source of the nonsense. The tales of the fabulous region had originated with the Iroquois chief Donnacona who related them to Jacques Cartier. Cartier was enchanted and ambitious and took Donnacona with him to France, where the Iroquois chief amazed the French king, François I, with his tales of this fabulous region. Lescarbot explained it all in 1618:

> Moreover, who is there, save a great fool, who would not rather see a forest belonging to himself, than a palace wherein he hath nothing? . . . especially as he had already resolved to carry the said chief Donnacona to France to recount to the King what he had seen in these western lands of the wonders of the world; for he assured us that he had been in the land of Saguenay, where is infinite gold, rubies, and other riches, and where the men are as white as in France, and clad in wool. He further said that he had seen another country, where the people do not eat, and have no fundament, and relieve themselves only by making water, and also reported that he had been in another country of the Picquenians, and other countries where the people have but one leg, and other marvels too long to relate. This chief is an old man, and as long as he can remember has never ceased to go from land to land both by river, stream, and trail.

Lescarbot's account comes from *The History of New France* (1907) as translated by W.L. Grant.

Researchers have suggested that the Kingdom of Saguenay was a tall tale meant to impress the King of France with visions of "a northern Peru." As Stephen Leacock expressed it, "All that Vasco da Gama found at Calicut Cartier thought he had found in this vast emptiness." There is also the argument that what the native guides were recalling, when they referred to mines being worked by tall men who wore shoes, were dim memories preserved in their oral traditions of the time when the land was occupied by their ancestors and by visiting Norsemen.

**Saint-Benoît-du-Lac/
Owls Head Mountain**

Overlooking the small monastery at Saint-Benoît-du-Lac and the habitat of Memphré in Lac Memphrémagog in the Eastern Townships is Owls Head Mountain. The peak of the mountain was used in the past as a triangulation station.

It is not generally known that at the top of the mountain there is a vale which sees each year the ritual re-enactment of the construction of King Solomon's Temple. Whenever Masons meet they recreate Solomon's Temple. The ritual at Owls Head is performed by members of the Ancient, Free and Accepted Masons. The annual, open-air lodge meeting held here is said to be unique in Masonry. Around the world members meet behind closed doors for reasons of concealment; this meeting is held out-of-doors at high noon. It is scheduled for the Saturday closest to St. John the Baptist's day, 24 June. The rite is restricted to Master Masons but is international in scope. In 1987, members came from three continents and fifty-seven cities.

Details of Masonic ritual are closely guarded, yet it is known that at Owls Head the Third Degree is re-enacted and the material is raised from the ground up, employing Jacob's Ladder, which takes one from the goat field to the crest of Owls Head Mountain.

**Saint-Bruno-de-Montarville/
The Apparition**

An apparition of the Virgin Mary was reported in an open field outside the town of St-Bruno-de-Montarville situated southeast of Montreal. According to Sheila Hervey in *Some Canadian Ghosts* (1973), six girls, ranging in age from four to thirteen, were involved in the actual sighting. The Virgin Mary appeared before them on 22 July 1968 while they were walking in the field at dusk.

Indepedently the girls maintained that they saw the Virgin Mary standing in the heavens between two clouds. "She was wearing a long white gown, a white veil and a blue mantle. The mantle was covered with innumerable stars." Two of the older girls spoke to her, and they were apparently told that the Virgin Mary would appear to them again in the same field at the same time but on 7 October. "She then disappeared into the growing dusk while a large choir of angels sang, 'Gloria, gloria.' Or so the children unanimously claimed."

When news of the apparition was carried by the press, more than twenty people came forward and maintained that they too had seen the apparition and received the same message. "On October 7, over 20,000 people gathered in the field in the cold, drizzling rain. Highway Number 9 was blocked for hours by parked and stalled vehicles." But the spectators had gathered in vain, for the Virgin Mary did not appear as promised, even to the suddenly saddened six girls.

Saint-Joseph-de-la-Rive/ A Miracle

The village of St-Joseph-de-la-Rive rests on the north shore of the St. Lawrence River near Ile aux Coudres. In the spring of 1896 it was saved from flooding in a particularly dramatic — or miraculous — manner, as described in the following account, reproduced in its entirety from the St. Catharines *Daily Standard*, 30 April 1896.

MIRACLE AT ST. JOSEPH
The Bridge and Village Saved From Destruction

Montreal, April 29. — An extraordinary miracle is reported by the *Courrier du Charlevoix*, a journal which a few weeks ago was commended to the faithful by Bishop Labrecque. Among the places that suffered most by the recent floods was the village of St. Joseph, near Baie St. Paul, County of Charlevoix. There the water rose so rapidly that the villagers had scarcely time to leave their houses, and for many hours there was reason to fear that the large heaps of ice gathered around the bridge would at any moment sweep away both the bridge and the whole village. It was then that the miracle took place, as reported by the *Courrier du Charlevoix*. At a moment when the heaps of ice around the bridge were most threatening the parish priest was standing on the bridge looking at the scene of the disaster. Some women came to him and begged of him to invoke Divine Providence with a view that the ice might move away without sweeping away the village and the bridge. The priest took a small statue of St. Joseph, patron saint of the parish, and threw it into the river, saying, "Save thyself and save us." Almost immediately the ice commenced to move on slowly. The fact that the bridge was not carried away when everybody said it was impossible to resist is attributed to a miracle. When the water had gone down Mr. Ferdinand Daniel found on the bank the little statue which hardly measured one inch in length. "Thus the words of the priest were realized, we were saved, and the little St. Joseph also," adds the *Courrier*.

Sainte-Anne-de-Beaupré/ New Lourdes

The shrine of Sainte-Anne-de-Beaupré, located northwest of Quebec City, has been called the Lourdes of North America. It is the largest Roman Catholic shrine in North America, a long-established place of pilgrimage, and the reputed site of a multitude of miraculous cures.

Three shipwrecked Breton sailors, washed ashore at the cape in 1638, acknowledged their deliverance by building a small wooden chapel close to the shore. It was the first of eight edifices to be erected in the vicinity. The present Basilicia of St. Anne, which is of striking Romanesque design and proportion, dates from 1926.

Virtually nothing is known of the life of Ste. Anne, the shrine's patron saint, and there are no references to her in the New Testament. She is honoured by Roman Catholics as "the mother of the Mother of God." From the earliest days the shrine dedicated to her glory enjoyed the distinction of being the site of miraculous cures. As St. Marie de l'Incarnation wrote in a letter of 30 September 1665, "There the paralyzed may be seen to walk, the blind receive their sight, and the sick, whatever be their malady, recover their health." Bishop Laval noted in 1670 that "a great number of miracles have already been worked through the intercession of Saint Anne."

The first recorded cure effected on the site was that of the stonemason Louis Guimond. Crippling rheumatism kept him from contributing his labour to the construction of the chapel in 1658. To demonstrate his devotion, he carried three pebbles to the chapel's foundation and deposited them there. He was instantly cured. Over the centuries hundreds of cures have been reported, and some of them have been medically examined. According to the codification of Pope Benedict XIV, for a cure to be judged a "first-class miracle," the sickness must be serious and organic, and the cure must be sudden and perfect. A number of seemingly miraculous interventions were described by Eugène Lefebvre in his book *A Land of Miracles for Three Hundred Years* (1958) prefaced by The Most Rev. Maurice Roy, Archbishop of Quebec. The author noted that in the year 1957 the shrine, which is managed by the Redemptorist Congregation, attracted some two million pilgrims and tourists for whom more than twenty thousand Masses were celebrated.

Roman Catholic worshippers seek out the Miraculous Statue of Ste. Anne with its glittering crown. Permission for coronation of the statue was granted by Pope Leo XIII in 1887. Behind the Miraculous Statue is the Major Relic. This is Ste. Anne's wristbone, the donation of Bishop Laval in 1670. In the vicinity are the twenty-eight steps known as the Holy Stairs and the Stations of the Cross.

In 1953, Cardinal Leger hailed Ste. Anne as "the Miracle Worker of Canada." Less in evidence in the 1980s than they were in the 1950s are displays of crutches, canes, and other prosthetic aids donated by the devout who dispensed with them on the spot. Sainte-Anne-de-Beaupré was the first of the two shrines to be visited by Pope John Paul II on his Canadian tour of 1984; the other was the Martyrs' Shrine outside Midland, Ontario, which also has the aura of a site of miraculous cures.

Sainte-Marthe-sur-le-Lac/ Bleeding Statue

In the private chapel of the Girouard family of Sainte-Marthe-sur-Lac, a town on the North Shore northwest of Montreal, there stands a statue of the Virgin Mary. It is made of plaster, painted in plain colours, differing in no way from hundreds or thousands of other mass-produced religious sculptures — except that members of the Girouard family claim that theirs bleeds.

Like many other "bleeding statues" in the United States, Ireland, and Yugoslavia, the face of the Girouard's effigy does not exude blood when sceptics are present, only in the presence of the faithful. When there is independent analysis of the substances said to be produced by such statues, the liquids are found to be not human blood at all, but animal blood or some readily available look-alike.

The phenomenon of the "bleeding statue" of Sainte-Marthe-sur-le-Lac occasioned a consideration of such "miracles" by Michael Higgins, a religious studies teacher at the University of St. Jerome's College, Waterloo, Ontario. As he observed in a column carried by the *Toronto Star* on 25 January 1986, the spectacle of a "bleeding statue" brings forth a variety of responses. "To the cynical it is yet another example of religious hysteria; to the credulous, always called the devoted for some reason, it is a privileged moment of divine disclosure. But for the majority it is simply a mystifying spectacle that succeeds more in demeaning than exhalting the religious sensibilities."

He went on to place such phenomena in a social and religious context:

Again and again, the Marian miracles and apparitions follow a particular pattern or prescribed formula. Exhortations to prayer, conversion and repentance—all of them in themselves of indisputable spiritual worth—are easily obscured by the extraordinary means of their transmission. Pre- and early adolescent children are often the special beneficiaries of the apparitions and they, in turn, become spokespersons for the Lady's message. Their innocence and disarming ways validate the authenticity of their experience for the onlookers.

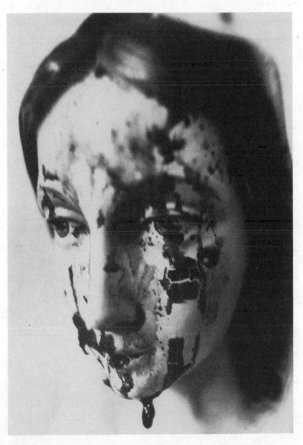

This statue of the Virgin Mary in a private home at Sainte-Marthe sur le lac, a town north of Montreal, was reported to have bled and wept. The photograph was taken on 10 January 1986. It was later learned that the blood came from an animal. [René Picard/La Presse/Canapress]

People come to these "sacred" sites determined to believe. The sceptical keep their distance and the ecclesiastical authorities shudder. For every miraculous manifestation the church approves, Lourdes in France, and Fatima in Portugal, for example, there are scores dismissed as spurious, fradulent or of ephemeral interest only. Church officials move with extreme caution. And rightly so!

Higgins noted the diminution of Marian Catholic piety in the wake of the Second Vatican Council (1962–65) and also the struggle of Christian feminists to reclaim or recover Mary for the Church. "And nowhere in Canada," he added, "is the tension between the Catholic feminists and their Mary with the Mary of the old order more acute than in Quebec." To Higgins, "these paranormal occurrences" have "their genesis or origin in despair."

> This depair results from the perception by many that their religion has become excessively rationalistic, a religion of propositions and debates that no longer speaks to the heart but only to the mind. When institutional religion does not give sufficient heed to the wants of the heart, the heart rebels. The sometimes catastrophic erosion of traditional forms of devotion in the Roman Catholic Church has led to a spiritual vertigo for many of the laity, and as a consequence they have simply not replaced the old habits of prayer with the new ones. . . .
>
> The restoration of the heart to religious practice will undercut such phenomena as Sainte-Marthe-sur-le-Lac. The "miracle" of the bleeding statue is more an act of rebellion than of faith. It would be folly to discount desperation, to laugh at the symptoms and misread the disease.

Shawville/
The Dagg Poltergeist

The case of the Dagg Poltergeist was exceptionally well documented by the reporter Percy Woodcock in the Brockville *Recorder and Times* for November 1889. A most lively account of the haunting, written by Lynn Harrington, appeared in *Early Canadian Life*, February 1980, under the title "Horrors: The Pesky Poltergeist of Pontiac County, P.Q., Canada's Own Amityville Horror." The events that the authors described began on 15 September 1889 and lasted for two months. They took place on the Dagg farmhouse seven miles outside the village of Shawville which lies in the Ottawa Valley west of Gatineau Park.

George Dagg, his wife Susan, and their two children, Mary Susan, four, and Johnny, two, inhabited a small clapboard farmhouse. Also living with the family and treated as a daughter was Dinah Maclean, eleven, a Scottish orphan. Trouble erupted when some money disappeared and turned up in an unexpected place. Then they found a trail of filth taken from the privy which was smeared on the front and back doors of the house, mixed with the sugar, and spread on the bedsheets. Pails of milk and crocks of butter were knocked over. Plates and bowls were hurled across the room. The sofa and the kitchen table overturned, seemingly when no one was touching them. The rocking chair moved all by itself. All the windows were smashed at the same time. Locks of hair from the children's heads were yanked and cut. Small fires broke out mysteriously throughout the house. Dinah, who alone could hear and sometimes see the poltergeist, was upset by the foul language that filled the air. No one was harmed but everyone was frightened.

Dagg journeyed to consult with Mrs. Elizabeth Barnes, known both as Mother Barnes and as the Witch of Plum Hollow, who resided in the small Ontario farming community of Plum Hollow located across the Ottawa River from Shawville. She was reputed to have "second sight." "Yes," she told Dagg, "an enemy has used witchcraft against your family. The culprit is a woman with two children." Dagg concluded that the villain was his neighbour, Old Mrs. Wallace. But when he returned to Shawville and accused the widow of placing the Dagg farmhouse under a spell, she denied all knowledge of the Black Art of witchcraft.

The only person present when all the disturbances took place was Dinah, who was uncharacteristically thin and white-faced with dark circles under her eyes. Then one afternoon the poltergeist began to speak. Dinah, her father, and the reporter Percy Woodcock were standing near the woodshed when this happened. They all heard a gruff voice address Dinah and inform her, "I'm the Devil. Get out of this or I'll break your neck." It proceeded to utter profanities. They quizzed the spirit for five hours and were joined by almost twenty neighbours. Later seventeen of the neighbours signed a statement that they had heard the mysterious voice. Only Dinah could see the poltergeist.

They summoned an Anglican priest who attempted to perform the rite of exorcism. But the Bible vanished from his hands. It was later found in the kitchen oven. Then the spirit announced that it would return the following Sunday, which it did to the delight of the neighbours who engaged it in conversation. The voice said it would leave for good at midnight, but the witnesses were so intrigued with its irreverent bursts of wit that they kept conversing with it until three the next morning.

Dinah and Mary Susan claimed they could see the noisy spirit and that it had assumed the form of a devil, complete with horns and spiked tail. When they woke up late Monday, all three children called their parents to see a white angel-like spirit in the sky. Their parents looked but could see nothing. Thereafter nothing is recorded of the Dagg Poltergeist.

Sherbrooke/
The Sherbrooke Inscriptions

The so-called Sherbrooke Inscriptions are among the treasures of the Musée de Séminaire Saint-Charles Borromée de Sherbrooke. Acquired about the year 1910 they are certainly the most curious of the museum's holdings.

The inscriptions are two rows of indecipherable characters. The characters were inscribed on both halves of the curious, pear-shaped boulder found in a farmer's field near the bank of the Saint-François River, outside Bromptonville, not far from Sherbrooke. The limestone boulder is not large; it measures approximately 3 feet by 1.5 feet by 0.5 feet. The earliest reference to the boulder goes back to about 1900. It is surmised that the inscriptions on the boulder are much, much older than that. It is even possible the inscriptions are really markings left by nature through the act of erosion. In the fall of 1966 they were drawn to the attention of a trained archaeologist with the Centre d'Etudes Nordiques at the Université Laval.

That archaeologist was Dr. Thomas E. Lee. Lee was regarded as a maverick archaeologist and dissident thinker by his colleagues for his strong views on the prehistory of Canada. For instance, he was prepared to argue that the ancestors of the present-day Indians arrived on this continent not five thousand years ago but fifty thousand years ago; that the oldest archaeological site in the Americas is one he located on Manitoulin Island; that the Viking settlement at L'Anse aux Meadows is not Norse but Basque; that

The Sherbrooke Inscriptions appear on the insides of the two halves of a pear-shape boulder. The boulder, which stands about three feet high, was found in a farmer's field near the bank of the Saint-François River in 1910, and now resides at Le Musée du Séminaire de Sherbrooke, Que. The markings are messages in "the Libyan language . . . a dialect of Ancient Egyptian," according to Barry Fell, the maverick epigrapher from Harvard, who added that they refer to an ancient expedition to the New World involving Lord Hiram, Hata, and Hanno, son of Tamu, personages otherwise unknown to history. Fell has declined to substantiate his claims. [Le Musée du Séminaire de Sherbrooke]

there exists indisputable proof that Norsemen colonized the Ungava Peninsula but that the archaeological establishment refuses to even examine it.

No one paid much attention to the Sherbrooke Inscriptions until Lee entered the picture. He copied the characters and circulated them among the scholars he knew would be interested in attempting to decipher them. For nine years there was no response. Then he sent a copy of the inscriptions to Barry Fell, and that act set off a remarkable chain of events which brought to Canadian attention another remarkable individual.

If Lee is an interesting person, Fell is a doubly interesting person. After retiring as head of the Department of Biology at Harvard University, Fell turned to his second interest, which was epigraphy, and studied ancient inscriptions to buttress his belief that the Americas were discovered and colonized well before Columbus by intrepid sailors and bold settlers from many parts of Europe and the East — Scandinavia, the Near, the Middle, and the Far East.

On 15 January 1975, Lee was astonished and delighted to receive a letter from Fell at Harvard. In it Fell identified the language in which the Sherbrooke Inscriptions were written and translated the characters in full. According to Fell, they were written in a dialect of Ancient Egyptian. The dialect was spoken in Libya about 500 B.C. "The Libyan language is a dialect of Ancient Egyptian. This was not known until 1974. If the inscriptions were known before, they cannot be forgeries."

So much for the preliminaries. What did the messages say? Here Fell was quite helpful. He found there were three messages and he translated all three. The first read: "Expedition that crossed [the sea] in the service of Lord Hiram to conquer territory." The second read: "Record by Hata who attained this limit on the river, moored his ship and engraved this rock." And the third read: "Hanno, son of Tamu, reached this mountain landmark."

It was as if a door had been opened or a curtain raised. Suddenly there was a whole new cast of characters with whom historians in the future would have to contend. Here was proof that ancient navigators,

hitherto unknown to historians, had set sail from the Mediterranean Sea, left far behind Gibraltar, and sailed across the mighty Atlantic. Not only had this expedition of unknown size crossed the ocean, it had journeyed up the St. Lawrence and reached the Saint-François River! Here was Lord Hiram who had sent forth from Carthage an expedition to the New World. Here was his navigator Hata who was keeping the expedition's all-important records. Here, finally, was Hanno who, because of his lineage, might well be a prince.

Four hundred and two days does not seem like a long time to an archaeologist. That is the length of time it took Lee to come to the conclusion that Fell was full of hot air. When he received the translation and explanation, Lee was overjoyed. But it did not take him long to write back to Fell, asking him for more particulars. How had he been able to identify the language and translate the inscriptions in record time? What dictionaries did he use? Were the messages unique, or were similar ones to be found elsewhere on the eastern coast of the United States?

From Harvard came silence. Professional colleagues who were sympathetic, like George Sotiroff, entered the picture with other interpretations of the characters. Perhaps they were, as Dr. Sotiroff suggested, characters written in ancient Bulgarian. If that was the case, their antiquity was established. The ancient mariners had hailed not from Carthage but from the Black Sea, even possibly Mongolia, at some time prior to 1500 B.C.

Such speculation, in light of Fell's silence, was hardly reassuring. Therefore it was with some reluctance that Lee offered the readers of the *Anthropological Journal of Canada*, Volume 14, Number 2, 1976, the following retraction, if that is the proper word. It was wittily titled, "Et Tu, Hanno?"

With something of sadness I say farewell to Hanno. I shall miss him. But he was never a comfortable fellow to have around. He was too elusive as he moved from century to century and place to place. Now he may roam at will, in company with St. Brendan and Prince Madoc.

The farewell was formal but perhaps not as final as might be expected in the circumstances. Brendan and Madoc, princes of church and state, continue to haunt the historical imagination. Hanno left the stage but only to lurk in the wings. He continued to crop up in subsequent issues of the *Journal*.

The issue of Volume 15, Number 3, gave Lee the opportunity to inform readers that 751 days had passed since Fell had produced his translations but not his explanations. The issue of Volume 16, Number 1, 1978, carried news that a geographer at the University of Sherbrooke had concluded that the inscriptions were not inscriptions at all but markings. "It turns out that chemical and physical erosion were the culprits, aided by a glacier!" The last reference to the affair appeared in Volume 16, Number 2, 1978. It seemed the geographer was misled and that markings are inscriptions after all. "The inscriptions are as obviously man-made as the carvings on a gravestone in a cemetery," concluded Lee.

In the meantime the Sherbrooke Inscriptions await translation and interpretation, if not explanation.

Ungava/
The Hammer of Thor and Imaha

Ungava, in the Inuktitut language, means "far away." The Ungava Peninsula of Northern Quebec is certainly far away from seventy-five per cent of Canadians who live within one hundred miles of the border with the United States. But it is not quite so far away from Greenland, a point not lost on Thomas E. Lee, the maverick anthropologist.

On an anthropological expedition to Ungava in 1964, Lee discovered an unusual stone monument that was standing on the north bank of the Payne Estuary some fifteen miles above the village of Payne Bay near the west coast of Ungava Bay. It had been standing there for a great many years, and no one in the area, whether Inuit or European, knew who had erected it. Inuit tradition held that it predated their occupation of the area.

It has a peculiar appearance. A vertical column or shaft is surmounted by a cross-member and a capstone.

The monument is large, the shaft being eight feet in height; the t-bar four-and-a-half feet long; and the capstone fourteen inches in height. The weight of the column was estimated to be about four thousand pounds.

Lee found it to be very impressive, very early European in appearance, and "a very presentable hammer." He described it in the *Anthropological Journal of Canada*, Volume 5, Number 3, 1967. He saw it as the handiwork of the Norse, not the Inuit, and ample proof of the occupation of the Ungava region a thousand or so years ago by Norsemen. "What can it be, if not a signpost for the European village at Payne Lake?" he asked, likening it in appearance to a hammer—albeit a gigantic one such as would be wielded by a Norse god like Thor.

Imaha, the Inuit word for "maybe," is the name given an archaeological site on Pamiok Island in Payne Bay on the west coast of Ungava Bay. The Inuit

The Hammer of Thor was so named by Thomas E. Lee, the archaeologist who discovered it on the north bank of the Payne Estuary in Ungava in 1964. No one knows whether the memorable stone monument is Inuit or European. It stands some eight feet in height and may well be, as Lee felt, pre-Cabotian. [Robert E. Lee]

reported some odd ruins, and an archaeological field party led by William Taylor of the National Museum of Canada confirmed their existence in July 1957.

In *Westviking: The Ancient Norse in Greenland and North America* (1965), the author Farley Mowat argued that the ruins show the hand of the Eskimo but also the skilled masonry of the Norse. The ruins consist of two burial vaults, a number of collapsed Eskimo food caches, and ruins of two types of buildings—circular tent rings of Eskimo origin, and a huge rectangular stone structure, measuring eighty feet long by thirty-one feet wide, enclosing a floor area slightly depressed below ground level. This was definitely non-Eskimo. The stone walls, slightly convex, had collapsed and were covered with moss. As Mowat concluded:

No archaeologist has so far cared to speculate in public on the possible origin of the great ruin at Imaha. Nothing comparable to it is known from any aboriginal culture so far discovered in the Canadian Arctic. Both in shape, size and apparent structure (including the convex wall plan) this ruin bears a close resemblance to a singularly massive Norse longhouse of the tenth or eleventh centuries. It is not too much to say that had it been found in Greenland, Iceland or in the north of Scotland or Ireland it would have been ascribed to the early Norse—at least on the basis of what can be determined of it without excavation. It should be also noted that the structure itself is only a short distance away from a small, perfectly protected harbour which is of a depth and general nature to have made it ideal for ships of the knorr type.

The Phantom Hunter *is the title of this large, striking, and deservedly popular work of art. It was painted in Sweden in 1888 by the artist W. Blair Bruce, a native of Hamilton, Ont. Bruce was inspired by an imaginative account of a hunter in the Quebec woods who was stalked by "a dusky figure" which left no footprints in the snow. To Theosophists the "figure" is an "astral body." [Art Gallery of Hamilton, Bruce Memorial, 1914]*

ONTARIO

Abitibi/
An Indian Clairvoyant

Abitibi is a small mining community near Cochrane in Northern Ontario. Ernest Thompson Seton, the naturalist, writing in *The Arctic Prairies* (1911), referred to an Indian clairvoyant at Abitibi. He heard about her from his friend Thomas Anderson, a fur trader.

> About 1879, when Anderson was at Abitibi, the winter packet used to leave Montreal January 2, each year, and arrive at Abitibi January 19. This year it did not come. The men were much bothered, as all plans were upset. After waiting about two weeks some of the Indians and half-breeds advised Anderson to consult the conjuring woman, Mash-kou-tay Ishquay (Prairie woman, a Flathead from Stuart Lake, B.C.). He went and paid her some tobacco. She drummed and conjured all night. She came in the morning and told him: "The packet is at the foot of a rapid now, where there is open water; the snow is deep and the travel heavy, but it will be here tomorrow when the sun is at that point."
>
> Sure enough, it all fell out as she had told. This woman married a Hudson's Bay man named MacDonald, and he brought her to Lachine, where she bore him three sons; then he died of smallpox, and Sir George Thompson gave orders that she should be sent up to Abitibi

and there pensioned for as long as she lived. She was about 75 at the time of the incident. She many times gave evidence of clairvoyant power. The priest said he "knew about it, and that she was helped by the devil."

Agawa Bay/
Inscription Rock

Centuries-old ochre figures adorn the face of Inscription Rock in Agawa Bay. Agawa Bay lies on the eastern shore of Lake Superior near the boundary of Lake Superior Provincial Park. The centuries may have diminished the vivid colours of the figures, but not their vital beauty. Yet the meaning of these fantastic images—a mounted man, a horned panther, a crested serpent, and other Algonkian symbols and designs— has been lost.

Even the site of Inscription Rock was lost for over a century, its very existence called into doubt. The fabled site of rock art was first described in 1851 by the American Indian agent and ethnologist Henry R. Schoolcraft. Although a resident of the Sault area, he had never seen it, having based his description on the accounts of Ojibway informants who said they had. The site was not rediscovered until the summer of 1959, when the native-art specialist, Selwyn Dewdney, armed with Schoolcraft's description and a detailed knowledge of the natural world and native ways, found the site. He recounted his emotions at the time in *Indian Rock Painting of the Great Lakes* (1962).

What took Dewdney years of scouting and canoeing to find may now be approached by canoe—or by automobile. A contemporary description of the site

Five persons in one canoe, two eel-like serpents, one lizard-like serpent with horns, one man on horseback, four circles, and one formation not unlike a cross . . . all these rock-art images may be readily discerned on Inscription Rock at Agawa Bay, Ont. The site is a tapestry of expressive forms and colours. The pale but beautiful hues reproduce badly, especially in black-and-white reproduction; but for centuries these images have withstood the elements. [Ontario Ministry of Tourism and Recreation]

appears in Wayland Drew's *Superior: The Haunted Shore* (1975).

A canoe approaches the pictographs by gentle degrees. First there are indecipherable drawings —ochre lines so slender and faint, so overshadowed by recent enamellings, that they could easily be missed. But they are pictographs beyond doubt, little harbingers, messages, prayers, or tributes. After them, past an indentation in the shore, Inscription Rock properly begins, a towering façade with a water-smoothed ledge where the painters stood. The first group of drawings consists of a canoe with two paddlers, a sturgeon, and a stiff-legged, horned quadruped with a long tail, and bristling back. Then comes a space, and then two beguiling figures dancing or making love; then an exuberant gathering of signs, circles, figures, and serpentine lines; then the main group of drawings. The crane and the whitefish may be totem signatures, calling cards, while others—the cartoon horseman, the bow-legged moose, and the trio of wraithlike canoeists— probably have a more specific message or a more potent magical capacity. But there is no doubt about the potency of the central figures —the undulating water snakes and the dragon-like monster they attend. These are among the most venerable manitos in Ojibway mythology. Together, Missikenahbik and Missipeshu, they symbolize all the latent power of the lake.

Algonquin Provincial Park/ The Ghost of Tom Thomson

Innumerable lakes and rivers lie within the boundaries of Algonquin Park, and one of them is reputed to be haunted by the ghost of Tom Thomson. The painter drowned in Canoe Lake, and it is said that on certain mornings, through the mist rising from this lake, one may discern his spectral form forever canoeing its nervous waters.

Tom Thomson (1877–1917), the artist whose paintings of the lakes and landscapes of Northern Ontario inspired the formation of the Group of Seven, was an expert woodsman and master canoeist who loved the great outdoors. He was in his fortieth year and in perfect health when he inexplicably drowned.

Thomson was a guest in Mowat Lodge, on the west shore of Canoe Lake. On the morning of 8 July 1917, he informed two park guides that he was leaving to go trout fishing on nearby Gill Lake. Off he went, paddling his favourite gray canoe in Canoe Lake. Eight days later his body was recovered from the waters of the lake. There was a gash on his right forehead and his fishing line was found wrapped sixteen or seventeen times around his left ankle. No water was found in his lungs. His canoe was never recovered.

Rumours circulated that Thomson's death was not the result of accident but of foul play. At the time of his death, it was said, he was involved with Winifred Trainor, the beautiful wife of a German-American summer resident of the area. Thomson had argued with her husband about the war being waged against Germany. They had then exchanged words about Winifred. Was he murdered by the German-American?

The mystery of Thomson's death was matched by the mystery of his burial place. Before the arrival of the family's instructions concerning the disposition of the body, the remains were placed in a casket and buried at the tiny hilltop cemetery at Canoe Lake. The following night the casket was disinterred by a stranger who worked alone by lantern-light through the night. Only later was it learned that the stranger was an undertaker named Churchill from nearby Huntsville who was acting on instructions from the Thomson family. Churchill had the casket conveyed to the family home at Leith, near Owen Sound. Once there it was opened in the presence of family members, the identity of the body was established, and the casket was reburied at the United Church Cemetery at Leith where it rests to this day.

The account presented above is based on the experiences and memories of members of Thomson's immediate family, as gleaned by the art collector Robert McMichael and recorded in his memoirs *One Man's Obsession* (1986).

The seeds of the mysteries or puzzles were planted early. The first biography of the painter, Blodwen Davies' *Tom Thomson* (1935), concluded: "Legend in the north says that he still lies on the brink of the hill overlooking Canoe Lake." The seeds were watered by Judge William T. Little who, in *The Tom Thomson Mystery* (1970), argued: "The mystery attending Tom Thomson's death and subsequent burial will never be solved short of an official opening of the Thomson family plot at the United Church Cemetery at Leith." As Sheila Hervey wrote in *Some Canadian Ghosts* (1973), "A disinterment of the body supposedly buried at Leith, Ontario, might help. It might determine if Tom's remains were ever transferred from the Park; it would not solve the mystery of his recurring ghost. Many claim that the spirit of Thomson lingers on in the Park, in the forest country he loved so well and where he died before his time."

Since that fatal day in 1917, numerous guides, fishermen, campers, and tourists have described the misty shapes they have seen moving across the waters of Canoe Lake. They report the progress of a lone, lean paddler in a gray canoe. Occasionally they see the canoe being beached near Hayhurst Point, but when they approach the point to look for the canoe, not only can it not be found but there are no signs of any human activity in the vicinity.

The painter was greatly loved by his fellow artists. J.E.H. MacDonald composed the moving inscription which appears on the Thomson Cairn, Canoe Lake. It was erected on 27 September 1917, and the wording is intriguing, especially the following lines:

> He lived humbly but passionately with the wild. It made him brother to all untamed things of nature. It drew him apart and revealed itself wonderfully to him. It sent him out from the woods only to show these revelations through his art. And it took him to itself at last.

The ghost of Tom Thomson, as well as his art, may be numbered among the "untamed things of nature."

An intriguing appendix was added to the Tom Thomson story by Roy MacGregor. The newspaperman has a special interest in the mystery. He discussed various theories about the death in "The Great Canoe Lake Mystery" in *Maclean's*, September 1973, and wrote *Shorelines: A Novel* (1980), which is based on the notion that Thomson was killed in a fistfight with his best friend and left behind a pregnant girlfriend.

MacGregor returned to the Thomson mystery on 23 January 1987 when he recalled in his column in the Ottawa *Citizen* how he had once met someone who knew the painter personally, had decided views about his death, and stated that he had seen Thomson's ghost not once but twice. That someone was a "bush bachelor" named Jimmy Stringer, and MacGregor met him in 1973 when Stringer was seventy-three years old. Stringer cast his memory back to the year 1917, when he was thirteen and growing up in the Park. He claimed that he knew Thomson well and that the artist had tried to teach him the rudiments of painting. Stringer also said that he had seen Thomson's ghost twice after his death. "Believe it, I seen him myself twice," he told MacGregor. Stringer promised to show MacGregor the site of the "secret grave" in which Thomson's remains would be found. But death intervened before the location of the site could be revealed.

MacGregor explained: "Jimmy fell asleep late in the afternoon and I never saw him again. Walking back across the ice to his Canoe Lake home he fell through and drowned, only a few paddle strokes from where Thomson himself had surfaced fifty-six years earlier."

Algonquin Provincial Park/ Algonquin Radio Telescope

The Search for Extra-terrestrial Intelligence, the acronym of which is SETI, has engaged the attention of radio astronomers in at least a dozen countries since the ground was broken by Dr. Frank D. Drake with Project OZMA at Green Bank, West Virginia, on 8 April 1960. In Canada, SETI exploration has been conducted on only two occasions by professional radio astronomers. The actual work was undertaken using the forty-six-metre telescope of the National Research Council's Herzberg Institute of Astrophysics at the Algonquin Radio Telescope, located about fifty miles northwest of Pembroke, Ontario, in Algonquin Provincial Park.

Dr. Alan H. Bridle and Dr. Paul A. Feldman conducted their search of seventy nearby solar-type stars in 1974–76. They scanned the spectre of these stars for a maser-like line of water vapour at 1.35 cm wavelength, the theory being that a "water line hole" would be a better "beacon" of life as we know it among the stars than the 21-cm wavelength of atomic hydrogen which informed opinion at the time held to be the best way to detect the "needle" in the "cosmic haystack."

Dr. Jacques P. Vallée (an Ottawa-based radio astronomer who is not to be confused with Jacques Vallee, the French-born and California based computer engineer, author, and UFOlogist) and Dr. Martine Simard-Normandin are both specialists in the linear polarization of cosmic radio sources. They argued that since cosmic linear polarization occurs naturally at low levels, any highly polarized signals that could be detected would imply artificial or intelligent modification of the radio source. They spent two hundred hours in their galactic search in 1982–83.

The results of the two SETI undertakings were both "negative" and "positive." They were negative in the sense that they failed to detect evidence of extra-terrestrial intelligence. But they were positive in the sense that they succeeded in sharpening the thinking of scientists engaged in using radio telescopes to search for evidence of intelligent beings beyond the confines of the planet Earth.

Alliston/ The Gibson-Atwood Ghost

In the early 1970s the novelists Graeme Gibson and Margaret Atwood moved into an old farmhouse not far from Alliston, a town southwest of Barrie. They had not been in the farmhouse six months when they began to realize that they were not its only occupants. The farmhouse was a frame building erected in the 1860s.

Gibson recalled how he was on the verge of sleep in the upstairs bedroom just before midnight on a cold winter night when he heard something downstairs.

"It wasn't a noise I could immediately identify. Then I heard someone in the vestibule. Almost immediately there was the sound of footsteps on our stairs. These were not the creakings or groaning that haunt old houses, but the very specific and unmistakable noise of a woman's shoes as she ascended towards the back of the house.

"Now it is important to emphasize several points. There had been no sound of a car on our curving drive, yet through my partially open window I could hear trucks half a mile away on Highway 89. Moreover, we'd recently acquired a stray Bluetick hound who insisted upon sleeping in a pile of hay in the drive shed. Max, as we'd named him, had proven himself a reassuring addition to our menagerie by baying alarums at every provocation—both real and imagined. Yet he'd made not a whimper. To top it off we'd had the locks changed; only Margaret and I had keys and she was miles away.

"And yet there was a woman in my house wearing solid shoes. I called, 'Hello!' in the darkness. 'Who's that?' I heard her reach the small window at the top of the stairs; then she began walking along the hall towards my bedroom door. She walked methodically, or so it seemed to me, with a kind of comfortable assurance in the dark. As if she was familiar with the house. Again I called out but there was no answer. Only the clear sound of heels on the pine floorboards.

"In retrospect I believe I remained in my bed out of puzzlement. If it had been a man's shoes I'd heard I'd have been more immediately apprehensive, and therefore self-protective. As it was I left it too late. She was almost to the door when it came to me with a genuine shiver (as if someone were walking on my grave?) that it was a ghost. . . .

"We had no bedside lamp, so the only light switch was on the wall beside the door which opened towards me and was ajar. In order to turn on that light I'd have to reach past eight or ten inches of dark space that contained whatever it was that waited out there. I'd like to say that I did so, that I went over to see who or what she was. But I didn't. In some fundamental way I didn't want to know.

"So I lay there while assuring myself that she could have no quarrel with me. We had not been in the house long enough. Anyway, try as I might, I could remember no instance of a so-called spirit actually harming anyone. Eventually I went to sleep.

"I told Margaret, of course. But as time passed we forgot about it, as one does. Perhaps I was melodramatic in my response to the sounds of the old house. Perhaps I'd drunk more than I'd thought; perhaps, as Scrooge protested, it was merely a scrap of undigested mutton. Certainly, without confirmation that would have been the end of it.

"Almost two years later we arranged with a new-found friend to mind the house while we went north for our annual escape into the bush. We had not told her about our 'ghost,' nor to my knowledge had we told anyone she might have known. Certainly she had no recollection of the story. . . .

"On our return we discovered that our friend had been visited not once, but three times, exactly as it had happened to me. The noise in the vestibule, the sound of footsteps on the stairs, and then in the hall. The alarming difference, for her, was that she took the footsteps to be those of a man. She didn't open the door either. Instead she threw herself against it to keep him out. But there had been no attempt to enter. . . .

"After moving back to Toronto we had a series of tenants before finally selling the farm. Each lasted for about a year before moving on. One day when I was visiting the second family, they were from Northern Ireland, the woman said, 'Tell us about the ghost.' I asked her to tell me first, whereupon she reported that her husband had been wakened by a woman who seemed to walk past him into a small room behind the bedroom. At first he'd thought it was his wife but immediately discovered she was still asleep beside him. Their bed was placed as ours had been, so whatever it was had apparently entered the room through the doorway from the hall.

"A married daughter was coming to visit and they had put a child's crib in the back room because it had logically seemed to be a nursery of some kind. We all wondered if it was the crib that had encouraged, permitted, or whatever, the 'spirit' to actually enter the bedroom.

"After that there were a number of incidents that are harder to verify. She appeared at least once again, and they were all convinced, for example, that the covers and pillows in the crib were moved about and some stuffed toys were rearranged.

"And then, about four years later, we met, once more, a young woman who had lived in our house as a mother's helper for almost a year. She told us that she had actually seen the woman from her bedroom which opened onto the hall at the top of the stairs. She says she called out, 'Hey, can I help you?' Neither young nor old, and wearing a plain, vaguely archaic blue dress, the apparition had seemed to pause, and then continued along the hall. There had been a great sadness about her. Our young friend hadn't said anything, at the time, because she feared we'd think she was nuts, or a witch, and she needed the work.

"While the unconfirmed episodes give convincing substance to this story, it has been the repetition of an almost identical experience that has forced me to believe that some ghostly phenomenon really was outside my door that night. . . . "

Baldoon/
The Baldoon Mystery

Baldoon is a small farming community, northwest of Chatham, which was originally settled by dispossessed Scots under Lord Selkirk. The Highlanders arrived in 1804 and left not long after. From the Scottish Highlands they undoubtedly brought with them their beliefs in spectres, in wraiths, and in those boisterous spirits known as poltergeists. Perhaps when they pushed on, they left those beliefs behind.

The Baldoon Mystery, the most celebrated of Upper Canada's hauntings, involved a poltergeist. During the three-year period between 1829 and 1831, visitors to the farmhouse of John McDonald and his family, near Baldoon, were witnesses to all manner of poltergeist-like disturbances. No reasonable explanation was ever offered for the hail of bullets, stones, lead pellets, water, and fire that descended upon members of the McDonald family. No visitor or family member was ever harmed but all were frightened. At one point the small wooden farmhouse heaved from its foundations; one night it was consumed in flames and burnt to the ground.

The Baldoon Mystery is not a "true" poltergeist haunting, for it was determined at the time that the origin of the disturbances was outside the house. It is said that the McDonalds were cursed by an old woman who lived not far away in "a Long, Low Log House." When this woman was denounced by Dr. Troyer, the celebrated Witch-Doctor who was brought in from Long Point to put things right, the happenings ceased.

A plaque on the bank of the Chenal Ecarté in Kent County marks the site of the ill-fated Highland colony of Baldoon, but it makes no mention of the haunting of the McDonald farmhouse. Researchers have yet to give this incident in Upper Canadian history — the only incident for which the tiny Scottish settlement is ever recalled—the attention it deserves. The dramatists have done better than the researchers, for James Reaney and C.H. Gervais have written a play, *The Baldoon Mystery*, about the incident.

It seems the single source for information on the

haunting is an anonymously written booklet which was privately issued some four decades after the events described. Research has established that it was originally published in 1871 as *The Belledoon Mysteries — an O'er True Story* and that the account was written and the testimonies were compiled by Neil T. McDonald, John's younger son. Since then it has been frequently printed under related titles. The booklet's account is a mixture of superstition, homilie, and romance. But it does include the testimonies of seven farmers of the region. Although these statements make for lively reading, they were gathered years after whatever events took place. Here, for instance, is the statement of James Johnson:

> During the years 1829–30–31, I lived within three miles of John T. McDonald's and I used to go and see the balls come through the window. Being young, it was great sport for me. I wore a Scotch cap at the time and I would gather the balls in it and take them home, and tell mother about the witch balls, as they were

This pen-and-ink sketch shows the John McDonald farmhouse at Baldoon, Kent County, U.C., about 1850. Twenty years earlier the lonely farmhouse was the setting for three terrifying years of poltergeist-like happenings during which it almost burnt down. The undated drawing is signed "Nick." [Frank Mann/C.H. Gervais]

called. She would make me throw them away, for she said the witches would come and take me with them. I said I would like no better fun. We used to see a stray goose with a black head and part of one wing black, swimming up and down the river, always quacking as if lost, but after McDonald shot it the mystery was solved. I have seen the furniture fly in all directions and the mush pot chased the dog from Canada to the State of Michigan. The pot had been absent for three days, and in four weeks we heard that the dog was found four miles west in Michigan and it never came back to Canada. Mr. McDonald used to trade at my father's store and was always upright in all his dealings.

As R.S. Lambert wrote in *Exploring the Supernatural* (1955), "There are many things we should like to know about the McDonald household which are not recorded."

Beardmore/
The Beardmore Relics

The Beardmore Relics is the name given to Norse artifacts that were unearthed — or buried and then unearthed—southwest of Beardmore, a settlement on the Blackwater River which runs into Lake Nipigon. In their day the cache was the centre of a storm of claims and counterclaims, discrepancy and disagreement. As the archaeologist A.D. Tushingham noted in *The Beardmore Relics: Hoax or History* (1966): "The Beardmore relics are either a practical joke — or a clue to one of the greatest adventures in Canadian history."

The public part of the story began on 3 December 1936, when James Edward Dodd, a CNR trainsman from Port Arthur (now part of Thunder Bay), sold a cache of iron artifacts to C.T. Currelly of the Royal Ontario Museum. The cache consisted of the remains of a sword, an axehead, and an oddly shaped bar of undetermined use. No questions have ever been raised about the authenticity of the artifacts, which experts agree originated in Norway and date from approximately A.D. 1000. What was questioned and continues to be questioned is their alleged discovery in Northern Ontario.

Dodd maintained that while prospecting southwest of Beardmore, on 24 May 1931, he dynamited a mess of roots and exposed the relics. Apparently he left them in place for two years before taking them to his home in Port Arthur, and then kept them in the cellar for another three years before offering them to ROM. Currelly accepted Dodd's account of the find and arranged for the relics to be displayed in the Museum. This met with delight from James W. Curran, editor of the Sault Ste. Marie *Star*, who lectured widely on the significance of the relics as proof of a Norse burial site in the region of the upper Great Lakes. He even published a book called *Here Was Vinland* (1939).

Archaeologists and others were dismayed at ROM's endorsement of the discovery, noting the discrepancies between Dodd's statement and the sworn statements of some of his friends and enemies

in Port Arthur and elsewhere. It emerged that they had seen the relics under different circumstances. Dodd altered his account a number of times, at one point backdating his find to 21 June 1930.

If he did not unearth the artifacts as he claimed, where did they come from? Critics maintained that originally they had belonged to a Port Arthur contractor, an immigrant from Norway, who had shown them to a number of people including Dodd. Indeed, the sale to ROM was concluded within a few months of the death of the contractor. Following a public inquiry in 1956, ROM withdrew the controversial objects from display and successfully sequestered them. Tushingham explained in 1966, "At present the Beardmore relics lie in storage at the Royal Ontario Museum, in that particular limbo reserved for objects of uncertain history."

Is there any proof that Norsemen visited Northern Ontario? Curran took delight in pointing to hard evidence, like the Beardmore Relics, and to soft evi-

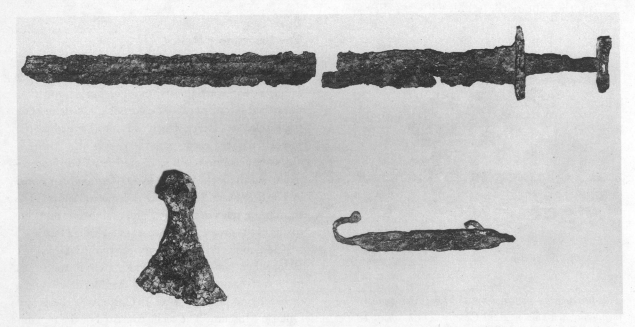

The Beardmore Relics are authentic Norse artifacts. But were they really found in Northern Ontario? Among the relics are fragments of a Viking sword and part of a large blade. In 1936 they were acquired by the Royal Ontario Museum from a CNR employee named James Edward Dodd who claimed that he had unearthed them five years earlier, while prospecting southwest of Beardmore. The claim was controversial, to say the least, for it implied, as one partisan of the relics expressed it, "A Norseman died in Ontario 900 years ago." [Royal Ontario Museum]

dence, like the fact that the word used by the James Bay Cree to refer to the white man really means "wooden boat man." Where did the notion of a wooden boat originate, he would argue, if not from the distinctive vessels used by early Norse colonists?

In a feat of associative thinking, Farley Mowat linked the Beardmore Relics with the Kensington Stone. In his book *Westviking: The Ancient Norse in Greenland and North America* (1965), he argued that the famous or infamous Kensington Stone — a rune-stone found by a Scandinavian farmer in Minnesota and accepted by some scientists as genuine and dismissed by others as a hoax — could be construed as proof of Norse penetration of the Great Plains. "If we admit the possibility that the Kensington Stone might have originated somewhere other than at Kensington, it becomes possible to link it with the Beardmore find of Norse weapons and artifacts," Mowat noted, siding with Dodds on the question of their authenticity. "A careful analysis of all the evidence does not give much support to the fraud theory, but the very mention of the word has been enough to throw the find into some discredit."

Mowat suggested that there was a Norse establishment on Hudson Strait and that one expedition sailed into Hudson Bay. "If they then continued south into James Bay and landed near the mouth of the Albany River, they would have been able to proceed by boat to within a short distance of Lake Nipigon."

Belleville/
Susanna Moodie and the Spirit World

The handsome stone cottage of Susanna Moodie and her husband Dunbar Moodie on Bridge Street in Belleville was in the late summer of 1855 the scene of Spiritualistic activity. If the stones of that cottage could speak, they would have at least two interesting tales to tell. One concerns the meeting between the pioneer writer and one of the two pioneers of the Spiritualism movement; the other, the meeting between the pioneer writer and hitherto unknown denizens of the spirit world.

Susanna Moodie viewed the world of the spirits sceptically. In the autumn of 1855 she addressed a long letter to her British publisher, Richard Bentley, in which she explained that like everyone else she was reading the latest book on the subject of Spiritualism. "There are some beautiful things in it," she wrote, "and some too absurd for a maniac with his eyes open to credit."

In her books Susanna Moodie ridiculed the notion that there could be spirits in the backwoods of the country. Yet her husband John Moodie was a practising spiritualist in Belleville in the 1850s, and she herself, as their recently discovered correspondence shows, covertly practised automatic writing and marvelled at the wonders of the Fox Sisters. The drawing is by the artist Don Evans who signs his work Isaac Bickerstaff. [Special Collections, University of Calgary Libraries]

127

Moodie was aware that the founders of the modern Spiritualism movement, the celebrated Fox Sisters, were natives of the nearby farming community of Consecon. In 1847, Margaret and Kate moved with their family to Hydesville, near Rochester, and the following year the spirit-rappings of the two farm girls attracted local then national and finally international attention. When Moodie learned that Kate, the younger of the two sisters, was in the vicinity to visit her old sister Elizabeth, who had remained in the Belleville area, she invited Kate to pay a visit. Moodie described this meeting in her drawing room in the late summer of 1855 in her letter to Bentley, which was published in *Susanna Moodie: Letters of a Lifetime* (1986) edited by Carl Ballstadt, Elizabeth Hopkins, and Michael Peterman.

Moodie skillfully described the impression Kate Fox made on her. She found the spiritualist:

A very lovely intellectual looking girl, with the most beautiful eyes I ever saw in a human head. Not black, but a sort of dark purple. She is certainly a witch, for you cannot help looking into the dream depths of those sweet violet eyes till you feel magnetized by them. The expression on her face is sad even to melancholy, but sweetly feminine. I do not believe that the raps are produced by spirits that have been of this world, but I cannot believe that she, with her pure spiritual face is capable of deceiving. She certainly does not procure these mysterious sounds by foot or hand, and though I cannot help thinking that they emanate from her mind and that she is herself the spirit, I believe she is perfectly unconscious of it herself.

Kate sensed Moodie's scepticism and offered to dispel her unbelief with a demonstration of spirit-rappings. She told Moodie to write a list of names of friends, living and dead, and run her pen down the list. Moodie did so and Kate requested the spirits to rap three times for every living friend and five times for every deceased friend. "I inwardly smiled at this," Moodie wrote. "Yet strange to say, they never once missed." She penned the name of a long deceased

friend and asked a question about her that no one else but the dead woman and Moodie would be able to answer. To Moodie's puzzlement, Kate's spirits answered the question correctly.

In the garden, raps were heard louder than ever. "The stranger vibrations of the knocks was to me the most unaccountable," she wrote. "It seemed as if a mysterious life was infused into the object from which the knocks proceeded." Kate's spirits then correctly read the inscription on the inside of the ring worn by Dunbar Moodie. He had to remove the ring to confirm the details, as he had forgotten precisely what was written there.

Following their meeting Susanna Moodie corresponded with Kate Fox, and in a subsequent letter to Richard Bentley, dated 22 January 1856, she described Kate as "a beautiful talented creature." Then she remarked upon a discovery of her own. "By the way," she added, "I can make the same raps, with my great toes, ankles, wrist joints and elbows. I found this out by accident. A girl, who has lived [as a] servant with me several years, tried it also, and she exceeds me in the loudness of these noises. Which so perfectly resembles those produced by the Mediums, that it has greatly surprised me."

Moodie returned to the subject of Spiritualism in her letter to Bentley of 2 May 1858. "Can such things be?" she asked, answering the question, as follows:

I was not only a sceptic, but a scorner. Yet, so many strange things have come under my own immediate knowledge, that though still doubtful on some points, I dare not now exclaim, as I once confidently did, "It is false. A mental puzzle. A delusion!" It is a mystery, strange, solemn and beautiful, and which, I now believe, contains nothing more nor less than a new revelation from God to man.

Moodie explained that she met a Scottish serving woman named Mary Williamson who "was a very powerful Medium for physical manifestations." She described how Williamson was able to levitate objects.

I have seen a large heavy English dining table,

rise in air repeatedly, without contact, have seen the leaf of the said table, fly up, and strike the snuffers out of my husband's hand, and put out the candles, have heard drums play, marital tunes where no instrument of the kind was to be found for miles, have been touched by unseen hands, and witnessed many curious phenomenon, which it is needless to my purpose, here to enumerate.

Then she described her own experience. In a depressed state, unable to make up her mind about spiritualistic matters, she placed her right hand upon a small table and said, "If there be any truth in this doctrine, let the so called spirits move my hand against my will off from this table, and lay it down in my lap!" As if acting on its own, her right hand was slowly wrenched up from the table and was laid down in her lap.

Moodie thereafter conducted experiments. Through a form of Ouija Board she contacted the spirit of Thomas Harral, a deceased editor friend. Then from Thomas Pringle, a deceased Scottish poet, she received a spirit communication, dated 22 June 1857, which predicted that blood would be let in the United States over the abolition of slavery.

On 6 July 1857, she learned: "God is a perfect Unity. The great circle and centre of existence. *Death*, is but the returning *wave of life* flowing back to Him. All created existence lives through and to Him, and no man lives for himself alone. He is a link in the chain of life, which would be broken without his ministration."

After receiving such messages and passing them on to Bentley, Moodie admitted her belief and her acceptance of the phenomenon of spirit communication. Then she added a surprising note that her older sister, Catharine Parr Traill, was also a believer. "My sister Mrs. Traill, is a very powerful Medium for these communications, and gets them in foreign languages. Her spirits often abuse, and call her very ugly names. Had I time, I could surprise you with some that she has received, but could not surprise you so much as she has been surprised herself."

She concluded, "Now, do not think me mad or possessed by evil spirits, like that great Medium of old St. Paul's. I could wish you altogether possessed by such a glorious madness."

Belleville/
Mary Edwards Merrill the Psychic

The life of Mary Edwards Merrill (1858–1880) is interesting but not as interesting as her death.

The talented young woman, who died at the tender age of twenty-one, was born in Picton but raised in Belleville. Mary was a model of inspiration for her sister, Flora, who was nine years her junior. In 1876 Mary graduated from Alexandra College—the ladies' wing of Belleville's Albert College—taking the highest honours in Mathematics and doing "nobly" in Natural Sciences. Benjamin Fish Austin was a fellow graduate who would cherish memories of Mary and in later life would keep them alive in a unique way.

Mary's death occurred in the following fashion. She was apparently in good health but she complained of feeling tired. About nine-thirty on Tuesday evening, 6 April 1880, she retired early. The following morning, about nine o'clock, her younger sister discovered Mary still in bed. Her body appeared to be lifeless but not yet cold. The family physician, Dr. Curlett, and the local coroner, Dr. B.S. Willson, were summoned. When they arrived they tried to take Mary's pulse but found none. She was pronounced dead. The County Attorney ordered an inquest and the jury members met later that day at 4:00 p.m. The jury declared that Mary Merrill had "died in a convulsion caused by a previous state of debility."

In the meantime, Mary's lifeless body lay under a sheet in a cold room of the family home. About eight-thirty that evening, Dr. Thomas E. Allen, a homeopathic physician and surgeon, who was apparently known to Mary and the family, arrived. He examined the body and found it to be warm. He had it lifted onto a bed and he applied warm water, water bottles, and warm irons. At 11:00 p.m. that evening, he declared that "he could discern a faint pulsation of the heart." Two non-medical witnesses later attested that they too had heard Mary's heart beat.

About seven o'clock on the following morning, Dr. Allen declared that the temperature of the comatose body had risen to sixty-seven degrees. Dr. Curlett, learning that there were some people who believed that Mary was still alive, attempted to enter the house and examine the body. He was turned away by Mary's father. So was the reporter for the Belleville *Intelligenser* who nevertheless continued to report the events in considerable detail. Dr. Allen summoned two specialists, Dr. Ridley and Dr. Tracy. Nothing is known of their qualifications. Between 1:00 and 2:00 p.m. that day, the three men conducted an examination. They pronounced Mary to be alive, though in a comatose state, with a temperature of seventy degrees.

Dr. Allen decided "to apply the test of electricity" and left to fetch a battery. When he returned, about seven o'clock that evening, he found "a coldness appeared over her face" and signs of rapid decomposition. He allowed the reporter to interview him. "The cause of death he says was a cataleptic fit which threw the patient into a trance, in which she died."

The funeral was held at the local Baptist Church on Saturday, 10 April, and the interment followed. The controversy did not pass quite so quickly. Column after column of the *Intelligenser* was filled with charge and countercharge, as Dr. Allen accused Dr. Curlett and Dr. Willson of carelessness, and Dr. Curlett and Dr. Willson called into question of professional and ethical competence of Dr. Allen and his two specialists. Finally the controversy died. But not so the memory of Mary.

In later life, Mary's younger sister, Flora, became a well-known suffragette and spiritualist. She is best known as Flora MacDonald Denison, and she kept alive the memory of Mary. In fact, she wrote a fictional version of Mary's life, stressing the young woman's spiritual and spiritualistic interests, even to the point of imparting to her fictional creation Mary Melville the brilliance of a child prodigy with such "psychic gifts" as telekinesis and levitation. She called it *Mary Melville — The Psychic* (1900). The publisher

was the Benjamin Fish Austin, Mary's old classmate, and he contributed the Foreword. In it he spoke of the real-life Mary and her "life of vast accomplishment."

The full story of Mary Edwards Merrill/Mary Melville is told by Cyril Greenland in "Mary Edwards Merrill . . . 'The Psychic' " in *Ontario History*, June 1976.

Bon Echo Provincial Park/ Myer's Treasure

Adjoining Mazinaw Lake in Bon Echo Provincial Park is Mississagagon Lake with its legend of Myer's Treasure. Silver hangs from its ceiling like stalactites or icicles, according to tales told before the turn of the century. The following account of the legend appeared on 22 August 1927 in the rotogravure section of a newspaper, the name of which is lost in the limbo of legend.

> There is a host of legends about the lost fortune of silver but the story that is most generally accepted is that it was bullion brought out of the district by the Indians and used in exchange for blankets, axes, whiskey and firearms and that they had stored much silver in a cave in the cliffs. The story goes that one John Myers, who kept a store at Myersville, often exchanged goods for the Indians' silver, but could never discover where the cache actually was. His son, however, was brought up with the Indians and, supplying them with whiskey, induced them to take him to the spot. The three of them went up the Moira River from Myersville to Loon Lake and across country to Bon Echo. Somewhere on top of the cliff they came upon two flat stones. By forcing these stones in opposite directions they discovered an opening about twelve inches in diameter, through which Myers forced himself. What the flame from his pine-pitch torch disclosed is doubtful, but there was silver in some form, so it is told, and immense quantities of it. Filling his pockets and a small bag with the treasure, the adventurer made mental note of the

location and commenced the return journey.

The lake was rough and the remains of the whiskey were lost. The two Indians, sobered by their waiting, became sorry for this action and fearful of the vengeance of their tribe. In an attempt to dispose of Myers, they upset the canoe and lost their own lives, while the survivor made a painful way back alone to Myersville, when he soon succumbed to pneumonia. Myers left a map and description of the location, and it is his map which up till quite recent years has led men to waste their years and substance on the supposed treasure of Bon Echo.

In 1860, George Merrill, grandfather of the present operator of Bon Echo Inn, Merrill Denison, well-known writer, and one John Bull, were among the first to make an attempt to wrest the secret from the Rock. Coming to the foot of the cliff which marks the jointure of the upper and lower Mazinaw Lakes, Bull took the southern face, while Merrill worked in the opposite direction, and is said to be the only man to ever see the cave again. Fearing however, that as Bull had once killed a man, his life would not be safe if his secret were known, he kept it to himself, and later the two men left, one discouraged and the other hoping to return again. He did return, but the great forest fires had so changed the topography of the top of the rock, that he was unable to locate the silver for a second time.

Later, a man named Van Asselstein becoming possessed of the map, mortgaged two excellent farms on the Kingston Road, and spent fourteen years prospecting on the rock to no avail. Then in 1911, two partners, Sills and Scott, were told by a spiritualist, the famous Anna Eva Fay, that they would find a hatchet dropped near the spot by John Myers. They spent over two thousand dollars (all they possessed) in the search, and sure enough found a rusty axehead with the initials J.M. stamped upon it, but they found nothing else.

Bon Echo has been a Provincial Park since 1961 when

the owner of this "wilderness estate," Merrill Denison (1893–1975), deeded it to the people of Ontario. The legend of Myers's Treasure survived well into the early 1930s, with Denison in the early 1970s recalling with glee the arrival of visitors, usually from the northeastern United States, who covertly unfolded their "treasure maps." Over the years he saw a multitude of roughly drawn charts of Mazinaw Lake. During his lifetime, no would-be prospector to his knowledge found so much as a splinter of wood or an ounce of silver.

Hugh F. Cochrane in *Gateway to Oblivion* (1980) equated the "caverns of silver" said to be at Bon Echo with the "city of Sagana" known by hearsay to the explorer Jacques Cartier as the abode of the men who flew in the sky like birds — or like "rabbit-men."

Bon Echo Provincial Park/ Old Walt

Bon Echo Provincial Park, situated north of Kingston, has a number of strange and peculiar features, not the least of which is the tradition that in one part of the park the acoustics are such that one can hear not one but nine separate echoes.

One of Bon Echo's unusual geographical features is the immense Precambrian rock which broods above Mazinaw Lake. The rock, which is a mile long and four hundred feet high, has been called "the Gibraltar of the North" and "Old Walt." The geological formation is a rich repository of rock art. In the distant past Algonkian Indians painted 135 ochre images on the rockface at waterlevel. While the meanings of these have been lost, there is some speculation that the image of "rabbit-man," a little human figure with immense ears, preserves the memory among the native people of the past of a humanoid being equipped either with wings or with antennae or with both.

A camp erected on the shore of Mazinaw Lake was operated first as a temperance camp and then during the 1910s and 1920s as Bon Echo Inn by the suffragette Flora MacDonald Denison and later by her son the writer Merrill Denison and his wife Muriel Denison. Flora arranged for the dedication of the great rock to the "democratic ideals" of the American poet Walt

131

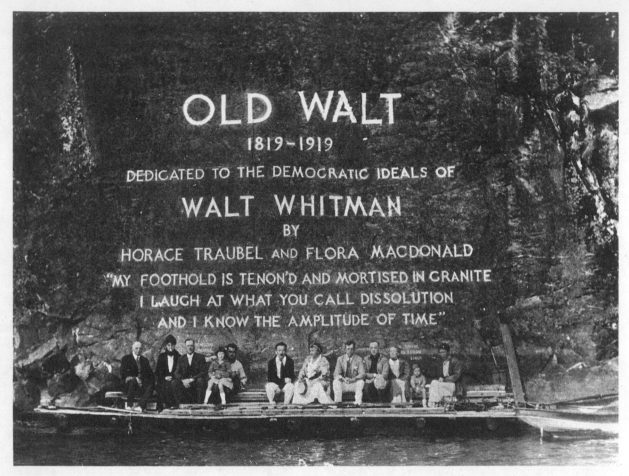

The centrepiece of Ontario's Bon Echo Provincial Park is Old Walt, an immense wall of granite, the face of which is inscribed with Walt Whitman's lines about immutability and immortality. The rock was dedicated on 25 August, 1919 in the presence of Horace L. Traubel, a close personal friend of the late poet. Three days later Traubel reported seeing the head and shoulders of Whitman above the brow of the rock, beckoning him to "come on." This was but the first in a series of visions that ended in Traubel's death at Bon Echo. [Griffin-Greenland Collection]

Whitman. The ceremony took place on 25 August 1919, and a year later the following lines were inscribed in foot-high characters on the rockface: "My foothold is tenon'd and mortised in granite / I laugh at what you call dissolution / And I know the amplitude of time." Henceforth the rock was known as "Old Walt."

Apparitions of Walt Whitman were seen by two guests of the Inn within days of the dedication of "Old Walt." Sitting on the verandah of Bon Echo Inn during the early evening of 28 August 1919, Horace L. Traubel, a close friend of Whitman, was astonished to see the head and shoulders of his beloved Walt Whitman appear above the brow of "Old Walt." The apparition, beckoning to him, whispered, "Come on."

The apparition appeared for the second time on 3 September 1919, but this time Whitman's spirit was in the company of two friends, the philosopher Dr. Richard Maurice Bucke and the free-thinker Robert G. Ingersoll, both deceased friends of Whitman and Traubel. This time Whitman said, "Come on, come on." Thereafter the rapidly failing Traubel reported seeing an eagle circling about "Old Walt," screaming before it disappeared into the moonlight.

Traubel took to his bed at Bon Echo Inn and was attended by Colonel L. Moore Cosgrave. At three in the morning, three days before he died, he suddenly started, staring about three feet above his bed. He motioned to the Colonel to look there too. According to the Colonel's testimony, there appeared a spectral light, faint at first, then bright, which advanced toward them, until it "touched" the two of them. Then the light was gone.

When Traubel died it was Flora's desire to bury him at Bon Echo close to "Old Walt." But Traubel's widow decided otherwise, so the body was transported by dead of night over the rocky road to the train station at Kaladar. In later years Denison spoke wonderingly of the eerie sight of St. Elmo's fire illuminating the corpse as it was taken through the dark woods by horse and cart to the station.

Flora preserved an account of these apparitions in an article in her magazine *Sunset at Bon Echo* (1920). But the fullest account was prepared and published by Walter Franklin Prince, the Harvard University psychologist and psychical investigator, who corresponded with all those concerned who were in a position to reply. Prince's balanced narrative in *Noted Witnesses for Psychic Occurrences* (1928) covers more than five pages.

Brockville/
Two Spirits in One

An old house in Brockville, on the St. Lawrence River between Kingston and Cornwall, may be the setting for the strange case of the two spirits that became one. The details that follow are derived from Sheila Harvey's *Some Canadian Ghosts* (1973).

The old fourteen-room house in question was built following the War of 1812 by Benjamin Chaffey who

designed Montreal's Victoria Bridge and the Morrisburg Canal. He and his wife Janet lived in their gracious home, which they called Somerset House, and Benjamin died here in the upstairs bedroom in 1867. They had been close in life and Janet was distraught with grief, crying in the halls for some time. Following Janet's death the house was occupied by a succession of families who reported no unusual occurrences.

The house became part of St. Alban's School, a private boarding school for boys, in the year 1900. The boisterous young scholars sensed nothing peculiar about the house. Then in the 1930s, one of the schoolmasters, an imaginative fellow who was given to drink, acquired the habit of blaming faults and foibles on "Gertrud"—a mischievous sprit of his own concoction. Before long Gertrud began "appearing" on the upstairs floors of the house. Students said they saw a woman who wore period clothes walking the halls. In the 1940s a cleaning woman said she heard a woman sobbing throughout the night. Gertrud remained a constant presence on the upstairs floors until the school closed in 1948.

Somerset House, set on a fifteen-acre estate, has since become a riding school. The present owners report the presence of not even a single spirit, neither a Janet, distraught over the death of her husband, nor a Gertrud, the mischievous spirit. However, in light of successful experiments in psychokinesis, like that involving "Philip, The Imaginary Ghost" it is conceivable that the spirit of Janet was waiting in the wings for a thought-form to inhabit and Gertrud supplied that. Perhaps the belief actualized the possibility. Maybe in Somerset House the two spirits became one.

Brockville/
The Phantom Invasion of 1915

The so-called Phantom Invasion of 1915 is among the best-documented of Canadian UFO sightings. This invasion of Canadian air space by a fleet of unidentified flying objects was studied in detail by Mr. X, a researcher based in Kingston, who published his find-

133

ings in the article "The Phantom Invasion of 1915" in *Early Canadian Life*, May 1979.

Mr. X set the scene:

> On the night of February 14th, about 9:15 p.m., many of the citizens of Brockville were startled to see the lights of aircraft crossing high over the St. Lawrence River and moving in the direction of Ottawa. The lights were seen by the Mayor and three of the city constables. The first of the unidentified aircraft flying rapidly overhead gave off the "unmistakable sounds of the whirling motor." About five minutes later, a second flying machine was heard. As it crossed the St. Lawrence from the direction of Morristown, New York, three balls of fire were seen to drop into the river. It was thought these might be bombs that landed harmlessly, but it was also remarked that they could have been flares used by the mysterious aviators to find their way in the dark. A few minutes later, another machine passed over the east end of Brockville, and soon after, another was crossing over the west end of Brockville.

Brockville Mayor Donaldson was one of many witnesses who saw "the mysterious invaders." The Mayor of Gananoque reported that two aircraft had been heard quite distinctly passing over his city, southwest of Brockville, but had not been seen. "Soon after, Mayor Donaldson telephoned the Prime Minister of Canada, Sir Robert Borden, to advise him that unidentified aircraft were seen crossing over Brockville from across the St. Lawrence in the direction of Ottawa. Borden notified the Chief of Staff and the Militia and suggested the Commissioner of the Dominion Police be notified."

The Chief of the Dominion Police, fearing the lights of Parliament Hill would shine forth like a beacon in the night for the daring aerial invaders, ordered the lights extinguished. "Blinds were ordered drawn, and life in the capital continued in an eerie darkness which marked the first blackout and air raid in Canada's history. Marksmen were dispatched to the roofs of government buildings and given orders to shoot down any aircraft approaching the city. The invaders were to be met with in force."

The invasion never took place. Soon there came an unexpected explanation for the phantom invasion.

> Word came out of Morristown, Ogdensburg, and Syracuse that the panic in Ottawa was the result of a prank by a few jokers in Morristown. It was said that three fire-balloons with fireworks attached were sent aloft from Morristown in celebration of the hundredth anniversary of the end of the War of 1812. The fireworks created the impression of aircraft lights and engines, falling balls of fire, and the powerful searchlight witnessed in Brockville. At first, Ottawa refused to believe this. Even the Dominion Observatory went so far as to explain that this was untenable since the prevailing winds were from the east and would not have carried the balloons in the northeasterly direction. However, the militia and police authorities in Ottawa contacted their American counterparts to investigate this story.

> On the morning of February 15th, Constable Storey of the Brockville Police Department found a paper balloon near Eastern Hospital, and soon afterwards a second paper balloon was found in eastern Brockville along the river. This news spread quickly across the telegraph lines so that the afternoon newspapers were able to laugh most loudly at how the morning newspapers and the politicians had been taken in by a few pranksters with toy balloons.

> Officialdom was reluctant to admit it had been the victim of a hoax.

As Mr. X noted, "Ottawa finally laughed off the 'scaeroplanes' as a case of war nerves on the part of Brockville's citizenry." However, strange aerial sights were being reported elsewhere. That same evening, residents of Richmond Hill, north of Toronto, reported to the police that a strange "aeroplane" was hovering over their homes. A resident of Guelph saw "three moving lights passing over the agricultural college." He called out to others and they too watched the spectacle. This occurred at a time when night flying, at least in Eastern Canada, was something of a rarity. "Were these phantom aircraft the result of hysteria and war nerves, or were they an unusual phenomenon which today would be classified as a UFO?"

Bracebridge/ Essiac

Essiac is an herbal cure for cancer, the best known of all in the country. Essiac is also a palindrome of the last name of Rene Caisse, the nurse who promoted its use. She first learned of it in 1922 from an Indian chief from Northern Ontario while she was a hospital nurse in Bracebridge. From the chief she learned of its potency, its list of ingredients, and its recipe. Apparently Essiac calls for the infusion of twenty-six herbs which are found in Northern Ontario. Between 1924 and 1938, Caisse privately administered the preparation to cancer patients and accumulated a sizeable collection of anecdotal histories of cures.

In 1938 an official medical commission was established to investigate Caisse's claims for Essiac. It was the conclusion of the commission that the evidence available did not support Essiac as a preparation of benefit in the treatment of cancer. Yet claims for Essiac continued to be heard over the years. Caisse refused to list the ingredients or the manner of preparation, but she did make limited quantities available for controlled clinical studies and scientifically controlled animal studies, yet never in sufficient quantity to permit continued testing.

Dr. K.J.R. Wightman, Medical Director of the Ontario Cancer Treatment and Research Foundation, which co-ordinated the studies, reported in the Canadian Medical Association *Journal*, 5 November 1977, as follows: "I am informed there is no evidence of any alteration in the disease process in any of these patients. (One series consisted of 40 patients, the other 25 patients.) These unequivocal negative statistics refute any claims made as to the efficiency of this cancer cure with the material provided in the suggested dose schedules."

Caisse's offer to deposit the formula with the Lieutenant-Governor of Ontario made the headlines but met with resistance. It has been anecdotally reported that the business executive Stephen Roman purchased the formula from Caisse — for a reported $1 million — and turned it over to the Resperin Corporation Limited under terms that have not been disclosed. As the Canadian Cancer Society noted in a position paper on Essiac prepared by its Executive Vice-President, R.A. Macbeth, M.D., the Resperin Corporation was associated with an unproven remedy for asthma which had some notoriety and was subsequently proscribed. Reports are that the Resperin Corporation plans its own clinical trials of Essiac.

It has also been reported that Essiac is currently being prepared in quantity by a prominent doctor in Port Perry who supplies it to members of the medical profession on request on an experimental (or non-therapeutic) basis.

Cave Springs/ Multiple Mysteries

Cave Springs, a region of multiple mysteries, is a hundred-acre tract of land located at the foot of the Niagara Escarpment southeast of Beamsville. The mysteries of the region were presented by William F. Rannie in his booklet *Cave Springs Farm in Lore and Legend* (1981).

The somewhat rocky tract was originally occupied by the Attiwandaronk. Because these Indians acted as a buffer between the Iroquois on the south and the Hurons on the north, Samuel de Champlain called them "la Nation neutre," the Neutral Nation. One of the few living legacies of the Neutrals that has survived to modern times is the name they gave the nearby falls: Niagara.

Part of their tract of land was turned into farmland by the Loyalists whose occupation commenced in 1798. It was said that during the War of 1812 disgruntled soldiers seized the payroll and deserted, hiding their unclaimed treasure in these parts.

Flashing lights on the crest of the Escarpment during World War I led some people to believe that

German spies were planted in the area. In 1981, about one-tenth of the tract was acquired by the Niagara Peninsula Conservation Authority. The rest remains in private hands.

The Adam Steps are a steep ascent that leads to the crest of the Escarpment. The steps reach a ledge close to the rim where an unspecified number of carved human heads were once visible. The archeologist Kenneth Kidd described the two heads then in place when he visited the site in 1948. They were carved in living rock and measured about six inches in height. The features were distinguished by flattened noses and thickened lips. "The heads had features closely resembling those often seen on protohistoric and early historic stone tobacco smoking pipes, so that I felt reasonably certain of the identity of their makers (late Iroquois and possibly Huron or Neutral)." A clay cast made of one of the heads in 1953 was subsequently presented to the Lundy's Lane Historical Society Museum in Niagara Falls. No heads are visible today. They were either removed by souvenir hunters or defaced by vandals.

The path to the Lost Cave, the storehouse of the artifacts of a vanished civilization, takes one along the trail of legend. One night in the 1900s, a farmer named Emerson Grobb stumbled into the Lost Cave and emerged the next morning with a clay vessel, which was subsequently donated to the Royal Ontario Museum. Local tradition maintains that the well-known archaeologist A.B. Skinner enriched the holdings of the Heye Foundation in New York with treasures taken from the Lost Cave.

Yet Rannie wrote, "Balanced against the loss of artifacts, however, is the intriguing fact that somewhere on the hillside at Cave Springs there exists today, and perhaps forever, a secret repository holding safe the remnants of a civilization that flourished on these acres long ago."

Tradition once held that in the Escarpment there lies an Underground Lake, an eerie chamber with subterranean rivers that connect it to Lakes Erie and Ontario. Recent research, however, shows that no substantial "lake" exists, though caves deep in the Escarpment's dolomite hold winter's runoff in large amounts, releasing the water slowly during the drier seasons that follow.

As Rannie concluded about this tract of multiple mysteries, "There is probably no other spot in the [Niagara] Peninsula as rich in folklore, in stories of what might have been, as Cave Springs Farm."

Chatham/ "Air Car"

A strange "air car" was sighted in the sky over Chatham Township, according to an item published in the Windsor *Record*, datelined Chatham, 7 March 1911:

A mysterious aircraft has been floating around this vicinity for some days. The air car, which is of enormous dimensions, has been sighted by several persons whose veracity goes unquestioned.

The strange part of the story is that this particular conveyance travels the ether without apparent planes and seems capable of staying up for days.

During the past three days it has been sighted from several villages around about but it has never been known to alight.

Last night it was seen by parties in Chatham Township when it was brilliant with lights. For a time it floated along about 100 feet from the earth's surface, then suddenly with a great whirring, it rose to a high altitude and soon disappeared in the distance.

Cobalt/ Old Yellow Top

Old Yellow Top is the affectionate nickname of a hairy ape-like creature which, according to newspaper reports published over the last eighty years, has been periodically sighted in the vicinity of the mines of the town of Cobalt. The creature derives its name from its most characteristic feature, a light-coloured mane of hair. Until the Second World War, it was called, simply, Yellow Top. But since the war, perhaps in deference to its longevity, it has been dubbed Old Yellow Top. The other nickname it is known by is "the Precambrian Shield Man," which suggests that it is a living legacy of the prehistoric past.

The first report of the creature was made in September 1906, when it was seen by a group of surprised men building the headframe of the Violet Mine. It was sighted the second time by two prospectors working their claims northeast of the Wettlaufer mine in July 1923. They saw "what looked like a bear picking at a blueberry patch." But one of the prospectors added, "It sure was like no bear that I have ever seen. Its head was kind of yellow and the rest of it was black like a bear, all covered with hair." The third account of its appearance is dated April 1946, when it was described by a woman and her son. They said they saw a dark hairy animal with a "light" head ambling off the tracks into the bush near Gillies Lake.

In the files of the North Bay *Nugget* there is a fourth report, dated 5 August 1970. The bus taking twenty-seven miners to the Cobalt Lode for the graveyard shift swerved, went out of control and almost plunged down a nearby rock cut. The driver had turned to avoid hitting a dark form which walked across the road. "At first I thought it was a big bear," the driver, Aimee Latreille, was quoted as saying. "But then it turned to face the headlights and I could see some light hair, almost down to its shoulders. It couldn't have been a bear." One of the miners at the front of the bus said he caught a glimpse of the creature. Larry Cormack said it "looked like a bear to me at first, but it didn't walk like one. It was kind of half stooped over. Maybe it was a wounded bear, I don't know." The miners in the bus were unhurt, but the description of Old Yellow Top suggested he had seen better days.

Consecon/
The Fox Sisters

Few people realize that the originators of the modern Spiritualist Movement were the Fox Sisters, two young girls from Upper Canada. Although the Fox Sisters did not originate the notion of "spirit communication with the dead" — that seems as old as civilization itself—they gave it a uniquely democratic (and one might say American) turn. To them is owed the past popularity of table-rapping and mediumism, and also the present vogue for what is essentially the same thing under the streamlined title: "trance-channelling." The fact that mediumship has always been fraught with fraud and deceit is also laid at their humble door.

The two sisters are Margaretta (Maggie) Fox, born 7 October 1833, died 8 March 1893, and Catherine (Katie) Fox, born 27 March 1837, died 2 July 1892. Their birthplace was Consecon, a small farming community southwest of Belleville. Their parents were a poor couple, John D. Fox, a farmer and blacksmith, and his wife Margaret. Maggie and Katie were the youngest of five children. There were three older children: two sisters, Elizabeth and Leah, and a brother, Daniel.

It was hard for the Fox Family to survive in Canada West, as Ontario was then known. Conditions looked more promising in upstate New York. So on 11 December 1847, the family emigrated, moving due south and establishing themselves in the farming community known at the time as Hydesville, located north of the town of Newark, Wayne County, New York. The farming community no longer exists, but the name Hydesville persists in the name of a country road. The original Fox Homestead stood by the intersection of Hydesville Road and Parker Road.

Elizabeth remained in the Belleville area and married a man named Ousterhout. Leah moved to Rochester where she married a fellow named Fish. Daniel lived and worked on a nearby farm. Both Leah and Daniel, like Maggie and Katie, made contributions to the birth of the Spiritualist Movement. Leah organized the *séances* conducted by her younger sisters, and Daniel devised a board and planchette to permit the spirits whom they had contacted to communicate through letters of the alphabet in addition to the noisy knocks and raps. It has been claimed he constructed a primitive form of the Ouija board.

This engraving depicts Kate and Maggie Fox, the famous (or infamous) Fox Sisters. The original "spirit-rappers" were two farm girls from Consecon, Upper Canada. Their fun and games in the family cottage at Hydesville, New York, the evening of 31 March 1848, marked the beginning of the modern Spiritualist Movement. [Dale News, Lily Dale, N.Y.]

The birthplace of the modern Spiritualist Movement was the Fox Cottage at Hydesville, N.Y. It is shown here with visitors at the doorway in a photograph taken in 1850. The original cottage was moved to the spiritualists' colony at Lily Dale, N.Y. A reconstruction of the cottage on the original site was single-handedly undertaken by John Drummond, a Canadian-born spiritualist in the late 1960s. It is the Drummond cottage that now stands on the site. [Dale News, Lily Dale, N.Y.]

The only members of the Fox family who remained at home were the parents and Maggie and Katie. They were members of the Methodist Episcopal Church and to all eyes were a happy family. The parents were devoted to each other and died seven months apart in 1865. The sisters, Maggie, fifteen and Katie, eleven, were in good health and even in good spirits. Perhaps they were feeling frisky, bored, confined, living in such close proximity with the parents in a two-room wooden farmhouse in the country during the winter. Whatever may have been behind it, early in the evening of 31 March 1848 the girls, playing games to amuse themselves and maybe to irk their parents began to communicate with raps and knocks — one for no, two for yes.

It seems that the Hydesville house was haunted and that unknown to the Fox family there was a body buried in the basement. The body was that of an itinerant peddlar named Charles B. Rosna who had been murdered by a previous occupant. Rosna's spirit was restless and took the opportunity to communicate with Maggie and Katie. According to later newspaper accounts, the basement was eventually dug up and human bones were discovered there.

Crowds of curious people from nearby communities flocked to the farmhouse to hear the mysterious raps and knocks which seemed to answer all questions. When Leah learned of the turn of events she brought Maggie and Katie to Rochester where she arranged *séances* to demonstrate the girls' gifts. Leah realized from the first what others only later learned: Spiritualism embraced all social classes and could be organized along paying lines. Public meetings were held at which the pros and cons of the girls' alleged abilities to communicate with the "spirit world" were hotly debated. One meeting ended in a near riot. In 1850 they moved to New York and for a time appeared as major attractions at P.T. Barnum's American Museum.

Thereafter Maggie and Katie — and to some extent Leah, who went on to marry well — gave public demonstrations and private consultations. In their heyday they were the world's best-known mediums. However, the life of the spiritualistic medium is not a happy one. The sisters took to drink. Maggie was drawn to Dr. Elisa Kent Kane, a wealthy and socially prominent physician. He was also an explorer, who made a name for himself in the Arctic. When he was not on his travels, he courted Maggie and tried to reform her. She should "come clean" and confess that the raps were done by the cracking of the toe knuckles, not by the spirits; he thought that the whole thing had gotten out of hand. Maggie maintained that they were secretly married, but by then Kane had died. In 1888, Maggie confessed in public that her life in spiritualism was all completely a fraud. Katie came clean three years later. But then Maggie retracted her confession, and Katie did the same. The Fox Sisters were never caught in fraud, but they confessed to it and later denied it.

Today the Fox Sisters are revered by those Spiritualists who cherish a sense of the Movement's history, and are studied by social historians, journalists, sceptics, feminists, and others with specialized interests. One legacy of the Fox Sisters is, surprisingly, the Fox Homestead.

By the turn of the century the original wooden cottage in Hydesville, where it all began in 1848, was in other hands and falling into a state of disrepair. A wealthy spiritualist acquired it in 1916 and had it transported to Lily Dale, the "spiritualist camp" on Lake Cassadagua in Chautauqua County in western New York State. Here it was reconstructed on a new foundation and used for *séances*. In 1938, the motion-picture photographers for Movietone News caught on film the sounds of rappings produced by the medium Flo Cottrell working in the cottage under the control of "Uncle Ike." In 1955, under mysterious circumstances, the cottage was burnt to the ground. Arson was suspected, but requests for further information directed to the Lily Dale Assembly have so far elicited no further details.

The original Hydesville site, bereft of the cottage, was marked by a granite marker erected at the personal expense of a wealthy Rochester spiritualist named Cadwallader. The inscription may still be read:

The Birthplace of
MODERN SPIRITUALISM
Upon This Site Stood
the Hydesville Cottage
the Home of the
FOX SISTERS
Through Whose Mediumship Communication
with the Spirit World was Established
March 31, 1848
There Is No Death
There Are No Dead
Placed Here by M.E. Cadwallader
Dec. 5, 1927

Visitors to the site will find a cottage—a reconstruction of the original—standing on the lot. The reconstruction is the work of a Canadian spiritualist named John Drummond. Not much is known of him.

Drummond was born in Canada of Acadian background and fought and suffered wounds in the Great War. Thereafter he worked principally as a carpenter but also as a farmer, mason, gold digger, grocery-store manager, librarian, newspaper correspondent, and postmaster. Early in 1950 he attended a spiritualist's circle in Toronto where he heard a prediction which changed his life. "I was told at meetings that I would live under the American flag and that I would come here," he recalled for the writer Herbert G. Jackson Jr. in the publication *D. & C.*, 14 September 1969. "I asked what I would be doing here and they said what I formerly did, and they were right."

Drummond bought a house in the Newark area and became secretary and treasurer of the local Ministry of Spiritual and Divine Science, the group which held the deed to the Hydesville site. He made his first visit to the property on the Labour Day weekend of 1953 and was saddened to find it so rundown. He became an American citizen and in the fall of 1967, working alone, he undertook the work of reconstruction. He was guided by old coloured postcards which showed the cottage as it was in its glory. He completed his work and the cottage was sublet. It caught fire in 1983.

In the summer of 1987, the building was derelict but still standing. Its walls were charred but the roof was intact. Torn curtains dangled from some of the windows and there was a television antenna and a lightning rod on the roof, but there were no signs of present occupancy. The doors and windows were boarded up. A Wayne County Sheriff's Notice and Warning was posted on each of the doors, condemning the structure. Almost lost amid the weeds and other growth on the front yard was the granite marker erected so long ago by M.E. Cadwallader. It most resembles a tombstone.

Behind the charred cottage may be seen part of the foundation of a modern building. Two low walls of cinderblocks create a corner with a head-high cornerstone. By parting the weeds one is able to read the inscription, part of which runs:

> The Birthplace and Shrine of
> Modern Spiritualism Corner-Stone
> The Ministry of Spiritualists
> Divine Science and Friends
> 4th July 1955

Why the modern structure? The spiritualists of the area decided that a world spiritualist's headquarters should be erected on the plot where it all began. They evolved plans for a centre in a handsome granite building with enough room for offices, a library, a museum, and an auditorium with one thousand seats. Subscriptions were taken and work was commenced — and abandoned shortly after the dedication of the cornerstone.

Cornwall/
"A Small Flame"

Cornwall was established on the St. Lawrence River by Loyalists in 1784. Settlers in the vicinity were soon perplexed by a phantom light which made its appearance late each year. The following description, "Natural Phenomenon in Cornwall," appeared in the Niagara *Gleaner* on 17 March 1828.

In the parish of St. Austel there is a singular phenomenon: it is the appearance of light near the Turnpike road at Hill Head, about three quarters of a mile West of the town. In the summer season it is rarely seen; but in the winter, particularly in the months of November and December, scarcely a dark night passes in which it is not visible. It appears of a yellow hue, and seems to resemble a small flame. It is generally stationary: and when it moves it wanders but little from its primitive spot sometimes mounting upwards, and then descending to the earth. As it had frequented this spot from time memorial it is now rendered so familiar, that it almost ceases to attract attention. It is somewhat remarkable, that, although many attempts have been made to discover it in the place of its appearance, every effort has hitherto failed of success. On approaching the spot, it becomes invisible to the pursuers, even while it remains luminous to those who watched it at a distance. To trace its exact abode, a level has been taken during its appearance which the curious have been guided in their researches the ensuring day; but nothing has ever been discovered.

Cornwall/
The Weeping Statuette

A twenty-seven inch statuette of Christ on the dresser in the bedroom of Leona Villeneuve began to "weep" Friday evening, 15 October 1937. Villeneuve, a thirty-year-old invalid suffering recurrent epilepsy and partial paralysis, noticed it "cry" for the first time after she had ended a nine-day prayer for recovery, promising in the prayer to return to the Ottawa convent of the Grey Sisters of The Cross to complete her education for holy orders.

An estimated two thousand people filed through the second-floor bedroom in her Cornwall home to witness the reported miracle. Many placed gifts of money at the foot of the statuette, according to the CP story filed and published in the Niagara Falls *Evening Review* on 21 October 1937. Moisture appeared on the head and shoulders of the image. Absorbent cotton, wrapped around the image to collect the drops of water, were snatched by visitors who apparently believed the moisture possessed virtue.

Miraculous cures were reported. For instance, Villeneuve's brother-in-law Harry Aubin claimed that the statuette healed his broken foot and that for the first time in four months he could walk without the assistance of his crutches. Villeneuve herself saw in the phenomenon recognition of the power and acceptance of her prayers.

The family physician expressed the opinion that moisture had condensed on the cool statuette from the warm air of the bedroom. The Cornwall clergy declined officially to express an opinion, but Catholic priests independently questioned were inclined to agree with the doctor.

Deep River/
"Sphere-shaped Lights"

The town of Deep River, located on the Ottawa River, was established as the residence community for the personnel employed by Atomic Energy of Canada at nearby Chalk River. Over the years reports of UFO activity over both the town of Deep River and the village of Chalk River with its nuclear reactors have been plentiful.

"Bright sphere-shaped lights have been travelling at phenomenal speeds through the trees and at least fifteen people have witnessed and recounted these bizarre occurrences. Sounds like science fiction? Apparently all of the fifteen witnesses have seen more than they're willing to say, but all steadfastly refuse to return to the area." So mysteriously wrote an Ottawa Valley resident Heather Pettipas in "Close Encounters of the Fourth Kind" in *Downstream: A Deep River and Area Literary/Art Review* (1983) compiled by P.A. Carver.

Deep River/
The Henry Hudson Rock

The curious story of the Henry Hudson Rock, found on the outskirts of the town of Deep River in the

No likeness of Henry Hudson is known. Yet no one who has ever seen the explorer's face in John Collier's historical painting, The Last Voyage of Henry Hudson, *will ever forget the English navigator's facial features: stark terror side-by-side with a Job-like acceptance of fate — being cast adrift with his son and faithful friends in James Bay in the winter of 1611. The image is a haunting one, befitting one around whom swirl so many legends. [Tate Gallery, London]*

1950s, has been briefly sketched by the contributors to *A History of Deep River*, a souvenir booklet issued in July 1970 to mark the Silver Jubilee of this Ottawa Valley town.

If one can visualize the castaway Henry Hudson and company making their way south from James Bay after their abandonment in the year 1611, either assisted or captured by Indians, then some realistic meaning can perhaps be given to the discovery made by a Chalk River resident in the 1950s. Just at the eastern limit of Deep River, a granite boulder was found, carrying the three-line legend:

H.H.
1 6 1 2
Captive

An expert from the British Museum examined the photographs of the inscription and on the basis of character formation pronounced it as "just right for the period."

The souvenir booklet was written by a committee; the section on the Henry Hudson Rock was contributed by Barry M. Mitchell, a technologist with the System Materials branch at the Chalk River Nuclear Laboratories. According to Mitchell, the man who found the rock within town limits on Highway 17 later moved to Brockville and took the rock with him. There it disappeared.

Joan Melvin, a columnist for the *North Renfrew Times*, has gathered much of the information on the Rock. A photograph of it appeared in that publication on 19 September 1962. It shows a large boulder which bears the above inscription in large letters.

Douglas Point/
UFO Sighting

The Douglas Point Nuclear Generating Station, located on the eastern shore of Lake Huron between Port Elgin and Kincardine, began producing nuclear energy in August 1967. The following press story about UFO sightings near the Generating Station appeared in the Toronto *Telegram*, 18 September 1967, and was quoted by Yurko Bondarchuk in *UFO: Sightings, Landings and Abductions* (1979):

Port Elgin, Ontario — This village has a fully-fledged flying saucer mystery on its hands but nobody wants to talk about it. At least seventeen people have seen a UFO over Lake Huron in the past week here in Bruce County, about 180 miles northwest of Toronto. One sighting rated an entry in the official log of the Douglas Point

Nuclear Generating Station of Ontario Hydro. Samuel Horton, superintendent of the Hydro station about ten miles south of Port Elgin, said between six and thirteen people at the plant sighted a saucer-shaped object last Monday, Sept. 11. The log entry reads: "On Monday, September 11, at 15:30 hours, (3:30 p.m.), a UFO was observed passing over the station in an easterly direction." Witnesses said they thought the object was part of an orbiting spacecraft until it seemed to hover over the lake about one mile and a half out and then dropped something into the water. One plant employee said he and others saw a similar craft return two nights later and for the next five nights search for the dropped object. One witness said he saw the craft hover near the station. Two others said they saw sparks coming from it over the lake. Selfridge Air Force Base [across the lake] did not investigate and made no radar contacts.

As Bondarchuk noted, "While reports of UFOs ejecting small objects are not uncommon, this case is unique in that the craft returned in an apparent effort to retrieve the object. This suspected attempt may indicate that the object was some form of device designed to gauge the emissions from the nuclear plant."

Lake Erie/
Erie Stones

Lake Erie is the fourth largest of the five Great Lakes. Its name, Erie, recalls the Erie Indians and means "long-tailed," a reference to a panther or a wildcat. It gave rise to the children's conundrum which goes like this:

Question: Which is the scariest of the Great Lakes?
Answer: Lake Erie . . . because it's so *eerie*!

Europeans in the seventeenth century yearned as much for a cure for cancer as do people in the twentieth. One celebrated "cancer cure" was the use of the so-called *Eriennes pierres* or Erie Stones. They were discovered and introduced to France and Germany by the physician and surgeon François Gendron. A French Jesuit who in 1640–47 resided at Sainte-Marie-among-the-Hurons, Gendron was the first physician to visit present-day Ontario.

Gendron described the Erie Stones and their curative properties in a letter he wrote to the Jesuit Superior in 1644: "The spray of these waters, rebounding from the foot of certain large rocks in that place, forms a stone, or rather a petrified salt, of a yellowish colour and of admirable virtue for the curing of sores, fistules, and malign ulcers." He found the stones on the shore of Lake Erie and below the Niagara cataract. He ground them into a powder and from the powder prepared an ointment which he took with him when he returned to France.

He administered the ointment to patients of the aristocracy and nobility. He found royal favour when he treated the breast cancer of the French-born Queen Anne of Austria. How effective the ointment was in this instance or other applications is not recorded. In composition the Erie Stones are a naturally occurring form of calcium carbonate—a placebo perhaps, a nostrum maybe, but not a cure.

Lake Erie/ The Great Snake

The so-called Great Snake of Lake Erie was reported as far back as 1819, when a naturalist, C.S. Rafinesque, referred to it in an article in *Philosophical Magazine*:

It appears that our large lakes have huge serpents or fishes, as well as the sea. On the 3rd of July, 1817, one was seen in Lake Erie, three miles from land, by the crew of a schooner, which was 35 or 40 feet long, one foot in diameter; its colour was a dark mahogany, nearly black. This account is very imperfect, and does not even notice if it had scales; therefore it must remain doubtful whether it was a snake or a fish. I am inclined to believe it was a fish, until otherwise

convinced: it might be a gigantic species of eel, or a species of the above genus *Octipos*. Until seen again, and better described, it may be recorded under the name of *Anquilla gigas* or *Gigantic Eel*.

Dwight Whalen, in his article on the snake-like monster or monsters of Lake Erie, published in the Buffalo *Courier-Express*, 2 August 1981, noted that the serpent seemed to be in hiding from 1817 until July 1892, when the Toledo-bound schooner *Madaline*, out of Buffalo, encountered a huge sea serpent thrashing upon the water. It was observed by the captain and all aboard the schooner at a distance of less than half a mile. A dispatch from Toledo, Ohio, carried in a St. Catharines, Ontario, newspaper, dated July 16 1892, gave an account of the close encounter:

Early Wednesday morning while the schooner *Madaline*, on its way from Buffalo to this city, was passing the Dumming about 130 miles east of here on Lake Erie, Capt. Woods saw about a half mile ahead the waters of the lake lashed into foam. Drawing near, to the surprise of the captain and all on board, a huge sea serpent wrestling about in the waters as if fighting with an unseen foe, was seen. It soon quieted down and lay at full length on the surface of the water. Capt. Woods' estimate is that the serpent was about fifty feet in length and not less than four feet in circumference of body. Its head projected from the water about four feet. He says it was a terrible looking object. It had viciously sparkling eyes and a large head. Fins were plainly seen, seemingly sufficiently large to assist the snake in propelling itself through the water. The body was dark brown in colour which was uniform all along.

Four people sitting on a rocky point at Crystal Beach near Fort Erie in the early evening of 5 May 1896 observed what was later called a "commotion" in Lake Erie some distance from the land.

Their idea was that the phenomenon was caused by a school of fish, as the disturbance in the water seemed to be almost continuous, and there was too much of it to be produced by one fish. The agitation came nearer. Finally one of the women exclaimed, "Why, it is all one fish." And so it appeared to all. There was one object, apparently, moving along the surface of the water towards a beach.

One of the four observers was a Captain Beecher. He answered all the questions of the inquisitive but unnamed reporter for the St. Catharines *Daily Standard*, 11 May 1896, who contributed the following account:

> It was not a mere fleeting glance of the serpent that was had by the four persons in the party, but they watched it for fully three-quarters of an hour, or until it was so dark that they could no longer distinguish the form. By this time it had retreated and was still retreating from the vicinity of the shore. The surface of the lake was comparatively smooth, and the serpent was so near to the party that they could distinctly see its eyes, which Capt. Beecher said looked as large as silver dollars. At times it would lie straight on the surface of the water with its whole length visible. Then it would lift its head and curl its body so that it would be visible only at intervals, where the humps projected above the surface. At times it would turn partly on its side, when it was plainly seen that the colour of the lower part of its body was much lighter than the back, which was dark brown or almost black. Its head looked like a dog's head, having a similar prominence above and back of the eyes. Its tail, however, was pointed, and like that of any monstrous land serpent.
>
> When Capt. Beecher threw a stone in its direction it would lunge fully 30 feet toward the stone, as it struck the water. In this way it turned in various directions in its efforts to catch the stones, evidently thinking they were something suitable for food. It spouted water fully four feet in the air, and kept "sloshin' around" in the water as if it were nervous or else enjoying itself hugely. Capt. Beecher says he will swear it was 35 feet long. It did not disappear from the surface, but just before dark it turned its head away from the shore and began to retreat.

Since then there have been numerous — almost innumerable — reports of such creatures in Lake Erie — "the ones that got away." Vertebrate zoologists point out that lake sturgeons of up to seven feet and more than three hundred pounds have been verified but these are tadpoles compared with the "Great Snake" of Lake Erie legend.

Fort Erie/ "Old McAfee"

One of the oldest burial grounds in the Fort Erie district is the McAfee Cemetery on Niagara Boulevard near Pleasant Point. It is the resting place of many United Empire Loyalists. Apparently well before the turn of the century a chapel or church which stood on the site burnt to the ground. Since then there have been reports of phosphorescent lights or "fire-balls." "One farmer even declared the ball to be a lantern in the hands of a grisly spectre and vouched for its having pursued him for a distance of more than half a mile. Only the speed of this steed, as he told it, saved him from being clutched to its fiery breath." The spectre is said to be that of "old McAfee" or "the Ghost of the McAfee." Horses and other animals are said to shy away from the burial ground. These legends are recounted in an unsigned article in the Niagara Falls *Evening Review*, 10 June 1933.

The spectre bears the name of Samuel McAfee, the local farmer who helped William Lyon Mackenzie escape to the United States in the aftermath of the Rebellion of 1837. McAfee disguised Mackenzie as an old woman, passed him off as a member of the family, and rowed the little rebel across the Niagara River to Buffalo. These details appeared in an article in the *Evening Review*, 27 October 1954, occasioned by the restoration of the old and neglected cemetery.

Gargantua/
"Major Spiritual Centre"

Gargantua is the name of a small community on a triangle of land overlooking Lake Superior west of Lake Superior Provincial Park. The author Wayland Drew has declared Gargantua to be one of the two most sacred places on the lake's eastern shore. The other is Agawa Bay which lies to the southeast. Inspiration for the name came from the nearby rock called the Devil's Chair on account of its shape and size.

As Drew wrote in *Superior: The Haunted Shore* (1975):

> The harbour has the lush and timeless atmosphere of a grotto, and is a fitting entrance to the assemblage of strange promontories and islands that surround the Gargantua Peninsula. The rock here is volcanic—soft, and porous. Where it meets the lake, waves have sculptured it on several levels, licking out seacaves, piercing promontories, and carving the northern extremities into sloping prows. In some places pillars stand severed from the shore, wrapped in creepers, and on the outcroppings ancient cedars crouch like bears, snouts to the wind.
>
> Gargantua is an enchanted landscape, and it is easy to see why it was a major spiritual centre for the Ojibway. From here Nanabozho presided over the moods of the lake and granted a calm journey to those who paid him homage.

Drew went on to refer to the Devil's Chair, citing a passage from Dr. John J. Bigsby's travel book *The Shoe and Canoe* in which the offshore rocks and ridges are described as rising starkly out of the water. "One of these is a rude pyramid from fifty to sixty feet high. Its strange shape, dark colour, and the surrounding gloom, have induced the Indians to worship it as an idol. It has given to the place the name of Gargantua."

Today this strange, lozenge-shaped rock is called the Devil's Chair. Drew concluded: "Viewed from one side it is a reclining man. Viewed from another, it becomes a bowl with a perpendicular opening at water level. Such a blend of masculine and feminine imagery would not have escaped the Ojibway imagination, ever alert for correspondences between the human body and the earth."

Georgian Bay/
The Mystery of the Waubuno

So huge is Georgian Bay (it is almost as large as Lake Ontario) that it has been called the Sixth Great Lake. Yet it is an extension of Lake Huron. Georgian Bay is also considered to be "the Graveyard of the Great Lakes." Innumerable ships of sail and steam have sailed its frequently turbulent waters only to disappear. The best-known doomed ship was the *Waubuno*. Its name is said to be the Algonkian word for "sorcerer."

The 150-foot, 200-ton sidewheeler regularly visited the small ports of Georgian Bay. It departed from Collingwood at 4:00 a.m., 22 November 1879. On its last scheduled trip of the season, it carried ten passengers, fourteen crew members, and a mixed cargo. It was headed for Parry Sound, but it ran into a November gale and never got farther than Christian Island. There it ran into a snowstorm and sank.

The cargo was washed ashore in the South Channel area, and four months later its hull was found overturned in the bay behind Moose Point. When the water is low near Wreck Island, the hull may be seen. Its anchor, recovered in 1962, is now part of the cenotaph at Parry Sound.

There are two enigmas connected with the *Waubuno*. One is the fate of the passengers and crew. No trace of their bodies or belongings was ever found. What is also enigmatic is the nightmare connected with the vessel's departure from Collingwood. The predictive nightmare was recalled by Frank Jones in the *Toronto Star* on 25 November 1979 to mark the centennial of the disaster.

Dr. and Mrs. W.H. Doupe, newlyweds from Mitchell, Ontario, were heading for the small community of McKellar, outside Parry Sound, where the doctor was to open his practice. The night before they were to board the *Waubuno*, the bride cried out in her sleep. She woke up, gripped with fear. She told

145

her husband how she had dreamt of being dragged down in the water, gasping for breath and life. Only with difficulty was he able to convince her to agree to cross Georgian Bay.

At the Collingwood wharf, as they waited to board the vessel, Mrs. Doupe shared her nightmare and fears with the other passengers. Some of them admitted to fears of their own, eyeing the choppy waters and the overcast sky, and headed back to the hotel. However, they were encouraged to return and board the vessel by another passenger, B.N. Fisher, editor and proprietor of the *North Star* at Parry Sound, who scoffed at their fears. But Mrs. Doupe was right to feel that disaster threatened her as her fears turned into a grim reality.

The Great Lakes/ Haunted HOMES

The Great Lakes consist of a system of five large bodies of water. As a unit they comprise the largest basin of fresh water on the surface of the planet. Each body of water is more an ''inland sea'' than it is a ''lake'' proper. Ranged in volume from the largest to the smallest, the five Great Lakes are Lake Superior, Lake Michigan, Lake Huron, Lake Erie, and Lake Ontario. Their names are easily recalled in the acronym HOMES, composed of the initial letters of their names. It may be said with some justice that these HOMES are haunted —by mysterious events if not mysterious beings.

The manifold mysteries of the Great Lakes are those of the sea and the sky. The sea's mysteries are those of ships and their treasures, mariners and strange creatures, wrecks, disappearances, and phantom vessels. The sky's mysteries are those of strange sights and flights involving aircraft and spacecraft. The presence of man is common to all the mysteries, whether they take place in the element of water or of air. But man, the greatest of all mysteries, is reduced to the height of a dwarf beside the gigantic forces of nature unleashed.

The Thunderbird and the Underwater Panther are dominant motifs worked into these woven medicine bags which were made and used by the Indians of the Central Great Lakes Region before the year 1800. The manitou motifs are vivid in colour; the nettlestalk fibres contrast with the yarns which were dyed green, purple, red, light blue, and yellow. The bags are part of the important Jasper Grant Collection. It is only distantly possible that the motifs of the Thunderbird and the Underwater Panther recall native memories of alien spacecraft and sea serpents from the depths. [National Museum of Ireland, Dublin]

Guelph/
A Bat Beneath the Belfry

The following news item, about a long-lived bat in St. James' Church, appeared in the *Kingston Whig*, 25 March 1915. It is reproduced verbatim.

Bat in Stone Wall
Creature Taken Out Alive
After Twenty-Three Years

Anyone who knows anything about bats or has had anything to do with these creatures realizes that they are very hard to kill, and that they will stand a lot of abuse. It is also known that they will live for long periods of time without food, and as soon as they are released will soon become active again. The latter has just been verified in a most peculiar manner in Guelph.

While some alterations were being made at St. James' Church it became necessary to make a hole in the stone wall of the church beneath the ground, the work being done by Mr. J. Benallick. When one of the masons was taking out some stones he was surprised to find a bat imbedded in the wall, which was 20 inches thick. It was covered with limestone and mortar, and the man naturally thought the bat was dead, but when he picked it up it felt warm and it was breathing. Mr. Art Hicks took charge of it, and put it in a box and later took it home with him. He put a glass over the box with a space left for air, and decided to watch it. During the night, however, the bat got out of the box and began to fly around the house.

Mr. Hicks got up, turned on the light, and endeavoured to capture it, but it got out of the window, and he thought that was the last of the bat. The following morning, however, when a member of the household went to shake a mat which was on the doorstep, the bat was found clinging to it, and it was killed and put into the stove, much to Mr. Hicks' regret. He says the bat was quite fat when found, but that it was very weak and could not have lived much longer.

There are no windows or other openings near where it was found, and the wall was erected twenty-three years ago.

Hamilton/
Disappearance of Rocco Perri

Rocco Perri called himself the King of the Bootleggers; indeed, he was Canada's equivalent of Chicago's Al Capone. Born in Plati, Calabria, in 1887, he emigrated at the age of thirteen and settled in Hamilton. Prohibition provided an unparalleled opportunity to turn a profit. Using his contacts and mob connections, he was able to oversee the foreign sale and domestic consumption of alcohol in the Niagara Peninsula and amass a considerable fortune.

Perri led something of a charmed life, managing for two decades to avoid prison and survive assassination attempts. He was living in Toronto to lessen the likelihood of the latter when, on 23 April 1944, he drove to Hamilton to visit his cousin Joseph Serge. Telling his host he had a headache, he left the house and went for a walk, never to return. The body was never found. Underworld rumour had it that he was "cement-coated" and dumped in Hamilton Bay. James Dubro quoted an RCMP officer in *Mob Rule: Inside the Canadian Mafia* who predicted: "His body will not turn up until the bay dries up."

Hamilton/
The Haunted House

They say ghosts never really go away. The same thing might be said about a good ghost story.

One Sunday night in June of 1971, Norm Bilotti was startled out of his sleep by the screaming of his wife Sherri who was lying in bed beside him. He opened his eyes and saw what was frightening her. The two of them could make out the long, black, gowned shape of a faceless spectre, which for a few seconds hovered a few feet above the bed, disappearing before the lights were turned on. They were shaken and could not explain their experience. Exactly twenty-eight days later the spectre appeared again in

147

the same way, but this time they could discern more detail. The spectre was a life-sized, legless woman, with bulging eyes and hair standing on end as though she were receiving an electric shock.

The phenomenon was reported in the press and it attracted wide interest. A professional psychic named Malcolm Bessent of the Human Dimensions Institute of Rosary Hill College in Buffalo came to examine the two-storey house on Upper Wellington Street. He was accompanied on his rounds by Bernard Baskin, a respected Hamilton rabbi with a special interest in witchcraft, Dr. A.S. MacPherson, former clinical director of the Hamilton Psychiatric Hospital, and John Bryden of the *Hamilton Spectator*.

Bessent in his tour of the house paused in the bedroom where the disturbances had occurred. He said that he sensed that the problems in the house were connected with the previous occupants, a family of four. He said that a woman had died a painful death in the house. The letters SA came to his mind and these could be the first letters in a name, perhaps hers. The sight of green and white flowers presented itself, as did the date August 1947.

According to the report by John Bryden in the *Hamilton Spectator* on 27 November 1971, the psychic was correct or close to the truth on some details but wide of the mark on others. A search of the title of the property revealed that it had been purchased in September 1947. The maiden name of the woman who had lived in the house was Flowers. She had not died in the house, but she had suffered a long, painful illness here. When she lapsed into unconsciousness, she was rushed to the local hospital where she died. She was the mother of four children. Someone suggested that the letters SA referred to the Salvation Army, as she and her husband were members of that organization.

The psychic did not establish any connection between the previous occupants and the spectre. But he did note that there was something odd about the bedroom area. "There's something about this house that this phenomenon is trying to attract attention to," Bessent claimed. "Maybe something under the floor. Definitely something has happened or is in this house that attention is being drawn to. I think something is concealed in this area—what, I don't know. I'm being drawn to it very strongly. It's the reason for the manifestation." An examination of the house revealed nothing unusual.

The spectre of the haunted house of Upper Wellington Street was a nine-day wonder. No further disturbances were reported for eleven years. But some stories will not die or go away for long.

The Bilottis eventually moved out of the house and it was slated to be demolished in October 1982. One member of the wrecking crew claimed that he heard strange sounds as he went about his noisy work. Then, between the walls on the second floor, workmen uncovered the upper half of a large tombstone, a marker meant for a double grave. One half was marked "Our Baby" and inscribed "Martha Louisa" with the date "1888." The other half was inscribed "Emma Grace" and dated "9 Nov. 1879." Mark McNeil of the Hamilton *Spectator* established in articles published on 23 and 26 October 1982 that the stones were the memorials to two infants, Martha Louisa Young and Emma Grace Young, who died and were buried in the local cemetery not far away. How their tombstones, which were missing from the cemetery, had ended up between the walls of the building, erected about 1942, was anyone's guess.

Hamilton/ Children's Accounts of Satanic Rites?

A child-custody hearing in a District Court in Hamilton took a bizarre turn when descriptions of child neglect and abuse were augmented by accounts of cannibalism, ritual murder, orgiastic rituals, graveyard rites, sadism, and satanism. The hearing, which turned into the longest and costliest in Canadian legal history, raised numerous social and psychological issues.

A distraught mother, estranged from both her husband and her lover, made a request to the Hamilton-Wentworth Children's Aid Society to provide temporary foster care for her two girls, both under the age of eight. This occurred on 7 February 1985. One year later she bore a third child, also a girl, so the outcome of the hearing ultimately affected the status of her three children.

The older children provided the foster parents with evidence of neglect and abuse but surprised them with dramatic and bizarre accounts of being lowered into graves and of participating in filmed sexual and satanic rites. Taped conversations with the older children were presented in court. On 30 March 1987, after eighteen months of hearings, 15,000 pages of transcripts, thousands of pages of evidence, appearances from sixty-one witnesses, and 142 exhibits, the District Court made the three children wards of the Crown. Six months later the Ontario Supreme Court dismissed the mother's appeal and all parental access to the three children was denied. There was no appeal to the Supreme Court of Canada.

There was clear evidence of neglect and abuse but not a shred of evidence to support the allegations of Satanism. No criminal charges were ever laid. Where did the children learn about such bizarre and gruesome behaviour? Why did they accuse their mother and her lover of engaging in such practices and subjecting them to them? Were the children inadvertently led into making such detailed accusations by carelessly phrased questions? Were their imaginations stimulated by horror movies on late-night television?

The parapsychologist A.R.G. Owen had an unexpected answer to these and related questions. He is the author of an unpublished study called "Morphogenetic Fields and Children" which places the Hamilton case in the context of similar cases reported from California and Minnesota in the 1980s, as documented by Charles Rappleye, an investigative reporter with the *L.A. Weekly.* Rappleye's account of these cases, which originally appeared in that publication, was reprinted as "Satanism and Child Abuse" by the editors of *Fate,* April 1987. What Dr. Owen added with his study was a consideration of Causative Formation, a hypothesis put forward by the British biologist Rupert Sheldrake:

These thoughts led us to contemplation of the possibility that Rupert Sheldrake's theory of Causative Formation — morphogenetic fields — might provide the answer to all of these phenomena. Is there a universal mind, easily accessible to children, from which they derive these various stories? Do they have access to knowledge which the adult world has forgotten how to access? Are the stories of Satanism and cannibalism some form of universal macabre game which children around the world are role-playing? Do they have real reincarnation memories, are these another game?

Owen explained that Sheldrake postulated that the universe functions not so much by fixed laws as by habit patterns. "The more deeply ingrained the habit, the more effectively timeless or 'absolute' it appears. These habit patterns are carried across both space and time by morphogenetric fields or 'M-fields.' These M-fields are highly detailed and carry tremendous amounts of 'information.' Living things tune in to appropriate sequences of physical, behavioural, and psychological M-fields throughout their life-cycles, through a process called 'morphic resonance' — the resonance of like upon like."

Owen suggested that children are naturally telepathic and that their often gruesome games, stories, and rhymes are transmitted across time and space.

Lake Huron/
The Fate of the *Griffon*

Lake Huron, the third-largest of the five Great Lakes, was not always so named. The lake was originally called Mer Douce, the sweetwater sea, and then Lac d'Orléans. Finally it was named after the nation of Indians who lived along its banks.

The Arms of Count Frontenac are supported by two heraldic griffons, so the *Griffon* was the name the explorer La Salle chose for the small barque which he ordered to be built for the exploration of the Great Lakes above Niagara Falls. (A griffin, griffon, or gryphon is a fabulous creature with an eagle's head and wings and a lion's body.) He had it constructed on Cayuga Creek which today is part of Niagara Falls, New York. The forty-five-ton, single-sailed ship, adorned with a flying griffon and armed with five small guns, was launched with the drinking of brandy and the singing of *Te Deums* on 7 August 1679.

The captain and his crew of some thirty men sailed the *Griffon* up the Niagara River, across Lake Erie and Lake Huron to Michilimackinac, and into Lake Michigan. It was loaded with furs at Green Bay, Wisconsin, and it commenced its return voyage. It was seen by Indians on Lake Huron on 20–21 September. Thereupon it disappeared. It has been surmised that the vessel capsized in a severe storm and the crew drowned, or that the crew mutinied and brought the ship to safe harbour before deserting with its valuable cargo.

For three centuries the *Griffon*'s fate was one of the minor mysteries of New France and of Great Lakes sailing. Over the years at least ten old wreckages were examined with a view to answering the question of the whereabouts of La Salle's ill-fated *Griffon*. Then what is in all likelihood the wreckage of the ship was found in a secluded cove on Russell Island, located at the point where Lake Huron turns into Georgian Bay, two miles northwest of Tobermory, the community on the trip of the Bruce Peninsula.

The white-oak remains of a forty-foot keel and various pieces of metal, all of which answer to historical descriptions of the *Griffon*, were discovered by a Tobermory fishermen, O.C. (Orrie) Vail, who informed the journalist Harrison John MacLean of his find. MacLean made the story his own and formally identified the wreckage in an exclusive for the Toronto *Telegram* on 16 August 1955. Most naval specialists and historians who examined the evidence agreed with MacLean, but not all.

As MacLean pointed out in his book *The Fate of the Griffon* (1974), there is a disinclination to take the discovery seriously. So to this day what are probably the remains of the *Griffon*, a ship which figured in the history of New France and the Great Lakes, rest in a shack at Tobermory.

Jacksons Point/ "Time Loss"

When Robert L. Ripley of "Believe It or Not!" fame called life "an odyssey of incredible oddities," he was not thinking of the Armstrong family. But the phrase does describe the odd events and eerie experiences that befell and befall Gerry Armstrong, his wife Susan, and their twin daughters Pamela and Wendy. These are not their real names but the names the community college lecturer and writer David Haisell gave them in the book he devoted to the family called *The Missing Seven Hours* (1978).

One day in 1953, when Gerry Armstrong was twelve years old and a student in London, England, he experienced a "time loss." To this day he has no memory of what happened to him during those seven waking hours which to him are unaccountably "missing." In 1959, on a trip outside London, he saw "a huge orange fireball" in the sky above a field. In 1963, he and his wife Susan, from the window of their London flat, saw what seemed to be a star "rippling" and "droning." Odd sights, sounds, and sensations abounded.

In 1972, the Armstrongs emigrated to Canada and settled at first in Mississauga, outside Toronto, and then at Jacksons Point. Apparently whatever had been "buzzing" them in England followed them to Canada and began "buzzing" them once they were settled on the shore of Lake Simcoe.

In October 1973, Susan and Gerry on two successive evenings over the lake saw a "red, pulsing glow." On a number of occasions Gerry reported a "bilocation," being in one location but being seen by a friend or a neighbour at the same time in another location a good distance away. The twins became blasé about the UFOs they saw. They were known to say, with dismay, "They're here again."

But the strangest and most unsettling occurrence of all was Gerry's "place and time loss." In November 1973, while driving in his car in the vicinity of Jacksons Point, he was perplexed to realize two things. He was not driving at all but was stopped beside the road helping some motorists who were strangers repair a tire. He was not in the vicinity of Jacksons Point but at the parking lot overlooking the Horseshoe Falls, some 180 miles distant. The strangers wanted him to get into their car and be driven to Vermont, but he managed to escape. At the nearest phone booth he placed a collect call to his wife. The call was placed at 6:30 p.m., and twenty minutes later he began the long drive back home. He believes he arrived in Jacksons Point in about one hour. He was hungry so he ate dinner in half an hour at the Jolly Roger restaurant before returning home at 8:00 p.m.

There is no way the drive between the two cities, with or without the meal at the Jolly Roger, could have been made in ninety minutes. Nor is there any way the car could have travelled to and from Niagara Falls on one tank of gas. Gerry did not buy gas along the way. Perhaps the trip did not take place. But if it was a delusion, how can one explain the collect telephone call which was made from Niagara Falls?

Haisell wrote about the Armstrongs: "They don't think of themselves as special, yet they recognize they are different from other people. They don't want to be, but are because of their experiences, and because of the effect their experiences have had on their lives."

Subsequent to the completion of the book about his life and experiences, Gerry consented to undergo regression hypnosis with a Toronto psychiatrist with a special interest in parapsychology. The texts and analyses of the two sessions were published in the first two issues of *Journal UFO*, a publication edited by Haisell. The editor wrote, "The contents of the transcripts seem to indicate that Armstrong had contact with non-human intelligences during the seven-hour period in question but, as with any case involving regressive hypnosis, the material must be carefully analyzed before any conclusions can be drawn, if indeed any can be drawn at all."

Under hypnosis, Gerry recalled the sensations, emotions, and thoughts that he had experienced one afternoon in the summer of 1953 when he was twelve years old and attending a summer camp in southeast England. He described what has come to be called "alien abduction." He saw a bright light and two strange beings who beckoned to him and floated him

toward them and into their round ship where there were other tall beings with whitish-grey skins, small mouths and prominent eyes. For a while he was left alone in a room. Then aliens entered and showed him a screen with a round red ball on it. Perhaps it was a planet, perhaps the planet Earth. Then he found himself in a dome with other children and a woman who wore around her neck a silver cross decorated with emeralds. She touched him and he fell asleep and he woke up while being carried back to where he had been. The beings bid him goodbye, saying that they shall "meet again . . . with others." Then sleep overcame him.

Such alien encounters have become commonplace in the 1980s. It is easy to dismiss an adult's hypnotically induced childhood recollections. It is especially easy to dismiss Gerry Armstrong's account when it is noted that the "alien abduction" occurred while the youngster smoked his first cigarette. It is a little harder to dismiss out of hand hundreds of somewhat similar experiences which were spontaneously recalled or remembered only under some form of pressure by people from all walks of life. The classic account of the alien-abduction scenario is *Communion: A True Story* (1987) written by Whitley Strieber. The account is described as a memoir and not a work of fiction, and the author takes pains to establish that he is describing memories and not imaginings of abductions which occurred at intervals throughout his life.

Kanata/
The Prophet of March

"This man was Henry Wentworth Monk, a Canadian whose character was compounded of elements we find in William Blake, Walt Whitman and Leo Tolstoy. He was an Anglo-Saxon forerunner of Theodore Hertzl, the founder of the Zionist movement."

So wrote the broadcaster and author R.S. Lambert in his biographical study of this unusual man. He called it *For the Time Is at Hand: An Account of the Prophecies of Henry Wentworth Monk, of Ottawa, Friend of the Jews, and Pioneer of World Peace* (1947).

Henry Wentworth Monk wore the mantle of the

Henry Wentworth Monk, the Prophet of March, was the perfect subject to sit for Holman Hunt, the Pre-Raphaelite artist, who painted this portrait of Monk in 1858. It depicts Monk in a Christ-like pose, holding in one hand the Holy Bible and in the other a rolled-up and sealed issue of the London Times, *symbolic of the relationship that Monk discerned between ancient Scripture and modern history—between prophecy and fulfillment.* [National Gallery of Canada]

prophet with dignity. He was a man obedient to the will of God and set himself the task of assisting the return of the Jewish People to Palestine. Peace would then reign with the establishment of the Kingdom of God on Earth. Over the years he would publish numerous texts and tracts to argue the inevitability of these actions taking place within his lifetime. He first used the phrase "United Nations" in 1880; he described the "Establishment of the United States of Europe" in 1896. He was a Zionist before the movement was founded. If a prophet is someone who bears moral witness to spiritual ideals in his own lifetime, Monk was a prophet.

Monk was born on 6 April 1827 at "Beechmount," the family fruit farm, located near Constance Lake in the Township of March, northwest of today's Kanata. He was only seven when he was sent to England for his primary education. He studied at

the cloister-like halls of Christ's Hospital, London, for seven years before being sent back to "Beechmount."

He assumed an ascetic appearance and gave some thought to the study of theology, with a view to entering the ministry, but he settled for the life of a fruit-farmer by day and a student of the Bible by night. He underwent some type of conversion experience in 1853, explaining that he had discovered "the key" to the Scriptures. Thereafter he referred to himself as a "true Israelite." He vowed never to trim his hair or beard until the Kingdom of God was established on Earth.

Through hard work and frugality he was able to afford a pilgrimage to the Holy Land in 1854–55. He spent eighteen months in Palestine, mostly at Ourtass, a Jewish agricultural colony which had been newly established near Bethlehem. It was here that he met and befriended Holman Hunt, the pre-Raphaelite painter. Hunt took one look at Monk and felt a thrill such as he had never before experienced. The young Canadian looked like Christ! It happened that a year earlier, in Surrey, England, Hunt had finished painting his major canvas, *The Light of the World*. This is the painting for which he is most fondly remembered. In it Christ is depicted as a tall and bearded young man, noble and handsome. The portrayal was much discussed in its day. Monk took the resemblance to be more than an omen; it was a prophetic fulfillment. The two of them would lead the world's Jews out of the Diaspora.

With some reluctance Monk returned to "Beechmount" where he completed the first of his numerous biblical tracts. He called it *A Simple Interpretation of the Revelation, Together with Three Lectures Lately Delivered in Canada and the United States of America on the Restoration of Judah and Israel, God and Man, Christianity* (1857). The next year, armed with his tract, Monk spent some time in London. He renewed his friendship with Hunt and he posed for a portrait (now in the National Gallery in Ottawa). It depicts Monk in a Christ-like pose, holding in one hand the Holy Bible and in he other a rolled-up and sealed issue of the London *Times*. The two publications were meant to symbolize the relationship which Monk discerned between the ancient Scripture and modern history, between prophecy and fulfillment.

In 1862 he returned to "Beechmount" where he worked on a new prophetic tract. Later that year he travelled to Washington, D.C., where he privately met with Abraham Lincoln. He was unable to convince the U.S. President to allow him to intervene in the Civil War.

In 1872 he could again afford to visit London. Here he met the art critic John Ruskin who subsidized the publication of Monk's manifesto *Our Future* which appeared later that year. Monk realized that to respond to the Darwinian challenge to biblical authority he had to sharpen his invective and revise his reasoning. In later years Ruskin would regard Monk as "an interesting and somewhat pathetic example of religious madness."

In 1875, Monk returned to Canada. As by this time the family fruit farm had been sold, he took up residence in Ottawa, where he established the "Palestine Restoration Fund" and encouraged subscribers to tithe one-tenth of their income to his support in his Christian endeavour to repatriate the homeless Jewish people.

He made his last trip to London in 1880. Here he published a sixteen-page booklet called *World Life, or the Future Existence and Development of the Aggregate Human Mind, in the Light of Modern Science* (1883) in which he marshalled all his arguments against the tide of scientism and materialism. In 1884, he left London for the last time and returned to Ottawa, penniless as usual. He devoted his final years to his double mission: "I now lift up the standard of the Peace of the World, and the Welfare of Canada." He died on 24 August 1896. It was Holman Hunt who had discerned greatness in the man and his mission who was most generous in his appraisal of the person and his achievement. "Every action of the community begins with a word," he said, "and who can say to-day that Monk did not bring men on the road towards the abolition of war. . . ."

Kempenfelt Bay/ Kelly

Kempenfelt Kelly is the name of the lake monster which is said to inhabit Kempenfelt Bay. The Bay is the westward extension of Lake Simcoe. No one remembers who first called the monster Kelly, or why, except that the alliteration makes for a memorable name.

It seems Lake Simcoe teems with sea serpents, which are frequently sighted making waves in Kempenfelt Bay and Cook's Bay. Each year visitors and citizens of Barrie, the city which overlooks the western tip of Kempenfelt Bay, report seeing a large, unidentified, aquatic creature in these waters. The Indians in the past maintained that powerful spirits resided in all deep waters. In the early 1800s, fur traders and British soldiers made the occasional marine sighting. But it was not until World War I that widespread reports accumulated of unidentified sea life in these waters. The creature in the lake was dubbed Igopogo in the 1950s, and the creature in the bay was called Kelly in the 1960s.

No two descriptions of Kempenfelt Kelly coincide. But Kathleen Kenna, writing in the *Toronto Star* on 4 April 1987, attempted a series of portraits: "Sightings of Kempenfelt Kelly, as the creature has come to be called, have included a serpent-like animal with a small head; a dinosaur-type beast with the head of a horse; a huge creature resembling a dolphin with flippers; and even a 10-metre mammal with large, gaping eyes, a fish-like tail and four fins with claws at the tips."

In 1976, the Barrie-based cartoonist John Beaulieu started to sketch Kelly as a huge, worm-like serpent with a couple of humps, a button nose, and appealing eyes. The Greater Barrie Chamber of Commerce began to promote Kelly as a tourist attraction. Now there are even Kempenfelt Kelly t-shirts. As yet no photographs exist of Kelly, but the creature was caught in a radar sounding by William W. Skrypetz from the Government Dock and Marina (Lefroy) on 13 June 1983 at approximately 3:30 p.m. The Skry-

153

petz sounding shows Kelly to be a long-necked, heavy-bodied creature with more than a passing likeness to the early photographs of Nessie, the monster of Scotland's Loch Ness.

Kenora/
Windigo Capital of the World

Kenora is a town in the Lake of the Woods region which could well be called the Windigo Capital of the World. Some two thousand native people live on eight Indian Reserves in this area of lakes and wooded hills, a remnant of glacial Lake Agassiz.

From this region come innumerable reports of the dreaded Windigo, the spirit or spectre of cannibalism among the Algonkian-speaking Indians. An Indian may be possessed by the spirit of cannibalism, or he may behold the giant cannibalistic spectre in the woods. The reports and accounts come not only from the lips of the Cree, Ojibway, and Sioux who have lived here, but also from the written records of explorers, traders, surveyors, missionaries, and writers well up into the modern period.

Some traditional accounts of meeting with the Windigo are retold by the native elder James Redsky in *Great Leader of the Ojibway: Misgwona-queb* (1972), edited by James R. Stevens. The explorer David Thompson on a case that took place at Lake of the Woods in March 1799. An Indian hunter who was about twenty-two years of age announced out of the blue that "he felt a strong inclination to eat his Sister . . . he must have human flesh to eat, and would have it." His behaviour otherwise was perfectly normal. The camp became alarmed, the band council met, and the decision was reached that the man must die. It was also decided that the hunter would have to be executed by his own father. The council felt that the father had been remiss in not securing the services of a medicine man in sufficient time to ward off the evil. What follows comes from *David Thompson's Narrative: 1784–1812* (1962), edited by Richard Glover:

> The young man was called, and told to sit down in the middle, there was no fire, which he did, he was then informed of the resolution taken,

to which he said "I am willing to die"; The unhappy Father arose, and placing a cord about his neck strangled him, to which he was quite passive; after about two hours, the body was carried to a large fire, and burned to Ashes, not the least bit of bone remaining. This was carefully done to prevent his soul and the evil spirit which possessed him from returning to this world; and appearing at his grave; which they believe the soul of those who are buried can, and may do, as having a claim to the bones of their bodies. It may be thought the Council acted a cruel part in ordering the father to put his Son to death, when they could have ordered it by the hands of another person. This was done, to prevent the law of retaliation; which had it been done by the hands of any other person, might have been made a pretext of revenge by those who were not the friends of the person who put him to death.

Algernon Blackwood, the British horror-story writer, travelled through the Lake of the Woods region in 1898. In his memoirs he described the lakes and woods as sacred sea and soil: "I saw dawn in a vale of the Indian Caucasus, I saw Panthea, Asia, fleeting dryads and troops of heavy fauns. Out of New York City into this primaeval wilderness produced intoxication." Yet here he learned of the spectre and here he set his classic story "The Wendigo" in the vicinity of Kenora, which appears in that story under its earlier name of Rat Portage.

Reports of the Windigo emerge from all the lands occupied by the Algonkian-speaking Indians. But the Lake of the Woods region seems to be particularly Windigo-infested. Witness the accounts found in *Windigo: An Anthology of Fact and Fantastic Fiction* (1982) edited by John Robert Colombo. Kenora, then, is the Windigo Capital of the World.

Kenora/
Ley Lines

It was the English antiquarian Alfred Watkins who made the simple yet surprising observation that the ancient spiritual sites in Britain lie in absolute alignment. As he showed in his book *The Old Straight Track* (1925), a "track" or line drawn to connect two separate but similarly named sites more often than not connects as well lesser-known and often forgotten sites that bear the same name. An instance is the St. Michael's Line which aligns about fifteen hitherto unrelated sites bearing the name of that patron saint, showing a conscious intent on the part of early planners. Brought into alignment may be prehistoric earthworks, megalithic structures, Celtic archeological works, man-made mounds, Christian shrines, even sites associated with King Arthur. Watkins' observation has been taken in hand by others and expanded into a full-blown theory of Ley Lines.

Geoffrey Ashe is not a proponent of Ley Lines, but he does have a Ley-like line of his own. He is a British writer who is especially interested in the lore and literature of King Arthur. He lived and worked in the Toronto area in the 1940s. Indeed, it was while reading a book about Glastonbury in the old Toronto Reference Library that he experienced "the force of a revelation," as he explained in *Miracles* (1978). His fascination for Arthur and the Ancient Wisdom proved too much for him so he abandoned Toronto for the Tor of Glastonbury. He devoted his efforts to researching and writing such books as *The Ancient Wisdom* (1977) and *Avalonian Quest* (1982).

Ashe offers only one Ley-like Line. It corresponds within one degree either way to the line of latitude 51°N. The line is the link between four equidistant yet otherwise unconnected points in the Northern Hemisphere. Two of the points are found in European Asia and Britain. The first point is Belukha, a mountain in the Altai range north of Mongolia, which is believed to correspond to a site of ancient wisdom. The second point is Glastonbury with all its Arthurian overtones and undercurrents. The other two points are found in North America. These are, surprisingly, Kenora, Ontario, and the Aleutian Island of Kiska in the Pacific.

"Neither of the two North American spots has any obvious significance," Ashe noted in *Avalonian Quest*. "Yet it is curious that all four quarterings, with a north-south deviation from the mean of only

a degree or so, gives places which are on land. If you try it with any appreciable different starting-point, in this latitutde or any other outside the polar regions, at least one of the steps will hit the sea."

Kenora is not the seat of all that is "high and holy" in the Arthurian tradition, but it does seem to be haunted. As the focal point of the Lake of the Woods region, it may be said to be haunted by the spirit of the dread Windigo. The shores are studded with Indian rock-art sites, many designed for the propitiation of spirits. As for Kiska, it is found in the Rat Island group in the Bering Sea. It lies northwest of the better-known Amchitka Island which was, despite public protests led by the Greenpeace activists, the site of underground nuclear tests conducted by the American military in 1965–71. The island was occupied by the Japanese during World War II but retaken in 1943.

Ashe admits that the nature of the characteristics shared by these four sites — Belukha, Glastonbury, Kenora, Kiska—is not particularly apparent. Yet they are linked by his global Ley-like Line.

Keswick/ Igopogo

Igopogo is the name that has been given to Lake Simcoe's monster, the cousin of the Okanagan Valley's Ogopogo and Lake Manitoba's Manipogo. The following report, from Keswick, on Lake Simcoe, was carried by the Oakville *Journal Record*, Saturday, 27 July 1963:

> A Presbyterian minister, a funeral director and their families are the latest to claim to have seen "Igopogo," the Lake Simcoe sea-serpent. The Rev. L.B. Williams of Mount Albert, and Neil Lathangue of Bradford, their wives and children were boating in the lake Monday when something came towards them. Mr. Lathangue said it was charcoal coloured, 30–70 feet long and had dorsal fins. Igopogo was first reported eleven years ago by an Indian trapper, and has since been described as a "dog-faced animal with a neck the diameter of a stove-pipe."

Kingston/
Kingstie

Due to its strategic location at the junction of the Great Lakes and the St. Lawrence River, Kingston has enjoyed more than its share of sea serpent sightings. There are newspaper accounts of monsters of the deep that go back to 1867, and no doubt some go back earlier, but the salient characteristic of the majority of the sightings in the Kingston area is that the serpents described, although monstrous in size, are not otherwise menacing. Indeed, despite their size, they seem to be rather silly creatures, and downright endearing, if these accounts are to be believed. Kingston's unusual serpent was nicknamed "Kingstie" in the 1980s, so the name is used here as a retronym.

The unnamed journalist who contributed "A Snake Story" to the Kingston *British Whig* on 29 August 1867 ridiculed the villagers at Sodus who held that they had seen the "old original" of sea serpents. He suggested that they had concocted the tale to "immortalize themselves" by the deed of capturing it! The Kingstie they invented was, apparently, a "snakeship . . . between 30 and 40 feet long, and as large round as a man's body."

On 14 September 1881, the *Kingston Whig* carried a story about "the nondescript amphibious animal, which has at regular intervals been disporting itself at the gulf and on the upper lakes," making its way into the Rideau Canal and surprising the crew and passengers of the streamer *Gipsy* en route from Ottawa to Kingston:

> The sportive creature made its appearance, of course, unexpectedly, and amazed the people with its immense proportions, unsightliness and graceless pranks in the water. The information respecting it is rather vague and indefinite, as usual in such cases, but it is said to have appeared, according to the bias on which it was viewed, to be between 25 ft and 40 ft in length, to have a body of peculiar shape and great circumference, a head as big as a small house, numerous feet,

and a tail so long and powerful that when in motion the water foamed and boiled up as a geyser and cast a spray which, one hundred yards distant, fell like heavy rain. The performance of this "critter" was regarded in ominous silence. Once its fierce glittering eyes, canopied by sharp flat horns, caught a glimpse of the steamer, and the serpent gave a tremendous lunge, the effect of which was to create a sea equal to that which the best gale on lake Erie could not bring about.

Apparently Captain Fleming of the *Gipsy* raced the serpent for some distance. The serpent won. The details appeared in the Toronto *Globe*, 16 September 1881.

Two men sailing the channel between Simcoe Island and Wolfe Island spotted a "peculiar looking object that showed its head about two feet out of water and then, with lightning rapidity, dove under and disappeared." The *Kingston Whig*, 11 June 1888, carried a description by one of the observers, Charles Staley. Staley's report was unusual in that it drew attention to the potential danger. "The sight of it has created alarm and the people in the locality are scared about going near the water." The report concluded, "It is said that the serpent has been seen before. It is big enough to carry off a baby."

Danger was also highlighted in a graphic way in the next sighting. As the Toronto *Globe* on 23 July 1892 noted, G. Parks and his wife, of Brakey's Bay, went for a sail in a skiff "and will never forget the outing."

> A serpent of huge proportions was heading for the boat. It held its head in the air and its eyes looked like balls of fire. It meant business, and Mr. Parks knew that if he did not make a defence he and his wife might be upset. Mr. Parks had a fish pole with him, and waited for the reptile. When it got near the boat the attack began, but Mr. Parks soon found out he had a mighty opponent. He had to pound the serpent for a long time before it would give up its attack. Finally it turned and disappeared in the water, making

a noise like a buzz saw. Mrs. Parks was greatly frightened.

But, the experiences of Staley and the Parkses to one side, Kingstie is a gentle creature. On 8 August 1931, the following story appeared in the Kingston *Whig-Standard*: "Kingston's famous sea serpent has put in an appearance again and if there has been any lingering doubt in the minds of any of the people hereabouts as to the bona fides of the serpent that doubt must now be effectually dissipated."

The author of the article was referring to the combined testimony of two medical doctors, R.R. MacGregor and Frank Bermingham, who "with their hands over their hearts, declare to this great family journal that they saw the serpent with their own eyes and that it is all that it has been described—and then some." Apparently the sighting took place from a private launch around midnight as they were returning from Alexandria Bay to the Yacht Club at Kingston:

> Contrary, they say, to the earlier published report, the serpent is not more than 30 feet long and its colour is neither green nor orange, as reported, but a changing hue, as though it were descended from the chameleon family. Thus when only the white sides of the launch showed the serpent likewise showed only white; when the green of the hull was revealed with the rolling of the launch the serpent likewise turned green, while when the flashlight of the boat was turned on it was revealed in a combination yellowish-golden hue. It had but one eye, right in the middle of its forehead, like the little girl with the little curl; and to balance this, as it were, it had two horns not merely a half foot long, as has been reported, but much longer (probably two feet) and spreading like the prongs of an antler.

As Lynn Jones concluded her article on "Our Forgotten Monster" in the Kingston *Whig-Standard* on 7 August 1980, "Long Live Kingstie!"

Kingston/ Mr. X the Consulting Resologist

A resident of Wolfe Island, south of Kingston, is a man with an unusual name: Mr. X. It is the gentleman's legal name. He adopted it in 1972 and professes to be a Consulting Resologist.

"There is as yet no science of Resology," noted naturalist Ivan T. Sanderson. "It is my contention that just such a science should be organized, and on the grounds of logic and necessity."

Mr. X studies "things." He is revising the works of the iconoclast Charles Fort; checking each and every reference is a mammoth undertaking comparable to finding sources for the allusions in *Finnegans Wake*. He collects accounts of anomalous phenomena. From newspapers, periodicals, books, and searches through museums and government files, he has found reports of more than 30 poltergeists, 97 lakes having monsters, over 250 reports of sea serpents and giant squid, 4600 UFO sightings—all in Canada! Activity of this sort may be seen as the expression of an obsessive and compulsive personality; but, it may be the legitimate attempt by a "completist" to demonstrate by sheer accumulation of data that many of the beliefs of society and science are based upon illusion and ignorance. What evidence cannot be properly explained is too often disregarded, he claims, for such taboo subjects challenge dogmatic beliefs and theories. "Meteorites and continental drift were once ridiculed and dismissed as nonsense by science," he notes, pointing to plenty of explanations of the source of the Sun's energy given by astronomers and physicists before atomic energy was suspected.

"During the period when Von Däniken's books were in all the bookstores, I felt it should be stated somewhere that mysterious phenomena are not only to be found at Stonehenge, in Egypt, on Easter Island, or in other remote places in the world. Such phenomena will be found everywhere. They are around us all the time."

Kitchener/
The Skull of Doom

One of the most mysterious and intriguing artifacts of all time is the so-called Skull of Doom, which was found in the British Honduras in 1924. As unlikely as it may seem, its principal home for the last two decades has been in the living-room of a suburban residence on Glen Avon Crescent in Kitchener, where it resides in a felt-lined case, attracting archaeologists, anthropologists, mineralogists, authors, journalists, spiritualists, and faith-healers from around the world.

The life-size quartz crystal skull has been photographed innumerable times with breath-taking results. Psychics have peered into its depths. It has served as the focal point for healing ceremonies. The book *The Crystal Skull* (1973) by Richard M. Garvin is one of many which has presented its history and mystery. The Toronto trance-channeller Carole Davis has looked into its interior and published the results

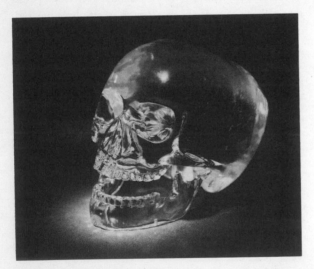

There is no gainsaying the dramatic appearance of the so-called Skull of Doom. The life-size crystal skull with moveable jaw was discovered in 1917 during the excavation of the ruins of the Mayan city of Lubaantun in British Honduras (now Belize). It is the property of Anna Mitchell-Hedges, a world traveller and adventurer. Since 1967 she has kept it at her home in Kitchener, Ont. [Hawkshead Services]

of her mediumship in *The Skull Speaks* (1985) edited by Brian Hadley-James.

The Mayan artifact was modelled on the skull of a mature female. Its weight is eleven pounds and seven ounces, and its measurements are seven inches high, five inches wide, and five inches deep. It has been dubbed the Skull of Doom, but the proper name, according to its custodian and owner, is the Crystal Skull of Dum or the Crystal Skull of Lubaantun. It has been also been referred to as ''an eye to elsewhere.''

The Crystal Skull is the personal property of Anna Mitchell-Hedges who was born Anna-Marie Le Guillon. In 1917, she was a ten-year-old orphan being raised by relatives in Port Colborne, Ontario, when she was befriended and adopted by a family acquaintance, F.A. Mitchell-Hedges, a British-born archaeologist, adventurer, and author of *Danger — My Ally* (1954). She accompanied Mitchell-Hedges on his ''digs,'' and in 1924 while excavating the ruins of the Mayan city of Lubaantun, in British Honduras (now Belize), she unearthed the skull. She made the incredible discovery, she says, on her seventeenth birthday — on New Year's Day of that year. The detachable jaw was missing but three months later was found not far away.

The later history of the skull is as melodramatic as its early history is dramatic. In 1927, the Mitchell-Hedges took it with them from British Honduras. In 1943 it was listed for auction at Sotheby's in London but at the last moment was withdrawn from sale. In his memoirs, Mitchell-Hedges wrote, ''How it came into my possession I have reason for not revealing.'' Even that cryptic sentence, as short as it is, was deleted from subsequent editions of the book.

Since 1967, the Crystal Skull has been the boon companion of Anna Mitchell-Hedges in Kitchener and elsewhere. In 1971–73, it was on loan to the Museum of the American Indian in New York. The skull is back in Kitchener (May 1987) but there are plans to establish the Anna Mitchell-Hedges Research and Exploration Association in London, England, and move the skull there to ensure its safety and availability for suitable services and study purposes.

There are many traditions about the Skull of Doom. Psychics maintain it possesses supernatural properties. It is believed Mayan priests employed it as a source of power and wielded that power to will death and destruction. There are theories about its origin: It is of modern manufacture and was planted in the jungle by the father to be the adopted daughter's birthday present; it is two hundred years old; it is four thousand years old; it is ageless, having been fashioned by aliens, its path having crossed that of the stars and Atlantis.

It is not, however, unique. There are six somewhat similar crystal skulls in the British Museum, in the Musée de l'Homme, and in private hands. The publicly displayed skulls are nowhere near as commanding in appearance as the Skull of Doom. Anna Mitchell-Hedges maintains, "Those skulls are dead or at least dormant, while mine is vibrantly alive." There is the belief that there are seven skulls in all, scattered around the world. Only when they are finally brought together will there be peace on earth.

Leeds County/
Spontaneous Human Combustion

"It strikes without warning, reducing its victim to an unrecognizable char," wrote Dwight Whalen. "It burns with macabre selectivity, often leaving nearby inflammables strangely untouched. It's a rare and grisly phenomenon known as Spontaneous Human Combustion."

This phenomenon — SHC for short — is not new to history or literature. Cases have been reported over the centuries and across many cultures, and even Charles Dickens made use of SHC as a literary device to suitably eliminate an unwanted evil-doer in *Bleak House*. Although alcohol is not part of the scenario, the suggestion that it was made excellent propaganda for the Temperance movement.

On 10 June 1828, Dr. Peter Schofield of Leeds County in southeastern Ontario delivered in Leeds the first Temperance address heard in Canada. To make his point, he described a case of SHC which he personally attended:

It was the case of a young man about twenty-five years old; he had been a habitual drinker for many years. I saw him about nine o'clock in the evening on which it happened; he was then, as usual, not drunk but full of liquor. About eleven, the same evening, I was called to see him. I found him literally roasted, from the crown of his head to the soles of his feet. He was discovered in a blacksmith's shop, just across the way from where he had been. The owner of the shop, all of a sudden, discovered a bright light in his shop, as though the whole building was in a general flame. He ran with the greatest precipitancy, and, on flinging open the door, discovered the man standing erect in the midst of a widely extended, silver-coloured blaze, bearing, as he described it, exactly the appearance of the wick of a burning candle in the midst of its own flame. The blacksmith seized him by the shoulder, and jerked him to the door, upon which the flame was instantly extinguished. There was no fire in the shop, neither was there any possibility of fire having been communicated to him from any external source. It was purely a case of spontaneous ignition. A general sloughing soon came on, and his flesh was consumed or removed in the dressing, leaving the bones and a few of the larger blood vessels standing. The blood, nevertheless, rallied around the heart, and maintained the vital spark until the thirteenth day, when he died, not only the most noisome, ill-featured, and dreadful picture that was ever presented to human view, but his shrieks, his cries and lamentations, were enough to rend the heart of adamant. He complained of no pain of body — his flesh was gone; he said he was suffering the torments of hell; that he was just upon its threshold, and should soon enter its dismal caverns; and, in this frame of mind, gave up the ghost.

Just who this man was, and where and when he died, was not said. The fatal fire, Dr. Schofield added, had not "been communicated . . . from any external source.'' His belief that alcohol was to blame may be farfetched, but not so the mystery itself. There is no scientific standing for SHC; nevertheless, this anecdotal account is probably the earliest recorded case in Canada. ''It's just the kind of story one might like to have a drink to forget,'' added Whalen, an investigator of the odd and unusual. Some further details appear in William Henry Leavitt's *History of Leeds and Grenville* (1972).

Lloydtown/
The Haunted Bookshop

Bookshops are haunted by book lovers. One shop that is said to be haunted by ''an authenticated apparition'' is the Country Bookshop in Lloydtown, a community south of Schomberg, which in turn is north of Metropolitan Toronto.

The Country Bookshop was opened in a remodelled barn in 1967 by Art Gray, a bibliophile whose specialty was Canadian history and pioneer life. He ran the shop until his death in 1984. It is currently being managed by his widow Audrey. The shop has over 15,000 volumes on its shelves.

''Our ghost is an authenticated apparition,'' Gray once told a reporter. ''She is a solid-looking figure. A lady in a cloak, hooded. You never see her face. She starts at twilight — at the walnut tree at the top of the driveway — and walks slowly, up or down. Many people have seen her. But she doesn't bother anyone. She's quite harmless, part of the family really.''

According to local tradition, there was a tragedy on the property in the early days of the last century. A young mother lost her little baby. She may have killed it herself, or it may have been taken from her. Whichever was the case, the baby was lost to her. The ghost is that of the young mother who even in death seems to be searching, looking about longingly as if for a lost child. The spirit is anything but malevolent. Apparently dogs wag their tails when the apparition is felt or seen.

One wonders if Audrey Gray has in stock a used copy of Christopher Morley's delightful volume *The Haunted Bookshop*.

London/
The Eldon House Ghost

Eldon House, one of London's oldest and most elegant homes, was built in 1834 by the merchant John Harris. It served many generations of the Harris family until it was donated to the city as a museum in 1960. It has been restored to its High Victorian splendour, with hand-carved furniture, oriental china, brocaded wallpaper, and safari souvenirs. It is not difficult to imagine the festive balls and parties held in its formal ballroom by John Harris and his seven daughters.

The following incident occurred one evening in 1856. One of the daughters, Sarah, was engaged to be married. Her fiancé was invited to their formal ball, but the gentleman was uncharacteristically late in arriving. Sarah kept glancing nervously at the entrance hall, fearing something was amiss. Finally, at 6:00 p.m., the gentleman appeared. He looked remote and distraught. He was dishevelled, and his clothes were muddy. Sarah greeted him and so did her father. But there was no reply. The apparition turned away and disappeared into the night.

The gentleman never did attend the party, but later that night his riderless horse appeared at the gate. The next day his body was found in a ford of the Thames River at the west end of Concession 4, London Township. He had been thrown by his horse and killed in the fall. His watch had stopped at 6:00 p.m.

Sarah's grief was genuine but brief. She eventually married the Hon. Robert Dalzell. Their marriage was happy and two of their daughters married earls.

London/
''A Wild Boy in the Woods''

The London *Free Press* published a report headed ''A Wild Boy in the Woods'' which drew attention to the ''wild child'' in the Gore district around London. The report was reprinted by the Niagara Falls *Evening Journal*, 27 June 1871.

He was first seen about two weeks ago, on the edge of a forest extending about a mile and a half, and situated about four miles from the city. Five residents of the neighbourhood, passing by the bush, saw him wandering aimlessly about, and made an effort to enter into conversation. But he no sooner saw them than he appeared to be very much frightened, and bounded off into the woods with the fleetness of a deer. He wore a peculiarly wild and haggard aspect, with nothing to cover him but a pair of dark pantaloons and a white shirt, both of which are torn and hanging in shreds to his person; one sleeve of the shirt was entirely gone. His hair all matted and awry lent him a lost and savage look. He has been seen on several occasions, but has always eluded his watchers, perhaps too timid to pursue him, and escaped from their sight into the depths of the wood. How he manages to subsist may be imagined from the fact that one day in the latter part of last week, an old resident whose name is in our possession, suddenly surprised him reclining on a knoll, and, Nebuchadnezzar-like, plucking the grass and herbs around him to eat. The old gentleman in question called to attract his attention, when the unfortunate demented being hastily arose, uttered a howl of dismay and rambled off as fast as he could into his shadowy retreat. On Friday evening a party of ten men went in pursuit, and scoured the bush thoroughly, but no trace of the wild boy could be found. It is supposed that he inhabits a cave which he has burrowed in some lonely place, and to which only his own instinct attracts him. On Saturday night a still larger party was to have been formed for the purpose, if possible, of ferreting out this strange being, and bringing him back to the walks of civilized life. The result, up to the hour of going to press, we have not learned, but as his conduct has created a strange sensation in the locality, and there seems a deep determination to hunt him down, and curtail his wild pranks, no doubt he will soon be captured. No one knows who he is, where he came from, or by what strange hallucination he has been prompted to run wild in the woods.

This is an excerpt of the full report. No subsequent report was found.

London/
Caroline Clare

Caroline Clare of London was an unusual woman: She was a "human magnet." She could, reportedly, draw metallic objects to her body without touching them. In the last thirty years, young Miss Clare has made cameo appearances in a string of books about the paranormal. These were written by Frank Edwards, Vincent Gaddis, Stanley Krippner, John Michell, and other authors who delight in oddities. In addition, she has played a minor role in not one but three of Colin Wilson's books.

As far as has been determined, this oddly talented young woman made her public *début* in an article called "Electrically Charged People" in *Fate* in August 1955. Here is what the author of the article, Henry Winfred Splitter, had to say about Caroline Clare, who is described as being a native "of Bondon, Ontario, Canada."

> In 1877 she was 17 years old and living with her parents and six brothers and sisters at No. 25, Second Rodney Concession in Bondon. She was a strapping girl, weighed 130 pounds and apparently was normal in every way. Suddenly, however, she became ill. Her appetite fell off and her weight dwindled to 87 pounds. Doctors found nothing wrong with her. Her body functions seemed unimpaired.
>
> After a few months another remarkable change took place in her condition. Fits or spasms came over her. When these subsided her eyes would be set and glazed, her body rigid. While in this state, she spoke eloquently, describing far-off scenes of great beauty although she had never done any travelling. Afterwards she appeared exhausted, was taciturn and surly and would not answer questions.
>
> This continued for about 18 months. Then the girl underwent another extraordinary

change. Although she did not gain weight, she appeared to rally. She became light-hearted and gay. Soon she was out of bed where she had spent most of her time and apparently as well as ever.

But now she constantly gave off electrical charges. No one could comfortably shake hands with her. By joining hands with a ring of 20 people she could give all of them a sharp shock.

Her body seemed to act as a magnet. When she moved to pick up a steel knife the blade would leap into her hand. A paper of needles would hang suspended from one of her fingers. So strong was this magnetism that she was unable to let go of any steel article she had picked up. It was necessary for a second person to pull the article away, while the girl stroked her arm vigorously from the wrist upward. Wooden spoons and other utensils had to be made for her to use at the table. . . .

All in all, Caroline's case was a most remarkable one and it attracted scores of investigators. Medical men were especially interested. A certain Doctor Tye wrote a paper on Caroline, for presentation before the Ontario Medical Association in the summer of 1879.

Caroline's six brothers and sisters showed no paranormal traits.

It is quite possible that poor Miss Clare was in possession of one ability even more surprising than "human magnetism" — that of nonexistence. The Ontario Medical Association published no report on her in 1879 or in contiguous years. Nor, as far as has been ascertained, did any other Ontario or Canadian medical journal of the day. There has never been a community named "Bondon" anywhere in the country.

Yet the reference to "a certain Doctor Tye" is verifiable. Willian Henry Tye was a physician from Chatham, Ontario, and an examiner in Histology and Physiology for the College of Physicians and Surgeons of Ontario from 1881 to 1885. But the references to Caroline Clare and her family seem to be faulty. As

W. Glen Curnoe, London Room Librarian, London Public Libraries, wrote on 29 December 1987:

> I cannot locate any such address as No. 25, Second Rodney Concession, for this area. However, there is a place called Rodney in Elgin County. There is a Romney Township in Kent County. Chatham is located in Kent County as well. I contacted the Chatham Public Library, and a search by their staff did not reveal any information about Caroline Clare in the Chatham area. I have had access to a researcher's computerized index to the 1871 Census for the City of London. A Caroline Clare is not listed, nor are there listings for six brothers and sisters of that surname. This does not rule out the existence of Caroline Clare and her family in the area surrounding the City of London. Lack of time and staff does not permit me to search the 1871 or the 1881 Census for the entire County of Middlesex. I am sorry that I have not been able to find any positive proof of the existence of Caroline Clare. Perhaps future research into Dr. Tye would either prove or disprove the existence of Caroline Clare.

In the meantime, it is a safe bet that for many years to come authors of books about the paranormal will continue to describe Miss Clare's wild talent for readers who will marvel in amazement — despite the fact that there is no evidence to date that she ever existed.

London/
The Death of Peg-Leg Brown

The account of the death of Peg-Leg Brown has so many interesting aspects, one hardly knows where to begin.

Marion Brown was an old-style desperado who was born in San Saba, Texas, of mixed Mexican-Texan ancestry. In one skirmish or other he lost a limb and sported a wooden leg. He was on the lam most of his life and the wooden leg did not slow him down in the least. Chance took him to London, Ontario, where he murdered Private Constable Michael Toohey of the London Police Force. He escaped to the United States where he was arrested for another crime and imprisoned in Texas. He escaped from that prison but was apprehended in the State of Washington, spirited across the international border, and tried for murder in London. He was found guilty and sentenced to be hanged.

Brown protested his innocence to the end. The official executioner arrived, supervised the erection of the gibbet in the yard of the Middlesex County Jail, and executed Brown according to plan sometime after eight o'clock in the morning of 17 May 1899. According to reports, at the critical moment of the springing of the trap door, the preacher began intoning, "Oh God, forgive us. Oh God, forgive our country." A bolt of lightning was followed by a bang of thunder as the onlookers scurried for shelter.

Brown had requested that his body be shipped to his sister in Texas for burial. Contrary to his wishes, but consistent with the custom of the day, the body was placed in a rough casket and buried in the jailyard. Legend has it that Brown's coffin never sank into the ground. Another story is that not a single blade of grass ever grew over his grave. His ghost was said to haunt the old Middlesex jail, "a story kept alive by oldtime jail guards, as well as newspaper editors seeking to impress youthful reporters," wrote L.N. Bronson in the London *Free Press*, 17 April 1985.

In May 1985, the parking lot behind the old Middlesex County jail was excavated. Found were the remains of a coffin and the bones of a one-legged man. "In traditional form, the head of the coffin pointed west toward the Thames River so the dead man could sit up and face his maker in the east," according to Dave Dauphinee in the London *Free Press*, 4 May 1985. It is said that Brown's peg-leg is on display in one area museum and the stetson he inadvertently left behind when he murdered Constable Toohey is in another.

In the proceedings the most dramatic part was played by the official executioner. His arrival and appearance were highlighted in the accounts of the day in the London *Free Press*. Other reporters covering other executions in different jurisdictions did the same. The visit of the enigmatic and somewhat mysterious figure of the Dominion's executioner was always newsworthy. Although as secretive and as closed mouthed as an embalmer, the man who hanged Brown was not averse to some publicity of his own.

He was an Englishman named John Robert Radclive and he had a grave sense of humour. But by 1912 he admitted to having bad dreams. "Now at night when I lie down, I start up with a roar as victim after victim comes up before me. I can see them on the trap, waiting a second before they face their Maker. They taunt me and haunt me until I am nearly crazy with an unearthly fear."

He was succeeded in 1913 by Arthur Bartholomew English, another Englishman brought over by the Department of Justice. Reclusive by nature, English effectively led a double life. His wife in Montreal thought he was a commercial traveller and had no idea what he did on his "travels." Until he retired in 1935, he used the *nom de guerre* Arthur Ellis. English took some philosophical pleasure in his trade. He agreed to allow the poet A.M. Klein to write his biography. Klein admitted to being fascinated with the man. English saw himself as a man with a mission. "I consider it the most sacred calling any man could have, since I am entrusted with carrying out the highest sentence our courts can pass." It is said that he drank and that occasionally he misjudged the condemned person's weight and decapitated the person.

With the abolition of capital punishment in 1967, the Radclives and the Englishes are no more. But the name Arthur Ellis lives on. Each year the Crime Writers of Canada makes an award to the author of the finest work of detective fiction published during the previous twelve months. It takes the form of a miniature gibbet. They call it the Arthur Ellis Award.

London/ Dr. Richard Maurice Bucke

Two sites in present-day London bring to mind the life and work of Dr. Richard Maurice Bucke, Canada's premier mystic.

O. R. M. Bucke in his library
From a Char. N. Elliott, Sept 1899

This photograph shows Dr. Richard Maurice Bucke seated behind the desk in his library on the grounds of the London Hospital for the Insane. The photograph is signed by Dr. Bucke who named the photographer and gave the month and year: Charles N. Elliott, Sept. 1899. Dr. Bucke, the author of Cosmic Consciousness, *died in 1902. The photographic portrait above Dr. Bucke's head is of his mentor, the American poet Walt Whitman. [University of Western Ontario Libraries]*

Dr. Bucke was not a mystic in the sense that he was a mysterious and meditative man. Quite the contrary. He was a man of practical affairs who made distinct contributions in the disparate fields of medicine, literature, and mysticism.

Richard Maurice Bucke (1837–1902), although born in England, was raised in a pioneer homestead on the outskirts of Hamilton. He was largely self-educated, reading widely in the extensive library maintained by his father who was a clergyman. In his youth he walked across the continent. When he decided on a medical career, he enrolled at McGill University. He graduated from the School of Medicine in 1862, then undertook postgraduate training in England and France. Upon his return in 1868 he married and opened a medical practice in Sarnia. He was appointed Superintendent of the Hamilton Asylum in 1876 where he proved to be an able administrator. The following year he was appointed Superintendent

of the newly opened London Hospital, which he ran until his death in 1902.

Bucke was an outstanding medical doctor and alienist. (The modern term for "alienist" is psychiatrist.) He helped to found the School of Medicine at what turned into the University of Western Ontario, and he served as President of the predecessor of the American Psychiatric Association. He was foremost in the promotion of the humane use of open restraint in the treatment of the insane. Controversial in his day as well as in our own was his use of surgery in the treatment of hysteria in women. But all his practices were in the mainstream of North American medical procedures of the day, when not in advance of them.

The poetry of the English Romantic poets was deeply meaningful to Dr. Bucke. But it was *Leaves of Grass* that changed his life. He felt so elated after reading Walt Whitman's transcendental lines that he went out of his way to visit the American bard at his home in Philadelphia in 1877. Whitman was then in his late fifties and the centre of a devoted following. The friendship culminated in Bucke devoting himself to the cause of Whitman. The cause included the composition of a biography, as no life of the Good Grey Poet had ever been written. To that end Bucke invited Whitman to come to London. The only foreign country ever visited by Whitman was Canada. The result of the visit was the publication of *Walt Whitman* (1883), the first formal biography of the poet. As Whitman rewrote much of what Bucke wrote, it could also be called a collaboration.

The association of the doctor and the poet did not end with the latter's death in Camden, New Jersey, in 1892. Bucke delivered an oration at the funeral and edited a number of Whitman's posthumously published books. Bucke found in the person and poetry of Whitman a confirmation of his belief that men and women may experience states of consciousness above and beyond ordinary self-awareness, that such states are a normal development in human evolution, and that these experiences will be more common in the future than they have been in the past.

Bucke's belief was a conviction founded on personal experience. He experienced an "illumination" in the spring of 1872 during a visit to London, England. The experience affected him profoundly, and he recalled it in the following, third-person account which appeared in his book *Cosmic Consciousness: A Study in the Evolution of the Human Mind* (1901).

> He and two friends had spent the evening reading Wordsworth, Shelley, Keats, Browning, and especially Whitman. They parted at midnight, and he had a long drive in a hansom. His mind, deeply under the influence of the ideas, images and emotions called up by the reading and talk of the evening, was calm and peaceful. He was in a state of quiet, almost passive, enjoyment.
>
> All at once, without warning of any kind, he found himself wrapped around, as it were, by a flame-coloured cloud. For an instant he thought of fire—some sudden conflagration in the great city. The next (instant) he knew that the light was within himself.
>
> Directly after there came upon him a sense of exultation, of immense joyousness, accompanied or immediately followed by an intellectual illumination quite impossible to describe. Into his brain streamed one momentary lightning-flash of the Brahmic Splendour which ever since lightened his life. Upon his heart fell one drop of the Brahmic Bliss, leaving thenceforward for always an aftertaste of Heaven.

As far as is known, Dr. Bucke was the first person to use the words "cosmic consciousness" to describe the ecstatic experience. His book *Cosmic Consciousness* appeared in 1901 and is a comprehensive case study of instances of the experience of illumination as recorded in the lives of many religious leaders and writers.

As Bucke saw it, three revolutionary changes were sweeping away the old and establishing the new. What he called "aerial navigation" was poised to transform the face of the planet and the nature of man's society. Economic relationships were being altered and would result in a more just redistribution of wealth. Finally, there was psychic change which would change man's perspective on everything. All these changes were inevitable. The final words in *Cosmic Consciousness* are the following:

> The simple truth is, that there has lived on the earth, "appearing at intervals," for thousands of years among ordinary men, the first faint beginnings of another race; walking the earth and breathing the air with us, but at the same time walking another earth and breathing another air of which we know little or nothing, but which is, all the same, our spiritual life, as its absence would be our spiritual death. This new race is in act of being born from us, and in the near future it will occupy and possess the earth.

The painter Lawren Harris is the only Canadian who is known to have written a review of *Cosmic Consciousness*. Harris's appreciation of the 1923 Dutton reprint appeared in *The Canadian Bookman*, February 1924, under the title "The Greatest Book by a Canadian and One Other." Harris was impressed by both the author and the book. "I know of no book by a Canadian writer with such nobility of thought, illuminated by so lofty a vision, nor one so rich in human kindness." He did not review it alone but together with the 1920 Manas Press edition of *Tertium Organum* by the Russian mystic and mathematician P.D. Ouspensky. A bold pen was needed to describe the two works, and Harris wielded it, concluding, "These two books belong to each other and should be read one after the other, the older one first."

Cosmic Consciousness was influential in its day and it finds numerous readers even today, having been continously in print since 1923. It is a remarkable legacy. It was a book written out of passionate conviction that the divisive doctrines of the world's religions would be "melted down" and that the result would be the ecstatic experience accompanied by a feeling for personal immortality. As he wrote in his last will and testament, "I cheerfully assign my Soul to God a part of whose unspeakable goodness I have seen and known.

London/
The Ghost of the Grand

The ghost of Ambrose Small is said to haunt the old and dignified Grand Theatre on Richmond Street. The Grand Theatre was owned by Small, a wealthy impresario and theatre owner. His disappearance in downtown Toronto remains as mysterious today as the day it occurred 2 December 1919.

Small owned more than ninety theatres in southern Ontario, but London's Grand was said to be his favourite. It opened in 1901 and, it seems, his spirit took up residence following his disappearance. Theatre folk are a superstitious lot so it is not surprising that if anything went awry during a production it was blamed on Ambrose, the Ghost of the Grand. As Mary Malone wrote in the *Toronto Star*, 4 May 1985:

> Ambrose stories are legion among actors. In death, as in life, he seems to prefer the ladies. An actress playing a Russian duchess found her jewellery kept falling off as she was about to go on stage.
>
> Ambrose's antics are not entirely mischevous. He is credited with saving the Grand's lovely proscenium and its painting of cavorting muses, by an unknown Italian artist, from destruction during the restoration of the theatre in the late 1970s.
>
> Although the entire façade, lobby, box office and back stage were rebuilt, every effort was made to preserve the Edwardian character of the audience area and the stage. One day a bulldozer that was clearing debris under the stage kept stalling unaccountably just inches from a particular section of an old wall. Upon further investigation, it was found the architects had miscalculated the site of the main retaining wall. It was generally agreed that Ambrose deserved thanks for preventing the bulldozer from knocking down the one wall that still held up the precious old proscenium arch.

London/
Shute Medical Clinic

The Shute Medical Clinic operates from a gracious old house on Princess Avenue in London. It was established in 1948 as a non-profit clinic by the Shute brothers, Wilfrid (1912-1982) and Evan (1907-1978), who were surgeons as well as proponents of Vitamin E. They anticipated by a good many years the present-day interest in megavitamin therapy and the widespread self-administration of Vitamin E.

Vitamin E (tocopherol) is an organic substance found in green leaves, peanut and corn oil, wheat germ, and eggs. Current biomedical opinion holds that the significance of Vitamin E in human nutrition is not clear. From 1932 on, Evan Shute experimented with the vitamin and administered it selectively to his patients, maintaining that it could increase fertility and alleviate cardiovascular difficulties, much to the dismay of the Canadian Medical Association and the Ontario College of Physicians and Surgeons. The two medical associations also objected to the formation of the Vitamine E Society on 22 June 1950 in Toronto. (It is interesting to note that one of its founding directors was Charles A. Grant who was granted posthumous fame as the hero of the CBC-TV production *Charlie Grant's War*.) Among the Clinic's benefactors were manufacturer W. Garfield Weston and publisher J. W. McConnell.

Linus Pauling, the American chemist and double Nobel laureate, contributed the Foreword to Evan Shute's *The Vitamin E Story: The Medical Memoirs of Evan Shute* (1985), in which he wrote: "It is clear that Dr. Shute believed he was responsible for a great medical discovery, the recognition of the value of a high intake of Vitamin E for the prevention and treatment of cardiovascular disease. I agree with his assessment."

Given a rough time by the medical establishment, Shute appended to his will a statement which begins: "As during my life-time my Country, Province and City, did nothing to aid or recognize my medical and scientific work, I desire no such recognition after my death. I do not care to be another Bethune. Therefore,

I urge and request my descendants to give no countenance to such recognition if it is later attempted. Canada is too careless of her sons, and does not give them the help they need when they need it."

Long Point/
Doctor Troyer

Long Point is a peninsula of land which extends some twenty-five kilometres into Lake Erie. The lore and legend of the "Doctor Who Was Afraid of Witches" extends equally far into the folklore of Norfolk County in southwestern Ontario.

The doctor was not a medical doctor at all, but an herbalist named John F. Troyer (1753–842). A Mennonite of Pennsylvania Dutch extraction, he was born in Somerset, Pennsylvania, the eldest son of thirteen children. In 1793 he trekked north, becoming the first permanent white settler in the area. He was a crack marksman, a good farmer, and a man skilled in smithing and dentistry, to name two trades he had mastered. It was said that he also had a talent for healing and a vast knowledge of herbal remedies. He was a fine figure of a man, with long white locks and a long flowing beard.

Troyer was no witch doctor; quite the contrary, he was a witch-hater, for he harboured an obsessive fear of witches and of witchery. He let others know that he had a detailed knowledge of witches and their ways and that their craft was to be feared and shunned. For their part, seductive witches plagued him by day and especially by night.

The log cabin he built for himself just east of the village of Port Rowan was decorated with hex signs and upside-down horseshoes to ward off the dark-eyed evil temptresses. At the foot of his bed he kept a "witch-trap" bolted to the floor and ready to snap shut. Neighbours said it was nothing more than a rusty bear-trap; certainly the "witch-trap" now on display at the Eva Brock Donly Museum in Simcoe caught more bears it its day than witches.

One night, he claimed, despite his precautions, a witch succeeded in transforming him into a horse. She rode him hard across the lake to Dunkirk. There he was hitched to a post and forced to watch a coven of witches as they performed their lewd sabbath dance. Then he was force-fed rye-straw. He was ill for days thereafter.

He performed incantations to raise evil spells. With his divining rod or dowsing stick he boasted he was able to locate running water and buried treasure. He was knowledgeable about the unseen world. When the Scots at Baldoon were perplexed over the poltergeist at the McDonald farm, he was summoned to lift the curse. He found a witch and not a poltergeist was the cause of the disturbances.

Long Point/
Buried Treasure

There are many tales of treasure buried in the Long Point area. One tale concerns Ramsay's gold. It seems about 1780 a fur-trader named Ramsay, his canoe heavy with gold, managed to evade Indians along the shore of Port Stanley. At a ridge near Long Point he buried the treasure, intending to return to claim it when the Indians no longer presented a problem. Ramsay never returned to claim his cache. Before the propitious moment presented itself, he may have died, or he may have tried to claim it but, as frequently happens, forgot its precise location.

Learning of the legend, John Troyer, through the practice of the "black arts," acquired knowledge of its locale. He invited young Simpson McCall to join him in the reclamation of the cache of gold. But McCall's parents refused to allow their eleven or twelve-year-old son to have anything to do with the dreaded Deacon. McCall did not assist Troyer but he later heard from his lips what had happened to the expedition. Troyer told McCall, and McCall told J.H. Coyne, who told the tale at an address to the Ontario History Society meeting in Norfold County "the other day," as reported in the Niagara Falls *Evening Review*, 19 October 1922. It seems Troyer and a young boy set out one evening in search of gold.

They went to Long Point, arriving just enough before dark to locate the spot where the treasure was. Then they waited until exactly midnight, and then started a procession, Deacon Troyer holding the open Bible before him, and his son following with a lighted candle, with spades, picks, etc. They dug down, and presently the pick struck metal. They got the pick under the lid of the box and pried it up. And then, at that moment a black shape rose up and assumed the form of a black dog, growing bigger and bigger, and they dropped their Bible and candle and rushed for the canoe, and never had any curiosity to return to the spot.

Mameigwess Lake/
Windigo and Maymaygwayshi

Selwyn Dewdney noted an "uncanny stillness" on Mameigwess Lake in Northern Ontario. He was there in search of rock art and found both the Cave of the Windigo and the image of Maymaygwayshi. He wrote about the experience in *Indian Rock Paintings of the Great Lakes* (1967).

He was informed that the Ojibway believe that at the east end of the lake "there was a devil at the foot of the cliff and they were not going past unless absolutely necessary." As a cave was known in the side of the cliff, Dewdney noted, "White residents say that a *Weyn-di-gow* is believed to inhabit this 'cave.' "

At nearby Indian Lake he found two images of little men which he identified as the *Maymaygwayshi*. The word has a number of meanings which depend entirely upon context. A Maymaygwayshi may be a gnome, ghost, spirit, merman, monkey, little hairy man, or sasquatch-like figure. It could even be taken to refer, as it has been, to the traditional description of the appearance of a Viking explorer who may have moved among the Indians in the distant past. Dewdney suggested that the best translation of the word is "Rockmedicine Man."

Authorities disagree on details, but some features of the Maymaygwayshi are common over wide areas. They are said to live behind waterside rock faces, especially those where cracks or shal-low caves suggest an entrance. They are fond of fish, and frequently—more out of mischief than need—steal fish from Indian nets . . . .

As they approach they put their heads down in the bottom of the canoe. Why? Because they are ashamed of their faces. In the south and east this is because their faces are covered with fur or hair — "like a monkey" one Nipigon Indian told me, holding his two hands up so finger and thumb encircled each eye. In the north and west there is no facial hair, the shame being due to lack of a soft part to the nose.

Specially gifted Ojibway shamans, I was told, had the power to enter the rock and exchange tobacco for an extremely potent "rock medicine." Many Indians to this day leave tobacco gifts on the ledges or in the water as they pass certain rocks — "for good luck," they usually explain.

Manitoulin Island/
Dreamer's Rock

Dreamer's Rock is a prospect point on the White Fish Indian Reserve, near Little Current, on the north shore of Manitoulin Island. The quartzite rock rises over 1650 feet above the level of Lake Ontario. It is sacred to the Anishnabec, as the Ojibway refer to themselves; the word means "the people."

On this rock for ages the Anishnabec have worshipped the Michi Manitou, the Great Spirit. From its vantage-point, Ojibway youth have fasted and prayed for a dream to learn the nature of their spirit guide, for Dreamer's Rock is the point of focus in the geography of their "dream quest."

Manitoulin Island/
Sheguiandah

The most controversial archaeological site in the country is the Sheguiandah site, a twenty-six acre hilltop quarry which extends into the modern Indian village of Sheguiandah at the northeastern corner of Manitoulin Island. The ancient quartzite quarry here was co-discovered in 1951 by Thomas E. Lee, an archae-ologist then in the employ of the National Museum of Man and subsequently something of a maverick with distinct views on the antiquity of early man in the Americas.

Lee maintained that Shequiandah was the richest and possibly the earliest known site of early man-made materials in the Americas. Working the various geological strata, he claimed that he had unearthed man-fashioned materials beneath glacial deposits, pro-viding evidence of early man's presence on Manitoulin Island in the interglacial periods — from 30,000 to 100,000 years before the present era — much earlier than granted by orthodox archaeologists. He described his finds and argued his views in dissident publications, like his own *Anthropological Journal of Canada*, and found some support for his findings and interpretations, but few if any from the National Museum of Man which soft-pedalled the significance of the Sheguiandah site. Today a new generation of archaeologist has begun to rework the site and view

The author Farley Mowat smiles at the archaeologist Thomas E. Lee who appraises the photographer in this snapshot. Mowat has adopted many unorthodox positions in such books as Westviking *(1965), including the notion that the Kensington Stone was carved in Northern Ontario. Lee is the discoverer of the archaeological site Sheguiandah on Manitoulin Island and of the Hammer of Thor in Ungava. [Robert E. Lee]*

with greater respect and charity Lee's views on its antiquity.

Yet judging by the reference to Shequiandah in a current textbook, the revisionists are moving with glacial speed. Ronald J. Mason wrote in *Great Lakes Archaeology* (1981) that "the Sheguiandah site was once touted to be of glacial or even preglacial age. There is not and never was much to support such a claim," adding that "the best available current esti-mated range is between approximately 8400 and 750 B.C."

Some day Sheguiandah will come into its own, and along with it the life and legacy of Thomas E. Lee. A controversial archaeologist and rogue anthropolo-gist, Dr. Thomas E. Lee (1915-1982) had a fiery tem-per and did not suffer fools at all. According to John Doig in "Storm over Ungava" in *The Canadian*, 3 March 1979, Lee first fell afoul of the establishment in 1951 when he failed a doctoral examination in anthropology at the University of Michigan. "He found the test unfair and fired off copies to several prominent anthropologists. The Michigan professors, who wielded wide influence over archaeology in North America, were displeased. When he later proudly refused to sit again for his Ph.D. they were furious and, Lee believes, never forgave him."

He was employed by the National Museum of Man from 1949 to 1959. During this time he stepped on a number of toes. For instance, there was the embar-rassment of the long-lost site of the Battle of Long Sault. French-Canadians patriotically assumed it would be found on the Quebec side of the Ottawa River. Lee dug up the ramparts and incautiously drew attention to the fact that this shrine of the Ancien Régime was on a farm near Hawksbury on the Ontario side of the river. The Historic Sites and Mon-uments Board of Canada was more politic and plaqued two sites—one in each province—stating that Adam Dollard's last stand took place "near here."

The fact that Lee championed the antiquity of the "Sheg" site on Mantoulin Island did him no profes-sional good. Nor did the fact that he published his own periodical, which he called the *Anthropological Journal of Canada*. He founded it in Ottawa in 1963, editing it with some brilliance for almost two decades. Back issues are a gold mine of dissident opinion and unorthodox information. From its pages was launched what was called "the Fell phase" of the appreciation of the mysterious Sherbrooke Inscriptions. The controversy did not help Lee's reputation, although he emerged from the ordeal with honour.

For almost eight years Lee was unemployed. Then he was appointed guest professor at Laval University's Centre of Northern Studies. Between 1966 and 1980, the Centre commissioned a dozen or so of his expeditions to Ungava. At Payne Lake and Payne Bay, he excavated a range of ruins which he linked with Inuit, Eskimo, Tunit, and even Norse occupancy. Among these ruins there stands the magnificent Hammer of Thor.

In all, Lee discovered some four hundred sites of archaeological interest. He was convinced that pre-Columbian voyages had been made across the Atlantic, but he had to reject almost every bit of evidence that was offered to him. The show of integrity and independence made him stand apart from both disciples and detractors.

Lake Michigan/
The American Lake

Lake Michigan, the second-largest of the Great Lakes, is an American lake for it is the only one of the five to lie solely within the borders of the United States.

This lake was the destination of the *Griffon*, the first ship to sail the Upper Great Lakes. Launched by LaSalle at Cayuga Creek in the Niagara River on 7 August 1679, it headed for Michilimackinac and then Green Bay. The barque, loaded with furs, disappeared sometime after leaving Green Bay on 20-22 September.

Over the centuries Lake Michigan has known its share of marine disasters and mysteries. Two of these are the sinking of the *Alpena*, a sidewheel steamer which went down the night of 15 October 1880, and the loss of the *Anna C. Minch*, a cargo carrier which sank on 11 November 1940.

Midland/
The Hurons and the Jesuits

In "the Heart of Huronia" on the outskirts of the town of Midland there stand Sainte-Marie-among-the-Hurons and the Martyrs' Shrine. The Ontario government was responsible for the historical reconstruction of this seventeenth-century French pallisaded fort and community; the Roman Catholic Church oversaw the erection of the shrine to honour the life and accomplishment of the Jesuit saints and martyrs. The structures harken back to the days when the Huron shamans battled with the Jesuit priests and missionaries in an epic confrontation between native spirituality and European religiosity.

The Hurons believed that the Jesuits and the Recollets who lived among them were sorcerers with powers superior to their own. After all, the missionaries with their pale faces and black robes could predict eclipses of the sun and the moon; they had access to advanced technology, like writing instruments and chiming clocks; they prayed for the sick and sometimes cured them; they prayed for rain and it often came. They performed elaborate rituals like the Mass, but kept secret some of their beliefs and rites like Communion, lest the natives conclude that consuming the body and blood of Jesus Christ was in any way a validation of their own ritual cannibalistic practices.

The Jesuits and the Recollets were seen as excellent practitioners of witchcraft, as noted by Bruce G. Trigger in *The Children of Aataentsic* (1976). Not that the Huron shamans were slouches, as witness the audacious appeal of the following curing ritual:

> The most sensational of all the curing rituals was the *andacwander*. To perform this ceremony, the unmarried people of the village assembled in the sick person's house and spent the night having sexual intercourse with the partner of their choice, while the patient watched and two shamans shook their tortoise shell rattles and sang. Sometimes a sick man might request a young girl to have intercourse with him. Although this

ceremony so shocked the Jesuits that they were hesitant even to mention it, it appears to have been a common one. This indicates the degree to which the Huron's concern for the welfare of members of their own society led them, in well-defined and short-lived contexts, to trangress even the most restrictive norms of their society.

The Jesuits and the Recollets were able to use their persuasive powers and their technology to convince the Hurons that their beliefs and practices were more powerful and practical than the traditional beliefs and practices.

There can be no doubt that the Huron regarded the Jesuits as shamans or sorcerers who controlled immense power and, therefore, had to be treated with great circumspection. Evidence of this power was perceived in their ability to transmit messages on pieces of paper, to control the weather, and to avoid or easily recover from illnesses that proved fatal to the Indians. The Jesuits further enhanced their reputation by predicting the lunar eclipses of 1637 and 1638, which made the Huron believe that they had caused these events to happen. The Jesuits also acquired prestige as the representatives of a people of recognized technological superiority.

The Huron word for those spirits, souls, or forces with the power to influence human beings is *oki*. The comparison of seventeenth-century European with aboriginal *oki* is far from farfetched.

When the Quieunonascaranas agreed to build a cabin for the Recollets in 1623, they asked the priests to stop the rain, which was excessive at the time . . . . After they had spent the night praying, the rain stopped and fine weather prevailed until the cabin was finished, after which it began to fall again. The Huron are reported to have regarded this as a proof of supernatural power and to have proclaimed everywhere the greatness of the spirit whom the Recollets invoked.

A Huron-style longhouse, erected for the Jesuits near Ihonatiria, consisted of a chapel, a living and working area (with a carpentry shop and a flour mill), and a store-room. The Hurons were intrigued.

The carpentry of this house, and the furnishings that the Jesuits brought with them, greatly interested the Huron. In particular, they were impressed by the European-style doors that were placed at the entrance to the cabin and between the first and second rooms, by the mill, and by the clock. Visitors took turns working the mill and believed that because the clock made a noise, it was alive. For this reason, they called it the Headman of the Day and enquired about the kind of food it ate and what it was saying. The Jesuits found that by telling the Huron that when it sounded four times it was telling them to leave, they could assure themselves of being left alone after four o'clock.

Then there is the equation of communion with cannibalism.

Because the Huron practised cannibalism, the Jesuits tried to keep their belief that the communion wafers were the body of Christ secret from all except those whose faith in Christianity had been well tested. In 1637 a rumor began to spread that the Jesuits had brought a corpse from France which they kept in a tabernacle in their chapel and that it was this corpse that was causing the Huron to die.

There were many skirmishes in the war between the Huron shamans and the Roman Catholic priests. The war could be said to culminate in the Armageddon-like confrontation between the Hurons and the Iroquois which led to the destruction of Saint-Marie-among-the-Hurons in 1649 and the retreat of the Hurons to Christian Island.

Jacques de Brébeuf, the Jesuit father who admitted that he had once been tempted in the woods by a demon in the guise of a beautiful temptress, whose blandishments he rejected, was martyred at St. Ignace on 16 March 1649. Among other tortures, the Iroquois poured boing water over him, a parody of the rite of baptism. Brébeuf's skull is preserved at the Indian chapel at Sainte-Marie-among-the-Hurons. His bones are interred at the Martyrs' Shrine.

Brébeuf and the other Jesuit Martyrs (Noël Chabanel, Antoine Daniel, Charles Garnier, Gabriel Lalemant, René Goupil, Isaac Joques, Jean de La Lande) were canonized by Pope Pius XII on 29 June 1930. They were proclaimed patron saints of Canada on 16 October 1940.

Midland/
Martyrs' Shrine

Roman Catholics hold the Martyrs' Shrine in special reverence. Pope John Paul II celebrated Mass at the Shrine in September 1984.

The shrine itself is situated on the crest of a hill overlooking Sainte-Marie-among-the-Hurons. On the grounds will be found a limestone church with twin spires; the Stations of the Cross; a spring said to have miraculous healing properties; and a grotto dedicated to Our Lady of Huronia, a patron saint of Sainte-Marie and Jesuit Martyrs. In the hierarchy of Canadian shrines, the Martyrs' Shrine ranks second in reports of miraculous cures. Pride of place is reserved for Sainte-Anne-de-Beaupré outside Quebec City.

Of interest is the newspaper report "Miraculous Cures among the Pilgrims" datelined Toronto 27 August 1928 and published that day in a number of newspapers, including the St. Catharines *Standard*. Here is the report in its entirety.

MIRACULOUS CURES AMONG THE PILGRIMS
Reported to Have Occurred at Shrine of Canadian Martyrs

FIRST OCCURRED BEFORE ARRIVAL
Visited Site of First Original Outpost of Christianity

TORONTO, Aug. 27. — Three miraculous cures at the shrine of the Martyrs near Midland, Ont., were reported by the members of the first pilgrimage party from the Province of Quebec, who reached Toronto last evening, after having spent the day at the spring. The party, which was approximately 190 in number, left Montreal in a special train Friday night and the first cure occurred on a C.N.R. sleeper shortly before the shrine was reached.

Among the members making the pilgrimage was Elie Bouchard, a clerk of Montreal, about 27 years of age, who had been suffering from total deafness and paralysis of the right arm. The attention of Father J. Dugas was drawn to him and he was told by a friend that when he arrived at the shrine to invoke the aid of the martyred Jesuit Fathers de Brebouf [sic] and Lallement [sic] to help him.

Suddenly to the surprise of all, Bouchard recovered his speech and the use of his arm, not only is he now able to talk but he can also write. The second miracle occurred at the shrine, and the cure was affected upon a boy aged 16 years, named Gerrard Henry, of Long Branch, Ont. He had been dumb for about six years, suffering from paralysis of the tongue and mouth and after touching the relics of Fathers de Brebouf and Lallement, fully recovered articulation.

His first words were spoken to this father, when he said: "I can talk now, daddy." The third miracle reported occurred to R. Burns aged 35, [of] Woodland, Ont., who was born deaf. He was praying at the grotto, distant from the church, when Father S. Bouvret of the shrine came to him and had him drink some water from the grotto. He announced then his hearing had been fully restored and was able to converse with his friends in a normal manner. The shrine of the martyrs is erected beside the site of Fort Ste. Marie. The first original outpost of Christianity in what was known as Huronia, it is noted for its martyrs who made the supreme sacrifice of the cross during the Iroquois conquest of the land.

Among the fathers who won the crown of martyrdom at the hands of the Six Nations warriors were two outstanding figures, Fathers de Brebouf and Lallemant, who were put to death with terrible torture March 16, 1649, at Fort St. Ignace, a distance of about three miles from Fort Ste. Marie. The relics of the two brave priests were subsequently brought back to the fort and their ashes were interred on the spot of their martyrdom. The Quebec party, which made the pilgrimage under the auspices of the Order of the Society of Jesus, left in their special train this morning for Niagara Falls where they will spend the day, returning at night, and on Tuesday will devote the day to visiting the Canadian National Exhibition, leaving the same night for Montreal.

Mississauga/
The Mississauga Blob

The Mississauga Blob is one of the happier names in the field of Fortean phenomena. It has a real ring to it.

Mississauga is a city located on Lake Ontario on the southwestern boundary of Metropolitan Toronto. The blob in question is a clump of something-or-other which fell down from the sky and landed with a sickening thud on the picnic table in the backyard of the family home of Traven Matchett on Melton Drive in Mississauga. It all happened late on a hot, sunny Saturday afternoon, 26 June 1979.

After hearing the thud, nineteen-year-old Donna Matchett let out a scream. "A cylindrical column of flame was shooting up from a molten green mass upon the centre of the table. Thinking quickly, she picked up a garden hose and doused the fire as her father ran up," explained Dwight Whalen in his study of the "fall" in *Pursuit*, First Quarter, 1981.

"The flame was like a blow torch, magnified, shooting up through the table," her father, Traven Matchett, a real estate broker, explained. He described the flame as very intense, reddish-orange in colour with yellow streaks, perfectly cylindrical, about eighteen inches high by eight inches wide. The fire was

immediately extinguished by the water. The extinguished mass shrank and solidified. It was a small, flat, dark green mass with a fibrous, pock-marked texture, weighing about four ounces.

Matchett phoned the control tower of the Toronto International Airport wondering if the flaming mass might have fallen from an airplane. Then he called the nearest Canadian Armed Forces base, the University of Toronto, and the Ontario Science Centre. But it was Saturday and he was advised to wait until Monday. The operator at the latter institution recommended that he call the press, so Matchett phoned the Toronto *Sun* which immediately sent a reporter.

Sunday's paper featured the story. That broke the logjam. "This place was like Grand Central Station," said Matchett, "and it was like that for a whole week. The story just zoomed across the country. Donna was giving interviews on the phone every three minutes. There were television cameras here, newsmen, it was

Traven Matchett and his daughter Donna examine the so-called Mississauga Blob. The afternoon of 26 June 1979, a molten green mass fell from the sky and landed on the picnic bench in the backyard of the Matchett home in Mississauga, Ont. It burst into bright reddish-orange flames which, when extinguished, left a "blob." No one in a position of authority expressed any interest until a local newspaper favoured it with front-page coverage. [Inland Publishing Co. Limited]

unbelievable the excitement there was around here over this thing.''

On Monday an inspector from the Ontario Ministry of the Environment arrived and took a sample of the green blob for analysis. The Ministry later reported that the blob was polyprophylene, a widely used chemical plastic in such items as plates, ashtrays, and frisbees. Then the Peel Regional Police arrived, questioned everyone, and departed with a sample of the blob for analysis by the centre of Forensic Sciences in Toronto. Matchett was refused a copy of their lab report as it was considered a confidential document. But the police let him read it three times. The gist of the report was that the composition of the blob was two different kinds of common plastic—polyprophylene and polystyrene—which burn with vigour. No trace of radioactivity was found.

One story attracts another. When the blob news story was published, Mrs. Dorothy Smith of Sherobee Drive, about a mile from Matchett's residence, came to him with a curious story. About a month before, she said, she found a solid, circular blob of plastic-like material in her own backyard. But unlike Matchett's green blob, hers was black. Matchett then showed her where his blob had melted between two planks of the picnic table onto his concrete patio blocks. There she saw a hardened, shiny, jet-black residue identical, she told him, to her blob.

Then Chuck Le Ber of nearby Brampton told much the same story. He had found a dark-coloured blob of what appeared to be hardened plastic in his backyard the previous April. Both blobs, however, met a fate hardly worthy of deadly invaders from space. They were thrown into the trash. Tom Grey, Canadian Director of the Northeastern UFO Organization, arrived and announced that his geiger counter indicated a very light but harmless radioactive reading, above the normal background level.

Matchett was not very impressed with the way the authorities responded to his call for help with the Mississauga Blob. ''What baffles me is that on a Saturday in June, if a spaceship loaded with little green men had landed in my backyard, nobody could have investigated it till Monday!'' He added, quoting a neighbour, ''Strange things happen in this world, and you may never find out what it is. It may be as mysterious twenty years from now as it is today.''

Mississauga/ Maha Yogi A.S. Narayana

Mississauga, west of Metropolitan Toronto, is the home of Maha Yogi A.S. Narayana. Not for nothing is he known as the Super Psychic and ''the businessman's psychic.'' At psychic fairs, where a psychic will rent a single booth to give ''readings,'' he reserves three booths in a row to fly the flag and create a super-sized exhibition area. His thrust is towards the world of business, and he boasts that he is registered with the Better Business Bureau. According to his promotional literature, in the year 1988 he charged $150 for a personal consultation, $300 for a business consultation, $3,000 for a corporate consultation, and $10,000 for an annual corporate retainer.

For his readings and predictions he boasts a ''success rate'' that ranges from seventy-five to ninety per cent, depending on the source cited. He also claims to be ''23 times'' as reliable as the ''average psychic,'' based on a statistical evaluation in terms of public predictions for the year 1979 conducted by a psychologist associated with the American Society for Psychical Research. He boasts that he ''holds a virtual world monopoly in paranormal futurology.''

By his own account the Maha Yogi is not Indian in background but Polish-German. He was born Alfred Schmielewski at Norkitten, Insterburgh, East Prussia, in 1928. At the tender age of seven he came under the influence of a master teacher who was touring Europe — Sri Bhagwan Sat Guru Babaji Maha Avatar Giri. Thereafter he graduated from the Academy of Fine Arts in Berlin. His psychic powers were so powerful that apparently even as a student he found he could predict where over Berlin the Allied bombers would drop their bombs.

Narayana gave an account of his special studies to Ajit Jain, a journalist with the Toronto weekly newspaper *India Abroad*. The 4 July 1986 issue outlines the numerous places Narayana has lived and studied the occult practices and beliefs of the native cultures. In his own words he is "the world's foremost authority in the field of world prophecy."

He emigrated from West Germany to Canada in 1961 and settled in Toronto where for some years he operated a yoga school. In 1973 he established the ESPON Corporation to place his psychic services at the disposal of the world of business and politics. In time he emerged as the country's best-known psychic. He was assisted by a commanding presence, a courtly manner, and a penchant for publicity. He always has a prediction or two for the journalist or columnist. He delights in jousting with debunkers like Henry Gordon, the magician and journalist.

The problem with predicting is that not all predictions come to pass; in fact, few do. As a predictor, Narayana has his "hits" but he also has his "misses." The former are eerie and uncanny, perhaps the products of lucky guesses or reasonable responses to the news and views of the day; the latter are ludicrous and make much more interesting reading, for they suggest a future which might have been.

What follows are selections of Narayana's predictions. They appear in three groups: "hits" and "near hits"; "misses"; and "some prophecies to think about." All the details come from duplicated press clippings, complete in themselves and dated, as supplied by Narayana. There are six predictions in each category. First, the "hits" and "near-hits."

• Brian Mulroney will become Canada's next Prime Minister. (25 September 1983)

• Yuri Andropov will not even be in power in another two years. (16 January 1983)

• The next election will be a "Conservative landslide and the Liberals will be finished. They'll never recover from the damage. They've frightened the wits out of the middle-class." (16 January 1983)

• "An explosion and a fire on board of a Challenger Space Craft will lead up to history's first outer-space rescue mission in 1986 or sooner." (16 November 1984)

• "In May, 1978, for instance, when the Dow Jones was at 850 and climbing, Narayana predicted it would slide to below 800 the following October. Sure enough, the Dow Jones started to decline on schedule, falling 116 points to 792.45 on October 31. Subsequently Narayana correctly pegged the rise in coffee futures, as well as fluctuations in the gold futures market and the Canadian dollar." (*The Financial Post Magazine*, 1 March 1984)

• "Pope John Paul has an 85% chance of dying, possibly by assassination, in 1981." (19 Sept. 1980)

Second, the "misses." [In brackets appear the Yogi's responses to this listing and the next listing when they were sent to him for his comments.]

• Jean Chrétien will be the opposition leader. (March 1982)

• The Canadian economic crisis will be so severe by the end of the year that the Senate will be virtually abolished. (22 February 1985)

• "He also foresees a federal election by next fall, a shift in power from Eastern Canada to Western Canada in the next five years and Joe Clark becoming Canadian ambassador to the United Nations." (25 September 1983) [He went into External Affairs.]

• Margaret Trudeau will become a television evangelist before 1983. "What else is left but God after Pierre Elliott Trudeau and the Rolling Stones?" (23 March 1982) [She was treated by a psychiatrist for hallucinating being the reincarnation of the Holy Virgin Mary.]

• Ronald Reagan may resign this year because of increasingly serious geriatric problems. (16 January 1983)

• All farm credit unions and banks will go under in 1986 and farm debts will have to be written off and converted into low interest and long-term bonds. (January–February 1986) [Most did and the Federal Deposit Corporation went virtually bankrupt.]

Third, here are some prophecies to think about [with the Yogi's comments added in brackets]:

• There will be no nuclear war. (22 February 1985)

• The Third World War is imminent and civilization will come to an end in this century. (3 June 1979)

• "We can expect to see a U.S.–Soviet alliance in the 1990s with unprecedented markets for American mass manufacturing. The U.S. and the Soviet Union will eventually unite to form a World Directorate." (22 February 1985) [Glasnost & Gorbachev]

• Gorbachev will probably get shot, John Turner will be out and gold will rise to $740 an ounce." (19 October 1986)

• Toronto will have a new CNE, which will be built over Lake Ontario within the next ten years. (January–February 1986)

• During his tenure, Mulroney "will succeed in restoring the economic health of this nation." And no small part will be played in that recovery by the introduction of freer trade between Canada and our leading trading partner, the United States. "It will," he predicts, "lead to a Golden Age for the Canadian economy—an age in which Canada will join the club of economic world powers." (30 May 1986)

One final item on prophecy and prediction. Narayana told Ajit Jain that he had completed work on a manuscript called *The Quintrains of Narayana*. The word "quintrain" is unusual; the word "quatrain" is familiar. Quatrains are four-line verses. Nostradamus is famous for writing them. Narayana is writing five-line verses, or quintrains. His manuscript bears the following subtitle: "Prophecies Till the Year 5000." Now who will be around to list the "hits" and "misses" of Narayana if the world "as we know it" is to end before the year 2000?

Mississauga/
The Cherry Hill House Ghost

Cherry Hill House is the oldest building in Mississauga. A restaurant and banquet hall reputed to be haunted, it stands at the intersection of Dundas Street and Cawthra Road.

Cherry Hill House was built as a residence by Joseph and Jane Silverthorne in 1807. Members of the Silverthorne family occupied the house until 1932 when it was rented to a Scottish family named Lindsay. When they vacated in 1972 it was in a dilapidated state. Nevertheless, it was acquired by a restaurant

chain the next year and restored. Part of the restoration consisted of moving the house onto a new foundation eight hundred feet from the old one. It was after this relocation that the hauntings were first reported. The restaurant chain opened its new restaurant in its new location on Halloween Night 1973, so there is always the suspicion that the earliest sightings were part of a publicity campaign. Subsequent sightings could be the result of superstition.

Following the relocation that summer, an outside security guard named Ron Land said he saw a white figure rise out of a pile of earth and brandish a sword. His dog Cindy shied away and Land fled. Workmen in the building reported the scattering of their tools. One restaurant manager said that he saw faces of old Indians floating out of the fireplace. Another manager described glimpsing the ghostly outline of a little girl who was running away. A Scottish carpenter fell down the attic stairs and broke a wrist, maintaining that he had been pushed.

Two explanations are offered for the hauntings and poltergeist-like activities. One is that the house was relocated onto an old Indian burial ground, thus angering the spirits. The other is that the new foundation blocks came from a nearby field that was once used as an old Indian burial ground, thus angering the spirits. The explanations appear in accounts of the haunting in two issues of the *Toronto Star*, 26 October 1980 and 14 January 1984. Since that date there have been repeated reports of strange sights, sounds, and movements at Cherry Hill House.

Moose Factory/
Strange Events

A series of strange events which reportedly happened in the sub-Arctic region around the southern shore of James Bay was described by Don Delaplante from Moose Factory to the Toronto *Telegram* on 21 October 1950. The events, which may or may not be related, took place over six months and included the following:

• Three Indians reported seeing "a water-going object" which they identified as a submarine, gray on top, black on the bottom, in James Bay near the mouth of the Moose River.

• A strange "red light" which hung almost stationary in the sky above Nemaska, a trading post in Quebec inland from Rupert's House, was observed by the factor and his assistant. They likened it to "a traffic stop light," denying that it was the light from a star.

• Indians west of Nemaska observed two "airplanes," one large and one small, which appeared to stand still in the sky over Northern Quebec.

• Three huge explosions, "like earthquakes," shook every building over a period of two or three minutes at Old Factory River.

• When observed by Indians, "strange white men" were seen to run and hide in the forest around Fort George.

These reports attracted the attention of the RCMP whose officers investigated them and filed their reports with the headquarters in Ottawa. "But nervousness prevails here," noted Delaplante, "for the vast unpatrolled coastline of James Bay and Hudson Bay makes a landing by any hostile invader an easy one."

New Hamburg/
Fifty-Pound Reptile

Members of the small farming community of New Hamburg, located between Kitchener and Stratford, complained to the chief of police about a strange creature seen on its streets. As zoologist Ivan T. Sanderson reported in "*Things*" (1967), for a period of three years in the early 1960s more than twenty of the townsfolk saw the creature which was variously described as large and "lizard-like."

When it was seen by the chief of police himself, he vowed that he would either capture it or, if necessary, shoot it. The town clerk and treasurer and others described it as greenish-brown in colour, with a scaled tail, about fifty pounds, four-legged but three-toed. It apparently lived in the Nith River which runs through the town.

As Sanderson concluded: "The point is, there are *no* fifty-pound reptiles [or amphibians] in Canada, and none matching this description with three toes anywhere else."

Niagara Falls/
The Mighty Thunderer

Niagara Falls in Ontario and Niagara Falls in New York may be twin cities but they are not twinned. Separating them is the Niagara River, perhaps the world's most famous short river, being only thirty-five miles long; linking them are the higher American Falls and the wider Canadian or Horseshoe Falls. Niagara Falls has been called "the Honeymoon Capital of the World" and "the World's Most Famous Address." The word Niagara may well be derived from *nia-gara*, "mighty thunderer," the last remaining word of the language spoken by the Neutral Indians. The Neutral nation occupied the region around the falls at the time of European contact. As their name suggests their foreign policy was one of neutrality. But because their traditional lands lay between those of the Huron and the Iroquois, the nation was attacked by the two groups and eliminated.

The earliest, first-person description of the Niagara Falls was written by Louis Hennepin, the missionary, who saw them for the first time on 6 December 1678. Hennepin overestimated their height by three hundred per cent. The American Falls are 167 feet high; to Hennepin "they plunge down a height of more than five hundred feet . . . in a fearful manner." Over the last three centuries the Mighty Thunderer has inspired no end of noble thoughts, like those of the English Poet Rupert Brooke in 1913: "I sit and stare at the thing and have the purest Nineteenth Century grandiose thoughts, about the Destiny of Man, the Irresistibility of Fate, the Doom of Nations, the fact that Death awaits us All, and so forth. Wordsworth Redivivus. Oh dear! Oh dear!"

Aleister Crowley, the Black Magician and so-called Wickedest Man in the World, visited the Falls on a trans-Canada trip in 1906. He was not much impressed with Canada. "Of all the loveless, lifeless lands that writhe beneath the wrath of God, condemn me to Canada!'' he wrote in his posthumously published book *The Confessions of Aleister Crowley: An Autohagiography* (1970). Yet the size and spirituality of the Falls cast a spell over him. ''They fascinate, as all things vast beyond computation invariably do. I felt that if I lived with them for even a short time they would completely obsess me and possibly lure me to end my life with their eternity. I felt the same about the mountains of India, the expanse of China, the solitude of the Sahara. I feel as if the better part of me belonged to them, as if my dearest destiny would be to live and die with them.''

Niagara Falls/
The Call of Niagara

Everyone who gazes upon the thundering Falls of Niagara is affected, each in their own way. Some are stirred to wonder and amazement; others find the monotony of the flow a crashing bore; and others, mesmerized by the motion and sound of the rushing water, feel an irresistible urge to throw themselves over the brink. Indeed many find the temptation to self-destruction at Niagara overpowering.

Death is intimately associated with the phenomenon of Niagara, and not only in physical terms. Dr. Ernest Jones was a neurologist and early Freudian and a Toronto resident in 1908–13. He published a paper on the dream-life of his Toronto patients in which he noted the presence in their dreams of images of spuming falls and plunging whirlpools, inspired by Niagara, symbols of phallic life and vulval death.

''The association between Niagara and death, especially suicide, is one that has been enforced by countless repeated experiences,'' Jones wrote in *Essays in Applied Psycho-Analysis*. ''It is not so generally known, however, that the association between it and birth is also very intimate. Niagara is a favourite honeymoon resort—possibly more so for Toronto people than for those of other places in the neighbourhood, on account of the romantic journey thither across the Lake of Ontario. So much is this so that Niagara town is commonly known—in Toronto at all events—as

Lewlawala, the Maid of the Mist, sacrificed her life for love. She plunged over the Falls of Niagara only to be rescued by He-No, the Thunderer, who resides at the foot of the mighty cataract in a mist-enshrouded cave. She lives there still, and may from time to time be discerned in the rainbow of the Falls. This image of Lewlawala appeared on a late-nineteenth century coloured postcard. The cut-line is incomplete. It should read in full: The Red Man's Fact — The White Man's Fancy.'' [Dwight Whalen]

'the Baby City,' from the high percentage of conceptions that date from a visit there.''

Long before Niagara became a honeymoon resort in the mid-1800s, Indians of the area spoke of Niagara in terms of death. An old legend tells of a suicidal Indian virgin who, rather than marry her hated betrothed, cast herself over the Falls in a canoe. Wondrously, she was saved in her plunge by the great god He-No the Thunderer, who lived behind the Falls, and took the maiden to live with him there.

Modern adaptations of this myth tell of the lovely Lewlawala, sent over the Falls by her father, Chief Eagle Eye, in a sacrificial plunge to He-No in hopes of ending a plague ravaging the Indian village. It became a double sacrifice when Lewlawala's father, filled with remorse, immediately followed his daughter over the brink. Another verson identifies Sahonwadi, Lewlawala's heart-broken lover, as the one who canoed over the Falls after her.

In all accounts only Lewlawala is saved, caught in the arms of the spirit He-No, or Hinum, the Thunderer, who is pleased with the sacrifice and ends her people's sufferings. For years afterwards a white birchbark canoe, brimming with ripe fruit and beautiful flowers, was sent over the brink as a symbolic offering to He-No. The ghostly form of Lewlawala, so the story goes, can sometimes be seen hovering, larger than life, in the great clouds of mist swirling up from the pit of the Horseshoe. Thus she became known as "The Maid of the Mist."

The Seneca and Neutral Indians who inhabited the Niagara region when the White Man came practised human sacrifice. Whether or not it took the form of ritualistically sending people to their deaths over the Falls is uncertain, but it is clear from their traditions that the Indians acknowledged in Niagara a seductive power to lure people to their doom.

"The Call of Niagara" still beckons today. People suffering from terminal disease, mental illness, traumatic loss, and anguish of every kind take their lives at Niagara in astonishing numbers. In fact, the statistics are appalling. It has been estimated that from twelve to fifteen people a year kill themselves by plunging over the Canadian end of the Horseshoe Falls at Table Rock, while from Prospect Point at the American Falls about sixteen people a year take the leap. If these figures are accurate, approximately thirty people every year — more than one every two weeks on average — deliberately end their lives in suicide plunges over Niagara Falls. Add to this total another thirty or so persons a year, who are prevented from

real or suspected suicide attempts at the Falls, and it becomes clear that Niagara can exert a deadly influence on the human mind.

The news media tend to downplay the phenomenon. Evidently the fear is that too much publicity will encourage even more people to take "the Niagara way out." Also, there is a fear of damaging public perception of Niagara as a recreational fun spot, as indeed it has been damaged in the eyes of countless horrified suicide witnesses. Tourism officials prefer not to talk about the subject, and Niagara guidebooks, to be sure, scrupulously avoid mentioning it. Traditionally known as "The Honeymoon Capital of the World," Niagara Falls can also claim to being "The Suicide Capital of the World." It has never demonstrated its deadly power more convincingly than when, according to Andy O'Brien's book *Daredevils of Niagara* (1964), a total of fifty-three people leaped over the Falls to their deaths in the immediate wake of the stock market crash of 1929.

Niagara's promise of instant annihilation has never been broken. Every suicide leap, without exception, has succeeded. Yet, strangely, an unknown number of these fatalities are almost certainly not true suicides. This is Niagara's most chilling feature. Even people with no thought of self-destruction can suddenly find themselves hurtling over the brink, gripped by a hypnotic siren call they are powerless to resist.

It can strike without warning. Mrs. Ellen King, rescued from the rapids above the brink of the American Falls, 20 September 1946, denied attempting to kill herself but could not explain how she came to be wading through the fast-moving water. "I was walking along the bank near the upper rapids on the American side," she recalled, "when I began to feel dizzy. The roar of the water became overpowering. It seemed to be drawing and inviting me. And then everything went blank. I remembered nothing until I woke up in the hospital hours later. The nurses had to tell me what had happened. At first I couldn't really believe what had happened but I knew that it was all possible because of the fascination I have always had for the Falls."

Canadian actress Margot Kidder, at Niagara to play

Lois Lane in the filming of the movie *Superman II,* also felt the Falls' hypnotic draw: "It's almost eerie, but you feel pulled to the water. It's so free and smooth-flowing and tranquil."

A Toronto *Star Weekly* article, published in the Niagara Falls *Evening Review,* 7 May 1923, reported the results of a psychological study done to determine the kind of personalities most vulnerable to Niagara's death lure. The effect of the Falls was studied on twenty people, ten of whom were selected for their "highly strung, nervous temperaments," while the other ten were of placid dispositions. One by one each person was allowed to gaze on the rushing waters at the precipice. Those of sanguine make-up felt no particular beckoning to "go with the flow," but seven of the tense, nervous types were noticeably affected. "One woman was unable to look at the waters more than two or three minutes at a time without experiencing that impelling, mysterious force that seemed to call her into its depths," said the *Star.* Most of the anxious group felt uncomfortable looking at the water, and safer when they backed away from the brink.

"What is this terrific appeal of Niagara?" asked the paper. "No other spectacle of nature seems to be able to exercise such control over those who gaze upon it. Is it a peculiar form of hypnotism, or does it affect only minds that are turbulent and on the verge of collapse?

"One girl who committed suicide at Niagara left the following note: 'These waters overpower me. I cannot resist them. Please forgive me.'

"Here was the case of a plain, sensitive soul called to death by a subtle but fierce appeal. How many lives have been snuffed out under the same circumstances?"

Undoubtedly many hundreds.

The article went on to advise that a "strong mind" is the best defence against the Falls' fatal attraction. "Those who fear and dread it had best stay away or else view it in the presence of a person who will remain unaffected."

That means, if one is the vulnerable type, one had better not view the Falls in the company of Dave Munday. A fifty-one-year-old mechanic from Caistor

Centre, Ontario, Munday has found the powerful "call of Niagara" irresistible, although he managed to escape it with his life. On 5 October 1985, he hurtled over the Horseshoe Falls encased in a custom-made barrel, becoming the tenth person in history to challenge the Horseshoe in a daredevil plunge.

The 167-foot drop knocked Munday unconscious, but the bruising crash failed to shake his obsession with Niagara. Returning on 11 October 1987, he successfully shot Niagara's Whirlpool Rapids in a barrel, making him the only living person to "double dare" Niagara.

Dave Munday is the latest of a rare, strange, and daring breed of adventurer who succumbs to Niagara's death lure in order to conquer it — or die trying. Those before Munday who have conquered the Horseshoe in barrels and rubber balls include Annie Edson Taylor (1901), Bobby Leach (1911), Jean Lussier (1928), William FitzGerald alias "Nathan Boya" (1961), Karel Soucek (1984), and Steve Trotter (1985). Three have been killed in daredevil duels with the Horseshoe: Charles Stephens (1920), George Stathakis (1930), and William "Red" Hill, Jr. (1951).

Only one person, in what has been christened "The Miracle of Niagara," has survived a Horseshoe plunge without a barrel or similar protective container. Roger Woodward, a boy of seven, tossed into the upper river in a boating mishap in 1960, was swept over the Falls and rescued by a Maid of the Mist tour boat, saved by the lifejacket he wore. Some, though, attribute his survival to divine intervention.

Woodward's ordeal was a terror beyond words. By contrast, Dave Munday's Horseshoe plunge was a life-long dream come true. He and others like him over the years have heard in the roar of the "Mighty Thunderer" a call to battle, as it were, an insistent voice urging them on, promising fame, money, and the highest experience of living if they would defeat Niagara's deadly power. Back in the 1800s death-defying funambulists danced on tightropes strung across the Niagara Gorge, amazingly without fatality. The rampaging Whirlpool Rapids, challenged by numerous adventurers since 1861, has swept six of them to their deaths. Nowadays stunting at Niagara, without special permission from Niagara Parks authorities, is outlawed, and under no circumstances are barrel-rides over the Falls permitted. Arrest and a fine ranging from $500 to $1500 faces anyone who performs this feat (assuming he or she survives to face charges), or anyone who even attempts the drop.

There is little else authorities can do. They know that if somebody feels the urge to plunge over the Falls, and cannot resist it, virtually nothing can stop him or her. There will always be wily Dave Mundays to elude the vigilant eye of the U.S. and Canadian Parks police, and although they are always alert for individuals acting suspiciously at the brinks of the Falls, police know that Niagara will inevitably reap an annual harvest of suicides. "The Call of Niagara" must be answered.

Niagara Falls/
The Curse of Devil's Hole

The Devil's Hole is located on the American side of the rocky Niagara Gorge about midway between the Whirlpool and Lewiston, N.Y. The hole-like cave is a gloomy, smoke-blackened chamber about twenty-five feet deep. Far above the river's edge, it was carved out of limestone ages ago. Together with winding gorge pathways and the grassy flat land above, it forms Devil's Hole State Park, a popular recreation locale visited in safety by thousands every year.

But, as Dwight Whalen explained in his article "The Curse of Devil's Hole" in the Niagara Falls *Gazette*, 24 January 1985, "Legend warns, and history proves, that Devil's Hole can bring devilish bad luck to the unwary. No other spot along the Niagara River, except for the deadly Falls themselves, has witnessed so much unexpected misfortune and tragedy."

The Senecas regarded the cave as the abode of the Evil Spirit. The explorer LaSalle, who arrived at Niagara in 1678, was allegedly warned by an Indian guide not to visit the cave for fear of disturbing its demon. LaSalle ignored the warning and ventured inside. Thereafter, it was noted, disastrous misfortunes plagued his explorations of the New World, culminating in his murder by mutineers in Lousiana in 1687.

A wagon-train of settlers escorted by British soldiers passing the cliff-top above the Devil's Hole was massacred by Senecas on 14 September 1763. A number of children have lost their footing here and plunged to their deaths. White men have reported being attacked by Indians near the cave. Indian bodies were found below it. Rockfalls were regularly reported in the vicinity, especially in connection with the Great Gorge Route, a scenic trolley line which had to be abandoned. Hours after riding on the line on 6 September 1901, U.S. President William McKinley was assassinated at the Pan American Exposition in Buffalo. On 1 July 1917 occurred the worst tragedy in Niagara River history. A train car carrying some fifty passengers derailed and plunged into the river above the rapids when a retaining wall below the tracks gave way. The hard-luck Great Gorge Route line was abandoned in the 1930s.

Whalen included in his account the spectre of a contemporary horror:

> Marvels of modern technology, not invisible bogeymen, capture our imaginations today. We live in the Age of Science. But we also are learning that progress, so-called, can have its own hidden horrors. Environmental experts tell us that hazardous chemical wastes from Niagara Falls dumpsites are seeping into the Niagara gorge and river. Bloody Run, which once ran red with the blood of slaughtered soldiers, now trickles into Devil's Hole contaminated with toxic chemicals.

Niagara Falls/
The Haunting of Lundy's Lane

From time to time observers report seeing a ghostly formation proceed across the field of battle known as Lundy's Lane. The formation consists of five old soldiers who are dressed in the manner of the Royal Scots. They limp across the battle field and then disappear in the distance.

It is presumed that they fell during the Battle of Lundy's Lane, a bloody incident in the War of 1812 which occurred on 25 July 1814. As Drummond Hill Cemetery now occupies part of the battlefield, it is presumed the five soldiers lie buried on the grounds.

Niagara Falls/
"A Ghost at Stamford"

The characteristics of the oral tradition of an earlier age may be determined in the account that follows which orginally appeared under the title "A Ghost at Stamford" in the Niagara Falls *Evening Journal* on 4 March 1872. The letters G.W.R.R. refer to the Great Western railroad crossing in Stamford Township.

> It is related by good authority that the ghost of the late Mr. Cale (a negro) is disturbing the peace and quiet of Stamford Township. The spectre first appeared to a German woman, who was greatly alarmed. She says his ghost-ship was clothed in the garments worn by Cale when on earth, had a haggard countenance, with flaming eyes, and was barefooted. The ghost was next seen by Mr. Berryman, who was very much frightened, and made lively time for home, arriving there in an exhausted condition. Mr. B. cannot be induced now to venture out after dark. The ghost walks barefooted from the G.W.R.R. crossing down to an old log house, which Cale formerly possessed, and back across Mr. Berryman's fields—a distance of half a mile. The footmarks in the snow have been seen by Mr. Foster and others, who positively declare that they are Cale's, because he was in the habit of going barefooted. Great consternation prevails in the vicinity among the people, more especially among the Celtic portion, who keep within doors at night. Why the ghost has returned to disturb the tranquility of the place is a query to the Celts. As one of them says: "He's been kilt, murdur'd, or hurt in some way." The reason assigned for the return of the ghost is that the affairs of the deceased were not settled as he desired when he died, and he has therefore come back to adjust matters.

Niagara Falls/
Houdini Magical Hall of Fame

The word "magic" has special meaning at the Houdini Magical Hall of Fame. The amusement parlour on Clifton Hill in Niagara Falls was opened on 6 June 1968 to exhibit the personal and theatrical effects of Harry Houdini (1874–1926), the most famous magician of the twentieth century and one of the greatest escape artists of all time. Some effects of the stage mentalist Joseph Dunninger are also on display.

As for the special meaning of the word "magic," perhaps it is wise to take a leaf from James Randi's book of tricks and distinguish between conjuring and magic. The former is trickery for the purpose of entertainment; the latter is trickery for the purpose of deception. The Amazing Randi describes himself not as a magician but as a conjurer; Houdini would doubtless agree with the designation, for he devoted many years to exposing fraudulent magicians.

Houdini died of complications following a blow to the abdomen delivered backstage at the Princess Theatre in Montreal. He died in Detroit on Halloween, 1926, after he had assured his wife that he would try to communicate with her from "the beyond." Whether he succeeded or not was for some years a hotly debated issue because various spirit mediums have maintained they were in receipt of his messages from the spirit world.

Throughout the English-speaking world (and perhaps beyond it), *séances* have been conducted each Halloween since 1926 for the purpose of contacting Houdini's spirit. Apparently the pursuit of his spirit was so popular on Halloween night 1973 that a total of sixty-three separate *séances* were scheduled! The great escape artist, with a choice of venues, chose none. Houdini himself was sceptical about the possibility of survival after death but was always willing to conduct an experiment and to scrutinize the protocols and procedures of others.

The first *séance* at the newly opened Houdini Magical Hall of Fame was staged on Halloween night 1968. The medium failed to communicate with anyone or anything. Some observers felt that the sessions were in bad taste and were nothing more than publicity stunts. Other observers argued that the sessions were consistent with Houdini's concern with survival and demonstrations of the fact that communication with the departed was a chimera. The willing participation of long-time friends of Houdini like Joseph Dunninger and Walter B. Gibson and of conjurers the calibre of James Randi lent authority to the latter view that some useful purpose was being served.

More than a dozen *séances* have been held in Niagara Falls, not all at the Houdini Magical Hall of Fame. A notable session was the one held at the Hall in 1974. As the medium Ann Fisher finished speaking, a pot of flowers and a book about Houdini fell from a shelf and crashed to the floor. The book was open at a page featuring a Houdini poster titled "Do Spirits Return?" While the incident was judged to be inconclusive, some of the participants felt that the whole thing had been neatly pre-arranged by the Amazing Randi.

For the session held at Lillie Langtry's night club in 1981, the medium Joanna Honsberger (sometimes called by the local press "the blonde witch of Niagara Falls" on account of her stunning coiffeur) arranged for fourteen chairs to be place on stage before the 150 or so observers. With the approach of midnight, six men and six women, all appropriately dressed in black, were seated. The medium took the thirteenth chair. The fourteenth remained empty, as it was reserved for Houdini, who was once more a no-show.

All of Houdini's appearances at Niagara Falls have been "live" ones. In his heyday he regularly performed his escape acts on both sides of the border. He was fascinated by the Falls themselves, and made an early silent motion picture called *The Man from Beyond* which culminated in a daring rescue on the Niagara River. At the time of his death Houdini was thinking about an escape act that had him nailed into a packing crate which would then be shoved over Niagara Falls. "So that the crowd can see that I am being nailed into the case, the nailing is done on a platform, into which I can slide after the box is nailed up," he confided to his notebook. "The best way would be to have the platform on a large wagon, which is drawn down to the landing place, where I get into the water according to opportunity. Or else

I get back into the box when placed on the wagon, and be found there, having failed to escape and being knocked out coming over the falls. This can be worked into an extra good idea and needs quite a bit or work." It is a pity he never had the opportunity to perfect what could be called the Great Niagara Falls Daredevil Escape!

Niagara Falls/
The Screaming Tunnel

A scene of horror and ghostly cries in legend, the Screaming Tunnel on the northern outskirts of Niag-

It is said that on certain nights the sounds of screams are heard coming from this railway tunnel on the outskirts of Niagara Falls. Known locally as the Screaming Tunnel, it was featured in the horror movie The Dead Zone. *In this photograph a figure, arms akimbo, stands 125 feet from the camera. [Hawkshead Services]*

ara Falls, Ontario has also been the scene of movie-making horror. Canadian film director David Cronenberg, impressed with the dank, creepy atmosphere of this CNR underpass, made it a murder site and the setting for a tense scene in his horror movie *The Dead Zone* (1983), based on Stephen King's novel of the same name. Other scenes of the film were shot at nearby Niagara-on-the-Lake.

The tunnel of rough cut stone, 16 feet high and 125 feet long, passes under a railway bed at an isolated spot off Warner Road, not far from an accident-plagued stretch of the Queen Elizabeth Highway known locally as the Sand Plant Hill. Many years ago, according to popular legend, a girl fleeing a nearby burning barn, her clothes ablaze, stumbled into the tunnel and died there, her agonized screams echoing off the tunnel's gloomy stones. And her death cries echo to this day. Strike a match inside the Screaming Tunnel, some say, listen quietly, and you can faintly hear the sound of the burning girl's screams.

Niagara Falls/
Psychic Predicts Rockslide

The Niagara region is know to Canadians as the Niagara Peninsula and to Americans as the Niagara Frontier. To Pat St. John, a Bridgewater, Connecticut, psychic certified by the Arthur Ford International School of Mediums, the Niagara region is known as a disaster area.

She was conducting a *séance* on 9 June 1979 when she had an unexpected vision that a "breakwater" or "dam" in the river above Niagara Falls would give way. The onrush of waters would flood the Gorge and capsize the *Maid of the Mist* tour boat, drowning deaf children aboard the vessel. She first publicly mentioned the vision on a local television program on 27 June. The prediction attracted local interest. Then, yielding to the media to give the precise date and time of the catastrophe, she predicted that the disaster would occur on 22 July at either four minutes before 5:00 p.m., or five minutes before 4:00 p.m.

A number of other psychics admitted to similar premonitions, and a local school board cancelled a trip

aboard the *Maid of the Mist* scheduled for a class of deaf students. Little attention was paid to the prediction until seismic sensors sounded at Terrapin Point at 6:06 p.m. on 13 July — Friday the Thirteenth. The next day the U.S. Army Corps of Engineers determined that the rocks above Terrapin Point, an area of Goat Island that had been closed to the public since 1971, had shifted at least a quarter-inch. The rock shift sparked international media interest and shifted attention away from a "breakwater" or a "dam" and onto Terrapin Point.

Pat St. John joined the crowd of spectators at Niagara Falls on Sunday, 22 July. The crowd totalled 155,000, about twice the usual size for a summer Sunday. Passengers aboard the *Maid of the Mist* included the mayors of the twin cities of Niagara Falls, Ontario, and Niagara Falls, New York. There was no disaster. Nothing unexpected happened. There was apprehension and curiosity, but no rockslide, flooding, or capsizing. Interviewed later by reporters, the psychic explained that she had been "pressured" by the media to come up with a specific date. The date was obviously wrong, she explained but the time of day was right. There would definitely be a rockslide and it would definitely occur at 4:56 p.m. "some day."

Members of the Jehovah's Witnesses, attending a convention in the area, stated their belief that Pat St. John was possessed of the devil. More to the point was the opinion of Paul Kurtz, Chairman of the Committee for the Scientific Investigation of Claims of the Paranormal. Interviewed by reporters, he noted, "It is common knowledge that the Falls is eroding and there have been numerous rock slides over the years. The fact that a sensor apparatus went off recently was coincidental." Kurtz added, "The public hears when psychics succeed, very rarely when they fail."

Niagara-on-the-Lake/
Burying Grounds

Niagara-on-the-Lake is picturesque, historic and haunted. It has more ghosts per capita than any other community in the country.

Butler's Rangers were a corps of Loyalist refugees raised by John Butler. When they were disbanded in 1784, Butler and many of his Rangers settled in the Niagara area. Now many of them lie in Butler's Burying Grounds at Niagara-on-the-Lake.

In *Pen Pictures of Early Pioneer Life in Upper Canada* (1905), by A "Canuck" (of the Fifth Generation), the author offered some general observations about the calibre of the Loyalist irregulars.

> The common saying that none of the Rangers were known to die a natural death was but one amongst the many other exaggerations as we know from ocular proof to the contrary. As has just been said, it is admitted that some of the Rangers were of a low type of men. But one black sheep or two should not be accepted as true representatives of a hardy, courageous and enterprising type of guerilla soldiers. Here is an instance that will explain our meaning: One of the Old Rangers, who lived alone on the Niagara, was the dread of the women and children in the neighbourhood on account of the frightful stories he told. When he died, it is said, the coffin would not stay in the ground, but one end kept coming to the surface. The superstitious people in the neighbourhood attributed this fact to his wickedness, whereas the real cause was quicksand!

Niagara-on-the-Lake/
Sobbing Sophia

Local tradition maintains that the sobs of Sobbing Sophia may be heard today, a century and three-quarters after they were caused.

Sophia was Miss Sophia Shaw, the fiancée of Major-General Sir Isaac Brock, the gallant young military commander and administrator of Upper Canada. The story goes that before setting out for the Battle of Queenston Heights, which took place on 13 October 1812, Brock paid his respects to the young Miss Shaw at her family's residence in Newark, as Niagara-on-the-Lake was then known. They kissed chastely and parted. Brock never returned from the battle, and Miss Shaw never recovered from the loss of her bethrothed.

Apparently she lived the rest of her life in barren spinsterhood. She was known to sob uncontrollably at the thought of her lost love. After the death of her parents, she remained in the family residence when it was managed by her brother and sister-in-law. When they moved elsewhere, she removed herself to Toronto where she died alone in a rented room. The original home was destroyed during the War of 1812, but another was erected on the original site. Subsequent occupants reported hearing strange, sobbing sounds which, tradition holds, are created by the inconsolable spirit of Miss Shaw — Sobbing Sophia.

Niagara-on-the-Lake/
The Ghostly Captain of the Oban Inn

Watching over the Oban Inn is said to be the ghost of Captain Duncan Mallory. It was Captain Mallory who built the handsome inn about 1824. It later served as a hostelry and, during the First Wolrd War, as an officer's mess. It was acquired by the Burroughs family in 1962, who completely restored it to its elegant Victorian décor and continue to operate it as a country-style inn.

The halls of the inn are said to reverberate with the footsteps of the ghost of Captain Mallory. The ghost is not seen, only heard at night. As it prowls the halls it probably takes pride in how well the inn has been maintained and operated. At other times another ghost is reported, this one being seen rather than heard. Guests and hired help have reported seeing the spectre of an old woman, somewhat dishevelled in dress and disorganized in demeanour. No one knows or has yet guessed her name or mission.

Niagara-on-the-Lake/
Butchery at the Buttery

The Buttery is a popular restaurant near the Shaw Festival's old Courthouse Theatre. Diners and restaurant help have reported "disturbances" in the basement and in the rooms on the second floor. It is maintained that the Buttery occupies a building which was erected on the former site of a private home in which cold-blooded murder was committed on 7 April 1850. The murder took place on the second floor and the body was buried in the basement. The particulars appeared in Jim Blundell's account in the St. Catharines *Standard,* 31 October 1981.

The victim was Lloyd Burns who is variously depicted as insane, drunken, or epileptic. He was a violent man but he went too far and attacked his long-suffering and pregnant wife Kate. Kate rebelled and with the help of her brother Philip crept up on Lloyd and threw him down the stairs to his death. They buried him in the basement. Kate was subsequently overcome with remorse and came to a bad end herself. It is her spirit that causes the "disturbances" that are reported in the Buttery.

It is not immediately apparent how much of this is fact and how much of it is fiction, for the details derive from a reconstruction of the past arranged by Geraldine Smith, a well-known Brampton psychic. She visited the Buttery on a number of occasions in 1981, went into a trance, established the cause of the problem, and exorcised the place so that today it is free of any "disturbances."

Niagara-on-the-Lake/
Elizabeth the Ghost

Elizabeth is the name given to the ghost which will not leave the historic Hawley-Breckenridge House in Niagara-on-the-Lake. The house was built in the Southern Colonial style in 1796. The earliest reports of it being haunted were made after 1899 when it was acquired by Major Charles Stanley Herring, an officer with the British Army in India. He reported seeing the ghost of a woman in a long grey dress who "disappeared like smoke" on at least one occasion.

The house was acquired by Aileen and Frank Hawley in 1953 who knew nothing of its ghostly occupant at the time of the purchase. Soon they grew accustomed to the knocker on the front door sounding and to raps on the back door when no one was there. They and their guests reported seeing the ghostly figure of a young woman on the main floor of the older parts of the building. She appeared to be in her thirties and she was wasp-waisted in the fashion of the time. She was wearing a long dress and had on a bonnet which was tied under her chin. She had a gentle face and she was called Elizabeth. A psychic who said she saw the spirit said it was the ghost of a woman who died in the house in the mid-1800s after devoting many years to the care of her parents. It appeared she did not relish leaving the house, preferring to die there than to leave it.

The haunted house was described by Michael Clarkson in the article "Gentle Ghost Visits Niagara Home" in the St. Catharines *Standard* on 30 October 1982. He quoted Mrs. Hawley on a typical appearance of Elizabeth. "She walks or stands for a few seconds, then disappears; but it's not a frightening experience. It's just as if she's checking to see if everything's okay."

Niagara-on-the-Lake/
Mystery Lights

Residents of Niagara-on-the-Lake were seeing so many strange and mysterious sights and lights in the skies above Lake Ontario in the 1975–80 period that they gave them little heed. It was the tourists attending the Shaw Festival who found them remarkable. The celestial shows were visible over the lake between Oakville and Oshawa and beyond. The lights were brighter than the planets and stars. They were always the same colour, deep orange. Their movements were executed at ultra-high speeds. The lights moved erratically around in the dusky sky, often making ninety-degree turns.

The mystery lights were repeatedly observed by numerous residents, among them Harry Picken, an aeronautical engineer and president of Genaire Limited, a St. Catharines-based firm which produces high-technology components for the Department of National Defence. Picken was a member of the American Institute of Aeronautics and Astronautics and the Canadian Aeronautics and Space Institute.

Harry Picken saw the lights for the first time at 9:30 p.m. on 9 April 1975. He described what he saw to John Dueck, a newsman with the Niagara *Advance,* 17 April 1975:

> There were three or four lights in the sky. At times they remained stationary; then they moved in an erratic way. They were [a] glowing, orange colour, and at times turned suddenly very bright, like a Roman candle, and then would go out again.
>
> The lights were certainly not those of an aircraft. Aircraft do not create lights of orange colour and are not of an intensity as these lights were. Through binoculars we could see aircraft flying above Toronto with much dimmer bluish and red lights. The landing lights create an altogether different effect. The illumination of the lights in the sky had an entirely different source than that of airplanes.

Picken said much the same to Paul Wilson of the Niagara Falls *Review* on 15 March 1980:

> They're seen most often in the winter months when there are high waves on the lake. Usually conditions are such that nobody in their right mind would be involved in manoeuvres. Rescue would be impossible. Besides, through my work I have a good idea of the activities of the air force. It's not them.
>
> These objects are not mirages. They move in a positive fashion as if controlled by some form of intelligence. And almost invariably their lights dim when aircraft pass overhead from Toronto. I offer no opinion. But I do say there are certain things we don't understand.

When he was interviewed by Michael Clarkson of the St. Catharines *Standard,* 11 October 1980, Picken stated: "What people are seeing cannot be explained away as physical phenomena . . . there's nothing in science to match it."

In the year 1800, as Clarkson noted, Mrs. Simcoe, wife of John Graves Simcoe, the first Lieutenant-Governor of Upper Canada, was the first person to observe (or at least mention) globes of light in the sky over the lake. In 1975, a right-angled, bar-like streak or band appeared in a Landsat satellite image of the Welland area of the lake. In the October 1981 issue, the editors of *Omni* published a photograph of an immensely long, cylindrical vehicle with portals and a rounded nose, light green and dull grey in colour. Over the years a host of UFOlogists have suggested that the mystery lights are really unidentified flying objects which come not from deep space but from the depths of Lake Ontario where there may be found a secret submarine UFO base.

Niagara-on-the-Lake/ The Spirit of the Angel Inn

The spirit of a British officer is said to haunt the Angel Inn, which is located at 224 Regent Street in Niagara-on-the-Lake. For some years the historic inn has been owned and operated by Florence LeDoux, a vivacious woman who was born and raised in the Niagara Peninsula and who admits to the occasional psychic experience.

In August 1987, Mrs. LeDoux related to the writer and researcher Dwight Whalen the full story of her involvement with the spirit of the British Officer, Captain Swayze.

"He was like family when we were kids," says Mrs. LeDoux, who was born at the Angel Inn, and whose great-great grandparents, she claims, witnessed Captain Swayze's death. "He's a mischievous, earth-bound spirit, earthbound through suffering."

As a young girl she remembers seeing chairs propelled across the room by an invisible force, and often dishes would noisily rattle in the cupboard for no apparent reason. Her grandmother, hearing the racket, would make Florence and the other children take the dishes out and wash them because she didn't want the family eating off plates that had been touched by a ghost. Eventually the children, whenever they heard the plates begin to rattle, would burst into singing to drown out the noise, and thus escape having to do the dishes.

Established in 1823 by Richard Howard, who supposedly named it "Angel" after his pet name for his wife, the Angel Inn was built where the Harmonious Coach House formerly stood, a three-room log cabin where Swayze was slain and which was largely burned when American forces torched Newark (Niagara-on-the-Lake) in 1813.

A British psychic visiting the Angel Inn some years ago told Mrs. LeDoux that she strongly felt Swayze's

The proprietoress Florence LeDoux is shown standing outside the Angel Inn, a popular restaurant and inn at Niagara-on-the-Lake, Ont. The inn is haunted, it is maintained, by the restless spirit of Captain Colin Swayze whose portrait hangs within. Swayze was a British officer tortured to death on this site by American invaders during the War of 1812. [Hawkshead Services]

presence. When she returned to England she began a genealogical search which surprisingly turned up a portrait of the captain. The painting now hangs in a corner of the inn where, according to the psychic, Swayze died. "I think he looks like our Prince of Wales," says Mrs. LeDoux, proudly. "Very handsome."

After several youths vandalized the painting one New Year's Eve, Mrs. LeDoux had it restored, but the artist complained that he couldn't eliminate a "teardrop" which had inexplicably appeared below Swayze's right eye. Three times he removed it, he said, but each time it returned. Finally, says Mrs. LeDoux, an Inn patron, thinking the teardrop was a blemish on the canvas, scratched it off, removing a tiny spot of paint underneath, and the tear has never reappeared.

Nor has Swayze himself ever appeared, unless one credits the tales of frightened cleaning women who claimed to have been startled by the sight of a "man in a red coat" in the ladies' room.

But the captain still makes his presence known by poltergeist antics. One night about three years ago Mrs. LeDoux was closing up the inn with her maître d', Bruce Cartwright, who had always scoffed at the story of Swayze's "ghost," when suddenly dishes began rattling, a cupboard door flew open, and three saucers floated out into the room. "They flew around the fireplace and landed on the bar," recalls Mrs. LeDoux, "one behind the other, like ducks, then fell on the floor and shattered." Mr. Cartwright's scoffing days were over.

Swayze's most recent disturbance occurred during the summer of 1987. One night, following a disagreement with Mrs. LeDoux after the inn closed, Mr. Cartwright was alone in the tavern when a metal beer stein, hanging from a nail in one of the hand-hewn ceiling beams, flew across the room and struck a post beside the bar where he was standing, missing his head by inches.

The stein still hangs on the peg from which it was hurled at Mr. Cartwright, its lip dented from impact with the post. Evidently Captain Swayze and Mrs. LeDoux are still "like family."

Lake Nipigon/
The Thunderbirds

The art of Norval Morrisseau is infused with the traditional teachings of the Ojibway of the Lake Nipigon area. The painter was born in 1932 at Sand Point Reserve, near Beardmore, and from his maternal grandfather, Moses Nanakonagos, he heard the stories, learned the lore, and was moved by the motifs. His Ojibway name is Copper Thunderbird.

Morrisseau was ostracized by the elders for making use of the motifs — including the so-called "x-ray style" which is so characteristic of the art of the Woodland Indians — but with the success of his first show at the Pollock Gallery in Toronto in 1962 and the tokens of respect paid by whites to the depiction of the traditional images, the opposition of the elders turned into praise. His courage and the boldness of his work inspired an entire generation of talented Woodland Indian artists.

Morrisseau described the massive bird-like beings known as the Thunderbirds in *Legends of My People, The Great Ojibway* (1965), edited by the native art specialist Selwyn Dewdney. When they blinked their eyes shot out lighting. When they flapped their wings thunder was heard.

I was told that the thunderbirds were believed to have a great nest on one of the mountains by Lake Superior. Some eighty-five years ago two young boys started to climb this mountain to find out if a thunderbird really was there although they had been told never to go up that mountain. When they got to the top they saw two big newly hatched birds who were still hairy and whose eyes blinked light like flashes of lightning. The frightened boys ran down the hill and told what they had seen. An Indian who in his youth had seen these boys died at Heron Bay some years ago. Later this same story was told to me by a relative who said that the birds moved away, where it is not known. Huge stone nests of these majestic birds are still seen in some parts of Ontario.

North Bay/
The NORAD Sightings

Two separate UFO sightings were reported by veteran RCAF airmen at the North Bay Air Force Base, one of five NORAD Control Centres on the North American continent. The nocturnal sightings were made outdoors in 1952.

Warrant Officer W.J. Yeo, a master telecommunications technician, and Sergeant D.V. Crandell, an instrument technician, spotted a luminous, disk-shaped craft streaking across the night sky on New Year's Day. They watched it make its way across the sky at a high altitude for more than eight minutes, changing direction from time to time.

Warrant Officer E.H. Rossell, an aircraft maintenance superintendent, and Flight Sergeant Reginald McRae observed a disk move across the sky at a terrific speed, reverse direction, and then disappear. This sighting was made at 8:30 p.m., 12 April.

The two sets of sightings by four experienced observers had a surprising effect. The Defence Research Board launched Project Second Storey, an interdepartmental committee to monitor existing government UFO research and establish new policy guidelines. This effect was noted by Yurko Bondarchuk in *UFO: Sightings, Landings and Abductions* (1979), who added: "Many critics feel Project Second Storey was ultimately instrumental in 'covering up' UFO research between 1954 and 1966."

Lake Ontario/
"Not the First One"

Lake Ontario, the smallest of the Great Lakes, has been likened in shape to an Indian moccasin. In fact, so has Lake Erie, the second-smallest of the five Lakes.

Not far from the mouth of the Niagara River, two youngsters reported "a hideous water snake, or serpent, of prodigious dimensions." The account comes from the *Farmers' Journal and Welland Canal Intelligencer,* 5 August 1829.

Lake Serpent.—A neighbour informs us, that his children (from 10 to 14 years old) were a few

189

days since playing on the lake shore, near the mouth of 10 mile creek, Grantham, when suddenly appeared in the water a few feet from the spot where they were standing, a hideous water snake, or serpent, of prodigious dimensions. According to their account, it must have been twenty or thirty feet in length, with a head ten or fifteen inches in diameter, and warts or bunches on it. On giving the alarm, it immediately turned and disappeared. — This, we believe, is not the first one of the kind that had been seen in Lake Ontario; and from what we can learn, here can be no doubt of the existence of such monsters in our inland seas.

Lake Ontario/
The Marysburgh Vortex

The Marysburgh Vortex is the name given by Hugh F. Cochrane to an area of Lake Ontario that is shaped like a funnel. It includes Wolfe Island where the Lake narrows into the Thousand Island region of the St. Lawrence River. Cochrane described the Marysburgh Vortex in terms of a "vile vortex" in *Gateway to Oblivion: The Great Lakes' Bermuda Triangle* (1980):

> This vortex, like the famed Bermuda Triangle, is a swath of water in the eastern end of the lake that has a long history of bizarre circumstances that have caused the loss of numerous ships and their crews. According to marine insurance records, the Great Lakes have a higher concentration of shipping accidents than any comparable area elsewhere. And it has held this unenviable position for over a hundred years.

He noted that there are fourteen known magnetic anomalies included on current navigational charts for the region. He described incident after incident of curious encounters and odd abandonments. Captain Charles Selleck of the *Lady Murray* in the spring of 1804 reported seeing a strange object beneath the surface of the water near the entrance to Presqu'ile Bay. "The huge stone monolith was standing upright like a giant tombstone in an incredible fifty fathoms of water!" Thereafter the ship vanished in a storm

and so did the "monolith." One abandonment was the seaworthy vessel the *Bavaria*. It was found crewless in May 1889 near the Main Duck Islands. "The only living thing on the ship was a canary that still chirped in its cage in one of the cabins." To Cochrane the region "outranks the Bermuda Triangle."

Orillia/
The Ghost of St. Columbkill's

St. Columbkill, one of the lesser-known saints in the Roman Catholic roster, has a church named in his honour set amid its own graveyard on the outskirts of Orillia. St. Columbkill's Roman Catholic Church is said to be haunted. Some of the details appeared in Jess Stearn's *The Search for the Girl with the Blue Eyes* (1968).

Around the turn of the century, it seems, Father Henry McPhillips, the pastor, whose body lies buried in the graveyard, died an untimely death. The story goes that he returns periodically to brood over the fortunes of his flock. One of his return appearances in the early 1960s was described by the Orillia *Packet and Times*:

> A shadowy figure floated across the gallery and, sitting down at the keyboard, started playing the organ. He played beautifully. Some of the watching girls screamed and fled but others stayed to see the figure vanish mysteriously into the belfry. The legendary "ghost" of St. Columbkill's Roman Catholic Church had returned.

One of the girls, a cleaning woman, described the appearance of the ghost: "We were all cleaning the church when suddenly this figure floated across the gallery and started playing the organ. It was dressed in a black choir gown and black hat with a white face. Only the eyes were visible." A carpenter saw it and lunged for it, but the figure eluded him and disappeared.

The position of the present pastor on the ghost is that it is all hearsay and gossip, for the church is not haunted.

Orillia/
Account of a Stigmatic

An interesting account of a stigmatic appears in the memoirs of Evan Shute, the Ontario medical doctor who practised in London and promoted the use of Vitamin E Therapy. The book referred to is *The Vitamin E Story: The Medical Memoirs of Evan Shute* (1985) edited by Dr. James C.M. Shute.

Dr. Shute joined a group which included some Roman Catholic priests and seminarians when they visited the forty-eight-year-old stigmatic, Mrs. Donald McIsaacs, in the bedroom of her farmhouse at Uptergrove, east of Orillia. The visit took place on 16 June 1952. Dr. Shute wrote:

> We all stood motionless in the stifling heat. Mrs. McIsaacs lay on the bed in a trance with her eyes closed and bloody smears on her forehead above the hairline and on the palms and backs of both hands. There were drops on her nightgown over her left breast on her pillow. There was no fresh bleeding, merely fresh smears and smudges. Mrs. McIsaacs was the only Canadian stigmatist there ever has been — someone who apparently bears wounds corresponding to those of the crucified Christ. This all began in 1939 when her feet began to bleed. She consulted her priest and he finally recognized it as a stigmata when her hands also began bleeding. Now on every Friday, but notably on Good Friday and on the first Friday of each month, she has three hours of Passion suffering.

Mrs. McIsaacs tossed about, occasionally twitching, relating in a clear monotone: "I see our beloved Saviour as the mob stones and blasphemes Him. He turns to bless them. His blessed mother turns to them urging them not to increase His suffering. She tells them that He has already suffered." She spoke for the two and a half hours they were there except when the rosary was being said. Dr. Shute observed:

> Everyone in the house seemed sincere and humble. They themselves undoubtedly had implicit belief in all that went on. I saw the fresh bloody smudges at close range. They certainly were bloodstained. The smudge on the dorsum of the last hand was a centimetre in diameter. There was no actual bleeding while I was there. Mrs. Rolland [a friend] said that sometimes her shoes were filled with blood and at times blood poured down from her eyes and forehead to stain her nightgown. She had a stigma on the left side under the heart and in the feet.

Mrs. McIsaac's wounds received a fair amount of media attention. *Maclean's* ran a story on the stigmatic on 15 September 1950. A Canadian Press news story appeared on 18 September 1950. *Time* published its story on 25 September 1950.

Orillia/
Dr. Rolph Alexander

During periods of drought, self-styled "rain-makers" do land-office business. During periods of heavy rainfall, mini-deluges, it is the "cloud-busters" who swing into action. History knows many "rain-makers" but not too many "cloud-busters." The former summon clouds through psychic means to produce downpours. The function has yet to be demonstrated in controlled circumstances. The latter dissipate clouds through psychic means. That function, too, has yet to be verified. One of the world's best-known "cloud-busters" was Dr. Rolph Alexander.

Dr. Rolph Alexander claimed to have the power to cause cloud dispersal through concentration. At one time the "cloud-buster" had a wide following, he was popular with the press, and his books, *Creative Realism: A New Method of Winning* (1954) and *The Power of the Mind* (1956), enjoyed a brief vogue. Alexander was born in New Zealand and ultimately settled in England. In the 1950s he was a resident of Orillia, and it was here that he gave frequent outdoor demonstrations of his supposed powers.

One demonstration was held at nearby Geneva Park on 12 September 1954. It was organized to demonstrate Alexander's theory of "Creative Realism." The event was covered by a CP reporter whose news story

191

appeared in the Niagara Falls *Evening Review*, 13 September 1954. As the reporter explained:

> He chose a cloud and then, claiming to bring his powers of energy transmission into use, concentrated on the cloud. It disappeared in about

three minutes. The same procedure was followed with two other clouds.

Several persons claimed they saw other clouds, not targets of Dr. Alexander's experiment, disappear at the same time. Dr. Alexander agreed that other clouds were probably being

Can "mind power" blast a cloud out of the sky? According to Rolph Alexander, it can. The author and native of New Zealand gave a public demonstration of his purported cloud-blasting at Orillia on 12 September 1954. There were more than fifty witnesses, including the mayor of the Ontario town, a group of reporters, and a news photographer who during the eight-minute demonstration took these four photos. A bystander selected the target cloud (circled), Alexander concentrated his "mind power," and the cloud disintegrated. Meteorologists maintain that fair-weather cumulus clouds disappear anyway. [Allen Spraggett]

broken up by atmospheric conditions, but said he doubted if any broke up as rapidly as his target clouds.

He said the experiment was to demonstrate his theory that the prefontal lobe of the brain can and does radiate some unknown form of energy that has never been measured by science, although the bio-electric energy from the rest of the brain has been found by the use of electrodes.

There is another reference to Alexander's "cloud-busting" in *The Search for the Girl with the Blue Eyes* (1968). The author Jess Stearn wrote:

> Actually, though, the more remote the area—the less intellectually oriented—the more open-minded its people appeared. With even the most routine Orillians, the psychic seemed taken for granted, local journalist Jim Pauk pointing out that this was not at all unusual on the Canadian frontier, where the harshness of the land seemed to demand intuitive rapport of the settler. Nothing of a clairvoyant nature apparently suprised anybody, though a healthy skepticism was everywhere apparent. Many were fascinated when Dr. Rolph Alexander, a notable metaphysician, stood confidently in Couchiching park, presumably dissolving overhead clouds with the magnetic action of his mind.

There is a debunking of Alexander by Denys Parsons in "Detective Work in Parapsychology" in *A Skeptic's Handbook of Parapsychology* (1985) edited by Paul Kurtz.

Orillia/
The Girl with the Blue Eyes

More people believe in the theory of reincarnation than in any other religious notion. It forms the backbone of Hinduism and Buddhism and of numerous other religions and spiritual systems. Its only rival in the race for global popularity is the theory of astrology.

In the Western world the notion that the soul or spirit of a person inhabits body after body, working out its *karma* from incarnation to incarnation, was brought to public attention and became a subject of controversy following the publication of the bestselling book *The Search for Bridey Murphy* and the subsequent release of excerpts from the long-play record associated with it.

The story of "the search for the girl with blue eyes" is really the search for the relationship between two girls with blue eyes. Perhaps in the story and in the search a point of difference is marked between the past-life memories of Canadians and the past-life memories of people from other parts of the world. When subjects elsewhere are hypnotized and regressed to recall their past identities and deeds, it seems they have exciting things to remember and breathless tales to tell. They were once Cleopatra, or at the very least they lived alongside the Nile. They were once Napoleon, or at the very least they took part in revolutionary activities. But when a teenage girl from Orillia is hypnotized and regressed, what does she recall? It turns out that in her previous existence she was an illiterate farm girl and childless housewife who lived her entire life in the Upper Canadian woods.

The tale which Jess Stearn told in *The Search for the Girl with the Blue Eyes* (1968) could begin in the year 1835 in Grey County, Upper Canada, but Stearn's account really begins on 15 February 1963. That was the day an advertisement appeared in the Personal Column of the *Toronto Star* which read as follows: "Anyone interested in assisting research of a case surpassing Bridey Murphy in importance and proven locally in Ontario. Contact M. Ganier, General Delivery, Orillia."

The advertisement caught the eye of David Manuel, a young, energetic, American-born editor with Doubleday Canada Ltd. He was motivated by a personal curiosity about the paranormal and a professional desire to return to the head office of Doubleday in Garden City, N.Y., and take over Doubleday's "occult list" where he could commission bestselling books on paranormal subjects by such writers as Jess Stearn.

The advertisement which drew attention to "the Canadian Bridey Murphy" was placed by Kenneth

MacIver of Orillia. MacIver was interested in hypnotism, and the Bridey Murphy case led him on 5 October 1962 to hypnotize his oldest daughter, thirteen-year-old Joanna MacIver. Joanna was a bright and lively teenager whose most arresting feature was a set of deep blue eyes. She went easily into a deep trance and then, almost by accident, regressed to a past life. To the astonishment of her father and other family members and neighbours, she answered their questions, seemingly recalling specific details of a past existence.

A note of caution should be sounded at this point. The subject of hypnotic regression is not one that is lightly explained. Even the practice of hypnotism, which was once called mesmerism, is little understood. One psychological theory of hypnotism is that it can be explained in terms of a behavioural pact, an implicit and voluntary agreement between the person acting as the hypnotist and the person acting as the hypnotee that the one will issue the orders and that the other will carry them out.

One should approach with additional caution the notions of "regression" and "past lives." It is a good question why anyone should recall a previous existence in a trance state which has been induced by hypnotic means but not during reverie or meditation or analysis. A clue to the answer might be the atmosphere in which most regression sessions take place. The ambience recalls that of the *séance,* where the medium is encouraged to manifest if not spirits from "the vast deep", then multiple personalities from the depths of the psyche.

The hypnotic regression sessions took place over a period of four years, and the details recalled by Joanna MacIver permitted her father to piece together the details of her past life. Apparently the daughter had lived before as Susan Ganier, born about 1835 near the town of Massie, in Grey County, west of Orillia. The life she lived was an unhappy and unfulfilled one. Susan was dominated and repressed by her father, a tenant farmer of French-Canadian background who was fearful the farming neighbours would learn of his ancestry. Her education was minimal. At the age of

seventeen she fell in love and married a local farmer, Tommy Marrow, and they lived happily on a farm on Lot 33 on the First Concession Line of Sydenham Township. Then after two years of married life Tommy was killed in an accident. That left Susan a childless widow at the age of nineteen. She had no prospects and no assets, her single point of beauty being her boundless blue eyes. She retreated into herself and died at the age of sixty-eight in 1903.

The portrait of Susan Ganier that emerged from the sessions seemed substantial enough and the fact that it was not the stuff of history seemed a point in its favour. Where did the details come from? Was Joanna MacIver a novelist in the making, unconsciously creating a character as credible as a minor one from the pages of an historical novel devoted to rural life in Upper Canada in the nineteenth century? Was her father, probably without knowing it, asking her leading questions, to which she was replying with ready answers, thereby fleshing out what is known to statisticians as an "artifact," a phantom effect that exists only because of distortions in the process of inquiry? Or was the subject delving deeply into the memories of a previous incarnation?

Many of these questions were asked by Jess Stearn when he was brought into the picture. David Manuel, sensing a bestselling book in the case of "the girl with the blue eyes," met the MacIvers and listened to the tape recordings they made of their regression sessions. He contacted Lee Barker, the Doubleday editor at Garden City, and they commissioned Jess Stearn to explore the situation and, if he felt the potential was there, devote a book to the case. Many of the details about Susan Ganier Marrow were gleaned from the early sessions with Kenneth MacIver. But Stearn sensed the need for an independent hypnotist and arranged for further regression sessions to be conducted by a hypnotist from New York.

There also were attempts to determine the factual basis in the nineteenth century for the memories or imaginings of the twentieth-century girl. The quest took Stearn to rural, township, county, and provincial halls of records. The quest also took Stearn with

Joanna and her father and sometimes David Manuel a number of times to the rough triangle of land called Cape Rich which juts out into Georgian Bay between Owen Sound on the west and Meaford on the east, where Susan lived almost all her life. Included in the region are such communities as Leith, Morley, Annan, and Silcote, as well as a Department of National Defence Tank Range. Just south of the area lies the community of Massie, where Susan was born. The entire region lies just over sixty miles west of Orillia where Joanna was born some forty-two years following the death of Susan.

No birth or death certificates could be found for Susan Marrow (née Ganier), although given the remoteness of the region during the period in question, this was not necessarily meaningful. Some details about the life of Thomas Marrow, a tenant farmer of the time, could be determined to be true. Taken by her father and Stearn to various locales which she had described in her regression sessions, she seemed to recall odd details that could be substaniated. They secured an affidavit from an octogenerian who recalled in his youth a meeting with a woman in her sixties who could have been the Susan in question.

Where does this leave the case of "the girl with the blue eyes?" It leaves it in a literary limbo. Perhaps because the book is more reasonable than many on the subject of reincarnation — it makes no claims, it comes to no conclusions — it remains a good read, expecially for anyone interested in the problems of psychical research. However, one problem with the book is that in researching and writing it Stearn could never decide just where he stood on these questions. Was he a hard-headed reporter? Or was he a psychical researcher set to prove a point or two? Reading between the lines one suspects that any beliefs he had concerning the field of the paranormal did not embrace the theory of reincarnation. The only conclusion he could come to in the book was that "death was no longer oblivion but promise."

Meanwhile, the participants moved on: David Manuel left for Garden City; Jess Stearn went on to write other books; and Joanne MacIver married and moved to Vancouver where she had the children denied Susan Ganier. Through it all Joanne remained unchanged. From the first she felt that she had lived before; at the end she felt the same. In fact, she had other stories to tell — not just Susan's life, but the lives of other people as well. It seems that she had previously lived not only as a childless widow in Upper Canada during the nineteenth century; but also as a farmer on the St. Lawrence River in 1792; as a slave in Virginia who fled with her child to Canada in 1701; and as a native of Africa in A.D. 784. She expressed her belief succinctly. "I'm as old as my memory," she said, "and as young as my body."

Ian Adams, the journalist and novelist, was intrigued with the "girl with the blue eyes." He was not so much interested in reincarnation as he was in how this interesting case was handled by the media and especially by Stearn. He wrote an article called "The Girl Who Lived More Than Once" which appeared in *Maclean's* in May 1968. He found a few details to add to the story that Stearn left out.

To draw attention to the case, Kenneth MacIver initially wrote to Morey Bernstein, the author of *The Search for Bridey Murphy,* asking advice. Bernstein, an amateur hypnotist and full-time businessman in Colorado, directed him to a former Canadian, Dr. Ian Stevenson, of the University of West Virginia, who is mentioned in the book only as "a prominent psychiatrist." As well as being a distinguished psychiatrist, Dr. Stevenson was a skilled hypnotist and a long-time student of cases of suspected reincarnation. He met with Joanna MacIver and tape recorded two sessions with her under hypnosis. With that Dr. Stevenson departed from the scene.

Nonplussed, Kenneth MacIver wrote a 22,000 word manuscript *à la* Bernstein about his findings. He sent it to Matie Molinaro, who heads a literary agency, and Molinaro submitted it to Doubleday, knowing their editor David Manuel's long-standing interest in the subject. What came of that was the commissioning of Stearn to write the book. According to Adams, Stearn received an advance of $100,000 for the book; the accuracy of this statement was subsequently denied by Doubleday, but the size of the advance was never announced. Stearn brought with him Joe Lampl, a hynotist and the founder of the Academy of Applied Mental Sciences in New York, and he conducted seven or eight sessions with Joanna under hypnosis.

Ian Adams found the book that Stearn wrote morally offensive, and Stearn's attitude particularly reprehensible. He rightly pointed out that Stearn cannot figure out where he stands. In one chapter he is as hard-headed (and often as knuckle-headed) as Hemingway; in the next, he admits to psychic intimations of his own, even playfully suggesting that in an earlier existence he had lived in Orillia. Adams noted a number of instances of Stearn's sexual suggestiveness, implying that he was closer to Joanna than she could remember. Then there is his pseudo-lyricism: "And in those eyes, you think to yourself, there are all the numbers of Ulyssean voyages to embark upon." At the same time Joanna was down-to-earth: "She was one of the warmest and gentlest people I had ever met." He never did know where he or anyone else stood on the subject of reincarnation.

Oshawa/
Millerites and Millennialists

Almost everyone feels that the world is rapidly going to the dogs, but the notion that the world is coming to an end—that the end of the world is at hand—is the particular obsession of fundamentalist Christian sectarians known as Millennialists. Attention these days seems fixed on A.D. 2000 as the year of grim reckoning. In sectarian circles in the nineteenth century, other dates were popular.

The fourteenth day of February 1843 was the doomsday of William Miller, an American farmer turned Bible scholar. Miller was a Baptist in New York State whose study of the Bible led him to evolve a doctrine of the imminent Second Coming. He founded a group called the Second Adventists, known as the Millerites, and published a tract in 1842 titled

Evidence from Scripture and History of the Second Coming of Christ about the Year 1843. His followers spread into Upper Canada or Canada West, as Ontario was then known. They too anticipated the Last Day.

Here is how the religiously educated Thomas Conant described the actions of the Canadian Millerites in *Upper Canada Sketches* (1898) as that dread day approached:

> During the winter of 1842–3 the Second Adventists, or Millerites, were preaching that the world would be all burnt up in February, 1843. Nightly meetings were held, generally in the schoolhouses. One E.H., about Prince Albert, Ont., owned a farm of one hundred acres and upwards, stocked with cattle and farm produce, as well as having implements of agriculture. So strongly did he embrace the Second Advent doctrines of the Millerites that he had not a doubt of the fire to come in February and burn all up, and in confirmation of his faith gave away his stock, implements and farm.
>
> Sarah Terwilligar, who lived about a mile east of Oshawa "corners," on the Kingston Road, made for herself wings of silk, and, on the night of the 14th February, jumped off the porch of her home, expecting to fly heavenward. Falling to the ground some fifteen feet, she was shaken up severely and rendered wholly unfit to attend at all to the fires that were expected to follow the next day.
>
> Mr. John Henry, on that 14th of February, was riding alone and met a man on horseback coming at the top of his speed. Accosting Mr. Henry he said, "Say, stranger, do you see that sign in the sky?" Mr. Henry looked up and saw only a sun-dog, frequently seen then and now in the winter season, and replied, "Yes, what of it?" "Well, that's the Lord coming tomorrow to burn the world up," and Mr. H. replied, "Get out! that's only a sun-dog." "Oh! you are an unbeliever," was the retort, as the man dug spurs into his horse's sides as if to ride away from the fire he felt so near.

Miller himself awaited the end of the world in flowing white muslin robes. When his prophecy failed, he returned to the pages of his Bible and soon realized his error. He had mistakenly followed the Hebrew instead of the Roman chronology. After further calculation, he established that the end of the world would occur on 22 October 1844. Even the failure of this prophecy did not dampen the ardour of his Millennialist-minded adherents. The well-known Seventh Day Adventists trace their lineage back to the Millerites.

Ottawa/
National Gallery of Art

There is a story told about one of the best-known paintings in the collection of the National Gallery of Art. The painting is a neo-classical composition in oil called *The Death of Wolfe.*

James Wolfe expired on the Plains of Abraham after taking Quebec on 13 September 1759. The popular image of him lying in the arms of his fellow officers, being observed by a crouching Indian, is derived from that painting which was conceived and executed in the heroic manner by Benjamin West, the fashionable London-based, historical painter.

When West completed *The Death of Wolfe* in London in 1770, it was immediately hailed as a masterpiece. He was commissioned to complete three other versions of it, one intended for George III. One reason for the acclaim was the fact that for the first time the figures in a major historical tableau were painted wearing the clothes of the day rather than draped in the traditional flowing gowns of Greece or Rome.

Lord Nelson was attracted to the painting and complimented West on its composition. Nelson was flattered when West promised to paint him in the same manner, should the occasion warrant. Replied Nelson, ''Then I hope to die in the next battle.'' And he did die in the next battle — victoriously at the Battle of Trafalgar in 1805. And West kept his part of the bargain, painting *The Death of Nelson* in the same manner as *The Death of Wolfe.*

Ottawa/
Lord Dufferin's Ghost Story

Lord Dufferin's Ghost Story is one of the classics in the literature of the supernatural, and a good story it is.

Frederick Temple Blackwood, first Marquess of Dufferin and Ava (1826–1902), served as Governor General of Canada in 1872–78. He was socially prominent, snobbish, politically astute, and something of a *littérateur*. After his appointment in Ottawa, he served as British viceroy or ambassador in Moscow, New Delhi, Rome, and Paris.

Lord Dufferin's Ghost Story, as recounted by Peter Underhill in *A Gazetteer of Scottish and Irish Ghosts: Frontiers of the Unknown* (1973), begins at Lord Dufferin's country home, Tullamore, not far from Wexford, County Wexford, Ireland. Shortly after midnight, unable to sleep, Lord Dufferin looked out the garden windows onto the moon-bathed lawn and saw the figure of a man carrying a long heavy box that looked a lot like a coffin. As the figure approached, Lord Dufferin could not help but recoil in horror at the malevolent features of the man. Inquiries the next morning failed to find anyone who knew anything about the sinister-looking stranger. But Lord Dufferin never forgot what he had seen. The spectre would always be there . . . .

Ten years later, in 1893, he was Ambassador to France and in the foyer of the Grand Hotel in Paris on his way to a diplomatic reception. With his aide beside him, he stepped into the lift that would take him and other diplomats to the fifth floor. He nodded to the other passengers and then glanced at the lift attendant. He was immediately overcome with horror. The face of the lift attendant bore the malevolent features of the figure he had seen that night in the garden! In a state of shock he stepped out of the lift, taking his aide with him.

The gates closed and the lift rose to the fifth floor when it suddenly stopped. Its cable snapped and the lift plunged and crashed. Some of the occupants were killed, others injured. Among the dead was the lift

197

attendant of whom nothing was known, for the hotel had hired him that very morning.

Lord Dufferin was in much demand as a public speaker, and on a number of occasions he told his famous Ghost Story. The French psychiatrist M.R. de Maratray learned of it and passed it on to the astronomer and psychical researcher Claude Flammarion who retold it in *Death and Its Mystery* (1920). That book has never been translated into English, so the tale, as recounted by researchers like R. DeWitt Miller in *Forgotten Mysteries* (1947), fails to take into account Flammarion's characterization of the story as "not indeed doubtful, but insufficiently reported." Nonetheless, the premonition became a prize piece, making its appearance in numerous books on the supernatural.

"Death Beckons Lord Dufferin!" is the title of one chapter in *Investigating the Unexplained* (1986) in which the author Melvin Harris debunks the story of the premonition. Although Lord Dufferin was in Paris in 1893, there was no diplomatic reception at the Grand Hotel. The tale was told much earlier about a frightful coachman at Glamis Castle by Lady Dufferin's grandfather. Lord Dufferin repeated the family tale directly relating it to himself.

In its earliest known appearance in print, in the English psychical publication *Light,* 16 April 1892, there is no reference at all to the Dufferins. Harris suggests that the present popularity of the tale stems from its retelling by a young politician, none other than Sir Harold Wilson, British Prime Minister in 1964–76! "In truth, though," Melvin concludes, "the whole account is nothing more than a grotesque pastiche of myth." Yet it remains a good story and a classic of its kind.

Ottawa/
D'Arcy McGee's Premonition

There is really no way to establish whether or not Thomas D'Arcy McGee had a premonition of his own death. But it has been suggested that he did. The Irish-born patriot, orator, and Father of Confederation was shot by an assassin in front of his flat in Ottawa the evening of 7 April 1868. At the time of his death he was in his early forties and at the peak of his power. He was shot because of the stand he took against the Fenians, and it was a Fenian, Patrick James Whelan, who was tried, convicted, and executed for the murder. Whelan maintained his innocence to the end.

D'Arcy McGee was possessed of a high Celtic imagination, so it is not improbable that he enjoyed premonitions and entertained such experiences. It is said that a month before his death he penned a poem which included the following lines;

> Friend of my soul, farewell to thee!
> Thy truth, thy trust, thy chivalry;
> And thine, so may my last end be!
> Miserere, Domine.

More intriguing is the dream that he had two days before his death. The details were recorded in Sir Joseph Pope's *Memoirs of the Right Hon. Sir John A. MacDonald* (1984). On Sunday, 5 April, McGee dined at the home of James Goodwin in Ottawa. After dinner he lay down on the sofa in the library to rest. He abruptly woke up from his reverie, pressed his hands to his head, and exclaimed: "I have had a fearful dream." Questioned about it he replied:

> I dreamed that I stood on the banks of the Niagara, where I saw two men in a boat being carried down by the current. I shouted to warn them of their danger, whereupon they pulled their oars and rowed up the stream, and I fell over the boiling abyss.

In relating the dream he seemed greatly distressed. Early in the morning of 7 April, he was shot while returning from a late session of the House of Commons.

Another tradition maintains that D'Arcy McGee was enamoured of the following lines of verse:

> In the time of my boyhood I had a strnge feeling,
> That I was to die in the noon of my day;
> Not quietly into the silent grave stealing,
> But torn, like a blasted oak, sudden away.

The lines are sometimes attributed to D'Arcy McGee himself but they probably derive from a poem titled "The Poet's Prophecy" written by the nineteenth-century Irish bard Gerald Griffin.

Who killed D'Arcy McGee? The question is a moot one. New light — or darkness — is shed on the issue by the following letter, which appeared in *The Globe* on 11 August 1887 over the signature "Outaouais." It was reprinted by Jack Kapica in *Shocked and Appalled: A Century of Letters to the Globe and Mail* (1985).

Now that the question: "Who shot McGee?" is being discussed anew in courts and journals, an autograph from Ghostland may be interesting to listen to.

A certain prominent Irishman in Ottawa, lately deceased, was an old friend of McGee, and a devout believer in spiritualism. Not long before his death I heard him tell, at a friend's dinner table, a strange tale, of which the following is the substance:

"When I was in Boston a few years ago I went to see a lady who professed to be a 'writing medium.' I said to her, 'I want to consult the spirit of D'Arcy McGee.' 'Who was he?' 'Oh, a Canadian politician whom I used to know.' She went into an apparent trance and soon began writing, rapidly, but fitfully. When she handed me the result my hair began to rise. It was McGee's own handwriting from beginning to end! It was in the ordinary form of a letter addressed to myself and dated — with the day of the month and the year only. I won't speak of all that was in it, but I'll tell you part of it. He said: — 'It was not Whelan who shot me — it was so-and-so,' naming a man I knew well, who has since died in a lunatic asylum. 'Whelan was there with him, but it was not he that fired the shot.'

"When I came home I went up to see Sir John, and showed him the letter, folded so that he could see neither date nor signature. I said, 'Do you know the handwriting?' 'Of course I do! That's poor McGee's.' 'Now look at the date and signature.' He did so and then said to me, with a very queer look, 'My God! What does this mean?' 'Then I told him all about it, just as I've told you. And we both felt very queer about it, too, I can tell you.'"

And so did the whole dinner party; for poor —'s sincerity and agitation were as evident as possible — and no mundane explanation occurred to anyone.

Ottawa/
Laurier House, House of Spirits

If ever there was a mansion that should be haunted, it is Laurier House. The three-storey brick mansion, erected in 1878, served as the residences of two Prime Ministers of Canada. It was occupied by Sir Wilfrid Laurier from 1897 until his death in 1919. His widow bequeathed it to William Lyon Mackenzie King, Laurier's successor as leader of the Liberal Party. King occupied it from 1923 to his death in 1950, naming it Laurier House and, in turn, willing the mansion and Kingsmere, his five-hundred-acre Gatineau country estate, to the government and people of Canada.

The third-floor study was Mackenzie King's favourite room. Here he entertained many distinguished visitors including Queen Elizabeth, Winston Churchill, Franklin D. Roosevelt, and Charles de Gaulle. This room contained a shrine to the memory of his mother, Isabel King, whose portrait was illuminated by a table lamp that was lit both day and night. Beside the lamp rested a photograph of the Prime Minister's grandfather, the rebel William Lyon Mackenzie. The original appearance of the study has been retained.

Haunted by the spirit of political endeavour, Laurier House was once possessed by other-worldly presences which are well-known to spiritualists as "discarnates" — disembodied personalities from the Beyond. It appears that the dead spoke and dictated their messages to Mackenzie King during the numerous *séances* he held in the parlour of Laurier House.

The spiritualistic life of William Lyon Mackenzie

Prime Minister William Lyon Mackenzie King is shown seated before the shrine dedicated to the memory of his mother, Isabel Grace King, at Laurier House, Ottawa. Mrs. King's portrait was painted by the portrait artist J.W.L. Forster. Laurier House was bequeathed to King in 1923 by Sir Wilfrid Laurier's widow. He lived here until his death in 1950. It was here, as C.P. Stacey observed a A Very Double Life, *that King conducted his experiments with "the little table," communicating with the spirits of the departed, including that of his late mother. [PAC C 75053/Life Magazine]*

King (1874–1950) has been well documented by C.P. Stacey in *A Very Double Life: The Private World of Mackenzie King* (1976). The historian based his account on the unpublished diaries and took a jaundiced view of this side of King's nature. "The reader is at liberty to believe, if he wishes, that King's messages actually came from the spirit world," he wrote. "My own opinion, I regret to say, is that they came subconsciously out of King's head." As the psycho-

biographer Joy E. Esberey suggested in *Knight of the Holy Spirit: A Study of William Lyon Mackenzie King* (1980): "In the context of King's neurosis it is suggested that spiritualism is best regarded as a defence mechanism directed to easing the tensions and anxieties aroused in the public world."

King embraced Spiritualism in 1932, when he was fifty-eight and between periods of leadership, but he had earlier attended sittings and *séances*. For instance, as early as 1925, he attended a sitting in Kingston with the medium Mrs. L. Bleaney. The following year, in London, England, he interviewed the noted spiritualist Sir Oliver Lodge. In 1932, at the home of a Mrs. Fulford in Brockville, he sat through a *séance* conducted by Mrs. Henrietta Wriedt, a well-known "direct-voice" medium from Detroit.

Laurier House was first used for a *séance* on 24 February 1932 when, "full of wonder & mystery," King communicated with his mother and his deceased friend H.A. Harper. Later, in June, he communicated with "the spirits of the departed" at Kingsmere. On 29 August 1933, on a Western trip, he conferred with T. Glen Hamilton, physician and politician, studied the latter's "spirit photographs," and communicated with Robert Louis Stevenson.

At Laurier House, on 13 November 1933, he explored the phenomenon of table-rapping with the Dominion Archivist, A.G. Doughty. Two knocks of the "little table" meant yes; one knock, no. King's spirit guide was Myers, the shade of Frederick W.H. Myers, the Cambridge scholar and author of *Human Personality and Its Survival of Bodily Death* (1901), who brought King in contact with Sir Wilfrid Laurier, Leonardo da Vinci, Lorenzo de' Medici, and Louis Pasteur. On 9 March 1934, King communicated with a long-dead Hindu priest named Koramura, Philip the Apostle, Alexander Mackenzie, Edward Blake, and William Lyon Mackenzie. On 6 October 1943, he reached Laurier and William Gladstone.

In Toronto, on 5 August 1942, a new medium introduced him to Laurier, Queen Victoria, Florence Nightingale, Anne Boleyn, and Sir Frederick Banting. In London, on 22 November 1947, through the agency of the London Spiritualist Alliance, he met another medium, Geraldine Cummins, who told King things about himself Stacey found remarkable. "The only explanation I can offer is that thought-transference in some form took place between King and the medium. It is much easier to believe in this happening between living people than to believe in communication between the dead and the living."

There is no indication that Mackenzie King's spiritualistic activities influenced in the least his political activities. Throughout his life, the public was unaware of his belief in communication with the Beyond. The first knowledge the public had of this side of the late Prime Minister's nature was Blair Fraser's article "The Secret Life of Mackenzie King, Spiritualist" which appeared in *Maclean's* on 15 December 1951. Fraser based his account on interviews with the London mediums, so he had no information on the table-rapping at Laurier House.

The late Leonard Brockington, who undertook

This undated vintage photograph shows William Lyon Mackenzie King standing with his beloved mother, Isabel Grace King, before a stone wall at Kingsmere, the country estate in the Gatineau hills that the future Prime Minister of Canada acquired in 1905. Devastated by the death of his mother, King maintained a shrine in her memory at Laurier House, and many times communicated with her spirit through mediums and the "little table." [PAC C-46560]

sensitive assignments for the governments of the day, was at one point dispatched to England to do what he could to silence the London mediums. If further details of Mackenzie King's spiritualistic practices were made public, it was felt that they could be politically embarrassing to the St. Laurent administration which sought to continue Mackenzie King's principles and policies. Brockington returned to Ottawa intimating that he had been successful. When asked how he had managed to stem the tide of further revelations, all he would say was that his maxim was as follows: "Never strike a happy medium."

Ottawa/ Parliament Hill

At the base of the Peace Tower, which soars like a spire above Parliament Hill, lies the Memorial Chamber which in 1927 was dedicated to the memory of the War Dead. The names of those Canadians who died in the wars in which Canada officially fought are inscribed in the chamber's four mammoth Books of Remembrance.

Here may be read the names of the 3,367 Canadians who died in the abortive raid on Dieppe. An Allied force, composed largely of Canadians, on 19 August 1942, launched a large-scale attack on Dieppe, the German-held seaport in northern France. The attackers withdrew in disarray. It was "a brave and bitter day."

What goes unnoted in the official accounts of the engagement is an auditory replay of the battle as experienced by two English women on a holiday near the seaport on 4 August 1951. Their account appeared as "The Dieppe Raid Case" by G.W. Lambert and Kathleen Gray in the *Journal* of the Society for Psychical Research, May–June 1952. The account is extremely detailed, as its truth lies in how closely what the two women experienced corresponded to what happened on the bloody beaches on that fateful morning.

The two women, identified as sisters-in-law, Mrs. Dorothy Norton and Miss Agnes Norton, spent the night of 4 August 1951 at a hotel not far from the beach at Puys, a village near Dieppe. Loud noises at a distance woke Dorothy at approximately 4:00 a.m. As the sounds which continued resembled those of an immense battle, she awakened Agnes at 4:20 and they both listened. The roar ebbed and flowed from the beach until 6:55 a.m. when all was quiet again.

They kept a log of the different sounds they heard and when they first heard them. For two hours their ears rang with a battle being waged but they could see none of it. It was as if the war was trapped in time. They heard men's cries, gunfire, dive-bombing, lulls, aircraft flying overhead, and then silence. Later that morning they learned they were the only occupants of the hotel to have heard anything at all.

Had they experienced an auditory hallucination? Was it a *folie à deux*? A different explanation was offered by R.A. Eades, writing in the *Journal* in September 1968. He suggested that what the sisters-in-law had experienced was the noisy operation of a dredger on a distant beach, modified by the wind and the sea and by whatever knowledge they had of the Dieppe raid, which admittedly was scanty. Yet an examination of the dredging schedule showed that there was no activity on the morning in question. So the question must be asked: Did two English women hear an auditory replay of the Dieppe raid one decade later?

Ottawa/
UFO Enthusiast

The country's leading proponent of flying saucers and unidentified flying objects was Wilbert B. Smith (1910–1962). Born in Lethbridge, Alberta, he graduated in electrical engineering from the University of British Columbia, receiving his B.Sc. in 1933 and his M.A.Sc. in 1934. He worked as a radio engineer with CJOR before joining the Department of Transport in 1939. His special concern was the technical matter of radio-frequency allocation. At the time of his death he was DOT's Superintendent of Radio Regulations Engineering.

Wilbert B. Smith, the country's leading flying saucer enthusiast, is shown seated behind the desk in his office at the Department of Communications in Ottawa. The photograph was taken in July 1950. Smith was an electrical engineer and a specialist in the technical aspects of radio broadcasting. At the time of his death in 1962, he was DOT's Superintendent of Radio Regulations Engineering. [Department of Communications]

Smith was plainly excited with the "flap" and "wave" of flying saucer sightings which followed the initial one made by Kenneth Arnold in 1947. Three years later he gained approval from DOT to establish Project Magnet to study how magnetic and gravitational principles might account for the reported flight patterns of flying saucers. He established his own "observation post" at Shirleys Bay, west of Ottawa. In 1952, when Project Magnet was co-opted by Project Second Storey and gradually wound down, Smith was permitted to continue with his work using government equipment, but on his own time.

By the late 1950s Smith had come to the conclusion that the peculiar flight patterns reported for flying saucers could only be explained by reference to some form of magnetic and gravitational force or action. Some areas of the Earth, he theorized, were areas of "reduced binding," and it should be possible to locate them with a "binding metre." He reasoned that alien astronauts were able to identify them and were in possession of some type of "antigravity device" which enabled them to propel their craft at supersonic speeds and execute astonishing manoeuvres.

Smith was interviewed at length about his theories by the American broadcaster and researcher Frank Edwards, and a report of the interview appeared in Edwards' book *Flying Saucers: Serious Business* (1966). Smith presented his own theories in *The New Science* (1964), in which he argued that his magnetic and gravitational interests constituted the basis of "a new science." In private he admitted to fellow investigators that he was in communication with UFO occupants. Arthur Bray referred to this in passing in his biographical entry on Smith in *The Encyclopedia of UFOs* (1980) edited by Ronald D. Story: "In the area of metaphysics, Smith claimed to communicate with occupants of UFOs through a contact who provided him with certain information. One instance pertained to areas of reduced binding in our atmosphere."

Peter M. Millman, an astrophysicist with the National Research Council and the official who was responsible for Project Second Storey, knew Smith quite well. On 13 May 1987 he described Smith for those who did not know him. Smith was a mild-mannered man and a sensible scientist with a personal interest in his work. He was very capable and designed an excellent form and file-card system for the reporting of data on UFOs. He believed near the end of his life that he was in contact with outer-space intelligences. These intelligences came originally from Venus, and he was put in contact with them through a medium in New Orleans. The equipment that he had at his disposal at Shirleys Bay, a storage shed turned into his installation, was of the old-fashioned, recording type.

Smith died of cancer in an Ottawa hospital at the age of fifty-two. Millman visited him a few days before his death. The dying man was very calm and relaxed. "He took his beliefs to death with him," Millman said. "He told me, 'I will soon be in a realm where I can associate with these people. Then I'll be certain to know more about it all'."

Ottawa/
UFO Reports and Files

The governments of only two countries in the world have taken flying saucers and unidentified flying objects seriously enough to study them and these are the governments of the United States and Canada.

Both a Department and an Agency of the Canadian federal government have undertaken studies of flying saucers or UFOs, as they came to be called. The bodies in question are the Department of Transport and the Defence Research Board. DOT undertook Project Magnet; the Defence Research Board established Project Second Storey.

In addition, since 1967, a Crown corporation has acted as the repository for Canadian UFO reports. Anyone who has seen a UFO and wishes to file a report on the sighting should send the report to the National Research Council of Canada, Herzberg Institute of Astrophysics, Ottawa, Canada K1A 0R6. The Herzberg Institute is NRC's laboratory division, and it maintains the reports in a file marked "Sightings, non-meteoric."

The first government agency to collect reports was the Department of Transport which began to do so in the early 1950s. DOT transferred its files and authority to the Canadian Forces Headquarters in 1965, where they were kept classified. Since they fell into the hands of the NRC in 1967, the reports have been open to the public. The reports are maintained in the file for three years before they are transferred to the Public Archives.

Allen G. McNamara, the scientist responsible for the NRC's file on UFOs, told David Miller of the *Toronto Star* on 8 July 1984 that between 1967 and 1984 more than 2000 reports were received. Therefore about 2.5 reports a week are received from all parts of the country. If one report is filed for every six sightings — a conservative ratio — then there are about thirteen sightings of UFOs each week in Canada.

The National Archives of Canada's Historical Resources Branch maintains the UFO Sighting Files.

The files for the years 1966–80 are available on microfilm through interlibrary loan. The names of individuals who filed sighting reports have been scored out to protect their privacy. More recent files are not yet available on microfilm, as the names have yet to be scored out, according to Brien Brothman, Archivist, Economic and Communication Records, Government Archives Division, in a letter written on 2 December 1987.

Ottawa/
Project Magnet

With a view toward discovering new technologies in unusual magnetic phenomena, Wilbert B. Smith of the Broadcast and Measurements Section, Telecommunications Division of the Ministry of Transport, sent a memorandum to Commander C.P. Edwards, Deputy Minister of Transport for Air Services. The memorandum suggested that a study of "geo-magnetics" could explain the extraordinary flight patterns observers claimed for flying saucers. Smith had learned on a visit to Washington, D.C., from a Defence Research Board liaison officer at the Canadian Embassy, that the Americans knew "flying saucers exist" and were studying them under the strictest secrecy. Smith's memorandum to Commander Edwards was dated 21 November 1950. Smith received Commander Edwards' "go ahead" on December 2.

Instead of building a "pilot power plant" for extracting energy from the Earth's magnetic field, as he expected to do, Smith spent a great deal of time collecting reports of flying saucer sightings and gathering surplus equipment for a flying saucer observatory at Shirleys Bay. Smith was instrumental in gathering reports from Department of Transport officials across Canada. He summarized the most interesting twenty-five sightings for the *Project Magnet Report*. The conclusion that Smith came to was that "the vehicles are probably extra-terrestrial." Such a conclusion from a private individual merited no particular attention, but coming in a government report required some explanation. As if that was not enough,

there was the publicity that followed his announcement that a flying saucer had been detected over Shirleys Bay on 8 August 1954. Neither the conclusion of his report nor the announced sighting pleased the Ministry of Transport.

Project Magnet, which was largely a part-time activity of Smith's, was officially ended in 1954 after running for four years. Although Smith was permitted to continue his work on flying saucers, he would henceforth do it in an unofficial capacity and on his own time. The work continued until his death in 1962.

Ottawa/
Project Second Storey Committee

Soon after the sight of "a bright amber disc" flying at terrific speeds over North Bay Air Station on 12 April 1952, Dr. O.M. Solandt, Chairman of the Defence Research Board, convened the first meeting of what was to become the Project Second Storey Committee.

The members of the Committee felt that because of their numbers the reported sightings could not be dismissed as "hallucinations" on the part of the public. It also felt that because of a heightened public awareness of flying saucers, created by banner headlines about sightings on 20 April, a "more active stand on the matter" was desired than the haphazard approach with which flying saucer reports were being gathered. The excitement of the first week, following the outbreak of reports across southern Ontario, and the publicity of the North Bay sighting, was reflected by two meetings of the Committee on 22 and 24 April 1952.

In addition to several Defence officials and intelligence officers, the Committee included Dr. Peter M. Millman of the Dominion Observatory and Wilbert B. Smith of the Telecommunications Division of the Ministry of Transport and author of the *Project Magnet Report*. As the public excitement ebbed, so did the optimism of the Committee. The meetings of 19 May and 17 November 1952, and the final meeting of 9 March 1953, were concerned with constructing a viable reporting form. No active investigation was contemplated. A "Summary Report" was issued by Dr. Millman on 21 November 1953, which concluded that the lack of "facts" did not lend much hope to a scientific investigation of flying saucer reports. "The committee as a whole has felt that owing to the impossibility of checking independently the details of the majority of the sightings, most of the observational material does not lend itself to a scientific method of investigation." Forms for receiving reports were made available to government agencies.

The "Summary Report" was the end of the Canadian Government's interesting but short history of involvement in the study and detection of flying saucers and UFOs. Since then the government has played no role except, through the National Research Council and the Public Archives, to maintain and keep a file of reports of sightings volunteered by the public.

Project Magnet and the Project Second Storey Committee may be seen in different ways. The undertakings seem innocent and simple by today's standards, yet they have the earmarks of the characteristics that are now associated with the 1950s, which was a decade of rapid technological growth coupled with anxieties connected with the hostilities of the Cold War. The Project Magnet report showed innocent enthusiasm and political *naïveté*. The deliberations of the Project Second Storey Committee seem, in retrospect at least, as a deliberate attempt to wind-up Project Magnet and wind-down the federal government's involvment with what has been called "UFOria."

Ottawa/
Vision of the Chapel

Gatineau Park is a national wilderness and recreation area north of Ottawa on the Quebec side of the Ottawa River. Anyone with an interest in Spiritualism will want to visit Kingsmere, the five-hundred-acre country estate in the Park owned by William Lyon Mackenzie King from 1905 to his death here on 22 July 1950. In his will he bequeathed the country estate in the Park to the nation.

Kingsmere consists of rolling countryside and King's summer home, known as Moorside, a small cottage, called Shady Hill, and structures that King in his diary variously described as "a ruin," "the Abbey Ruin," "the Temple," "the Cloisters," and a "vision of the chapel." In 1934, Mackenzie King started to collect architectural remnants from various structures and sites, including the British Parliament Buildings, and combining them so that his "ruins" over the years acquired a mock-mediaeval appearance

Should the spiritualists of the country ever decide to establish a central shrine, that cenacle should be erected in Gatineau Park. On his property in this national wilderness and recreation area north of Ottawa, William Lyon Mackenzie King began work on what is variously known as "the Abbey ruin," "the Temple," "the Cloisters," "the vision of the chapel." In 1934 he commenced collecting architectural rubble from Europe and America for his "ruin." It was left unfinished at the time of his death here on 22 July 1950. The ruins have an eerie effect on many visitors. [National Capital Commission]

and the patina of age. They were still growing at the time of their creator's death.

Mackenzie King, a convinced spiritualist in his later years, conducted *séances* at Shady Hill in June 1932 and contacted "the spirits of the departed," as the historian C.P. Stacey noted in *A Very Double Life: The Private World of Mackenzie King* (1976). It is interesting to note it was shortly after he embraced Spiritualism that Mackenzie King commenced acquiring his remnants and accumulating his ruins. Perhaps he yearned for a sense of antiquity, which Rupert Brooke among others found so wanting in Canada. Or he may have given expression to his desire for a religious or mystical experience — a "vision of the chapel."

The ruins have aged with good grace. They appear picturesque to tourists but they affect some people in an eerie way. They deeply moved the poet Gwendolyn MacEwen who first heard about them and saw them in the early 1960s. MacEwen was in Ottawa to read her poems. When the evening reading was over, one of her hosts, a practical-minded person and not a poet, suggested she might enjoy a late-night ride to Kingsmere to see the ruins. "I had no preconceived notion about the ruins. In fact, I had never even heard of them. But my imagination can do anything!"

By the time they reached the Park it was close to midnight. They parked the car and began walking towards the ruins when a thunderstorm suddenly struck. Light rain began to fall, and in the distance the ruins were momentarily lit by a flash of lightning. They quickened their pace in order to reach their destination before the rain began to pelt down. Then lightning struck again, brilliantly illuminating the ruins right in front of them. They froze dead in their tracks. They felt very cold. Time stood still. There was a figure standing within the arch, illuminated in the night. "Did you see that?" the host asked MacEwen. "I don't want to talk about it," the poet replied. It was eerie.

By this time they had turned around and were racing through the pelting rain to the car. They drove back to Ottawa in silence. Even recalling the experience almost a quarter-century later in August 1987,

the poet felt fright. "There was something about that figure. It still chills my blood!"

Ottawa/
Arthur Bray and UFOlogy

Arthur Bray is a leading light in the field of UFOlogy in Canada. For many years he has been a beacon on the Ottawa scene.

Born in Ottawa in 1925, Bray joined the Royal Canadian Air Force in 1943, fulfilling his boyhood dream by qualifying as a pilot. In 1945 he transferred to the Navy and held numerous posts ashore and afloat. He wrote the technical safety manual for Naval Aviation. He retired from the Navy as a Lieutenant Commander in 1971. He then joined the Canada Safety Council, where he promoted the development of the National Standard on non-verbal warning signs for workplace safety. In 1986 he became Director of Corporate Affairs at the Council.

Bray became interested in UFOs in 1947 when he read about numerous sightings by technically qualified people. "I wondered what strange things might be sharing the sky with me. The more I read, the more interested I became, and eventually developed my study into an avocation." He taught a course on UFOs at Algonquin College in Ottawa and is a member of the Academy of Independent Scholars and the Aerial Phenomena Research Organization. He is the author of two thoughtful books: *Science, the Public and the UFO* (1967) and *The UFO Connection* (1979).

"My position is that UFOs are entirely real and constitute a major scientific and political enigma," he explained, when Ronald D. Story, editor of *The Encyclopedia of UFOs*, asked him for a statement of his beliefs. "As to their nature, I feel the evidence shows that in some cases they are craft, both manned and remote-controlled, some of which may orginate from a parallel universe, and others from other stellar systems."

Bray possesses a private library of 3500 volumes of UFO literature, plus many hundreds of reports, proceedings, scientific journals, and news clippings. He was one of the mainstays of the Ottawa New Sciences Club.

Ottawa/
The Ottawa New Sciences Club

Originally formed as the Ottawa Flying Saucer Club in the late 1950s, the Ottawa New Sciences Club was so named in the summer of 1963 to reflect the extension of the club's area of interest to other scientific and metaphysical subjects. The choice of the new title was an indirect tribute to the club's late founder, Wilbert B. Smith, who spent some of the latter years of his life writing a highly technical treatise on what he termed "The New Science."

The group was formed very informally as a means of discussion, and from the desire to have the opportunity to exchange ideas with others similarly interested. Smith was always against the principle of an "organized" club. He wanted merely an informal discussion group. When the group formalized itself Smith went along with it very reluctantly, although he gladly shared his home and his table with club members and anyone else who was interested.

In March 1960 the club issued its first quarterly newsletter, *Topside,* which was edited by Mrs. Carol Halford-Watkins. *Topside* was a form of communication for those who were unable to attend meetings regularly. It kept them up to date on new developments in the UFO field and related subject areas. Approximately thirty people attended each meeting in the early years. The club eventually disbanded, and the last issue of *Topside,* Number 35, was issued in 1971.

Some idea of the range of discussion at the meetings may be gleaned from *The Boys from Topside* (1969), edited by Timothy Green Beckley. Many of the chapters were articles of Smith's that had appeared elsewhere. Some offered information of a technical nature which orginated not with Smith but with "the Space Brothers."

> The messages were received by a specially-selected intermediary through direct telepathic communication with the Space Brothers — and

since mental telepathy and ESP are now accepted facts by many Earth scientists who have made a serious study of these phenomena, it should not be too difficult for skeptics to accept that if thought transference is possible at great distance on this planet, then the exchange of pure thought between any intelligent beings must be equally possible throughout the wider distance of Outer Space. Natural Laws of the Cosmos are not confined to this planet alone.

What is interesting to note is the fact that the club moved from a study of flying saucers to an appreciation of the UFO phenomenon—from physics to psychology, from hardware to software. In fact, the movement of the club anticipated the thinking of the Franco-American scientist and humanist Jacques Vallee, who later went the same route in his highly influential book *Passport to Magonia: From Folklore to Flying Saucers* (1969).

Ottawa/
NCR's UFOs

Unidentified Flying Objects (UFOs) apparently buzzed the National Capital Region (NCR) the evening of 4 March 1969.

UFOs were spotted directly above the Parliament Buildings on Parliament Hill and Rideau Hall. Yurko Bondarchuk in *UFO: Sightings, Landings and Abductions* (1979) quoted the testimony of an RCMP constable stationed near the Privy Council entrance the evening of March 4:

> At 7:45 p.m., an object was seen from Parliament Hill, going through the sky at a terrific rate of speed, heading from south to north. This object stopped and appeared to hover in the sky over Hull. It gradually moved in a northwest direction and at 9:34 p.m. disappeared from view. It appeared to be round in shape and much smaller than the moon in size.

The object was seen by six other RCMP officers at various locations on Parliament Hill.

Later that evening an RCMP contable patrolling the part of Sussex Drive between Rideau Hall, the Governor General's Residence, and 24 Sussex Drive, the Prime Minister's Residence, observed flashing red lights:

> At approximately 10:00 p.m., while on foot patrol from the police lodge at Government House to the prime minister's residence, I noticed two rather bright flashing red lights in the sky. At first glance, I assumed they were aircraft but could hear no sounds of engines. One of these lights proceeded east and was lost from view within a minute or less, while the other one travelled in a westerly direction. These lights were first seen directly overhead at a point slightly inside the gates to Government House and were very bright red. No definite shape could be distinguished nor was there any type of trail visible behind these lights.

Three months later, on 5 June, at 10:12 p.m., three RCMP constables and three tourists on Parliament Hill were surprised to see a luminous craft hovering over the Ottawa River behind the Parliament Buildings. Bondarchuk noted, "They watched as the vessel emitted a dazzling array of lights, changing from red to green to red to white." At 10:10 p.m., "all the lights on Parliament Hill — East, West and Centre Blocks—went out . . . Ontario Hydro was notified, but . . . the cause could not be ascertained at the time." Then the UFO moved eastward "with an up and down ping-pong-ball-like trajectory," finally settling above eastern Hull and Pointe-Gatineau across the river. It proceeded west and then disappeared from sight behind high buildings.

Bondarchuk commented on the lack of official interest in the incidents which he found disturbing. "It is equally disturbing that neither the sighting nor the blackout received noticeable press coverage. A check of subsequent editions of the Ottawa *Journal* and the Ottawa *Citizen* failed to reveal any reference to either event. Whether this omission was intentional or accidental does not alter the fact that while two potentially explosive events were taking place, the public was left virtually in the dark."

Ottawa/
The Dinosauroid

Dale A. Russell is a paleobiologist with the National Museum of Natural Sciences whose genius lies in scientific speculation.

Russell is respected in paleobiological circles for his views on the extinction of the dinosaurs. Two orders of large reptiles—Saurischia (lizard-hipped) and Ornithischia (bird-hipped)—dominated the Earth during the Mesozoic era (225 to 63 million years ago). Then the orders perished. Whatever caused their extinction also affected about three-quarters of all known animal species. Russell has argued that the cause was a cosmic catastrophy. The "sudden death" was caused by the consequences of the collision of the Earth and an asteroid.

After speculating on the death of the dinosaurs, Russell turned his powers of speculation on the possible consequences of the continued existence and evolution of the dinosaurs. He chose a versatile lizard-hipped beast, a Cretaceous theropod called *Stenonychosaurus* (or *Troodon*) *inequalis,* and reconstructed it in scale-model form, complete with flesh and facial features. Then he imagined the form the body would take after millions of years of evolution. Had the creature lived to evolve, it may well have turned into Russell's "hypothetical dinosauroid." The subject is discussed in the paper *Reconstructions of the Small Cretaceous Theropod Stenonychosaurus inequalis and a Hypothetic Dinosauroid* (1982) by Russell and R. Séguin.

The resulting creature, for a descendant of a dinosaur, is surprisingly humanoid in appearance. Its body is supported by two legs and it has two arms. The appendages have four toes and three fingers apiece, however. There is a somewhat small, bird-shaped head. What catches the attention are the immensely large eyeballs with vertical pupils. The man-like beast stands nine feet tall. In appearance it resembles nothing more than the human-looking aliens conceived by science-fiction writers and drawn by pulp-magazine illustrators. In passing, the hypothetical dinosauroid also bears an uncanny resemblance to the "critters" from UFOs as described by "abductees."

Russell has speculated on the evolution of intelligence itself, both human and extra-human. In the paper "Exponential Evolution: Implications for Intelligent Extraterrestrial Life," published in *Advances in Space Research*, Vol. 3, No. 9, 1983, he suggested a strange symmetry. "Changes in the physical universe become less rapid as time increases from the Big Bang. Changes in biological complexity may be most rapid at such later times. This lends a unique and symmetrical importance to early and late universal times." He compared human and non-human intelligences and asked the question, "Is there a peculiar set of adaptive attributes enabling the anthropoid-humanoid form to interact with materials and organisms on the surface of the Earth in such a manner as to optimize selection for intelligence?"

Russell placed the consequences of "exponential evolution" in the context of the search for extraterrestrial intelligence and its consequences: "A vigorous and unsuccessful SETI program might imply that our planetary environment has been unusually favourable for the evolution of life, or grounds for pessimism concerning the survival of intelligence. Long-term trends in the evolution of complexity and recently high rates of encephalization on Earth indicate that an accelerating shower of intelligent organisms could be occurring from biospheres throughout the cosmos."

Penetanguishene/ Giants Tomb Island

Giants Tomb Island is an irregularly shaped island located in Georgian Bay near the entrance to Penetanguishene Bay. It is said to be the sepulchre of the mysterious giant Ki-chi-ki-wa-na, or Rockman.

Rockman was born at Hudson Bay, and the Hurons of long ago maintained that he was so immense that he could throw icebergs around the way the Indians could throw snowballs. The last of his race, he travelled south in search of giants his own size but found none. He slipped on a fish and fell on the rocky shore, shattering the rocks into thirty thousand pieces, thus creating that many islands in Georgian Bay.

He spent his final years on Giants Tomb Island.

The unicorn is a fabulous beast which if it could speak would boast a number of Canadian connections. The narwhal of the Far North may have given birth to this creature's legend; it certainly supplied Queen Elizabeth I with her "horn of the unicorn." The beast appears as the symbol of France on the Canadian Coat of Arms. Here, sculpted in stone, it guards the entranceway to the Centre Block, Parliament Hill, Ottawa. [Dwight Whalen]

When the Indians discovered his dead body they covered it with boulders, reserving for his immense head a special high flat rock. Indians in historical times have paid tribute to his spirit, leaving tobacco and other offerings for him, but only during the daylight hours, never at night, for fear that their presence would disturb his rest.

The legend of Rockman is kept alive these days by the Huron people, but the white men know Rockman hardly at all. The details recalled here come from an article called "Indians of Huronia in the Old Days Were Very Superstitious" published in the Niagara Falls *Evening Review* on 9 July 1921. The article concludes with the following tale about the lighthouse keeper on nearby Christian Island:

> A story is told which illustrates the reality of their superstition. The lighthouse keeper of Christian Island visited the Giant's Tomb on a tour of exploration. While he was on the island a steam yacht passed and blew a loud blast on its siren. The Indians on Christian Island did not see the yacht but they heard the strange noise which it made. Immediately they decided that Ki-chi-ki-wa-na had been disturbed. He was protesting thus against the invasion of his tomb by a white man and nothing would persuade the Indians to allow the innocent lighthouse keeper to return to his home on Christian Island until the yacht chanced to pass by again and they heard and saw at the same time.

Penetanguishene/ Brûlé's Death

Etienne Brûlé was the original *coureur-de-bois* whose "native ways" infuriated Samuel de Champlain and the Jesuits. He was a fur trader, explorer, and translator, and he became the first white person to see three of the five Great Lakes — Ontario, Huron, and Superior.

He was forty-one years old in June 1633 and living with the Hurons when he was tortured and slain at the encampment of Toanché, west of Penetanguish-

ene. Jesuit and Recollet accounts maintain that he was barbarously and treacherously murdered. The account of Gabriel Sagard goes further and adds that Brûlé's body was eaten by the Hurons. The theory of Bruce G. Trigger in *The Children of Aataentsic: A History of the Huron People to 1660* (1976) is that the slaying of Brûlé was an act of political assassination occasioned by intertribal rivalry.

There are numerous stories told about Brûlé. One is that when he realized that he was to be sacrificed, he fell to his knees to pray to Jesus. But the only prayer he could remember from his childhood was Grace before Meals, so he mumbled those words. There was a terrific thunderstorm at the time of his death that caused many fires. A curse was visited upon the entire Bear Clan whose members had killed him. The chief of the clan was ostracized by his own people. Smallpox killed many and others survived only by abandoning their village. Members maintained that the spectre of a woman, believed to be Brûlé's sister, wandered through the forest at night breathing the smallpox pestilence. Great care was taken to burn the Frenchman's remains along with his corpse and scatter the ashes and bury the bones in various holes deep in the earth so no one would ever find them.

Peterborough/ Manly Palmer Hall

One of the world's most prolific authors of mystical texts is a native of Peterborough, Ontario. Not only is he a native of Peterborough, but he is the founder of a major occult religious organization.

The man in question is Manly Palmer Hall who was born in 1901 in Peterborough but taken to the United States by his parents three years later. In 1934 he became the founder and president of the Philosophical Research Society, Inc., of Los Angeles. The PRS is centre for occult and religious thinking and has a publication program second to none.

According to *Contemporary Authors* (1980), Volumes 93–96, Hall is also a member of the International Society for General Semantics, the American Federation of Astrologers, and the American Society for Psychical Research. The list of his "writings" includes two hundred individual books which were issued by the PRS, the majority in multiple reprintings. Probably his best-known book is *The Secret Teachings of All Ages: An Encyclopedia Outline of Masonic, Hermetic, Quabbalistic, and Rosicrucian Symbolical Philosophy — Being an Interpretaion of the Secret Teachings Concealed Within the Rituals, Allegories, and*

Shown in this photograph is Manly Palmer Hall, president and founder of the Philosophical Research Society, Inc. The organization, established in Los Angeles in 1934, has grown into an institution. Hall was born in Peterborough, Ont., but raised in the United States. He became a noted lecturer on spiritual, mystical, and occult subjects and one of the most prolific of all authors of such texts. [The Philosophical Research Society, Inc.]

Mysteries of All Ages. Under that title the book went through nineteen printings to 1973; under an earlier title, issued in 1928, it went through ten printings.

Manly Palmer Hall of the Philosophical Research Society must be the most prolific if least known of transmitters of "the secret teachings of all ages." As he expressed his credo in the booklet *The Little World of PRS: A Field Tour of the Philosophical Research Society:* "I have carefully avoided personal publicity. After all, I am only trying to carry on a torch that was lighted long ago by those far wiser than I."

Petroglyphs Provincial Park/ Rock Art

Petroglyphs Provincial Park, northeast of Peterborough, is the largest single concentration of prehistoric rock carvings in Canada. Between A.D. 900 and 1400, Algonkian-speaking Indians carved some 900 stylized images onto the outcrop of crystalline limestone. The limestone is sometimes called "white marble," and the inscribed part comprises an oval area approximately 180 feet in length and 100 feet in width. One-third of the glyphs are readily identifiable; two-thirds are obscure in meaning or significance.

The locale of this sacred site of rock art was lost by the Ojibway descendants of the Algonkian-speaking Indian carvers. Charles Kingam, a member of the Peterborough Historical Society, stumbled upon the isolated site in 1924. Although he described it to others, the site was forgotten once again. In May 1954 three geologists came upon it by accident. Later that summer archaeologists at the Unversity of Toronto mounted an expedition to map the site. Petroglyphs Provincial Park was opened in 1972.

The standard analysis of these remarkable glyphs is *Sacred Art of the Algonkians: A Study of the Peterborough Petroglyphs* (1973) written by Joan M. Vastokas and Romas K. Vastokas. In their study this art historian and archaeologist at Trent University in Peterborough discussed the carved images under the following eight headings: sun figures, shaman figures, squatting figures, thunderbirds, snakes, figures of birds and reptiles and animals, and boats.

211

Over 900 separate images have been carved in the outcrop of limestone on a promontory northeast of Peterborough. The site is called Petroglyphs Provincial Park, and it is the largest single concentration of prehistoric rock carvings in Canada. The glyphs have attracted the scholarly eye of Joan M. and Romas K. Vastokas as well as the free-wheeling imagination of Barry Fell. An epigrapher with an enthusiasm for the notion of pre-Columbian exploration of the Americas, Fell has interpreted the glyphs in such a fashion as to tell the tale of a Nordic King named Woden-lithi (who is otherwise unknown to history) who traded in the region about 1700 B.C. [Ontario Ministry of Tourism and Recreation]

They concluded, "The images engraved here are not the projections of man, imposing his will upon his surroundings. Instead, they render visible the hidden meanings in nature whose significance it has been the shaman's task to conjure up and capture in stone."

The interesting (and somewhat surprising question) of whether or not the Peterborough Petroglyphs constitute a "mysterious" site was raised by Joan M. Vastokas in a private communication dated 14 June 1987. Dr. Vastokas explained:

> The petroglyph site is a concrete expression of Agonkian Indian religous beliefs and practices and to include them along with dubious and, at least, inexplicable phenomena would be an insult to native people. There is just too much written about rock art that borders on the kooky, such as by Von Däniken and Barry Fell. In the former case, the carvings are expressions of men from outer space; in the latter, the Peterborough Petroglyph site in particular is inspired by Viking copper-traders.
>
> As we tried very carefully to demonstrate in our book, the only thing "mysterious" about the Petroglyphs is that they are prehistoric in date and, like most things prehistoric, we do not have all the details we would like about function and meaning. The petroglyphs, however, are firmly imbedded in a long-standing tradition of pictorial communication and are aligned with innumerable other rock art sites throughout North America and Asia and with other modes of pictorial expression in the Great Lakes area.

Perhaps the best reason for the inclusion of rock-art sites in a book of mysterious sites is the fact that the traditional religious beliefs and practices of the native peoples strike the non-native as strange and wonderful when not specifically mysterious.

The reference to Barry Fell is to the Professor Emeritus of Biology at Harvard University who in his retirement became an esthusiast for the theory that Northern Europeans and Near Easterners engaged in the pre-Columbian exploration and colonization of the Americas. He studied ancient inscriptions and read into or out of them novel confirmations of his theories.

In his book *Bronze Age American* (1982), he argued at considerable length that the glyphs found at the Peterborough site are not images but letters cut "in the Tifinag and ogam consaine alphabets, using an early form of the Norse tongue." He was aware that in their book *Sacred Art of the Algonkians* the Vastokases had treated the images as artwork and admitted to finding the book "valuable for its treatment of the Algonquian art at the site."

Fell proceeded to evolve a grandiose theory of his own, one that permitted him to interpret the glyphs in light of the theory of the Norse colonization of North America. It presupposes the existence of Woden-lithi, "a Nordic king, perhaps of Jutish origin, who established a trading colony in Ontario ca. 1700 B.C. The name means 'servants of Odin.'" The surmise is best stated in his own words in the following passage and left there.

> Some seventeen centuries before the time of Christ a Nordic king named Woden-lithi sailed across the Atlantic and entered the St. Lawrence River. He reached the neighbourhood of where Toronto now stands, and established a trading colony with a religious and commercial center at the place that is now known as Petroglyphs Park, at Peterborough. His homeland was Norway, his capital at Ringerike, west of the head of Oslo Fjord. He remained in Canada for five months, from April to September, trading his cargo of woven material for copper ingots obtained from the local Algonquians . . . . He left behind an inscription that records his visit, his religious beliefs, a standard of measures for cloth and cordage, and an astronomical observatory for determining the dates of the Yule and pagan Easter festivals. Having provided his colonists with these essentials, he sailed back to Scandinavia and thereafter disappears into the limbo of unwritten Bronze Age history. The king's inscription gives his Scandinavian title

only and makes no claim to the discovery of the Americas nor to conquest of territory. Clearly he was not the first visitor to the Americas from Europe. . . .

Pickering/
UFOs and Ontario Hydro

The Pickering Nuclear Generating Plant at Pickering, east of Toronto, is owned and operated by Ontario Hydro and is one of the world's largest nuclear power generating facilities. Security personnel at the Plant reported seeing clusters of bright red pulsating objects in the sky on two nights, 31 December 1974 and 4 February 1975.

On both occasions the balls of light were observed to hover in the night sky above Lake Ontario for about half an hour. The incidents were described by Yurko Bondarchuk in *UFO: Sightings, Landings and Abductions* who noted that at the time of the two sightings Reactor Number 3 was temporarily disabled. He offered the suggestion that the UFOs might be on a "spy" mission.

Pickering/
Dennis Prophet

Dennis Prophet's life was changed when he saw his first UFO.

An RCAF veteran and the operator of an automobile dealership in West Hill, near Pickering, a town east of Toronto, Prophet had no interest in unidentified flying objects until 16 January 1974. That was the night that he experienced his first sighting. "When you've seen what I have seen and what my family has seen, you've got to believe," he explained.

It was the sight of an oval, orange glowing object in the sky toward the east that excited him. He was talking with an employee on a cold night outside his West Hill dealership when they saw the UFO.

It was at an altitude of about 1,500 feet. It appeared to be hovering over the Cherrywood Hydro lines in Pickering, Ont. After watching

it hovering there for about 10 minutes, we noticed it coming closer to us. As it came closer, we observed a ribbon of light that appeared to be revolving on the top, which indicated that it had some form of cabin or observation tower on the top of it.

To define more clearly the ribbon of light, it appeared like a miniature rainbow revolving around the top of an observation deck. While hovering, it maintained the same altitude. Being an extremely cold night, the employee suggested that we step back into the showroom and for other reasons I felt the same way.

While observing the object at very close range for a further 5 minutes, we saw it slowly begin to rise, accelerating in a spiral pattern to an altitude of some 4,000 to 4,500 feet, where it stopped for a moment, hovering, then started to move across the sky to the north.

The object was observed for a further 10 minutes by my employee and another witness, my wife. I had called home and asked her to look into the sky to see if she could spot the object, which she did for some 10 minutes as it headed in a northerly direction still at an altitude of about 4,500 feet. The whole sighting lasted from 11 p.m. to 11:25 p.m. It seemed in the range of a quarter of a mile away.

That was simply the first in a series of sightings, many of which were spotted in the vicinity of the Pickering nuclear power plant.

Prophet equipped and modified a van for UFO tracking purposes. "It's a 1974 Dodge Royal Sportsman, soon to be a $15,000 UFO research unit complete with a dome for observational purposes, a telephone, a number of binoculars of various power, spotting scopes, including a Schmidt-Celestron 8-inch casgrain telescope for night viewing." The quotations come from Gene Duplantier's Foreword to Prophet's own illustrated pamphlet *The Amazing West Hill–Pickering Sightings* (1975). Duplantier added, "Since 1974, he has seen several hundred strange objects in the night skies but only nineteen that could be classified as genuine UFOs." Prophet soon joined the MUFON (Mutual UFO Network), a U.S. based organization, and planned to establish a Canadian group with the same aims. He proposed to call it the Reptune Research Organization.

There is a reference in his booklet to Henry McKay, the provincial director for MUFON, an electrician by training. Elsewhere McKay predicted, "Some time before 1977, I'm confident that I'll have a face-to-face meeting with extraterrestrial creatures who've landed their craft on Ontario soil. These creatures are exploring Earth, just as we're sending out craft to investigate the Moon, Venus, and Mars."

McKay quoted J. Allen Hynek, the scientist who established the Center for UFO Studies in Illinois and who coined the phrase "close encounters of the third kind." Apparently Hynek once said, "I don't know why, but there are more UFO sightings in Canada than anywhere else in the world."

Picton/
Dowsers

The practice of dowsing for water was wide-spread throughout Upper Canada and water witches or dowsers were familiar figures in farming communities in the last century.

Water witching attracted the attention of Canniff Haight, a native of Adolphustown and later a chemist in Picton, who recalled the custom from the days of his youth in the Bay of Quinte area when he wrote his book of reminiscences, *Country Life in Canada Fifty Years Ago* (1885).

> Another peculiar notion prevailed with respect to discovering the proper place to dig wells. There were certain persons, I do not remember what they were called, whether water doctors or water witches, who professed to be able, with the aid of a small hazel crotched twig, which was held firmly in both hands with the crotch inverted, to tell where a well should be sunk with a certainty of finding water. The process was simply to walk about with the twig thus

> held, and when the right place was reached, the forked twig would turn downwards, however firmly held; and on the strength of this digging would be commenced in the place indicated. A curious feature about this was that there were but few in whose hands the experiment would work, and hence the water discoverer was a person of some repute. I never myself witnessed the performance, but it was of common occurrence.

Psychics like Uri Geller maintain they are able to dowse not only for water but also for oil, precious metal, and buried treasure. They cover the ground in question by foot, by car, or by air, and some of them even dowse by map, suspending a pendulum or branch over a large-scale map and having it "twig." No matter how it is practised, dowsing has never been demonstrated under controlled circumstances. James Randi made this point after he challenged dowsers to prove their powers experimentally. The results are described in his book *Flim-Flam!* (1985).

Plum Hollow/
The Witch of Plum Hollow

The small farming community of Plum Hollow in Leeds County is located northwest of Brockville. Its most celebrated resident was Mrs. Elizabeth Barnes (1880–1888), an Irish-born woman whose psychic abilities — clairvoyance, fortune-telling, witching — were fabled far and wide. She claimed that because she was "the seventh daughter of the seventh daughter" she was blessed with "second sight" and "the sixth sense." She was treated with wary respect and some fear by the farmers in the community who called her Mother Barnes. Her log house is still standing, but her burial site is unmarked in the Sheldon Cemetery.

Mrs. Barnes was consulted for her witching powers to banish the poltergeist at the Dagg family farm, Shawville, Quebec. She figures in at least two literary works of interest. Thaddeus W.H. Leavitt, the founder and editor of the *Brockville Times,* wrote a novel of adventure, mystery, and the supernatural called *The*

Witch of Plum Hollow (1892). More recent is the dramatic work by Dorothy Morgan titled *The Witch of Plum Hollow: A One-Act Play on a Canadian Legend* (1977).

Mrs. Elizabeth Barnes, shown here in a contemporary drawing, lived in Plum Hollow. Her fame as a witch went well beyond the borders of Ontario's Leeds County. In the 1880s she was known far and wide as Mother Barnes or the Witch of Plum Hollow. She was barely five feet in height, yet her eyes were sharp and penetrating, wrote Ruth Mackenzie in Leeds and Grenville: Their First Two Hundred Years *(1967). [McClelland & Stewart]*

Port Colborne/
Hopkins' Tomb

After a varied and adventurous life Samuel Hopkins died in Port Colborne at the age of seventy-seven on 12 October 1899. In a sense he never died but still lives on.

An affluent and rather vain businessman, his will provided for the construction and maintenance of an imposing mausoleum in Oakwood Cemetery, on Lakeshore Road, west of Port Colborne. A twin-columned mausoleum was duly erected and inscribed

"S. Hopkins 1899." With the demise of his descendants, the mauseoleum fell into disrepair.

It is said that to this day Hopkins' faithful dog may be seen on the steps leading up to the mausoleum, guarding his late master's final resting place. It is locally maintained that the tomb is cursed for three youths who attempted to break into the tomb came to bad ends. All three had accidents: The first fellow lost his life in an automobile crash; the second lost his arm in an accident; and the third lost his leg below the knee in a motorcycle accident. As Arlene Lessard noted in "The History and Horrors of Hopkins' Tomb," *Alive and Well,* November 1981:

> Well known by the residents of Port Colborne, this tomb has long been associated with tales of ghosts and strange happenings. In order to break the supposed curse of the tomb a person must walk around the tomb seven times and knock on the door in passing each time. This feat was apparently attempted by a fellow who found that by the third time around, he started to hear loud noises from inside and felt thumping of the earth beneath his feet. He had in his possession a tire iron which was hastily thrown at the door during his retreat. (Is a tire iron really the appropriate weapon to use on a ghost?) After regaining some of his nerve, he started searching for the tire iron and found it in the bushes—red hot.

One rumour was that Hopkins' ghost would appear at the entrance to the tomb at the Spring Equinox. A group of students and curiosity seekers gathered but nothing happened. In 1981 a *séance* was held in front of the tomb. The session was interrupted by the spirit of the cemetery's irate caretaker who ordered the students off the property. The curse of Hopkins' tomb seems to be that it attracts the curious.

Port Hope/
"Spiders' Threads"

Spherical objects described as flying saucers were observed over the town of Port Hope, east of Oshawa.

Observed to accompany them were "spiders' threads." The following statement was made by P.L. Lewis of Port Hope.

Sunday, September 26, 1948. Port Hope, Ontario. This day was warm and the sky cloudless. We had had dinner in the garden and I was lying on my back on the lawn, my head just in the shade of the house, when I was startled to see an object resembling a star moving rapidly across the sky. The time was 2 o'clock Eastern Standard Time.

At first it was easy to imagine that recent reports of "Flying Saucers" had not been exaggerated.

More of these objects came sailing into view over the ridge of house, only to disappear when nearly overhead. With field glasses I was able to see that each was approximately spherical, the centre being rather brighter than the edges. The glasses also showed quite a number at such heights that they were invisible to the naked eye.

With only a gull flying in the sky for comparison, I should estimate the elevation of the lower objects to be about 300 ft. and the higher ones 2,000 ft; the size was about one foot in diameter and the speed about 50 m.p.h., in a direction SW to NE.

Also visible every now and then were long threads, apparently from spiders. Some of these were seen to reflect the light over a length of three or four yards, but any one piece may of course have been longer. Each was more or less horizontal, moving at right angles to its length. In one case an elongated tangled mass of these gave the appearance of a frayed silken cord. These threads appeared only in the lower levels.

It is reasonably certain that these objects were balls of spiders' threads, possibly with thistledown entangled in them, but the way in which they caught the rays of the sun and shone so brightly was very striking. P.L. Lewis

P.L. Lewis was a personal friend of P.R. Bishop whose report, "Cobwebs or Flying Saucers," appeared in *Weather,* 4:121–122, 1949. Bishop noted, in reference to the flying saucers, "No one else seems to have seen them on this occasion, but perhaps Mr. Lewis was the only one to be taking horizontal, post-prandial repose at the time." The statement is reproduced from *Handbook of Unusual Natural Phenomena* (1978) compiled by William R. Corliss.

In Fortean literature the phenomenon of "spiders' threads" is better known as "angel hair."

Princeton/
Margery the Medium

Mina Crandon (1888–1941) was one of the century's most colourful mediums and certainly its most beautiful. She was born Mina Stinson on a farm on the outskirts of Princeton, which is an agricultural community mid-way between Woodstock and Brantford. In 1904, Mina and her brother Walter, who was five years her junior, and the rest of the family moved to Boston.

In her prime, Mina was a beautiful blonde of pleasing disposition, so when she divorced her first husband, a green-grocer, she was able to attract the attentions and the hand in marriage of a considerably older man, Dr. LeRoy G. Crandon, a distinguished surgeon and member of the Harvard Medical School. During the 1920s and 1930s they resided at Crandon House, Number Ten Lime Street, Knob Hill, Boston. It was on the second floor of this mansion in Boston's most exclusive area that she and her husband later conducted their soirée-like *séances.*

When Dr. Crandon became interested in psychical phenomena, Mina followed suit and they were both delighted to realize that she had a talent for physical mediumship. Within a year Mina was producing such effects as bells, apports, deports, fingerprints, and cross-correspondences. They felt so confident of her powers that they offered to demonstrate Mina's abilities before a panel of experts convened by *Scientific American* in order to claim the magazine's standing offer of $2,500 to anyone who could produce psychic effect under close observation.

The magician and debunker Houdini was a member

of the panel which met at Number Ten Lime Street on 23 July 1924 and on subsequent occasions until 25 August to test Mina's abilities. She claimed she was assisted by the spirit of Walter, who was killed in a train accident somewhere in Ontario in 1911, but Houdini was able to prove to the satisfaction of the other members of the panel that the phenomena were fraudulent and that Mina was cheating with the connivance of her husband.

In February 1925, *Scientific American* exposed the Crandons. Their American career was ended though they did practise briefly in England. Dr. Crandon died in ill-health in 1938. Mina died an alcoholic in 1941. Mina's story is told by Thomas R. Tietze in *Margery* (1973).

Tietze has a few words for Walter, Mina's spirit-control. In the tradition of guides to the spirit world, Walter had a mind of his own. Tietz wrote, "Walter was not the most spiritual of spirits." It seems that Walter was uninhibited and years younger than Mina and would express himself in language Mina would never use, even in her non-trance moments. It seems Walter was also a poet. He may not be the first poet whose work was posthumously published but he was undoubtedly the first Canadian poet whose work was posthumously composed. Walter Steward Stinson dictated to Mina the following lines from his poem "The Voyageur":

> There is a plan far greater than the plan you know,
> There is a landscape broader than the one you see,
> There is a haven where storm tossed souls may go,
> You call it death — we, immortality.

The full text appears in *The Trials of Truth* (1930) by Jenny O'Hara Pincock.

Pukaskwa River/ In Search of the Curious

Pukaskwa National Park lies off the eastern shore of Lake Superior. Here the gorge of the Pukaskwa River and the beaches of Lake Superior are of special interest to the reader or traveller in search of the curious.

The legend of the gorge in all its disquieting grandeur is well told by Wayland Drew in *Superior: The Haunted Shore* (1975):

> Only one story, however, truly captures the sense of menace in the gorge at Pukaskwa. According to this legend, a marauder once stole a young woman from her father's lodge at Michipicoten and fled with her along the north shore, hotly pursued by her kinsmen. When he reached this river he turned inland, but finding the woman a serious encumbrance and enraged that he could not escape with her, he killed her. The story concludes by telling how the soul of the girl was transformed into a white doe of such radiance that the sight of her caused death, and how to this day, a peril to all who journey on the river, she roams in search of her murderer.

High up on the barren cobble beaches of Lake Superior are remnants of old structures, the Pukaskwa Cairns and the Pukaskwa Pits. The Pukaskaw Cairns are arranged in curious patterns. "One beach has forty-seven in two meandering lines," according to Drew. "No one knows who built them, or when. We know only, from the patterns of lichen growth on them, that most are at least several centuries old.

At least as intriguing are the shallow depressions known as the Pukaskwa Pits often found alongside the cairns. "They were made simply by removing the boulders from round sections of beach, varying in diameter from three to seventeen feet, and in depth from a few inches to about four feet. Some pits have walls roughly three feet high above the ground level." Drew noted that they were ideal for overnight shelters to give protection from the cold winds off the lake and for sentry points from which to observe the approach by water of hostile parties.

The strange pits seem to have had another purpose. "A few Pukaskwa Pits seem placed for maximum exposure to the elements. These are usually the highest and the smallest, situated on the most remote beaches. They were very probably vision pits, retreats for shamans and for youths on their first and most important quest.'' Drew is eloquent on the subject:

> To understand their use, imagine yourself travelling on the lake in another time, drawn by a glimpse of a plateau across a bay. At first it is unclear in drifting fog, but seen closer it is unmistakably an upland beach, a sterile band, paler green than the surrounding forest, paler grey than the dark lake. There is no movement on it, although a man sits erect in its centre, a tiny, vulnerable figure gazing out to the place where lake and sky join together. What he hears you do not hear; what he sees you do not see. If you are tired and hungry, he silently reminds you that there are journeys which do not begin until the body is forgotten. If you are frightened of the winter circling with the wind, he reminds you that the human dread behind such fears can be confronted, can be disarmed and absorbed in unknown repositories of courage. A seer, he is alone by choice. Time to him is nothing. Perhaps he will return among his people, perhaps not.

Queenston/
The Great Northeast Blackout

The northeastern region of Canada and the United States was plunged into blackness late in the day of 9 November 1965. The Great Northeast Blackout, the worst in history, affected thirty million people, one-sixth of the population of the North American continent, in eight American states and the eastern portion of Ontario. Electrical power which went off at 5:16 p.m. was restored within three hours in most parts of the province. New York City was without power well into the early hours of the next morning. The Blackout gave rise to a great deal of lore, including the belief that the birthrate in New York increased sharply nine months after the Blackout. Doris Day and Steve Allen starred in a 1968 motion picture based on the incident called *Where Were You When the Lights Went Out?*

The Blackout has been studied by a score of authors, including Yurko Bondarchuk in *UFO: Sightings, Landings and Abductions* (1979); John G. Fuller in *Aliens in the Skies: The New UFO Battle of the Scientists* (1969); and Frank Edwards in *Flying Saucers: Serious Business* (1966). A number of authors including Bondarchuk point out that there were reports of UFO activity in the vicinity of hydro installations at the time of the Blackout.

The official investigation pinpointed the problem —the malfunction of a backup relay on one of the six lines linking the mammoth Sir Adam Beck No. 2 Generating Station at Queenston, Ontario, north of Niagara Falls, with the rest of the Eastern power grid. A sudden surge of power tripped the circuit breaker and the backup relay failed. The overflow of power leaped to the other five lines, the relays of which overloaded and tripped their circuit breakers. The process continued along lines in New York State until the entire grid of thirty-one interconnected power utilities had broken down.

Where did the sudden surge of power come from? ''To this day that question has remained unanswered,'' wrote Bondarchuk. Donald E. Keyhoe maintained that ''a giant craft, estimated at well over one hundred feet in diameter,'' appeared to be positioned directly over the Clay substation, a strategic installation that channelled power from Niagara Falls to New York City. Early explanations for the Blackout had pinpointed this very substation as the cause of the power failure. And Edwards noted there was UFO activity in the Syracuse area at the time of the Blackout. A scientist and UFO researcher James M. McCampbell, in *Ufology: New Insights from Science and Common Sense* (1973), maintained that the power-grid breakdown was UFO-caused, that Canadian and America hydro authorities knew this, and that they were ''covering up.''

Bay of Quinte/
Dark Days

Dark Days occur for whatever reason when there is daytime darkness. The phenomenon is so striking that it evokes the emotions of fear and terror, not to men-

219

tion awe and wonder. The Bay of Quinte area experienced at least two Dark Days, as recorded by Canniff Haight in *Country Life in Canada Fifty Years Ago* (1885).

> In the year 1780, on the 14th day of October, and again in July, 1814, a most remarkable phenomenon occurred, the like of which was never before witnessed in the country. "At noonday a pitchy darkness completely obscured the light of the sun, continuing for about ten minutes at a time, and being frequently repeated during the afternoon. In the interval between each mysterious eclipse, dense masses of black clouds streaked with yellow drove athwart the darkened sky, with fitful gusts of wind. Thunder, lightning, black rain, and showers of ashes added to the terrors of the scene, and when the sun appeared its colour was a bright red." The people were filled with fear, and thought that the end of the world was at hand. These two periods are known as the "dark days."

Rainy River/ "The Mound-Builders"

"The most spectular prehistoric native monument in all of Canada is a burial mound on Rainy River," noted the archaeologist W.A. Kenyon in *Mounds of Sacred Earth: Burial Mounds of Ontario* (1986).

The mounds along the Rainy River between Fort Frances and Rainy River were mentioned in passing by Henry Youle Hind on his Red River exploring expedition of 1857. He compared the country-side around the tumuli to "a neglected Indian garden." In 1884 the historian George Bryce described twenty-one separate mounds and expressed the feeling that they were the work of northward-moving Indians and not the handiwork of some earlier non-Indian race of "mound-builders."

The notion that the architects of the mounds in Manitoba and Ontario were a race of "mound-builders," a people otherwise unknown to history, was dismissed in an article by C.N. Bell. (His article,

misleadingly titled "The Mound-Builders in Canada," appeared in the *Proceedings of the Canadian Institute,* Vol. 3, No. 1, 1886.)

In 1957 W.A. Kenyon excavated five mounds on the northern bank of Rainy River and one on Oak Point Island at the eastern end of Rainy Lake. The latter site produced a total of 3596 small glass beads, all round or tubular specimens in black, white, and blue. When he examined the skeletal remains, he learned that a typical skull had a circular opening about two inches in diameter in the occipital region at the back of the head.

> In northwestern Ontario, the skulls that have openings in their occipital regions are reasonably clear evidence of power transfer. The individuals whose skulls were opened would have had some unusual and highly valued personal characteristics; the occipital openings made it possible to remove their brains and to transfer those characteristics from the dead to the living. This would have been accomplished through a religious ceremony that included eating the brain that was the seat of such wondrous powers. The eating, of course, could have been either actual or symbolic. In either event, the highly valued qualities would not be lost to the band through death but would be preserved through reincarnation.

He also found evidence of the "masking" of skulls. The eye and nose sockets of a typical skull were packed with clay. A shell bead was pressed into the wet clay of each eye socket to simulate a pupil. The entire skull was lightly dusted with red ochre. Skulls so treated acquired an eerie, somewhat mask-like appearance.

Kenyon came to the conclusion that the primary function of the mounds was not the funerary function but "was to mark the locations of sacred places and to establish territorial occupation. The sites they occupied were used as ceremonial centres for the loosely organized bands that occupied the surrounding areas." He observed the importance of delineating "sacred places":

Here in Ontario, as throughout much of the world, the process was never completed. For the Precambrian rocks of northern Ontario are still dotted with pictographs and petroglyphs — cabalistic figures from remotest antiquity. In southern Ontario, on the other hand, these ancient symbols were superseded by more recent deities who presided over rituals such as the Green Corn ceremony. In the modern world, the pictographs and petroglyphs seem strangely out of place. We find them in odd nooks and crannies of the landscape, on isolated rock faces in northern Ontario, deep in the caves of Spain and France, or in remote corners of Africa. We recognize them as belonging to a different world, one that is rapidly fading from sight. And it is quite fitting, perhaps, that they should disappear with the cultures they symbolized and sustained throughout countless centuries. For even gods are mortal. After millennia, our own gods are showing signs of weariness. Christianity, with its pastoral symbolism, is beginning to feel uncomfortable in the concrete and plastic jungles we have built around us.

St. Catharines/
Practical Physician

The announcement read: "The Public are respectfully invited to witness the Wonderful Cures performed every morning at the Hall . . . No Surgical Operations Performed! Chronic Diseases Cured! Acute Pain Instantly Relieved! The Lame Walk! The Blind See! The Deaf Hear! Over 200,000 Patients Treated in Eleven Years." It continued:

Synopsis of His Philosophy. He treats all manner of diseases by calling to his aid and properly directing the electric currents and nervous forces, without using minerals or questionable drugs. The philosophy of his treatment may be briefly stated thus: Force is spirit in motion. Vital force is organic motion, or the proper movement of organized particles as they pass to and from the human system. Disease, in a word, is obstruction — the result of an impaired vital force, and it is at least accompanied, if not caused, by deranged organic motion. — These derangements can only be radically removed by inducing a recurrence of the normal or healthy action. A cure can only be effected by calling in the aid of these electro/magnetic or vital forces, which are concerned in all organic changes.

The advertisement announced the appearance of Dr. J. Ruttley of New York City, Practical Physician. It was carried by the St. Catharines *Evening Journal*, 5 October 1868. The self-styled Dr. Ruttley held healing sessions each morning at the Town Hall in St. Catharines. At least one of these sessions was interestingly interrupted, to judge by the following column in the *Evening Journal*, 10 October 1868:

Dr. Ruttley at Work — One of the most extraordinary scenes we have ever witnessed took place at the Town Hall, this morning. A man calling himself Dr. Ruttley, who professes to cure the lame, blind and halt by laying on of hand, &c., while publicly manipulating the afflicted credulous, was charged by a man name O.P. Dodge, with being a bigamist, a humbug, and a fraud on the public. He asserted that Ruttley came from Mitchell, Ontario, where he had a wife living, and that he is now married to a woman from Painsville, Ohio. He also charged him with certain nefarious transactions in Baltimore and offered $100 if he would go to the United States, where Ruttley is wanted. Ruttley thereupon rose in his might, and hurled back the "lying perjured statements of O.P. Dodge." Ruttley then acknowledged the sole impeachment on the bigamy questions, and exhibited the knife with which he at first intended to stab to the heart the lecherous Methodist class leader whom he caught in the act of adultery. He called O.P. Dodge foul names, and used such blasphemous and obscene language as to cause many respectable females to retire from the hall. Shortly afterwards, one of his rheumatic

221

patients, named Richard Tuite, faced him on the stage and denounced him as a humbug. During the time we were in the hall there was no case of cure, or even benefit, beyond what temporary relief can be had from a magnetic shock. If people are credulous enough to have faith in a man who professes to derive miraculous powers from Heaven to heal the sick, all we can say is that they deserve to be fleeced. We consider the thing a bare-faced fraud.

St. Catharines/
Three Dozen Séances

In the twilight of the *séance* parlour, events occur or seem to occur which are seldom if ever reconsidered in the light of day. Something of an exception to that rule was observed in 1928–29 at the residence of Mrs. Jenny O'Hara Pincock in St. Catharines, Ontario.

In the darkened parlour of Mrs. Pincock's residence at 47 Church Street almost three-dozen *séances* were held over a period of nine months. Complete minutes of the sessions were taken, and exceedingly detailed records of the proceedings were published in the form of a 396-page book called *The Trials of Truth* (1930). The book was compiled by Mrs. Pincock and includes a foreword by B.F. Austin, the spiritualist from Belleville who settled in Los Angeles. In fact, the book bears the publishing imprint of the spiritualist, for it was issued in 1930 by the Austin Publishing Company, Los Angeles, California.

Austin in his foreword has strong and stirring words to say on behalf of Mrs. Pincock and the witnesses who contributed to this book:

Their united testimony is to the proof of the most stupendous fact, the most amazing truth, that can possibly enter the mind of man—a fact that alters the whole outlook of the individual from life and destiny—a fact that is fundament to any system of religion or morality and one of supreme personal import to every man everywhere.

What Austin meant by the "most amazing truth" is proof of what spiritualists call "survival after death" and "spirit-return."

The proofs were very important to Jenny O'Hara Pincock. Tragedy struck her four times in a row. Mrs. Pincock, a young housewife in St. Catharines, endured three miscarriages and no live births. Then, in May 1928, she suffered the death of her husband, Robert Newton Pincock, a native of Newfoundland. During their years of marriage, they had given consideration to the possible truth of spiritualism, without coming to any conclusion about the matter.

Four months following the death of her husband, Mrs. Pincock arranged to hold the first *séance* in the series on 6 September 1928. All of the sessions were held in her residence in St. Catharines, except for two at the home of a friend in Hamilton, Ontario, and one at the spiritualist camp at Lily Dale, New York. Although the series concluded on 23 June 1929, it might be said to have culminated in the publication of *The Trials of Truth*.

The circle consisted of Mrs. Pincock and from six to twelve of her friends and relatives. The medium was Mr. William Cartheuser, "well-known at the American Society of Physical Research," who seems to have commuted between his home in New York and St. Catharines for the sittings. No session was held without a bowl of water, a bouquet of fresh flowers, and a musical instrument—a trumpet, a violin, or a guitar. Occasionally an instrument would be played, apparently by a spirit.

A typical session would begin with the recital of prayers and the singing of hymns. If the conditions were favourable, the "the marvellous manifestations" would follow. The manifestations were not of the sensational variety, like those reported from some *séances,* but simple messages from "the beyond." The "direct-voice" medium would establish contact with his spirit-guide and hear from him or her or it through the medium of the trumpet. The medium had a number of spirit-guides, including a squaw named Bright Moon, her husband a brave called Tall Pine, and another brave known as White Bear. It was always a great moment when Mrs. Pincock could record, "Then my husband came through." His voice and the voices of many others who had "passed over" came through, sometimes strongly, sometimes weakly, with individual messages of consolation and encouragement. The sessions would last an hour or take up an entire morning or afternoon. Then, abruptly, the contact would be broken. "Water was spinkled as a final blessing. The trumpet fell."

Some sessions were "pregnant with evidence and marvellous manifestations," wrote Mrs. Pincock. "It has been humanly impossible, rather, for the author to do more than touch the fringe of the evidential matter which has come through from the invisible entities." Evidence that Mrs. Pincock described as "evidential" and regarded as providential might be described by others as circumstantial. One member of the circle was informed that her mother who was living in a distant city was suffering problems with her shoulder; the following week the daughter received a letter from her mother complaining of neuritis in the shoulder.

Some voices were more philosophical than others. They were willing to answer the religious questions posed by members of the circle on such matters as the divinity of Jesus, the divine inspiration of selected passages in the Bible, the relationship between the Christian church and the Spiritualist faith, the inevitablity of progress, and the movement toward internationalism.

It may be hoped that the revelations from the three dozen *séances* brought Mrs. Pincock some degree of relief for her suffering. Whether or not they did, they certainly placed her sorrows in a spiritual or spiritualistic context. She explained that she emerged from the experience with the conviction that there is life after death — personal survival — and that this was a conviction she did not receive in the Christian churches of the day. Evidence of the conviction is not "revealed through material means. For proof of survival lies principally in the simple, personal evidence of invisible entities. Such proof shall always appeal to the sincere, intelligent and unprejudiced minds of earth."

St. Lawrence River/
Under the Sea

Aultsville, Dickinson's Landing, Farran's Point, Milles Roches, and Moulinette are the names of the submerged communities of the St. Lawrence. In 1958 these long-established communities in southeastern Ontario were abandoned and flooded to permit the opening of the St. Lawrence Seaway the following year. To these communities should be added two more, Iroquois and Morrisburg, parts of which were also lost forever in the flooding.

It has been said that seafarers on the Seaway, when they pass over the places where these communities formerly flourished, are witnesses to strange sights and sounds. They report seeing lights from the depths of the waters and hearing murmurs from among the waves.

Edgar Cayce, who gave "psychic readings" while in a state between a sleep and a trance, had information to impart about the St. Lawrence Seaway. During the reading he gave on 13 August 1941, the following message was recorded: "The waters of the lakes [Great Lakes] will empty into the Gulf [Gulf of Mexico], rather than the waterway over which such discussions have been recently made [the St. Lawrence Seaway]. It would be well if the waterway were prepared, but not for that purpose for which it is at present being considered." Cayce was convinced that the course of the river and the purpose of the seaway would be altered by an "earth change" which would occur between 1941 and 1998. These and similar prophecies of catastrophe appear in *Earth Changes Update* (1980) by Hugh Lynn Cayce.

St. Thomas/
Angela the Ghost of Alma

The city of St. Thomas, south of London, is associated in the minds of collectors of the curious with Jumbo, the circus elephant, who on 15 September 1885 was mortally wounded in his encounter with a Grand Trunk locomotive speeding through St. Thomas. The city is also associated with Alma College, a long-established girl's school.

As "resident presence" of the college is Angela the Ghost of Alma. "The origin of Angela is lost in antiquity; however, her presence is still celebrated each Hallowe'en by the students," wrote Eileen Sonin in *ESPecially Ghosts* (1970). Apparently Angela, a well-established "resident presence" by 1930, haunts Ivory Tower, one of two towers at the south end of the building. "Of the many stories about Angela, a persistent one seemed to concern an unpopular music teacher who was locked in a cupboard up there by the girls." However, the school's records which go back to 1881 include no reference to a teacher named Angela.

St. Thomas/
Premonition of a Death

Did the telegraph operator of the Grand Trunk Railway have a premontion in a dream of the death of another worker, a brakeman, a week or so before he was killed on the job? The incident was described in great detail by the Rev. B.F. Austin, Principal of Alma College, in his book *Glimpses of the Unseen* (1898). Austin's book is a five-hundred-page collection of accounts which establish the reality of psychical phenomena, including Spiritualism. Austin believed that the telegraph operator had a premonition of the death.

At 10:30 a.m., 3 May 1893, Edward Thomson, a nineteen-year-old brakeman employed on the Grand Trunk Railway, was killed twelve miles west of the city of St. Thomas. At the time of his death he was working on a stretch of track that was new to him. It was a freak accident. He slipped and fell between two cars and was crushed to death.

The premonition occurred "a week or ten days before" the accident. One night in late April, possibly on the 28th, James Finch, the night telegraph operator and a friend of Thomson's, was not on duty but in bed, asleep and dreaming. In his dream he was operating the telegraph. The flow of messages was interrupted by an urgent message which read: "Teddy Thomson is killed. Tell his mother." Finch did not

tell Thomson's mother, but he did tell members of his family and some friends. Apparently Finch was not the only person to receive a premonition about this time. "The thing was felt as an actual thing by four or five persons" between that time and the time of the lethal accident. Austin added, "The single circumstance of Finch's prophecy would, perhaps, have been treated as a mere accident—a strange coincidence and nothing more—if it had not happened that other members of the family, one of them hundreds of miles away, had received 'warnings' of the danger that hovered over the young man."

Austin went on to described the interest shown in the case by Dr. Richard Maurice Bucke, Superintendent of the Asylum at London, north of St. Thomas, who was working on a book about intuitive experiences and who went to the trouble of writing to witnesses and others, requesting that they describe the incident in greater detail. Bucke accumulated a number of first- and second-hand accounts and expressed the belief that the "faculty of second sight is hereditary" and that the ability flowed through the veins of the Thomson family in particular. Austin's conclusion was that "mortals are permitted to witness in advance the machinery of destiny at work shaping the predetermined and inevitable events which make the web of human life."

St. Thomas/
Spiritualism and Christianity

Spiritualism and Christianity collided quite dramatically in June 1899 when a Methodist minister was tried on four charges of heresy, found guilty of three, and subsequently expelled from the ministry.

The clergyman was the Rev. Benjamin Fish Austin (1850–1933) who through his preaching and his publications was briefly the country's most controversial spiritualist. Austin was born in Brighton, Ontario, and educated at Albert College in Belleville. He graduated in 1877 and a fellow student was Mary Edwards Merrill, the prodigy whose bold beliefs, brief life, and odd death would inspire Flora MacDonald Denison to write a fictionalized biography which was later prefaced and published by Austin.

Austin graduated in divinity and served in the Methodist Episcopal congregation at Prescott before assuming the principalship of Alma Ladies' College in St. Thomas. The liberalization of Austin's thought from Christian dogmatism through the spirit of scientific inquiry into the realms of spiritualism has been traced by the historian Ramsay Cook in *The Regenerators: Social Criticism in Late Victorian English Canada* (1985). Austin resigned the principalship of the college in 1897 but continued as a clergyman, reconciling Christian spirituality with spiritualistic principles. He spoke as one who had had his share of psychical experiences and as a hypnotist and healer. He felt spiritualism augmented Christianity and that his pastoral work was the better for his beliefs. He could allay fears of death by affirming "spirit return," for instance.

Then four charges of heresy were laid against him by a fellow minister, the Rev. A.H. Goring of Port Stanley. Goring cited a sermon which Austin had delivered in May 1899 and thereafter published in which he denied the doctrine of eternal punishment, questioned Christ's divinity, denied the doctrine of Christ as God's final revelation, and upheld the fraudulent system of spiritualism.

The charges were formally considered by the General Conference of the Methodist Church meeting in Toronto in June 1899. In a written defence, Austin denied the first three charges but admitted that he was a spiritualist, adding that he rejected all its fraudulent forms. The Conference sustained all the charges but the first. Austin had not denied the doctrine of eternal punishment. Austin could not be both a spiritualist and a Methodist clergyman. He was expelled from the ministry for heresy.

The Annual Conference of the Methodist Church met later that month in Windsor. Austin addressed the body, speaking for three and a half hours. He refuted the charges against him and defended his spiritualist beliefs. He argued that the Church should recognize the Higher Criticism of the Bible and the Theory of Evolution. He claimed, "The Prophets of the olden time and the Psychics of today are one and the same."

The arguments and the rhetoric were to no avail. The Conference was one vote short of unanimity in affirming the expulsion order.

Austin wrote, edited, and published several books of spiritualist interest. Finding the climate of opinion in Canada uncongenial, and unable to earn a living to support himself and his large family, he emigrated to the United States. He served as pastor of spiritualist churches in Rochester, New York, and Los Angeles, California. He died in the latter city in 1933.

B.F. Austin was ahead of his time. But it took almost a century for Canadian churchmen to admit Christian Spiritualists to their company. In the 1980s the United Church of Canada recognizes the spiritualistic ministry within its congregations. But not all Christian groups are so lenient — or lax. The Anglican Church of Canada is more strict. In the 1960s it withdrew clerical status from the Rev. Ernest Harrison who had publicized his position that it is possible for there to be a "church without God."

Sault Ste. Marie/ The Great Turtle

The fur trader Alexander Henry the Elder witnessed the operation of the Great Turtle, the oracle of the Ojibways, at Sault Ste. Marie in 1764. He described the consultation in his book *Travels and Adventures in Canada and the Indian Territories. Between the Years 1760 and 1776* (1809).

As Henry recalled, the Ojibway were in a quandary. Should they attack the English or not? The elders consulted the Great Turtle to aid in their deliberations. They did so in much the same manner that the Ancient Greeks consulted the Delphic Oracle for direction in matters of state. The Great Turtle was Mikinak, the spirit of the Shaking Tent. A large wigwam of moosehide was erected, and that evening the medicine men entered the tent which immediately began to shake violently. Alexander Henry heard a pandemonium of sounds, shrieks, and words. After some time there was a cry that sounded like that of a young puppy.

225

The chief medicine man announced the Great Turtle was present.

The spirit was asked if the English at Fort Niagara were massing to attack. The tent shook violently. There was a piercing cry, then a silence that lasted for a quarter of an hour. It was explained that during this time Mikinak was flying over Lake Huron, visiting Fort Niagara, visiting Montreal, and flying back. When the sounds resumed, the medicine man spoke: "At Fort Niagara the Great Turtle has seen no great number of Red Coats. But on going down the St. Lawrence to Montreal, he has found the river there covered with boats, and the boats filled with Red Coats with guns, in number like the leaves of the trees. He has seen them on their way upstream, coming to make war upon the Indians."

When asked if the leader of the Red Coats, Sir William Johnson, would receive a peaceful party of Ojibways, the Great Turtle replied in the affirmative. This information was met with joy. Thereafter the oracle answered personal questions, including one from Alexander Henry. "O Great Turtle, shall I soon revisit my own country?" he asked. The spirit replied, "Take courage, white man, no harm will come to you. In the end you will reach your friends and return in safety to your own country."

The Great Turtle would prove to be right on both accounts. Alexander Henry suspected trickery. "But such was the skill displayed in the performance, or such my deficiency of penetration, that I made no discoveries, but came away as I went, with no more than those general surmises which will naturally be entertained by every reader."

Scotland/
Small Balls of Fire

The following letter was sent by J.R. Malcolm, M.D., from Scotland, a community southwest of Brantford. It was published in the Toronto *Globe* on 6 May 1890. It was republished by Jack Kapica, editor of *Shocked & Appalled: A Century of Letters to The Globe & Mail* (1985). It deals with a problem that is timeless — Fortean "fire-balls."

The appearance last evening for the third time of a luminous ball of fire in the streets of this village induces me to ask yourself or some of your scientific correspondents a few practical questions. But, in order to explain myself, I will first give a short description of the last appearance of this phenomenon, as described by a reliable gentleman living near the Baptist church in this village: — "On the evening of the 29th inst., as I was in a rear room of my residence without a light, I was surprised by the sudden illumination of the room to an extraordinary extent. I looked out the window, and, seeing a bright light a few rods up the street, seized my hat and ran out to ascertain its cause. On nearing it, at a distance of about a rod, a luminous ball about the size of my closed hand appeared lying on the ground and bounding along the highway in front of me, making a hissing noise and sparkling each time it struck the earth and bounded along. I followed it and approached it, but, when within about two yards of it, it suddenly moved away northward at a very rapid pace, as fast or faster than a running horse, leaving a peculiar odor not unlike burning powder, and disappearing over the hills north of the church. The centre portion of the luminous body was of a very white color, like the calcium or electric light, and appeared to be without substance. This was surrounded by a bright red light, which in turn was enveloped by a voluminous smoke. The wind was blowing strongly from the north at the time, and this went rapidly against the wind as I approached it. It was followed by both pedestrians and horsemen, but could not be overtaken."

The locality where these balls have appeared three times within ten days is of a sandy loam and gravely soil, about forty rods from the cemetery, and about fifty rods from a spring coming out below the knoll on which the church and cemetery are situated.

Can it be possible, Mr. Editor, that the phosphorated, carbonated, or sulphurated hydrogen gases have travelled around or through the base of the knoll a distance of forty or fifty rods without being disseminated; and, becoming ignited, spontaneously producing the ignis fatuus so much dreaded by the superstitious of the olden times; and would either of these gases or a mixture of them produce a light of sufficient brilliance to illuminate the side of the church to enable people to count the clapboards at a distance of a quarter of a mile away?

Again, could a fireball of that description travel in the face of a strong wind at that speed? Or might there have been a strong undercurrent under the hills in a contrary direction to that of the main superstratum above?

I take it for granted, Mr. Editor, that the fact of none of the three appearing to have material substance or to have fallen from above precludes the idea of their being of meteoric origin.

Apologizing for trespassing on your valuable space, I am, yours very truly,

J.R. Malcolm, M.D.
Scotland, Ontario

Lake Scugog/
The Ghost Rider

Strange lights seen on Scugog Island, which lies in Lake Scugog, north of Oshawa, have given rise to the legend of the Ghost Rider of Scugog Island. According to Jim Shrigley of the Oshawa *Times,* 13 July 1984, "Local legend says the spirit of a dead motorcyclist is so possessed with the love of speed, it will ride a lonely section of the island forever."

Observers on the south shore of the mainland maintain that at night they can see on the island an iridescent white light race a mile or so a few feet above the level of the road. The light resembles the headlight of a motorcycle and appears to halt near the spot where a motorcyclist was reportedly killed in an accident many years ago. Seconds later the white light blinks out and a bright light, round and red, said to resemble the tail-light of a motorcycle, fades away into the distance. Neither the bike nor the cyclist is seen, only the white then the red light.

Two psychics visited the scene in December 1982 and agreed that a motorcycle accident had occurred at the intersection where the light is said to halt. Apparently in the early 1950s the motorcycle driver, an eighteen-year-old youth with sandy hair, was speeding and struck the huge boulder by the side of the road. He was thrown from his vehicle and killed. The location in question is a north-south sideroad off Durham Road 7 which runs between the ninth and tenth concession roads.

Critics and sceptics maintain that the legend is a tall tale meant to explain the lights which are merely the reflection of automobile headlights from the Purple Hills area about four miles south of Lake Scugog. They claim the legend is as old as the phenomenon which was first reported about 1979.

Serpent Mounds Provincial Park/
"Alien"

The archaeologist W.A. Kenyon felt that serpent mounds in Canada were "strangely out of place." Here is what he wrote in *Mounds of Sacred Earth: Burial Mounds of Ontario* (1986):

If we stand on the north shore of Rice Lake, for example, and look at the ancient serpent resting quietly in its grove of oaks, our minds drift spontaneously to the south; for the Serpent Mound is an alien form — the only one of its kind in Canada — and its nearest relative, almost a quarter of a mile long, sits on a high bluff overlooking a small stream in Adams County, Ohio. Originally, we feel, these serpents must have been conceived in the jungles of Central American or Mexico. As they moved north, their ranks gradually thinned, for the harsh climate of the higher northern latitudes is not suitable for tropical serpents. And so the last surviving member of that strange breed came to rest in Ontario, on the flank of the Precambrian Shield.

227

The serpentine mounds are found in Serpent Mounds Provincial Park located on Rice Lake southeast of Peterborough. At one time the mounds were believed by the local inhabitants, both Indian and European, to be earthwork that had been raised as a defence against the marauding Iroquois from New York State.

In 1896 archaeologists established that the mounds or tumuli served as a burial site. Yet the skeletal remains that have been found are so few in number as to suggest that they were erected to serve additional purposes. The materials have been dated to the first three centuries of the Christian era. The mounds were constructed not by a mysterious non-Indian race of migrant Mound-Builders, as once believed, but by the Adena and Hopewell peoples of the north, ancestors of the present-day Indians.

The principal Serpent Mound is a sinuous structure with head and tail. From the air it resembles an immense spermatozoa more than it does some sort of sea serpent. It measures 194 feet in length and an average 25 feet in width. It is surrounded by eight other mounds, low oval or circular structures with major diameters. These other mounds were vividly described by the archaeologist David Boyle as "eggs."

Sharon/
Children of Peace

The Sharon Temple of the Children of Peace is a beautiful and symbolic prayer hall which was erected over a period of seven years (1825–32) at Sharon, a community north of Newmarket, by David Willson and his followers, unorthodox Quakers who equated vocal and instrumental music with prayer.

Willson's followers were formally known as the Children of Peace and informally called the Davidites. He led them from New York State to Upper Canada where they farmed and prospered. They prayed and sang in their square wooden temple of symbolic design. Its tiers represent the Trinity; the twelve pillars recall the Apostles; four additional pillars recall Willson's four virtues (Faith, Hope, Love, Charity). There are illustrations on the walls of the Setting Sun and Armageddon. The temple's centrepiece is a wooden model of the Ark of the Covenant, familiar enough from Biblical illustration and the movie *Raiders of the Lost Ark*. A curving Jacob's Ladder leads from the gallery floor to the music gallery.

Following Willson's death in 1866, the temple fell into a state of disrepair. It was fully restored by the York Pioneer and Historical Society in 1957. It now serves as the setting for the annual Sharon Music Festival — and as a reminder of a peace-loving Christian sect that has long disappeared from the face of the Earth.

Shirleys Bay/
"Flying Saucer Sighting Station"

The world's first "flying saucer sighting station" was established in November 1953 at Shirleys Bay, a community on the Ottawa River, east of Ottawa and north of Kanata. The station was an integral part of Project Magnet, a study of UFOs undertaken by the Department of Transport (DOT) which was set up under the direction of Wilbert B. Smith, then senior radio engineer, Broadcast and Measurements Section, and UFOlogist.

"This station consisted of a small wooden Defence Research Board (DRB) building, containing some highly sophisticated instrumentation specially adapted to detect flying saucers. These instruments were: a gamma-ray counter, a magnetometre, a radio receiver, and a recording gravimetre. These four instruments produced traces on a multiple-pen graphical recorder which was checked periodically to note any disturbances."

So wrote Arthur Bray in his entry on Project Magnet in *The Encyclopedia of UFOs* (1980) edited by Ronald D. Story. The station was established to note any anomalous aerial behaviour, and there was just such behaviour. "At 3:01 P.M., August 8, 1954, the station registered a definite disturbance, quite different from disturbances registered by passing aircraft. Smith and his colleagues were alerted by a built-in alarm system. Regrettably, heavy fog prevailed and it was impossible to see anything overhead. The recorded evidence, however, indicated that something strange had flown within feet of the station.''

DOT officially folded Project Magnet on 20 August 1954, but permitted Smith to continue to use its facilities on his own time at no expense to the government. At the time of his death in December 1962, Smith believed it was possible to determine areas of "reduced binding." He was working on the development of an "antigravity device" and felt himself to be on the verge of an important discovery in the physics of UFO flight.

The world's first "flying saucer sighting station" was established by Wilbert B. Smith on the compound maintained by the Communications Research Centre of the Department of Communications at Shirleys Bay, outside Ottawa. The station was opened in November 1953 but was in operation for less than a year. At 3:01 p.m. on 8 August 1954, its automatic equipment registered a disturbance of some sort in the atmosphere. A bulletin was issued to the effect that the disturbance the station had recorded had been caused by a "flying saucer," a mysterious, newsworthy, but nevertheless bureaucratically embarrassing form of transport. This led to the decision of the Department of Transport later that month to discontinue Smith's shoestring operation. [Department of Communications]

Sioux Lookout/ Radar Station

Reports of extensive UFO activity in the vicinity of the Canadian Forces Radar Station at Sioux Lookout in northwestern Ontario led to a question about UFO activity being asked in the House of Commons.

On 12 December 1968, during question period, the Member of Parliament for Kenora-Rainy River, John Reid, rose and directed a question to the Parliamentary Secretary to the Minister of National Defence. "Shortly after my last visit to Sioux Lookout, I was told by telephone, and in person, that there had been a large number of sightings there," he explained, and then proceeded to read from an article published in the Sioux Lookout *Daily Bulletin,* 29 November, which described "a big light in the sky, which kept changing colour" seen by a number of people in the area. The article described the UFO as "a flat circular object of bright greenish hue, which appeared to be pulsating." Apparently it travelled at conventional speed for an airborne object.

"That brings me to the point of my question, Mr. Speaker. We do have this very extensive facility at Sioux Lookout that is operated by the Department of National Defence. Surely if anything was in the sky over that period, records would be kept by this most efficient establishment . . . .Therefore, I would like to ask the parliamentary secretary whether he could release some of this supposedly confidential information for the benefit of the Canadian public. The Christmas holiday season is fast approaching, but I do not want to receive the answer from the parliamentary secretary that it was Santa Claus trying out his reindeer in anticipation of Christmas."

The Parliamentary Secretary to the Minister of National Defence rose in reply. He confirmed that strange lights had been reported but explained that none had been picked up by radar screens at Sioux Lookout. "There probably will be some unidentified flying objects picked up by that radar station," he concluded. "There is some evidence that these will eventually be identified as a space vehicle propelled by eight unknown objects!''

Six Nations Reserve/
Belief Systems

The native peoples' traditional way of life is maintained from generation to generation as much as possible in the modern era on the Indian Reserves and at the Eskimo Co-operatives. Exceptionally meaningful oral legend and myth, customs and practices, are kept alive by the 9500 Indians who live on the Six Nations Reserve, located on the banks of the Grand River, southeast of Brantford, probably more than elsewhere in the country. The Reserves are depositories and distribution points for age-old belief systems which strike the non-native as non-Western. Many of them seem Eastern and positively pagan and shamanistic in origin.

The Six Nations Reserve keeps alive the tradition of Dekanahwideh, the founder of the Iroquois Confederacy, who was born of a virgin mother, near the present site of Kingston, Ontario, raised in a family of Mohawks, wandered for many years in the West, and returned on a boat of stone. He summoned the leaders of the warring nations, and with the help of the semi-legendary Hiawatha, he founded the Great Peace, also called the Iroquois Confederacy, which was the union of the Five (later the Six) Nations. He uprooted the tallest pine tree, and into the cavity he ordered the chiefs to cast down their weapons of war. He buried these weapons and replanted the tree, naming it the Great Tree of Peace and calling on its branches to shelter them forever. He ordered the Eagle to perch upon its tallest branch, and watch over the nations of the Confederacy. Dekanahwideh said unto them, "If the Great Peace should fail, call on my name in the bushes, and I will return." Uttering these words of promise, he embarked on his boat of stone and sailed on the Great Lakes and vanished in the West.

The Iroquois Confederacy has endured to this day. It is said that at various times resolutions have been introduced and debated in the council chambers of the Six Nations Reserve as to whether or not to request the return of Dekanahwideh. The Indians of North America still regard the eagle as their special symbol, the U.S. government's symbolic use of it being a usurpation.

The early explorers described with astonishment the concepts and customs of the Indians. When the Jesuit missionaries arrived and observed the rites and rituals of the Iroquois, they condemned them as works of the devil. One Jesuit, more open-minded than most, was Pierre-François-Xavier de Charlevoix who in 1721 witnessed and described the so-called Festival of Dreams. In one account this is called *Ononharoia,* "turning the brain upside down." The festival was held for fifteen days each year, commencing about 22 February. During this period the Iroquois gave themselves licence to act out their dreams, desires, and deepest fantasies with impunity. As Charlevoix wrote in his anonymously translated *History and General Description of New France* (1744):

> I know not if Religion has ever any Share in what they generally call *the Festival of Dreams,* and which the *Iroquois,* and some others, have more properly called *the turning of the Brain.* This is a Kind of *Bacchanal,* which commonly lasts fifteen Days, and is celebrated about the End of Winter.

There are further details: all forms of folly were permitted; destruction was countenanced; individuals could opt out if they remained out of the way; participants tried to guess each other's dreams; everything taken or broken was returned or repaired at the great feast which ended the festival. "But when the Festival is over, every Thing must be forgot." Charlevoix added that some participants acted reasonably but that others acted outrageously, using the festival as the occasion to settle long-standing grievances.

The Festival of Dreams is not an affair of the past. "It may interest you to know that this ritual is still observed at Ohsweken in the Iroquois Longhouse religion, the present wrter having participated in it," wrote Wm. Guy Spittal in a letter written on 17 March 1980. "However, it no longer assumes the rather dramatic proportions of earlier times. Dreams are still guessed and charms made as a result of it."

Spittal is the owner and operator of Iroqrafts at Ohsweken on the Six Nations Reserve.

The anthropologist Bruce G. Trigger discussed the significance of the Festival of Dreams held for only three days by the Hurons in his major work, *The Children of Aataentsic: A History of the Huron People to 1660* (1976):

> The main Huron winter festival, the *Ononharoia*, belongs to the general category of soul-curing rituals. It was celebrated at least once a year in every large village. The main reason was either that many people in the village felt ill or depressed, or that some important individual was unwell. This boisterous celebration, which lasted three days, began with people breaking into houses, where they proceeded to upset furniture, break pots, and toss firebrands about. Following this, people who felt ill dreamed of objects, then went about the villiage propounding riddles and seeking to find someone who could guess what these objects were and give them to them. During this period, they were showered with many presents in the hope that one of them would fulfill their dream. If they were finally given what they were looking for, it was a sign that all their troubles were over. After the festival, all presents were returned, except those that were answers to dreams.

Whether it cured souls or not, the Festival of Dreams was one way to waive the "blahs" of February. Since 1978, the Heritage Canada Foundation has been promoting the idea of a statutory holiday to fall on the third Monday in February. It would celebrate the social past, the same way Canada Day celebrates the political past. The notion was to name the holiday after Sir John A. Macdonald, but since the first Prime Minister of Canada was born in January, not February, and since no one seems to know on which day he was born, the 10th or the 11th of the month, it might be more appropriate to designate a statutory holiday to honour the native people of Canada and to name it the Festival of Dreams.

Steep Rock Lake/ Humanoid Creatures

Just north of Atikokan lies the small mining community of Steep Rock Lake. Atikokan has the head office of Steep Rock Iron Mines Limited which at one time issued for its employees *The Steep Rock Echo*. The September and October 1950 issues of that house publication carried an unusual story about little humanoid creatures from a flying saucer. Frank Edwards, the American broadcaster and author of *Flying Saucers — Serious Business* (1966), stated that this narrative was the earliest credible account of little humanoid creatures of which he was aware. What is recounted is what happened to a company executive and his wife while picnicking on the shore of Steep Rock Lake the afternoon of 2 July 1950.

The couple were relaxing behind some rocks near the cove at Sawbill Bay when they heard what sounded like a dynamite blast. But they were miles from any mining operation, so the husband climbed the rock and later described what he saw on the waters of the Bay about twelve hundred feet away.

> Looking through a cleft in the rock I could see a large shiny object resting on the water in the curve of the far shoreline, not a quarter of a mile across the top end of the narrows. I scrambled quickly back to where my wife was. She took one look at me and said, "What's wrong?" I tried to be calm and told her of what I had seen. Then we both climbed back up and looked through the opening. The thing was still there. It looked like two huge saucers stuck together, one upside down on top of the other. Round, black-edged ports appeared to be about four feet apart around the edge. As the bottom was resting on the water or very close to it, it was impossible for us to see the underside.
>
> The top had what looked like hatch covers open . . . and moving slowly around over its surface were about ten queer-looking little figures. Rotating slowly from a central position and about eight feet in the air was a hoop-shaped

object. As it rotated to a point directly opposite us it stopped — and so did the figures. Everything seemed to be concentrated on the opening we were looking through. We instinctively ducked behind the stone at that moment. Looking down over my right shoulder to see how we could best get down I caught a movement in the bushes. Directly opposite us, on the far side of our cove, a deer had come down to drink. The figures and the hoop were facing the deer. As the circle, or hoop, began to rotate again it did not stop at the deer as before. My wife and I would count twenty and duck. We feel that the rock before us shielded us from the action of the hoop.

We could both see that the hooplike thing was being operated by a figure on a small stand directly beneath it. This figure had on what appeared to be a bright red skull cap or helmet. All the others wore dark blue headpieces. All were about the same size: We estimated three and a half to four feet in height. All were dressed the same, with a shiny metallic appearing substance over the chest and their legs and arms covered with a darker material. At that distance we could not make out any features — if they had any.

The most noticeable thing was that they moved like automatons, and did not turn around — that is right around as we do — but they had to turn their feet in order to change direction . . . .

I watched one of these figures pick up the end of a flexible hose (a very vivid green) and lift it while facing one way, then laboriously turn the feet around in order to walk the opposite direction. During all this my wife and I could hear a steady humming sound. They seemed to be drawing in water through one hose and discharging something into the water through another hose.

We had to duck again because of that rotating hoop and when we looked again everything was gone from the surface of the object and it was beginning to rise from the water. It was about eight feet in the air. The water where it had rested was reddish blue, tinged with gold. The thing looked to be about fifteen feet thick at the centre and about twelve feet thick at the rim. There was a rush of wind as it streaked away at about forty-five degrees and was quickly lost in the distance. By having lined it up with two trees on the opposite shore I estimated that it was about forty-eight feet in diameter.

Edwards added that "the strange experience at Steep Rock Lake was to recur many times in the ensuing years," as little humanoid creatures were to continue to put in appearances.

The story, as well, would recur and be retold a number of times. Jacques Vallee for one summarized it in his "A Century of UFO Landings (1868–1968)" which appears in *Passport to Magonia* (1969). Alas, the story is a hoax, as the Scarborough researcher Robert T. Badgley learned when he wrote to the president of Steep Rock Iron Mines Limited in Atikokan. On 2 December 1974, he received a letter from the office of the president which told of the origin of the story in the *Echo* and of its subsequent history. "The story was entirely fictitious and written solely for the amusement of our somewhat isolated community. It was picked up by an American magazine at the time with resultant publicity."

Sturgeon Lake/
The Cross on the Moon

It all began on 25 October 1939 when one W. Ellis, of Omemee, wrote to the newspaper to state that his sister, Mrs. W.A. Fell, who owned and operated Felpark Lodge at Long Beach, Sturgeon Lake, near Peterborough, "saw a cross on the moon about 11 p.m. quite distinctly. It was visible for several minutes. When she told me about it I thought it quite unusual, and decided to write to your paper about it. Others may have seen it also."

Others did see it, or something like it. F. Kent Hamilton, of Hamilton, wrote on 6 November to state, "Your correspondent can be of good cheer, the world is not coming to an end. Any time she wants to see a cross on the moon again, tell her to pick a nice moonlight night and look through an ordinary window screen and the cross will appear."

Mrs. Thos. O'Neill, of Ottawa, wrote on 10 November to say that she, her husband, and a friend, while in Trenton, had "noticed the moon a peculiar shape at times." On 16 November, M. Levason, of no given place, recalled for the *Globe*'s readers that he twice saw "the moon on a cross" while stationed at St. Peter's Mission, Lesser Slave Lake, Alberta, in 1917. "A reflection of light, probably about a foot wide to our eyes, in the form of a gigantic cross, with a full moon in the centre where the beams meet; and strangely enough the lower part or foot was as if broken unevenly at the extreme end. The mission staff all witnessed this phenomenon without window or screens between them. . . ."

On 17 November, Laurence Hyde, of no address, wrote to say that he and his girl-friend "saw a double moon; one seemed to slide rapidly toward the western horizon, while the other [seemed to] slide toward the east, though not as fast as the western refraction." It gave them "quite a turn at the time." A. Graham, of Toronto, read that letter and on 23 November wrote to say that he and a friend also saw "a double moon" and "a peculiar ruddy glow seemed to light up the heavens until both moons disappeared." He went on to say, "My friend has been very unwell since that time and will not venture out after sundown."

Someone signing him or herself Moonie, on 24 November, claimed he saw "eight moons dancing" in front of him one New Year's Eve. He found it peculiar but concluded that the phenomenon was due to light refraction. Someone calling himself "Amateur Astrologist" wrote on 29 November to suggest that Moonie's eight dancing moons might have been due to "refracted moonshine."

On 1 December, E.D. Sewell, of Toronto, raised the level of the discussion by recounting his experience as a surveyor on the shores of Red Lake. Sewell described one evening seeing the moon assume "a

strange appearance: it seemed to be square, and not round as it should be." Through his telescope the corners of the square lunar orb appeared to be on fire. The next evening the moon appeared "like a triangle" with three fiery points. "I recount it at this time in case any of your readers should be interested in the event." Edith Willcock Smith, of Toronto, wrote on 4 December, recommending that the correspondents read the book *Wind, Sand and Stars* by the French airman Antoine de Saint-Exupéry who once described the moon as a "pallid ember."

The correspondence concluded on 11 December with a longish letter from A.S.C. Tebbit, of Wellandport. A person of broad reading, he drew attention to *New Lands* by Charles Fort and to a passage in Deuteronomy about the moon. He noted with approval Fort's view that (as Tebbit expressed it) "the moon is an independent luminary; its rays quite different from sunlight." He then quoted Deuteronomy 33:14: "And for the precious fruits brought forth by the sun. And for the precious things put forth by the moon." His conclusion was that man had gone wrong when he rejected "the cosmogony of Genesis" and put in its place "a theory whose roots lie in the speculations of a heathen philosopher named Pythagoras, who flourished around 500 B.C. The fruit is seen in such Godless systems as fascism, nazism and communism; whether we realize it or not, these anti-God ideologies are the final outcome of men's rejection of God's truth."

The complete correspondence appears in *Shocked & Appalled: A Century of Letters to The Globe and Mail* (1985), edited by Jack Kapica.

Sudbury/
Lunar Landscape?

The Sudbury Basin was created by the impact of a huge meteor some two billion years ago. The cataclysm resulted in high concentrations of nickel, copper, and iron ore. So the mineral wealth and some topographical features of present-day Sudbury are the twin legacies of the crashlanding of a three-mile-in diameter meteorite from Outer Space.

A debate among geologists was raised over the pockmarked surface of the moon. Was it volcanic or meteoritic in origin? Geologists at the National Aeronautics and Space Administration (NASA) in Houston, Texas, argued that one way to determine the cause was to compare known meteoritic conditions on the earth's surface with conditions on the lunar surface. Since the Sudbury Basin was of known meteorite origin, and since the airless lunar surface may well have sustained innumerable bombardments by meteorites, there might well be geological similarities between the impact area in Sudbury and comparable areas on the moon.

In July 1971, Apollo 16 astronauts John Young and Charles Duke spent three days exploring geological features in the vicinity of High Falls, Creighton, and Kelly Lake. On the lunar walk in April 1972, Young and Duke spotted breccias (coarse-grained rocks composed of angular fragments of other rocks, evidence of impact and not volcanic action) and also shatter cones (cone-shaped features associated with meteorite impacts which indicate that shock waves have travelled through the rock). They knew what to look for, having observed breccias and shatter cones at Sudbury.

Geology was well served, so NASA in May 1972 arranged for astronauts Eugene Cernan and Harrison Schmitt to travel to Sudbury for their geological studies. On their lunar walk, Cernan and Schmitt were able to substantiate the findings of the two earlier astronauts concerning breccias and shatter cones in a different lunar sector, the Valley of Taurus-Littrow.

Schmitt, who holds a doctorate in geology, was the first and last scientist-astronaut to fly on an Apollo mission. He was also the last man to walk on the lunar surface. In January 1987, he returned to Sudbury to visit Science North. On that occasion he commented: "The Sudbury Basin represents the effects of a large meteor impact. There are certain detailed rock features that we felt it was critical to understand. Nobody ever said we came here because Sudbury looked like it was on the moon. We came here because you had some things here that we might find on the moon."

So the Apollo astronauts did not travel to Sudbury to train but to study. They did not learn their moonwalk on the "moonscape" of the Sudbury Basin. Such distinctions are dear to the heart of the Regional Municipality of Sudbury, which is proud of its program to promote "the greening" of Sudbury.

If the landscape of the moon is to be compared with any portion of the Earth's surface, it should be with the Arctic. The lunar topography somewhat resembles the topography of the Far North. It has been pointed out that the area of the surface of the moon is almost identical with the area of the Arctic regions.

Sudbury/
The Sudbury Incident

What did observers see over the city of Sudbury the night of 11 November 1975? Did they see UFOs? Did the radar screens of the NORAD station at nearby Falconbridge really respond to the presence of UFOs in the sky over Sudbury?

These are some of the questions raised by Philip J. Klass in *UFOs: The Public Deceived* (1983). More to the point, after gathering existing first-hand evidence, he came to an independent conclusion. Perhaps because his answers to these questions are plausible, they are not calculated to bring satisfaction to those predisposed to belief in UFOs.

The commander at the Falconbridge radar station was notified at 5:45 a.m. that the station had received a number of reports of UFOs over Sudbury. The commander observed, "All reports were similar in that three to four objects, described as bright, round objects with no apparent velocity, were sighted over the city of Sudbury." As the Falconbridge personnel had not noted any unidentified targets on their long-range surveillance radar, they decided to turn on their height-finder radar and look for targets in the direction of Sudbury.

In doing so they observed a target at an altitude of about 36,000 feet moving slowly from west to east. Station personnel, sent outside to watch the lights in the sky, reported that one of them "appeared to ascend at a high rate of speed. Simultaneously . . . the height finder reported a change in altitude . . . from 36,000 feet to 72,000 feet in a matter of two minutes.''

The commander discussed the persistent radar target with NORAD officials. The 23rd Region decided to dispatch two F-106 interceptors from Selfridge AFB, Michigan, to investigate. By now it was broad daylight but the pilots could find no craft-like objects, only high-altitude clouds laden with ice crystals that reflected the sunlight. Such clouds were capable of returning radar energy and producing blips on the Falconbridge height-finder radar.

In the opinion of the commander, this could account for the "anomalous propagation." As for the lighted objects seen in the night sky with the naked eye, Klass concluded: "This is not surprising, considering that a very bright Jupiter was visible after 2:30 a.m. local time. On the night of October 20, NBC-TV, whose programs can be seen by Canadians living near the U.S. border, had rekindled interest in UFOs with a dramatic two-hour film recounting the alleged UFO abduction of Betty and Barney Hill.''

Therefore, to answer the questions posed above, observers in Sudbury saw the planet Jupiter; they did not see UFOs; and the radar screens at Falconbridge independently responded with blips from ice crystals, not alien spacecraft.

No UFOlogist is going to accept any conclusion supplied by Philip J. Klass. No matter how knowledgeable and reasonable Klass may sound, they argue, he is a charter member of the Committee for the Scientific Investigation of Claims of the Paranormal (CSICOPS), the principal sceptical group. One student of such matters has compared Klass with the surgeon who finds it necessary to boast that he has not lost a patient yet. The reader should examine *Clear Intent: The Government Coverup of the UFO Experience* (1984) for a point of view on the Sudbury incident at variance with Klass's. The authors of this book, Lawrence Fawcett and Barry J. Greenwood, take pains to point out the "considerable concern" expressed by governments in the United States and Canada to "the UFO phenomena." They find that the Sudbury incident was responsible for "probably one of the most significant modern examples of suspicious unknown air activity possibly affecting national security.''

Sudbury/
Theorist of Space-Time Transients

One of the few scientists in Canada whose research directly clarifies paranormal experiences and events is Michael A. Persinger. A full professor of psychology and coordinator of the Behavioural Neuroscience Programme at Laurentian University in Sudbury, Persinger was born in 1945 in Jacksonville, Florida. He took his B.A. at the University of Wisconsin, his M.A. at the University of Tennessee, and his Ph.D. at the University of Manitoba, whereupon he joined Laurentian University.

Persinger is a tireless researcher. His *curriculum vitae* lists approximately one hundred technical papers that have appeared in scientific journals. In addition, he is the author of six books, the most widely reviewed being *Space-time Transients and Unusual Events* (1977), which was written with G.F. Lafrenière. Forthcoming from Praeger in New York is *Neuropsychological Bases of God Beliefs*.

Persinger's special contribution is establishing a relationship between ill-understood natural forces and so-called "Fortean events." He defines clusters and patterns in his micro and macro reports. One of his micro studies is titled "Strong Temporal Relationships between Inclusive Seismic Measures and UFO Reports within Washington State" (which appeared in *Perceptual and Motor Skills* in 1984). It established a positive correlation between high levels of seismic activity—stress and strain within the earth's crust—and numerous reports of UFOs with special attention to their luminosity.

A macro study was called "Are Earth Faults at Fault in Some Poltergeist-like Episodes." It appeared in *The Journal of the American Society for Psychical Research* in 1986 and it examined recurrent spontaneous psychokinesis (RSPK) which it found to be directly related to tectonogonic forces (TFs) which include electromagnetic and seismic activity. The human body is an organic semiconductor and is affected by TFs through mechanisms yet to be explained. There is a connection between TFs and temporal lobe disorders. Such disorders are classically related to such paranormal experiences as "haunt episodes" — enhanced phosphence occurrence, and piloerection. A specific case of poltergeist activity in a Sudbury apartment in 1975 is thus established within a wider context of generalized disturbances.

Persinger is treating the supernatural as if it were a special case of the natural, and his research is taking him toward predictability and replicability. Indeed, he has recently completed a 450-page manuscript with the intriguing title "Predicting UFO Events and Experiences." By determining the causes of parapsychological phenomena he is erasing the need for such terms as "acausal" or "sychronicity" and finding scientific significance in the terms in the vocabulary of the parapsychologist.

"Before we discovered radioactivity, uranium was just an ugly black rock," he told Olivia Ward of the *Toronto Star* on 23 September 1979. Have you ever had a psychic experience of your own, she asked him, and he replied in the negative. He had never experienced one. "In fact," he added, "I'm psychic dead space." Sounds like another field of study altogether.

Lake Superior/
Symbolic Geography

Lake Superior is superior to the other four Great Lakes in size. It also has a symbolic shape, as noted by William Ashworth:

> Seen on a map, Lake Superior bears a striking resemblance to the head of an immense wolf. The nose lies at Duluth; the neck is truncated by the long curved shoreline stretching east 180 miles from Marquette, Michigan, to the U.S.-Canadian border at Sault Ste. Marie. The great ruff of fur around the neck is separated from the lower jaw by the bulk of the Keweenaw Peninsula; the lower lip ends at Ashland, Wisconsin; and the ears are up around Nipigon, Ontario.
>
> Isle Royale is the eye.

Ashworth made this observation in *The Late, Great Lakes: An Environmental History* (1986). Whatever horrors Lake Superior and the other Great Lakes held

in the past and hold in the present for mariners and fishermen and aviators count as nothing beside the horrors that man daily inflicts upon these waters in the form of pollutants and toxic substances.

The Ojibway believe that the icy depths of Lake Superior are the home of Mishipeshu, the Great Lynx, the most dangerous of all the underwater monsters. With its dragon-like tail it whips up the waves and clouds to create terrible storms. It sucks down ships and snatches planes from the air.

Lake Superior/
Aboriginal or Alien Copper Mines?

The extensive deposits of copper on the northern shore of Lake Superior were mined in the prehistoric past. The extent of the mining and the ancestry of the miners are matters of debate not only among academic historians but also among Fortean "rehistorians."

As early as 1700 B.C., copper from this region was exchanged for Scandinavian woollen goods by Woden-lithi, the Norse king who established his trading colony at the site of the Peterborough Petroglyphs. That at least is the theory of Barry Fell in *Bronze Age America* (1982). As for the primitive mines themselves, let the last words be those of Charles Fort, who along with Robert L. Ripley was one of the world's greatest collectors of oddities. In his ample volume *The Book of the Damned* (1919), Fort anticipated by a half-century the "ancient astronaut" theory now identified with Erich von Däniken. Fort wrote:

> It is difficult to accept that the remarkable, the very extensive, copper mines in the region of Lake Superior were ever the works of American aborigines. Despite the astonishing extent of these mines, nothing has ever been found to indicate that the region was ever inhabited by permanent dwellers — . . . "not a vestige of a dwelling, a skeleton, or a bone has been found." The Indians have no traditions relating to the mines. . . . I think that we've had visitors: that they have come here for copper, for instance.

Lake Superior/
Ancient Records

Throughout history there are rumours and reports of the existence of secret repositories of ancient learning. In these hidden libraries are preserved for the ages ancient records and books of secret knowledge and ageless wisdom-literature. It makes no difference whether these storehouses of divine and human knowledge are found or not found in some inaccessible lamasery in Tibet, in the forgotten caverns and caves in the Gobi Desert, in the unknown chambers beneath the Pyramids of Egypt, or even in the Vatican's so-called secret archives, their first and perhaps sole centre will be found in the imagination of man.

Are there any respositories of ancient records in Canada? Are there secret libraries of ageless learning in this country? Interestingly and intriguingly, the answer is yes. The question is answered positively by the Ojibway author and missionary George Copway (1818–1863), who was born of Chippewa parents in the Rice Lake area of Ontario, being given the Indian name of Kagigegabo, which means "He Who Stands Forever." He served his people as a Wesleyan missionary and wrote a number of books on his background and native spirituality.

He dispelled the notion that the Indian people lacked the means to record their history and knowledge and were thus unable to pass them on to future generations. For one thing, the elders could commit to memory their thoughts and traditional tales, and on special occasions recite them, thus passing them from one generation to another. For another thing, they could also preserve such information in the form of "picture writing." In this form of communication, ideas are visualized and images are drawn. The images, which may appear to be childishly simple, are really highly stylized when they are cut into or painted onto rock. Imagery that is more detailed is drawn on long birchbark scrolls which are then carefully preserved.

The interpretation of such imagery requires special instruction. Schools of secret initiation were established within the traditional medicine societies. Indians who were knowledgeable about such imagery maintained that the native system of "picture writing" was superior to the white man's written letters. Using his written letters, the white man is able to sound out and read specific words, but often their meaning is in doubt, especially when words change their meanings over the years. The native, interpreting the "picture writing," is able to recall the essential meaning of the picture, not a specific word, for he is required to express the meaning in his own words, suitable for the time and place. Thus the Indian imagery preserved the spirit, whereas the white man's writing preserved the letter of the law.

Most Indian Nations of the West have places in which they deposit the records that are said to have orginated their worship. The Ojibways have three such depositories near the waters of Lake Superior. Ten of the wisest and most venerable of the Nation dwell near these, and are appointed guardians over them.

Fifteen years intervene between each opening. At the end of that time, if any vacancies have been caused by death, others are chosen in the spring of the year, who, about the month of August, are called to witness the opening of the depositories. As they are being opened, all the information known respecting them is given to the new members; then the articles are placed before them. After this, the plates are closely examined, and if any have begun to decay they are taken out; an exact facsimile is made and placed in its stead. The old one is divided equally among the wise men. It is very highly valued for having been deposited; as a sacred article, every fibre of it is considered sacred; and whoever uses it may be made wise. It is considered efficacious for any good purpose it may be put to.

These records are written on slate rock, copper, lead and on the bark of birch trees. The record is said to be a transcript of what the Great Spirit gave to the Indian after the flood, and by the hands of wise men has been transmitted to other parts of the country ever since. Here is a code of moral laws which the Indian calls "a path made by the Great Spirit."

This passage was written by Ojibway chief George Copway, privy to the sacred traditions of his people. It appeared in *Indian Life and Indian History* (1858).

It is doubtful that such practices as were described by Copway continue into modern times, though it is laudatory if they do. Today the oral trandition must strain to compete with the electronic media. The tradition of "picture writing" may seem incompatible beside — yet be oddly complementary to — such an artifact of the most advanced technology possible in the late twentieth century as, say, the Voyager Interstellar Record, with its pictograph-like outline drawings, which is the first man-made object ever to leave the Solar System.

Lake Superior/
The Man Who Saw a Mermaid

History does not recall Venant St. Germain, Esq., of Repentigny, Merchant and Voyageur, as an employee of the North West Company, although that is what he was. History recalls him (when it does) as the man who saw a mermaid in Lake Superior. To ensure as much as possible that his testimony would not be discounted or dismissed, Venant St. Germain appeared before two judges of the Court of King's Bench in Montreal and swore an affidavit to this effect on 13 November 1812. The document was published under the heading "A Mermaid in Lake Superior" in *The Canadian Magazine,* May 1824.

In the affidavit, Venant St. Germain stated that shortly after sundown on 3 May 1782, while returning from Grand Portage to Michilimackinac, at the south end of the Isle Paté, he saw "an animal in the water, which appeared to him to have the upper part of its body, above the waist, formed exactly like that of a human being. It had the half of its body out of the water, and the novelty of so extraordinary a spectacle, excited his attention, and led him to examine it carefully."

When he did so he saw that "the body of the animal" seemed to be about the size of a child of seven or eight years of age. "The deponent distinctly saw the features of the countenance, which bore an exact resemblance to those of the human face." He was able to examine the figure for a space of three or four minutes. An attempt to seize the figure was thwarted by the protests of his Indian woman companion who expressed "the superstitious belief among the Indians, that the God of the Waters had fixed upon this for his residence."

Nowhere in the affidavit did Venant St. Germain call the "animal" a "mermaid." Nor did he describe any characteristically female features of the animal's countenance or torso. It was the editor of *The Canadian Magazine* who reprinted the affidavit who referred to the affidavit as "a proof of the existence of the mermaid."

Lake Superior/
The Fate of the *Bannockburn*

The last person to see the *Bannockburn* was Captain James McMaugh of the *Algonquin.* At the time — 21 November 1902 — the 245-foot steamer was moving through the choppy water on Lake Superior about fifty miles southeast of Passage Island. The *Bannockburn,* under Captain George R. Wood of Port Dalhousie, had been loaded with grain at Port Arthur and was heading in the direction of Caribou Island. The weather was gusty and hazy. As the steamer disappeared, McMaugh remarked to his first mate, "I must say, that vessel certainly has gotten out of sight remarkably quickly."

The words proved prophetic for the steamer was never seen again. It simply vanished along with its crew of twenty seamen. Rumours immediately circulated. It had been sighted opposite Michipicoten Island. It was stranded on Caribou Island twenty-two miles to the south. Alas, the lighthouse on that reef-ridden island was out!

It was Captain McMaugh's opinion that the steamer had burst its boilers and sunk not far from the point at which he had last seen it. All that was ever recovered of the *Bannockburn* was a single life preserver and lone oar found on the south shore of Lake Superior many months later. Yet perhaps it did not disappear for good but continued to reappear as a phantom ship. As Dwight Boyer wrote in *Ghost Ships of the Great Lakes* (1968), "On stormy nights, several sailors claimed to have seen the *Bannockburn,* buffeting her way down Lake Superior, her lamps blinking in the storm scud, while in the darkened pilothouse her master looked vainly for the welcoming flash of Caribou Island Light."

The single lasting memorial to recall the ill-fated *Bannockburn* — the ship known as "The Flying Dutchman of Lake Superior" — is the tablet in St. John's Anglican Church in Port Dalhousie. The wording on the table reads as follows:

In Memoriam. Capt. George Richard Wood, Born March 9, 1865. Died Nov. 22, 1902. Erected by His Brother, John W. Wood.

Lake Superior/
The Wreck of the *Edmund Fitzgerald*

One cannot think about the *Edmund Fitzgerald* without hearing in the mind the haunting words and music of Gordon Lightfoot's ballad "The Wreck of the Edmund Fitzgerald" with its lilting refrain about "the gales of November."

The *Edmund Fitzgerald* was the largest ship ever lost on the Great Lakes and the latest in their long line of ghost ships. The "queen" among the lake freighters, it was 729 feet long and on its last voyage it was carrying 26,116 gross tons of iron ore pellets. It was taking them from Superior, Wisconsin, to Detroit, Michigan. There were twenty-nine seamen aboard, including Captain Ernest McSorley. It sailed into stormy weather and final radio contact was made at 7:10 p.m. It sank in two minutes on 10 November 1975 close to Whitefish Bay at the southeastern end of Lake Superior. The exact site is known. The vessel is said to be on the seabed, split in two, straddling the Canada-U.S. boundary.

The cause of the sudden sinking could have been leaking vents and hatchways or a split in the hull caused by brushing against shoals. Captain James Wilson of the U.S. Coast Guard's Board of Inquiry a year after the accident said: "The *Fitzgerald* went down with all hands on deck. She had, as old timers would tell you, 'sailed through a crack in the lake.' "

Superior has its share of superstitions. Sailors are aware of "the three sisters" and "the gales of November." The sisters are a trio of killer waves known to sweep across waters swamping whatever lies ahead of them. The "gales of November" are particularly fierce storms which descend on the Lake on the eleventh month of the year. Any reference to the eleventh day of the eleventh month recalls Armistice Day; on Superior it recalls anniversaries of sinkings and drownings. The eleventh has been called Superior's "unlucky day."

The vessel was an American one, built in the United States and chartered in Cleveland, Ohio. It bore the name of a Great Lakes steamer skipper who was the grandfather of the chairman and president of the Northwest Mutual Life Insurance Co. of Milwaukee, the owners of the "Big Fitz." The book that tells the whole story is *Gales of November: The Sinking of the Edmund Fitzgerald* (1981) by Robert J. Hemming.

Gordon Lightfoot was deeply moved by the fate of the crew members and the plight of their families. He composed "The Wreck of the Edmund Fitzgerald" and arranged for a portion of the earnings of the ballad be directed to the families of the victims of this marine disaster.

Swastika/
The Twisted Cross

To the ancient Hindus the swastika was a symbol of good luck and good health. It took the form of a cross with equal arms and cross-arms, the latter so placed as to suggest the figure was rotating in a clockwise direction. The symbol was used as a motif on ancient Indian monuments. It was believed to have magical properties.

Swastika was also the name of a small mining community outside Kirkland Lake in Northern Ontario. Who chose it or why it was chosen is unknown, but the place name first appeared in print in 1906. With the adoption of the swastika as the emblem of the Nazi Party in Germany in the 1930s, the word and symbol became an embarrassment. In point of fact, the Nazis turned the traditional swastika around. Their *Hakenkreuz* (hooked or twisted cross) had cross-arms so placed as to suggest motion in a counter-clockwise direction. Any Hindu would see this as a symbol of bad luck and poor health.

And so it proved to be to the Nazi Party and to its leader Adolf Hitler. The Ontario place name almost ceased to exist. After World War II broke out, the Ontario Premier Mitch Hepburn decide the name was unpatriotic, so he lobbied to change the name of the post office to Winston, in honour of the British wartime leader Winston Churchill. But the inhabitants of Swastika thought otherwise, and at a public meeting on 13 September 1940 resisted the change. Speakers pointed out that their use of the name predated the Nazi Party's use and would postdate it as well. They maintained that their patriotism was second to none.

The proud inhabitants were right on both accounts. They won the day and the name remained in place. Expansion during the 1950s accomplished what Hepburn was unable to do, and Swastika was absorbed into greater Kirkland Lake, with the attendant loss of the name. Yet there does seem to be an unusual connection between the Ontario place name and the German twisted cross. As unlikely as it might seem, the place name may have inspired the Nazi use. It is an irony of history that the peaceful community probably contributed the twisted cross to the arsenal of Nazi symbology.

It came about in this fashion. Historians are silent on when and why Adolf Hitler adopted and adapted the symbol. Yet occult symbology was nothing new to Hitler who from his youth had occult leanings. He may have seen the swastika in quasi-mystical publications. Or it has been argued that he may have learned about the twisted cross from Unity Mitford, his "Nordic goddess," who undoubtedly heard about it from her father, Lord Redesdale, the eccentric British peer who for some time resided in a log cabin just outside Swastika, Ontario.

Thorah/
The Fire-Spook

The "fire-spook" is what R.S. Lambert called Jennie L. Bramwell in his book *Exploring the Supernatural: The Weird in Canadian Folklore* (1955).

Jennie L. Bramwell, an orphan from England, was raised in an orphanage in Belleville. She was adopted by the Dawsons, a childless couple who lived on a farm at Thorah, near Beaverton. There were no problems until 1891 when Jennie, then fourteen years old, came down with meningitis. Her recovery was slow and accompanied by an extended period of drowsiness. Then, beginning on 25 October, and continuing for some weeks, a series of small fires broke out in the house. The conflagrations occurred seemingly at random and without cause. They were easily extinguished. One day the Dawsons extinguished a total of fifty little fires.

Neighbours and reporters for Toronto newspapers who visited the farm and witnessed the mindless incendiary activity had no explanation other than that they were caused by Jennie. But the fires broke out whether or not Jennie was in the vicinity. "By this time the Dawsons had lost all patience with their adopted daughter," Lambert wrote. "They arranged for her return to the Belleville Orphanage, and thereafter had peace." And that is about all that is known of Jennie L. Bramwell, the "fire-spook."

Thorold/
"Welsh Lullabies Are Heard"

The city of Thorold is located on the Welland Canal south of St. Catharines. The Bishop Fuller House, east of the Thorold Tunnel, is a twenty-one room mansion built in 1820. The mansion is unoccupied.

Not only is it uneconomical to maintain but it has also been described as haunted.

According to its owner Bill Davis, who resides in a modern house on the same lot, the ghost of a young woman clad in a pioneer gown is occasionally seen in the mansion. If approached, she vanishes, leaving behind the scent of lavender. On at least one occasion at night, a lighted candle was observed to travel through the air, unsupported by human hand, moving from room to room on the second floor. More eerie than the scent of lavender and the sight of a lit candle is the sound of singing. At dusk there are reports that Welsh lullabies are heard as if being sung by a young girl.

Paul Cosen, writing in the St. Catharines *Standard*, 19 July 1974, quoted Bill Davis, the house's owner: "Where the supernatural is concerned, leave well enough alone and mind your own business."

Thunder Bay/
The Sleeping Giant

Thunder Bay is located near the northern tip of Lake Superior. From Hillcrest Park there is a fine view of the bay and the long peninsula which is Sibley Provincial Park. From a distance the landform of the peninsula bears a striking resemblance to a giant prone figure with hands folded across the chest as if at rest.

The rocky peninsula is a thousand feet high and seven miles long and is called the Giant's Tomb or the Sleeping Giant. The Ojibway called the figure by the name of Nanabozho. He was their trickster hero who was "more than human." He stole fire for man, raised the Canadian Shield, refashioned the world following the Flood, fought his enemies the Windigos, entered the belly of the Great Sturgeon, made an ally of the Thunderbird, created the Midéwewin or Medicine Society, invented rock art, and fell into a long sleep from which he will awaken to save his people yet again.

The notion is not a new one that there are heroes of the past who will save the world in the future.

They are not really dead but lie in a long sleep and will one day at the appointed time arise from their night of sleep into the day of judgement and punish their enemies, reward their friends and bring about the great happiness. It is a notion found in many cultures.

Thunder Bay/
Silver Islet Mine

In its day the mine on Silver Islet, the skull-shaped island off Sibley Peninsula's Sleeping Giant, was one of the world's leading silver producers. It yielded silver of unsurpassed purity, but the lode took the miners under the floor of Lake Superior. Seepage through the rocks and then flooding of the shafts became major problems. The lode was still a strong producer in 1888 when the mining operations were suspended and the mine was closed by its Detroit owner, Alexander Sibley.

The rumour is still current that in about 1869 a group of miners, disgruntled with the disparity between their low wages and the owners' high profits, stole three barrels of pure silver and secreted them in a cave on the property. Despite repeated attempts to locate the natural hiding place and its valuable silver treasure, no trace has been found to this day. The rumour is recalled by Ronald Wrigley in "Lost Treasure of the Silver Islet Mine" in *Canadian Treasure Trails* (1976) edited by T.W. Paterson.

Toronto/
Old Fort York

There are stories that spectral stragglers from the War of 1812 wage long-forgotten battles at Old Fort York.

Fort York was the military post built by the British at York, today's Toronto, in 1793. American invaders attacked via Lake Ontario and took the fort on 27 April 1813. Many lives were lost, including that of the American General Zebulon Pike. The fort was set aflame but was rebuilt in 1816. The present-day reconstruction, which lies on land somewhat to the north of the orginal post, was undertaken in the 1930s and is operated as a museum of military life.

Touring Old Fort York one would have to be deaf not to hear the sound of feet marching to the martial music of the fife and drum. Visitors claim that they have seen ghostly soldiers dressed in American uniforms of the nineteenth century standing at the base of the flagpole. Guides maintain that invisible hands attempt to push them off the walls and parapets. Maintenance personnel complain about the sound of stomping feet which reverberates throughout the former sleeping quarters on stormy nights. These "disturbances" suggest that American "forces" still occupy the British-Canadian fort!

Toronto/
The Gibraltar Point Ghost

The Gibraltar Point Lighthouse was erected on Toronto Island in 1808 on the orders of Governor John Graves Simcoe. The tower overlooks Lake Ontario and is the oldest historical landmark in Toronto still standing on its orginal site. Although it no longer functions as a beacon, the structure is maintained by the Toronto Historical Board for architectural as well as historical reasons.

It is widely believed that the lighthouse is haunted by the ghost of its first keeper, a rather morose individual named J.P. Rademuller, who lived in a cabin beside the tower. The cabin has long been gone but the lighthouse remains. The story goes that on the dark and stormy night of 2 January 1815 the keeper was disturbed by a group of carousing soldiers, guards from nearby Fort York, who wanted some of his bootleg beer. When he refused to oblige, they chased him up the spiral staircase of the lighthouse to the top-deck. They caught him, knocked him unconscious with a rock and then threw him over the edge.

To hide their villainy, they chopped up the body and buried the pieces over the grounds. Some of the bones were discovered by a later keeper Joe Durnan in 1893. Durnan maintained that he could hear moans and on misty nights that he could see Rademuller's spectre seeking its lost limbs. Others swear that his ghost is said to ascend and descend the spiral staircase

in order to light the lamp on dark and stormy nights.

"What kid, wandering around the lighthouse, hasn't fantasized about coming back alone, at midnight, to discover once and for all the true fate of poor old Rademuller?"

Toronto/
Montgomery's Prophecy

There is an interesting prophecy connected with the aftermath of the Rebellion of 1837 in Upper Canada. The prophecy was made by John Montgomery, the proprietor of Montgomery's Tavern on the northern extension of Yonge Street, the rallying point for the rebel farmers led by William Lyon Mackenzie.

When the Rebellion was put down, Montgomery was arrested and charged with high treason. He appeared before Chief Justice John Beverley Robinson in the dock of the York (now Toronto) court house on 2 April 1838. He heard the Chief Justice pronounce him guilty. "John Montgomery, you have been found guilty of high treason. Have you anything to say before the judgement of the court is passed upon you?"

"I have," replied Montgomery bitterly. "I have not had a fair trial. There are witnesses here who have sworn my life away. The perjured evidence of William Gymer, William Crew, and David Bridgeford will haunt them in after years. These perjurers will never die a natural death; and when you, sir, and the jury shall have died and perished in hell's flames, John Montgomery will yet be living on Yonge Street."

The feelings of the Chief Justice are unknown. But eight days later he sentenced Montgomery to death. The sentence was eventually commuted to imprisonment. Montgomery soon escaped from prison and resided in the United States until he was pardoned. Then he returned to Toronto where he lived until his death in 1879 in his ninety-sixth year.

The historian Edwin C. Guillet, writing in *The Lives and Times of the Patriots* (1938), commented on Montgomery's prophecy. "An obituary notice in the Picton *Times* of January 29, 1880, is the basis of the alleged address to the court, which had been one of his favourite stories as an old man. The prophecy was partially fulfilled, for one man shot himself and another cut his throat, and Montgomery outlived judge, jurors, witnesses, and prosecutors.''

Toronto/
The University College Ghost

One building in Toronto which impressed Oscar Wilde when he visited the city in 1883 was University College. He particularly admired the Norman entranceway to the academic building which was erected in the Gothic Revival manner in 1857–58 and restored following the fire of 1890. If ever a building deserved a ghost of its own, it is University College which is garnished with gargoyles and such medievalisms as cloisters and corridors, ballustrades and buttresses, even a chapter house with a rose window.

Wilde would have enjoyed hearing the story of the ghost that stalks the corridors of University College. It was in Canada, after all, that he met the young woman artist who drew his picture—the picture that inspired his masterful horror novel *The Picture of Dorian Gray*. But there is no record that anyone told Wilde the story of the rivalry between Ivan Reznikoff and Paul Diabolos over the woman the two men loved. It is a shame because the first appearance of the ghost preceded Wilde's visit by about a decade.

One misty night in the 1870s, a young student named Allen Aylesworth—later Sir Allen, a prominent lawyer—was walking alone across the campus when he encountered the tall figure of a man whose bearded head was topped with a tall hat.

''Cold night,'' said Aylesworth.

''It's always cold with me,'' replied the figure cryptically.

Aylesworth invited the strange man into his quarters, and as they sat before the fire, the guest introduced himself as a Russian named Ivan Reznikoff. He went on to recount the story of how he and another stonemason, a carter named Paul Diabolos, were engaged in the construction of University College. One afternoon they were busy carving a pair of gargoyles when the Greek pointed to the grotesque face which he had finished and the smiling face on which the Russian was still working.

''Does that remind you of anyone?'' the Greek asked.

The Russian shook his head.

''It's supposed to be you!'' the Greek continued. ''See, mine! It's laughing behind your back at your smiling face!''

''Why?'' asked the Russian.

The Greek then launched into a wild account of how Susie, the beautiful daughter of the local publican, was inconstant in her affections. She might be engaged to the Russian, but she was secretly seeing the Greek!

The Russian said nothing but that night he spied on Susie and, sure enough, she was consorting with the Greek. In a rage the Russian picked up a double-headed axe and swung it at the Greek. The axe missed but left a gash in the thick oak panel of the Chapter House door. Later that night the Greek crept up on the Russian and knifed him to death, disposing of the body by dropping it down the unfinished stairwell.

Aylesworth listened to the story with mounting interest. Was this tall mysterious figure the Russian? Was it the ghost of the Russian? Aylesworth never found out. When he looked up, the figure had vanished.

In the aftermath of the fire of 1890 which gutted University College, workmen uncovered in the stairwell the remains of a man — skull and bones — and, inexplicably, a silver buckle. Guides point out to visitors to the college the gash on the door and the twin gargoyles, one grinning, the other grimacing — images of Paul Diabolos and Ivan Reznikoff.

One wonders what Oscar Wilde would have made of the story.

Toronto/
The Ghost of Mrs. Howard

From time to time the gray, misty figure of Mrs. Jemima Howard is said to appear from the second-storey front window of Colborne Lodge in High Park. A shawl covers the head of the figure, which nevertheless appears to be staring across Colborne Lodge Drive and pointing to the little cemetery which lies there. In the cemetery lie the bodies of Mrs. Howard and her husband John Howard.

John Howard was an important surveyor, architect, and engineer. He resided with his wife in Colborne Lodge and when he died in 1890 by the terms of his will he left forty-five acres to the City of Toronto to be developed into a public park. This grew into High Park. Mrs. Howard predeceased her husband, dying in 1877. Her last years were spent confined to the second-floor bedroom. She was suffering from some form of mental illness and died in that room of breast cancer. Her last days were spent staring out of the window onto the cemetery. Apparently her ghost continues the melancholy vigil.

Colborne Lodge is now a museum run by the Toronto Historical Board. The ghost of Mrs. Howard was first reported (by a policeman on a motorcycle) in early 1970. The reports attracted the attention of Herbert A. Graham who reported on the situation in "Old Houses Remember," *Fate,* October 1971. He wrote:

> The house has four upstairs bedrooms — one large master bedroom at the front, two smaller ones at each side of a hall and another at the end of the hall toward the back. Having visited this last one many times, I long had known that it has a strange atmosphere but on this visit it felt particularly weird. The room was empty of any living entity. It contained nothing more than its usual four-poster bed, bureau, washstand and, beside one window, a table on which lies an open Bible. Yet I was certain I shared the room with somebody — somebody I couldn't see but whose presence I felt. An odd smell pervaded the air like that of a bedroom too long slept in with the windows shut. For once I did not linger but quickly went downstairs.

Toronto/
The Theosophical Society

The word *theosophy* combines the Greek words for "divine" and "wisdom." The Theosophical Society was formed in New York by Madame H.P. Blavatsky and others. It has three aims: "to form a nucleus of the Universal Brotherhood of Humanity," "to encourage the study of comparative religion, philosophy, and science," and "to investigate the unexplained laws of nature and the powers latent in man." Theosophy is colourfully replete with pre-Adamic races, reincarnation, karma, secret wisdom, esoteric sections, and the Masters or Adepts of the Great White Brotherhood.

Helena Petrovna Blavatsky (1831–1891), the founder of the Theosophical Society in New York in 1875 and the author of many occult tomes including *The Secret Doctrine,* was vague about her background and extensive world travels. However, it is known that she visited Quebec City in the late summer or early fall of 1851.

In the Quebec capital she sought out Indian chiefs and conversed with them about their secret oral traditions. She was disappointed to learn that the native traditions were being lost and dismayed to realize that one of the natives had pilfered her pair of expensive leather boots.

Three months before her death Madame Blavatsky signed the charter of the Theosophical Society of Canada. The document is dated 25 February 1891 and it bears the signatures of a number of prominent Torontonians. Two signatures retain special interest—those of Algernon Blackwood and Albert E.S. Smythe. Blackwood served as the Corresponding Secretary and went on to become one of Britain's finest authors of horror fiction. The Canadian bush is the setting for some of his most atmospheric stories like "The Wendigo." Smythe was a newspaper editor who played an active role in the Society and published his own little magazine, *The Lamp,* until he assumed editorship of the Society's official monthly journal, *The Canadian Theosophist,* which is still appearing albeit on a quarterly basis. To the world at large Smythe is best remembered as the father of the sportsman Conn Smythe.

It was during the 1920s that the T.S. was most influential, combining culture, nationalism, and mysticism. The Society had a profound effect on Lawren Harris, the intellectual leader of the Group of Seven. Theosophical ideas led Harris from representational painting to abstraction; similar doctrines had similar ends in Europe, with the work of Kandinsky and other abstractionists, and in Asia with the mystical paintings of Nicholas Roerich.

The Society also influenced Roy Mitchell, the theatre director and innovative thinker, who led the Arts and Letters Players of Toronto in 1905 and became the first director of Hart House Theatre in 1919.

Some members saw the Society in Canada as having the special mission of safeguarding the home of the first "root race," known as "the Imperishable Sacred Land," believed to be at the North Pole. Others felt more simply that as the North was a place of both sanctuary and sanctity, Canadians were duty-bound to represent such ideals to the world at large. A strong influence on the Society in Canada was the poetic transcendentalism of Walt Whitman. Other influences came from the books and monographs issued by the Blavatsky Institute which was established by the lecturer George Lazenby and others. Among its numerous books were *The Bhagavad Gita* (1937), "a conflation from all available English translations" done by Smythe, and *Theosophy in Action* (1951) by Roy Mitchell.

The T.S. sponsored public addresses by visiting Theosophists. Annie Besant, the suffragette who succeeded Madame Blavatsky as the world leader, spoke to audiences in Toronto in the years 1893, 1907, and 1926. She gave four talks in the city in 1926, two of which were held in Massey Hall. That was a mistake, according to the *Evening Telegram* on 1 November 1926, for nine-tenths of the Hall's three thousand seats were empty. Nevertheless she spoke and conducted a service on behalf of the Liberal Catholic Church and the Order of the Star of the East, T.S. offshoots.

She was then in her eightieth year. She wore the Sign of Solomon ring bequeathed her by Madame Blavatsky, and she delivered the following benediction to the audience, one especially meaningful to members of the Toronto Lodge: "May the blessings of our Masters rest on us all, illuminating our minds, and filling our hearts with love."

One reason for the poor attendance was Besant's avowal of the Liberal Catholic Church and the Order of the Star of the East. The two organizations were established within Theosophy by C.W. Leadbeater, who declared himself to be a Bishop of the Church and the leader of the international Order which he had founded as a vehicle for "the next world saviour," a young Indian youth named Jiddu Krishnamurti. Krishnamurti later dissolved the Order and led his own disciples. Many Theosophists were wary of Leadbeater, especially after the scandal caused by the discovery of the so-called Cipher Letter which is also known as the Toronto Letter.

On a lecture tour, Leadbeater arrived in Toronto in 1906, accompanied by a handicapped, fourteen-year-old boy named Robin Pettit. When they had vacated their rooms in the house in which they were lodged, a suspicious housekeeper lighted upon a letter that they had inadvertently left behind. It was typewritten and unsigned and composed in cipher. The simple code was easily broken. It seemed that the letter was written by Leadbeater and addressed to Robin. It included the following passage which was judged offensive in its implication of homosexuality: "Glad sensation is so pleasant. Thousand kisses darling." The text is discussed by Mary Lutyens in *Krishnamurti: The Years of Awakening* (1975) and by Arthur H. Nethercot in *The Last Four Lives of Annie Besant* (1963). Revelation of the letter's contents coupled with other indiscretions of Leadbeater's led to his resignation from the Society.

Toronto/
Haunted Queen's Park

Queen's Park is the name of the Legislative Building of the Province of Ontario. A bulky building of pink sandstone designed in the Romanesque Revival style, it occupies the site of an old lunatic asylum which was demolished in the 1880s. Queen's Park was formally opened on 4 April 1893.

The five-storey building is the haunt of both politicians and spirits. There are reports that ghosts have been seen descending the Grand Staircase and standing in the darkened Legislative Chamber. They haunt the Lieutenant-Governor's Suite and the offices occupied by the Premier, the Speaker, and the Clerk of the

House, as well as the dark storage areas in the basement, near the tunnel which passes beneath Queen's Park and connects the Legislative Building with the eastern block offices.

The political journalist Claire Hoy, in his biography *Bill Davis* (1985), surveyed the spirit population of the building, and found the host to include one male and three female ghosts. The male ghost haunting Queen's Park is the spectre of an old soldier who is seen from time to time strutting in full regimental dress and frowning. The female ghosts, inmates of the long-demolished asylum, are a motley threesome. The first is gowned in white with streaming hair; the second wears a checkered dress which obscures her head; the third hangs from a hook in the basement of the building. All these ghosts have been reportedly seen by sober legislators and custodians in various parts of the Legislative Building over the years.

Toronto/
The Phantom Ship of Etobicoke

"Call them old-wives' tales, sailors' myths, hallucinations, metaphysical manifestations, or what you will, the fact remains that knowledgeable and reputable people have experienced strange and seemingly unexplainable sights and sounds and, while they cannot account for the visual and audible phenomena revealed to them, they can most certainly vouch for their existence." In this way the journalist Dwight Boyer in *Ghost Ships of the Great Lakes* (1968) introduced the "remarkable experience" reported by Rowley W. Murphy, the distinguished Canadian illustrator and historian of the Great Lakes.

The experience occurred to Rowley and ten other yachtsmen on Lake Ontario near the mouth of Etobicoke Creek about 1:30 a.m. one clear, moonlit night in August 1910. Rowley called it an "appearance from the past." He was awakened from sleep by four blasts on a steamer's whistle. He saw, approximately half a mile off shore, a steamer heading west-south-west at half speed.

She was considerably smaller than the three famous Upper Lakers, *China, India,* and *Japan.*

. . . She was not as small as *Lake Michigan*, but like her, did appear to be of all wooden construction. However, there were many in the past, of quite related design and size. The vessel seen had white topsails and deckhouses, and appeared to be grey below her main deck, like the Welland Canal-sized freighters. . . .

Her chime whistle was a good one, but was reduced in volume . . . and was sounded continuously for perhaps ten minutes. Very soon all hands now watching on the beach decided that something should be done. So a dinghy was quickly hauled over from the basin and, with a crew of four made up from some of those aboard the three yachts, started to row out with all speed to the vessel in distress, to give her what assistance might be possible.

As the boys in the dinghy reached the area where something definite should have been seen, there was nothing there beyond clear and powerful moonlight, a few gulls wakened from sleep . . . but something else, impossible to ignore. This was a succession of long curving ripples in a more or less circular pattern, which just might have been the last appearance of those caused by the foundering of a steamer many years before on a night of similar beauty. In any case, the four in the dinghy returned in about an hour, reporting also small scraps of wreckage which were probably just old driftwood, seldom seen with any fresh breezes blowing.

Dwight Boyer concluded with questions of his own.

What, indeed, did the eleven yachtsmen see that night? Was some supernatural manifestation projected before them in the moonlight on Lake Ontario? Did some unearthly power cause an old steamer to rise from her grave to live once more her final minutes afloat? Or did eleven sober and dependable citizens, against incalculable odds of coincidence, all suffer the same hallucination at the same time? Not likely. Whatever the name of the phantom ship looming so eerily in the moonlight, something was there, beyond a doubt. And it was thoroughly consistent with the stories told by many old sailors, before and since, of spectre ships of the past riding the seas once more. The incident cited by Rowley W. Murphy and verified by ten companions of unquestioned integrity gives them credibility and substance.

Such is the unnamed Phantom Ship of Etobicoke.

Toronto/
Albert Durrant Watson

Albert Durrant Watson (1859–1926) was at one and the same time a poet and a physician, a Methodist and a Whitmanite, a spiritualist and a Theosophist, a psychical researcher and an astronomer. An active fellow of the Royal Astronomical Society, he was also the founder of the short-lived Association for Psychical Research of Canada. He was the author of over twenty books, including a *Poetical Works* published by the Ryerson Press in 1924.

Watson was the author of three books based on spiritualism and psychical research. From these books it is possible to piece together something of his philosophy of the beyond. They are: *The Twentieth Plane: A Psychic Revelation*, *Birth through Death: The Ethics of The Twentieth Plane*, and *Mediums and Mystics: A Study in Spiritual Laws and Psychic Forces* (1923). The first and second books were published by McClelland & Stewart; the third, written with the assistance of the journalist Margaret Lawrence, was issued by the Ryerson Press.

Although interested in mediumship, Watson did not feel himself to be psychic. So he engaged the services of Louis Benjamin, a Chicago-born, Toronto-raised, self-educated young man with psychic gifts. Benjamin operated the Ouija board or delivered "trance-addresses" during the *séances* which were held over the years in the parlour of Watson's home on Euclid Avenue in Toronto. Watson believed himself to be in communication with the spirits of the departed who called themselves "the Humble Ones of the Twentieth Plane."

The Twentieth Plane is or was a place that abounded in good spirits with familiar names. For instance, Benjamin contacted the poetic spirit of Samuel Taylor Coleridge and was able to communicate with him. The deceased English poet was impressed with the seriousness shown by Watson and Benjamin, and he offered to contribute a preface to the second volume of their findings. The offer was accepted, the words were transmitted and transcribed, and the preface was duly published. So this little-known volume came complete with a hitherto-unknown prose-work signed by S.T.C.

The third volume contributed little to one's knowledge of the Beyond beyond the fact that a "sea of Universal Consciousness" exists and that minds swim in it. Apparently the "Humble Ones" took these *séances* as a golden opportunity to inform the living of the fate of the dead. Not only did the spirits of the dead approve Watson's plans to publish their privileged communications, they set up a Publication Committee on the Twentieth Plane. The committee consisted of four notables: Abraham Lincoln, Ralph Waldo Emerson, Walt Whitman, and Robert G. Ingersoll.

It is a comforting thought to realize that Canadian literature, although it may be ignored on the earthly plane, is widely read on the Twentieth Plane. It seems that John Keats enjoys reading the poems of Robert Norwood, whose writing is now entirely out of fashion and out of print. Tennyson, though regrettably unfamiliar with the poems of W.W. Campbell, is familiar with Bliss Carman's poetry. Whitman is not reading much these days, but he does bless Helen and Henry Saunders, Toronto-based collectors of his works; he even thanks them with the words, "I love to remember that they are living in the spirit of my teaching."

Little information is available on the short-lived Canadian Association for Psychical Research. The society was founded in Toronto about 1908 along the lines of the original Society for Psychical Research (launched in London in 1882) and the American Society for Psychical Research (established in Boston, later New York, in 1884). The Canadian Association is often described as the child of Albert Durrant Watson but his name does not appear in the Association's executive and officer roster which was published in *Secular Thought,* August 1908. The roster is reproduced by the historian Ramsay Cook in *The Regenerators* (1985). Cook also reprinted the aim of the Canadian Association:

> It is the purpose of the Society that all investigations shall be systematically and skillfully conducted and results faithfully recorded; and such reports, whether the work of individual members, branch societies or committees of the parent body or branches, shall be placed with the board of directors of the parent society to deal with. The new society, following the parent bodies in England and the States, will investigate dreams, apparitions, clairvoyance, discarnate spirits, the influence of the mind on mind, and other like subjects.

If it published a Journal or a Proceedings, no record has been found of them. Even the name of the Canadian Association varies from time to time. It is sometimes given as the Canadian Association for Psychical Research or as the Society for Psychical Research of Canada. If Albert Durrant Watson was not one of the original founders, he came to be identified with the society and served in the early 1920s as its last president. No doubt, for further information, one should turn to "the Humble Ones of the Twentieth Plane."

Toronto/
Chant's Meteors

The father of Canadian astronomy is the title bestowed on C.A. Chant (1865–1956), the distinguished astronomer and astrophysicist at the University of Toronto. Among his many contributions to the field of astronomy was the establishment of the David Dunlap Observatory at Richmond Hill, Ontario. He died at the age of ninety-one at Observatory House, close to this instrument, Canada's largest optical telescope.

Professor Chant missed the observation of a lifetime when he was otherwise engaged the evening of 9 February 1913. If only he had known in advance what was going to happen that Sunday evening! Then he would have been ready to make precise observations of the event that was to unfold over Toronto at 9:05 p.m. Eastern Standard Time.

That evening there was a spectacular meteoric display. A stream of meteors travelled in apparent formation and illuminated the night sky for 3.3 minutes. The procession was first observed at Mortlach, Saskatchewan. It proceeded west in a stately fashion over Saskatchewan, Minnesota, Michigan, Southern Ontario, New York State, the southeast Atlantic, Bermuda, and Brazil's Cape São Roque. Some observers heard the sound of distant thunder. Astronomers called the shower the Cyrillids after St. Cyril of Alexandria on whose feast day the lights had been observed.

Professor Chant was able to compensate for missing the main event by reconstructing precisely what had happened.

> It was not my good fortune to be an eye-witness of the phenomenon, but when, a few minutes after it had passed, telephone messages were received describing it, I realized that there had been a very exceptional occurrence. Yet it was only on the following day, after interviewing various observers and reading the reports in the newspapers, that the truly extraordinary nature of the display was recognized. I then decided to investigate the matter.

Chant collected more than one hundred descriptions from eye-witnesses and then compared and contrasted them. He discussed the sighting of the meteors under the headings of General Description, Path, Height, Speed, Size, and Other Meteors Seen Within a Few Hours of the Great Display. His findings were published in two issues of *The Journal of the Royal Astronomical Society of Canada,* May–June 1913 and November–December 1913.

What the descriptions of eye-witnesses had in common was a sense of the wonder of the display plus the play of the imagination:

> To most observers the outstanding feature of the phenomenon was the slow, majestic motion of the bodies; and almost equally remarkable was the perfect formation which they retained. Many compared them to a fleet of airships, with lights on either side and forward and aft; but airmen will have to practise many years before they will be able to preserve such perfect order. Others, again, likened them to great battleships, attended by cruisers and destroyers. Should these bodies strike the earth they might prove destroyers indeed! Still others thought they resembled a brilliantly lighted passenger train, travelling in sections and seen from a distance of several miles. The flight of the meteors has also been compared to that of a flock of wild geese; to a number of men or horses in a race, and to a school of fish, startled and darting off in a single direction.

Professor Chant's scientific description of the phenomenon may be contrasted with the opinion of the broadcaster and author Frank Edwards writing in *Strange World* (1964).

> The simplest explanation which covers all the known facts in this case — and the only conclusion that *does* cover all the facts — is that these things were under intelligent direction. . . . In 1913 it would have been difficult, perhaps impossible, for many persons to have accepted the conclusion that the earth had been visited even briefly by intelligently directed craft of extra-terrestrial origin. Yet that conclusion, and that alone, seems to fit the evidence of that unforgettable night.

Toronto/
The Disappearance of Ambrose Small

The most famous missing person in Canadian history is Ambrose Small. His disappearance earned him enduring if posthumous fame in the form of a legend and an entry in Charles Fort's *Wild Talents* (1932):

> Upon December 2, 1919, Ambrose Small, of Toronto, Canada, disappeared. He was known to have been in his office, in the Toronto Grand Opera House, of which he was the owner, between five and six o'clock, the evening of December 2nd. Nobody saw him leave his office. Nobody — at least nobody whose testimony can be accepted — saw him, this evening, outside the building. There were stories of a woman in the case. But Ambrose Small disappeared and left more than a million dollars behind.

Fort collected such oddities. According to the humourist H. Allen Smith, Fort would call attention to the disappearances of Ambrose Bierce in Mexico and of Ambrose Small in Toronto, all the while suggesting, "Somebody is collecting Ambroses."

At the time of his disappearance Small was at the height of his career. He was fifty-three years old, the owner of theatres in seven Ontario cities, the controller of bookings in sixty-two other houses, and a self-made millionaire. The day before his disappearance he sold his theatrical holdings for $1.7 million. The day of his disappearance, he met with his lawyer and friend F.W.M. Flock in his office at the Grand Opera House near Adelaide and Yonge Streets. Flock left at 5:30 p.m., the last person known to the police to have set eyes on Small. The disappearance of the prominent businessman under these odd circumstances caught the public's imagination. There was an extensive police investigation that came to naught. The case remained unsolved, not being officially closed until 1960.

The week of Small's disappearance the Grand Opera House was playing *Revelations of a Wife*. The play attracted full houses but the theme supplied no clues. Theresa Small felt that her missing husband had fallen into the hands of a "designing woman" but there were no likely candidates. The police did discover that "Amby" had, in addition to his office in the building, a "private secret room" with its own entrance. It was no doubt useful for assignations and the settling of gambling debts, but it yielded no leads.

Sir Arthur Conan Doyle, contacted by reporters

on a New York visit, showed enough initial interest in the case to generate the headline "World's Greatest Detective to Solve Small Case." (Perhaps it was too "small" for Doyle, for nothing came of the Holmesian inquiry.)

Spirit mediums claimed they had contacted Small or his spirit. He was a victim of amnesia. He was starting his life over again in foreign parts. He was abducted by his private secretary. He was murdered by gamblers or gangsters. Theatre folk reported seeing him in unlikely places. Harry Blackstone, the famous magician, signed an affidavit which read, "On April 8th, 1920, I saw Amby playing roulette in a gambling casino in Juarez, Mexico." A weird wail was reported by janitors emanating from the cellar floor of the Opera House's furnace room. He was a prisoner in the lime-kilns near Brampton, Ontario. The police received a telephone call from a man in Wisconsin who claimed he was the missing millionaire, but who turned out to be an escaped lunatic. From Vienna came a psychic detective, Max A. Langsner, who said he would solve the case. Through "thought waves" he determined in 1928 that Small's body was burning or burnt in the house in Montreal.

"The final curtain may be down on the most bizarre melodrama in Canadian theatrical history — but who can be sure? The ghost of Ambrose Small has never rested quietly." So wrote Murray Rutherford in "Where's Ambrose Small?" in *Early Canadian Life,* October 1978.

Toronto/
The Whereabouts of Peking Man

Peking Man is the name given to an important ancestor of modern man. The skull and bones of Peking Man were uncovered in 1929 at Chou Kou Tien (Zhoukoudian), southwest of Peking, by a team of archaeologists headed by Davidson Black. Black, a Toronto anthropologist, was head of the Cenozoic Research Laboratory of Peking Medical Union College. A member of the archaeological team was the famous Jesuit metaphysician Pierre Teilhard de Chardin.

For the next five years Black studied the fragments of skull and bones. He succeeded in identifying and describing a new species of ancient human. He called his discovery Peking Man, *Sinanthropus pekinensis,* and for the accomplishment he received many honours. He died unexpectedly in Peking in 1934. It is said that he died in the Cenozoic Research Laboratory with the skull of Peking Man clutched in his hands.

The fate of Peking Man is one of the ironies of history. This human-like individual died almost a million years ago. His bones lay undisturbed for all that time until they were uncovered in 1929. They were studied intensively for a dozen years. Then they vanished from the face of the earth. They have not been seen since 1941 despite an extensive search.

A great deal has been written about the disappearance of the valuable remains. Dora Hood told the basic story in *Davidson Black: A Biography* (1964). Subsequent events were grippingly described by Christopher Janus in *The Search for Peking Man* (1975). What happened was that the invasion by the Japanese in 1937 closed down Peking Medical Union College. But the bones were packed and a company of American Marines was instructed to move the bones in lockers to Chinwangtao. They then would be shipped to the United States. The precious cargo disappeared en route and has not been seen since then.

The People's Republic of China has long wanted the remains returned, suspecting that they are being kept under wraps in Tokyo, Taipei, or New York. The search for the bones took a new turn in 1972 when a Greek-American businessman named Christopher Janus visited Peking and was encouraged to take up the cause. Janus offered a reward for their return which he kept increasing until it reached the sum of $100,000.

Over the next ten years he travelled around the world following innumerable blind leads. He did acquire one substantial piece of evidence which led him to suspect for a long time that the bones had left China, crossed the Pacific, and were somewhere in the eastern United States. A cryptic phone call from a mysterious woman resulted in a meeting on the observation deck of the Empire State Building. The woman refused to be identified but gave Janus a photograph of some of the bones in a Marine's locker. Thereafter there was no further contact. He was unable to locate the mysterious woman, who may well have been the wife of a Marine who knew the whereabouts of the bones. He suspected the woman lived in some fear for her life.

Eventually he withdrew the offer of the reward. Now no one, including Janus, has any idea of the present whereabouts of Peking Man.

Toronto/
R.S. Lambert

A man who especially relished the supernatural in Canada was Richard Stanton Lambert. The reading public knew him as R.S. Lambert, and his friends referred to him as Rex.

Lambert was born at Kingston-on-Thames, England, in 1894, the son of a prominent Liberal Member of Parliament. He attended Repton School and Wadham College, Oxford, where he took his M.A., and commenced an eventful career in adult education, journalism, and broadcasting. He wrote for *The Economist* in 1914–15, served as a founder of the British Institute for Adult Education, and taught at the Universities of Sheffield and London. In 1927, he joined the British Broadcasting Corporation, and the following year became the founding editor of *The Listener*.

Lambert edited the BBC's cultural weekly for a decade before resigning the editorship and leaving England permanently. Why he did this is instructive. Lambert's passionate interest in psychical research led him to the Isle of Man to consider a case of possession or poltergeist. The controversial case involved Gef, the Talking Mongoose. The controversy concerned whether or not the mongoose possessed the power of speech. Lambert collaborated on a book about Gef with Harry Price, the celebrated ghost-hunter who was not averse to seeing his name in the headlines. *The Haunting of Cashen's Gap* (1936), their book on the case, was a nine-day wonder. It led an outspoken BBC Governor to question Lambert's sanity. He did so publicly, and Lambert, feeling that his judgement

R.S. Lambert is shown at his desk in the CBC's Radio Building in Toronto in January 1945. In 1939, in the wake of a successful lawsuit for slander involving Geff the Talking Mongoose, he left England for Canada. He joined the Canadian Broadcasting Corporation at the right time to assist broadcasters on "the home front." He became an authority on school broadcasting in Canada. Two of his forty books are For the Time Is at Hand *(1947), the life and times of Henry Wentworth Monk, and* Exploring the Supernatural *(1954). [Mrs. Jessica Riddell]*

was being called into question, as well as the validity of psychical research, launched a civil suit. Lambert won the suit and an award, but thereafter his position with the public broadcasting corporation was untenable.

Leaving the BBC in April 1939, he emigrated to Canada and in late September joined the Canadian Broadcasting Corporation in Toronto. He published almost thirty books, including biographies and histories, textbooks, and travel books, volumes of history and social studies. One of his children's books won the Governor General's Award for Literature. Eleven years following his retirement he and his wife settled in Victoria, British Columbia, where he died in 1981.

Lambert is best remembered in this country as the

251

author of *Exploring the Supernatural: The Weird in Canadian Folklore* (1955). This pioneering study was originally published in London and Toronto in 1954; it has remained in print in paperback in Canada to this day. Less influential but no less worthy is *For the Time Is at Hand* (1947), the first and so far only biographical study of Henry Wentworth Monk, the Prophet of March.

The only Canadian book with which *Exploring the Supernatural* may be compared is *Psychic Mysteries of Canada* (1975) by A.R.G. Owen. Both Lambert and Owen were born in Britain. Whereas Lambert was a man-of-letters deeply affected by the supernatural, Owen is a scientist with an intellectual interest in "recent developments in the field known as psychical research, or parapsychology." Whereas Lambert told the story of the "Fire-Spook of Caledonia Mills," Owen discussed the tabulated characteristics of "poltergeists." Two decades of psychical research have separated the two books. These are decades during which "the supernatural," which was described by authors, was transformed by researchers into such entities or qualities as "psi," "ESP," and "PK." Did science, during the years between 1955 and 1975, finally replace superstition? Or was the supernatural only temporarily displaced by the pseudo-science known as "parapsychology?"

Not only are the books characteristic of their periods; they are characteristic of different temperaments. If Lambert and Owen were attracted to the same subject of study—a subject like Gef the Talking Mongoose—Lambert would marvel at what it said, while Owen would wonder about how it said it.

Toronto/
Mackenzie House

The most celebrated haunted house in Metropolitan Toronto and perhaps in all of Canada is Mackenzie House. This is the name of a Georgian-style residence at 82 Bond Street built in the 1850s and occupied by William Lyon Mackenzie (1795–1861) from 1859 to his death in the second-floor bedroom on 28 August 1861.

Mackenzie House is Toronto's best-known haunted house. William Lyon Mackenzie, the rebel leader of the Rebellion of 1837, died in the second-floor bedroom on 28 August 1861. His grandson, Prime Minister W.L. Mackenzie King, was a secretive spiritualist. The historic building is administered by the Toronto Historical Board, and its official policy is that the house is not haunted. Yet a succession of live-in caretaking couples reported disturbances and both a séance and an exorcism took place in Mackenzie House in 1960. The pen-and-ink sketch is reproduced from an official brochure. [Toronto Historical Board]

The three-storey residence fell on hard times following Mackenzie's death and was slated for demolition in 1936 when it was acquired as an historic site. Since 1960 it has been owned and operated as a museum by the Toronto Historical Board. The residence is decorated in the manner of the 1860s and displays much Mackenzie memorabilia, including his Bible. A flat-bed printing press, like the one he used for his newspapers, is in working condition in the basement. There are no records or reports of psychic disturbances in Mackenzie House in the early years. All the accounts stem from the seven-year period 1956–62.

The residence was presented to Mackenzie by his friends "as a mark of esteem and in recognition of his public services" in 1859. So he occupied the house for only two years before dying a bitter and unhappy man. His youngest daughter Isabel Grace lived a lot longer in the house, dying there in 1873. She was the mother of Mackenzie King.

The first inkling that the building was haunted came from the first live-in caretaking couple, Mr. and Mrs. Charles Edmunds, who occupied the flat on the third floor from August 1956 to April 1960. That period of time was long enough, as far as Mrs. Edmunds was concerned. She was so frightened while she lived in the house, she said, that she lost forty pounds.

"We hadn't been here long when I heard the footsteps going up the stairs," she said. "I called to my husband. He wasn't there. There was no one else in the house. But I heard feet on the stairs." Mr. Edmunds was less bothered by the noises on the stairs than his wife, but he heard them too.

Then Mrs. Edmunds had a frightening experience. "One night I woke up about midnight, though I am normally a good sleeper," she explained. "I saw a lady standing over my bed. She wasn't at the side but the head, leaning over me. There is no room for anyone to stand where she was. The bed is pushed against the wall. She was hanging down like a shadow but I could see her clearly. Something seemed to touch me on the shoulder to wake me up. She had long hair hanging down in front of her shoulders. Not black or gray or white, but dark brown. She had a long narrow face."

About a year later the phantom lady returned and this time she struck Mrs. Edmunds in the eye. In the morning she found that her left eye was darkened and bloodshot. At odd times she caught glimpses of a woman in nineteenth-century attire with long, cascading hair moving through the corridors and rooms. In the kitchen the rocking chair rocked of its own accord. On eight or nine occasions, she said, she saw a small, bald-headed man in a frock coat standing in one of the second-floor bedrooms. At the time she did not know that Mackenzie wore a bright red wig to hide his bald pate. The couple heard the heavy thump of footsteps, as if someone were walking around in heavy boots. From the basement they complained of a rumbling and shaking sound.

The Edmunds were succeeded by Mr. and Mrs. Alex Dobban. The new caretaking couple arrived in April 1960 and first noticed the disturbances that had plagued their predecessors that June. That very month they moved out of the house into an apartment which they rented elsewhere, but they continued to tend the house until replacements could be found.

The Dobbans complained of footsteps on the stairs and a rumbling which Mrs. Dobban took to be caused by someone or something operating the flat-bed press in the basement. She clearly heard the piano being played in the parlour when no one else was in the house. "It wasn't a tune," Mrs. Dobban said. "It was just as if someone was hitting the keys with closed fists or a child playing the piano."

A *séance* was organized by the *Toronto Star*. Six mediums and one reporter met in the dining room, under a large oil painting of Mackenzie, but there was no communication with the spirit world. Then the rite of exorcism was performed by Archdeacon John Frank of Holy Trinity Anglican Church. This was held on 2 July 1960. As Sheila Hervey explained in *Some Canadian Ghosts* (1973), the priest, accompanied by a reporter, toured the house praying in each room. "In his prayers he asked that the disturbing spirits leave the Homestead forever. He also asked God to visit the house and drive from it all torment, unhappiness and fear. He prayed for Mackenzie and added another prayer that 'this house may long stand as a monument to those who pioneered in this country.' "

Thereafter the caretakers lived off the premises and the disturbances ceased—more or less. During renovations in 1962, the workmen complained of strange, poltergeist-like meddling. The foreman reported that things were moved at night, despite the fact that the house was locked up and there were no signs of a break-in. One morning a hangman's noose dangled over the stairway.

Even four years later there were unexplained things happening. A new caretaker, Mrs. Winnifred McCleary, complained that the toilet flushed by itself and that from time to time she could feel arms encircling her. As she explained in November 1966, "You knew you weren't alone."

Since then there have been few if any accounts of disturbances in Mackenzie House. It should be added that there has always been a facetious side to the haunting. It was long suspected that the ghostly happenings were reported as a form of free advertising to draw attention to Toronto's new historical attraction. However, far from taking pleasure in the building's ghostly past, the Toronto Historical Board downplays the reports of ghosts. Visitors are guided from room to room by young women who draw attention to points of historical, social, and cultural interest. But they make no reference to the events of the psychic past unless specifically asked about them.

Toronto/
The Haunted Old City Hall

Toronto's Old City Hall is a red sandstone building with a slender 260-foot tower. It was opened in 1898 and served as the jucicial and municipal headquarters for the City of Toronto and the County of York until 1966. The Old City Hall is reputed to be haunted, unlike the New City Hall which, completed in 1964, has yet to acquire its host of ghosts.

Like any older building, the Old City Hall has it share of creaky stairways, reverberating corridors, and draughty hallways. Perhaps these may be pressed to account for the eerie presences felt by Provincial Judge S. Tupper Bigelow who in 1965 told the press that when he walked down the hallways he could hear footsteps behind him and from time to time could feel his judicial robe being tugged:

> My office was located on the second floor. I began using the staircase which is a convenient way to go downstairs to our common room. On more than one occasion, I have heard these footsteps. I couldn't see anything, but I could feel my robes being plucked. There was no chance that the robes might have caught on anything as I walked downstairs.

Judge Bigelow was not the only person to report strange sounds on the stairways. As Sheila Hervey noted in *Some Canadian Ghosts* (1973):

> Judge Peter Wilch also used the staircase. He, too, heard the mysterious footsteps. On one occasion he heard them ahead of him on the stairs. It is difficult to imagine a dignified judge chasing up a flight of stairs after an unseen intruder. But that is exactly what Judge Wilch did. Following the sounds he went right to the top floor. He began a careful search of the entire area. The place was empty. There was no one there.

Some caretakers who have worked for years in the building have felt nothing, but others who have worked equally long in its draughty corridors maintain that presences may be felt throughout the building. John Carey, operations manager of the Metro property department, was quoted by Kathleen Kenna in the *Toronto Star,* 26 September 1983, as saying, "I don't believe in ghosts, but there's something weird about the northwest attic." Other people mention the cellars, which are said to reverberate with the moans of former prisoners in the detention areas, or Courtroom 33, where capital trials were regularly held.

One Halloween night in the early 1980s, a *Toronto Star* reporter and her sister decided to test the truth that the building was and remains haunted. They camped out in Courtroom 33. Although they wanted to spend the night there, they were frightened by the many "weird sounds" and "cool fogs." At one point they felt their feet were "glued" to the floor. They lasted until 4:00 a.m. when they left for home and a good night's sleep. They never did prove that the Old City Hall is haunted; only that it feels haunted.

Toronto/
The Avro Car

Do UFOs or unidentified flying objects exist? Of course. Innumerable, yet-to-be identified objects are flying through the sky right now. But do flying saucers exist? Of course. Two of them were constructed and launched in Toronto in 1961. Surely beside the point is the fact that the pair of vehicles were experimental models which worked poorly and that the project was promptly cancelled! Flying saucers exist, or did exist, in this sense anyway.

The A.V. Roe Company, a large aircraft manufacturer at Malton, developed plans for an aircraft with the dual capability of vertical take-off and landing and high forward speed. The plans called for a kind of airborne hovercraft that was circular — disc-shaped or saucer-shaped — in design. In February 1953, the Canadian Ministry of Defence Production awarded Avro a grant of $400,000 to develop its plans. Then the U.S. Army and U.S. Air Force jointly commissioned the production of two prototypes. It was reported that the total cost was $10 million. The vehicles were designed to climb vertically into the upper atmosphere and then quickly attain a horizontal speed of 1600 miles an hour.

The two vehicles were designated VZ-9Z Avro Car. The first prototype made its first untethered flight at Malton on 16 May 1961, piloted by W.J. (Spud)

This is the clearest photograph ever taken of a flying saucer. The craft in question is shown hovering a few feet above the tarmac in front of the A.V. Roe Company at Malton, Ont. This undated photograph was taken sometime between late 1959 and late 1961. The Avro company designed and built an experimental, prototype flying saucer, named the Avro Car, under contract to the U.S. Army. The saucer-shaped craft, eighteen feet in diameter, was powered by three turbo-jet engines which drove the central fan and provided a peripheral air curtain and ground cushion for VTOL operation and then for forward flight. The Avro Car was a permanent exhibit at the U.S. Army Transportation Museum at Fort Eustus, Virginia, until June 1986 when it was repatriated by the National Aviation Museum in Ottawa. [U.S. Army Transportation Museum]

Potocki. The Avro Car measured 18 feet in diameter and weighed 6000 pounds. It was powered by three turbo-jet engines located in the centre of the vehicle. It was designed to carry two pilots and one observer. It rose four feet above the ground and was said to be capable of forward movement at 350 miles an hour. However, there were severe stability problems. The first untethered flight was recorded on colour film fifteen minutes in length.

The vehicles were judged to be inherently unstable so the project was abandoned in December 1961. One of the Avro Cars was scrapped. The other was donated to the Smithsonian Institution in Washington, D.C., which in turn donated it to the U.S. Army's Transportation Museum, Fort Eustis, Virginia, where for many years the "flying saucer" was a prized exhibit. The Avro Car, the sole man-made flying saucer, was "repatriated" in June 1986. Now it is displayed at the National Aviation Museum in Ottawa.

Toronto/
The Etobicoke Poltergeist

The so-called Etobicoke Poltergeist was a dweller in the attic of a large, three-storey house on Prince Edward Drive in Etobicoke, a city in the western end of Metropolitan Toronto. The house was built as a farmhouse in the 1880s, when the district was entirely rural. Today the area is suburban. The poltergeist was a noisy and obnoxious one, as Sheila Hervey noted in her book *Some Canadian Ghosts* (1973). She changed the names of the human occupants of the house to spare their families further publicity, a practice followed in this entry.

In May 1968, the house was occupied by various members of the Craighill and Bullen families. Living on the main floor were Edward Craighill, his wife, and their daughter Anne, aged ten. The second floor was occupied by their older daughter Diana, twenty-seven, her husband John Bullen, and their two small daughters. The basement was rented to a bachelor schoolteacher.

Early one night Diana woke to hear heavy footsteps in the attic. "I heard the footsteps, thump, thump, thump. Next I heard screeching laughter. It sounded like a middle-aged woman was right in the room with me." She awakened John who heard the strange sounds. Everyone else in the house was asleep at the time and heard nothing. The couple searched the attic but found nothing. The next morning, while still half-asleep, Mrs. Bullen felt someone standing over her. Nobody was to be seen but she felt a sudden chill. The thumping was heard again the next night.

Two nights later, at 12:30 a.m., the Bullens heard footsteps and the screeching laughter. John spoke and ordered whatever it was to keep quiet. There was quiet then until 4:00 a.m. when Fluffy the cat walked out the bedroom toward the attic door. "The Bullens heard a thump as if the cat had been kicked and then the cat screamed as if in terror or pain. This was followed by screaming which sounded human, and then by horrible laughter."

John found the cat leaning against the wall, stunned, its fur standing straight out as if it had been given an electric shock. The cat recovered but they slept poorly the rest of the night. The next morning there were no sounds but that afternoon Diana was alone in the house and heard footsteps in the attic. That was most unusual because up to that point sounds were heard only at night. She summoned a neighbour who came armed with a .22 calibre rifle. The attic floor appeared to be illuminated. The neighbour explored the attic but could find nothing.

The press learned of the poltergeist in the attic. John Downing and John Gault of the Toronto *Telegram* arrived late that day and decided to spend the night in the attic. To determine whether anyone or anything was walking across the attic floor, they sprinkled flour on it. At 3:30 a.m. they heard the phantom footfall but when they checked the flour-covered floor they found no footprints.

The following evening an exorcism was performed in the attic by the Rev. Tom Bartlett of the Star of Progress Spiritualist Church. "It was, by this time, dusk and the attic was gloomy. The door to the attic was closed on him. He stood for a few minutes in silence and then, glancing slightly to his left, he saw a brown, egg-shaped form. It was luminous, providing its own light.'' He later said the phantom form measured about four feet by two feet and moved in slow motion back and forth.

Bartlett summoned his wife Pat who described the sight as ''a brownish yard-stick about two or three inches wide.'' Pat experienced a sharp pain in her stomach and chest, and a thump was heard by others throughout the house. Reporters and others stood at the foot of the stairs and reported that they saw the attic door illuminated. Everyone felt intensely cold. The exorcism was performed but Diana went into a semi-faint that lasted half an hour. And at 4:00 footsteps were heard once more.

The next evening the reporters returned and everyone heard the footsteps and felt a series of cold waves passing through the house. Mrs. Craighill smelled perfume. Anne became hysterical, and Mrs. Craighill broke down. A crowd collected outside the house and four policemen were dispatched to keep order. Shortly thereafter the families moved out of the house and the manifestations ceased.

What to make of the Etobicoke Poltergeist? Sheila Hervey quotes the view of the spiritualists, Tom and Pat Bartlett:

> The Bartletts, however, had their own theory. They still felt that the disturbance was caused by a thought form. It was found out that an elderly woman once lived in the house and was expert at fortune-telling. She became rather peculiar in old age, however, and took to sitting at the dormer window in the attic to shout songs at the passersby. Neighbours complained about the noise, and the woman was forced to move. She was alive at the time of the Craighill haunting, living some miles from the Etobicoke house. She had some idea that she was ''keeping the house for her son.'' The poltergeist activity in that house was caused by the ghost form or thought form of a person not yet dead, but miles away, thinking about past experiences which she wanted to relive.

Toronto/ Psychic Archaeology

J. Norman Emerson (1917–1978) was the country's leading archaeologist as well as its leading proponent of ''intuitive archaeology.'' He was called the Father of Canadian Archaeology; he held a doctorate in archaeology; he was the principal archaeologist at the University of Toronto for thirty years, where he established the first program for Canadian archaeologists; he was the founding vice-president and former president of the Canadian Archaeological Association; and he was a recognized authority on Huron and Iroquois culture.

How did a man like Emerson come to embrace the use of psychics in the practice of his profession? ''It is my conviction,'' he told the members of the Canadian Archaeological Association at its annual meeting in March 1973, ''that I have received knowledge without archaeological artifacts and archaeological sites from a psychic informant who relates this information to me without any evidence of the conscious use of reasoning.'' No doubt his colleagues were surprised, and those who were not surprised were dismayed. He left them with no doubt as to where he stood: ''By means of the intuitive and parapsychological a whole new vista of man and his past stands ready to be grasped. As an anthropologist and as an archaeologist trained in these fields, it makes sense to me to seize the opportunity to pursue and study the data thus provided. This should take first priority.''

George McMullen was a former carpenter and real estate salesman, with a Grade 9 education and no apparent knowledge of Indian artifacts, who demonstrated psychometric abilities. Now the psychometrist is someone who is able, or believes himself to be able, to receive psychic impressions from an object. Thus he acquires knowledge of the object's past which is known through no other means. McMullin felt he had this ability since childhood.

At his home in Peterborough in 1969, McMullen gave Emerson a reading of an Indian relic. McMullen described the object as a pipestem, made a drawing of its original shape, and described the maker of the

257

pipe and also the living conditions at the time. He told Emerson the object was found within a hundred miles of Toronto. The pipestem had been dug up at Black Creek Pioneer Village, outside Toronto. The drawing was correct for the time period. Emerson was impressed.

For the next seven years McMullen accompanied Emerson on archaeological digs throughout Ontario and Quebec. At Warminster, near Orillia, McMullen described a visit to the spot centuries ago by men in bandanas and pigtails, and days later the same men dressed in lace-cuffed shirts, silk vests, and ostrich-plume hats. The men answered the description of explorer Samuel de Champlain and his companions who were known to be in the area and presumably at the site in 1615. On another occasion, McMullen walked over a site near Toronto while others put stakes in the ground behind him. When the site was excavated, it was found that the stakes were within inches of outlines of structures built and destroyed more than nine centuries earlier. There is no uncontested evidence that McMullen led Emerson to discover any previously unknown sites, but he painted verbal pictures of native lifestyles which Emerson found convincing.

After Emerson's death, McMullen travelled off and on for three years with Hugh Lynn Cayce, son of Edgar Cayce, the Sleeping Prophet, throughout Iran, Israel, and Egypt. It is said he detected a water system beneath the Sphinx. Again it is hard to say from the published accounts whether or not anything was detected by psychic means. McMullen then joined the American adventurer Stephan [sic] A. Schwartz in a commerical undertaking to use science and parapsychology to locate new archaeological sites. Schwartz described their work in his book *The Secret Vaults of Time: Psychic Archaeology and the Quest for Man's Beginnings* (1978). According to the article by Claire Gerus called "A Feel for the Past," which appeared in *Maclean's*, 22 September 1980, McMullen identified the former site of Cleopatra's Palace, outside Alexandria. Searching for the ancient lost city of Marea, they discovered priceless Byzantine mosaics. Once again, the claims are many but the proofs are few if any.

McMullen eventually retired to Nanaimo, British Columbia.

The psychics and sceptics remain as divided as ever on the subject of psychic or intuitive archaeology. The former recall that Emerson exclaimed: "We are just at the beginning." The latter remember his professional maxim: "The truth's in the digging."

Toronto/
TV Séance and Allen Spraggett

The world's first televised *séance* was shown on the national CTV Network on 17 September 1967. It was arranged by the broadcaster and journalist Allen Spraggett, who acted as moderator or host for the sensational affair.

The *séance* was taped live for three hours on 3 September 1967, two weeks prior to its airing. Then it was edited down to about thirty-five minutes and shown on CTV's principal public-affairs program, "W5." The host of that show, Ken Cavanaugh, invited Spraggett, then religion editor of the *Toronto Star*, to introduce his two American guests: James A. Pike and Arthur Ford. Pike was the most controversial clergyman of the day, a maverick Episcopalian bishop who espoused radical causes which in retrospect seem tame if not traditional. Arthur Ford was an old-style spiritualistic medium in his seventies — no trance-channeller he.

After the introduction and some conversation, Pike expressed remorse over the fate of his son, James Pike Jr., who had committed suicide a year earlier. Ford fell into a trance, and contacted his spirit-guide, an entity known as Fletcher. Ford believed Fletcher to be the shade of a French-Canadian Catholic soldier who was killed in World War I. Apparently they had met as youngsters at Fort Pierce, Florida. Fletcher contacted the spirit of Pike's son. They conversed for some minutes.

Pike was visibly moved, and when the trance-session was over he averred that the *séance* had produced information that only his son could have known. Pike did not let the matter rest. Some months later he arranged for another sitting with Ford, and

Allen Spraggett was throughout the Sixties and Seventies the country's best-known broadcaster and writer about "the unexplained." Here he is shown in the fall of 1976 on the set of his popular CBC-TV show Beyond Reason, *establishing a point for the benefit of a guest. His guest on this occasion was Mrs. Virginia Morrow who achieved a measure of fame as Virginia Tighe, the woman who seemed to recall details of a previous existence as an Irish woman named Bridey Murphy. [Memory Lane/CBC]*

the results of that sitting convinced Pike. Thereupon he declared himself to be a spiritualist.

The *séance* briefly focused world attention on Pike, spiritualism, Ford, Spraggett, and Pike's son's spirit. The headline on the front page of *The New York Times* read: PIKE ASSERTS HE GOT MESSAGES FROM DEAD SON AT TV SÉANCE. It may well be that this televised *séance*

was the single most reported *séance* in the history of spiritualism, eclipsing in fame if not in importance two landmark sessions: the private affair held in the Fox Homestead, at Hydesville, New York, on 31 March 1844, which launched the modern movement; the widely cited one held in Ashley Place, London, on 16 December 1868, at which the Anglo-Scottish medium D.D. Home apparently levitated around a room and out a second-storey window.

The Pike-Ford affair consolidated the position of Allen Spraggett as the best-known public proponent of parapsychology in the country and one of the best known on the continent. A sprightly figure of a man, Spraggett was born in Toronto on 26 March 1932. He was ordained a minister in the Open Door Evangelical Churches in 1954. Thereafter he graduated from Queen's University in Kingston and made a name for himself as a young preacher and pastor who delivered hell-fire sermons in small communities such as Feversham, Collingwood, and Hamilton. Then, as his theology liberalized, he applied for admission to the United Church of Canada and was assigned a pastoral charge in small Eastern Ontario communities like Toledo, Plum Hollow, and Rock Springs. He might have become a noted fundamentalist preacher. Instead, he left the pulpit for the press, the Holy Spirit for the world of spiritualism.

Spraggett was religion editor of the *Toronto Star* in 1962–69, a daily columnist in 1969–71, and the author of a weekly syndicated column titled "The Unexplained" in 1972–77. He was a popular radio broadcaster and the host of two network television shows, Global's "ESP — Extra-Special People" and CBC-TV's "Beyond Reason." He was also the founding president of the Toronto Society for Psychical Research. Over the years he wrote one dozen popular books:

• *The Unexplained* (New York: New American Library, 1967).

• *The Gift Within: Experiences of a Spiritual Medium* (New York: New American Library, 1970), with James Wilkie.

• *The Bishop Pike Story* (New York: New American Library, 1970).

- *Kathryn Kuhlman: The Woman Who Believes in Miracles* (New York: World Publishing Company, 1970).
- *Probing the Unexplained* (New York: World Publishing Company, 1971).
- *Arthur Ford: The Man Who Talked with the Dead* (New York: New American Library, 1973), written with William V. Rauscher.
- *The World of the Unexplained* (New York: New American Library, 1974).
- *The Spiritual Frontier* (Garden City, N.Y.: Doubleday, 1975), with William V. Rauscher.
- *The Psychic Mafia* (New York: St. Martin's Press, 1976), with M. Lamar Keene.
- *New Worlds of the Unexplained* (New York: New American Library, 1976).
- *Ross Peterson: The New Edgar Cayce* (Garden City, N.Y.: Doubleday, 1977).
- *The Case for Immortality* (New York: New American Library, 1979).

Relevations of fraud in spiritualist circles do not dismay Spraggett. He knows only too well that the literature of psychical research is fraught with deception. In fact, his book *The Psychic Mafia* is unique in the twentieth century in that it exposes the trickery of fraudulent mediums in pursuit of the dollar. Yet when he learned that some of the information which Ford had introduced into his *séances* derived from research and not from Fletcher — even some of the information used in the Pike-Ford *séance* — he resiliently and bravely concluded that Ford was a "gifted psychic who for various reasons, scrutable and inscrutable, fell back on trickery when he felt he had to."

Spraggett's career suffered a setback on 22 February 1979 when he was charged with two accounts of gross indecency involving teenage males in Winnipeg, Manitoba. After a thirteen-month delay, caused by the judicial process, the case was heard in a single day. Spraggett was acquitted on 3 April 1980, and the judge in his decision declared that the evidence was suspect and that the accused would be leaving the courtroom with his character "unimpeached." This occurred on the Thursday before Good Friday, and Spraggett expressed a wish in the spirit of Easter to

the CP reporter who interviewed him: "The media was very zealous in reporting my crucifixion a year ago. I hope they are just as zealous in reporting my resurrection."

Perhaps what sustained Allen Spraggett throughout the ordeal was a sense of the fact that the stars were on his side. The truth of astrology consoled him. He found in the heavens a place in the universe. In point of fact, he defined himself as a "neo-astrologer" — one who recognizes the importance of both the causal and the acausal factors in human destiny. As he told the reporter Nancy Reynolds, who interviewed him for the Niagara Falls *Review* on 24 August 1976, "Our universe is vastly more mysterious than science has grasped. There are no accidents in the universe. I believe there is a cosmic plan for us and this belief is based on facts not on faith."

Since then Spraggett has been busy. For two years he was "resident astrologer" at CFNY Radio, hosting a daily morning open-line program. In 1985 he hosted a daily, one-hour, open-line astrology and occult program on CFRN-TV in Alberta. He acts as personal and corporate astrological consultant. He has completed an occult thriller employing "the known data of parapsychology and showing that truth is more terrifying than the fantasies of Hollywood movies." He is planning to write a humorous account of his family's life in the parsonage. (He and his wife are happily married and have five children; he defines himself as "a devout practising heterosexual.") A book of his personal and professional experiences is in the wings. It will describe the mediums and psychics he has met — and he has met most of them — and it will be called, inevitably, *Confessions of a Ghost Hunter.*

Toronto/
A Thanatological Experience

What does the conscious person experience at the moment of death? In the absence of a scientific answer to that question, folk beliefs abound. Traditionally, the dying person watches as scenes from his or her life unfold; then the spirit separates from the body and surveys it dispassionately before journeying into realms of radiance.

Something approaching the latter, near-death experience was recorded by a patient in the Coronary Unit of the Toronto General Hospital. The details were set down by the patient himself at the request of his two doctors. Then they added their own observations and published the account under the heading "Cardiac Arrest Remembered" in the Correspondence Column of the *Canadian Medical Association Journal*, 22 May 1971.

A sixty-eight-year-old male patient suffered a myocardial infarction and remembered in detail the events surrounding his cardiac arrest. At the request of his physicians, R.L. MacMillan and K.W.G. Brown of the Coronary Unit of the Toronto General Hospital, he set down his recollection of his experiences.

"I do not have words to express how vivid the experience was. The main thing that stands out is the clarity of my thoughts during the episode." The patient continued, "It seemed at times that I was having a 'dual' sensation — actually experiencing certain things yet at the same time 'seeing' myself during these experiences."

The patient even saw his own body "face to face" as though in a mirror. "Almost immediately I saw myself leave my body, coming out through my head and shoulders." The new body appeared less than substantial. "The 'body' leaving me was not exactly in vapour form, yet it seemed to expand very slightly once it was clear of me. It was somewhat transparent, for I could see my other 'body' through it. Watching this I thought, 'So this is what happens when you die' (although no thought of being dead presented itself to me)."

The patient felt the exquisite sensation of "floating in a bright, pale yellow light — a very delightful feeling . . . I continued to float, enjoying the most beautiful tranquil sensation. I had never experienced such a delightful sensation and have no words to describe it." This bliss was short-lived, being followed by "sledge-hammer blows to my left side." The patient was responding to treatment. "Immediately I was in control of all my faculties and recognized the doctors and nurses around me."

The patient concluded, "I have read about heart transplants where it is claimed the brain dies before the heart stops. In my case, my brain must have been working after my heart stopped beating for me to experience these sensations. . . . If death comes to a heart patient in this manner, no one has cause to worry about it."

Toronto/
The Hilarion Series

"The Hilarion Series" is a series of texts published by Marcus Books of Agincourt. The texts were "dictated telepathically through M.B. Cooke by a source identifying itself as Hilarion," according to the catalogue issued by the publisher. Further details are supplied by the same publisher's bimonthly newsletter *Lightline: A Channel for Esoteric Truth and Information*, in which it says: "Hilarion is an ascended Master who is responsible for the Fifth Ray manifestation on our planet. He speaks through many channels on the earth at this time, Maurice B. Cooke being one of them."

Maurice B. Cooke is a what used to be called a medium but which is now termed a channeller. Cooke is really the pseudonym of a successful Toronto engineer and patent lawyer. If the name Hilarion recalls one of H.P. Blavatsky's Masters of nineteenth-century Tibet, the publications are strictly contemporary. They have the look and feel of New Age publications — a seamless and somewhat synthetic amalgam of positive thinking, parapsychology, oriental wisdom, occultism, and a symbolic reading of "the patterns of life."

From 1975 to the end of 1987, Hilarion dictated to Cooke and Marcus Books issued to the public sixteen separate books which have sold in excess of 100,000 copies. One senses that to read one is to have read them all. *Seasons of the Spirit* (1979) and *Symbols* (1980) are typical publications. Each has about one hundred pages. The texts are easy to read and the exposition is clear and concerned, characteristics not usually found in "dictated" writing. Each ends with the injunction: "May the peace and blessing of all the higher beings who care for humanity's struggle be with you forevermore. OM MANI PADME HUM."

Hilarion must be unique among the ascended Masters in that he sees the spiritual importance to the world of the Great Lakes and Southern Ontario. In *Symbols* he notes that the Great Lakes "have been placed in their precise positions for a special purpose, namely to protect the area known as Southern Ontario from negative aetheric influences coming from other parts of the world. In particular, there is much negativity of this kind emanating constantly from the larger cities in the eastern U.S.A. . . . " Toronto in particular is a protected spot:

> . . . the souls incarnated into that city, and those who are attracted to it as a place to live and work, are among the most evolved on this planet. Of course, there are individual exceptions to this generalization, but in the main, the spiritual level of its people is higher than for any other city of comparable size in the world. . . .

> In the years of trial which are now descending upon the earth, it is expected that the Toronto region will be the first to embrace the new ideas and new approaches which will characterize the Age of Love following the Tribulation.

According to the questions and answers in *Lightline*, No. 10-11, the country itself possesses a spiritual mission.

> Canada is meant to be a great unifying force for the human family, after the terrible years of the Tribulation have passed. She must take up the task of showing the world how different groups, with different languages and backgrounds, can learn to live together in harmony and brotherhood.

It cannot be denied that Hilarion—whether he resides in Tibet or Toronto, in Kanada or Canada — gives expression to a vision denied most Canadians.

Toronto/
Ian Currie and Past Lives

"You cannot die," Ian Currie states with the abruptness of a person who has little time to spend on disputation. He is one of the continent's leading and most conspicuous past-life therapists. His own definition of himself is as a parapsychologist who is specifically interested in establishing "survival evidence" —proof of life after death.

He was born (this time around) in 1936 in Vancouver. He took his Bachelor's in English and Anthropology and his Master's in Sociology at the University of British Columbia. He spent two decades teaching Sociology at the University of Toronto and the University of Guelph. Then he left the academic life far behind.

Since the summer of 1985 he has functioned as a full-time parapsychologist. Each week he sees between ten and twenty clients for past-life sessions. Each session is two hours in length. A single session is usually sufficient, though some clients have been known to require as many as six sessions. Currie does not generally employ hypnotic regression, but establishes a slight drowsiness in the client, this state of reverie usually being sufficient to permit brief access to the storehouse of past-life memory, the record of reincarnations. Currie keeps detailed records of the proceedings and the entire process is tape recorded. The client receives a tape for their own use. Roughly ninety per cent of his clients are female.

Currie is a systematic thinker. He discussed eight forms of evidence of previous lives in his book *You Cannot Die: The Incredible Findings of a Century of Research on Death* (1979) For the revised edition he plans to discuss four more forms. Concisely expressed the twelve forms of "survival evidence" are as follows:

1. Apparitions of the living and the dead.
2. Hauntings by the dead.
3. Out-of-body experiences.
4. Deathbed visions.
5. Near-death experiences.

6. Possession experiences
7. Memories of reincarnations, conscious and subconscious.
8. Mediumistic communication with the dead.
9. Photographic effects.
10. Electronic voice effects.
11. Kinetic effects at the instant of death.
12. Signs of intention to communicate after the event.

Currie's work is not limited to the reclamation of buried memories of past lives, but extends to restoring the integrity of human life today. He performs the rite of exorcism with the psychic Carole Davis. "Ten per cent of all houses are haunted," he says. "Of the sixty cases of exorcism that we have performed, only one was delusional; all the other houses were truly haunted. Sixty per cent of the spirits did not realize that they are dead. Eighty-three per cent of the spirits suffered precipitous death. There are prayers to be said against the possibility of a sudden death."

Do regression therapists actualize latent memories or do they liberate lively fantasies? The jury is still out . . .

Toronto/
New Horizons Research Foundation

The New Horizons Research Foundation was established in Toronto in July 1970 as "a non-profit organization whose purpose is to promote research on the frontiers of science and disseminate information." Among its founders were A.R.G. Owen, a respected Cambridge biologist and noted authority on the subject of poltergeists, and his author-wife Iris M. Owen.

Throughout the 1970s, members of this group were an extraordinarily active lot — sprightly if not spirited. They met in a Rosedale residence and sponsored the First Canadian Conference on Psychokinesis and Related Phenomena in Toronto, 18–22 June 1975. The first issue of *New Horizons* (the Journal of the New Horizons Research Foundation, incorporating the Transactions of the Toronto Society for Psychical Research Foundation) appeared in summer 1972. It

The Owens are the best-loved and most-active couple in parapsychological circles in this country. A.R.G. Owen (who is better known as George) was a mathematician at Cambridge and a contributor to that university's tradition of psychical research. In 1970, at the invitation of the venture capitalist Ben Webster, he and his wife Iris M. Owen came to Canada and settled in Toronto where they established the New Horizons Research Foundation and the Toronto Society for Psychical Research (TSPR). They retired from active involvement in the field on 31 December 1987. [Hawkshead Services]

was "published occasionally" until fall 1978.

In 1971, Iris Owen established the Toronto Premonitions Bureau. It was modelled on the first such bureau, opened in London in 1967, and on one later established in New York City. Its purpose was to register premonitions submitted by Canadians — a kind of patent office for predictors.

The Foundation served as a focal point in Toronto and a forum for the country for investigatory and theoretical work in the field once called psychical research and now known as parapsychology. The academic standing of the Owens guaranteed that the Foundation's activities would meet respectable and scientifically acceptable standards. The couple produced two remarkable books. The first is A.R.G.

Owen's *Psychic Mysteries of Canada* (1975). The American edition was titled and subtitled *Psychic Mysteries of The North: Discoveries from the Maritime Provinces and Beyond* (1976). It sheds scientific light on such traditional subjects as poltergeists and hauntings and on such contemporary wrinkles as force fields and psychic archaeology. The second important book is Iris Owen's *Conjuring Up Philip: An Adventure in Psychokinesis*. It describes an experiment that is so special and suggestive of new directions in parapsychological research that it deserves description and discussion in a section of its own.

The learned societies of academia were the models for the New Horizons Research Foundation. Its founders were intimately familiar with the British and American Societies for Psychical Research, not to mention the American Parapsychological Association. During its salad days the small Canadian foundation made a marked national contribution to an international field of study. As Dr. Owen observed in 1975: "In the past few years the Canadian contribution to psychical research has been a distinguished one, and the relatively small number of people concerned in it can take pride in what has been achieved."

In a sense the Toronto Society for Psychical Research (TSPR), established by A.R.G. Owen, Allen Spraggett, and others was the successor of the Canadian Association for Psychical Research. This short-lived organization was established in Toronto about 1908 and was identified in its later years with the Toronto physician, poet, and spiritualist Albert Durrant Watson.

The New Horizon Research Foundation and its subsidiary, the Toronto Society for Psychical Research, ceased to function, 31 December 1987.

Toronto/
The Philip Phenomenon

The New Horizons Research Foundation will long be remembered as the sponsor of what has been called the Philip Phenomenon. A.R.G. Owen discussed the phenomenon in *Psychic Mysteries of Canada* (1975), and Iris M. Owen called it "An Adventure in Psychokinesis" in *Conjuring Up Philip* (1976), the lively book she and Margaret Sparrow devoted to this equally lively landmark experiment.

The Philip Phenomenon sheds new light on spiritualism, *séances*, poltergeistery, and psychokinesis (or PK, the alleged ability to affect objects through mental means). Sceptics are inclined to see the Philip Phenomenon in light of playing with a Ouija board.

In 1972, eight members of the Society for Psychical Research, whose membership overlapped with that of the New Horizons Research Foundation, decided to explore the convention of the *séance*. They were curious about such questions as the following: Can a *séance* be conducted in a brightly lighted room rather than in a darkened parlour? Is it possible for a group of interested people, who claim no psychic abilities or mediumistic powers, to bring about a manifestation? Is the manifestation the end result of their combined efforts or the product of some outside force? It is to their credit that the members were able to find unexpected answers to these questions.

"The group was an ordinary cross-section of the population," wrote A.R.G. Owen, "an accountant, an engineer, an industrial designer, a scientific research assistant, and four housewives. None of them claims to be a medium. Psychical research is just one of their many diverse interests." What attitude did they take? "The point is that though by nature they were all sceptical and scientific, they were also truly open-minded. One could say that the group's point of view was that one cannot absolutely deny the existence of phenomena that one has not taken the trouble to look for."

They tried to summon up an apparition or a ghost. When their efforts failed, they decided to create their own ghost. They concocted one whom they called Philip of Diddington Manor, an English Cavalier at the time of Cromwell, and they gave him both a wife and a lover. Married to the frigid Dorothea, he was secretly in love with the gypsy girl Margo. Learning of their liaison, Dorothea accused Margo of witchcraft and watched as she burnt at the stake. Philip, the coward, was stricken with remorse and took his own life. Such was the fictitious biography of Philip of

Diddington Manor. There never was a Manor by that name, but Diddington Hall is a small mansion in Warwickshire, England. One member of the group had once seen it, but it had no ghost and no one named Philip was ever associated with it.

Members of the group met each week for a year and produced no effects. Their solemn, serious meditations resulted in no raps, no table levitations, no voices, and no materializations. In August 1973 they decided that if solemnity was ineffective perhaps joviality would work. It did. They produced raps.

The first experience was the "feeling" of raps in the table. "Feeling" is the right word because these raps were definitely felt rather than heard at this initial stage, and also because the group was making a degree of noise at the time and would not necessarily have been able to hear the raps if they were audible.

Philip himself adopted the procedure of one rap for yes and two for no with slight, hesitant knocks when the answer was doubtful or the question apparently not understood. He would also give a loud series of raps for a song which he approved and very soon adopted the habit of actually beating time to favoured songs. Members addressed questions to the table and the table responded. No one expected that when questioned about his mistress Philip would deny ever loving the gypsy girl Margo.

After some four weeks of sittings when raps were produced, one night suddenly the table started to move and it moved around the room in random fashion. The sitters were forced to vacate their chairs and follow it.

On one occasion the group invited Philip to flip the table right over.

Whereupon the table immediately tilted and, with all hands on top of it, gave a curious little "flip" and landed completely upside down with all four legs in the air. (It should be stated that the group were all standing up at the time, and so there was no question of a push with the knees — there was nothing underneath the table.)

Visitors were invited into the room.

Prior to hearing the raps and seeing the table movements the visitors were highly sceptical but went away satisfied that these happenings were produced paranormally and not by the group members tapping with hands, feet, or knees.

If it is the case that the physical force which makes the raps and table movements is generated by the group members themselves, then it is a case of collective psychokinesis or, as one might say, PK by committee.

The Philip research does not necessarily validate the full spiritualist assumption that the presence of a disembodied spirit is necessary for physical phenomena to occur in the séance room. This is because, in this instance at least, the operative factor is not the actual spirit of Philip but, instead, the *idea* of Philip in the minds of the group members.

Iris M. Owen added the following thoughts to her account of the phenomenon:

It is our contention that the joint thought projection acquired by our Toronto group is either the same force or similar to the force that is projected in a poltergeist situation. In the typical poltergeist disturbance the force or energy is projected, often unconsciously, by just one person, who for some reason or another (in many cases the frustrated tensions of pubescence or adolescence) acquires a superabundance of energy.

In the Philip experiment the group learned to combine their focus of interest upon a single object, so that whatever mental or psychological processes they employed were powerful enough to produce raps and movements in the table. The whole experiment has been part of a learning process for the group, requiring both time and patience. Once acquired, however, the force now seems at their disposal whenever they wish to use it. The question to be asked now is whether any group of people who are similarly oriented and willing to give of their time regularly can acquire the same skill. We believe that other groups can be taught and motivated to acquire the same skills.

Toronto/
IAO Research Centre

The only public astrology library in the world is the IAO Research Centre's Library of Divine Sciences, Parapsychology, and the Healing Arts. This library is a sprawling collection of more than 10,000 books and periodicals on these arcane subjects located at 9½ Casimir Street, Toronto.

According to Robin Armstrong, the professional astrologer who is the founder of the IAO Research Centre, the letters IAO are not an abbreviation but a cryptic cabbalistic code name for Jesus which is encountered not just in Christianity but in other cultural traditions as well. The Centre's collection of books grew out of Armstrong's personal library, but reached its present size through donations from over three hundred like-minded individuals. It continues to grow at the rate of some five hundred titles a year.

Armstrong was born in Montreal in 1946 and studied mathematics and chemistry at Sir George Williams University. Initially attracted to the I Ching, he began in 1970 to teach himself the principles of astrology. Now he casts horoscopes with the assistance of a computer and teaches the subject and the practice to others. "I teach astrology as a language, as a means of conceiving and perceiving," he told an interviewer on 2 October 1987.

Science and mathematics are languages that evolved from astrological perceptions. Scientists espouse objectivity in the perception of the universe and dismiss subjectivity. Astrologists perceive that life is both subjective and objective. Where do we begin? Where do we fit in? Where do we go? Einstein's Theory of Relativ-

ity is an affirmation of astrological principles because nothing changes without it affecting us.

Astrology is concerned with both uniquenesses and differences. Over everyone's head is a different star; underneath everyone's feet is the same earth. There are two genetic codes: the physical, genetic one and the social, cultural one. A person's horoscope is his social, cultural one. What astrology uniquely has to offer is 'time perspective' — clear, concise measurements of time-periods in one's life.

Robin Armstrong feels that astrology is a true humanistic discipline. Throughout history and around the world, astrological thinking has affected every aspect of human life in the same way the stars continue to influence men and women every moment of the day and night. He feels that the casting of a horoscope is both a science and an art.

Toronto/
The Legion Ghost

It may well be that the ghost of a soldier haunts a Legion Hall in the west end of Toronto. The haunted hall is located in an old, three-storey house at 515 Royal York Road south of the Queensway, which is the meeting place of the Mimico and Humber Bay Branch No. 217 of the Royal Canadian Legion. Bootlegging and gambling figure in the house's past, but the ghost seems to be connected with either the First or Second World War.

One Saturday evening before Christmas 1985, the country artist Donna Dunlop was singing in the Club Room, which is located in the basement of the house. After performing her first set of songs, she took a break. To escape the noise and the smoke, she climbed the flights of stairs leading to the third floor where the rooms are used for storage. Flags, standards, wreaths, wheelchairs, and memorabilia connected with the annual Remembrance Day parades are stored there.

Was there also a ghost on the third floor? "I was

alone but I just felt another presence," she recalled on 24 March 1987. "I didn't see anything but I felt the presence of a young man. In my mind's eye he was a young soldier. He was there and he knew that I was there. He was not menacing. He was a friendly presence. But it was an eerie experience!"

Somewhat shaken, the singer returned to the Club Room where she sang her second set of songs. When it came time to take the next break, however, she did not return to the third floor. Nor did she mention her experience to anyone. Some months later she was invited to perform again at the Hall. She was not really surprised when she overheard a group of Legionnaires discussing their ghost.

Over the years many men and women had felt a presence of "a young man . . . a young soldier." Whenever he puts in an appearance, there is a chill in the air.

"Since then I have performed many times at the Hall. I have even climbed the stairs to the third floor. But I only go halfway up to that floor. Sometimes I sit on the stairs but I never turn my back to the top of the stairs. I periodically glance up. And when I sing at the Hall, I usually include in my program 'The Ghost of Bras d'Or,' the folksong by Charlie MacKinnon. You can hear it on the album *Calling All You Nova Scotians*. It's the most moving song about a Canadian ghost. Whenever I sing it I think of that young man, that young soldier."

Toronto/
The Amazing Randi

The world's leading debunker of the pretensions of psychics and others is the Amazing Randi. This is the stage name of the conjurer, escape artist, author, and psychic debunker known as James Randi.

Randi does not call himself a magician. What he calls himself is a conjurer. The words imply different things. The conjurer capitalizes on the power of illusion and the audience's anticipation to create effects. Although these effects appear to defy reason and natural explanation, they are really brought about by

skill and intelligence, in short, trickery. That is how the conjurer works. The magician, in Randi's view, attributes his effects to the possession of magical powers, or allows his audience to come to this conclusion. The magician does so despite the fact that the presence of such powers has never been demonstrated in controlled circumstances. The mentalist is a magician,

James Randi is shown displaying his personal check for $10,000. The Toronto-born conjuror, escape artist, and debunker of psychical claims is known professionally as the Amazing Randi. He made the following standing offer in 1964: "I will pay the sum of $10,000 (U.S.) to any person who can demonstrate any paranormal ability under satisfactory observing conditions." Randi has taken on his shoulders the mantle of the late Harry Houdini who spent decades exposing fraudulent mediums. Randi delights in duplicating the feats of Uri Geller and others who dupe parapsychologists. He nurses a special hate for self-styled faith-healers. [The Toronto Star]

like Kreskin or Dunninger, who specializes in mind-reading acts.

Not all popular magicians imply that they are in the possession of psychic powers or are practitioners of the so-called Black Arts, of course, but some of the great performers of the past did so. And so do a number of practitioners in the present. For every Houdini who disavowed the supernatural, there was a Dunninger who fostered the illusion that he was in possession of telepathic powers. For every new-wave "master illusionist" like Doug Henning, there is a New Age mentalist like Kreskin who speaks and writes about the unexplained psychic powers within him.

The Amazing Randi was born Randall Zwinge at the Toronto General Hospital in 1928. He grew up at the family home in North Toronto. When he was twelve years old he lived for a year in Hamilton then it was Toronto again. Thereafter he called Montreal home. At the age of seventeen, he contributed a fake astrology column to the tabloid *Midnight*, signing it "Zo-ran." Even as a youngster he turned the art of quibbling into the science of questioning. He scrutinized claims of all kinds, whether psychic or not. He referred to this in an article titled "The Role of Conjurers in Psi Research" which appeared in *A Skeptic's Handbook of Parapsychology* (1985) edited by Paul Kurtz:

> I recall that, when I was a child in Canada, a certain company who made baking powder adopted a rather clever ruse to degrade the competition. They announced, "Our product is made without the use of alum!" and they immediately won over my mother as a customer. When I asked her if the other manufacturers put alum in their baking soda, she was a bit puzzled by my question. She had merely made an unconscious assumption that they did. This very gambit is well know to conjurers — and to "psychics" as well. One popular American "mentalist" is heard to declare, "Why, if I wanted to, I could perform *all* of these demonstrations by trickery!" And the audience jumps into the trap by assuming that at least some of the items are *not* performed by trickery. Wrong.

Randi made his stage début as a conjurer performing in Montreal night clubs. He moved to the United States in 1948 and now makes his permanent home in Sunrise, Florida. But he is seldom there, for he travels widely, performing on campuses and in theatres as a conjurer and escape artist. He has probably wiggled out of as many straitjackets as Houdini. Since the 1960s he has been in demand as a lecturer on paranormal claims and a debunker of parapsychologists and faith healers. Even Houdini would have marvelled at how deftly Randi unmasked the faith-healer the Rev. Peter Popoff on Johnny Carson's "Tonight" show.

Through the use of a videotape, Randi showed viewers how Popoff performed the "Gift of Knowledge" stunt. Popoff explained that the voice of God gave him detailed knowledge of the lives and illnesses of members of the studio audience. Randi revealed that while Popoff was on stage, impressing the audience with his knowledge, his wife was backstage privately broadcasting to him the information he was sharing with the audience. She employed a small transmitter; his "hearing aid" was actually a tiny receiving set. The "Gift of Knowledge" was coming to Popoff on 39.170 megahertz. Randi could not find a single instance in which Popoff or any televangelist or any faith-healer had cured anyone of anything.

In fact, Randi has issued the most famous challenge in the history of the rational inquiry into psychic claims. In his memoirs *Flim-Flam!*—there are two editions with different subtitles—*Flim-Flam! The Truth about Unicorns, Parapsychology and Other Delusions* (1980) and *Flim-Flam! Psychics, ESP, Unicorns and Other Delusions* (1985)—he wrote, "I am always in possession of my check in the amount of $10,000, payable to any person or group that can perform *one* paranormal feat of *any* kind under the proper observing conditions." The challenge itself was published as the Appendix to *The Faith Healers* (1987).

Randi has not neglected Toronto in his travels. As he wrote in *Flim-Flam!*:

> In Canada I have investigated such "psychics" as Rita Burns, whose fame rests almost entirely upon the enthusiastic hyperbole of one newspaper reporter who quoted endorsements made by the Royal Ontario Museum. Officials of the museum denied the statements only when I visited and questioned them. Rita had claimed to be working with that august organization, using her supposed powers to identify odd artifacts. Her performance was much less than successful, though her press coverage indicated quite the opposite. After extracting certain sums from a few Canadian businessmen for her "psychic" advice, she declined to meet me on a television program to examine her claims. This is an unfinished investigation that also needs more attention.

On a visit to his hometown to address a meeting of the Committee for the Scientific Investigation of the Claims of the Paranormal, 14 November 1987, he said that he did not "grow up" in Toronto. "I did not grow up and I never plan to grow up," he said, "I am having too much fun doing what I most want to do." He recalled that as a youngster he had explored the ravines of the Don Valley. On one occasion he came upon a rock with some graffiti written on it. The graffiti read: QUESTION AUTHORITY! Randi was impressed. He thought about it for a moment, then added a line of his own: WHY SHOULD I?

Walkerton/
The Nocturnal Light Case

The Walkerton Nocturnal Light Case is the well-documented account of the curious movements of a highly luminous object. It ranged across the countryside and then hovered around a large tree which it appeared to examine. The movements were observed and the case was reported by a professional astronomer and his brother.

The sighting occurred on a country road outside the town of Walkerton in western Ontario. It lasted about an hour, ending around 2:00 a.m. on a summer morning in 1960. The case was considered in detail by J. Allen Hynek in *The UFO Experience: A Scientific Inquiry* (1971). What Hynek as a veteran UFOlogist found unusual about the case was "the small estimated linear size" of the light.

The report that follows was made eleven years after the event. "The reporter, who today is a professional astronomer, did not wish to report it earlier because he was unwilling to expose himself to ridicule."

> The tree was about 100 yards distant and about 120 feet high. The object, which subtended an angle of about 1/4 degrees (giving it a physical diameter of less than 3 feet), appeared circular in shape and was thus probably a spheroid. It was highly luminous against the dark sky background and changed colour through the whole visible spectral range with a period of 2 seconds (rather an irregular period). Because it was rather bright, I may have slightly overestimated the angular size, and 1/4 degrees should perhaps be considered an upper limit. A lower limit would certainly be 1/8 degrees.
>
> The object appeared to be examining the tree rather closely. It circled the upper branches, ranging from 50 to 100 feet off the ground, passing *in front of* the tree, then clearly visible *through* the branches on passing behind the tree again. It continued this apparent "observation" of the tree for several minutes while we watched. Then, anxious for a picture, we climbed the perimeter fence and started slowly toward the tree facing due west. We had not gone more than 10 feet before it "noticed" us and, noiselessly accelerating at a very high rate, headed almost directly south, disappearing over the horizon (on a *slightly* rising trajectory) in about 2-1/2 seconds. (I consider my length and time estimates to be quite reliable as I was actively engaged in track and field at the time and thus

quite competent at this type of estimation. Even under such exceptional circumstances, these figures are most probably within ∓ 20 percent.)

Several observations about the object:

1. It was certainly too small to contain human life;

2. It had no apparent physical surface features apart from the circular shape it presented — possibly because the "surface" was highly luminous;

3. It moved *deliberately* and *purposefully* in its "inspection" of the tree, pausing slightly at apparent "points of interest" and giving the distinct impression of possessing "intelligent" behavior;

4. Its motion was completely silent, even the final rapid acceleration;

5. It was definitely *not* any natural physical phenomenon I have ever encountered or read about (I'm sure you are familiar with what I refer to — "marsh gas" and the like);

6. It was definitely *not* a distant astronomical object. It was clearly visible alternately *through* the branches of the tree and *obscuring* the branches of the tree, fixing its distance quite exactly;

7. It was definitely seen by competent witnesses (including several police officers) besides myself; and

8. On acceleration from the tree it almost certainly should have exceeded the speed of sound. There was no acoustical disturbance whatever. (My uncle attempted to take a picture of it as it accelerated but the result was not good enough to publish due to our excessive distance from the object and its rapid motion, which combined to produce a very faint blurred image.)

The salient points to consider are these: the object appeared to be governed by some intelligence, and it did not behave as would a physical phenomenon as we understand it.

Walpole Island/
The Tecumseh Cairn

During his life the Shawnee chief Tecumseh sought to unite the Indian tribes of North America against the westward expansion of the whites. He prophesied that in the fullness of time this would happen, and there is a tradition among the native people that he will return to lead his Shawnee people along the path and achieve his long-awaited victory. In the meantime his remains lie in the Tecumseh Cairn at the Walpole Island Indian Reserve on Walpole Island, St. Clair River. Therein lies a story . . .

In the War of 1812, Tecumseh allied himself with the British, and was killed . . . at the battle of Thames, in Ontario, on October 5, 1813. Armed with a war club, Tecumseh was killed in close combat with Colonel Richard M. Johnson (who was later vice-president from 1837–41 in President Van Buren's administration) who shot him in the chest with his pistol. After the battle, the Shawnees buried Tecumseh in a secret place on a bank beside a creek, distant from the battlefield. Some years later, they returned, intending to exhume the body and take it to Oklahoma for burial suitable for one of his importance. But the creek had often overflowed, obliterating evidence as to the exact spot of burial. Rather than make an extended search at that time, the Indians left the spot. In September 1941, however, his bones were disinterred, re-assembled, and placed in a cairn of stones on the bank of the St. Clair River, on Walpole Island Indian Reserve, Ontario. It remains a Shawnee tradition that Tecumseh will one day return and that at that time all Indian tribes will be united.

These details come from Robert B. Dickerson, Jr.'s *Final Placement: A Guide to the Deaths, Funerals, and Burials of Famous Americans* (1982). There is a plaque at Thames to mark the site where Tecumseh fell in battle.

In those days to be a great chief one had to be a great shaman. Tecumseh was both the war chief and the chief medicine man of the Shawnees. With his half-brother, known as The Prophet, he preached the return to native religion and traditional values. He saw his own mission as that of halting the American advance on Indian lands. The War of 1812 was the opportunity he needed to rally his Indian brothers behind the Crown against the Republic.

There is a tradition that Tecumseh cursed the Creek Indians and uttered a prophecy. The year was 1811. His powerful oratory failed to move the Creeks. There were five thousand of them but they would not unite with him against the Americans. "You do not believe the Great Spirit has sent me," he declared. "You shall know. I shall stamp my foot and the earth will tremble." After he had uttered those words, he stamped his foot and departed.

But the stamp of that foot echoed throughout the earth and the curse or prophecy was realized two months later. On 16 December 1811, the earth quaked. There were three tremendous shocks. An area fifty thousand miles square, which included the land of the Creeks, reeled with what was called "the greatest earthquake in the history of man."

As Angus Hall wrote about Tecumseh's curse or prophecy in *Signs of Things to Come* (1975), "It has been cited as an awesome example of the power of the shaman—who can not only foresee the future but, in some cases, make it come about through what magic no one else knows."

Warwick/
"Three Men"

Warwick is a farming community located east of Sarnia. A farmer working in his field in the vicinity of Warwick reported seeing the unusual sight of three men on a cloud sailing through the sky, one following the other.

The farmer, Charles Cooper, looked up from his work in the middle of the afternoon of 3 October 1843. According to his testimony, included by Eli Curtis in the booklet *Wonderful Phenomena: Wonders of the Age!* (1850), he beheld "a remarkable rainbow." It disappeared and was replaced by a rumbling sound.

The sound seemed to approach from the west. Then he saw the cloud. As he recalled:

> I beheld a cloud of very remarkable appearance approaching, and underneath it, the appearance of three men, perfectly white, sailing through the air, one following the other, the foremost one appearing a little the largest. My surprise was great, and concluding that I was deceived, I watched them carefully. They still approached me underneath the cloud, and came directly over my head, little higher up than the tops of the trees, so that I could view every feature as perfectly as one standing directly before me. I could see nothing but a milk-white body, with extended arms, destitute of motion, while they continued to utter doleful moans, which, I found as they approached, to be the distant roar that first attracted my attention. These moans sounded much like Wo — Wo–Wo! I watched them until they passed out of sight.

It is difficult to make much of this account. But it was corroborated by two other residents of the area who saw much the same sight: Robert Meneray, a youngster, who was four miles west of Cooper; and Charles Demster, an adult, who was two miles east of Cooper. Demster added the detail that the figures appeared to have belts around their bodies. Many people in the communities in the vicinity of Warwick heard the rumbling sounds but did not look up to see the cloud and the strange men. The publisher of the booklet, Eli Curtis, placed Cooper's testimony and others in the context of millennialism. He described his own publication as being "carefully compiled."

Waterdown/
The McCarthy Photos

There is strong endorsement of the so-called McCarthy Photos in Yurko Bondarchuk's *UFO: Sightings, Landings and Abductions* (1979). These are still photographs of an apparently immense, fast-moving object which were taken at 1:30 p.m., on 18 March 1975, in a field five miles north of Waterdown.

The photographer was Pat McCarthy, a nineteen-year-old native of nearby Hamilton who wanted to take some pictures of hawks in flight but instead caught sight of a UFO and succeeded in capturing it on film. The photographs were developed in the lab of the Hamilton *Spectator* and subsequently reproduced in the widely read *Bulletin* of the Aerial Phenomena Research Association, Tucson, Arizona.

According to Bondarchuk the "three-photo sequence shows a massive sombrero-shaped vessel, much larger than a jumbo jet, zig-zagging across the sky. The spectacular black-and-white shots have been subjected to every conceivable evaluation test and have withstood repeated scrutiny. The experts are unanimous: the prints are bona fide representations of an airborne craft; not man-made in origin." He includes them among "the most respected UFO photos ever taken anywhere."

Waterloo County/
The Fire-Letter

The Pennsylvania Dutch Mennonites and other farmers who settled in Waterloo County in the 1830s introduced into this farming community in south-central Ontario a great many superstitious beliefs and practices. A number of these survived well into the 1940s, when one could still see freshly repainted hex signs on the sides of barns and hear mumblings about the apocryphal *Sixth and Seventh Books of Moses.*

There was also the tradition of the Fire-Letter which could keep oneself and one's property safe from conflagration. A hand-copied or letterpress-printed Fire-Letter could be found nailed to the interior wall of the barn or preserved between the pages of the family Bible. The text was in German Gothic but a translation of parts of the traditional Fire-Letter appears in Blodwen Davies' *A String of Amber: The Heritage of the Mennonites* (1973).

Apparently the text was set down and printed by Alexander Bauman in Konigsberg, Prussia, in 1715. It seems six gypsies had been hanged for their crimes, and the seventh, a certain "Christian gypsy king from Egypt," was awaiting his turn when a great fire broke out in Konigsberg. As it was believed the gypsies could command the element of fire, the king was released to show his power to "talk the fire down." This he did in half an hour. The king of Prussia was so impressed he ordered that the gypsy's life be saved and that his prayer be committed to print. Here is part of the prayer:

We welcome you, Fiery Guest, don't take more than you have, this I count you, Fire, for a penance in the name of the Father, the Son and the Holy Ghost.

I command you, Fire, by God's power, which does all things and is able to do all things, you must cease and not proceed. As the true Christ stood in Jordan where he was baptized by John, the Holy man.

This I count you, Fire, for a penance in the name of the Holy Trinity.

I command you, Fire, in the power of God to lay down your flames.

If you keep this letter in your house, then you will have no fires, no lightning will strike you; also if a pregnant woman carries this letter neither she nor her seed can be hurt through witchcraft or ghost. Also if you keep this letter in your house, or carry it with you, you will certainly be protected from possession and pestilence.

Wiarton/
Spirit Rock

Spirit Rock is a forbidding craig on the rocky cliff which overlooks Colpoys Bay near the town of Wiarton on Georgian Bay. The legend of Spirit Rock is preserved at nearby Cape Croker Indian Reserve.

An Objibway maiden was seized by a band of Iroquois hunters and enslaved. The maiden was not only beautiful, she was also a gifted singer. She caught the eye of a young Iroquois chief as she sang the songs of her own people in captivity. Without tribal consent he released her from bondage and married her. His fellow warriors were so incensed and insulted that on the next hunting trip to the peninsula they seized the opportunity to push him over the cliff at the point now called Spirit Rock.

The grief-stricken widow was left free to wander and eventually found her way back to her own people. But she was now a pariah to them, too, for she had willingly married an enemy of her people. Ordered out of the camp, she returned to Spirit Rock where she leapt to her death.

The legend was recalled by Gerald Wright in the *Kitchener-Waterloo Record* on 25 October 1985. Wright cited the findings of W.G. Cheshire, a Wiarton historian, who concluded the story was based on an incident that occurred about a century before the first white settlement of the area. The skeletons of a man and a woman of Indian origin were discovered at the base of the craig in 1890.

From a distance the crest of the rock bears a slight resemblance to a human face with foliage forming its Indian-style headdress. It is reported that at the water's edge one may hear mournful sounds and songs. The site of Spirit Rock is marked by a plaque erected by the Wiarton & District Chamber of Commerce.

Williamsburg/ Dr. Mahlone Locke

Williamsburg is a small community located northwest of Morrisburg. For almost four decades the medical needs of the farmers of the area were met by the local country physician and surgeon, Dr. Mahlone Locke. He practised general medicine but over the years he acquired the reputation as a "miracle worker."

Mahlone William Locke (1881–1942) was born the son of a farmer at Dixon's Corners, just west of Williamsburg. When he was a youngster a travelling preacher advised him to attend university. He did so, graduating from Queen's University in Kingston with an M.D. in 1904. He undertook postgraduate work at the University of Edinburgh and Glasgow University, where he specialized in what he began to call "manipulative surgery." He came to the conclu-

sion that by manipulating the foot he was able to relieve if not cure some types of rheumatism and arthritis as well as other afflictions and promote general well-being.

Returning to Williamsburg in 1908, Dr. Locke bought a medical practice, complete with horse and buggy. His patients were poor but he was known to charge only one dollar a consultation, often waiving fees entirely when the fee proved excessive. At the same time he became known for his practice of "manipulative surgery" — popularly referred to as "feet twisting" — and his reputation as a "miracle worker" grew beyond the bounds of the community. Imaginative magazine journalists like Rex Beach made his name synonymous with "miracle cures" throughout North America. Beach even wrote a book called *The Hands of Dr. Locke* (1934).

It is said that Williamsburg — with a population of three hundred and fifty souls in the 1930s — had to contend with one thousand visitors a day, six days a week. Patients came in wheelchairs and on crutches from all over the Continent and Europe. They lined up in front of the doctor's frame house and he treated them on the lawn. He sat outdoors from six o'clock in the morning to midnight most days, taking brief breaks in order to nap.

He would ask each patient in turn to describe his symptoms. Then he would take the patient's foot into his strong hands and twist. The twisting produced a wince and the sound of bones cracking and a jolt but no real pain. Many patients said they experienced immediate relief from their symptoms. The patient was charged one dollar for the treatment.

Dr. Locke claimed no special supernatural or miraculous powers. He once wrote, "The foot is the foundation of the body and carries a heavy load every day. If the foundation of a building becomes weak or injured, the whole area above is in danger and is usually affected." His views are familiar enough to chiropractors, masseurs, and physiotherapists. Psychiatrists will note the "placebo effect" of the physician's forceful personality and wide reputation as a miracle healer. But as John Picton noted in his article on Dr. Locke in the *Toronto Star*, 8 July 1984, today's medical profession would not take lightly the practices of Dr. Mahlone Locke.

Windsor/
Symbolic Geography

Primary school children quickly inform their teacher that the continents of South America and Africa "fit together." Secondary school children direct the geography teacher's attention to the fact that Italy looks like "a boot"; that France has the shape of "a square," "a rectangle," or a "rhombus"; that the continents of South America and Africa are "skulls looking to the right," and so on.

Symbolic geography is the name given to the study of patterns or images which may be discerned or discovered in geographic areas of the globe. Some of these symbolic representations can be quite farfetched; witness Paul Theroux's description of Britain as a pig surmounted by a witch. Others appear reasonable, at least until closely examined, like the surmise of Rudolf Steiner, the Anthroposophist who noted that the mountain-chains in the Eastern Hemisphere run horizontally, whereas those in the Western Hemisphere run vertically.

It is a commonplace observation that Canada assumes the shape of the left hand, palm down, fingers stretched wide. The thumb is the Atlantic Provinces; the index finger, Quebec; the third finger, Ontario; the ring finger, the Prairie Provinces; and the baby finger, British Columbia. It was Northrop Frye who first observed that while the United States possesses an eastern seaboard, Canada lacks one, owning instead the gaping maw of the Gulf of St. Lawrence. The Gulf itself is a starfish stretching west. Robert L. Ripley pointed out that New Brunswick, when inverted, assumes the shape of its discoverer, John Cabot. Hudson Bay is a miniature outline of the continent of Africa.

The Great Lakes are characteristically shaped. Lake Superior has been likened to a massive wolf's head facing west. Lake Michigan with its twin bays resembles nothing more than a bloated but detumesced penis flanked by a pair of shrivelled testes. Lakes Erie and

Ontario appear from the air like a couple of sportive whales. That leaves Lake Huron with Georgian Bay which could only be indecipherable ink-blots designed by the Swiss psychiatrist Hermann Rorschach!

Windsor, Canada's southernmost city, is as good a point as any from which to identify and illustrate what has been called the Ontario Elephant. Specifically, when the map is turned ninety degrees clockwise, the section of southern Ontario enclosed within the Great Lakes resembles an elephant. The tip of the trumpeting trunk is Windsor; the heart is Stratford; the front feet are Niagara Falls; the armpit is Hamilton; the sex organs are Toronto; the elephant's piddle is Lake Simcoe; the anus is Owen Sound (sorry that!); the tail ends in Tobermorey. Although not the largest province, Ontario becomes an elephantine place.

The theory of Continental Drift, once anathema to scientists, is today completely accepted. The truth is that scientists should give some consideration to replacing it with the theory of Continental Drip. If the Mercator Projection of the map of the world is inverted, the continents appear to "drip" from the South Pole, forming immense "teardrops." The theory of Continental Drift thus "rains" supreme!

Windsor/
Wildfire

Wildfires are mysterious fires that ignite of their own accord. Vincent H. Gaddis studied the physical or psychical aspects of the phenomenon in *Mysterious Fires and Lights* (1967). Here is his account of the wildfires near Windsor.

> One of the most astonishing outbreaks of wildfire occurred in December 1941, at the recently opened $55,000 Dominion Golf and Country Club near Windsor, Ontario. It started at about 1 a.m. when a customer ran out of the cloakroom shouting: "Hey, a piece of paper in there just caught on fire for no reason at all."
>
> Nicholas White, the owner and manager, started for the cloakroom to investigate when he was interrupted by the cry of a waiter who

was pointing at a flaming tablecloth. White ran to the kitchen and seized a fire extinguisher. When he returned, tablecloths all over the dining room were covered with tiny dancing blue flames. The waiters grabbed water-filled pitchers and joined White with his extinguisher in running from table to table dousing the fires.

The matter seemed under control when White was again startled by shouts from the kitchen. All the towels on a rack there had burst into bluish flames. When a bar rag was similarly affected, White dashed into his office to call the Windsor Fire Department. From the desk drawer he pulled out the phone book, and as he opened it, flames emerged. The operator completed his call.

Mrs. White, ill in one of the ten second-floor bedrooms, came to the top of the stairs to ask what all the commotion was about. Suddenly she screamed. The curtains in her room were on fire. White and his waiters rushed upstairs and found little blue fires breaking out in seven of the bedrooms. By the time firemen arrived, a total of forty-three fires had been extinguished.

The next morning the Province of Ontario Fire Marshal and an insurance investigator arrived at the club. Employees were busy cleaning up the debris, and one placed his broom against a table several feet from the officials.

"Do you mean to tell me that various things just burst into flames?" the insurance man asked White. "For example, like that broom over there?" He stopped, leaped from his chair and shouted: "Put out that broom! It's on fire!"

There were a few more scattered fires during the morning, then the phenomenon ended.

Gaddis based his account on the coverage given the wildfire by James S. Pooler, staff writer for the Detroit *Free Press*; an article in *Fate*, June 1958; and Frank Edwards' story in *Strange World* (1964).

Woodstock/
The Haunted Courthouse

The old Oxford County Courthouse may well be haunted. Construction workers making repairs to the building in 1982 complained that their tools were disappearing from one place and reappearing in another, and that lights were blinking off and on of their own accord.

One explanation for the disturbances is that the Courthouse is haunted by the ghost of the murderer Thomas Cook. Cook was the first person to be hanged in Oxford County. The execution which took place in 1860 was botched. Cook's head was torn from his body by the death fall. Cook's family at Innerkip supplied a coffin for the return of the body. The unscrupulous undertaker returned it sealed but empty. It was buried at Innerkip. In the meantime he turned the body over to medical students for practice in dissection. After the cadaver had served its medical purpose, it was carted to the local dump. When the bones were accidentally exposed about forty years later, the authorities arranged for them to be buried in an unmarked grave.

Cook's death mask was removed from the door of the county jail for fear it would be damaged by vandals and was stored in the Courthouse basement shortly before the first hauntings were reported. A photograph taken of the reconstruction work apparently revealed the hazy outline of a face in a tunnel leading to an old air duct. It has been suggested that the construction work "disturbed" Thomas Cook who has begun to protest.

275

MANITOBA

Athapapuskow Lake/
Conjurers as Surgeons

The explorer Samuel Hearne observed Chipewyan conjurers acting as surgeons on his native guides in the vicinity of Athapapuskow Lake in Northern Manitoba. He gives new meaning to the phrase "the breath of life" in the account of a native medical operation in the entry for August 1771 in *A Journey from Prince of Wales's Fort in Hudson's Bay to the Northern Ocean* (1795) edited by Richard Glover in 1958:

> Several of the Indians being very ill, the conjurers, who are always the doctors, and pretend to perform great cures, began to try their skill to effect their recovery. Here it is necessary to remark, that they use no medicine either for internal or external complaints, but perform all their cures by charms. In ordinary cases, sucking the part affected, blowing, and singing to it; haughing, spitting, and at the same time uttering a heap of unintelligible jargon, compose the whole process of the cure. For some inward complaints; such as, griping in the intestines, difficulty of making water, &c., it is very common to see those jugglers blowing into the *anus*, or into the parts adjacent, till their eyes are almost starting out of their heads: and this operation is performed indifferently on all, without regard either to age or sex. The accumulation of so large a quantity of wind is at times apt to occasion some extraordinary emotions, which are not easily suppressed by a sick person; and as there is no vent for it but by the channel through which it was conveyed thither, it sometimes occasions an odd scene between the doctor and his patient; which I once wantonly called an engagement, but for which I was afterward exceedingly sorry, as it highly offended several of the Indians; particularly the juggler and the sick person, both of whom were men I much esteemed, and, except in the moment of levity, it had ever been no less my inclination than my interest to show them every respect that my situation would admit.

The antics of the medicine-men may have been amusing to Hearne, but he failed to report on the post-operative condition of the patients. However, he did conclude his account of native medical practices among the Chipewyans with a detailed description of the operation of the "conjuring-house," or Shaking Tent, which he found quite intriguing.

Beausejour/
"Overgrown Ape"

Between Beausejour, which is northeast of Winnipeg, and Lac du Bonnet, which is northeast of Beausejour, lies a region of many sasquatch sightings.

A man from Lac du Bonnet described the appearance of an "overgrown ape or monkey" about six foot six inches, with dark hair or fur, on the road to Pointe du Bois one night in July 1974. A youth saw and heard a huge, hairy thing thumping on the trunk of his car as he made a U-turn on a road near Beausejour one night in June 1975. Another youth reported a seven- or eight-foot creature approaching his stopped car on the road between Beausejour and Lac du Bonnet. The creature left fifteen-inch footprints in the snow which could be followed for more than seven miles. These and other reports from the region come from John Green's *Sasquatch: The Apes Among Us* (1978).

Berens River/
Psychic Shamans

The region around the Berens River which flows into Lake Winnipeg is occupied by the Saulteaux or Ojibway Indians. The American anthropologist Alfred Irving Hollowell who worked among these bands was unable to attend a *séance* organized by a shaman, but one of his informants reported what had occurred, and the account appeared in Hollowell's study *The Role of Conjuring in Saulteaux Society* (1942). The following account comes from D. Scott Rogo's article "Shamans: The World's Greatest Psychics?" in *Fate*, September 1983.

> Hollowell reported that one of his informants was present at a seance intended to locate her son who had been missing for a week. As the seance progressed, the voice of the young man spoke through the entranced shaman, said he was fine and even described where he was camped. The woman left the seance feeling comforted.
>
> The young man came home two days later. It turned out that during the night of the seance he had been asleep at the very location indicated through the shaman; yet he had no idea that his "soul" had been called forth by the conjurer's power.

Carman/
"Charlie Redstar"

A mysterious red light appeared in the sky at night in the vicinity of Carman in the 1970s and attracted considerable attention. It was dubbed "Charlie Redstar, the visitor from outer space," and was caught by photographers, including a television film crew, according to Chris Rutkowski who collected accounts of the sightings, two of which appear as "UFO Stories" in Edith Fowke's *Tales Told in Canada* (1986).

> "A large red light . . . seemed to be bouncing up and down in the sky from occasion to occasion" about two miles north of Carman, 13 May 1975. It moved erratically and changed in intensity. It seemed to hover about fifty feet above the road. It was spotted again on 10 July 1976 when it "went from the brilliant white to a very intense orange . . . rather than being a ball, he now gave the appearance of a small domed saucer."

These accounts are unusual if not unique in that the UFO is personified and actually given a name.

Cedar Lake/
Sasquatch Sightings

Sasquatch sightings south of Cedar Lake were reported following the construction of the new road through the bush country. The road connects the small community of Easterville with the highway that leads north to Grand Rapids. Cedar Lake lies west of the northern part of Lake Winnipeg.

John Green in *Sasquatch: The Apes Among Us* (1978) reports on some of the sightings on the road renowned for its sasquatch sightings. On 23 August 1968, three men stopped their car about four miles west of the junction of Highway 6 because they saw "something" walk out of the bush about a hundred yards away and onto the road. It walked like a man but was much too large and covered all over with short hair. "The men left hurriedly." Two days later, near the Easterville end of the road, two other men spotted a similar creature. "They too drove off in a hurry."

Indian residents of Easterville and three non-Indian

teachers at the Easterville school all reported sightings while driving along the road, usually at night. One observer described a dark man-like figure hurdling over willows and small bushes with long strides. Another compared the creature with the colour and size of a moose yet it jumped over things like a man. A third slammed on the car's brakes to avoid hitting a dark thing, estimated to stand nine feet tall, extremely broad, with a flat-profiled face.

The Indians at Easterville whisper about the windigo; the non-Indians joke about the sasquatch.

Churchill/
Voodoo at the Prince of Wales's Fort

Samuel Hearne, the fur trader and explorer, served as chief of the Prince of Wales's Fort from 1776 to 1782 when he was forced to surrender to the French. The fort was located at the mouth of the Churchill River on Hudson Bay. In its partially reconstructed form today it is known as Fort Prince of Wales.

Hearne was interested in the practices of the Chipewyan conjurers or medicine-men and their apparent voodoo-like ability to cast fatal spells. He affixed to the entry for November 1771 in *A Journey from Prince of Wales's Fort in Hudson's Bay to the Northern Ocean* (1795) a note to the effect that his friend and guide Matonabbee beseeched him to employ the "art" to seek "secret revenge" against an enemy.

> . . . Matonabbee, (who always thought me possessed of this art,) on his arrival at Prince of Wales's Fort in the Winter of 1778, informed me, that a man whom I had never seen but once, had treated him in such a manner that he was afraid of his life; in consequence of which he pressed me very much to kill him, though I was then several thousands of miles distant: On which, to please this great man to whom I owed so much, and not expecting that any harm could possibly arise from it, I drew a rough sketch of two human figures on a piece of paper, in the attitude of wrestling: in the hand of one of them, I drew the figure of a bayonet pointing to the breast of the other. This is me, said I to Matonabbee, pointing to the figure which was holding the bayonet; and the other, is your enemy. Opposite to those figures I drew a pine-tree, over which I placed a large human eye, and out of the tree projected a human hand. This paper I gave to Matonabbee, with instructions to make it as publicly known as possible. Sure enough, the following year, when he came in to trade, he informed me that the man was dead, though at that time he was not less than three hundred miles from Prince of Wales's Fort. He assured me that the man was in perfect health when he heard of my design against him; but almost immediately afterwards became quite gloomy, and refusing all kind of sustenance, in a very few days died. After this I was frequently applied to on the same account, both by Matonabbee and other leading Indians, but never thought proper to comply with their requests, by which means I not only preserved the credit I gained on the first attempt, but always kept them in awe, and in some degree of respect and obedience to me. In fact, strange as it may appear, it is almost absolutely necessary that the chiefs at this place should profess something a little supernatural, to be able to deal with those people.

Cloverdale/
The Miracle Worker

The farming community Cloverdale, located northwest of Selkirk, briefly came to national attention when the Canadian Press news service ran two stories on its "miracle worker." The reports appeared in the Niagara Falls *Evening Review* on 20 and 27 October 1934. Far more detailed coverage appeared in the Winnipeg *Free Press*, 13–27 October 1934.

The faith healer was a farmer named John Love. The slightly built man called himself "Doctor" Love and claimed he exercised no powers of his own, only that of "the word," not "the word of God," but just "the word." According to the news reports, he was very popular and powerful. Over a period of six weeks he drew to his simple log farmhouse a total of ten thousand people. "In the unkept yard of Dr. Love little knots of people huddled over bonfires . . . sitting or lying on wet boards the crippled folk and their friends talked in subdued tones as the chilly winds whirled across the prairie."

Curiosity seekers as well as sick people congregated in his yard. The wife of the "miracle worker" would emerge, select someone at random from the yard, and lead that person into the house. "Mystery shrouds his beliefs and doctrine and his mode of cure is as unkown as his art. Whether his power by psychological, spiritual or even sorcery is just now debated in all kinds of places by all manner of people."

One man said his sight and hearing were restored after two treatments. One woman claimed that after twelve years of partial paralysis she was now able to walk without her "stick." The sleeplessness of a former school caretaker was now a thing of the past, and a man with a crippled hand discovered it was "almost as good as the other." A boy journeyed to Cloverdale to ascertain if it would be worthwhile to bring his bed-ridden mother all the way to the farm. He "was told to return home as his mother was better." One reporter noted, "He accepts no payment but the offerings of the afflicted he has waited on have almost filled a damp root-house in the yard."

Falcon Lake/
The Falcon Lake Encounter

One of the most intriguing accounts of a close encounter with a UFO occurred on the afternoon of 20 May 1967 in the woods near Falcon Lake, Whiteshell Provincial Park. The encounter is not conclusive evidence of the existence of UFOs but it has all the earmarks of a "classic case."

The following account appeared in Coral and Jim Lorenzen's *Encounters with UFO Occupants* (1976):

> Steve Michalak is a Polish-born industrial mechanic living in Winnipeg, Canada. A chance meeting with a UFO on the ground while prospecting in a wild area in the vicinity of Falcon Lake, Manitoba, which is about 75 miles east of

Winnipeg, resulted in strange second- and third-degree burns on his chest and a minor burn on his face. After several years the burn scars are still evident, and he claims that they occasionally become reddened as though the burns are recurring.

The incident took place at 12:13 p.m. on May 20, 1967, when Michalak's attention was arrested by the noise of a number of geese which had been aroused when he first arrived in the area, but they quieted down shortly after becoming used to his presence. Michalak looked up to see what was disturbing the birds and saw two red objects approaching at about 14 to 15 degrees from the horizontal and on a heading of 240 degrees. The first was about 15 feet above the ground and the second slightly higher and they approached at very high speed. The first object came to rest on the ground, blowing leaves and rock lichen from the landing spot. Michalak was crouching in the bush, examining a rock sample and out of sight of the object. The second object hovered for a few seconds, then took off at high speed.

The machine just sat on the ground for the next half hour and radiated heat in "rainbow-like" colours. While airborne it had been a dull red colour, but when on the ground it had the appearance of stainless steel. During the period that it sat on the ground Michalak took out pencil and paper and sketched the object. After about 25 minutes a square door with rounded edges opened and a "fantastic" purple light emanated from the opening. He pulled his welding glasses down over his eyes and was then able to see flashing red, green, and blue lights inside the object but could not discern whether or not they were on a control panel. At this time, Michalak said, he heard a high-pitched whining sound like that of a motor running at high speed and smelled an odour resembling that of a burned-out electrical motor and heard a "whooshing" sound as if air was being taken in and expelled. Michalak then approached the machine, noting

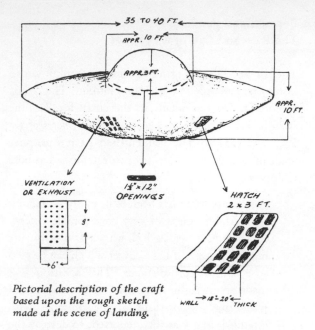

Pictorial description of the craft based upon the rough sketch made at the scene of landing.

This is Stephen Michalak's sketch of what he saw at Falcon Lake in 1967. It shows a saucer-shaped craft between thirty-five and forty feet in diameter with a grill-like ventilation or exhaust system as well as bands of rectangle-shaped apertures. The sketch is reproduced from Canadian UFO Report, *May-June 1969. [John Magor]*

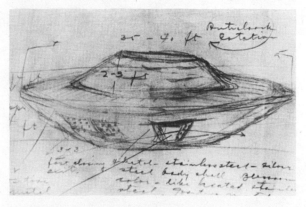

This pencil sketch was also executed by Steve Michalak to show the appearance and possible dimensions of the UFO that he encountered on 20 May 1967 at Falcon Lake, Man. The ports and gateway are clearly visible and the clockwise rotation of the saucer-shaped vehicle is indicated. The drawing was completed shortly after the Falcon Lake Encounter, one of the most puzzling in the history of UFOs in Canada. [Fortean Picture Library]

the heat that radiated from it. He claims he heard the sound of voices, so he spoke to it but got no answer. He tried English, Russian, German, Italian, and Polish. While he was talking the sound of the motor stopped, he heard voices again, and the door closed and moved out to become flush with the outside of the object. Although he saw the door and knew it was there, he said, when it closed there was no evidence of an opening or seam nor were there any seams or rivets of any kind visible over the rest of the vehicle.

Michalak then reached out and touched the side of the object with a canvas-base, rubber-coated glove, which melted and slipped off the surface. As he looked down at the glove, the machine began to move in a counter-clockwise direction and he was blown to the left by a blast of hot air or exhaust which set his clothes on fire. The machine then took off in the direction from which it came.

After putting out the fire on his clothes, Michalak packed his gear into his briefcase and headed back for the highway. He felt dizzy occasionally but went into town, called the Royal [Canadian] Mounted Police at Falcon, but they told him they could do nothing about it. When he went to the Misericordia Hospital for treatment, he told the doctors who treated him that he had been burned by airplane exhaust.

Mrs. Michalak was one of the first to note her husband's odd condition. He could not keep food in his stomach, was nauseated and vomiting and had a strange odour about him, which she said, "Seemed to come from inside." When he did begin to eat and accommodate food on the fourth day after his experience, he seemed to derive no nourishment from it for he lost a total of 22 pounds. Blood counts were taken and the lymphocyte count was down considerably below normal.

That, in essence, is Michalak's story. Because it is a one-witness case it would ordinarily not be considered to be the best, but Michalak's reputation, the burned glove and shirt, added substance to his claim. Additionally, when Field Investigators James B. Thompson, Edward Barker, and Brian Cannon investigated, they found the circular area where leaves and lichen had been blown away, indicating that something might have hovered above the ground even if it had not landed. Examination of the glove and shirt yielded nothing — there was no residue of any kind which could contribute anything to the case. Examination of the landing site gave us no further clues either.

The most detailed description of the Falcon Lake Encounter was published by the Winnipeg researcher Chris Rutkowski. It appeared in three parts in the June, August, and October 1981 issues of *Flying Saucer Review*. Rutkowski is an associate of the Centre for UFO Studies at Evanston, Illinois, and Secretary and Librarian of the Winnipeg Centre of the Royal Astronomical Society of Canada. His study concluded with these comments:

> Today, over thirteen years after his experience, Michalak remains convinced he had encountered something he wasn't supposed to see. His convictions are firmly entrenched. He has read several books about UFOs since 1967, and is still frustrated by not knowing what happened to him.
>
> It is interesting to note that Michalak has reported another UFO sighting. It occurred in northwestern Ontario several years ago, while standing near a lake. He said that he observed "the same thing" as he had seen at Falcon Lake, though at a much greater distance from him, flying through the sky.
>
> Are "they" keeping an eye on him? Or is Michalak simply one of those people who is now encouraged to look skyward for unusual things?
>
> The mystery continues.

Fort Chipewyan/ The Rise and Fall of a Prophet

The rise and fall of a prophet otherwise unknown to history was recorded by Sir John Franklin. The Arctic explorer noted the details in the entry for 21 June 1820 in his *Narrative of a Journey to the Shores of the Polar Sea* (1823). The unidentified native prophet made his appearance at the fur fort established at Fort Chipewyan on Lake Athabaska.

> Fort Chipewyan has been built many years, and is an establishment of very considerable extent, conspicuously situated on a rocky point on the northern shore; it has a tower which can be seen at a considerable distance. This addition was made about eight years ago, for the purpose of watching the motions of the Indians, who intended, as it was then reported, to destroy the house of all its inhabitants. They had been instigated to this rash design by the delusive stories of one among them, who had acquired great influence over his companions by his supposed skill in necromancy. This fellow had prophesied that there would soon be a complete change in the face of their country; that fertility and plenty would succeed to the present sterility; and that the present race of white inhabitants, unless they became subservient to the Indians, would be removed, and their place be filled by other traders, who would supply their wants in every possible manner. The poor deluded wretches, imagining they would hasten this happy change by destroying their present traders, of whose submission there was no prospect, threatened to extirpate them.

It is unfortunate that Franklin did not bother to record the subsequent fate of this remarkable prophet, who may or may not have been "skilled in necromancy," but who did succeed in predicting the fate that befell his Chipewyan people.

In the reported prophecy there are elements that recall the notion of the Cargo Cult of Micronesia. The belief was prevalent among certain primitive peoples that once, a long time ago, an alien people arrived on their shores. These people were strange, and they brought with them even stranger goods. But they had to depart suddenly, and when they left they left behind their strange goods for the people to use. They promised that they would return and that when they did they would bring with them more strange goods for the people to use. Erich von Däniken and others who hold the "ancient astronaut" theory that the Earth was visited in the past by "the star people" are able to make much of the Cargo Cult and might find elements of it not only in Micronesia but also among the Chipewyans of the Canadian North.

Fort Walsh/
The Vanishing Village

Sir Cecil Edward Denny was an original member of the North West Mounted Police. He joined in 1874 an resigned in 1881, becoming an Indian agent and archivist. An odd incident occurred to him while he was stationed at Forth Walsh in the Cypress Hills area. He described it in his memoirs which were written in 1905 but published posthumously as *The Riders of the Plains: A Reminiscence of the Early and Exciting Days of the North-west* (1935).

It occurred about four o'clock one afternoon in summer 1875. He was boating on the Oldman River about fifteen miles from Fort Walsh when he was overtaken by a fierce storm and strong winds. Amid the sudden lightning and thunder, he beached his boat to wait out the storm. During a lull he could hear in the distance the rhythm of drums and the familiar chanting of Indians, "Hi-ya, hi-ya, hi-ya-ya." He staggered through the rain and wind towards the sounds. In the distance he could dimly discern a camp of teepees. They were in a circle about a hundred yards away, brightly coloured, as if illuminated by the sun. Not only were there teepees but there were also Cree men and women moving about as if unaffected by the storm with its wind, thunder, and lightning.

As he approached the settlement, he found himself engulfed in a cocoon of a flickering, blueish flame. Then he was hurled to the ground, senseless. He had

to lie there, helplessly, while the storm raged. When it abated he rose to his feet and staggered in the direction of the village, only to find that it had vanished. He examined the ground as well as he could but he could find in the immediate vicinity no traces of any encampment.

Denny was badly shaken. The storm resumed its fury so he left his boat where it was and walked back to Fort Walsh, arriving there around midnight, exhausted. The next day he returned to the site of the vanished village. Again he found no signs of recent habitation, but this time in the clear weather he could discern a few rings of stone overgrown with grass where there had once been an encampment. He also found bleached human bones scattered about. From his guide he learned that here had once been a Cree Village there which had been sacked and burned by the Blackfoot who slaughtered every last inhabitant.

Landry Lake/
The Uchtmann Tracks

The so-called Uchtmann Tracks are photographs of three giant footprints twenty-one inches long and seven inches wide. The tracks were discovered by accident in an old ant hill on a limestone ridge on the shore of Landry Lake, which lies southeast of The Pas. The photographs were taken on 9 September 1974 by their discoverer, R.H. Uchtmann, a provincial conservation officer, who sent the evidence to the Manitoba Museum of Man, along with an explanatory letter.

The Uchtmann Tracks and the interesting letter appear in John Green's *Sasquatch: The Apes Among Us* (1978). Uchtmann referred to the tracks as "some human footprints," yet he wondered about the size of the human that left those prints. He explained:

> I was moose hunting at the time I found the three tracks. My impression at the time was that they were not man made and that they fitted no animals in the area. They were sharp and clear at the time and were made after the rainfall on September 25 . . . . There is the possibility of

someone having made the prints but this strikes me as being highly unlikely. The prints were approximately 1/4 mile from a bush trail passable to vehicles. Back along the road 200 yards is a dike across a creek on the north end of Landry Lake. It seems more likely that someone creating a hoax would have placed the prints on the dike where there would be more chance of seeing them.

Lake Manitoba/
Manipogo

The Assiniboine who populated the marshy shores of Lake Manitoba named it after the Manitou, or Spirit, and according to native tradition the voice of the Manitou may be heard in the rushing of its waters at the narrows. Native tradition also holds that the lake has long been the haunt of "the big snake" — a lake monster now known as Manipogo.

The popular press made much of the so-called McLeod Expedition which travelled to the north end of Lake Manitoba in search of lake monsters. It was essentially one man's private pleasure trip undertaken the last weekend in July 1960 to interview some Manitobans who had recently reported seeing odd creatures in the lake. The "expedition" bore the name of J.A. McLeod, a zoologist at the University of Manitoba in Brandon, who for some time had collected reports of sightings.

Seventeen or so holidayers reported seeing an immense serpent undulating in the waters of the lake the afternoon of 12 August 1960. The holidayers were on a beach five miles north of Toutes Aides, which is a small community north of Ste. Rose du Lac. One of the observers, a provincial land inspector named Tom Locke has been credited with popularizing the name "Manipogo," a portmanteau term which combines the name of the Province of Manitoba and British Columbia's well-known lake monster Ogopogo. Locke attempted to take motion pictures of what he saw but found he had run out of film. The beach where the 1960 sighting occurred is now known as Manipogo Beach.

Dick Vincent, a radio news commentator from Pembina, North Dakota, took a series of 35 mm photographs of Manipogo swimming in the waters of Lake Manitoba near the mouth of the Waterhen River at 4:00 p.m. on 13 August 1962. The clearest photograph, published in the Winnipeg *Free Press* on 15 August 1962, shows what appears to be a long, snake-like creature in the water. The body of the creature was estimated to be a foot thick, twelve feet in length above the water, and from fifty to seventy-five yards from the camera. It was seen by about twenty people for about fifteen minutes in all.

Another widely reported sighting was made in August 1964 by Ralph Sanderson and his family north of Toutes Aides who spotted a twin-humped, greenish-black creature with a tail. The creature was perhaps sixteen feet in length. It surfaced and out-swam their outboard motorboat before disappearing in the distance.

The 1960s were the halcyon years of Lake Manitoba's Manipogo. Although there are earlier and later reports, the sightings of the Sixties were richer and more plentiful than for any other decade.

Norway House/
Shaking Tent

The artist and explorer Paul Kane, travelling in the vicinity of Norway House, observed how the Cree in his party erected and operated the Shaking Tent. It was no mystery to him, for as he recorded on 27 July 1848 in his book *Wanderings of an Artist among the Indians of North America* (1859), the tent was rocked and shaken not by Manitou but by man.

In the evening our Indians constructed a jonglerie, or medicine lodge, the main object of which was to procure a fair wind for next day. For this purpose they first drive ten or twelve poles, nine or ten feet long, into the ground, enclosing a circular area of about three feet in diameter, with a boat sail open at the top. The medicine-man, one of whom is generally found in every brigade, gets inside and commences shaking the poles violently, rattling his medicinal rattle, and singing hoarse incantations to the Great Spirit for a fair wind. Being unable to sleep on account of the discordant noises, I wrapped a blanket about me, and went out into the woods, where they were holding their midnight orgies, and lay down amongst those on the outside of the medicine lodge, to witness the proceedings. I had no sooner done so than the incantations at once ceased, and the performer explained that a white man was present. How he ascertained this fact I am at a loss to surmise, as it was pitch dark at the time, and he was enclosed in a narrow tent, without any apparent opening through which he could espy me, even had it been light enough to distinguish one person from another.

A trader from Norway House told Kane that "a Canadian once had the temerity to peep under the covering which enclosed the jonglerie, but that he got such a fright that he never fairly recovered from it, nor could he ever be prevailed upon to tell what it was that had so appalled him." Kane concluded his account of the Shaking Tent by noting, "on the next day we had a fair wind, for which the medicine-man of course took all the credit."

Norway House/
The Windigo Trial

An unusual capital murder trial was held at Norway House on 7 October 1907. Charged with the slaying of a native woman named Wahsakapeequay were Jack Fiddler, the eighty-seven-year-old shaman and leader of the Sucker clan, and his younger brother Joseph Fiddler, a member of the same clan from the upper Severn River in Northwestern Ontario.

The trial was unusual in that the two accused Cree pleaded guilty to the charge and gave as their reason for the murder the fact that the woman was a Windigo, and hence a danger to the community. They described the woman, who was Joseph Fiddler's daughter-in-law, as demented and possessed of the

cannibalistic Windigo spirit. As she was a menace to herself and to her fellow Cree, native tradition required that she be executed. Jack Fiddler explained that over the years he had confronted and killed some fourteen Windigos! The Crown established that the

The Windigo is the spirit of cannibalism among the Algonkian-speaking Indians. This painting of the Windigo was done in tempera in 1965 by Norval Morrisseau. The Ojibway artist defied the elders in his community when he began to make use of the traditional motifs in his bold artwork. [Glenbow Museum]

standards of white morality and justice were unfamiliar to the members of the Sucker clan, none of whom spoke English.

The trial lasted one day with the six-man jury finding the two Cree guilty of murder with the recommendation for mercy. An order-in-council commuted their sentences to life imprisonment. Jack Fiddler spent 101 days in confinement, no more. He managed to escape custody in January 1908, strangling himself beneath a tree outside Norway House. The tree is standing to this day. Joseph Fiddler was transferred to Stony Mountain prison, where he died in 1909. He never did learn that three days earlier he had been granted a pardon.

An unusual account of the Windigo trial is presented from the native viewpoint by Chief Thomas Fiddler and James R. Stevens in *Killing the Shamen* (1985).

Poplar River/
The RCMP Report

The Poplar River Indian Reserve is located south of Norway House on the east coast of Lake Winnipeg. The chief of the reserve, bothered by reports of "a large hairy animal that walks on two legs," alerted the RCMP detachment at Norway House. Officers of the detachment made an investigation, and then sent the following report by telex to the Force's Vancouver Lower Mainland Division. The text is reproduced by John Green in *Sasquatch: The Apes Among Us* (1978).

> It was reported to our office on the 26 July 76 by the chief of the Poplar River Indian Band that many of his people have sighted on the reserve many times a large hairy animal that walks on two legs. Poplar River is located approx. 76 miles to the south of Norway House. An investigation was conducted and the results are as follows:
>
> Several people were interviewed and they all stated that the animal was approximately seven to eight feet tall and was very broad at the shoulders. It had the general body structure of a man

only many times larger. A foot cast was taken of the foot impression that was left behind by the so-called monster and is held at this detachment. It measures 16 inches by five inches, and has only three toes. Its fur is a glossy gray colour and it has white hair on its head. They stated that it was very powerfully built and one man reported that he saw it swimming. To date there have been no further reports of sightings in our area. It should be noted that this so-called monster seemed very inquisitive towards the people and would come around the houses on the settlement and look in doors and windows.

St François Xavier/
The White Horse

The legend of the White Horse is preserved in the name of the White Horse Plain and recalled by the twelve-foot statue of a sparkling white horse which was erected at St. François Xavier on the Trans Canada Highway west of Winnipeg.

In the 1690s, the hand of a beautiful daughter of a Cree Chief was sought by two suitors, a Cree chief from Lake Winnipegosis and a Sioux chief from Devil's Lake. The Cree was favoured because he had offered a beautiful pure white horse, a Blanc Diablo from Mexico. The prospect of such a gift was irresistible and the father succumbed.

Shortly after the horse was presented to the prospective father-in-law and the Cree claimed his bride, the rejected suitor with his escort of Sioux warriors was seen thundering across the prairies. Everyone fled. The Cree helped his bride mount the white horse, he leapt onto his grey steed, and they rode furiously westward with the Sioux and his party in hot pursuit.

Despite its speed and endurance, the white horse became the undoing of the fleeing couple. They doubled back to mislead their pursuers and hid in the prairie bluffs, but once they were again on the open plain, the white horse was the mark that betrayed them. Finally, at a point just east of the present village of St. François Xavier, Sioux arrows killed the young couple. The grey mount was caught but the white horse escaped and roamed the plain for years, thus giving its name to the region.

Because they believed the soul of the girl had passed into its body, the Indians feared to approach the horse. Eventually the belief grew that the ghostly form of the white horse would haunt the plain forever. That ghost is today a statue of the white horse.

Whiteshell Provincial Park/
Petroforms

The "petroforms" in Whiteshell Provincial Park are mysterious-looking mosaics in the form of snakes, fish, turtles, birds, and geometric forms. They were traced in the bedrock at Bannock Point midway between Betula Lake and Nutimik Lake. The petroforms occupy an area of nine acres. They were so shaped by a prehistoric people who lived in the southeastern part of the province between 500 B.C. and A.D. 800.

It is believed that strange effigies were connected with the Grand Medicine Society (the Midéwiwin) of the Ojibway. They probably played a role in the annual initiation ceremony conducted in the autumn to renew "spirit power." The Society's elders presided over the secret ritual, each "armed" with a medicine bag containing herbs and a *migis*, or white shell, symbolizing "spirit power." After chanting and dancing, the initiate to the Society was shot through with "spirit power." He immediately collapsed, unconscious. When he awoke, if he was to be accepted into the Society, a white shell was found in his mouth. The new member then added his *migis* to his medicine bag as a symbol of "spirit power."

Winnipeg/
Prophet of the New World

The development of the prairies owes much to the Métis leader and prophet Louis Riel (1844–1885). It is intriguing to view Riel against the private panorama of his beliefs, as revealed by Thomas Flanagan in his study of the man's mystical side, *Louis "David" Riel: Prophet of the New World* (1979), rather than to see

him as the pawn or prime mover of vast social and political forces which found expression in the Red River Rebellion of 1869–70 and the North-West Rebellion of 1884–85.

"Some go mystical and some go mad," noted A.M. Klein. Perhaps Riel went in both directions. On 8 December 1875, he acquired a mystical sense of mission. He was attending Mass at St. Patrick's Church in Washington, D.C., when he was overcome by "an immense sadness of spirit." Thereupon he assumed the mantle of prophet and acquired a mystical sense of mission. He called himself "David" (he enclosed the prophet's name within quotation marks as if citing from the Old Testament). Perhaps in consequence of entertaining such notions, he spent the period from 6 March 1876 to 23 January 1878 as an inmate of asylums at Longue Pointe and Beauport, Quebec.

Riel proclaimed his Provisional Government at Fort Garry on 19 March 1870. His private perception of his public mission was to save the Métis people, to renew the Catholic Church from within, and to prophesy and predict what would occur in the millennia ahead. He foresaw that the Papacy would migrate by stages from Rome to Montreal, commencing in 1876. Then 457 years later it would move farther west to St. Boniface. This would occur in the year A.D. 2333. The Second Coming of Jesus Christ was destined to happen in A.D. 4209.

In his millennial thinking, Riel was influenced by his own visions, by his reading of the Old Testament, and by motley insights ranging from Métis folk beliefs to the *Celestial Book of Revelations* by the fourteenth century mystic Bridget of Sweden. To Riel, the Métis were the descendants of the ancient Hebrews. The heavens were to be renamed, beginning with the North Star which would be called Henrietta. The days of the week were also renamed — Sunday would thenceforth be known as Vive Aurore, etc. As Flanagan explained:

> Calling himself the "Prophet of the New World," he did exactly what a prophet should do (the role is clearly described in the Old Tes-

tament). He saw visions and heard voices. He made predictions about the future, he called men to repentance, he promised to work miracles. He was "charismatic" in the strict sense of that much-abused term; that is, his claim to lead was based on the visible manifestations of the anointing of the Holy Spirit — miracles, revelations, prophecies, and sanctity. Riel slipped into the messianic role at times, as when he styled himself the redeemer of the Jews or when he speculated on his own resurrection.

Riel was hanged for treason in Regina on 16 November 1885. He prophecied that his body would rise on the third day, but it only lay in state for two days in Riel House, 330 River Road, St. Vital. Riel was buried in the churchyard of the Basilica in St. Boniface, where a brown granite tombstone, inscribed "Riel/ 16 Novembre 1885," marks his final resting place. But there is no certainty that if his grave were opened today his body would be found there. Riel may not have risen from the dead, but there is a tradition in St. Boniface that his body was secretely reburied elsewhere, and that at any one time only two or three trusted Métis elders know its true location.

Winnipeg/
The Haunted House

George H. Ham made a name for himself as a journalist and raconteur; in later years he served as the advertising manager of the Canadian Pacific Railway. In 1877, when he was a thirty-year-old journalist and resident of Winnipeg, he and his wife moved into what he called in his autobiography, *Reminiscences of a Raconteur* (1921), "the haunted house."

They took possession of a little house, just south of old Grace Church on Main Street. Tradition held that it was built on an old Indian burial ground. "During the night queer noises were heard," he wrote. "The stove in the adjoining room rattled like mad, and investigation proved nothing. There was no wind or anything else visible that should cause a commotion. A door would slam and on going to it, it

was found wide open. One night there was a loud noise as if some tinware hanging up on the wall in the kitchen had fallen . . . and so it went on."

The basement was the source of one problem. "One time the cellar was filled with water coming from where, goodness only knows, though it was said that there was a slough through that property years ago. Anyway the cellar was full of water, and it had to be bailed out." Ham procrastinated so his wife engaged some local boys to do the bailing. "But lo and behold, when the trap door was opened, there wasn't a drop of water in the blooming cellar. It was dry as a tin horn. . . . We never ascertained whence came the water or where it went, but by this time I had got accustomed to the prances and pranks of the house and didn't care a continental."

In due course the Hams moved out and the next tenants found the house not to their liking. "The building was removed to the north end, and some years after, on recognizing it, I called to see if the noises still continued. But they wouldn't let me in."

"I don't pretend to be able to explain the queer noises," Ham concluded. "Whether they were the spirits of the past and gone, Indian braves showing their displeasure at our intrusion in their domain, or were caused by some peculiarity in the construction of the house and its environments, I can not offer an opinion. But, as we got accustomed to them, they didn't disturb us at all, and we got rather proud of our ghostly guests whose board and lodging cost us nothing."

Winnipeg/
The *Titanic* Premonition

The evening of 14 April 1912 was (to employ a phrase popularized by the journalist Walter Lord) "a night to remember." That was the evening the *Titanic* struck an iceberg and sank, marking the world's greatest peacetime marine disaster. The precise location of the disaster was determined only on 1 September 1985. The *Titanic* went down at 11:40 p.m. at a point in the North Atlantic 367 nautical miles southeast of Cape Race, Newfoundland.

The aptly named *Titanic* was the White Star's premier luxury liner, the largest and most modern ship afloat, and it was making its maiden voyage from London to New York. On board were 2207 persons, and more than half of them — 1513 — perished in the disaster. In Halifax's Fairview Cemetery, one hundred and twenty-five numbered graves marked the resting places of bodies recovered but never identified or claimed.

Whenever an event of titanic proportions occurs, someone comes forth to claim that he or she had foretold it. Such predictions are usually instances of nothing more mysterious than retrospective or self-fulfilling prophecies. Martin Gardner, the mathematician and author, analyzed a number of claims of psychic premonitions of the ship's sinking in *The Wreck of the Titanic Foretold?* (1986) and found them all wanting. One premonition which he did not analyze was the intriguing one reported from Winnipeg.

On the North Atlantic it was early Sunday evening; in Manitoba it was early Sunday afternoon. The *Titanic* was two hours away from its rendezvous with the iceberg. The Rev. Charles Morgan, minister of Rosedale Methodist Church, Winnipeg, was in his study. He drew up a list of hymns to be sung at the service and then stretched out on the couch. He suddenly felt very tired and took a short nap. Word would not reach Manitoba of the disaster that was about to unfold on the high seas until early Monday morning.

It seems he drifted off into a trance-like sleep which lasted for twenty minutes or so. It was a troubled sleep, one in which he heard sounds and voices, sounds like the crash of rushing water, voices like cries for help. And above the din he could detect the strains of an old hymn, a hymn which he had not recalled hearing sung for years. It began "Hearing, Father, while we pray to Thee,/For those in peril on the sea."

The nightmare of the vision so unsettled him that while he was conducting the early evening service, the minister confided to the congregation that he felt full of fear and apprehension. He asked the congregation to sing "Hearing, Father, while we pray to Thee,/For those in peril on the sea."

It was the next morning before Winnipeggers learned of the sinking of the *Titanic*. Then they also learned that about two hours before the *Titanic* struck its iceberg, at the Sunday evening services held in the second-class dining room of the ship, the Rev. Ernest Carter led his congregant passengers in the singing of "Hearing, Father, while we pray to Thee,/For those in peril on the sea."

Did the Rev. Charles Morgan experience a premonition of the sinking of the *Titanic*? Dr. Ian Stevenson believes the experience to be an instance of a precognitive experience. For no known reason, through no known agency, the minister had telepathic foreknowledge of the drama on the high seas. Stevenson reported on the *Titanic* premonition in the first of two papers on paranormal experiences associated with the *Titanic*. These were published in the *Journal of the American Society for Psychical Research* in October 1960 and July 1965.

Winnipeg/
The Hamilton Circle

Asked to name the most important psychical researcher Canada has ever known, no one would go wrong naming Dr. T. Glen Hamilton. As a psychical researcher, he made notable contributions in such areas as the study of telepathy and telekinesis, the production of teleplasm or ectoplasm, and what might be called "spirit photography." At the same time, as a public figure, he made substantial contributions in the spheres of medicine, university teaching, and government. He tried to keep in focus both the foreground of spiritualism and the background of science. His was an attempt to square the circle, so to speak.

Thomas Glendenning Hamilton was born in Agincourt, Ontario, in 1873, and raised on a homestead in the West. Upon graduation from the Manitoba Medical College, he practised medicine in Winnipeg. In 1915–20 he served as a Conservative member in the Manitoba Legislature. Then he served as President of the Manitoba Medical Association. He held many other positions, including that of Elder in the Presbyterian Church. His interest in psychical research,

The "spirit photography" of Dr. T. Glen Hamilton is the surprising legacy of the life and work of a distinguished Winnipeg physician, professor of medicine, and public figure. The legacy takes the physical form of nineteen cartons of papers and photographic plates which now form the T. Glendenning Hamilton Collection in the Department of Archives & Special Collections at the University of Manitoba in Winnipeg.

Of particular interest to students of psychical research are Dr. Hamilton's glass-plate negatives. Some 300 of these were exposed between the years 1918 and 1934. They offer the researcher a graphic record of the effects associated with physical mediumship during the séances of the day. Among the effects caught on film are psychokinesis (specifically table levitation) and the production of ectoplasm or teleplasm (a substance believed to extrude from the medium's bodily orifices).

All the photographs which follow come from the Department of Archives and Special Collections, the University of Manitoba.

Array of cameras to record effects produced during séances.

Photographic portrait of Dr. T. Glen Hamilton.

Table levitation, 5 April 1925.

Table levitation, 16 April 1926.

The Lucy teleplasm, 10 March 1930.

The ship teleplasm, 4 June 1930.

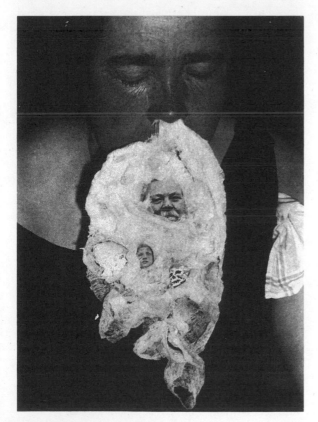

The Doyle teleplasm, 27 June 1932.

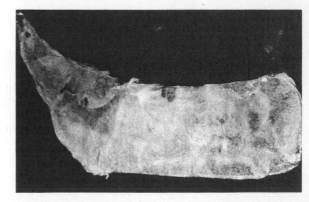

A mass of teleplasm, with faces, 29 June 1930.

sparked by an interest in the Patience Worth phenomenon, blossomed in the years 1918–34. Mediumship was socially acceptable on most levels of society at the time, in much the same way that trance-channelling is vogueish in show business circles in the 1980s.

Dr. Hamilton specialized in the study of "phenomena" — specifically rapping, psychokinesis, ectoplasm, and materializations under controlled circumstances. In the words of Kathryn F. Dean, the author of the excellent *Register of the Thomas Glendenning Hamilton Collection* (1980):

> TGH was particularly suited, both by training and by temperament, to conduct investigations. While psychic phenomena have been known under one name or another in every recorded society, the questionable claims (some of which read like adventures in the absurd) of those who conducted their investigations under loose (if not fradulent) experimental conditions, produced a skepticism on the part of many. There are few subjects which have aroused more bitter controversy. Dr. Hamilton, however, was interested in certain basic issues: 1) Do we have paranormal abilities, potentials for awareness and communication and action that we do not fully realize? 2) Can they be observed, measured and evaluated? 3) Are these abilities psychological or physical or both? 4) Do these capabilities continue to function after the experience of physical death? In other words, "Is there survival after death?"

The Hamilton Circle conducted its *séances* not in the first-floor parlour but in the second-floor bedroom of the doctor's mansion on Henderson Highway in Winnipeg's fashionable Westgate district. Family members, friends, and visitors met weekly for sessions which centred around the mediumship of middle-aged women — identified by initials or first names — women of limited education.

Experiments in telepathy (or thought transferrence) were conducted in 1918–21. Telekinesis (or movement at a distance) was explored in 1921–28. The production of teleplasm (a quasi-material substance better known as ectoplasm) was attained in 1928–33. But sombre research did not dominate the afternoon or evening sessions. Dr. Hamilton, a photographer as well as a spiritualist, took pleasure in combining his two interests. Through "spirit-photography" he was able to keep a visible, physical record of the phenomena produced. Almost three hundred black-and-white still photographs taken of the mediums and their effects remain his most characteristic contribution to the field of psychical research — and also the most difficult to consistently explain.

Sympathetic souls travelling through Winnipeg were invited to the session. Sir Arthur Conan Doyle, touring America to promote the spiritualist cause, joined the Hamilton Circle in July 1922. The medium on that occasion was Mrs. Elizabeth Poole. She "charged" the table by placing her hands on it for a moment. The table was then put inside a cabinet shaped like a phone booth and the lights were turned off. Two of the group held Mrs. Poole's hands. Doyle stood in front of the cabinet. The table moved violently up and down and lunged at Doyle, who was so impressed that he described the evening at length in his travel book, *Our Second American Adventure* (1923). He returned to visit the Hamilton Circle two more times — following his death.

Another sympathetic visitor was William Lyon Mackenzie King who joined the Hamilton Circle for an afternoon session on 29 August 1933. As he confided to his diary, according to C.P. Stacey in *A Very Double Life: The Private World of Mackenzie King* (1976): "The afternoon was quite the most remarkable one . . . I believe absolutely in all that Hamilton & his wife & daughter told me." As the leader of the Opposition, he was perhaps in need of some encouragement. The circle contacted the spirit of the late Robert Louis Stevenson and he supplied some words of encouragement. The author of *Treasure Island* was popular with spiritualists. On an earlier occasion (17 February 1927), R.L.S. or his spirit informed the Hamilton Circle: "It is good work you are doing for your fellow-man. Commence again. R.L.S."

The collection of astonishing photographs produced by the Hamilton Circle is the principal claim on contemporary interest. The first photo of a teleplastic mass'' emanating from the mouth of Mrs. Y. was taken by William Creighton, M.D., on 20 March 1927. Then there was the remarkable photograph of 27 October 1929, which showed a face amid the teleplasm; the features resembled those of Raymond, Oliver Lodge's dead son, but a Raymond older than his years. Thereafter there was no shortage of ectoplasm—globs, strings of it—protruding from all the orifices of the female mediums. Then it all came to an end. Dr. Hamilton died on 7 April 1935.

The voluminous manuscripts and many photographs were deeded to the Libraries of the University of Manitoba in 1979 by Dr. Hamilton's daughter, Mrs. Margaret Hamilton Bach, herself a spiritualist. But they are only part of this remarkable legacy. Another part of it is his own book, *Intention and Survival*, which was concerned not so much with the proof of spiritualism as with the proof supplied by spiritualism: survival after death. He was working on this manuscript at the time of his death, and it was edited by his son, J.D. Hamilton and published posthumously in 1942 by Macmillan of Canada. The full title is *Intention and Survival: Psychical Research Studies and the Bearing of Intentional Actions by Trance Personalities on the Problem of Human Survival*. It concluded on a personal and positive note: ''That our small share in this unfoldment may lead to still greater discoveries is my greatest hope. How far off these great days are I cannot venture to surmise, but that they will come, I am certain.''

Winnipeg/
Sir Arthur and the Spirits

The British author Sir Arthur Conan Doyle and his wife travelled across the United States and Canada on a lecture tour in 1922, addressing spiritualists, not specifically readers of the Sherlock Holmes stories who no doubt attended some of the lectures. In Winnipeg he spoke and attended two *séances*, which he described in *Our Second American Adventure* (1923). One of the mediums, who produced both physical and mental effects, impressed him mightily. The other medium worked on a spiritual plane and impressed him with her sincerity and devotion. He does not indentify the leader of the first circle, but it was obviously Dr. T. Glendenning Hamilton.

On our first night in Winnipeg we attended a circle for psychical research which has been conducted for two years by a group of scientific men who have obtained remarkable results. The medium is a small, pleasant-faced woman from the Western Highlands of Scotland. Her psychic gifts are both mental and physical. The circle, which contained ten persons, including my wife and myself, placed their hands, or one hand each, upon a small table, part of which was illuminated by phosphorus so as to give some light. It was violently agitated, and this process was described as ''charging it.'' It was then pushed back into a small cabinet made of four hung curtains with an opening in front. Out of this the table came clattering again and again entirely on its own, with no sitter touching it. I stood by the slit in the curtain in subdued red light and I watched the table within. One moment it was quiescent. A moment later it was like a restless dog in a kennel, springing, tossing, beating up against the spoorts, and finally bounding out with a velocity which caused me to get quickly out of the way. It ended up rising up in the air while our finger-tips were on it and remaining up for an appreciable period. . . .

On the mental side the peculiarity of the sittings is that little quotations which can be traced to R.L. Stevenson's works are rapped out by the medium. So far as is known, the little Scotch woman knows nothing normally of R.L.S., because she is not of a literary turn. Quotation after quotation has been actually verified. One curious line came through which has not yet been located. It is: ''It will come at last like grey hairs and coffin nails.'' It sounds like Stevenson, but I cannot place it.

The second *séance* of a religious nature was described at length and gave the Doyles a good sense of the people who lived in Winnipeg.

> When I considered the wonderful psychical phenomena of the one circle seen with my own eyes and the religious atmosphere of the other, I came away with the conclusion that Winnipeg stands very high among the places we have visited for its psychic possibilities. There are several Spiritualist Churches and a number of local mediums of good repute.

Winnipeg/
The Pogue Carburetor

A *motif* familiar to folklorists throughout the industrialized world is the urban legend of the Economical Car. If the average automobile can go twenty-five miles on a gallon of gas, the Economical Car can travel two hundred and fifty miles on a gallon of gas. The secret of the Economical Car is its wonderfully advanced fuel-efficient engine. The only problem is that the invention has scared the vested interests — the gas and oil producers who fear a disastrous drop in the consumption of fuel. But they have been successful in convincing the automotive manufacturers to scrap their plans to introduce the Economical Car. All would be well except every so often an independent inventor stumbles upon the secret of the wonderfully advanced engine and tries to build the Economical Car.

A Winnipegger named Charles Nelson Pogue made national headlines in 1937 with his announcement that after seventeen years of experimentation he had finally developed an incredibly fuel-efficient carburetor. On an automobile engine it could deliver 200 miles on a gallon of gas. It was said to vaporize fuel ten times more efficiently than the standard carburetor, thus eliminating waste and releasing ten times more energy. Engineers and businessmen attended demonstrations and marvelled at the amazing device. Pogue fitted the carburetor on his eight-cylinder Ford, and

one of his backers drove the 1819 miles from Winnipeg to Vancouver on 14 gallons of gas — 130 miles to the gallon. It was independently tested by Ford of Canada and it did better than Pogue had claimed — it achieved 25.7 miles per pint, or 205 miles per gallon. The U.S. Patent Office issued several patents on the device, and Pogue planned to retire on the royalties he would earn.

But that was the end of the story, rather than its beginning. George Gamester suggested a possible scenario in the *Toronto Star* in 1978:

> Then, as quickly as they had popped up, Pogue and his invention dropped out of sight. Dark rumours about oil companies suppressing the device circulated, and nothing more was heard until 1941, when the Canadian Army announced the carburetor had been tested and found unsatisfactory.
>
> These days, with the world's petroleum reserves shrinking fast, Pogue's brainchild could be a godsend. But, according to a Winnipeg writer who knew Pogue, it had a fatal flaw: It created so much heat in the engine that cylinders, pistons and valves were burned to ashes.
>
> And Pogue? What's he up to now?
>
> Well, there's a Charles Nelson Pogue listed in the Winnipeg phone directory. But when we called to ask him about his invention, he replied: ''I have nothing to say, nothing at all. Goodbye.''

Four years later Pogue was still not talking. When John Picton, another *Toronto Star* writer, phoned him in 1982, all the retired inventor would say before hanging up was, ''That was a long time ago. I'm not feeling very well today.''

The bold heading on the full-page advertisement in the June 1982 issue of *Psychology Today* catches the eye. It reads: CARBURETOR GETS 200 MPG! The capital letters, almost an inch in height, were drawing attention not to the Pogue Carburetor but to a forty-eight page booklet *about* the Pogue Carburetor. For $4.95 (plus $1.00 postage and handling) — U.S. currency — the reader would receive *Secrets of The 200 MPG Carburetor* (1980, 8th ed., 1982) by Allan Wallace.

What Wallace does in his booklet is discuss a whole series of carburetor designs, with special reference to the Pogue Carburetor. He reproduces three quasi-technical drawings of Pogue's device as well as an endorsement of the device in the form of a letter from the Winnipeg Branch of the Ford Motor Comanpy of Canada Limited, dated 30 April 1936. There never was a Winnipeg Branch, and Ford officials today deny any knowledge of the carburetor.

It is possible that the Pogue Carburetor was a hoax or practical joke that got out of hand; a fraud that never got off the ground; or a device that never got the mileage it was supposed to. What is most unlikely is that Pogue invented a contraption which would have revolutionized the automotive industry had it not been suppressed by the gas and oil industry. What is quite likely is that Charles Nelson Pogue did invent something of importance — the urban legend known as the Economical Car.

Winnipeg/
The Playful Organ

An inexplicable or at least unexplained event of some beauty and melody took place in St. John's Anglican Cathedral in Winnipeg. It happened in the Chapel during a service late one Sunday afternoon in December 1953, and was witnessed by a dozen members of the congregation, the curate, and the rector.

When the Rev. H.J. Skynner, Curate of the Cathedral, began to read a passage from the Epistles, a note sounded on the pipe organ. "It was clear, rather like that of a flute," wrote Sheila Hervey in *Some Canadian Ghosts* (1973). "The single note was followed by others, forming a pattern of sound. The tune was not familiar but it was melodious." The Very Rev. J.O. Anderson, Dean of Rupert's Land and Rector of St. John's, was surprised. "He looked at the organ and could see the manual clearly, but nobody was playing the instrument. All the members of the congregation were witness to the fact that the organ was playing with nobody at the keyboard. The music continued throughout the service, about twenty minutes in all. It played entirely on the flute stop and at no time did more than one pipe sound."

After the service the pipe organ was examined by experts who found that all the valves on the organ were securely stopped. "The wind could not have made sounds in the pipes; in fact, the organ could not logically make any sound at all." That Sunday afternoon it had been, indeed, a playful organ.

Winnipeg/
Sensory Deprivation

Work in the field of Sensory Deprivation, or SD, commenced within the Department of Psychology at the University of Winnipeg in Manitoba under the direction of John P. Zubek, Research Professor of Psychology and Director of the university's Sensory Deprivation Lavoratory. As another researcher Peter Suedfeld explained in "Introduction and Historical Background," a contribution to Zubek's collection of scientific papers, *Sensory Deprivation: Fifteen Years of Research* (1969):

> With a number of graduate students, technicians, and consultants, Zubek has used deprivation of unusually long durations (7 to 14 days) and varying modalities, with many dependent variable measures, to produce approximately 30 publications to date. His major interest is on the neurophysiological mechanisms involved, and the laboratory at the University of Manitoba, Winnipeg, Canada, is known for its unique physical design (a large translucent plexiglas dome, suggested by an aircraft cover).

Zubek was associated with the original series of experiments in "perceptual isolation" which were conducted at McGill University and concluded in 1954. He commenced his own work at the University of Manitoba in 1959.

In the 1950s and 1960s there were twenty-three centres conducting research in SD. In Canada work was underway at the Allan Memorial Institute, at McGill University, and at the University of Winnipeg. There were fourteen centres in the United States and a number in Europe. The work in North America proceeded under grants from national governments and not all the results were published. What began as an attempt to determine the extents and limits of the "brainwashing" techniques being employed by the Chinese Communists became in time an academic area within the discipline of Psychology.

Work at Winnipeg proceeded under the "large translucent plexiglas dome" of the isolation chamber or in an immobilization box which was seven feet long, twenty-eight inches wide, eighteen inches deep, and lined with a thick layer of foam rubber cut in the shape of a human figure, with the head held in a padded head-holding device. Subjects spent hours or days on end alone in the isolation chamber or in the immobilization box. Zubek made a discovery about duration. He learned, "A considerable body of evidence indicates that a 2-day period frequently produces greater behavioural changes than either a shorter or a longer duration."

Experiments were conducted with selected stimuli and also with the Ganzfeld screen — a uniform, featureless field. Changes in the subject's physiology, personality, drives, needs, desires, cognition, and perception were noted and measured. "Subjects who have been exposed to a prolonged period of isolation frequently appear dull, sluggish, and not very alert," Zubek noted. One of his contributions was to correct the early conclusions of the McGill team. Dramatic perceptual disorder followed isolation among the subjects at Montreal; this was not so with the subjects at Winnipeg.

The researcher Marvin Zuckerman came to the following conclusion: "Sensory variety is not just the spice of life; it is the bread of life." SD work relates directly to the conditions that face astronauts and could shed light on the hallucinations of shamans, psychics, and mystics. Work continues at the University of Winnipeg, where it is no longer known as SD. The new name is Restricted Environmental Stimulation — REST for short.

Lake Winnipeg/
Mother Damnable

Not much is known of this native seer or witch. Wampohama was her native name, but she was known to the English as Mother Damnable. It is believed that she was born among the Hurons and that she married a Huron chief about 1648. She lived the life of a recluse and was treated like a shaman by the Cree on the shore of Lake Winnipeg, where her death was recorded about the year 1700.

Wampohama's legacy to the world is a perplexing one. On her death-bed she dictated a series of dark and obscure prophecies or predictions. These were published in booklet form in Western Canada in 1882, 182 years after her death. The full title of the booklet is *A Short Account of the Old Indian Witch, Wampohama, better known to the early settlers as Mother Damnable, Together with her Extraordinary Prophecies, already partially fulfilled, concerning the Future Destinies of What are Now Winnipeg, Manitoba, and the Great North-West.*

Here are a few of the dark prophecies or predictions, with possible interpretations, said to be uttered by Wampohama or Mother Damnable from her deathbed.

> All the land to the west of this shall remain wild and unpeopled for two hundred years. Then it shall give food to the eastern tribes of men. [The phrase "west of this" is taken to mean west of Winnipeg; "two hundred years" would bring the year to 1900, when the West began producing wheat which was exported to the East.]

> All the world shall one day be divided into two great countries; one of these shall almost destroy itself, but shall afterwards become greater than before. [It is assumed that Mother Damnable meant North America when she said "all the world" and that she was referring to the American Civil War.]

> A country shall rise up that shall take its name from the great Master of Life, and shall be blessed by him and shall prosper, and shall spread to the west and fill the western country with white men; and the face of the country shall be divided like crystal. [As "Master of Life" would be Manitou, so this might be a prophecy of the birth of Manitoba; "divided like crystal" might be an imaginative image for surveyors' sections.]

Lake Winnipeg/
Skrimsi

There are Cree legends about the fabulous serpents that inhabit the depths of Lake Winnipeg, the sixth largest freshwater lake in the country. The Icelanders who settled in the vicinity of Gimli in 1875 reported that there were *skrimsi* in the waters of the lake, skrimsi being Icelandic for "sea creatures" of a fabulous size and shape.

An early sighting of a serpent-like creature in Cedar Lake, which flows into Lake Winnipeg at Grand Rapids, was made in September 1909 at Graves Point. The fur trader Valentine McKay was in his canoe when he heard "a rumble like distant thunder." He rounded the point and was astonished to see on the glossy surface of the water, four hundred yards from shore, a huge creature travelling over two miles an hour. It had a dark upper surface which glistened in the sun, and part of its body projected about four feet in the air vertically. The water around the creature was considerably disturbed.

Lake Winnipegosis/
The Red Deer Point "Spook"

From a fishing camp at Red Deer Point on Lake Winnipegosis came the following account of a "spook" or poltergeist. The account has been reproduced in its entirety from the 17 March 1898 issue of the Winnipeg *Fress Press*.

GHOSTS IN THE NORTH
A Fisherman's Story of Midnight "Spooks"
Perfect Pandemonium Prevails in a Winnipegosis
Fishing Camp —
"Spirit" Will Not Speak

The following letter reached the *Free Press* by the Dauphin mail and is given space, as the writer thereof appears to be perfectly sincere in his statements that "spooks" — probably Andree ghosts — are rambling about in the northern portions of our province:

To the Editor of the *Free Press*.

Sir,—With your permission, I would like to give your readers a brief account of some strange phenomena existing at present in this fishing camp, near Red Deer Point, in this camp, about thirty-five miles from Winnipegosis station. The first time we noticed anything was on Wednesday, the 9th inst. There were five of us in the camp at the time, D.S. Nichols, of Mossy River, D.H. Mason, of Alliston, Ont., two Norwegians and myself. We were seated round the table shortly after 9 p.m., when we heard a loud, rasping noise at one of the windows, which was kept up almost continuously until nearly midnight. At intervals, also, we could hear what appeared to be something dragging along the roof, and a rattling and banging of the pipes. We could find nothing to account for these noises, though we did out best to do so. The next night, about the same time, we heard the ringing of a small bell, apparently near the stable. We were expecting our foreman back from the station, and thought nothing of this at first, although he had no bell on his horse when he left. We heard it again shortly after, and as no one appeared, we went out to see and though it was clear moonlight, we could discover nothing. The bell rang again; this time close to the camp. Then it rang inside the camp, and has done so every night more or less frequently, and is ringing to-night more than ever, having commenced about two hours earlier. The same noises went on as before, but more loudly. On Friday night tin dishes were thrown off the wall and the shelves with considerable force. Just after we had blown out our lamp about 11 p.m., it seemed as if all the boots and rubbers in the camp were being thrown about and the noise on the roof was very loud. Mr. A. Stewart, of Birtle, foreman for Mr. P. McArthur, of Westbourne, whose logging camp is near us, was with us on Friday night a part of the time, and on Saturday night several of his men came over to see for themselves, so that we had plenty of witnesses

297

for the still more curious freaks of that night. Dishes were thrown all over the floor, a heavy iron stove lid lifted, was several times thrown off the stove, three or four feet out on the floor, and a dipper was not only thrown out of the pot, but replaced. A hat of one of McArthur's men, hanging on a nail about five feet from him, was put on his head, and shortly after thrown off. While I was writing the paper was pulled out of my hand, and a large German stocking was flung twice into the air, the last time hitting me on the head. However to be brief the climax was reached about 10.30 p.m. I had noticed for some time previously a slight oscillation of the table and a corresponding oscillation of the lamp. Suddenly the lamp went out, and then it was pandemonium let loose. Everything in the camp seemed to be on the move, the blows on the window were delivered with apparently sledge-hammer force; the stoves rattled and shook, while the roof noise was very loud and there was also a loud knocking at the door. This happened three times, and then gradually the disturbances became less and ceased as usual shortly before midnight. It is now 10 p.m. and things are again on the move, amongst others, two large pillows have been flung out on the floor. If any of your readers could furnish me with a satisfactory solution of these occurrences I would be much obliged. I have several times asked the spirit, if it be a spirit, to speak, but receive no answer. In conclusion, I may say I am nearly 21 years in the country and am known to a good many, among others, Dr. E. Benson, who, I think, would vouch for my credibility.

A.C. O'BEIRNE.

Winnipegosis, Man. March 13.

SASKATCHEWAN

Beechy/
"Murder on His Mind"

The little auditorium at Beechy, a village southwest of Saskatoon, was the scene of a real-life drama the evening of 10 December 1932. The somewhat complicated tale was told by the broadcaster and journalist Frank Edwards in "Murder on His Mind" in *Strange People* (1961).

That evening the townsfolk were being entertained by Professor Gladstone, Mentalist. The so-called mentalist apparently departed from the script and informed the astonished audience that the farmer Scotty McLauchlin, who had been missing from the small community for four years, had been brutally murdered. Pointing to a person in the audience whom he had never met, the mentalist added that together they would find the body. The person turned out to be an off-duty RCMP officer, Constable Carey.

The publicity that followed the mentalist's public remarks led to the RCMP reopening the case of the missing man. Carey introduced the mentalist to the farmers in the community who had known McLauchlin. They reconstructed McLauchlin's last days and, according to Edwards's account, the mentalist was able to locate the corpse in a barn, reconstruct the events that led to the murder, and identify the murderer. The guilty party confessed, was tried, and was convicted in the court at Kindersley. Edwards concluded his account with these words:

And what of Professor Gladstone? As a result of the widespread publicity given to the case of Scotty McLauchlin, he was much in demand and played for many years on the stage. But he was never again able to duplicate his performance at Beechy, Saskatchewan, on that bleak December night in 1932, when the mentalist solved a murder for the Royal [Canadian] Mounted Police.

Cabri Lake/
The Human Effigy

In a field near Cabri Lake, in west-central Saskatchewan, will be found the Human Effigy.

At some point in the past boulders were so arranged as to represent in outline form a colossal male figure. The figure may be that of a shaman or a hunter who is standing his ground, as if in awe or defiance, both arms raised, fingers spread apart. The head is a concentration of boulders; from the crown emerges some sort of extension. The figure is decidedly male; irregular sized boulders represent a penis and testicles. The total form is visible only from the air.

The height of the figure, from the soles of its feet to top of its head, is about twenty-eight feet. The span of the feet measures in the neighbourhood of fifteen feet. There may be published descriptions of the Human Effigy at Cabri but these have not been located. A drawing of the figure appears in *Tracking Ancient Hunters: Prehistoric Archaeology in Saskatchewan* (1983), edited by Henry T. Epp and Ian Dyck.

The Human Effigy is an arrangement of boulders found near Cabri Lake, Sask. The pen-and-ink drawing displays the arrangement from an aerial perspective. The height of the figure is approximately eight feet, its stride almost five feet. It is not known when the Human Effigy was constructed. [Saskatchewan Archaeological Society, 1983]

Frenchman River/ Medicine Wheel

Nothing is permanent in this world. Even structures as gigantic as the Indian Medicine Wheels, which stand on isolated knolls and lonely bluffs across the prairies and plains, are subject to the depredations of the weather and of man. The poet Archibald MacLeish suggested, "The mountains over Asia move." It is equally true that the medicine wheels, known since shortly before the turn of the century, are in danger of receding from view.

This is especially so concerning the Canuck Medicine Wheel. It was described by Alice B. and Thomas F. Kehoe in *Solstice-aligned Boulder Configurations in Saskatchewan* (1979):

> In the area south of the Frenchman River Valley in which the Canuck Medicine Wheel . . . had been reported, a low rock cairn was located. This cairn lies on a south-facing hill slope about three miles south of the Valley, in rolling topography. Two short rock lines, about twenty feet long, radiate from the cairn, one line approximately north, the other east-northeast. This cairn and lines would not have been suitably situated for astronomical observations, and do not seem to be significant to this study. A careful foot survey of the section on which the Canuck Wheel was said to lie failed to find that configuration, but did cross several recently-ploughed fields. The man presently farming this land could not recall seeing the configuration recorded by Watson, and the previous owners, now retired, were unsure of the nature of the "grave" visited by the Sasktachewan Museum crew some years ago. Whether the observed cairn and lines were part of the Canuck Wheel, disturbed since Watson's mapping, or whether the Canuck Wheel is now the impressive recent pile of rocks in the fence corner of the ploughed section, could not be determined.

Hughton/ The Hughton Medicine Wheel

The Hughton Medicine Wheel was named after the community of Hughton which lies south of Rosetown. The wheel itself lies on the edge of a rolling plateau south of Hughton. It has a large central cairn, twenty-four feet in diameter, a peripheral circle of stones, and a break in the circle through which a "walkway" passes. The "walkway" leads northeast and is slightly funnel-shaped. A third line, shorter than the outer two, runs between them. According to Alice B. and Thomas F. Kehoe in *Solstice-aligned Boulder Configurations in Saskatchewan* (1979), "Neither calculation nor observation at the site showed any apparent solar or stellar alignments." Have the boulders been moved or removed?

A serious problem with the Hughton configuration was the assessment of disturbance. Several persons in the district have been concerned over the preservation of the monument, and have attempted to restore some loose rocks to what is believed to have been their original position. According to a local historian, Oscar Lindell, whose family homesteaded near the site, when he first saw the configuration, about 1926, there were five "walkways," one in each cardinal direction as well as the existing northeast one. Each "walkway," as remembered by Mr. Lindell, was three to four feet long and about two feet wide, except for the northeast one which was larger (now measures not quite twenty feet long and eleven-one-one-half feet wide). Mr Lindell's father, who saw the configuration shortly after he came to the district in 1912, told his son that until 1913 or 1914, the central cairn was a truncated cone of rocks capped by a tipi-like set of poles, from the top of which a "very beautiful tribal emblem" — not further described — was hung. The elder Mr. Lindell believed that Indians took down the "tribal emblem" when the district began filling with settlers. If the Lindells are correct, it is no longer possible to validly judge astronomical alignments in the Hughton "Wheel."

A test excavation made at the edge of the central cairn in May 1971 disclosed potsherds, projectile points, stone scrapers, skull and bone fragments that were possibly human, which was summarized as indicating a date of the seventeenth or eighteenth centuries.

Kerrobert/
The Mystery Inscription

The so-called Mystery Inscription appears on a large boulder found at the bottom of a buffalo wallow in the vicinity of Kerrobert, the town in southern Saskatchewan east of the Alberta border. The boulder measures about three by four feet and is two feet high. Its smooth upper edges indicate that the buffalo which once roamed the prairies used it as a rubbing stone.

Chiselled figures on the flat upper surface are apparently quite old. The area was settled in the 1900s, yet the inscription reads: "July 1, 1791." If it was inscribed at that time, it could be the handiwork of an employee of the Hudson's Bay Company. Yet there is no record that any traders were in the district in that period. Anthony Henday, the first white man to reach the Rockies from the east, did so in 1754–55, but his route did not take him so far south.

Langenburg/
The Rapeseed Swirls

A curious incident occurred on 1 September 1974 in a field of rapeseed on the farm of Edwin Fuhr outside Langenburg, a town southeast of Yorkton. The incident involved the sighting of five UFOs and the "rapeseed swirls" they left behind. The affair was discussed by J. Allen Hynek and Jacques Vallee in *The Edge of Reality* (1975). Photographs of the rapeseed swirls appear in Yurko Bondarchuk's *UFO: Sightings, Landings and Abductions* (1979).

Edwin Fuhr, a rapeseed farmer, was swatching a field when he came upon five dome-shaped objects the colour of stainless steel that were revolving and hovering a foot or so above the ground. "From one of them, something was probing around the grass," he later told an interviewer. "It was like, oh, I would say, the size of a fifty-cent piece, *it looked like a probe*, and the grass was all twisted and you could see marks like something had jumped here and there, all over."

The objects suddenly rose about two hundred feet and stopped in midair and stopped spinning. They emitted blasts of vapour, the downward pressure of which flattened the rape that had been standing. Then they sped away, leaving five perfectly round rings of flattened rapeseed in the field below, swirled in a clockwise direction. The RCMP prepared a report on the sighting which noted: ''There were five distinct circles caused by something exerting what had to be heavy air or exhaust pressure over the high grass.''

Masefield/ Millennial Sect

H.G. Wells described in his short story ''The Lord of the Dynamos'' a cult that had but one believer. The community of Masefield, a small farming community located due south of Swift Current and just north of the Montana Border, boasted one cult with three believers.

''Wally,'' the name given to the replica of the Woolly Mammoth in the Saskatchewan town of Kyle, was erected to commemorate the discovery in 1964 of a Woolly Mammoth skeleton five kilometres west of Kyle. The twelve-hundred-year-old bones are exhibited in both the Saskatchewan Museum of Natural History in Regina and the National Museum of Canada in Ottawa. Kyle's ''Wally'' stands 9' 11'' in height, weighs 1749 pounds, and was created in 1981 by the Saskatoon artist Don Foulds. The replica stands in Wally Park and is dedicated to the past, present, and future citizens of Kyle as a symbol of community pride. It reminds one and all of the Biblical reminder that there ''were giants in the earth.'' [Town of Kyle/Eric L. Chambers]

The Regina *Leader* on 28 September 1929 ran a news story about the three-person millennial sect. ''It is headed by Archie Chandler, his brother, Sid Chandler, and the latter's wife. They have erected a large tent on the side of one of the many hills so characteristic of the district, and here they are awaiting the coming of Christ and the end of the world on November 6.''

The account explained that on their camping ground they stored ten tons of flour and three thousand bushels of rolled oats ready for grinding.

So positive of the coming of Christ are the Chandler Brothers, the most influential and up-to-date farmers in the Masefield district, that they have sold all their holdings and stock and are using the proceeds for carrying on their propaganda.

Their tented home, amid a sea of hills, is the centre of attraction to travellers from far and near. Their evident sincerity, and courteous behaviour, have made strong impressions on many of the visitors, and at the same time caused many a head to wag in derision.

Two years ago Archie and Sid Chandler became convinced that the prophecies of the Bible were about to be fulfilled, and following out the injunction of sacred script started to prepare for the advent of the Messiah. A tent was put up in the hills and there Archie started the cult, that for a time had a number of followers. As the months went by and the dates set for the momentous event passed, the brothers decided that they would abandon the ways of the world, and make better preparations. . . .

While services have been carried on at the tent for two years, it is only since the early part of June that the Chandlers have gone to live in the tent. The two children of Sid Chandler are members of the cult, and the five people are now housed in the tent, in preparation for the end of the world. Of late weeks not one of the former followers of the cult have attended any services, and it is believed they have given up their beliefs, leaving the two brothers to carry on their work alone.

Fifteen years ago the Chandler brothers came from England, from a well-to-do and highly placed family. The two men were well educated at the higher schools and arrived in Canada well equipped to carry on the pioneer work in the south country. They prospered, and gathered together a fair competence. Two years ago, their religious beliefs on the second coming of Christ and the end of the world became pronounced, hence their active working in the hope of informing the world of their prediction.

The Last Day — 6 November 1929 — fell on a Wednesday. Neither the Regina *Leader* nor the Canadian Press news services, which carried the story nationally, interviewed the Chandlers on Doomsday Plus One.

Milk River/
Petrographs

The petroglyphs in the Valley of the Milk River, which lies across the southern part of Southern Alberta, attracted the attention of Barry Fell. He is a founder of the Epigraphic Society, an organization devoted to the interpretation of ancient inscriptions which is based in San Diego, California, and the author of a series of books which argue that there is epigraphic evidence for the pre-Columbian colonization of the Americas.

The petroglyphs cut in the soft bedrock of the valley of the Milk River are seen by anthropologists and others as a range of expressive images rather than as a script. Fell argued in *Bronze Age America* (1982) that like other inscriptions scattered across North America the images are letters of ogam and words of old Nordic. He wrote: "As we have already seen, the ogam alphabet that for so long has been supposed to be exclusively Celtic script was in fact well known in Nordic countries as early as the Bronze Age. This fact accounts for the otherwise untranslatable ogam inscriptions that occur in the Western Plains and as

far west as the valley of the Milk River in Alberta, Canada."

Minton/
The Minton Turtle

The Minton Turtle is an Indian medicine wheel which was constructed on a knoll overlooking the Big Muddy River Valley in south-central Saskatchewan, west of the village of Minton. It takes the form of a figure of a turtle 130 feet long. It is composed of a line of small rounded boulders which form an ovoid body with four curved lines as legs (the rear two

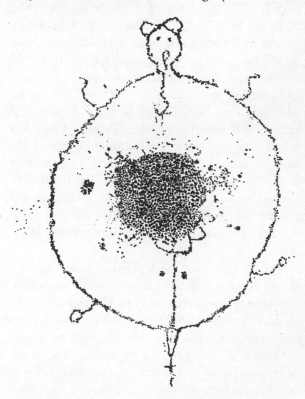

The Minton Turtle is an unusual Indian Medicine Wheel in that the figure has the shape of a turtle. The figure, outlined in small rounded boulders, measures 130 feet from head to tail. The centre is a concentration of loose stones some thirty feet in diameter. The Minton Turtle lies across a knoll overlooking the Big Muddy River Valley near Minton, Sask. [Saskatchewan Archaeological Society, 1983]

ending in circular feet), a short neck, and a round head. The head has a pair of large rounded ears, "dot" eyes, and a round mouth from which a question mark-shaped "lifeline" leads into the upper portion of the body.

The centre of the body is occupied by a cairn of loose stones thirty feet in diameter. From the rear of this cairn a line of stones leads to the point on the circle opposite the head. A triangular tail projects from the circle at this point and ends in a cross. There is a pair of small mounds of stones, one on either side of the line through the rear of the body (possibly meant to represent testicles), a larger mound of stones in the middle of the right side of the body (assuming the turtle lies on its back), a smaller cluster of stones in a "sunburst" pattern diagonally opposite that mound on the left side of the body, and a small mound of stones outside the body on the left side.

According to calculations, observers standing on specified cairns and following given sightlines would be able to observe the summer solstice's sunrise and sunset. The principal axis of the turtle aligns with the rising of Sirius. "An observer standing at the junction of the body line with the body circle at the base of the tail, or on the cross at the end of the tail, and looking east, would sight the heliacal rising of Sirius at summer solstice over the approximate centre of the central cairn."

The quotation and the descriptions appear in Alice B. and Thomas F. Kehoe's *Solstice-aligned Boulder Configurations in Saskatchewan* (1979). "Incidentally," the authors observed, "the Minton configuration appears to represent a turtle, but it might have been constructed as an effigy of another animal. Over much of the world, Sirius is called the Dog Star, and it is not difficult for the junior author to see a dog rather than a turtle in the configuration."

Moose Mountain/
Medicine Wheel

The Moose Mountain Medicine Wheel was constructed on the summit of the highest hill it its area.

The configuration of boulders lies seven miles north of the village of Kisbey not far from the southwest boundary of Moose Mountain Provincial Park. The construction consists of a central cairn, thirty feet in diameter, constructed of loose rounded boulders. From the central cairn radiate five lines of small rounded boulders, each line ending in a circle of stones, each about three feet in diameter. An elliptical circle of stones, sixty-two feet by fifty feet, surrounds the central cairn.

The Moose Mountain Medicine Wheel was first reported in 1896. The only larger such wheel in the world is the one at Majorville, Alberta. The Moose Mountain wheel shares a number of features with the Big Horn Medicine Wheel in Wyoming, which is the largest in the United States. John A. Eddy, an authority on archaeo-astronomy, found many alignments in common. In fact, it has been suggested that the two wheels are in alignment. Based on possible astronomical alignments, the Moose Mountain Medicine Wheel was constructed about A.D. 1 or sometime during the eighteenth or nineteenth centuries. The latitude in the dating is discussed by Alice B. and Thomas F. Kehoe in *Solstice-aligned Boulder Configurations in Saskatchewan* (1979).

Dr. Eddy, the scientist who referred to the Big Horn Medicine Wheel as "the American Stonehenge," is with the High Altitude Observatory, Boulder, Colorado. He is the author of the paper "Archaeo-astronomy of North America: Cliffs, Mounds, and Medicine Wheels" included in the collection *In Search of Ancient Astronomies* (1978) edited by E.C. Krupp. Here Dr. Eddy noted the following:

Cairns of the Moose Mountian wheel appear in position to mark the same celestial features as those at the Big Horn wheel: sunrise at summer solstice and the rising of Aldebaran, Rigel, and Sirius. A small group of rocks arranged in the form of a sun symbol, with short rays, was found at the end of the Moose Mountain wheel's summer solstice sunrise spoke. . . . The Moose Mountain site may predate the Big Horn wheel by one thousand years or more.

A note of caution was sounded by Michael W. Ovenden and David A. Rodger in an article called "Megaliths and Medicine Wheels" in the *Proceedings* of the Eleventh Annual Conference, Archaeological Association of Calgary, 1981:

> A stick stuck in the ground can be used as a marker for any direction that you choose, provided that you allow yourself the freedom to choose your observing location accordingly. So the Moose Mountain wheel *could have* been used to sight the Sun, or anything else for that matter. . . . The fact remains that the reason for believing that the Moose Mountain Medicine Wheel was solstitially oriented is an alleged alignment which does not work today.

From southern Manitoba to southern Arizona more than fifty medicine wheels may be found, and it is likely that more of these oddly eloquent structures will be discovered. Some of them are in "alignment" not only with the sun and the stars but also with each other, suggesting stone-age man's wide knowledge of the lay and the extent of the land. Medicine wheels have been called "sky calendars," and archaeo-astronomers, with the assistance of computers, have shown that their principal "sightlines" may mark the dawning and setting points of the summer solstice. As megalithic observatories, they parallel in structure and function the stone observatories across the Atlantic, like Britain's Stonehenge and Carnac in Brittany.

Native traditions hold that the North American medicine wheels were constructed by a previous people for purposes related to the cycle of the sun. Indeed in structure they resemble in some particulars the floor plans of the Sun Dance lodges of the Plains Indians. In other particulars, notably in the man-sized caverns or fissures created by the boulders, they imply the architecture of "vision sites." Not to be ignored is the simple fact that in the past some of the wheels served a mortuary function. As they had manifold uses in the past, they have varied uses in the present. They convey other meanings and messages in the twentieth century. To the Indian they harken back to lost native knowledge and technologies, and to the non-native they evoke a sense of the mystery of man and the heavens.

The astronomer and writer Terence Dickinson had the following comment to make about cultural chauvinism in "The Mystery of the Medicine Wheels" in *Science Forum*, March-April 1979:

> It flies against some firmly accepted ideas to suggest that thousands of years before Euclid was inventing modern geometry in Greece, North American Indians and the early Britons, among others, were using his principles to build stone monuments for a purpose still obscure. But this concept, along with other recent insights into our ancestors, is telling us that we have probably underestimated their cultural and intellectual sophistication — perhaps by a wide margin.

Okotoks/ Big Rock

The large glacial erratic south of the town of Okotoks is known as Big Rock. So large is the quartzite boulder that it is said to be the world's largest erratic — an erratic being an out-of-place rock. The town southeast of Calgary was named Okotoks after the Blackfoot word *okotoks* which means "big rock."

Big Rock, which is split in two parts, is estimated to weigh 18,000 tons. Indian pictographs were painted beneath its protecting ledges, and the Blackfoot Indians have a legend of how the great rock rolled in anger, splitting itself in half and breaking off in smaller pieces which may be seen lying about.

Qu'Appelle River/ "Who Calls?"

There is a Cree legend about love and loss set in the beautiful valley of the Qu'Appelle River. The river flows west of Regina through a valley renowned for its echoes.

The story is told of a Cree brave who paddled his birch-bark canoe through the river valley at night to claim a beautiful Cree maiden as his bride. In the darkness he heard a girl's voice utter his name. "Qu'appelle?" he cried out. "Who calls?" There was no answer. Then he heard the voice utter his name again. When he reached the village, he learned to his sorrow that the maiden had died. Her dying words were his name.

Ever since then, according to Ella Elizabeth Clark, who retells the tale in *Indian Legends of Canada* (1960), travellers on the river have heard a voice ask, "Who calls?"

Rama/
The Grotto

The Grotto of Our Lady of Lourdes in the village of Rama, in the east-central part of the province, annually attracts thousands of pilgrims in mid-August. They come to see the shrine which is modelled after the original grotto at Lourdes in the south of France.

The grotto was constructed next to St. Anthony's Roman Catholic Church in 1939-40 by an Anthony Sylla, an Oblate priest, who had visited the site in France where in 1858 the fourteen-year-old Bernadette Soubirous had reported seeing apparitions of the Virgin Mary. The first pilgrimage to the grotto at Rama took place during the Second World War, on 14-15 August 1941, the latter day being the Feast of the Assumption of the Virgin Mary into Heaven.

Pilgrims may admire and pray before many impressive statues, including one of Our Lady of Grace and another of St. Bernadette of Lourdes which faces the grotto itself. Surrounding the site are the fourteen Stations of the Cross representing stops along Jesus's way as he walked through Jerusalem to Calvary.

Regina/
"Dirigible-Shaped"

The eight-man crew of a Canadian Forces Hercules C-130E observed a "dirigible-shaped" craft during a routine flight from Namao Air Force Base, north of Edmonton, to Rivers Air Force Base in southwestern Manitoba. The sighting occurred over Regina at 2:52 a.m., 16 August 1968. The captain advised the Winnipeg RCAF Centre of the sighting and also requested that U.S. air control in Montana be notified, according to Yurko Bondarchuk in *UFO: Sightings, Landings and Abductions* (1979) who quoted the captain and crew's report to Canadian Forces Headquarters in Ottawa:

> Observed by seven man crew and by Captain through twelve-power field glasses. Appeared as elongated sphere or dirigible-shaped with five or six rectangular-shaped dark patches on side. No gondola or tail. Aluminum or similar surfaces reflected the sun. No contrail from UFO, although Air Canada Flight 851 contrail observed continuously from 2:00 a.m. to 3:00 a.m. UFO was visible to naked eye of crew for about one and a half minutes, then it shrank rapidly in size and disappeared to the southwest very, very rapidly. It reappeared faintly twice in the next five minutes to four crew members, probably due to reflected light.

As Bondarchuk noted, "This case is noteworthy because it involves eight reliable specialists, who were unanimous in their account of what they had viewed."

Regina/
"Universcope"

Donald S. Johnston, a resident of Regina and a professional rainmaker, was the subject of a CP story which appeared in the Niagara Falls *Evening Review*, 29 July 1950. The story described Johnston as "a professional moisture manufacturer" and described the tool of his trade, his "universcope."

According to Johnston, it is the moon and not the sun that affects the weather the most. With his "universcope" — a contraption about the size of a small electric fan — he can control the moisture in the atmosphere. The affair consists of two magnets, pivoted one upon the other, which sway back and forth like a metronome.

"The magnets produce electric-magnetic forces

which draw electrical powers from the moon, causing the moisture to condense and fall as rain,'' Johnston told the reporter. He maintained that his machine could coax moisture-bearing clouds from the Pacific Ocean or the Gulf of Mexico, depending on the position of the moon.

Johnston said he was able to raise the level of a lake at a summer resort. On another occasion officials of a western rodeo hired him for a demonstration then impounded his machine to help ensure clear weather. ''Johnston operated his machine in Calgary the week preceding the annual Stampede,'' the reporter noted. ''Everyone breathed a sign of relief when he left before the start of the show. But it rained anyway during Stampede week — after the Stoney Indians, in a fit of pique, held a rain-dance.''

This drawing of Louis Riel was made in pencil by a Lieutenant-Colonel Irwin. It was done in 1885, the year the Métis leader was executed in Regina for the crime of high treason. The eyes are particularly rivetting, suggesting that the mind is somewhere else. [PAC C 22242]

St. Laurent-Grandin/ The Métis Lourdes

St. Laurent-Grandin, north of Batoche, is a farming community established in 1873 on the shore of the South Saskatchewan River.

The ''Métis Lourdes'' was inspired by the vision of the Virgin Mary who appeared to the French peasant girl Bernadette Soubirous in France in 1858. Reports of the miraculous cures wrought by the Virgin Mary were brought from faraway France to the tiny community of Métis farmers at St. Laurent by Brother Piquet, a Roman Catholic priest who arrived in 1879. Struck by the resemblance between the site near the spring in the St. Laurent hillside and the grotto of Our Lady of Lourdes in the Hautes-Pyrénées region of France, he worked to establish a shrine on the Prairies.

Help came from an unexpected quarter. Charles Nolin, a former member of the Manitoba Legislature, pledged to donate a statue of Our Lady of Lourdes to the shrine if his wife, who was suffering from a disease the doctors were unable to cure, was helped. But allow Arlene and Robin Karpan to continue the story. They are the authors of *Saskatchewan Guide to Historic Sites of the North West Rebellion* (1985):

> On December 16, 1884, a religious novena began and the Lourdes water was applied to Mrs. Nolin's ailing body. She reported a burning sensation, followed by a feeling of comfort. She made a complete recovery from her illness and lived to the age of seventy-nine. Mr. Nolin made good his promise, and placed the statue of St. Laurent on November 1, 1885, just a few months after the fateful battle at nearby Batoche.

In the years following the North West Rebellion, St. Laurent became known as a religious centre and a shrine for cures. According to the Karpans, ''In 1893, Brother Guillet, who was crippled in one leg, made a pilgrimage to the shrine and was cured. Thus began the custom of walking from Duck Lake to St. Laurent. The first organized pilgrimage took place in 1905, and it has been an annual tradition for thousands of people ever since.''

Two pilgrimages to the Métis Lourdes are arranged each year and they are held on 15-16 July and on the Saturday and Sunday closest to 15 August. Close to the log church of St. Laurent stands a large Christ on the Cross, which marks the site of an early reported miracle. A plaque on the back of the life-size crucifix explains: "Here appeared the shadow of the cross showing a close outline of our crucified Lord." In 1890, apparently, a miraculous shadow darkened the interior of the convent that once stood on this ground. It darkened the interior for several days and was witnessed by many people who could find no rational explanation for the phenomenon.

The statue and the grotto are situated in a heavily wooded area. Near the base of the hill appears the original statue of Our Lady of Lourdes donated by the grateful Charles Nolin in 1885. The inscription on the base reads: "Don de Mme C. Nolin." Across the trail from the statue will be found the grotto and sanctuary which have been rebuilt over the years, most recently in 1951. A circular trail through the trees takes one through the Stations of the Cross and to the other side of the grotto. Yet another trail leads one to the edge of a cliff overlooking the South Saskatchewan River and a ravine, a place of particular beauty long frequented by the Indian and Métis.

South Saskatchewan River/ Medicine Wheel

On the north rim of the South Saskatchewan River Valley, just inside the Saskatchewan border and east of the town of Empress, Alberta, lies the Roy Rivers Medicine Wheel. This configuration of boulders was named after a local farmer Roy Rivers who has safeguarded the Indian medicine wheel. Mr. Rivers, with his daughter, Mrs. Velma Booker, runs the farm where the site is found.

The shape of the Roy Rivers Medicine Wheel is a circle broken on the south by an opening from which a parallel pair of lines of stones leads inward to a large central cairn. On the northwestern portion of the circle lies a smaller but prominent cairn of stones, and within the circle are 15 still smaller cairns, each about

3 feet in diameter and 1.5 feet high, incompletely surrounding the central cairn. Also within the circle, like the small cairns approximately midway between the central cairn and the peripheral circle, is a figure constructed of stones 1.5 feet or smaller in diameter. When it was mapped some years ago, this figure was assumed to represent a man. But closer examination in 1975 suggested that it might be a "sunburst" with one radiating line disturbed from position.

It was observed on 24 June 1975 that the sun at summer solstice set directly over this figure for an observer stationed on the central cairn. No other solar or stellar alignments were apparent at this site. The information above came from Alice B. and Thomas F. Kehoe's *Solstice-aligned Boulder Configurations in Saskatchewan* (1979).

Tipperary Creek/ Medicine Wheel

Tipperary Creek, a small valley on the bank of the South Saskatchewan River, is located north of Saskatoon. In the valley are a total of fifteen prehistoric sites, including a medicine wheel.

The wheel is a circle of stones twenty feet in diameter, surrounded by an outer ring of fifty feet and marked by three outlying cairns. The wheel was built within the last 1500 years, estimated Ernie Walker, archaeologist at the University of Saskatoon. "You can find virtually every type of archaeological site encountered in the Northern Plains in this small area," he told the Canadian Press. "It is a continuum that leads right into the coming of the pioneers. The occurrence of these sites within walking distance of each other in a completely natural setting adjacent to a major urban area is unprecedented."

The Tipperary Creek site includes, besides the medicine wheel, a buffalo drop, tipi rings, and habitation sites (including the remains of a 1903 homestead). One dig revealed no fewer than fourteen successive layers of artifacts, including teeth and bones, trade beads, ceramics, fire-cracked rock, fragments of a clam shell, and a bone needle.

According to the CP story published in the *Toronto*

Star, 18 March 1984, the Saskatchewan government is to declare the area a provincial heritage site.

Turtle Lake/
The Turtle Lake Terror

The Turtle Lake Terror takes its name from Turtle Lake in southwestern Saskatchewan. In winter, it tears huge holes in the nets of local fishermen. In summer, it frightens swimmers and boaters. According to the Canadian Press story carried by the Niagara Falls *Review*, 31 January 1979, the huge monster has three humps, a long neck, and the head of a horse, pig, or dog, depending on the report of the observer. The Turtle Lake Terror has been dismissed as being a large sturgeon. There are reports of a monster appearing in the lake since the mid-1920s.

Weyburn/
The Word "Psychedelic"

It is a curious fact that the word "psychedelic" was coined not in Los Angeles or in Zurich, where one might expect to find its first use, but in Weyburn, a city which lies southeast of Regina. The word means "mind-expanding," and was introduced to characterize the disorienting effects of certain psychoactive substances, some of which were being tested by Dr. Humphry Osmond and Dr. Abram Hoffer, psychiatrists engaged in such research at the Weyburn Psychiatric Hospital.

The word first appeared in print in a scientific paper written by Dr. Osmond in 1957. The title of the paper was "A Review of the Clinical Effects of Psychotomimetic Agents." At that time Dr. Osmond was director of psychiatric research in the department of public health in Saskatoon. Dr. Hoffer was professor of psychiatry at the University of Saskatchewan. At Weyburn they were experimenting with mescaline, a natural form of the synthesized hallucinogenic drug Lysergic Acid Diethylamide (or LSD).

It was Dr. Osmond who administered mescaline to Aldous Huxley. The essayist and novelist was then living in Hollywood, California, where he was trying to understand the visionary or mystical experience and trying to place it in a clinical context. After he took mescaline and had the sensation he wrote two slim books in which he described the experience and explored the personal, social, and spiritual consequences of this new type of drug-taking. These books were *The Doors of Perception* (1954) and *The Gates of Heaven and Hell* (1956). Through these doors, these gates, marched the so-called Psychedelic Movement of the 1960s.

Huxley took to the drug, but not to Dr. Osmond's term. He rejected the word "psychedelic," which he found to be a garbled mixture of Greek and Latin. In his place he proposed his own term, "phanerothyme," meaning "to reveal the soul." Dr. Osmond was not impressed. In response, according to Michael Horowitz and Cynthia Palmer, editors of Huxley's *Moksha: Writings on Psychedelics and the Visionary Experience, 1931-1963* (1977), he composed a ditty to argue his case. This is how it ran: "To make this mundane world sublime, / Take half a gram of phanerothyme. / To sink in Hell or soar angelic, / You'll need a pinch of psychedelic."

Had not Dr. Osmond's term caught on, social historians would be referring not to the Psychedelic Movement, which sounds rather expansive, but to the Phanerothyme Movement, which sounds rather medicinal.

Yorkton/
The Girl of the Crossroads

The city of Yorkton, in the eastern part of the province, is more renowned for the Yorkton International Film Festival (which is devoted to documentary rather than feature films) than it is for psychic manifestations. Yet it has experienced one or two of the latter and these predate the founding of the Festival in 1950. The most memorable concerns the Girl of the Crossroads.

The ghost of a small girl three or four years old was commonly seen at the crossroads near the Telsky Farm on the outskirts of Yorkton. The girl appeared to be unattended and stood for long periods of time at the side of the road. No one saw her come or go; she was either there or not. Should someone approach to question her, she would vanish. She was seen for decades yet never appeared to age. "The people in the community came to accept her presence," wrote Sheila Hervey in *Some Canadian Ghosts* (1973). "No explanation was ever found to account for this child's sporadic appearances."

ALBERTA

Banff/
The Lost Room

Banff Springs Hotel, which overlooks the stunning, picturesque beauty of the Bow Valley, was built by the Canadian Pacific Railway in 1888. The story goes that in the early 1900s, when the new wings were being added, the architects made a serious error, leaving space for a room with no doors or windows. They revised the blueprints to disguise their error and instructed the builders and workers to seal off the area and keep quiet about it. When the new wings were burnt in the fire of 1926, the lost room was eventually found.

It was empty, of course, but attention was drawn to its location along one of the corridors which had long been the focus of eerie disturbances. Night watchmen complained that a shadowy figure flitted down this hall. There were rumours of service being supplied by an elderly bellhop, when all the bellhops in the employ of the hotel were young.

The hotel's Rob Roy Lounge is said to have numerous ghostly guests. Besides the apparition of a bride who fell down a stairway and broke her neck, guests and staff have reported a headless bagpiper, disembodied carollers in the men's room, and a deceased barkeeper who informs imbibers when they have had enough to drink.

Some of these details appear in Linda Curtis's article in the Calgary *Herald*, 28 April 1983.

Big Horn/
Silent Watcher

Big Horn Dam is located not far from the Big Horn Indian Reserve on the North Saskatchewan River. The dam has or had a "silent watcher," as John Green reports in *Sasquatch: The Apes Among Us* (1978). The morning of 24 August, 1969 a construction worker at the dam site noticed:

> . . . a dark figure on the high bank over half a mile away and 300 feet above him. It looked like a large man standing watching what was going on. The figure stayed there for about half an hour, sitting down part of the time, and walking a considerable distance along the edge of the bank before it disappeared in the trees. Before it left the number of men watching it had increased to five. Although it was on the same side of the river as they were there was a loop of the river between them, so they could not readily approach it. They did try waving to it, without result. They thought it was too big for a man, but did not appreciate its real size until two of them went over where it had been. Using the small trees in the background for comparison the other men, still watching from below, estimated that the creature was at least 12 feet high and likely 15 feet. No footprints were found.

One wonders what the Big Horn Dam looked like to the "silent watcher."

Calgary/
The Deane House

The Deane House is a three-storey, porched house dating back to 1906. As the only surviving building from the original Fort Calgary site, it was recently restored and reopened by Alberta Culture. It is said to be haunted. It certainly has had a chequered past.

The house was named after Richard Burton Deane, Superintendent of the Royal North West Mounted Police. Although he disliked the house, he lived in it until 1914, when it was acquired by the Grand Trunk Pacific Railway for use as a railway station and station-master's house. It was moved to a new location that year and moved again in 1929. Remodelled and refurbished, it became a rooming house known as the Gaspé Lodge. In 1973 it was taken over by the Dandelion Co-op for artists' and authors' studios.

Rumours that the Deane House was haunted circulated between the years 1979 and 1985 when it was deserted. From time to time a woman who was said to resemble Mrs. Deane was seen standing on the enclosed porch. It was said that the murder-suicide of a husband and wife took place at the time it was called Gaspé Lodge. There is the suggestion that the house now stands on an Indian burial ground. Haunted houses burst into flames from time to time. In 1985, there was a fire in the attic and on the third floor, but firemen were fortunately able to bring it under control.

Monika Tremblay, a Calgary psychic, toured the house in 1982 and described her impressions to a television audience as "terrifying." She said, "As I walked through the front room, it felt like I was walking on Jello, and then I actually witnessed the murder. Right before my eyes, I saw a man chasing a woman with an axe. He then bludgeoned her to death while two children hid in fright in a secret compartment in the kitchen." She also described someone bleeding and stumbling down the steps. In the living room, she saw an old man sitting in a rocking chair, smoking a pipe, and staring out of the window. Her description matched that of Superin-tendent Deane, the original resident. In the basement, the psychic claimed she encountered an old Indian spirit which said: "This is a secret burial ground — please don't disturb us."

There have been no further reports of spirits or spectres since 1986, when the house was opened to the public as a tearoom and historical museum.

Calgary/
The Coste House

The Coste House is the name of a twenty-eight room mansion built in 1913 on Amherst Street in Mount Royal. From 1946 to 1958, it served as the headquarters of the Allied Arts Council. It is said to be haunted.

According to Debra Cummings, columnist for the *Calgary Sun*, 13 March 1987, the mansion was abandoned during the Depression and fell into ruin over the years. It was renovated and during the twelve years it was used as an arts centre there were stories that it was haunted by a ghostly Dr. Carmichael who wandered its corridors, flitted from room to room, slammed doors, and creaked floor boards.

"Some say Coste left an attendant who later died in the dwelling," Cummings added. "Others claim the house sits on an Indian burial site."

Calgary/
The Haunted Firehalls

There is a tradition in Calgary that two of its old firehalls are haunted by phantom horses. The stations in question are No. 3 (East Calgary) and No. 6 (Hillhurst).

William G. Ritchie was a Captain with the Calgary Fire Department. He joined the Department in 1911 and served until retirement in 1951. He died four years later, but during his life as a firefighter, he saw the transition from horse-drawn rigs to motorized vehicles. Horses were finally replaced about 1925. Captain Ritchie was stationed at both firehalls, serv-

The Calgary Fire Department maintains two old firehalls which, according to local tradition, are haunted by teams of phantom horses. The horses are heard to clomp whenever a fire breaks out in the vicinity. The sounds of the phantom horses were reported from 1942 to 1945 at Firehall No. 6 at Hillhurst, shown here as it appeared in 1987. [W. Ritchie Benedict]

ing first at No. 3. From 1942 to 1945, he worked at No. 6. He claimed that the firemen of both stations —and among them he included himself—could hear the sounds of phantom horses.

"My father told me about an odd phenomenon that would often occur just before the alarm would ring for a fire," his daughter Muriel H. Ritchie recalled in 1987. "Both he and the other firemen on the second floor would hear the feet of horses clomping down below where the horses were formerly quartered. I understand this happened at both No 3 (which today is a modern restaurant) and No. 6 (which is now used for equipment storage)."

Calgary/
The Capitol Hill House

The following report on the Capitol Hill House was prepared by W. Ritchie Benedict, a Calgary writer

and researcher with a special interest in the paranormal.

A small, nondescript bungalow located in the Capitol Hill district of Calgary was the scene of a bizarre disappearance in March 1929. Thomas C. Hall, a recluse, vanished. Nineteen years later his remains were found below the floorboards of the house, semi-mummified in the soil. He had been shot in the head. Although the police identified a suspect — a friend who had often played cards with Hall—there was no proof he was the murderer.

That should have been the end of it, but it wasn't. The body was found in 1948. Cecil Pearce, the owner of the house from 1948 to 1956, reported that before the discovery of the corpse his three daughters had complained that "a mysterious clammy hand" had poked one of them. Also prior to the grisly discovery was the experience of another previous owner, Elizabeth Irish, who often complained of feeling uneasy in the house. As late as August 1982, Rick Passey, a young steelworker who lived there, complained of unexplained knockings at the front door.

Edith Taylor, who had lived in the neighbourhood for forty years, always felt there was something unnatural about the house. She recalled that not long after the discovery of the body a horrible thing had happened. The families that lived in three houses which were set in the shape of a triangle on land once used by Hall to graze his horses—he was a teamster—all reported the deaths of children. She said Hall's house had been a source of bad luck to everyone who has lived there. Families were always breaking up. In one instance, a husband chased his wife around the block with a knife.

Calgary/
The Canmore Opera House

The Canmore Opera House was used in 1898 by miners at Canmore for concerts and band practices. Later it served as a hospital and retirement home for miners, until it was shut down in 1960 and five years later moved to Calgary, where it is part of the city's Heritage Park.

The Opera House was put to good use by various musical and dramatic groups from 1965 to 1985. It was during the summer of 1975 that performers and employees alike began to note that a number of odd things were happening. The administrative director of Alberta Theatre Projects was quoted as saying: "I'm reluctant to state we have a ghost, but a large number of staff people claim to have either seen or heard what they say is a ghost." She herself saw nothing, but added: "I've had a feeling there was something present and heard someone walking upstairs in the building when there was definitely no one else around. It's not a publicity stunt either! There have been a lot of incidents that we haven't been able to explain."

Many of the incidents centre around a young man with long blond hair who is dressed in turn-of-the-century clothing. An historian employed by Heritage Park noted that the young man in question who seems to enjoy eavesdropping on the theatrical productions fits the description of Sam Livingstone, a homesteader on the grounds of Heritage Park, who died in 1897. Since he was an Irishman, the suggestion is that his spirit likes to listen to the musicals now and then.

Two directors of Alberta Psychic Society spent a night at the Opera House during the winter of 1974-75. The next morning they claimed that they felt "some kind of presence there." They determined that the presence was persistent but not malevolent.

The last known report of anyone sensing anyone or anything was in the early 1980s when, during a theatrical performance, two actresses complained to the stage manager about a stranger who had been allowed backstage. They said they saw a man sitting on the stairs. When the stage manager checked, there was no trace of anyone.

It is difficult to know whether or not such manifestations will continue since the Opera House is no longer in use for theatrical presentations. If the managers of Heritage Park decide to shut down the Opera House, then (to paraphrase Shirley Jackson), "What ever walks there will walk alone."

Calgary/ The Third Eye

Calgary was the last home of Cyril Henry Hoskins (1911-1981), the Englishman from Devon who became the centre of a controversy when, as T. Lobsang Rampa, he published a book called *The Third Eye* (1956). The bestselling book purported to be the autobiography of a Tibetan monk whose clairvoyant powers had been activated by an operation performed in a lamasery in Tibet. The identity of the author was kept secret by Sir Stanley Unwin who published the book, and remained a secret until a firm of private detectives was engaged by irate scholars to run the author down, which they did in short order.

The book was controversial for two reasons. It described in some detail a medically impossible operation. While a student of Buddhism in the lamasery, the author claims he had a hole bored into his forehead in order to "activate" the pineal gland. This gland is identified as the Third Eye which releases clairvoyant powers. The book was also controversial because its details of everyday life in Tibet divided the scholarly community. Some scholars argued that they could only be derived from first-hand experience; other scholars maintained that they had been cribbed from travel books.

The controversy was decided against the author when the Cyril Henry Hoskins/T. Lobsang Rampa connection was demonstrated. Few readers bought Hoskins's ingenious if inevitable explanation that both sides were right: he himself had never been to Tibet but the author of the book had, for when he wrote the book his body was taken over by the spirit of the Tibetan monk to whom all that was described had occurred. The press levelled charges of fraud against the author with the appearance of each new Rampa book. There were nineteen in all, but soon readers stopped buying them in quantity, and they began to appear only in paperback editions issued by lesser-known mass-market publishers.

To escape the negative publicity and high tax rates in England, Hoskins settled in Ireland and then in Canada. He arrived in Canada in 1958, legally changed his name to T. Lobsang Rampa—the T standing for Tuesday—and became a Canadian citizen in 1973. He lived briefly in a number of towns and cities, including Tecumseh (near Windsor), Fort Erie, Prescott, Saint John, Montreal (in Habitat in 1967), and Vancouver before settling in Calgary. He and his wife loved that city. His book *As It Was*! (1976) bears a unique inscription: "Dedicated to the City of Calgary, where I have had peace and quiet and freedom from interference in my personal affairs. Thank you, City of Calgary."

The last seven years of his life he spent occupying a two-bedroom apartment overlooking the downtown area but lacking a view of the Rockies. In failing health, he had a motorized wheelchair which he drove along 8th Avenue S.W., particularly on weekends when there was little downtown traffic. He died on Sunday, 25 January 1981, and was cremated the following day. There is no burial or memorial site. He was survived by his widow, an author in her own right. As Mama San Ra-ab Rampa, she wrote at least two mystic books, *Pussy Willow* (1976) and *Tigerlily* (1978).

The saga of the man with or without "the third eye" is a fascinatingly grotesque story of the willingness of readers to accept the most outrageous things when they are found between the covers of hardbound books and when they conform to their expectations, no matter how extraordinary or sensationalistic they may be.

Camrose/
"Fairy Circles"

Folklorists are familiar with "fairy circles," which are circular paths in fields and woods made by the trampling of feet, specifically those of the fairy-folk. Specialists in urban lore are familiar with the circular patterns in another context. They crop up in UFO literature, where the presence of a ring is generally held to be evidence of the landing of an unidentified flying object. Botanists know them too but as fungal infections.

The Camrose circles or rings are well known to UFOlogists. Researcher W.K. Allan investigated and photographed several strange circles on the ground in the vicinity of Camrose in August 1966. Each ring measured between thirty-three and thirty-six feet in diameter. "The imprinted bands, which eventually turned to an off-white colour, were about six inches wide."

The first discovery of rings on the farm of Edgar Shielker at Camrose was dismissed by some authorities as caused by fungus, yet others, like Larry Williams, the district agriculturalist, said of the sight, "I certainly can't account for it; I was expecting to find 'fairy circles' when I went out there, but it doesn't have any of the usual symptoms." He found the circles too regular for fungus growth, adding, "I've never seen anything like the depressed rings and imprints on the turf."

W.K. Allan reasoned that an incredible weight or pressure had to be applied to leave a permanent indentation in the pasture. "Where the pasture had a slope, one of the rings was in the form of an ellipse with the long axis in the direction of maximum slope. Since the level rings were circular, this suggests the effect was due to a horizontal circular source above the ground." The quotations come from *UFOs Over the Americas* (1968) by Jim and Coral Lorenzen.

Cardson/
Mormons and the Ten Lost Tribes

The town of Cardson, southwest of Lethbridge, was founded by a group of Mormon settlers who trekked from Utah to the Canadian prairies in 1887. They were led to that part of the prairies by Charles Ora Card, the son-in-law of Brigham Young. The community was named in his honour. For sixty-odd years it was the site of Canada's single Mormon temple, an immense and imposing white granite building erected in 1913-23 in the shape of a Maltese cross.

Mormons are members of the Church of Jesus Christ of Latter-day Saints, a religion which was founded in Upper State New York in 1830 and which has been called the first true (non-native) religion of American origin. Joseph Smith, the founder, and

315

Brigham Young, his successor, both proselytized in Upper Canada. Members accept as inspired words both the Bible and the Book of Mormon. They see the latter as a continuation of the Bible — specifically its account of the fate of the House of Israel in America.

One of the mysteries of history has always been: What happened to the Ten Lost Tribes of Israel? The simple answer is, they were either annihilated or assimilated into the vast Assyrian empire. According to the Bible they went into "another land." But according to the Book of Mormon, their fate was otherwise. They left the Middle East and immigrated to the Americas. Once there they introduced their advanced ideas, notably monotheism, and assimilated into the native populations. They divided into two warring camps, and on the Hill of Cumorrah, near present-day Palmyra, New York, they fought a terrific, Armageddon-like battle.

The notion that the Indians of North and South America are the descendants of the members of the Ten Lost Tribes of Israel has a long and circuitous history. Descendants of the northern kingdom, who otherwise disappeared from history, have been "located" in numerous places, including Mesopotamia, Ethiopia, Turkey, Persia, Afghanistan, Arabia, and Africa. No so long ago Arthur Koestler argued that the Khazars were the descendants of the Ten Lost Tribes.

From 1492 on, the indigenous peoples of Peru, Yucatan, and Mexico were scrutinized for their "Jewishness." When the seaboard was more fully explored, speculation expanded to more northern and western tribal groups. The notion had special appeal to early Americans like Cotton Mather, Roger Williams, and William Penn, and to eccentric Englishmen. To varying degrees they inspected the physiognomy, language, customs, traditions, practices, and beliefs of the North American Indian groups for what they could regard as "proofs" of their Israelite origin. Any parallel practices were cited as unassailable evidence. Specially favoured groups were the Ojibway, the Algonquins, and the Mandans.

The question was even considered by the Jesuit missionary and author Pierre-François Xavier de Charlevois, who travelled through New France between 1720 and 1723. He heard many stories from travellers about parellel Indian-Israelite practices, but he dismissed them as evidence of "a very lively Imagination." The Church of Jesus Christ of Latter-day Saints is the only religion to make the Israelite-Indian connection a matter of dogma — so far, at least.

Dinosaur Provincial Park/ Mass Death

Dinosaur Provincial Park lies northeast of Brooks in the Badlands of Alberta along the Red Deer River Valley. The park's "bone beds" are the sites of mass deaths for the area's dinosaur population. The mass extinction occurred at the end of the Mesozoic era about 65 million years ago, and the causes are still being debated. It is interesting to note that the dinosaur, as ancient as it is, was unknown to science until the year 1824.

Since 1910, Alberta's fossil deposits have yielded over 500 museum-quality dinosaur skeletons, including skeletons of Tyrannosaurus rex (the most popular of all the dinosaurs), Albertosaurus (named after the province in which its remains are found), and Stenonychosaurus (also called Troödon and believed to be the most intelligent of all the prehistoric beasts).

Two bone beds of importance today are the Centrosaurus Bone Bed, which covers 2990 square yards and contains the remains of at least seventy members of the genus Centrosaurus, and the Pachyrhinosaurus Bone Bed which is smaller. Although only about 19 square yards of the latter have been excavated, the area has yielded five skeletons. Both beds were discovered in the 1970s. The horned, plant-eating Centrosaurus was first described by Lawrence Lambe in 1904, and the smaller, bone-nosed Pachyrhinosaurus by Charles Sternberg in 1950.

Some of the world's richest dinosaur bone beds are in Dinosaur Provincial Park which has been designated by UNESCO a World Heritage Site. Much of the fossil material excavated resides in the Tyrrell Museum of Palaeontology located in nearby Drumheller.

Penelope the Plesiosaur was the name given this life-size replica of a prehistoric beast by the visitors to Calgary's Dinosaur Park. The long-necked Plesiosaurus was a marine reptile which flourished in the Alberta region some 130 million years ago. Penelope was commissioned by the Calgary Zoo in the early 1930s and constructed from reinforced concrete by John Kanerva, a local handyman. Kanerva ultimately built more than fifty models of such beasts for the zoo. Kanerva once said, "The dinosaurs were created before God, you know." [Travel Alberta]

Edmonton/
The Last Sun Dance

The Sun Dance was performed by the Cree and Black-foot Indians on the river-flats in the heart of the area now known as the City of Edmonton. The six-day ceremony was observed in the late 1870s by the young Richard Hardisty (1871-1942), the first white child born in Rupert's Land. He never forgot the event, and in later years he referred to it as "The Last Sun-dance." This was the title of a posthumously published account reprinted by Edith Fowke in *Folklore of Canada* (1976).

About one hundred braves sat around an "Idol Pole" decorated with streamers. Six braves who had signalled their willingness to face the ordeal of the test of torture to prove their bravery as warriors invoked the presence of the Sun. A pointed stick about four inches long was selected for each youth. Hardisty explained, "Now the medicine man gathers as much of the flesh of the youth's chest as he can between his thumb and forefinger, forcing the stick through the flesh." When each youth was skewered, the sticks were linked to the pole and the pole was raised and slowly turned.

The drums beat, the medicine man cavorts, the war whoop rings out, there is a frenzy of movement and sound. The young men, their legs extended, their bodies thrown back, their

317

weight carried by that portion of their flesh punctured by the stick, sway back and forth, blood streaming down their bodies from their wounds, sweat pouring from them. They leap and tumble, but utter no sound. The agony must continue until the flesh is torn through and they are free.

In less than fifteen minutes of agony, the youths were free of the skewers and were welcomed into the community of warriors. Over the six-day period, forty-eight young men endured such torture to prove their manhood.

Hardisty wrote about other aspects of the Sun Dance—the food, the drink, the contests, the drums, the medicine men—and concluded:

> I had spent much of the time during the week running about, taking in everything to be seen. Yet on the morning following the last day of the festival I was up early and out on the balcony of the Big House. I looked over the flat, there was no sign of life—the flat was deserted. Nothing but the skeleton of the Sun Temple was to be seen.
>
> The Camp had moved at dawn.

Edmonton/
UFO's and the Canada Council

At one time it was the policy of the Canada Council to announce the names of its new award-holders and to include with the press release thumbnail descriptions of the projects that their adjudicators had found worthy. The policy is no longer in force because the press took the descriptions as open invitations to ridicule some of the projects sight unseen. So the Council was subsidizing a Marxist scholar with a grant of one thousand dollars? Three thousand dollars was going to the City of Vancouver to employ a "town-fool"? Someone was to receive five thousand dollars to investigate flying saucers? Wherever would it all end?

The Canada Council made the latter award in 1975 in its Explorations Programme, which was designed to take a broad view of the cultural horizon by encouraging projects of study and creation outside the usual disciplines and regular categories of competition. The award "to investigate flying saucers," as the press would have it, was made to John Brent Musgrave.

Musgrave is currently an Educational Consultant in Edmonton. He was born in 1941 in Minneapolis, Minnesota, and studied at the University of Chicago and Yale University. At the time of the grant he was a freelance writer. Now he is the author of the sixty-six page report *UFO Occupants and Critters: The Patterns in Canada* (1979), the preface to which makes the following point:

> As part of their Explorations Programme, the Canada Council awarded me a grant in 1975 to help prepare a book on the history of the UFO phenomenon across Canada. The purpose of this proposed work was, and is, at least twofold; to document the social history of a phenomenon, and to collect as many UFO case histories, past and present, that have been reported in Canada. This small book is in part a progress report on one kind of case history being collected for this on-going project.

Musgrave examined almost one hundred Canadian eyewitness reports of UFO "occupants and critters." Probably Musgrave's most original contribution to this field of study consists of his grouping of the reports into nine categories which begin with Type 0 (insufficient information). The picturesque terms he uses for Types 1 through 8 are: Fly-by; stopping for the view; stroller—no UFO; stroller—UFO; tourist; pit-stop; peeping tom; molester/contact.

Since the appearance of his report, one of the categories — Musgrave's Type 8 (molester/contact), which corresponds to J. Allen Hynek's "Close Encounters of the Third Kind"—has literally "taken off." Witness the success of books like *Communion: A True Story* (1987) by Whitley Strieber, a horror-story author. They suggest that certain human beings have been selected by nonhumans — aliens or critters — and irregularly but repeatedly subjected to extensive physical examination and psychological probing over extended periods of time for purposes which remain incomprehensible. Extreme disorientation is one of the costs of the experience; memory loss and hallucinations are others. These "abductees" in an earlier age would have been described as "haunted," "possessed," or "damned."

Musgrave is less interested in the nonhuman abduction scenario than he is in the nature of "the UFO experience." When asked by Ronald D. Storey for a statement for *The Encyclopedia of UFOs* (1980), he replied: "UFO reports are . . . empirical observations from folk wisdom and tradition. They represent real events; but few scientists are willing to use them as starting points or keys for understanding the world. It goes against their training and practice."

He was also quoted by the *Edmonton Journal* on 23 July 1976 : "What we're investigating is a new global phenomenon that's worthy of scientific study . . . and, in all probability, the crafts come from elsewhere. But that is only a good working hypothesis."

Fort Macleod/ Childerhose Photographs

A cross-Canada speed record was set by RCAF Squadron Leader Robert J. Childerhose and Flight Lieutenant Ralph Innis in their F-86 Sabre jet in August 1956. They established a speed record of five hours which remained unchallenged for over ten years. But when their flight is recalled it is usually in connection with their report and photographs of a UFO.

While flying at an altitude of 36,000 feet over southern Alberta on 23 August, they spotted a glowing mass in the vicinity of thunder clouds over the town of Fort Macleod. Childerhose succeeded in photographing what could be an instance of "ball lightning." An analysis of the so-called Childerhose Photographs shows an "intensely brilliant oval-shaped object, which emitted a plasma-like glow from its underside."

This is the well-known Childerhose Photograph of a UFO. It was taken by RCAF Squadron Leader Robert J. (Chick) Childerhose on 23 August 1956. At the time it was taken he was flying a F-86 Sabre jet at an altitude of 36,000 feet. Amid the clouds over the southern Alberta town of Fort Macleod, he saw and photographed in colour a bright, white, glowing, plasma-like object, oval in shape. The sighting was widely reported at the time and the Childerhose Photograph was widely reproduced. [R.J. Childerhose]

319

Frog Lake/
The Massacre and the Mystery

The Frog Lake Massacre, an incident in the North West Rebellion, took place on 2 April 1885. Wandering Spirit, with a band of Big Bear's Cree, murdered two priests and a number of settlers at Frog Lake, north of the North Saskatchewan River.

The events surrounding the massacre were not without their mystery, according to Theresa Gowanlock who was nineteen years old when she survived the massacre. She recalled the events immediately thereafter in *Two Months in the Camp of Big Bear: The Life and Adventures of Theresa Gowanlock and Theresa Delaney* (1885). The mystery connected with the event is recorded in books of mysteries but not in histories. For instance, Warren Smith retold the story in the chapter titled "The Vision that Stopped a Rebellion" in *Strange Powers of Mind* (1968).

The Indian Reserve near Onion Lake, west of Fort Pitt, was the setting for the events prior to the massacre. In late March, the Cree leaders met here and demanded open rebellion against the white settlers and the militia. Big Bear cautioned against an uprising. The pow-wow was joined by a fat old woman with unkempt black hair who uttered a series of incantations and went into a trance. She too cautioned against rebellion. "No brave can move fast enough to outrun the soldiers who have a thousand bullets for every Indian brave."

The situation was unstable. A few days later, the morning of 2 April, the warriors surrounded the homestead of John Delaney. They took ten captives, including Theresa Gowanlock, and led them to the church at Frog Lake, where two priests, conducting Mass, quickly concluded the divine service. Then the warriors murdered all the male prisoners, including the two priests. Young Theresa Gowanlock and Mrs. Theresa Delaney, the wife of settler John Delaney, were spared to watch the mutilation of the bodies. The settlement was looted and the church was set afire.

The two women captives were taken to Onion Lake where the old woman appeared again, Cassan-dra-like, to predict that no good would come of the rebellion. Fearful of the militia's revenge, the Cree took to the country, dragging their two captives with them. Even in retreat the old woman would not keep quiet but predicted destruction. Big Bear ordered her killed. She was dragged into the bushes and axed to death, her body being left for the wolves.

In late May the Cree were still on the run. One cloudy morning, Theresa Gowanlock reported that the Cree observed the clouds part and an image of the church of Frog Lake appear in the sky. The church was observed to burst into flame. A rider on a white horse galloped up to the flaming church and dismounted, stretching out his hand as if to bless the fiery church. Then the clouds closed over the vision.

"We are doomed," Big Bear cried out. "Our world of beauty has vanished forever." The warriors began to quarrel and threaten one another. They were heedless of the approaching militia. Two days later they were surrounded by the militia at Frenchman's Butte. Some warriors fled, others were killed. Big Bear surrendered in July and was tried and sentenced to two years' imprisonment. He died almost immediately upon his release.

Gleichen/
Ancient Sacrificial Stone

A curious object, an ancient sacrificial stone, was found somewhere on the Prairies and described by Jean L'Heureux, a government interpreter at the Blackfoot Indian Reserve near the town of Gleichen.

The stone is a rough boulder approximately fourteen inches in circumference with a planed surface oddly engraved with the figures of a shining star and a crescent moon. L'Heureux wrote a descriptive paper on the strange stone the year of its discovery, 1882, which was read before the British Association for the Advancement of Science meeting in Montreal. He called it a "marked stone—Kitsipokotoks—and also a Kekip-Sesoators, relating it directly to the sacrificial stones of the Toltecs and the Aztecs. It is uncertain whether it was inscribed in the Alberta District or brought there by the Nahuas or mound-builders of old.

L'Heureux described the place where it was found. "Elevated two hundred feet above the level of the surrounding plain, Kekip-Sesoaters, the hill of the Blood Sacrifice, stands like a huge pyramidal Mound commanding an extensive view of both Red Deer and Bow River valleys." He referred to the site as "the Altar of the Temple of Nature," suggesting it was the stone upon which the Blood Indians performed their sacrifices, like the ritual excision of a finger, a limb, or a heart. He went as far as to supply a translation of a traditional invocation which would likely be intoned above the stone: "Hail, O Episors, O Morning Star, Lord of the Night! Hail! Hear me! Regard me from above. To Thee I give of my blood. I give of my flesh. Glorious is Thy coming, all powerful in battle, Son of the Sun! I worship Thee. Hear my prayer. Grant me my petition, O Episors."

L'Heureux presented the stone to Governor General Lord Lorne who in turn deposited it with the museum authorities in Ottawa. It is now part of the holdings of the National Museum of Civilization, formerly the National Museum of Man. The stone remains something of an enigma according to an article on it which reprints L'Heureux's scholarly paper in the *Alberta Historical Review*, Autumn 1959.

Highwood River/ UFO Photographs

The Smith Colour UFO Photographs are two photos of a circular, shiny object in flight. They were taken at 5:30 p.m., 3 July 1967, by Warren P. Smith, who was prospecting in the mountainous wooded area of Highwood River with two friends, Lorne Grovue, and Craig Dunn. Highwood River is some 80 miles southwest of Calgary.

This UFO sighting and the accompanying photos constitute a "classic case." Smith, the photographer, made the following statement under oath:

At the time of the sighting, we were walking and facing in an easterly direction when we sighted an object no higher than 2,000 feet and

at a distance not any farther than a couple of miles. It was travelling towards us, gradually losing altitude, passing in front of us, and as it passed slightly out of view behind some trees, it then reappeared and hovered in the open sky and something of a much smaller size fell from the craft. I, Warren P. Smith, took two (2) pictures of this strange craft and *swear* to the best of my knowledge that there were no other humans in that area and that there was no camera trickery involved.

Smith's statement was quoted by Paul Grescoe in *Weekend Magazine*, 25 May 1968. The colour photographs were examined by J. Allen Hynek, consultant to the USAF's Project Blue Book, who detected no signs of trickery. In fact, Hynek called one of the photos the "best Daylight Disc photograph I have personally investigated." The photographs were then studied by the Defence Photo Interpretation Centre of the Department of National Defence in Ottawa.

Yurko Bondarchuk, who reproduced them in black and white in *UFO: Sightings, Landings and Abductions* (1979), published the evaluation of Colonel W.W. Turner for the Chief of Defence Staff on 17 November 1967:

Unfortunately, it has not been possible to identify or explain the object shown in the two photographs. However, it may be of interest to note that the Department of National Defence and other interested agencies in UFOs have received a number of photographs of unusual aerial sightings that can neither be identified nor explained.

The letter was then deposited with the Herzberg Institute of Astrophysics, Planetary Sciences Section, National Research Council, Non-Meteoritic Sightings File.

Given the importance of these photos to UFOlogy, it is interesting to compare the above information with what is found in *Scientific Study of Unidentified Flying Objects* (1970) by Edward U. Condon, director; Daniel S. Gillmor, editor. That study is better known as the Condon Report. Here is Condon's abstract:

321

The witness and two companions reportedly sighted and took two photographs of an object described as shiny, and approximately 25-ft. in diameter. The craft reportedly dropped a small object, which when recovered was reported to be composed of solder, aluminum, and magne-

The Smith Colour UFO Photographs are two 35 mm exposures which show the progress of an unidentified flying, disc-shaped object. The photographs were taken by Warren P. Smith of Calgary and two friends in the wooded Highwood River area southwest of Calgary at 5:30 p.m., 3 July 1967. After examining the negatives the UFOlogist J. Allen Hynek called the photographs "the archetype of the Daylight Disc." Whatever the nature of the object that was photographed, it was high in the sky and it moved with dispatch. In the original colour photographs the difference between the densities of the swollen clouds and the moving object is apparent; the difference is lost in black-and-white reproduction.
[Wendelle C. Stevens]

sium. A report by the Royal Canadian Air Force implied substantial evidence that the sighting was authentic and that the object was, subject to certain assumptions, 40 to 50 in. diameter. Although the case was widely described, both in the press and by several investigators, as being exceptionally strong, examination of the original photographs and the circumstances indicates no evidence of probative value for the existence of unusual aircraft. Only the sworn testimony of the witnesses could be described as making this case more impressive than most others.

It is useful to include yet another account, that of the above-mentioned scientist and UFOlogist J. Allen Hynek, the author of *The UFO Experience: A Scientific Inquiry* (1974). Hynek examined both original negatives, tested them, tested the camera, interviewed all three observers and obtained affidavits from two witnesses. He also flew over the Highwood region. Here is his description of the sighting:

Warren Smith and two of his companions, who prospect as a hobby, were returning from a weekend prospecting mission when, at about 5:30 p.m. on a fairly clear July day, the youngest of the three, a teenaged boy, drew his companions' attention to what at first everyone thought was a plane in trouble. No noise was heard, so they thought that the engines had been cut off. As soon as it was apparent that the object had no wings and was gliding smoothly downward, the men abandoned the airplane hypothesis.

Even before this, however, Warren Smith, who remembered that he had a loaded colour camera in his pack, called excitedly for it and started photographing. He thought that the object was an aircraft heading for a crash, and it crossed his mind that the photograph could be sold to the newspapers on their return. (This was the only time in which the idea of monetary gain entered their thinking, as far as I could gather.) One picture was reportedly obtained as the object came down toward the trees in the foreground, behind which the object soon disappeared. Then, the men reported, the object reappeared from behind the trees and ascended towards the clouds. The observers also reported that the object dropped some material, but this report was never fully substantiated.

The entire incident took some 25 seconds. The only tangible evidence we have are the two colour photographs — taken, unfortunately, with a fixed focus camera—both of which contained real images and gave no evidence whatever of having been tampered with.

The remote possibility exists that quite independently of Smith and his companions and without their knowledge, someone in the "bush" had at that moment "launched" a "platter," which Smith was "fortunate" enough to have been on hand to photograph. Yet we have both the word of Smith that the disc was first seen to descend and *then* to ascend and disappear into the clouds and the established sequence in the negatives, which shows that the stipulated descending photograph was taken first. One could argue, even then, that the invisible platter-tosser had tossed twice and that Smith photographed the descent of the first one and the ascent of the second, some 15 seconds or so later, but we have the word of the reporters (who in this case must have been independent of the tossers) that this was definitely not the case. In any event, close examination of the cloud structure shows that the two photographs were taken in close succession; even a brief interlude would have resulted in minor but detectable changes in the cloud edges. None is perceivable.

Hynek's conclusion is that this is a "classic case," for he wrote, "The Smith photographs portray quite well the archetype of the Daylight Disc . . . ."

Highwood Mountain Range/ Lost Lemon Mine

The fabulous Lost Lemon Mine may someday be found in the rocky foothills of the Highwood Mountain Range. Until that time, would-be prospectors and students of such lore will have to be content with the mysterious, romantic, and bloody tales inspired by the search for gold in those rugged hills.

Senator Daniel Riley, journalist Tom Primrose, and historian Hugh Dempsey contributed to the monograph *The Lost Lemon Mine: Greatest Mystery of the Canadian Rockies* (n.d.) which examined the legend of the Lost Lemon Mine and found it wanting—but exciting.

The story begins in March or April 1870 with a group of gold prospectors setting out from Montana to explore Alberta's Highwood Mountain Range. Two of the prospectors, Frank Lemon and a man known only as Blackjack, separated from the main party. They headed towards Tobacco Plains and beyond it they found a lush valley. By chance they stumbled on a mother-lode of ore. That night they celebrated and then fought over whether they should leave and stake their claim or remain and work their diggings. Lemon grew hysterical and axed Blackjack to death.

Unknown to Lemon the slaying was observed by two Stoney braves, William and Daniel Bendow, who contributed to Lemon's state of hysteria by making frightening noises through the rest of the night. In the morning Lemon sped off to Tobacco Plains. The braves ransacked Lemon's campsite and then returned to their reservation at Morley. There they reported the events of the previous night to their chief, Bearspaw, who swore them to secrecy lest news of the gold strike bring hordes of white men to their land. The Stoneys have kept the secret to this day.

At Tobacco Plains, Lemon made his confession to a would-be priest known as Father Jean L'Heureux. The unscrupulous L'Heureux coaxed from Lemon precise directions to the scene of the crime, and then dispatched a half-breed confederate, John McDougall, to the site. Once there McDougall buried Blackjack's body under a mound of stones. But the Stoney braves still had the scene under surveillance, and as soon as McDougall departed they hid the body and scattered the stones.

Lemon agreed to lead a party of prospectors to the site, but as he approached the scene of his crime he became increasingly unhinged. When he could not locate Blackjack's body or the mother-lode he grew hysterical. In the meantime, McDougall agreed to lead his own party to the site. But on the way he stopped at Fort Kipp, a notorious whisky-fort, where he drank himself into a stupor, then died.

L'Heureux mounted his own expedition but its progress was halted by a forest fire. Lemon agreed to lead yet another expedition but it too had to be abandoned when the prospector grew increasingly agitated as they approached the site of the slaying. Thereafter Lemon and L'Heureux abandoned their efforts to locate the mine. The quest was taken up by an American rancher and prospector named Lafayette French who on his first attempt to find the mother-lode was stricken by a mysterious illness which the Indians ascribed to a "hoodoo."

French devoted the next fifteen years of his life to the search. At first he followed a crudely drawn map

prepared by Lemon but it proved to be useless. He turned to other means, including intimidation and bribery. He threatened and then bribed William Bendow, the Stoney brave who had witnessed the slaying so many years earlier. Bendow agreed to lead French to the site. But on the way there the brave had second thoughts and refused to proceed farther. Then he died under mysterious circumstances, attributed by members of his tribe to the wrath of Wahcondah. Nevertheless, French would not abandon his quest. He wandered the area until he found what he believed to be the mother-lode. He scribbled a letter which he intended to send to a friend at Fort Benton. It was found on his body the night he died in the winter of 1912.

Even his death was dramatic. The last night of his life he returned from the Highwood Mountain Range and took refuge in an old log cabin at Emerson's Cross. It went up in flames, but French succeeded in escaping by crawling through the snow the two or so miles to the bunkhouse of the Beddington Ranch (the one later acquired by the Duke of Windsor). He died that night in the bunkhouse. His last words were: "I know all about the Lost Lemon Mine now."

Iron Creek/
The Manitou Stone

The Manitou Stone is one of a number of exhibits in the Provincial Museum in Edmonton. The story of this unusual iron meteorite is a fascinating blend of legend and history, native spirituality and Christian religiosity.

According to Blackfoot and Cree tradition, in the distant past the Manitou Stone blazed across the night sky and crashed into the bank of Battle River, north of present-day Lacombe. The Plains Indians who recovered it regarded it as a gift of the Manitou. The shiny iron stone, for all its pockmarks, seemed to feature the profile of a man's face, the Face of the Manitou. The stone was taken to a high hill, sometimes called Iron Stone in its honour, where it was venerated and treasured as a talisman.

The Manitou Stone was seen by the trader, Alexander Henry the Younger, on 2 September 1810 at White Earth House east of present-day Pakan. Then it was described by two travellers, W.B. Cheadle and Viscount Milton, in *The North-West Passage by Land* (1865). Their travel book records the Indian and Métis belief that the Manitou Stone, far from being inert, possesses power and continues to increase in weight and size.

Then in 1864 the missionary, the Rev. George M. McDougall, established a Methodist mission to the Crees at Victoria, later called Pakan, between Fort Pitt and Fort Edmonton. Two years thereafter, against native protests, he arranged for his son David to remove the Manitou Stone from its hilltop site over-

The profile of "the face of Manitou" may be discerned along the right-hand edge of the Iron Creek Meteorite. For an unknown period of time it was venerated by the Blackfoot Indians as their Manitou Stone. It was seized by Methodist missionaries in 1866 and ultimately taken to Toronto. It is now on display at the Provincial Museum of Alberta. [Provincial Museum of Alberta]

looking Iron Creek, northeast of present-day Killam, to the Victoria Mission House, where it was seen lying in the yard by Sir William Francis Butler who described it in *The Great Lone Land* (1872) as "a curious block of metal of immense weight; it was rugged, deeply indented, and polished on the outer edges of the indentations by the wear and friction of many years."

Butler went on to note that the stone was venerated by the Indians "over a vast territory" and that their medicine-men predicted that no end of catastrophies would befall the People of the Plains should their stone be kept from them. Butler added, "Never, probably, since the first trader had reached the country, had so many afflictions of war, famine, and plague fallen upon the Crees and the Blackfeet as during the year which succeeded the useless removal of their Manitou Stone from the lone hilltop upon which the skies had cast it." To these three afflictions, he might have added a fourth, the failure of the buffalo to return.

When the Manitou Stone became Methodist property it came to be regarded as an object of superstitious awe and of scientific interest, and lost whatever power it once may have possessed. It also began to travel widely. It was transported to Red River, and then to Victoria College in Cobourg, Ontario. For many years it was on display at the Royal Ontario Museum in Toronto. It remains the property of Victoria College at the University of Toronto and is on long-term loan to the Provincial Museum of Alberta. It is known to geologists as the Iron Creek Meteorite.

The meteorite was weighed by the Provincial Museum upon its arrival in 1973. Its main mass is 320 pounds, which makes it Canada's largest meteorite. To this mass must be added small portions removed and sent out to various museums world-wide. The total weight of these pieces is twenty-four ounces. In composition it is over ninety-one per cent iron, about eight per cent nickel, with traces of cobalt. It takes the shape of a low cone, nine inches high and twenty-two inches in diameter. Modern scientific opinion holds that the meteorite originally landed on a hill outside the present-day village of Lougheed near the bank of the Iron Creek.

Jasper/
"The Track of a Large Animal"

The explorer and geographer David Thompson was in the vicinity of present-day Jasper on 7 January 1811 when he came upon an extraordinary set of footprints. He described the discovery in detail in his journal, which went unpublished until 1916.

> Continuing our journey in the afternoon we came on the track of a large animal, the snow about six inches deep on the ice; I measured it; four large toes each of four inches in length to each a short claw; the ball of the foot sunk three inches lower than the toes, the hinder part of the foot did not mark well, the length fourteen inches, by eight inches in breadth, walking from north to south, and having passed about six hours. We were in no humour to follow him: the Men and Indians would have it to be a young mammoth and I held it to be the track of a large old grizled Bear; yet the shortness of the nails, the ball of the foot, and its great size was not that of Bear, otherwise that of a very large old Bear, his claws worn away; this the Indians would not allow. Saw several tracks of Moose Deer.

The prints were very much on Thompson's mind when he returned to the site later that year. Then he saw the beast, for as he wrote in his journal on October 5:

> I now recur to what I have already noticed in the early part of last winter, when proceeding up the Athabasca River to cross the Mountains, in company with . . . Men and four hunters, on one of the channels of the River we came to the track of a large animal, which measured fourteen inches in length by eight inches in breadth by a tape line. As the snow was about six inches in depth the track was well defined, and we could see it for a full one hundred yards from us, this animal was proceeding from north to south. We did not attempt to follow it, we had no time for

> it and the Hunters, eager as they are to follow and shoot every animal made no attempt to follow this beast, for what could the balls of our fowling guns do against such an animal. Report from old times had made the head branches of this River, and the Mountains in the vicinity the abode of one, or more, very large animals, to which I never appeared to give credence; for these reports appeared to arise from that fondness for the marvellous so common to mankind; but the sight of the track of that large beast staggered me, and I often thought of it, yet never could bring myself to believe such an animal existed, but thought it might be the track of some monster Bear.

Two passages are reprinted from *David Thompson's Narrative of His Explorations in Western America, 1794-1812* (1916), edited by J.B. Tyrrell.

The great mammals of the past are the mastodons. The word "mastodon" is the name for any one of a number of prehistoric mammals of the extinct genus *Mammul*, from which it is believed the modern elephant developed. During the Miocene era, mastodons rose in the Old World and spread to the New World. They died out at the end of that era in the Old, but in the New they survived well into the late Pleistocene or Ice Age.

One mastodon that roamed the Northern Hemisphere was the Siberian Mammoth or Woolly Mammoth. This large, prehistoric, elephant-like creature stood nine feet tall, wore a coat of long shaggy hair, and used upward-curving tusks. Its appearance is familiar today through the cave paintings of Cro-Magnon man. Its ivory tusks are commonly found in Siberia, and from time to time the carcass of a Woolly Mammoth is recovered from the permafrost of the Arctic. There are even instances of the carcass being thawed out and eaten — once at a banquet during a scientific convention in Europe; once on site by starving peasants. The species is now extinct. It is generally held that the Woolly Mammoth was extinct during the entire historical period, but sightings reported by native and non-native observers would tend to question that belief.

Lesser Slave Lake/
Veridical Dream

A veridical or truthful dream was reported by Warren Smith in his book *Strange Powers of the Mind* (1968). The story of the prophetic dream is recounted in the chapter called "The Dead Man's Message," but no source is cited.

One night in England in September 1904, George Hayward dreamed that his brother Edward Hayward, who was in Edmonton, Alberta, had been shot by a balding man with a moustache. In the dream, Edward's body was burnt in a fire and the remains were pitched into the lake. George was disturbed by the clarity of the dream and passed on to the Canadian authorities an account of what he had "seen." The police in Edmonton were impressed, for there was no way that George could have known at that time that his brother was missing.

George's detailed dream led to the arrest, trial, and conviction of Charles King, a balding, moustached confidence man. It seems King met Edward in a hotel in Edmonton and convinced him that he knew the location of a gold mine on the shores of Lesser Slave Lake. King convinced Edward to outfit an expedition. Once they arrived there and King was unable to produce the gold-bearing ore, Edward was murdered in the fashion "seen" in the veridical dream thousands of miles away.

Lethbridge/
The Medicine Stone

The first white settlers who came to Lethbridge were aware of a granite boulder in the bottom of the Belly (now Oldman) River bottom which had special significance to the native people. It was called *Mek-kio-towaqhs* by the Bloods and the Medicine Stone by the whites. The Rev. John Maclean recorded one version of the stone's history in 1882:

> On the river flat at the mouth of one of the ravines at Lethbridge, not many yards distant from the coal mine, lies a stone, which often-times I have seen painted and surrounded by

numerous Indian trinkets which had been given it by the Indians. The Blood Indians called it Mikiotouqse (The Red Stone). Tradition states that a long time ago a young man lay down beside this stone and fell asleep, and as he lay there he dreamed that the stone spoke to him and said, "Am I the Red Stone?" And the young man said, "Yes, you are the Red Stone." When he awoke he felt that this must be a mysterious stone that could thus converse with him, and he made offerings to it. Until the present day these offerings are made, the Indians believing that by giving it reverence they will be blessed in all things that concern them in this life.

In the 1930s white workmen hauled the Medicine Stone away to be used to reinforce a partial weir then in use near the waterworks. In 1984 the stone was identified, removed, and relocated in Indian Battle Park close to its original site. The actual location of the original site is covered by thirty or so feet of fill as it is now the Third Avenue Extension.

"Also, it is hardly necessary to add that we are not absolutely sure we have the original Medicine Stone," wrote the local historian Alex Johnston in a letter on 18 September 1987. "Every now and then someone surfaces who knows the exact location of the original and, if we will pay him, he will direct us to the proper place. My own opinion is that the stone we have is as close to the original as we are ever going to get. The stone had been set up in Indian Battle Park, near where it traditionally stood, and its significance is indicated on a plaque."

The story of the stone was published in *Lethbridge: A Centennial History* (1985) by Alex Johnston and Andy A. den Otter.

Majorville/
Medicine Wheel

The highest hill in the vicinity of Majorville, a small prairie community southeast of Calgary, is the site of an ancient medicine wheel. There is some evidence to suggest that this wheel was in continuous use from 2500 B.C. to perhaps A.D. 1500. As Suzanne Zwarun wrote in "Medicine Wheels Decoded," *Weekend Magazine* 25 July 1977, "The Majorville wheel is 1,000 years older than Stonehenge."

The wheel is formed of boulders and takes the shape of an off-centre circle a hundred feet in diameter with twenty-eight spokes radiating from the hub, some of which end in smaller cairns. The hub is an impressive accumulation of boulders, measuring thirty feet in diameter, six feet in height, and weighing some fifty tons. It was discovered in 1960 and is the largest such structure in North America.

Evidence suggests that the medicine wheel was used as an archaic astronomical observatory. Its alignments probably measured the summer solstice and marked the rising of Aldebaran, Rigel, and Sirius. It "points" in the direction of the Moose Mountain Medicine Wheel in Saskatchewan.

Mannville/
The Murderer and the Mentalist

The broadcaster and journalist Frank Edwards tells the story of "The Mentalist Who Solved Murders" in *Strange People* (1961). Apparently there was a multiple murder in the farmhouse of the wealthy Booher family outside the farming community of Mannville, east of Edmonton, in 1928, and a mentalist from Vancouver, who was brought in to find the murder weapon, was instrumental in breaking the case.

The RCMP arrived at the farmhouse to find that three people had been shot to death. The victims were the wife of Henry Booher, the elder son Fred, and two hired hands, William Roysk and Gabe Goromby. The police surmised that the murderer was the younger Booher son, Vernon, twenty-one. They reasoned that he had shot his mother because she had objected to his relationship with a young girl from Mannville and then shot the others when they tried to apprehend him. But Vernon steadfastly refused to confess, and short of the murder weapon the police felt they had a poor case against their suspect.

According to Edwards, the RCMP in Edmonton sought the services of Maximillian Langsner, a Viennese-born mentalist and resident of Vancouver who

claimed past success in solving crimes by reading the thoughts of criminals. The RCMP asked Langsner to locate the rifle and he agreed. The mentalist arrived and joined Vernon in his jail cell and simply stared at the prisoner. Vernon squirmed but he would not be "psyched out."

After four hours and forty minutes, Langsner emerged from the cell with a smile on his face. He informed the officers that he had telepathically located the murder weapon. He sketched a picture of a clump of bushes near the farmhouse, which he had never visited, and said there would be found the rifle. He accompanied the police to the site which they had no difficulty locating. Hidden in the bushes they found the .303 Enfield. There were no useable fingerprints on the rifle, but when the suspect was confronted with the murder weapon, which he thought he had so carefully hidden, he was so shaken that he broke down and confessed.

Vernon was tried, found guilty, and hanged. "Langsner was paid for his strange services . . . and was last heard of shortly before the outbreak of World War II when he left for a tour of the Middle East," wrote Edwards, concluding the tale of the Murderer and the Mentalist.

Colin Wilson, writing in *The Psychic Detectives: The Story of Psychometry and Paranormal Crime Detection* (1987), called this case "one of the most puzzling murder cases in Canadian history." Wilson based his account of the case on a variety of popular sources. "With the single exception of Langsner's intervention in the Booher case," he noted, "I can think of no murder case—or, for that matter, any other criminal case—that was actually solved by a clairvoyant."

Medicine Hat/
Ghost Trains

It is a matter of record that a head-on collision occurred on 8 July 1908 between the engine for the Spokane Flyer and a passenger train from Lethbridge on the CPR line two miles out of Medicine Hat. The Lethbridge locomotive was thrown off the tracks and its baggage car was demolished. Seven men were killed, including the two engineers, the Flyer's Jim Nicholson and the Lethbridge train's Bob Twohey. At the inquest it was established that Nicholson was at fault, having neglected to check that the Lethbridge train had left on time, which it had not.

There were two premonitions of the disaster, and both were witnessed by the railway fireman, Gus Day. The first incident took place two months before the crash. At eleven o'clock one night, Twohey was guiding his engine over the same CPR track two miles out of Medicine Hat. Then something astonishing happened. "A huge blinding spotlight suddenly appeared in front of him. He shouted for the fireman, Gus Day, to jump but it was too late. Twohey fully expected to die. To his amazement, the approaching train veered to the right and flashed past his engine, its whistle blowing. The coach windows were lit and he saw passengers looking out. Now here's the frightening part. *There was only a single rail line running through those hills.*"

That was the first appearance of the Ghost Train. There was no collision—indeed, there was no second train!—but the experience so frightened Twohey that he decided to stay off the trains for a while. One month later and on the same stretch of track the Ghost Train put in its second appearance. Twohey was not at the throttle, having chosen yard work instead, but his friend Nicholson was, and Day was stoking the engine. The same astonishing thing happened. "A dazzling light, a shrieking whistle, and passengers peering out of lighted windows as a train that didn't exist sped past on tracks that didn't exist."

Shortly thereafter the fatal collision occurred. Day was firing up an engine in the yard when he learned of the crash and deaths of his two friends, Nicholson and Twohey. Day pondered the fact that both Nicholson and Twohey had seen the Ghost Train and both were dead. He himself was the only person to see both Ghost Trains.

That was the end of the Ghost Trains, at least as far as Day was concerned. He saw them no more. He kept his peace until his retirement in British Columbia in the 1930s. Reading in a magazine about a ghost train in Colorado, he remembered his experience and

recalled it for a reporter. The story is told by Ted Ferguson in *Sentimental Journey: An Oral History of Train Travel in Canada.* (1985).

Milk River/
The Hoodoo Petroglyphs

The Milk River, which rises in Montana and flows through the southeast corner of Alberta, is the sole Canadian river to flow south and empty into the drainage basin of the Gulf of Mexico. The river has cut an impressive canyon with steep walls and imposing sandstone columns called hoodoos through Alberta's Dry Belt region. Some of the hoodoos bear petroglyph-like inscriptions.

William R. McGlone and Phillip M. Leonard, authors of *Ancient Celtic America* (1986), discuss the inscriptions in terms of Ogham, the writing system of the Ancient Celts. They claim that in 1855 James Doty, the first white visitor to the area to record seeing the petroglyphs, learned from the Indians that the rocks had been inscribed many years earlier by white men. The authors note that Barry Fell, the epigrapher, took an interest in the inscriptions, and they quote his translations of the Ogham script.

According to Fell's reading of the petroglyphs, they are concerned with divination. One of the inscriptions reads: "Diseases. Times of flood. Omens of disaster. Death in battle. Withering of corn cobs and prairie." Another reads: "Birds bring good luck. Eastern quarter. Here is good luck. The secret writings interpret the auguries of the geese, from the gabble, its when, its whence, and its whither."

Fell's reading is not lacking in oracular poetry, but it is doubtful that any other scholar would read them in the same way, if the scholar could read them at all. It is possible that the meaning of the petroglyphs will never be understood.

Morley/
Ghost of White Eagle

There are three Stony Reserves at Morley, northwest of Calgary. The Indians on the reserves have the legend of "Ghost River," which was recounted by John H. Hutton in the Calgary *Daily Herald* and reprinted by the Montreal *Gazette* on 30 January 1934.

In certain seasons of the year one may see the ghost of White Eagle wearing his flowing white robes, astride his great white stallion, followed by his white dog, emerging from the mist on the peaks of the Ghost Hills and moving along the shores of Ghost Lake and Ghost River and disappearing into the heart of Devil's Head Mountain.

It seems White Eagle led his Stony people to safety and prosperity in the Morley area following their humiliating defeat on the plains at the hands of the Cree and Blackfoot. Yet White Eagle yearned for revenge and found it when their traditional enemies attacked them in their mountainous stronghold. White Eagle was wounded but as he lay dying he instructed his warriors to bury him on the peak of Devil's Head Mountain and as they did so to loosen the boulders there. The attacking warriors were caught in the avalanche and killed. Thus did White Eagle die avenged. His ghost continues to gloat as it patrols the peaks and the shores to this day.

Pincher Creek/
Medicine Wheel

"There is here a cairn of concentric circles of stones and radiating lines," wrote the naturalist Sir J.W. Dawson in 1885. "I have not seen it, and therefore cannot describe it in detail." The cairn crests Sundial Hill which lies sixty kilometres northeast of Pincher Creek in southwestern Alberta.

Mapped in 1975, the site was described by Michael Wilson, an archaeologist with the University of Calgary: "The Sundial Butte wheel has two concentric circles around a large central cairn, with a 'pathway' or 'vestibule' bounded by two sub-parallel spokes that extend in a southeasterly direction." Wilson went on to consider the significance of this site and similar sites in his scholarly paper "Sun Dances, Thirst Dances, and Medicine Wheels: A Search for Alternative Hypotheses" in the *Proceedings* of the Eleventh

Annual Conference, Archaeological Association of the University of Calgary, 1981.

Wilson noted that the Plains Indians during the proto-historical and historical periods erected the medicine wheels, tipi rings, and similar sites across the prairies and plains of North America for many different reasons. The constructions were often of a composite nature, and over the centuries met one or more of a number of uses as burial chambers, memorial sites, structures for the "vision quest," landmarks, stone-age observatories, sites for ritual and ceremonial dances like the sun dance and the thirst dance, and "master symbols" which express and share the traditional wisdom in symbolic form.

Carl Jung would have noted the overall pattern of the medicine wheel, so much like that of the mandala. In point of fact, the designation "medicine wheel" is catchy but misleading. "Circle," "ring," or "hoop" would be more in keeping, given the cultural development of the Plains Indians when they erected these "medicine wheels."

The Rocky Mountains/
Sacred Sites

The Rocky Mountains were formed during the Mesozoic and Early Cenozoic eras in a series of upheavals that took place over hundreds of thousands of years some 58 million years ago. The range extends 3000 miles from central New Mexico to northwest Alaska. In Canada the Rocky Mountains extend 750 miles from the international border along the provincial border between British Columbia and Alberta to the Basin of the Liard River. The chain divides the continent, the Prairies to the east, the Rocky Mountain trench on the west. The highest peak in the Canadian range is Mount Robson which rises 12,972 feet.

The spectacular size and appearance of the gigantic mountains — from their cavernous valleys and rivers to their snow-white peaks and domes — impress everyone. To the natives who inhabited the foothills, they were "the shining mountains." To the French they were *les montagnes de roche*. The first known

"One of the most spectacular natural features of North America is a gigantic gash, 50 miles wide in places, running from the northern wilds of British Columbia down into Montana. It is the Rocky Mountain Trench, source of the great Columbia River," wrote John Magor in Canadian UFO Report, *Vol. 2, No. 3, 1971. "A landscape of magnificent contrast from its fertile bed to its snow-brushed peaks, the Trench looks like a playground of gods. And perhaps it truly is, for here there is a seemingly endless record of visits from the sky." [B.C. Government Air Photograph/Department of Lands, Forests & Water]*

European to see them in the distance was the Hudson's Bay Company agent Anthony Henday, who saw them on 17 October 1754 near present-day Innisfall, Alberta. They have an ancient look but, as instances of orogeny, they are relatively young. Even so, the novelist Frederick Niven wrote in 1920, "The Rockies run the length of the continent, and are in league with Eternity."

It is said that Madame H.P. Blavatsky claimed that hidden in the vastness of the Rocky Mountains lies a secret sanctuary where ancient adepts and sages live to this day, preserving the "secret doctrine," and guiding the destiny of the planet. No written record of Blavatsky's remark has ever been found. Yet the art critic F.B. Houser, in an address called "Some Thoughts on National Consciousness" published in *The Canadian Theosophist*, 15 July 1927, observed that "occult centres" may be found amid the Rocky Mountains:

> Across the northern regions of Canada and down through the Cordilleran area of the North American continent, that area comprising the ridge known as the Rocky Mountains, are sacred and occult centres of the earth. The most ancient traditions of the North American Indian speak of them. They are hinted at in the letters of Mahatmas and by Madame Blavatsky whom we have reason to believe visited some of them. Some time, if not now, these places will likely become active spiritual centres for the development of the promised new race. In the meantime their very presence is inspiring to contemplate and their occult influence on the life of our people is probably far more extensive and deep than we at present believe.

It is apparent that the existence of these "sacred and occult centres of the earth" was unappreciated by Aleister Crowley, the English "black magician" and self-styled "Great Beast." He travelled by train across the country in 1906, confiding his feelings in his memoirs which were posthumously published as *The Confessions of Aleister Crowley: An Autohagiography* (1970): "The Rockies have no majesty; they do not

elevate the mind to contemplation of Almighty God any more than they warm the heart by seeming sentinals to watch over the habitations of one's fellow men."

Sir Edwin Arnold, the British mystic and poet who penned the vastly influential life of Buddha in verse titled *The Light of Asia* (1879), crossed the Rockies in 1903, and exclaimed: "These vast ranges exceed in grandeur the Himalayas, the Alps and the Andes, all of which I have seen."

John Magor and other UFO researchers have taken to describing the Rocky Mountain Trench — the immensely long valley along the western wall of the range — as "the Playground of Gods." Innumerable UFO sightings are reported along the Trench.

The native people hold the land in liege from their predecessors to their ancestors. The Stony chief John Snow wrote in *The Mountains Are Our Sacred Places* (1977):

> . . . the Rocky Mountains are precious and sacred to us. We knew every trail and mountain pass in this area. We had special ceremonial and religious areas in the mountains. In the olden days some of the neighbouring tribes called us the "People of the Shining Mountains." These mountains are our temples, our sanctuaries, and our resting places. They are a place of hope, a place of vision, a place of refuge, a very special and holy place where the Great Spirit speaks for us. *Therefore, these mountains are our sacred places.*

St. Paul/
UFO Landing Pad

The world's first UFO Landing Pad was erected by the citizens of the town of St. Paul, northeast of Edmonton. It was built as a Centennial project in 1967, is decorated with provincial and territorial flags, and includes a time capsule to be opened on 3 June 2067. Although used for civic functions, it has yet to be employed by aliens.

The pad takes the form of a raised platform, forty feet in length, which resembles both a helicopter landing pad and an old-fashioned bandstand. A sign at the foot of the stairs leading up to the pad bears an inspired message:

> The area under the world's first UFO Landing Pad was designated international by the town of St. Paul as a symbol of our faith that mankind will maintain the outer universe free from national wars and strife. That future travel in space will be safe for all intergalactic beings. All visitors from Earth or otherwise are welcome to this territory and to the town of St. Paul.

To mark the International Year of the Child, the citizens of St. Paul raised a substantial sum of money for the missions of Mother Teresa in Calcutta. Mother Teresa arrived to accept the donation on 25 June 1982. It was formally presented to her on the platform of the UFO Landing Pad. Not only did she acknowledge the gift but she referred to the unique structure by saying, "If there is sickness in outer space, we will go there too." There is a photograph of the presentation ceremony in Douglas Curran's book *In Advance of the Landing: Folk Concepts of Outer Space* (1985).

Lac Ste. Anne/ Curative Properties

Lac Ste. Anne is both a lake and a community — a small community, with a population of thirty-four in the 1981 census—northwest of Edmonton. Here the Shrine of Ste. Anne, which was named after Ste. Anne de Beaupré, attracts large numbers of native Indians from across Canada. Their pilgrimage culminates on the saint's feast-day, 26 July. The shrine is visited by thousands of pilgrims each year, many of whom bathe in the lake which is held to have curative properties.

Suffield/ The Ellis Site

The Suffield Military Reserve is located north of Medicine Hat on land that includes what is known to archaeologists as the Ellis Site. This is a prehistoric burial lodge and medicine wheel which lie on land that overlooks the valley of the South Saskatchewan River.

The Ellis Site was described by John H. Brumley of Ethos Consultants Ltd. in a paper called "The Ellis Site: A Late Prehistoric Burial Lodge/Medicine Wheel Site in Southeastern Alberta" included in *Contributions to Plains Prehistory* (1985), edited by David Burley. It consists of two small stone cairns, thirteen stone circles or "tipi rings," along with a single medicine wheel. This medicine wheel is composed of a central stone ring from the margins of which ten or eleven stone lines radiate outwards in various directions for a distance of from forty-seven to sixty-three feet.

The site was discovered and recorded in 1971 by W.J. Bryne while evaluating the archaeological significance of the Suffield Reserve and the effects of proposed long-term military training activities and of oil and gas development activities. "To date," he wrote, "as a result of both programs, over 1650 archaeological sites have been located and recorded on the reserve and over 90 sites subjected to detailed mapping and/or excavation." Fragments of human skeletal materials were recovered from its central hub. From various dating techniques, archaeologists have

The world's first UFO Landing Pad was built at St. Paul, Alberta, in 1967. Erected as a Centennial project, it consists of a raised platform large enough to land a helicopter, an arena and a baseball park. The complex serves as a focus for civic functions, if not alien landings. [Travel Alberta]

determined that the medicine wheel dates from about A.D. 1430. Native traditions imply that it was erected by the ancestors of today's Blackfoot.

The site was visited in 1975 by Dr. Richard Forbis, and archaeologist at the University of Calgary, and Dr. John A. Eddy, the first scientist to suggest that the New World "wheels" might, like the Old World "circles," function as Stone Age observatories. But they were unable to determine any significant astronomical alignments for the spokes of this medicine wheel.

The designation "medicine wheel" is well worth examining. Native people believe that all things possess some form of power — *orenda* to the Iroquois, *manitou* to the Algonkian-speakers, and *wakanda* to the Sioux—and their words for "power" are sometimes translated "medicine." The characteristic cairn configuration resembles a gigantic cartwheel with a hub and radiating spokes. The designation "medicine wheel" was first used in the late nineteenth century to refer to aboriginal surface stone structures found on the northern plains and prairies, being applied first to the Bighorn Medicine Wheel which is located atop Medicine Mountain near Sheridan, Wyoming. The designation "medicine circle" or "medicine ring" or perhaps "medicine hoop" would be more appropriate than "medicine wheel" as the use of the wheel is not identified with the North American Indians.

Structures as huge as Medicine Wheels had to meet multiple needs, including serving social and sacred functions. It has been shown that European neolithic structures, like Stonehenge on Salisbury Plain in England, were constructed along lines that permitted them to be used as megalithic observatories. Ever since the U.S. mathematician Gerald S. Hawkins published *Stonehenge Decoded* (1965), it has been commonplace to give consideration to any neolithic structure's possible archaeo-astronomical function. The notion was introduced to North American archaeology in 1977 by the U.S. astronomer John A. Eddy. In an address to the American Association for the Advancement of Science, he advanced the theory that the Big Horn Medicine Wheel in Wyoming was constructed along

such lines as to permit primitive calendar-making in pre-Columbian America.

Today access to the Ellis Site, which is also known as the British Block, is restricted to military personnel.

Suffield/
RCAF Chases UFOs

Has an RCAF interceptor jet ever chased a UFO? Were chases ever a routine practice in the late 1950s? Were the chases really co-ordinated by the Defence Research Board Experimental Station at Suffield in southeastern Alberta?

All these things happened, according to Donald E. Keyhoe, retired U.S. Major and flying saucer enthusiast. Pilots of the RCAF (now the Canadian Armed Forces Air Command) *did* give chase to UFOs "hundreds" of times, and there *was* a secret landing site at Suffield. Keyhoe made these claims in his book *Aliens from Space* (1974):

> Though jet pursuits are the usual method for capture attempts, at least one country has tried a different plan. In 1954, U.S. Air Force intelligence learned that Canada had set up a top-secret project, after Royal Canadian Air Force pilots had failed to bring down a UFO. Hoping to lure aliens into landing, the Defence Research Board established a restricted landing field near its experimental station at Suffield, Alberta. All RCAF and commercial pilots were banned from the area. But there was nothing to indicate that the restricted field was reserved for the alien machines and none came near the area. Even if the aliens had known, they might not have risked landing, after hundreds of earlier chases by the RCAF.

Keyhoe did not explain how he learned of this "top-secret project" and of "chases" in the "hundreds." Researcher Yurko Bondarchuk, writing in *UFO: Sightings, Landings and Abductions* (1979), commented on "Major Keyhoe's impeccable credibility" and implied a possible cover-up by the Department of National Defence.

Taber/
The Taber Child

The partial skeleton of a four-month-old child was discovered in 1961 by a geological survey party at a bluff along the Oldman River, near the community of Taber in Southern Alberta. The find was significant for a number of reasons. It was the oldest human skeleton ever discovered in Canada, and it was among the oldest bones — rather than fossils — unearthed in the Americas.

It was dated as being between 30,000 and 60,000 years old. This analysis was based on its position in preglacial strata. However, subsequent analysis based on its composition led the National Museum of Man in Ottawa to announce on 9 March 1982 that the bone fragment was not quite so old or early as previously believed.

It appears that the Taber Child is a mere stripling. The skeleton dates from 3500 B. C., making it not even 6000 years old.

Viking/
The Ribstones

The so-called Ribstones rest in a field southeast of Viking, a town that lies southeast of Edmonton.

Among North America's oldest sculptures, the Ribstones are two quartzite rocks which resemble a pair of buffalo, with backbones and ribs clearly defined on each rock. The larger of the two, which measures fifty inches in length, twenty inches in width and the same in height, resembles a bull buffalo, and the smaller a cow buffalo. It is estimated they were carved a thousand years ago.

The Ribstones remain important in Cree hunting rituals to this day. As Ted. J. Brasser explained in *"Bo'Jou, Neejee!" Profiles of Canadian Indian Art* (1976):

> The Plains Indians believed that a strong relationship existed between these sacred rocks and the buffalo spirits. The Lord of the Buffalo Spirits himself resided in a huge boulder on Ribstone Hill in Alberta; all other sacred rocks were

believed to be its descendants. Marine fossils and other oddly shaped stones were used as magical charms by the Blackfoot. Set in wads of buffalo wool, these "buffalo stones" were placed in front of the shaman, who rubbed them with red paint while he "called" the buffalo. The stones were believed to be alive: they grew, produced offspring in the shape of smaller stones and, like the buffalo, grew heavy in summertime. Although more elaborately decorated than the buffalo stones of the Blackfoot, the sacred stones of the Crow Indians figured in the same spiritual context. Not surprisingly, the buffalo loomed large in the symbolism of the Plains Indian hunters.

Writing-on-Stone Provincial Park/
Carvings

The petroglyphs found in Writing-on-Stone Provincial Park, south of Lethbridge, are a form of "writing" that may forever be indecipherable. What the carvings on the sandstone cliffs on both banks of the Milk River in the Park are meant to preserve or convey may never be known.

Such rock art may be a record of the presence of Asians in North America in pre-Columbian times. Such at least is the view of Henriette Mertz, an American lawyer and student of "unsolved mysteries." Writing in *Pale Ink: Two Ancient Records of Chinese Exploration in America* (1953, rev. ed. 1972), she notes that in two classical Chinese texts there are detailed references to voyages across a wide, Pacific-like sea to a broad and mountainous land rather like western North America. The two texts are "Classic of Mountains and Sea," compiled by the scholar Yu at the request of the Emperor Shu, traditionally dated to 2250 B.C.; and "Fu-Sang," written by Hwui Shan, also called Hoei Shin, a Buddhist monk who left the Court of China for "the East" — to North Americans it is "the West" — traditionally in A.D. 499.

The rock art found at Writing-on-Stone Provincial Park, which Mertz specifically mentions in drawing the routes taken in the interior of North America by the author of "Classic of Mountains and Sea," remain as enigmatic as the Chinese texts remain ambiguous. If the Chinese Buddhist monk Hwui Shan proselytized and explored in the wilds of North America, as did the Jesuits more than a millennium later, then his descriptions of towering mountains and gigantic trees could be first-hand descriptions of features of West Coast geography. In fact, he named the new continent Fu-Sang, which may be translated from the Chinese to mean *fir tree*. Did the Ancient Chinese know British Columbia as the land of the fir tree? The glyphs in Writing-on-Stone Provincial Park spark such speculation.

BRITISH COLUMBIA

Agassiz/
Sasquatch Researcher

The small community of Agassiz, close to the Harrison Hot Springs, bears the name of the Swiss-American scientist Louis Agassiz. Agassiz was a geologist, and while John Green is not a geologist, he is as careful as a scientist must be in his own chosen field, which is sasquatch research.

John Green is a veteran newspaperman and former publisher of the weekly Agassiz-Harrison *Advance*. He has written three reports on sasquatch sightings. These are *On the Track of the Sasquatch* (1969, 1980), *The Sasquatch File* (1970), and *Year of the Sasquatch* (1970), all issued by Cheam Publishing, Agassiz, B.C. His definitive work is *Sasquatch: The Apes Among Us* (1978).

If anyone knows anything about the sasquatch it is Green. Although he has yet to see a sasquatch himself, he has studied almost 3000 reports of sightings of man-like monsters from around the world, and some 700 descriptions of giant footprints. Yet he began his address "What Is The Sasquatch?" at the Conference on Anthropology of the Unknown at the University of British Columbia in 1978 with a surprising admission: "Whether a real creature is responsible for the many eyewitness reports of giant hairy bipeds in North America has not been established, and that may remain the case for many years."

He went on to suggest that a "constant picture" does emerge from the reports. "The reports portray not a semi-human, but an upright ape; not an endangered remnant of a species, but an extremely widespread and secure population; not a fearful monster, but a remarkably inoffensive animal."

John Green, veteran newspaperman, sasquatch enthusiast, and author of Sasquatch: The Apes Among Us *(1978), is shown here holding in his hands a copy of a pair of beautifully detailed casts of tracks made in 1976 by Bob Titmus near the Skeena River not far from Terrace, B.C. The tracks, found by children, were 15.5 inches long and 6.5 inches wide, with an average stride of 6.5 feet. [John Green]*

337

What do sasquatches look like? Green summarized his findings:

1. They are significantly larger than humans.
2. They are solitary creatures.
3. Their hairiness is of the animal, not the human sort.
4. The proportions of their limbs are more human-like than ape-like.
5. From the shoulders up there is less resemblance to the average human.
6. They are omnivorous.
7. They are largely nocturnal.
8. They are not active in cold weather.
9. The make considerable use of water.

To these nine observations, Green added three general conclusions. First, the sasquatch is not normally a dangerous animal. Second, the relationship between the sasquatch and *Homo sapiens* has not been proven to be any closer than that between our species and the other great apes, except in shared posture and means of locomotion. Third, the sasquatch is not an endangered species in most of its range.

In 1978, Green wrote, "The fascination of the subject, for me, involves the very thing that I am most inclined to complain about—that the scientific world ignores it." There are signs that this is changing, thanks in great part to Green's own work. If anyone is "owed" a sasquatch sighting, it is John Green, the Agassiz of sasquatch researchers.

Ashcroft/
The Tunguska Effect

Readers of Fortean literature are familiar with the Tunguska Event — the terrific explosion that took place in the vicinity of Siberia's Tunguska River at 7:15 a.m. on 22 June 1908. Scientists mounted expeditions to the remote area to determine the cause of the blast which levelled trees for miles around. Although the Tunguska Event was never fully explained, the most likely cause of the explosion was the impact of a meteor. Among the less likely explanations is the suggestion that the explosion resulted from the collision in mid-air of matter and anti-matter.

The Tunguska Effect was repeated on a smaller scale in Western Canada the night of 31 March 1965. An explosion affected an area of nearly one million square kilometres. The sky was lit up, there was a thunderous roar, windows were rattled and broken, and "black rain" fell on freshly fallen snow over a wide area.

The effect was observed in mid-air by Phil Miller, a Canadian Pacific Airline pilot, who was first officer on a flight from Prince George to Vancouver. "For three to four seconds the sky was completely illuminated as if it were total daylight on a bright, sunny morning," he told Nat Cole of the *Vancouver Sun* on 1 April 1965. "We could see the horizon all around us, the snow on the mountains below and a light blue sky above.

"It was a moonless night, quite dark. We had come out of the clouds and were in the clear. The stars were visible. We had just gone by Ashcroft and were about 20 miles south of there. It was exactly 9:46 p.m. Gradually, the sky started to get light. It was like a sunrise. It got brighter until it was like total daylight. We could see ahead down past Mount Baker and east to Princeton. It was the brightest light, other than sunlight, that I have ever seen."

Miller estimated the light took between three and four seconds to reach full intensity and remained bright for the same period of time. "Then over a period of another two or three seconds it slowly dulled down. It was like a sunset — the light changed from white to yellow to red. There was a slight flicker as it died off."

Miller saw no fireball, heard no sounds, and felt no turbulence, although these sights and effects were noted by residents of the interior of the province. Some thought that a huge bomb had been dropped or that it was the end of the world. In a Canadian Press story published on the same day, one spokesman for the Dominion Astrophysical Observatory at Victoria explained that the disturbance was caused by a meteor or fireball, while another independently suggested that its cause was a U.S. space satellite re-entering Earth's atmosphere. Sightings were reported as far afield as Saskatoon, Saskatchewan; Peace River,

Alberta; Helena, Montana; Spokane, Washington; Vancouver and Sandspit, Queen Charlotte Islands, British Columbia.

Bella Coola/
The Boqs

The Bella Coola Indians maintain a tradition about a hairy, man-like animal. To this day it may be encountered in the wooded valleys in the coastal region of Burke Channel. They refer to this dwarfish and mischievous creature as the Boqs.

"This beast somewhat resembles a man, its hands especially, and the region around the eyes being distinctly human," noted the anthropologist T.F. McIlwraith in "Certain Beliefs of the Bella Coola Indians Concerning Animals," *Ontario Archaeological Report of 1924-25*. "It walks on its hind legs, in a stooping posture, its long arms swinging below its knees: in height it is rather less than the average man. With the exception of its face, the entire body is covered with long hair, the growth being especially profuse on the chest, which is large, corresponding to the great strength of the animal." The boqs makes life difficult for the Indian by menacing him in the woods. When angered the boqs may be heard to shriek and whistle.

Bella Coola/
Native Psychic Surgery

There is a vivid description of a native psychic surgical operation which was performed by the medicine-man of the Bella Coola Indians, as observed and described by Sir Alexander Mackenzie. It appears in his journal entry for 19 July 1793. The West Coast natives turned to Mackenzie for medicine or treatment, but when these failed, as they often did, the patients would return to the traditional ways.

Mackenzie saw a chief's son who was emaciated and suffered from "a violent ulcer in the small of his back, in the foulest state that can be imagined." Mackenzie administered a few drops of Turlington's balsam in some water" and left him. The patient turned to the medicine-men of the band.

On my return I found the native physicians busy in practising their skill and art on the patient. They blew on him, and then whistled; at times they pressed their extended fingers, with all their strength on his stomach; they also put their fore fingers doubled into his mouth, and spouted water from their own with great violence into his face. To suppose these operations the wretched sufferer was held up in a sitting posture; and when they were concluded, he was laid down and covered with a new robe made of the skins of the lynx.

Mackenzie added, "I could not conjecture what would be the end of this ceremony . . . the scene afflicted me and I left." The passage is reproduced from a longer account in *The Journals and Letters of Sir Alexander Mackenzie* (1970) edited by W. Kaye Lamb.

The practice of psychic surgery has been associated with native peoples both here and in South America.

Bishop's Cove/
Monkey-like Wild Man

Bishop's Cove is a fishing community, north of Vancouver, on the west coast of British Columbia. It once was the haunt of a monkey-like wild man, according to the following report which appeared in the Vancouver *Province* on 8 March 1907:

A monkey-like wild man who appears on the beach at night, who howls in an unearthly fashion between intervals of exertion at clam digging, has been the cause of depopulating an Indian village, according to reports of officers of the steamer Capilano, which reached port last night from the north.

The Capilano on her trip north put in to Bishop's Cove where there is a small Indian settlement. As soon as the steamer appeared in sight the inhabitants put off from the shore in canoes and clambered on board the Capilano in a state of terror over what they called a monkey covered with long hair and standing about five

339

feet high which came out on the beach at night to dig clams and howl.

The Indians say that they have tried to shoot it but failed, which added to their superstitious fears. The officers of the vessel heard some animals howling along the shore at night but are not prepared to swear that it was the voice of the midnight visitor who has so frightened the Indians.

The journalist John Green in *Sasquatch: The Apes Among Us* (1978), in reporting this and similar cases, asks the following question and answers it: "What can be said about these old stories? Not too much beyond the fact that they exist."

Campbell River/ "Monkey Man"

The historian the Rev. Bruce McKelvie preserved this account of a "monkey man" in the Campbell River area. It is reprinted from John Green's *Sasquatch: The Apes Among Us* (1978).

> One of the most outstanding timber cruisers who ever operated in British Columbia, Mike King was a fine type of man with an enviable reputation for reliability. He told of being in the Campbell River locality of Vancouver Island. He was alone, for his Indian packers refused to accompany him into that particular area, being afraid of the "monkey men" of the forest. It was late afternoon when he saw the "man-beast" bending over a water hole, washing some roots, which he placed in two neat piles. When appraised of Mr. King's presence, the creature gave a startled cry and started up a hillside. He stopped at some distance and looked back at the timber cruiser, while Mike King kept "it" covered with his rifle. Mr. King described the sasquatch as being "covered with reddish-brown hair, and his arms were peculiarly long and were used freely in climbing and in bush running; while the trail showed a distinct human foot, but with phenomenally long and spreading toes."

Cassiar Mountains/ Ancient Chinese Coins

One of the most curious and suggestive of discoveries ever recorded in Canada was made by miners working in the Cassiar Mountains in the northwestern part of the province. In 1882, they uncovered a cache of coins which had their origin in Ancient China.

All that is known of the discovery appears in the following item written by James Deans and published in the *American Naturalist*, 18:98-99, 1884. It was reprinted under the title "Chinese Coins in British Columbia" in *Ancient Man: A Handbook of Puzzling Artifacts* (1978) compiled by William R. Corliss:

> In the summer if 1882 a miner found on DeFoe (Deorse?) creek, Cassiar district, Br. Columbia, thirty Chinese coins in the auriferous sand, twenty-five feet below the surface. They appeared to have been strung, but on taking them up the miner let them drop apart. The earth above and around them was as compact as any in the neighbourhood. One of these coins I examined at the store of Chu Chong in Victoria. Neither in metal nor markings did it resemble the modern coins, but in its figures looked more like an Aztec calendar. So far as I can make out the markings, this is a Chinese chronological cycle of sixty years, invented by the Emperor Huungti, 2637 B.C., and circulated in this form to make his people remember it.

The present whereabouts of the cache of coins is unknown. Coins were used by the Ancient Chinese but not as early as the year 2637 B.C.

Equally intriguing is an account of an earlier discovery of Chinese coins. This find was made in the Chilcotin River area in the interior in the days when the province was still a colony. The account titled "An Indian Antiquity" appeared in the Niagara *Herald*, 25 July 1801:

> A piece of copper coin has lately been discovered in opening a spring in the village of Chillicothe, in the North Western territory. Impressions

upon paper of both sides of this coin have been sent by John S. Willis, esq., to a gentleman in Philadelphia. They appear to be Chinese characters. Upon presenting them to Mr. Peale, for his museum, he produced four pieces of copper coin procured at different times from China, which are exactly similar to the one found in the spring at Chillicothe, as far as a judgement can be formed from comparing them with the impressions of the latter upon paper. — The Chillicothe coin is now in the possession of governor St. Clair.

Did the ancient Chinese sail along the West Coast of the province and penetrate the interior of British Columbia? Only time and any future finds will tell.

Chehalis Indian Reserve/ "Sasquatch"

The Chehalis Indian Reserve is located at a number of locations along the Harrison River in the vicinity of Chilliwack. It was from here that the word "sasquatch" was introduced to the world.

Someone or something left this enlarged print in August 1977 in the soil of northern British Columbia near the village of Chetwynd. If the giant print was made by a sasquatch, the creature has four toes rather than five. [Vancouver Sun/ Canapress]

Sasquatch is an Anglicization of the Coast Salish word for a huge, hairy-looking creature said to live in the Coast Mountains of British Columbia, where Indians occasionally encountered it. The word was popularized in a number of newspaper and magazine articles written in the 1920s by John W. Burns, a school teacher on the Chehalis Indian Reserve. Burns was quite taken with the idea of the "wild mountain men."

Burns's article "Introducing B.C.'s Hairy Giants" was published in *Maclean's* on 1 April 1921. Publication of the piece on April Fool's Day may have been a coincidence or a jest on the part of the Toronto editors. Whatever the case, the word acquired national usage when it was announced that Harrison Hot Springs would host a "Sasquatch Hunt" to mark the B.C. Centennial of 1958. Like the sasquatch, which is never there when most wanted, the hunt was never held. Yet the word was accepted as the name or description of the Canadian cousin of California's Bigfoot, Nepal's Yeti, the Himalayas' Abominable Snowman, and Siberia's Almasti.

Further details may be found in Wayne Suttles' "Sasquatch: The Testimony of Tradition" in *Manlike Monsters on Trial* (1980) edited by Marjorie M. Halpin and Michael M. Ames.

Chilliwack/
Portrait of a Ghost

When Douglas and Hetty Frederickson bought a twelve-room house on William Street North in the city of Chilliwack in December 1965, they were surprised to find that they were not the only tenants. According to Sheila Hervey in *Some Canadian Ghosts* (1973), the experience ultimately drove Doug, a logger, and Hetty, a painter, to move to Sayward on Vancouver Island.

Hetty had a series of vivid nightmares about a woman lying on the floor of the attic. In the dream the woman wore a red dress covered with yellow flowers and her face was contorted in terror. Bureau drawers kept opening and closing by themselves. An old bedstead moved of its own accord. One night she saw what appeared to be a misty figure standing by the window. In May 1966, Hetty began to sketch the woman she had glimpsed, but as she painted the woman's face in the portrait kept changing into that of a man.

Press reports of the disturbances in the Frederickson house led a previous occupant to report that about ten years earlier a man had committed suicide in the house. Another report had it that a woman had been killed in the house and cemented into the chimney. The publicity attracted the public in droves. One Sunday over seven hundred visitors turned up hoping to tour the house! For this reason the Fredericksons moved to Sayward and the house stood empty for some time.

The house was rented from 1968 to 1972 by a group of musicians, none of whom had any strange experiences to report. Then a family purchased the house and their children reported recurring nightmares. Everyone heard doors banging for no reason, and the family dog would cower and whimper with fear in a corner. The new occupants believe that three separate ghosts occupy the house with them — a female spirit, a child-like male spirit, and a presence in darkened hallways which sends cold chills up people's spines and keeps them rooted to the spot.

Hetty's painting was donated to the Haunted House exhibit organized by Station CKNW in Vancouver. The show was mounted to raise money for the radio station's orphan's fund. The painting, eight feet by five feet, in oranges and blacks, depicts a woman — not a man — staring through a bedroom window. Her arms are folded. Her left eye and the left side of her face are painted in but there is nothing on the right side of her face.

As Sheila Hervey concluded, "There are still no satisfactory explanations for the hauntings in Chilliwack; perhaps there never will be."

Chilliwack Lake/
That "Thing"

Charles Flood was one of a group of three prospectors in the mountains of the Chilliwack Lake area in 1915.

Flood came from Hope, and the others, Donald McRae and Green Hicks, both came from nearby Agassiz. Exploring the Holy Cross Mountains, they found alligators in Alligator Lake. (Actually they were black lizards about twice the size of normal lizards.) At Cougar Lake, a mile away, they saw something more interesting. The following account comes from John Green's *Sasquatch: The Apes Among Us* (1978):

> While we were travelling through the dense berry growth, Green Hicks suddenly stopped us and drew our attention to a large, light brown creature about eight feet high, standing on its hind legs (standing upright) pulling the berry bushes with one hand or paw toward him and putting berries in his mouth with the other hand or paw.
>
> I stood still wondering and McRae and Green Hicks were arguing. Hicks said "it is a wild man" and McCrae said "it is a bear." The creature heard us and suddenly disappeared in the brush around 200 yards away. As far as I am concerned the strange creature looked more like a human being, we had seen several black and brown bears on the trip, and that "thing" looked altogether different. Huge brown bear are known to be in Alaska, but have never been seen in southern British Columbia.
>
> . . . I never have seen anything like this creature before or after this incident in 1915, in all my days of hunting and prospecting in British Columbia.

Christina Lake/ "Flying Object"

The credit for drawing public attention to the remarkable "Flying Object" pictograph at Christina Lake in southeastern British Columbia goes to John Magor. Magor, a veteran journalist, was at the time the publisher of the *Canadian UFO Report*. He linked the pictograph with the world of UFOlogy in the cover story he wrote for the *Report*, Vol. 2, No. 6, 1973,

running two black-and-white photographs and even a pen-and-ink sketch based on the image.

Magor came across the "Flying Object" pictograph on the rockface of a secluded natural alcove overlooking Christina Lake. He was overcome with emotion when he saw it for the first time, and the memory of the event continues to move him. The image is reddish orange in colour, and it seems to depict a flying object. The area it covers measures 28.3 inches horizontally and 31.8 inches vertically. Calcite has almost obscured two outer figures which stand below the principal image.

The Christina Lake Pictograph must be one of the loveliest and most suggestive of all native-art images. It is reddish-orange in colour and painted on buff-coloured rock. The image measures 28.3 inches horizontally and 31.8 inches vertically. It was painted by the Salish people in a natural alcove, or grotto, overlooking Christina Lake in southeastern British Columbia. The overall effect is delicate, almost mystical. [John Magor]

343

The site was first recorded by John Corner in his self-published book *Pictographs in the Interior of British Columbia* (1967). Corner connected it with the Indian story of the youth who tumbled into the lake from the cliff above and whose body was never recovered. The elders decided that he was the prisoner of evil spirits. Some of the figures on the rocks in the vicinity were drawn to ward off unwanted visitors.

Magor feels the pictograph has a deeper purpose. "Our relief at finding the spot at all was replaced by a feeling that some strong spiritual quality lingered here. We found ourselves comparing the grotto to a recess in an ancient church containing a sacred panel."

He continued:

> This particular artist, perhaps superior to others, showed great skill in conveying the idea of something extraordinary in the air. Because of its comparative size, it is obviously not a bird and just as obviously because of its shape (perhaps that is why he retained the winged look) it is not the sun. But the touch of real brilliance is in the use of those four human figures. Not only do they lend size and height to the object but, by their suggestion of a worshipful attitude, create the impression that this was an event of rare spiritual importance. We can assume the people they represent thought a god had come to visit, just as ancient scriptures—if we care to make the interpretation — describe visits elsewhere by gods in their chariots.

Magor studied the vivid and noble image for some time and came to the conclusion that it was painted by the ancestors of the Interior Salish some three hundred years ago. The image was certainly painted before the year 1860 when the natives ceased to create rock art of any sort. "We are almost certainly looking at pictographs in the 300-year bracket or beyond," he wrote. "Not only has the formula gone but so has the practice. The art of pictographs is now so remote it has no place at all among the relic customs still remembered and acted out by native communities."

Because of its age the Flying Object pictograph does not depict a primitive airplane. Because of its schematic nature it may have symbolic value. But it is also possible that the native artist sought to recall an event of signal importance, the landing of a strange aerial craft. "If, however, we give him credit for good reporting of an amazing event in which a flying object appears, there is immediate plausible meaning to the lines emanating from the object and the attitude of its witnesses. Understandable, too, is the selection of a separate site to describe such an extraordinary incident.

"In the case of our primitive artist, there is no chance at all the pictograph is a fake but, to equalize matters, we may doubt that a flying saucer was what he saw. It is easier to settle for symbols."

Whether it depicts a UFO that has landed near the rocky shores of Christina Lake or it preserves some

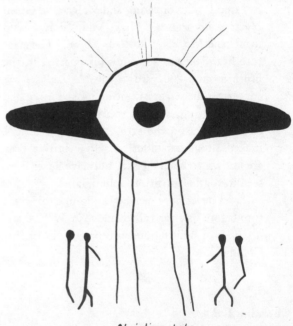

Christina Lake

The existence of the Christina Lake Pictograph was brought to public attention by the journalist John Magor. He dubbed it the "flying object" pictograph and reproduced photographs and diagrams of it in Canadian UFO Report, *Vol. 2, No. 6, 1973. The artist Lesley Footner prepared a pen-and-ink version of the pictograph which dramatically enhanced the "flying object" aspect of the pictograph. [John Magor]*

tribal tradition unconnected with the stars will probably never be known.

"Our purpose is simply to have a part in writing what may be the most important news story of our time." So explained John Magor who, more than anyone else in Canada, could and should be called *the* UFO reporter.

John Magor was born in Passaic, N.J., of Canadian parents. He graduated from the Columbia School of

"Our purpose is simply to have a part in writing what may be the most important news story of our time," explained John Magor. The veteran journalist was the publisher and editor of the widely admired Canadian UFO Report *and is the author of two books,* Our UFO Visitors *(1977) and* Aliens Above, Always *(1983). [Hawkshead Services]*

Journalism in 1937 and served with the RCAF in World War II. He is a professional journalist. He has been a freelance contributor to newspapers and magazines, the British United Press' parliamentary correspondent in Ottawa, and the publisher of both the Prince Rupert *Daily News* and the Cowichan *Leader.*

From his home in Duncan on Vancouver Island, he launched the journal *Canadian UFO Report* in 1968 — on the very day a U.S. investigating committee announced that flying saucers were not worth bothering about. The *Report*, which appeared on a quarterly basis until 1979, sought to supplement with Canadian coverage the widely reported phenomena in the skies over other countries.

He is the author of two books. The first is *Our UFO Visitors* (1977) which is devoted to Canadian encounters. The second, *Aliens Above, Always: A UFO Report* (1983), bears the intriguing dedication: "This study is dedicated to the developing association between us and our UFO visitors which, though still barely recognized, may set us on an utterly new course in history. While some observers have said these visitors are a passing fancy, signs persist they will be here always."

Magor has had "two good UFO sightings," both over Vancouver Island in 1971.

Columbia River/
Indian Prophetess

The famous surveyor David Thompson encountered an Indian prophetess on Rainy Lake, near the Upper Columbia River, in July 1809. He left a description in his journal.

> The day after my arrival a lady conjuress made her appearance; she was well dressed, of twenty-five years of age; she had her medicine bag, and bore in her hands a conjuring stick about 4½ feet in length, 1½ inches wide at the foot and three inches at the top, by one inch in thickness. One side was painted black, with rude carved figures of birds, animals, and insects filled with vermilion; the other side was painted red with

carved figures in black. She had set herself up for a prophetess, and gradually had gained, by her shrewdness, some influence among the natives as a dreamer, and expounder of dreams. She recollected me before I did her, and gave a haughty look of defiance, as much to say, I am now out of your power. Some six years before this she was living with one of my men and his wife, but became so common that I had to send her to her relations; as all the Indian men are married, a courtesan is neglected by the men and hated by the women. She had turned prophetess for a livelihood, and found fools enough to support her; there is scarce a character in civilized society that has not something like it among these rude people.

Two years later on the banks of the Columbia River, en route to Astoria, Thompson encountered the same unusual woman dressed like a male and accompanied by a young female lover. He described the woman's appearance in the entry in his narrative for 28 July 1811.

A fine morning; to my surprise, very early, apparently a young man, well dressed in leather, carrying a Bow and Quiver of Arrows, with his Wife, a young woman in good clothing, came to my tent door and requested me to give them my protection; somewhat at a loss what answer to give, on looking at them, in the Man I recognised the Woman who three years ago was the wife of Boisverd, a Canadian and my servant; her conduct then was so loose that I had then requested him to send her away to her friends, but the Kootanaes were also displeased with her; she left them, and found her way from Tribe to Tribe to the Sea. She became a prophetess, declared her sex changed, that she was now a Man, dressed, and armed herself as such, and also took a young woman to Wife, of whom she pretended to be very jealous: when with the Chinooks, as a prophetess, she predicted diseases to them, which made some of them threaten her life, she found it necessary for her safety to endea-

vour to return to her own country at the head of this River.

Thompson and his native interpreter were so impressed with the young woman that they described her to the next group of Indians they met along the way. The following month, on 2 August, the explorer noted "the story of the Woman that carried a Bow and Arrows and had a Wife, was to them a romance to which they paid great attention and my Interpreter took pleasure in relating it."

The passage appeared in *David Thompson's Narrative of His Explorations in Western America: 1784-1812* (1916) edited by J.B. Tyrrell. It was Tyrrell who first noted that the remarkable young woman was also described by Sir John Franklin in his *Narrative of a Second Expedition to the Shores of the Polar Sea* (1928).

Franklin's account was written at Fort Chipewyan, April 1827, and referred to a Mr. Stewart who was the Hudson's Bay Company's chief factor there.

I mentioned in my former Narrative, that the northern Indians had cherished a belief for some years, that a great change was about to take place in the natural order of things, and that among other advantages arising from it, their own condition of life was to be materially bettered. This story, I was now informed by Mr. Stewart, originated with a woman, whose history appears to me deserving of a short notice.

While living at the N.W. Company's Post, on the Columbia River, as the wife of one of the Canadian servants, she formed a sudden resolution of becoming a warrior; and throwing aside her female dress, she clothed herself in a suitable manner. Having procured a gun, a bow and arrows, and a horse, she sallied forth to join a party of her countrymen then going to war; and, in her first essay, displayed so much courage as to attract general regard, which was so much heightened by her subsequent feats of bravery, that many young men put themselves under her command.

Their example was soon generally followed, and, at length, she became the principal leader of the tribe, under the designation of the "Man-like Woman." Being young, and of a delicate frame, her followers attributed her exploits to the possession of supernatural power, and, therefore, received whatever she said with implicit faith. To maintain her influence during peace, the lady thought proper to invent the above-mentioned prediction, which was quickly spread through the whole northern district.

At a later period in her life, our heroine undertook to convey a packet of importance from the Company's Post on the Columbia to that in New Caledonia, through a tract of country which had not, at that time, been passed by the traders, and which was known to be infested by several hostile tribes. She chose for her companion another woman, whom she passed off as her wife. They were attacked by a party of Indians and though the Manlike Woman received a

"A new world was in a manner before me . . . ." So marvelled David Thompson in his journal on 10 January 1811. The surveyor and mapmaker of the Northwest faithfully recorded the sights and sounds of all the lifeforms he encountered on his travels. Crossing half a continent, he kept coming across the tracks of animals unknown to zoologists but apparently known to his native informants. This sketch by artist C.W. Jefferys depicts Thompson in the act of establishing the latitude and longitude. [Metropolitan Toronto Library]

wound in the breast, she accomplished her object, and returned to Columbia with answers to the letters. When last seen by the traders, she had collected volunteers for another war excursion, in which she received a mortal wound. The faith of the Indians was shaken by her death, and soon afterwards the whole story she had invented fell to discredit.

The two passages are of considerable interest because they describe a highly individual person (who remains nameless, alas) and also some of the forces that led her to adopt the habit and costume of the prophetess, medicine-man, conjurer, or shaman.

Cowichan Bay/ Chief Dan George

In the 1960s, Chief Dan George (1899-1981) emerged as the most eloquent of the native spokesmen. He was a Squamish chief in his own right, an inspired orator, a fine published poet, and a film actor of immense dignity. He died in a North Vancouver hospital on 23 September 1981 and was buried at the Burrard Reserve in North Vancouver.

The story of the curse first came to light in a Canadian Press story filed in Victoria on 9 December 1981. According to the news story, Chief Dan George addressed a gathering in the small coastal community of Cowichan Bay in March 1972. It was not a pleasant speech, for it culminated in an angry litany of the sins committed by the province's forest industry and concluded in a curse. Afterwards he was approached by a member of the audience, Nora Maxwell of Vancouver Island, who spoke with the Chief and asked him to repeat the invocation for her private diary. He did so and she wrote it down, but he made her promise to reveal it only after his death.

According to Nora Maxwell's account and a subsequent news story in the *Toronto Star*, 12 December 1981, the Indian chief uttered these words in conclusion:

Then the final blasphemy—the loggers, the rapers, the spoilers come in with their screaming

347

saws and their cruel steel cables, and they mutilate and wreak havoc in the place of the Great Spirit and they destroy his creation which is the great forest.

Theirs is the cruellest abortion of all because they destroy not a few weeks of growth but one hundred, five hundred, one thousand years of growth. And they do it with greed and with wantonness, and they leave the forest a broken, humiliated, mutilated thing and they do it for their god Mammon.

May they be cursed unto the fourth and fifth generation. May their seed be cursed and may they find their profits turn to ashes in their mouths, that they cannot sell their product of their filthy hands.

Certainly the British Columbia forest industry went into a steep decline over the subsequent years, culminating in violent clashes between government-backed loggers and Haida-backed protesters on South Moresby Island.

Cowichan District/
The Encounter

A practical nurse at the Cowichan District Hospital reported seeing a UFO and its two occupants from the second floor of the east wing of the hospital. At 5:00 a.m. on 5 January 1970, while attending a patient, Doreen Kendall pulled open the drapes of the ward window and was astonished to see a circular UFO with a transparent dome hovering in the air about forty feet away. A summary of her sighting prepared by the Aerial Phenomena Research Association (APRO) appears in *The Encyclopedia of UFOs* (1980) edited by Ronald D. Story:

A "saucer," resembling a sphere, around which was a circular air foil with lights on the rim, was hovering about sixty feet off the ground over a small patio. She estimated it to be about fifty feet in diameter, and that it was hovering at about the level of the third or children's floor, at about sixty feet from the hospital wall. When

first seen, it was tilted toward her position, so that she could see inside of the upper portion, which she felt was illumined from below rather than above. The top portion was transparent and the light at the bottom (which she saw later) was red.

Inside the transparent "bubble" or "cupola," she claimed to observe two human-appearing entities. At first, they were visible from the side and only from the waist up, but when the object tipped toward the hospital she saw their complete forms. Both were standing, one apparently behind the other, and each stood in front of a stool with a back on it. The occupant farthest to her right was facing what appeared to be a chrome instrument panel comprised of large and small "circles" (possibly dials), which were brilliantly lit. She felt that both of the "men" were over six feet tall and noted that they were both well built.

As the object hovered, the man on Mrs. Kendall's left turned toward her, then extended his hand and touched the back of the man near the instrument panel, who reached down and grabbed a rodlike device with a ball on the top extremity, which protruded from the floor. She compared the latter to the joy stick of an airplane. The man moved the "stick" up, then down, at which the disk tilted toward her, and she obtained a good view of the interior, including the men.

She said that the hand of the man, who apparently alerted the other to her presence, was flesh-coloured and human-appearing. Both wore dark clothing, and their features were concealed by some kind of headgear. The latter seemed to be similar to the material of the rest of their clothing.

Nurse Kendall summoned her co-worker, Nurse Frieda Wilson, who asked, "What on earth is that?" Nurse Kendall replied, "I guess it's a flying saucer." They summoned three other nurses who arrived in time to watch the lights of the disc-shaped craft disappear to the northeast.

Nurse Kendall later said that she had not been afraid, but was curious. She had the impression that the disc was having mechanical trouble. The APRO calls incident the "Cowichan (Canada) Encounter."

Duncan/
Granger Taylor's Flying Saucer

The Granger Taylor Flying Saucer rests on stilts in the backyard of the Taylor home at Duncan on Vancouver Island. It is a mute memorial to its builder, young Granger Taylor.

"He built his spaceship out of two satellite receiving dishes and outfitted it with a television, a couch, and a wood-burning stove. He became obsessed with finding out how flying saucers were powered, spending hours sitting in the ship thinking and often sleeping there," wrote Douglas Curran in his book *In Advance of the Landing: Folk Concepts of Outer Space* (1985).

Then one November night in 1980 Granger Taylor simply disappeared. He left behind a yard strewn with old tractors, machine engines, vintage automobiles, a bulldozer, as well as a note which read: "Dear Mother and Father, I have gone away to walk aboard an alien ship, as recurring dreams assured a 42 month interstellar voyage to explore the vast universe, then return. I am leaving behind all my possessions to you as I will no longer require the use of any. Please use the instructions in my will as a guide to help. Love, Granger." The forty-two months were up in May 1984 and his parents, Jim and Grace Taylor, leave the back door unlocked in case their son shows up. But he never has.

Granger Taylor left school in the eighth grade and found work as a mechanic's helper, showing a flair for repairing machinery. At the age of fourteen he built a one-cylinder car which is on display at the Duncan Forest Museum. He constructed a replica of a World War II fighter plane, and he left behind his silver-and-red flying saucer. He told a friend a month before he disappeared that he was in mental contact with someone from another galaxy and that he was in receipt of an invitation to go on a trip through the Solar System.

"On the night that Granger disappeared," wrote Curran, "a storm struck the central part of Vancouver Island. Hurricane winds were reported and electrical power was knocked out. Granger vanished, along with his blue pick-up truck.

"After four years of 'exhaustive checks' of hospital, passport, employment, and vehicle records, the Royal Canadian Mounted Police have not uncovered a single clue as to the whereabouts of Granger Taylor. 'I can hardly believe Granger's off in a spaceship,' his father said. 'But if there is a flying object out there, he's the one to find it.' "

Duncan/
UFO Sighting

Mr. and Mrs. William Marshall and their daughter and her friend, both students at the University of Victoria, were witnesses to a UFO sighting at the Marshall home in Duncan, Vancouver Island. It took place during the evening of 7 March 1969. Mrs. Marshall's testimony was carried by the *Canadian UFO Report*, May-June 1969, and reprinted by Yurko Bondarchuk in *UFO: Sightings, Landings and Abductions* (1979):

[The object] appeared to be looking for something, speeding up and then slowing down, almost to a standstill. It passed over Mount Prevost, and turned east until it was over the large B.C. Hydro generating station [Georgia Thermal Generating Plant] about four or five miles north of Duncan. By seeing the lights, we were able to ascertain that the UFO hovered over the plant. It hovered over the generating station for about fifteen minutes, and then returned over Mount Prevost again in a westerly direction for a time. It again turned and came straight towards our house, and as it passed over us we could see quite plainly its shape as it was flying at a much lower altitude than previously, and its light threw their gleams onto the object. It was round in shape, and we could plainly see it rotating. It had four lights, one green, one red, one yellow and the other white. After passing slowly over our house, it hovered around for a few more minutes, then speeded up and headed rapidly in an eastern direction towards where I believe Vancouver is situated from here. I timed how long the UFO was in this area—forty minutes.

Bondarchuk concluded that because the craft hovered over the Marshall home, "It would seem that the UFO, presumably manned, had detected that its presence was being observed by members of the Marshall household."

Eve River/
The UFO Experience

The Eve River flows into Johnstone Strait on the northeastern shore of Vancouver Island. Dave and Hannah McRoberts of Campbell River took a photograph of a mountaintop with white clouds behind it from the Eve River Rest Area just before noon in October 1981. When the film was developed, the mountain and clouds were in focus but to their astonishment so was a bright, silvery disc, not unlike a UFO.

The McRoberts received so many requests for their

This is a black-and-white reproduction of a colour photograph of a mountaintop overlooking the Eve River Rest Area on the north shore of Vancouver Island. The snapshot was taken in October 1981 by Hannah McRoberts who was intent on getting a picture of the mountain. At the time neither she nor her companions saw anything unusual in the sky, so her surprise was great when the processed film showed a metallic-looking UFO above the mountain. [Fortean Picture Library]

photograph, they began to sell enlargements—$5 for a five-by-eight, $10 for an eight-by-ten — according to Edward Regis, Jr., in "Anti-Matter," *Omni*, March 1985, who quoted Hannah McRoberts as saying, "I believed in flying saucers before I took the picture, and I still believe in them, even more so. We've put the picture under a microscope, and there's no way that the object can be anything else. The scary part is, once you've had a UFO experience, you're supposed to have another. I keep looking at the mountains and waiting for a UFO to come."

Grand Rapids/
A Premonition or Prophecy

The Overlanders of 1862 were a group of settlers who travelled from Fort Garry, Manitoba, to the present city of Prince George, British Columbia. They travelled overland in Red River carts, using mules and packhorses to cross the Rocky Mountains. It was a tremendous ordeal for the 142 stalwart Overlanders, including two women and two children.

Not all of them made it. One Overlander drowned shooting the Grand Rapids of the Upper Fraser River on 30 September 1862. He was a young married man named J. Carpenter. He might have had a premonition that he was going to drown because the previous night he scribbled in his diary what fate had in store for him. In it he referred to his wife in Toronto. The wording of the note — surely a premonition if not a self-fulfilling prophecy — was recalled by Carpenter's companion, Richard H. Alexander, who was eighteen at the time. It is quoted by Mark Sweeten Wade in *The Overlanders of '61* (1931).

> I forgot to tell you that Carpenter wrote something in his diary just before starting, which on examination proved to be the following, as nearly as I can recollect, "Arrived this day at the cañon at 10 A.M., and drowned running the canoe down; God keep my poor wife!" Was it not strange? He was not much of a swimmer and clung to the canoe which I think was sucked down under and held under the rocks, at least we never saw it again.

Haney/
The Haney Boulder

A large granite boulder found near Haney, a small community outside Vancouver, has unusual markings which may or may not date from the Bronze Age.

Bruce Macdonald, a zoologist and amateur epigrapher with the University of British Columbia, discovered the boulder by accident on the bank of Spring Creek outside Haney in 1979. At first he mistook the markings for bulldozer scratches. Then he copied and sent them to Barry Fell, professor emeritus of Harvard University, president of the Epigraphic Society, and enthusiast of Bronze Age inscriptions.

Fell identified the markings as being an inscription carved in North Iberic, a script related to Arabic. According to the CP story carried by the Niagara Falls *Review*, 4 April 1983, the inscription had a definite purpose. It stated that the water of the creek was uncontaminated and was drinkable. If Fell is right, what were North Iberic-inscribing people doing on the West Coast of Canada during the Bronze Age?

Harrison River/
Medicine Man

The following account of an encounter between an Indian medicine-man named Frank Dan and a sasquatch was said by J.W. Burns, who collected it, to have occurred in July 1936 along Morris Creek, a small tributary of the Harrison River which lies generally north of Chilliwack. The folklore-like account is reproduced from Ivan T. Sanderson's *Abominable Snowmen: Legend Come to Life* (1977):

> It was a lovely day, the clear waters of the creek shimmered in the bright sunshine and reflected the wild surroundings of cliff, trees, and vagrant cloud. A languid breeze wafted across the rocky gullies. Frank's canoe was gliding like a happy vision along the mountain stream. The Indian was busy hooking one fish after another hungry fish that had been liberated only a few days before from some hatchery. But the Indian was

351

happy as he pulled them in and sang his medicine song. Then, without warning, a rock was hurled from the shelving slope above, falling with a fearful splash within a few feet of his canoe, almost swamping the frail craft. Startled out of his skin, Frank glanced upward, and to his amazement beheld a weird looking creature, covered with hair, leaping from rock to rock down the wild declivity with the agility of a mountain goat. Frank recognized the hairy creature instantly. It was a Sasquatch. He knew it was one of the giants — he had met them on several occasions in past years, once on his own doorstep. But those were a timid sort and not unruly like the gent he was now facing.

Frank called upon his medicine powers, sula, and similar spirits to protect him. There was an immediate response to his appeal. The air throbbed and some huge boulders slid down the rocky mountain side, making a noise like the crack of doom. This was to frighten away the Sasquatch. But the giant was not to be frightened by falling rocks. Instead he hurried down the declivity carrying a great stone, probably weighing a ton or more, under his great hairy arm, which Frank guessed — just a rough guess — was at least two yards in length. Reaching a point of vantage — a jutting ledge that hung far out over the water — he hurled it with all his might, this time missing the canoe by a narrow margin, filling it with water and drenching the poor frightened occupant with a cloud of spray.

Some idea of the size of the boulder may be gained from the fact that its huge bulk blocked the channel. Later it was dredged out by Jack Penny on the authority of the department of

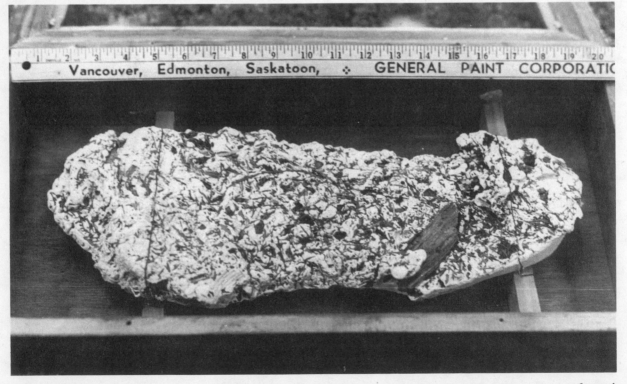

Seventeen-inch footprints were found in the dense bush near the community of Kaslo in the West Kootenay area of British Columbia. A plaster cast was made of one of the prints in December 1978 by Roy Green of Kaslo, who said he was convinced that the prints were not a hoax. [Nelson News/Canapress]

hinterland navigation. It may now be seen on the tenth floor of the Vancouver Public Museum in the department of "Curious Rocks". . . .

The giant now posed upon the other ledge in an attitude of wild majesty as if he were monarch of these foreboding haunts, shaking a colossal fist at the "great medicine man" who sat awe-struck and shuddering in the canoe, which he was trying to bail out with his shoe. The Indian saw the Sasquatch was in a towering rage, a passion that caused the great man to exude a repugnant odour, which was carried down to the canoe by a wisp of wind. The smell made Frank dizzy and his eyes began to smart and pop. Frank never smelt anything in his whole medicine career like it. It was more repelling than the stench of moccasin oil gone rotten. Indeed, it was so nasty that the fish quitted the pools and nooks and headed in schools for the Harrison River. The Indian, believing the giant was about to dive into the water and attack him, cast off his fishing lines and paddled away as fast as he was able.

Kamloops/
Divining a Lost Mine

There is an intriguing but anecdotal account of how an adventurous diviner tried — and failed — to locate a lost mine in the vicinity of Kamloops.

The diviner or dowser in question is Evelyn Penrose, who told the story in a sketchy way in her autobiography, *Adventure Unlimited* (1958). It was Penrose's belief that she had inherited the gift of divining for subterranean waters and minerals from her father, a wealthy landowner who possessed the same ability. She was born near St. Ives, Cornwall, in the early 1880s. A legacy permitted her to travel at will and she did so. She lived for a time in California, Hawaii, and British Columbia before settling in Western Australia in the 1950s. She made her Canadian home in Victoria.

Apparently during a period of drought in the 1930s, the British Columbia government employed her as province's official water-diviner. Governments have been known to do stranger things. By her own account she visited 249 homesteads on the mainland and the island and successfully dowsed 392 water locations. But she was restless and ever on the lookout for new adventures. When she learned that in the Kamloops area there was a lost gold mine which had been cursed by "Red Indians," she went there, hired an experienced woodsman as a guide, and ventured into the woods in search of the mine. She immediately felt she had plunged into an evil domain. She was frightened and the woodsman lost his bearings for more than twenty-four hours. He later explained, "I was like a man walking in a fog and I couldn't see properly either. All my knowledge of the forest was gone. There's something mighty queer up there. I half-believe you're right. The Indians may have done something funny to this place."

But they were rescued and she returned to Victoria, quite ill. From a professor of anthropology, who was knowledgeable about native ways and the history of the Kamloops area, she learned that her intuitions had been right. The mine was not only lost, it was cursed. The mine was on Indian land and they had worked it for their own needs until the white man had ejected them and worked it for themselves. The Indians then placed a curse on the land and thus "sealed off" the mine. The white miners suffered sickness and accident and there was even a tunnel collapse. Over the years even its locale was forgotten. The curse proved effective on Penrose, as well as on the miners. She wrote that it "took many weeks, many curious ceremonies, and much earnest prayer to break it and set me free and it was a long time before I was well again."

Penrose could dowse without any equipment whatsoever, using only her bare hands. She did not even have to travel to the area that was to be divined. With a plumb-bob suspended from a string, she would dowse over a map of the area and thus identify sources of subterranean waters and minerals. Further particulars appeared in her autobiography and also in Walter Kempthorne's article "Evelyn Penrose's Lifetime of Dowsing," *Fate*, June 1969.

Kanaka Bar/
The Kettle Valley Express

Canadian Pacific's Kettle Valley Express, No. 12, left Vancouver on New Year's Eve, 1924, and headed east into a blizzard. "Her regular route, up through the famous Coquilhalla pass and down by way of the Okanagan Valley from Hope to Nelson had long since disappeared under a blanket of closely packed snow," explained Gillmore Stevens in "The Kettle Valley Express Mystery," *Railroad Stories*, December 1934. "There was only one thing left to do; route her over the main line north to a station called Spencer's Bridge and detour back down to Brodie, which was on her regular run."

The express train was seven miles out of North Bend approaching Kanaka Bar on the Fraser River when the engineer heard two distinct blasts, the emergency whistle. He halted the train and examined the track and then questioned the crew. There seemed to be no reason to stop, and none of the trainmen admitted to pulling the "monkey line" to signal a halt. "Had the engineer been alone in the cab he might have been accused of dreaming. But the fireman had heard it just as plainly as the hogger."

No sooner had they started up than they again heard the two distinct blasts. Again the engineer stopped, to check the track. There "standing on the track, squarely in the path of the oncoming express, stood another locomotive. Without lights, no signals displayed, and as silent as a tomb, it was motionless, not ten feet from the pilot of the stalled express."

The solitary engine had been abandoned outside Kanaka. There was an explanation for that. But a head-on collision had been avoided. What about the warnings? "In the investigation which followed no light was thrown on the mystery of how the signal cord on the express had been pulled as she roared through the darkness. It was a mystery, and it still is." Such is the mystery of the Kettle Valley Express.

Kelowna/
Two Likenesses of Ogopogo

Kelowna, a city located on the east shore of Okanagan Lake, is said to be the Indian word for "grizzly bear." In Kelowna, there are two likenesses of Ogopogo, the creature said to inhabit Okanagan Lake.

At the entrance to the Kelowna City Park there is a statue of the serpent-like creature with two horns, two green humps, and a single red forked tongue. The image of Ogopogo looks down from the totem pole carved by Oliver Jackson in 1955 and erected to mark the city's fiftieth anniversary.

It was from Kelowna that John Fisher, the broadcaster and publicist, on behalf of the Canadian Tourist Association, of which he was an ex-director, offered $5000 for an authenticated photograph of Ogopogo. At the time there were no claimants.

Ogopogo may be viewed in the main park in downtown Kelowna, B.C., if not in the waters of nearby Okanagan Lake. This effigy of the lake monster measures about twenty-five feet in length, sports a horselike head with erect ears and twin horns, and disports its snake-like body of coils, scales, and fin-like spikes in its own tiny pool, unaccountably drained in this photograph taken in April 1988. [Don Weixl Photo]

According to Ian Mullgrew, writing in the *Globe and Mail*, 12 August 1985, "Even Lloyd's, the London insurance cartel, is betting $1-million against anyone catching Ogopogo. But the backers have hedged their bet by ensuring you can collect the money only if you catch him on a rod and line, cage him and have him authenticated by a Vancouver-based zoologist."

Keremeos/
Old Spanish Mound

Legend has it that the weapons, armour, and remains of long-dead Spanish soldiers, members of an ill-fated expedition which was ambushed and annihilated by the Similkameen Indians almost two centuries ago, lie buried in the Spanish Mound, a low-lying grassy mound in the Similkameen River valley not far from Keremeos. As N.L. Barlee explained in *Gold Creeks and Ghost Towns* (1970):

> The Indians say that sometime near the middle of the 18th century, a band of strange-looking men with white faces and wearing "metal" clothes marched up the Similkameen from the south and set up camp near Keremeos. They remained at this campsite until an altercation erupted between an Indian and a soldier; the quarrel quickly turned into a small-scale battle between the natives and the whites. In this fray, the Spanish managed to inflict heavy losses on the Indians, and afterwards the Spaniards, along with several Indian prisoners taken as carriers, retreated to the northeast and disappeared up the valley of Keremeos Creek.

The strange column made its way over the flats at the foot of Okanagan Lake, near present-day Penticton, and then followed the old eastside trail north to a point slightly north of present-day Kelowna, where they erected quarters and wintered. The following spring, their numbers diminished, they retraced their steps southward to the upper reaches of Keremeos Creek.

> They marched out of the hills and camped on a small flat overlooking Keremeos Creek near where that stream enters the valley proper. Forewarned, the Similkameen tribe waited and when the unsuspecting Spaniards finally struck camp and moved off down the valley they were suddenly ambushed in overwhelming numbers; and after a sharp and bloody battle the Indians slaughtered them to the last man.

> After this epic struggle, according to the legend, the Similkameen then buried the despised white strangers with most of their armour and weapons in a small mound somewhere between the last Spanish camp and the Keremye'us Indian village, and they lie there to this day, in this long lost and unmarked burial place — the legendary "Spanish Mound."

Although no written records support the Spanish expedition theory, it is bolstered by the oral tradition and a number of artifacts found in the vicinity. Pictographic images of the so-called Prisoner Paintings found on a nearby boulder depict what look like riders on horses and roped prisoners or bearers. A rare cache of old copper armour resembles old Spanish mail. A study of the foundations of a dilapidated cedar structure, discovered in 1863 at Mill Creek northeast of Kelowna, indicates that the logs were cut with iron axes. It is known that Spanish ships in the eighteenth century were wrecked close to the mouth of the Columbia River.

As Barlee concluded, "The evidence is circumstantial but it is also highly intriguing. The old mystery remains unsolved."

Leechtown/
The Mystery Tunnel

In the absence of evidence there are tales in abundance that tell about the Mystery Tunnel in the historic Jordan Meadows–Leechtown region, which is located in the vicinity of the Sooke River west of Victoria on Vancouver Island.

The story goes that a veteran prospector named Ed Mullard, working his way through the bush, was astonished to find carved rock stairs which led him down to an archway carved into the face of a bluff and down again into a subterranean cellar. The Mystery Tunnel continued farther down into the darkness, but Mullard had only matches with him for illumination and had to turn back. In later years he described the tunnel as neither a natural cave nor a mine, and tried to relocate it but never with success.

Mullard died in May 1959, and on the Remembrance Day weekend the Victoria *Daily Colonist* sponsored an expedition in search of the Mystery Tunnel. Members of the expedition explored the most likely candidate, Survey Mountain, but found no rocky stairway. As noted by T.W. Paterson in "Mystery Tunnel of Leechtown" in *Canadian Treasure Trails* (1976), there are tales that the Mystery Tunnel was the work of Spanish explorers and conquistadores who before they withdrew from the West Coast in 1795 constructed a stronghold for their golden treasure, booty from their empire in Central and South America. Mullard maintained he had recovered a bar of Spanish gold from the site but never produced it. Paterson wrote:

> Yet the rumours persist: rumours of a "Spanish" cannon lost in Jordan Meadows; of a bronze tablet in the fork of a tree; of mystic symbols and ancient dates carved in tree trunks on the Island's west coast; of a Spanish monastery and massacre at Sooke's Boneyard Lake; of a beautiful "Madonna" carved into stone beside the Leech River. Fascinating as they are, they just do not hold up under close inspection.

And yet two ancient swords, one shaped like a cutlass, were found near the Sooke Potholes. Preliminary research has suggested they could be of Spanish origin.

Mica Mountain/ The Wild Thing

William Roe was a hunter and trapper working on the highway near Tête Jaune Cache. One day in October 1955, he climbed Mica Mountain in the Monashee range, close to the Alberta border, to see an old deserted mine. What happened next was reported by

Roe in a long statement he prepared for John Green, author of *Sasquatch: The Apes Among Us* (1978). Here are some excerpts:

> I came in sight of the mine about three o'clock in the afternoon after an easy climb. I had just come out of a patch of low brush into a clearing when I saw what I thought was a grizzly bear, in the bush on the other side. . . .
>
> I could see part of the animal's head and the top of one shoulder. A moment later it raised up and stepped out into the opening. Then I saw it was not a bear.
>
> This, to the best of my recollection, is what the creature looked like and how it acted as it

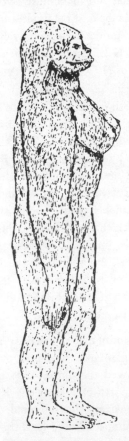

This sketch of a female sasquatch was drawn by William Roe's daughter under his direction. It is a likeness of the hairy monster that he saw in 1955 on Mica Mountain, B.C. [John Green]

came across the clearing directly toward me. My first impression was of a huge man, about six feet tall, almost three feet wide, and probably weighing somewhere near three hundred pounds. It was covered from head to foot with dark brown silver-tipped hair. But as it came closer I saw by its breasts that it was female.

And yet, its torso was not curved like a female's. Its broad frame was straight from shoulder to hip. Its arms were much thicker than a man's arms, and longer, reaching almost to its knees. Its feet were broader proportionately than a man's, about five inches wide at the front and tapering to much thinner heels. When it walked it placed the heel of its foot down first, and I could see the grey-brown skin or hide on the soles of its feet.

It came to the edge of the bush I was hiding in, within twenty feet of me, and squatted down on its haunches. Reaching out its hands it pulled the branches of bushes toward it and stripped the leaves with its teeth. Its lips curled flexibly around the leaves as it ate. I was close enough to see that its teeth were white and even.

Finally the wild thing must have got my scent, for it looked directly at me through an opening in the brush. A look of amazement crossed its face. It looked so comical at the moment I had to grin. Still in a crouched position, it backed up three or four short steps, then straightened up to its full height and started to walk rapidly back the way it had come. For a moment it watched me over its shoulder as it went, not exactly afraid, but as though it wanted no contact with anything strange.

The thought came to me that if I shot it, I would possibly have a specimen of great interest to scientists the world over. . . .

I levelled my rifle. The creature was still walking rapidly away, again turning its head to look in my direction. I lowered the rifle. Although I have called the creature "it," I now felt that it was a human being and I knew I would never forgive myself if I killed it.

Roe gives further details about the appearance of the female creature and its habitat, but sheds no further light on the mystery of the sasquatch.

Nanaimo/
The Brother Twelve

The Brother Twelve was the title and name assumed by Edward Arthur Wilson (1871–1943), a charismatic cult leader and confidence man also known as The Chela, The Great Guru, Swami Siva, and (simply) The Master. Although born in Wyoming, a village east of Sarnia, Ontario, he operated on the West Coast and called himself The Brother Twelve, professing to be in psychic rapport with eleven previous "Masters" of "The Great White Council."

At Cedar-by-the-Sea, near Nanaimo, on the east coast of Vancouver Island, in 1926 he established a commune for like-minded followers. In all, some two hundred adherents turned their wealth over to him, took part in the weekly fertility rites, and subscribed to the occult-sounding principles of the Aquarian Foundation, formed the following year to fight "The Invisible Empire of Evil" which seemed to be a compound of Judaism and Catholicism.

The commune was supposedly founded on the principles of free love and communism, naturopathy and vague but voguish "eastern" esoteric wisdom. Members even issued a publication titled *The Chalice*. But its principles were really the practices of its founder, and Wilson was all of the following: swindler, embezzler, sexual exhibitionist, charismatic cult leader, father figure, messianic medium *manqué*, and unbalanced personality. The local police were repeatedly summoned to separate the warring factions and they charged Wilson with a variety of offences. The group disbanded in confusion in 1934.

Nine years later Wilson died in Brisbane, Australia, penniless and broken. The story of Wilson's "love cult" was told more in sorrow than in anger by his straight-laced brother, the Rev. Herbert Emmerson Wilson, in *Canada's False Prophet: The Notorious Brother Twelve* (1967). (The biography was "ghost" written by the pulp writer Thomas P. Kelley.)

The Brother Twelve has long departed to the reward reserved for "swindling swamis." But they remember him well with some affection and wonder on Vancouver Island, and relish such details of his "love cult" as the antics of the whip-wielding Madame Zee, his "soul-mate." Fifty years later the novelist Jack Hodgins drew on details of the Brother Twelve's commune for his lively novel *The Invention of the World* (1977).

But there is something else they relish on Vancou-ver Island and that is the tale of the buried treasure of The Brother Twelve. It seems that before he fled the commune and left it in disarray, he hid a cache of gold. It is claimed that he had an immense quantity of gold dust which he poured into jars then packed into wooden crates. There were forty-five crates in all, and these were buried in the woods behind the commune at Cedar-by-the-Sea. And unless someone has found them in the intervening years, that is where they still are.

Has the snowman's cap blown away or does this snapshot capture the flight of a UFO? The photograph is not a prank shot but the first in a series of four taken from different vantage-points which depict the UFO or whatever it is disappearing into the distance. They were taken in February 1975 at Nanaimo, B.C. The photographer, sixteen-year-old Lance Willet, completed his snowman and was snapping a picture of it when the sombrero-type UFO flew into and out of view. [John Magor]

Nass and Skeena Rivers/ "Buddhist Dirges"

Are the traditional songs sung by the Northwest Coast Indians really Buddhist dirges? This question was asked and answered in the affirmative by Marius Barbeau. For the distinguished folklorist, the matter became a pet subject.

In 1920, Barbeau first noted the melodic resemblance between traditional funerary songs sung by Buddhists in Asia and those sung by Indians on the reserves along the banks of the Nass and Skeena Rivers in northern British Columbia. "The tune scaled a high curve, touched a top note, then dropped over

wide intervals to the bottom, where it droned leisurely."

Barbeau reasoned that the songs came from "a common Asiatic source" — India, China, Japan, Mongolia—through Siberia, across the Bering Strait, and into Alaska and the northwest coast of Canada— the route taken by the Asian migrants themselves. In addition to their songs, they brought with them their clan structure, totemic system, and characteristic, one-sided drum.

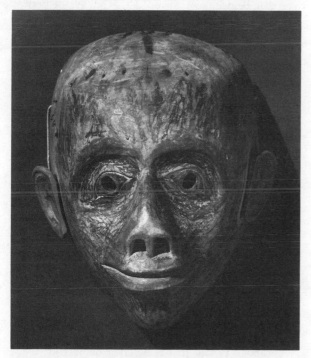

What does this Niska Monkey Mask really represent? Monkeys? Images or memories of sasquatch-like creatures on the West Coast? "Mask, wooden, representing a monkey, used at feasts. British Columbia, Nass River. From Marius Barbeau, September 1927." Barbeau, the distinguished ethnologist and collector, supplied the artifact along with its scant documentation to the ROM's Department of Ethnology. [Royal Ontario Museum, Toronto]

This Tsimshian "monkey mask" was carved from red cedar and worn on ceremonial occasions by the Niska Indians of the Nass River area of northern British Columbia. The mask was collected by the anthropologist G.T. Emmons about 1914. The following question is worthy of Erich von Dañiken: "Do the mask's features represent and recall the visage of the sasquatch, the wild creature of the woods?" [Peabody Museum, Harvard University, Photograph by Hillel Burger/Copyright (c) President & Fellows of Harvard College, 1977/All Rights Reserved]

Nelson/
"It Sure Was Curious"

John Bringsli, a veteran woodsman and hunter, met a curious man-like animal or animal-like man in the woods north of Nelson, where he lived. He recalled the encounter for John Green, the reporter and sasquatch-hunter.

On 7 August 1962, at seven-thirty in the morning, Bringsli was picking berries on an old logging road near Lemon Creek, not far from Kokanee Glacier Provincial Park. Half kneeling, he looked up and saw a strange animal. "At first I thought it was, like, a bear, but then I looked closer at it and realized it

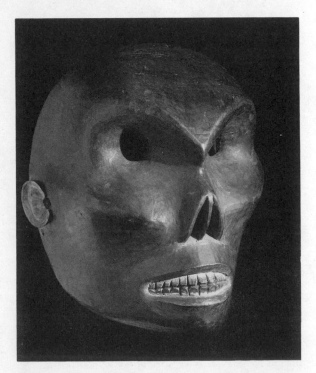

This Tsimshian mask has deeply sunk eyesockets, pointy nostrils, clenched teeth, high cheekbones, and tiny ears. Its description in the catalogue is stark: "Ape-like face." It seems the mask was carved to evoke the terror of the unknown. Does it preserve the appearance of strange wild creatures of the British Columbia interior? [Courtesy of the British Columbia Provincial Museum, Victoria, British Columbia]

wasn't an animal, it was more like a human being. It was coated in steel-grey hair and it was very tall. I would say between seven and nine feet. An enormous size." It walked upright. "It had an enormous set of arms on it. Believe me, I was so close I could see the nails on its fingers."

Bringsli was frightened. "It looked terrible at me, like a terrific human being." But it was as interested in Bringsli as Bringsli was frightened of it. "Its head was cocked to the side like it was trying to figure out what I was doing, who I was . . . I wouldn't say it looked menacing at all, that way, but it sure was curious to see what I was doing."

"Well naturally a man like me hadn't seen a thing like that before, so I dropped the bucket of berries and I took off. I came out this logging road, you know how old logging trails are, trees felled across it here and there, I never even saw them, I went over them, and got into my car and took off. I don't remember much till two or three miles down the road that I really came to."

Okanagan Lake/
The Home of Ogopogo

British Columbians may boast that there are more strange creatures in their province than anywhere else in the country and perhaps anywhere on the continent. By "strange creatures" are meant not human beings but creatures of land and lake which are unknown to modern science. The monsters of the land are led by the sasquatches. The schools of monsters of the deep are led by Ogopogo, the best-known of all the strange creatures of Canada.

Ogopogo is said to be the chief denizen of Okanagan Lake in the Okanagan Valley. The lake is 69 miles long and varies from .75 of a mile to 2.5 miles in width. It covers an area of 127 square miles and drains through the Okanagan River into the Columbia River. The lake was formed at the close of the last ice age about 10,000 years ago. Members of the Okanagan tribe of the Interior Salish were the inhabitants of the valley to greet the Scottish fur-trader David Stuart who arrived in 1814, the first known white person to enter the valley. There are large Indian reserves in the valley, and the area is noted for its fruit farming and its holiday attractions. One of the latter is Ogopogo.

Each summer tens of thousands of tourists arrive to the shores of Okanagan Lake. Many of them hope to catch a glimpse of Ogopogo, but fewer expect to. All of them may see effigies of the lake monster in the cities of Kelowna and Vernon. In addition, the Department of Recreation and Conservation has erected an official marker on Highway 97, south of Peachland, roughly halfway between Vernon and Kelowna. The marker singles out Squally Point on

Okanagan Lake which it identifies as "Ogopogo's Home." The inscription reads:

OGOPOGO'S HOME

Before the unimaginative, practical white man came, the fearsome lake monster, N'ha-a-itk, was well known to the primitive, superstitious Indians. His home was believed to be a cave at Squally Point, and small animals were carried in the canoes to appease the serpent.

Ogopogo still is seen each year—but now by white men!

The B.C. Department of Recreation and Conservation erected this plaque on the eastern shore of Okanagan Lake between Peachland and Penticton, B.C. The plaque identifies the location of "Ogopogo's Home" at Squally Point. The area, remarkable for its fruit and vegetable production, is renowned for its "lake monster" sightings. [Don Weixl Photo]

The sign was raised in the 1950s. Today the racist wording of the inscription would bring acute embarrassment to the Department of Recreation and Conservation.

Ogopogo is usually identified as Canada's Loch Ness monster, but the reverse is true, for it is Nessie who should be identified as Scotland's Ogopogo. While references to the Great Orme in the Scottish loch go back to the sixth century, the period of modern sightings really began with an article that appeared under the heading "Strange Spectacle on Loch Ness —What Is It?" published in the *Inverness Courier* on 2 May 1933. Then familiar photographs of the "monster" were published around the world. The photos showed a prehistoric-looking creature with a small head and long neck or a simple, serpentine form which appeared to undulate on the loch's surface.

Native references to the creature in the depths of Okanagan Lake give it many names, among them the Salish *Na-ha-ha-itk* and "snake in the lake" and the Chinook "wicked one" and "great beast in the lake." Modern sightings begin in the 1860s, with the first white settlers in the Okanagan Valley. One of the earliest dated sightings occurred in July 1890 when Captain Thomas Shorts was passing Squally Point aboard the steamer *Jubilee* and saw a creature fifteen feet long, with a head like a ram, and fins thin enough for the sun to shine through. By 1925 sightings had

Edward Fletcher of Vancouver believes that he has photographs of Ogopogo rippling across Okanagan Lake, the loch-like lake in the interior of British Columbia. On 3 August 1976, Fletcher was in his motor boat and came within fifteen feet of the "strange creature" which seemed to stretch out some seventy feet. The image is shown on Fletcher's television screen. [Colin Price/Vancouver Province/Canapress]

become so common that hunting parties were formed in various cities to run down the creature, whether fish or animal.

Ogopogo was named before Nessie was described as a "monster." It is maintained that on 23 August 1926, at a luncheon meeting of the Rotary club in Vernon, a member named Bill Brimblecombe sang a parody of an English music-hall song with new lyrics hailing the Vancouver Board of Trade party. The lyrics were adapted by H.F. Beattie, an amateur actor, and they went:

> I'm looking for the Ogopogo,
> The bunny-hugging Ogopogo.
> His mother was a mutton,
> His father was a whale.
> I'm going to put a little bit of salt on his tail.
> I'm looking for the Ogopogo.

The phrase "bunny-hugging" refers to a popular dance of the 1920s. This is the origin of the name according to Mary Moon, author of *Ogopogo: The Okanagan Mystery* (1977). It is possible that the creature's name was in the air in more ways than one. A craze popular from the time it was launched in August 1921 was the Pogo Stick, a springloaded pole with crossbars for hands and feet on which children and even adults went hopping around.

Approximately fifty-five seconds of 8 mm colour film were taken of movement in the water by Art Folden, a millworker, in August 1968. He thus became the first person to capture Ogopogo on motion-picture film. The Folden Film received its first public screening at nearby Kelowna on 2 February 1970.

The shooting locale of the Folden Film was Highway 97 just south of Peachland, on the west side of Okanagan Lake in the interior of the province. The film, which shows serpent-like movements across the surface of the lake, is taken as visual evidence that the lake is the watery home of a sea serpent.

Four frames of the Folden Film were reproduced in monochrome in Arlene B. Gaal's *Beneath the Depths* (1976) who explained: "The film quality is not too sharp, but something definitely submerges three times

and moves several hundred yards at speeds ranging from a slow cruise to fairly quickly."

Pitt Lake/ "A Human-shaped Head"

Two prospectors, in the mountains northwest of Pitt Lake, in June 1965, encountered some fresh tracks in the snow. "The prints were enormous, twice as long as their own boots and as wide as a boot is long," wrote John Green in *Sasquatch: The Apes Among Us*

Footprints left in the ground may be cast in plaster. But when prints are made in the snow they are ephemeral. Here is a news photograph which shows a young woman on 17 March 1977 pointing out a print left in the snow by a large-footed creature, perhaps a sasquatch. [Les Bazso/Vancouver Province/Canapress]

363

(1978). "They were perfectly flat and showed four clear toe impressions, with the big toe on the inside of the foot like a man's. The stride was double a man's stride. Snow in the bottom of the prints was tinted pink."

The prospectors followed the tracks until, in the trees on the other side of a lake, they saw a figure standing and watching them.

> The thing was auburn in colour except for its hands, where the colour lightened gradually almost to yellow. As sketched on the spot it had a human-shaped head set directly on very square shoulders and its forearms and hands bulged like canoe paddles. It was swaying slightly as if shifting from foot to foot, and its hanging arms swayed too. They couldn't make out its face because of the distance, but the features seemed flat. It was just noon, and they sat down and had a cigarette and a chocolate bar while they watched it and tried to estimate its size. Counting the sets of branches on the evergreens where it stood and comparing them with those on their side of the lake, they decided it was between ten and fourteen feet tall. It just continued standing there, so finally they went on. When they came back later there were more tracks around, but the animal was gone.

The following day the prospectors saw more tracks, but never again did they see the creature with "a human-shaped head."

Pitt Lake/
Slumach's Lost Mine

Slumach's Lost Mine is the best known of British Columbia's legendary mines. It is said to have claimed twenty-three lives over its century-long history.

Near Pitt River at the head of Pitt Lake northeast of Vancouver, a sixty-year-old Salish Indian named Slumach shot and killed a half-breed prospector named Louis Bee. Slumach was hanged for the offence at New Westminster on 16 January 1891. These details come from T.W. Paterson's article "Legend of the Lost Creek Mine" published in *Canadian Treasure*, Vol. 2, No. 2, Summer 1974. And so do the legends that follow.

Slumach is credited with the discovery of a fabulously rich gold deposit northwest of Pitt Lake, the location of which he refused to divulge to anyone. He would travel to the deposit, work the lode, and return with gold nuggets worth a fortune. Each time he went he took a "squaw" with him; each time he returned he came back alone. In all he claimed he had silenced eight women to ensure that the site of the mine remained a secret. Some he stabbed; others he shot with bullets cast in gold.

The day before his execution, a squaw arrived with a canoe laden with gold in an attempt to buy his freedom. That is one tale. Another is that the day of his execution he confided to his son the location of the mine. But the condemned father cautioned his intemperate son, "Go only when times are bad." At first the son obeyed his father's injunction. Then he grew careless. Once, while drunk, he visited the site in the presence of a half-breed prospector. Both the son and the prospector came to bad ends.

The half-breed is sometimes identified with an actual American prospector, John Jackson, who made trips to the site in 1901–03. Before his sudden death at New Westminster, the prospector sketched two maps of the mine which he passed on to friends. The maps have long histories, and each has resulted in prospecting trips and tragic deaths. It is known that one crude map turned up in Seattle in the 1950s, another in Vancouver in the 1970s.

According to Jack Khahtsahlano, a Salish chief who claimed he knew Slumach's son, not only has the site of Slumach's mine been lost, but the site is cursed. While it may be found again, it will never be found by a white man.

Prince Rupert/
The Metlakatla Man

The full-sized outline of the Metlakatla Man is preserved in intalgio in the rockface on the southwestern tip of Robertson Point, near the Indian community of Metlakatla on the Tsimpsean 2 Reserve, just west of Prince Rupert on the province's northwest coast.

According to Tsimshian tradition, long ago a chief declared he was going to visit the sky. He disappeared and reappeared some days later, explaining that he would have stayed longer in the sky but there was no food up there and he was hungry.

He further explained that in returning he had fallen through the sky and struck the earth with some force. To prove it, he led the Indians to the sculptured rockface and pointed to the dent he had made in his descent. "Of course he really made it himself while hiding," the news reporter added. "The Dominion Archaeologist has made a plaster mold and sent it to the National Museum of Canada." Such is the story of the Metlakatla Man.

According to David J. W. Archer, who contributed the entry on "Metlakatla Pass Sites" to *The Canadian Encyclopedia*, "The area is noted for its density of archaeological sites; archaeologists have discovered 40

The Man Who Fell from Heaven is what the newspaperman and UFO enthusiast John Magor has dubbed the Metlakatla Man. Preserved in rock in intaglio form is the full-size outline of a recumbent human being. The Metlakatla Man may be found on the southwestern tip of Robertson Point, west of Prince Rupert, B.C. Stories about the origin of Metlakatla Man are found in the traditions of the Tsimshian Indians whose reserve is close by. [John Magor]

sites along its shores — 27 are shell middens which represent the remains of ancient Indian villages; 13 are petroglyph or rock art sites, which consist of low-relief carvings and boulders or rock outcrops. The people who occupied the area of the time of European contact were the Coast Tsimshian." The Metlakatla Pass, or Venn Passage, on the northern coast, has been occupied for approximately 5000 years.

Queen Charlotte Islands/ Chinese Jewish Immigration

Is there any evidence of ancient Chinese Jewish immigration on the West Coast, specifically the Queen Charlotte Islands? There is some speculation, but no real evidence, as Eric Downton noted in *Pacific Challenge: Canada's Future in the New Asia* (1986):

> Perhaps the most fascinating speculation concerning early Asian migration to the territory now known as British Columbia is the possibility that Jews from China accidentally landed there at the close of the thirteenth century. The existence of a flourishing and influential Jewish community in China almost a thousand years ago is a confirmed fact. The late Father Jean Marie Le Jeune, who pioneered linguistic studies among the Indians of British Columbia, recorded that he found Hebraic words in native languages west of the Rockies, and that some Coast Indian ceremonial rites are strongly suggestive of Hebraic ceremonies and usages. To account for the possible appearance of Chinese Jews in North America, a theory has been developed on the unsuccessful attempt by the powerful Mongol ruler, Kublai Khan, to invade Japan from ports in China and Korea in A.D. 1281. A typhoon scattered the Mongols' armada. Speculation suggests that junks carrying a Jewish contingent in Kublai Khan's army were blown by the typhoon out across the Pacific to finally make landfall off the North American coast, perhaps in the area of the Queen Charlotte Islands.

In the absence of evidence, wonders never cease.

Queen Charlotte Islands/
Haida and Mu

The Queen Charlotte Islands consist of about 150 islands which lie in a scimitar-shaped archipelago off the north coast of British Columbia. Because of their isolation and their escape from glaciation, the plant life resembles that of some faraway places like Ireland and Japan, and the land mammals and some birdlife are unique subspecies.

Parts of the Islands have been inhabited for at least 2000 years. The old Haida village of Ninstints, the centrepiece of Anthony Island Provincial Park, before it was abandoned in the 1880s, had an exceptional stand of totem poles which were the crown and glory of the native art of the Northwest Coast. The poles not now rotting were removed to museums in the South. At its height the Haida nation numbered some 6000 people. By 1915 the number had fallen to 588 individuals. Today it has risen to 5700 men, women, and children. Ninstints was added to UNESCO'S list of World Heritage Sites.

"The Babirussa, as everyone knows, is an animal of the hog tribe, inhabiting only Celebes and the adjacent islands," explained F.W. True in *Science*, 4:34, 1884, reproduced in *Ancient Man: A Handbook of Puzzling Artifacts* (1978) compiled by William R. Corliss. Celebes is an Indonesian island. A pair of tusks of the Babirussa were excavated in August 1883 from the grave of an old Indian medicine-man near the northwest end of Graham Island. "The question then arises, How did these teeth come into the possession of the Indian doctor, who died some fifty years since at an advanced age?" The author suggested that the tusks were trade goods found on the wreck of a Japanese junk that had made its way across the Pacific to the Queen Charlotte Islands some time before the turn of the nineteenth century.

James Churchward, the English author and mystic principally responsible for the published descriptions of the mysterious island-continent of Mu, which supposedly stretched from the Bering Strait to Australia before sinking into the Pacific Ocean some 14,000 years ago, was said to be inhabited by the prehistoric Uighurs people, of whom, according to Churchward, the present-day Haida are the proud descendants. Apparently the Haida carve their totem poles in dim memory of those poles originally erected on Mu. The claim is recalled by Peter Kolosimo in *Not of This World* (1971).

Race Rocks/
Zone of Silence

Is there a Zone of Silence in the waters off the southern tip of Vancouver Island? The question has been raised many times since the turn of the century, and it continues to be asked at a time when radar has usurped the function of lighthouses and foghorns.

The region in question lies south of the lighthouse and foghorn at Race Rocks, where a narrow channel separates the Pacific Ocean and the Strait of Juan de Fuca. The channel is an area of treacherous sailing. From the days of sail to the age of steam, many a vessel was lost in the rock-strewn channel, and many a sea captain argued in his defence before a court of inquiry that the foghorn failed to penetrate the "region of inaudibility." The zone has thus been described as "acoustically dead."

Bruce Levett, a West Coast CP staff writer, discussed the Zone of Silence in an article carried on 26 March 1956 by the Niagara Falls *Evening Review*. In it he quoted the remarks of J.H. Hamilton, of Victoria, who noted:

> As long ago as 1930, the existence of a silent zone was disproved and the cause of the inaudibility of the foghorn ascertained. It is true the sound of the foghorn was not heard within a certain small sector which was found to be due to the fact it was screened or shut off by a large rock and a small building.
>
> After an on-the-spot investigation by the Dominion hydrographic officers, the foghorn was raised 30 feet. No strandings have occurred since then.

Levett wrote, "With radar sweeping a path through the fog for modern-day vessels, Race Rocks has lost much of its air of mystery.'' Yet he concluded, ''Whatever the answer — an excuse for faulty navigation, a sound-shielding rock or an unnatural phenomenon — the legend persists.''

Richmond/
Psychic Photography

It should be noted that ''psychic photography'' has nothing to do with ''spirit photography.'' The distinction made by students of the two subjects is that the former is regarded as a process, the latter as a product. ''Psychic photography'' may be defined as the process whereby a photographer claims through the use of ''psi'' or psychic powers the ability to produce photographic images with or without the use of the camera lens. ''Spirit photography'' may be defined as the study of images preserved in photographic form of apparitions, spectres, or ghosts. The photographer seldom makes any psychic claims of his own, maintaining that the images were caught accidentally. Yet they are generally taken in such places as haunted houses and ancient chapels, though they are sometimes taken at *séances*.

The world's leading psychic photographer is a former elevator operator from Evanston, Illinois, named Ted Serios. Following an illness, he claimed the peculiar ability to influence photographic film through nonphysical means. What he does is hold a Polaroid camera at arm's length, stare into the lens, concentrate, and release the shutter. The exposures that result are often photographically and pictorially unsettling. The images are not at all what anyone expected, including, perhaps, Serios. His critics, of whom there are many, note that in the process he makes use of a ''gizmo'' as a ''concentration aid.'' This is a short tube which is not always made available for immediate examination.

Ted Serios's main proponent is Jule Eisenbud, a Colorado-based psychiatrist who is also active as a parapsychologist. Eisenbud is most widely known as the author of a book called *The World of Ted Serios* (1967). One of the psychic photographer's most memorable images is reproduced in this illustrated study

of the ''wild talent.'' The image was produced in a sitting in 1963, and it shows, in a blurry sort of way, the airplane hangar at the RCMP's Air Division in Rockcliffe, Ottawa. Not only is the building skewed, but the large letters on the outside wall reveal a misspelling. Instead of ''CANADIAN'' the letters read ''CAINADAIN.''

The Canadian contribution to spirit photography has been a major one—witness the photographs taken by Dr. T. Glendenning Hamilton in Winnipeg in the 1920s—but the contribution of Canadians to psychic photography has been a minimal one except for the work of Dorothy Izatt. Mrs. Izatt is a British-born Canadian and resident of Richmond, B.C. She produces her psychically derived imagery on single frames of 8 mm movie film.

John Magor, a journalist with a scientific background, has described Mrs. Izatt's psychic photography in *Aliens Above, Always* (1983):

> Without any special facilities or training, she has produced images so strange yet containing such definable forms, they give one the feeling of peering into another world, which perhaps is true. Although she has readily allowed experts to examine her pictures and equipment (she favours a simple Keystone XL movie camera and sends all her film out for processing), the mystery remains unsolved.
>
> It may well be that the secret is within Dorothy herself, for her psychic aptitude is pronounced, a trait that she and her six sisters seem to have inherited from their father. She remembers that as a girl in Hong Kong, where they grew up, she could see vision-like pictures on the walls of her room.
>
> Now a young-looking mother and grandmother, she is far removed from any tangible association with the occult, yet her unusual qualities persist perhaps more strongly than ever. For instance, there is the wide spectrum of her sight. While she can see the auras of living things, as can others of her kind, there is more to it than that. After she and her husband had a microwave

oven installed in their kitchen, she remarked on the beauty of the colours it sent out when the heat was turned on. Only then did she learn that the microwaves were invisible to others!

In 1974 she started taking her pictures. She loads Kodak Ektachrome film into one of her Super 8 cameras — the Keystone XL, the Minolta XL, or the Sankyo Seiki XL. She aims the camera at the night sky from the window of her bedroom or the balcony of her house. She shoots a single frame from time to time. The reel of film is sent to a commercial laboratory and developed. When it comes back, it is found to be blank — except for single frames here and there that are exposed with unexpected imagery. There is no movement or continuity in the imagery. Indeed, there is no ready explanation for the presence of the luminescent images at all.

It seems that some protean, plasma-like alien presence in the sky manifests itself for an instant or for some time for the camera of this unusual woman. But

"This object beamed its light into my bedroom and made it look like daylight. I watched it for a while and saw it change from a round object to the shape you see in my photograph. It stayed in sight for approximately 10 minutes, then dimmed its light and disappeared." It was taken at 5:30 a.m., 20 Oct. 1980.

These are some of the images that Dorothy Izatt, of Richmond, B.C., captures on film. Black and white reproduction does not do justice to the colourful forms which are so mysterious yet strangely beautiful.

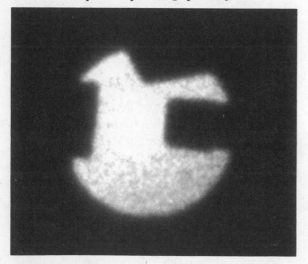

The large moon-like image, yellow on black, is one of a series taken with a zoom lens at 9:20 p.m., 28 March 1980.

This ovoid object, so reminiscent of the traditional form of the UFO, altered its shape from large to small to large again. The image was exposed on film at 1:38 a.m., 14 March 1983.

that is not the full story, for the photographer also *sees* the images that she is photographing.

Observers of the photographic procedure include J. Allen Hynek, the man who coined the phrase "close encounters of the third kind," and Jule Eisenbud, the psychiatrist who studied the "thoughtography" of Ted Serios. It was Eisenbud who suggested that the images she captures on film are the projections of her own thoughts. But it is Izatt's belief that the images are created by UFOs and their occupants in response to her desire to photograph them. She believes that UFOs are a form of the etheric energy which pervades the universe. She senses that earlier she has lived in Atlantis.

When asked what the power of taking such mysterious movies has done for her, she replied that the ability has helped her as a person. "It has made me a more serious person. It has changed me, made me better. It has never never failed me, and I try never to fail it."

Roberts Creek/ "Sea Lions"

The novelist Hubert Evans (1892–1986) saw "Sea Lions" in the Strait of Georgia. The sighting took place when Evans was living in the community of Roberts Creek, which overlooks the waters of the Strait of Georgia, northwest of Vancouver. He recalled the sighting for the writer Howard White who recorded the conversation in "The Cadborosaurus Meets Hubert Evans," *Raincoast Chronicles Sixteen: Collector's Edition II* (1983).

Evans and White were sitting and talking in the same house at Roberts Creek some fifty years later when they heard a news report on the radio about the Loch Ness Monster.

> "We had one here, you know."
> "One what?"
> "A sea serpent. Or some sort of sea creature quite similar to the way they describe that one over there."
> "No!"

"Well, I've never told many people, but it's a fact," he said. "It was in 1932, right out there where you're looking. I was up on the back lot with Dick Reeve, our neighbour, working on the road—that same one you drove in on to get here. Bob Stephens, the old Scot from down the beach—he's dead these many years—came puffing up the hill and said, 'By God now, you've got to come down and see what you make of this. We've had the glass on it for half an hour. It's the damnedest thing.'

"It was late afternoon with the water dead calm just as it is now, and the sun was low so the water was just a sheet of gold. And here, out just beyond that deadhead, was a series of bumps breaking the water, all in dark silhouette, and circled with ripples.

"'Sea lions,' I said. 'They run in a line like that sometimes.'

"'Just you keep watching,' old Scotty said. And just a minute or so later, along at the end of this series of bumps, up out of the water comes a shaft—this was all in silhouette, so we couldn't see detail, although the outlines were very clear—up, up, up until it must have been six or eight feet out of the water. There was a spare buoy out on the reef then, which was about twelve inches through, and I could see this thing was about the same thickness — certainly no smaller.

"'You know, it could be a log,' I said. I'd seen a crooked log sometimes scatch in the current and roll, so a limb comes up like that — when you see something you don't know what to make of, you keep trying to explain it by the things you know.

"But right there as we stood watching, none of us breathing a word, the top end of this shaft began to elongate horizontally, until we were presented with the profile of a head, very much like a horse's in general shape, with eye bumps, nostrils, and something in the way of ears or horns. The neighbour down the way said it had stuff hanging down like hair but I didn't see that. I tell you, it was a feeling, watching that head come round as if to look at us. It just put the hair up on the back of your neck.''

Howard White added a tribute to the integrity of Evans: ''He is the sort of person who, if he tells you the Cadborosaurus exists, you suddenly discover you believe in Cadborosauruses. I would be hard put to say which is more remarkable.''

Rossland/
"Strange Aerial Body"

Rossland, a city near the American border, was part of what has been called the Airship Wave of 1896. In the latter half of that year and during the next, Americans in the western states reported sightings of strange aerial phenomena, ranging from processions of luminous bodies through the night sky to fleets of articulated flying machines streaming through the sky during the day. Today these sightings would constitute a UFO flap, but the Airship Wave took place before UFOs and Flying Saucers; indeed, it predated by eight years the historic flight of the Wright Brothers at Kitty Hawk.

A newspaper report dated 12 August 1896 recalls what is known. ''It told of a strange aerial body that approached the town, paused momentarily above a nearby mountain peak, made seven wide circles in the sky, and then sped away on a straight course. The thing was described as a 'luminous ball of fire that glowed amidst a halo of variegated colours.' The object took a quarter of an hour to complete its man-oeuvres and was watched by many citizens of Ross-land.'' The report comes from Loren E. Gross's ''Airship Wave of 1896'' in *The Encyclopedia of UFOs* edited by Ronald D. Story (1980).

Ruby Creek/
"The Sasquatch Is After Me!"

The Ruby Creek Indian Reserve adjoins the Fraser River northeast of Harrison Hot Spings, and the farm-house of George and Jeannie Chapman was in 1942 located a few miles north of Ruby Creek.

One day one of the Chapman children, playing in the field, started yelling about ''a big cow coming out of the woods.'' Mrs. Chapman was in the house but rushed out to see what was wrong. She saw approaching the house a man-like creature about eight feet tall all covered with dark hair. It had a flat face and was neither a cow nor a bear. Terrified, she called her children and fled. She found her husband, a rail-road maintenance worker, and explained her panic, ''The sasquatch is after me!''

A group of men went to the farm to investigate, and they found huge tracks that crossed the field to the house, went around to a shed where a barrel of fish had been dumped, then down to the river and back across the field to the mountains. The footprints were huge. A cast was made and the imprint was found to be sixteen inches long, four inches across at the heel, and eight inches across the ball. The weight had crushed whatever was underfoot. The weight of the creature was estimated to be between eight hundred and a thousand pounds. It stepped over a fence more than four feet high without breaking stride.

John Green explained in *Sasquatch: The Apes Among Us* (1978), ''For an Indian to see a sasquatch was believed to be very bad luck; in fact, the observer was in danger of dying.'' Mrs. Chapman survived but she never quite recovered from the scare.

Saanich/
The Spirit of the Hanging Judge

Sir Matthew Baillie Begbie (1819–1894), an Old Country barrister, was appointed chief justice of the mainland of British Columbia in 1866. He was nick-named ''the Hanging Judge'' for his fair but summary decisions.

Is the spirit of the Hanging Judge still hanging around? Jean Kozocari believes that in some sense Sir Matthew's spirit remains on the earthly plane. Kozo-cari, a native of Victoria, is a practitioner of wicca. In the company of two mediums, she visited a bun-galow believed to be haunted or disturbed. The own-ers and occupants of the bungalow, which was built

370

in the 1950s in Saanich, north of Victoria, had a long list of complaints about the place — swarms of flies, plagues of rats, strange noises, and peculiar movements. They said they felt that the bungalow was in some sense "unliveable." Kozocari and the mediums immediately felt that something was awry.

Kozocari's first visit took place on Father's Day 1980. Over the next three years she made repeat visits to the house until it was acquired by new owners. During her visits she noted the disturbances. Whatever was affecting the house resisted the rite of exorcism. Dowsers came up with nothing. At one point the letter M was found scratched into the silver of a large mirror mounted on a bedroom wall.

Kozocari sensed that the disturbances emanated from the basement of the house where it rested on solid rock. The rock oozed an oily, aluminum-coloured substance. There seemed to be no rhyme or reason to the disturbances. In researching the history of the property, Kozocari learned that the property had once been owned by Sir Matthew Baillie Begbie. In those days it was simply a tract of land without any dwellings. Apparently Sir Matthew was quite attached to the property, and from time to time would ride out to visit it, sitting for hours on the large rock and staring out into space.

Kozocari took a number of photographs of the bungalow. They were clear except where it rested on the rock. Here all detail was lost behind a peculiar pillar of white. One final photographic negative, taken of the house as a whole, was found to depict a curly-haired, white-bearded man sporting a cowboy-like hat: the very image of the older Sir Matthew.

Did the M in the mirror stand for Matthew? Kozocari believes that it does and that his spirit was responsible for the disturbances. "His very strong presence made it possible for other and later things to manifest."

Sechelt/
"A Shaggy-haired Creature"

A huge hairy creature was seen by a drill-rig operator on the extension of a logging road near Mile Nine on Chapman Creek not far from Sechelt. About seven-thirty on a morning in June 1973, the operator had taken his rig to the end of the road and climbed on top of a huge log to look over the grade ahead.

Across the clearing he saw a shaggy-haired creature about 150 or 200 feet away, standing on two legs. "Besides being covered with hair, it seemed to have a goatee. It appeared to be larger than a man, and it was jumping up and down, with its arms bowed out at its sides," noted John Green in *Sasquatch: The Apes Among Us* (1978). "The witness looked for a place to run to, but glanced back and saw the creature 'do a somersault off the log to the lower side of the road cut.' Then the man leaped onto the drill rig and started to drive it away in reverse . . . and then told his boss that he would not work alone on the road anymore.

"When the men returned to the site they found some footprints in mud, only one of which was much good. All the witnesses agreed that it looked more humanlike than bearlike. The man who saw the creature did not say that it was a sasquatch, but he insisted that it was not a bear."

Silver Creek/
Sasquatch Wrestlers

Sasquatch wrestlers were spotted by Burns Yeomans, a veteran prospector, working the headwaters of Silver Creek, not far from Harrison Hot Springs, in August of 1939 or 1940. Yeomans told his story to sasquatch-hunter John Green in 1965, recalling that from the peak of a mountain he and a fellow prospector could see into an open valley about three-quarters of a mile below and beyond them.

The sight he found unforgettable was of four or five dark and hairy men-like beings, standing upright, wrestling. They were knocking one another to the ground in a playful rather than a vengeful manner. He watched the sasquatch wrestling match for about half an hour, until the participants tired of their sport and disappeared into the woods. Yeomans estimated that the wrestlers stood about seven feet tall and each weighed about four hundred pounds.

South Pender Island/
Gulf Island Monster

What could be dubbed the Gulf Island Monster was spotted on South Pender Island, one of the Gulf Islands in the Strait of Georgia.

The creature was seen about eleven o'clock on the morning of 4 February 1934 by two duck hunters, Cyril H. Andrews and Norman Georgeson, who later swore an affidavit about the sighting. At the time of the sighting they were on the rocks near Gowland Head.

Andrews looked down into the water and was astounded to see a long, snakelike object just below the surface. Apparently this experience did not deter the hunters, for shortly thereafter they brought down a duck close by. The duck was not dead, but it was wounded severely, and the hunters attempted to retrieve the wounded animal by means of a small boat. Just as they approached the duck a head and two loops or segments came clear of the water. Then the whole thing except the head, which remained just out of the water, sank. The monster then opened its large mouth, seized the duck, and swallowed it. Numbers of sea gulls swooped down at the creature, which snapped at them when they came too close. Shortly after this it sank below the surface.

The head of the creature resembled a horse without ears or nostrils. The tongue came to a point, and its teeth were fishlike. In color it was a gray-brown with a darker brown stripe running along the body slightly to one side. (Presumably, there was a corresponding stripe on the other side.)

Immediately after the episode Andrews phoned the local justice of the peace, G.F. Parkyn, who came along some fifteen minutes later. About ten minutes after Parkyn arrived, the creature's head and part of the body broke the water about 18 meters (twenty yards) from shore, swimming in an undulating manner away from

it. The head did not appear to come clear of the water; it seemed to rest on the surface; about 4 meters (twelve feet) of the body behind the head showed, and the body had an estimated diameter of $\frac{2}{3}$ meter (two feet). On this occasion the creature was seen by twelve residents of South Pender Island.

Andrews, who was only 3 meters (ten feet) from the animal when it gulped down the duck, estimated the overall length of the animal at 12 metres (forty feet) and its diameter at the thickest part about $\frac{2}{3}$ to 1 meter (two to three feet). The body gradually tapered toward the tail. He estimated the head to be about 1 meter (three feet) long and $\frac{2}{3}$ meter (two feet) wide.

One could hardly ask for a better set of anecdotal observations, in laymen's terms, of the primitive snakelike whales known as zeuglodons . . . a variety of related forms roamed the seas as recently as the Miocene, twenty-five million years ago, reaching lengths up to 21 meters (seventy feet).

The description appeared in *Searching for Hidden Animals* (1980) written by the marine scientist Roy P. Mackal.

Squamish/
"It Did Have Hands"

An unusual animal was spotted on the road north of Squamish by a highway maintenance foreman. He prepared a report for his superintendent who passed it on to the B.C. Provincial Museum.

One afternoon in January 1970, the foreman was driving north of Squamish; around a slight curve in the road he saw "a large hairy animal" that "got up on its hind legs and ran across the road in an upright position." He judged it to stand at least seven feet and weigh 250 pounds. It had a prominent stomach. There was a shag of reddish-brown hair all over its body from the shoulders down. The hair on its head was quite short and darker brown in colour. "It didn't have a bear's face, it had more of a flat face like a person or a monkey.'' He was perhaps one hundred feet away from the animal when, noting the approaching driver, it ''just scurried right across the road and up the bank here on the other side, in the upright position like a man would run, and it did run, it didn't waste any time at all.''

An unusual feature of the sighting is that the animal was carrying its food. ''I'm not sure how many fingers but it did have hands and in the right hand it was carrying what appeared to be a fish, a ten-inch fish.'' John Green, in *Sasquatch: The Apes Among Us* (1978), added: ''Nearest water is a river running far down below the road in a steep canyon, so if the creature was indeed carrying a fish it seems probable that it was not for its own consumption.''

Toba Inlet/
The Ostman Abduction

The strangest sasquatch story of all is the one told by Albert Ostman, the logger and experienced woodsman who left a detailed account in writing of his abduction, captivity, and escape from a family of four sasquatches in 1924. As strange as it may seem, his story has a strong narrative appeal and may well be true in part if not in whole.

Ostman was prospecting about twenty-five miles northeast of Toba Inlet, on the mainland coast, and was in the habit of sleeping with his belongings, which included cans of provisions and a Winchester rifle, snug beside him in his sleeping bag. He was rudely awakened one night by being hoisted onto the shoulder of a hairy creature and being carried on a journey that lasted some three hours. He was numb when they arrived at their destination, a small valley surrounded by high mountains.

Here Ostman was held captive but not otherwise harmed by a family of four sasquatches. The family members were the eight-foot male who had abducted him, a female who must have weighed between five hundred and six hundred pounds, and two young sasquatches of each sex. They were hairy naked apelike creatures who subsisted on a vegetarian diet. Ostman took an interest in their appearance and way

of life, introducing them to canned milk and tins of snuff. But they had no intention of allowing him to leave, so he bided his time and on the sixth day of captivity he made his escape, firing the Winchester to frighten them. He took his bearings from the position of the sun and made his way on foot to Salmon Arm Branch, Sechelt Inlet, and then to Vancouver.

This was Ostman's last prospecting trip and his sole experience with the sasquatch. Although he told his tale to a couple of people, no one would believe him, so he simply stopped telling it. In 1957, however, he wrote out his account in longhand in a scribbler and agreed to be interviewed extensively by John Green, who recounts Ostman's experience in *Sasquatch: The Apes Among Us* (1978). Green added: ''Albert Ostman is dead now, but I enjoyed his friendship for more than a dozen years, and he gave me no reason to consider him a liar.''

Rene Dahinden (left) converses with Albert Ostman outside the latter's cabin at Fort Langley, B.C. The interview took place in the summer of 1957. Ostman recounted how he had been abducted and held captive by a family of sasquatches in the interior of British Columbia. In his lap he holds the notebook in which he wrote down the story of his 1924 kidnapping. Dahinden holds a copy of Ralph Izzard's book Yeti. *[Rene Dahinden/Fortean Picture Library]*

373

Vancouver/
The Headless Brakeman

It is said the CPR yards at the foot of Granville Street have been haunted by a Headless Brakeman since 1928. That was the year Hub Clark, a railway brakeman, literally lost his head in the yards. One dark and rainy night he slipped and fell off a freight train and his head hit the rails next to the freight track. He was knocked unconscious and a passenger train, speeding down the track, severed his head from his body, two inches below the Adam's apple. Thereafter stories circulated about how a headless man in railway overalls was seen in the yard on dark and rainy nights. Apparently for years Vancouver railwaymen joked, "Don't throw your pumpkin away after Hallowe'en, Hub Clark can use it." The Headless Brakeman was last sighted on a dark and rainy night darting between boxcars in 1942 by a railway worker. The story is told by Ted Ferguson in *Sentimental Journey: An Oral History of Train Travel in Canada* (1985).

Vancouver/
Cults and Occults

Not for nothing has British Columbia been called "California North." The Canadian province shares with the American state of California a position on the Pacific Coast and a reputation for fostering a range of cults and sects which appear, at least to outsiders, as somewhat bizarre. One of these bizarre cults was mentioned by I. Hexham, R.F. Currie, and J.B. Townsend in their article on "New Religious Movements" in Volume II of *The Canadian Encyclopedia*.

> Probably considered the most notorious is the Children of God, or "the Love Family." The group originated with David Berg, a Pentecostal evangelist, as a California "Jesus people" group in 1968. Berg's movement arrived in 1971 in Vancouver, where it grew relatively rapidly. Berg changed his name to Moses David and claimed to receive "revelations" from God that

included visions of the end of Western society. Eventually the group formed a series of colonies that went underground as a result of adverse publicity and the exposure of their allegedly perverse sexual practices. At its height the Children of God had around 8000 members. In 1983 it likely had under 2000 worldwide, with about 50 in Canada.

Another bizarre group which the authors discuss in their article is the Kabalarians.

> A uniquely Canadian movement is the Kabalarian Philosophy. Founded in Vancouver in 1930 by Alfred J. Parker (1897–1964), it blends Eastern and Western thinking, and teaches an understanding of mind and cycles based on mathematics. Its practices include vegetarian diets and physical exercises similar to those of Yoga.

A precept of the Kabalarians is numerology—the letters of one's name bear numerical values which affect that person for good or ill.

Vancouver/
The Pursuit of Major Sumerford

The story of the improbable, accidental, or destined pursuit by lightning of Major Sumerford was told by Vincent H. Gaddis in *Mysterious Fires and Lights* (1967), who based his account on Albert A. Brandt's "Lightning to the End" from *Fate*, April–May 1952.

> Probably no man was ever more relentlessly pursued by lightning than Major R. Sumerford, late of Vancouver, British Columbia, Canada. His enemy first struck in 1918, in Flanders, while the major was on patrol. He was hit by a bolt that killed his horse and left him paralyzed from the waist down. An invalid, he returned to his home in Vancouver, and eventually recovered enough to walk with the aid of two canes.
>
> In 1924, the major and three friends went on a fishing trip to a mountain lake. His friends left to get some supplies, leaving the major sitting

under a tree. A sudden storm blew up. Lightning struck the tree, and his friends returned to find his right side paralyzed. He was removed to a hospital, and it required more than two years for him to recover.

One day during the summer of 1930, Major Sumerford was walking with friends in a Vancouver park. Again there was a sudden storm. The group hurried toward the canopy of a refreshment stand, but before the major could reach shelter, he was felled by a bolt. This time he was permanently paralyzed and confined to a wheelchair until he died two years later.

But even death did not stop the grim pursuit. On a July night in 1934, a violent electrical storm raged over Vancouver. A bolt struck in a cemetery, completely destroying a single tombstone. The shattered stone had marked the grave of former British cavalry officer, Major Sumerford.

Vancouver/
The Orenda Expedition

The notion that ancient people sailed across the oceans of the world and thereby populated its islands and continents was merely a theory until 1947. That was the year the Norwegian adventurer Thor Heyerdahl constructed a balsa-wood raft, which he named *Kon-Tiki* after an Inca deity, and with five companions aboard it set sail from the west coast of South America to islands east of Tahiti. His voyage proved that ancient people from America could have colonized Polynesia.

The voyage of the Haida canoe *Orenda* was designed to show that the ancient Haida were not only a seafaring people but also an ocean-faring people. It was already known that the Haida in their dugout canoes up to seventy feet in length, some of them twin-hulled, conducted raiding expeditions as far south as the State of Washington. But it was not known how far they could travel in their large canoes.

Three non-Haida — Geordie Tocher, Gerhard Kie-

sel, Richard Tomkies — proved that a Haida canoe could carry three people from Vancouver as far across the Pacific as Hawaii. The adventurers set off on 14 May 1978 in a forty-two foot dugout canoe, cut from cedar according to native instructions preserved by Franz Boas, and rigged with a sail. They arrived seventy-six days later in Honolulu on 28 July.

The Orenda Expedition demonstrated that in the past it was technically feasible for the Haida to have colonized the islands in the Pacific and then the South Seas, including Australia and New Zealand. According to the tradition of the indigenous Hawaiian people, as recorded by Karin Lind in "First Hawaiians Could Have Migrated from B.C.," *Canadian Geographic*, March 1978, the natives erected their houses to face the East because, they said, "That is where we come from." Their tradition told them that their forefathers had come from a land where the leaves of the trees disappeared for half the year. Could that land be Vancouver Island, the home of the Haida?

Vancouver/
Rainbow Warrior

The prophecy of a native North American Indian was behind the naming of the Greenpeace protest vessel *Rainbow Warrior*. This vessel was the converted trawler used as its flagship by anti-nuclear Greenpeace activists to protest the testing of nuclear devices by the French government in Polynesia. French security service agents retaliated on 10 July 1985 by dynamiting and sinking the vessel with the loss of one life in the harbour at Auckland, New Zealand. Two of the agents responsible were captured, tried, convicted, and imprisoned by the New Zealand government.

The Greenpeace Movement grew out of the Don't Make a Wave Committee which was formed in Vancouver in 1970 to protest U.S. nuclear tests at Amchitkas. The following year the Greenpeace Foundation was established, and it now has chapters throughout the Western world. As for the naming of the *Rainbow Warrior*, which had formerly been known as the *Phyllis Cormack*, the imaginative act was done by the

Greenpeace activist, chronicler, and novelist Robert Hunter. In his book *Warriors of the Rainbow: A Chronicle of the Greenpeace Movement* (1979), he described what led to the naming of the vessel.

> I had on board a copy of a well-worn pamphlet containing a collection of North American Indian prophecies and myths. It had been given to me, rather mysteriously, by a Jewish dulcimer maker who described himself as a gypsy and predicted that the book would reveal a "path" that would affect my life. It contained one particular prophecy made some two hundred years ago by an old Cree grandmother named Eyes of Fire, who saw a time coming when the birds would fall out of the skies, the fish would be poisoned in their streams, the deer would drop in their tracks in the forest, and the seas would be "blackened" — all thanks to the White Man's greed and technology. At that time, the Indian people would have all but completely lost their spirit. They would find it again, and they would begin to teach the White Man how to have reverence for Mother Earth. Together, using the symbol of the rainbow, all the races of the world would band together to spread the great Indian teaching and go forth — Warriors of the Rainbow—to bring an end to the destruction and desecration of sacred Earth.

The book that Robert Hunter was fortuitously reading at the time of the renaming of the vessel was *Warriors of the Rainbow: Strange and Prophetic Dreams of the Indians* (1962) by William Willoya and Vinson Brown.

Vernon/
Likeness of Ogopogo

Vernon is a city near the north end of Okanagan Lake. A likeness of Ogopogo, the creature said to inhabit the lake, may be found in the city's Polson Park. It takes the form of a green-coloured, serpentine fountain. Water shoots out of the serpent's wide-open mouth.

No doubt children of all ages take delight in this effigy of Ogopogo. The alligator-like head, made of reinforced concrete, rises above the ripply waters of the duck pond in Vernon's Polsen Park. The city of Vernon is situated on the shore of Okanagan Lake, B.C. The depths of this loch-like lake are reputed to be the habitat of Canada's most celebrated lake monster. Ogopogo was a household name in Western Canada long before Nessie was photographed in Scotland's Loch Ness. [Don Weixl Photo]

Victoria/
Psychic Surgery

Psychic surgery is said to be regularly practised in the Republic of the Philippines and in some of the republics of Latin America. It involves performing medical operations on patients without the use of knives, anaesthesia, or incisions. The medical establishment and stage magicians agree that the practice is nothing more than faith fealing with the addition of sleight-of-hand, and the practitioners of psychic surgery are really charlatans and conjurers.

Psychic surgery was apparently known to the natives of the West Coast in the mid-nineteenth century. Paul Kane, the explorer and painter, described a pseudo-medical operation performed by medicine-men of the Clal-lums band near Fort Victoria in May 1848. The following account comes from his book *Wanderings of an Artist among the Indians of North America* (1859).

About 10 o'clock at night I strolled into the village, and on hearing a great noise in one of the lodges I entered it, and found an old woman supporting one of the handsomest Indian girls I had ever seen. She was in a state of nudity. Cross-legged and naked, in the middle of the room sat the medicine-man, with a wooden dish of water before him; twelve or fifteen other men were sitting round the lodge. The object in view was to cure the girl of a disease affecting her side. As soon as my presence was noticed a space was cleared for me to sit down. The officiating medicine-man appeared in a state of profuse perspiration from the exertions he had used, and soon took his seat among the rest as if quite exhausted; a younger medicine-man then took his place in front of the bowl, and close beside the patient. Throwing off his blanket he commenced singing and gesticulating in the most violent manner, whilst the others kept time by beating with little sticks on hollow wooden bowls and drums, singing continually. After exercising himself in this manner for about half an hour, until the perspiration ran down his body, he darted suddenly upon the young woman, catching hold of her side with his teeth and shaking her for a few minutes, while the patient seemed to suffer great agony. He then relinquished his hold, and cried out he had got it, at the same time holding her hands to his mouth; after which he plunged them in the water and pretended to hold down with great difficulty the disease which he had extracted, lest

it might spring out and return to its victim.

At length, having obtained the mastery over it, he turned round to me in an exulting manner, and held something up between the finger and thumb of each hand, which had the appearance of a piece of cartilage, whereupon one of the Indians sharpened his knife, and divided it in two, leaving one end in each hand. One of the pieces he threw into the water, and the other into the fire, accompanying the action with a diabolical noise, which none but a medicine-man can make. After which he got up perfectly satisfied with himself, although the poor patient seemed to be anything but relieved by the violent treatment she had undergone.

Victoria/
The Ghost Photograph

Displayed in the Archives of the Parliament Buildings in Victoria is its famous — or notorious — Ghost Photograph. One glance at its ghostly image permits one to come to the conclusion that an apparition put in an appearance in the group portrait. It is a matter of historical record that the photograph was taken on 12 December 1864, and that it shows all eleven members of the First Legislative Council at New Westminster, British Columbia, plus the Clerk. The gentlemen posed for their group portrait on the outside stairs of the wood-frame building. That is, eleven of the twelve did.

Charles Good, the Clerk, swore that he was unavoidably absent on the day the photograph was taken. Yet there is his image, second from the right. The gentlemen are (from left to right): Henry Holbrook, George A. Walkem, W.O. Hamley, Charles Brew, H.M. Ball, A.N. Birch, C.W. Franks, Peter O'Reilly, Walter Moberly, J.A.R. Homer, Charles Good, H.P.P. Crease. An examination of Good's image reveals it to be unique in that unlike the others it is slightly blurry and somewhat transparent.

Not much is remembered of Charles Good. He was born in Dorset, England, attended Oxford, and

The Ghost Photograph is among the permanent displays of the Provincial Archives of British Columbia. It is an eye-catcher. Eleven gentlemen appear in the photograph. Or is it twelve? The photograph was taken on 12 December 1864 outside the Colonial Government Buildings at New Westminster, B.C. The names of the eleven (or twelve) gentlemen are all known. At the far right is H.P.P. Crease. Second from the right is J.A.R. Homer. The semi-transparent gentleman is Charles Good who is on record as being too ill to attend the formal session "in person." [B.C. Provincial Archives]

shortly afterwards settled on the West Coast. He was appointed Chief Clerk in the Office of the Colonial Secretary in 1859. When the Legislative Council was established, Good became its Clerk and held that appointment until 1867 when he was promoted to the position of Assistant Colonial Secretary. He became Acting Colonial Secretary and, following Confederation, Assistant (later Deputy) Provincial Secretary and Clerk to the Legislative Assembly. He

retired to Devon. The date of his death is unknown. One would judge him to be a responsible person and an important colonial official in 1865 when the photographic portrait was taken. Today his life and career are forgotten by all but West Coast historians; only his hazy image in the so-called Ghost Photograph brings him to mind.

The information which follows comes from an article published in *Two Words*, 5 March 1955. According to the article, the group photograph was scheduled to be taken on 13 January 1865. But the date was delayed out of deference to the state of Good's health. He was unwell; indeed, the rumour had circulated that he had died. The taking of the photograph was delayed eight days, until 21 January. Good was still confined to his sick bed and unable to be there "in person." Nevertheless the councillors posed without their clerk. The picture was snapped and developed. When Good recovered he was shown the print and no one was more surprised than Charles Good to see his own face in it.

Allen Spraggett in *The Unexplained* (1967) discussed the Ghost Photograph, viewing it as yet more evidence for "the unexplained." Good was sick at the time and thus perhaps in closer-than-normal contact with his psychic self. He wished so hard to be there "in person" that he unconsciously projected his astral body to the place in question to be there "in spirit." Thus the image in question is not that of the "ghost" of Good, for Good was very much alive and a ghost is the appearance of someone dead. Instead, it is the "apparition" of Good, the likeness of a living person. According to Spraggett, this is an instance of "spirit-photography."

After more than a century and a quarter it is difficult if not impossible to establish the whereabouts of Good on the day of the sitting, whenever that was, for even that is in some doubt. Yet an examination of the Journals of the Legislative Council suggests that Good was in attendance and discharging his official duties as Clerk throughout the month of January. Therefore, he was in good health and not at all ill. He was probably in attendance for the sitting. Why then is his image so ghost-like? It appears somewhat blurry and transparent, and the apparent reason for this is that Good's image is "underexposed." He was a busy man and he was late for the sitting. He slipped into place later than the rest of the gentlemen, taking his place somewhat behind them. Photographic plates were slow in those days, and the photographer had to take a long "time" exposure. Hence it was no "spirit-photograph." It was a "time" exposure and Good was not "on time."

Good no doubt chuckled over the photograph when he saw it. The practical man that he was, he would have chuckled all the harder, had he known that visitors to the Archives of the Parliament Buildings in Victoria were marvelling at the ghostly image of himself more than a century and a quarter later!

Victoria/
"Caddy, King of the Coast"

The first important sighting of a sea serpent in Victoria's Cadboro Bay, on the southeast coast of Victoria Island, occurred on Sunday, 8 October 1933. Major W.H. Langley, a barrister and then the clerk of the Legislature, sailing past Chatham Island about 1:30 p.m. in his sloop *Dorothy*, spotted a serpent "nearly eighty feet long and as wide as the average automobile." Langley described it as greenish brown in colour, with a serrated body, "every bit as big as a whale but entirely different from a whale in many respects." As Langley had spent some time on whaling vessels, his report was taken seriously.

Three days later Langley's sighting was reported in the *Victoria Times* by the newsman Archie Willis, who subsequently staked out the serpent and made it his "beat." The serpent was subsequently given the name Cadborosaurus, a combination of Cadboro Bay, its habitat, and *saurus*, Latin for "lizard." Willis himself attributed the memorable coinage to Richard L. Pocock of the rival newspaper, the Victoria *Daily Colonist*. Quite quickly Cadborosaurus, or Caddy for short, became King of the Coast. For regal honours, Caddy had and has only one rival in the West, and that is Ogopogo, who is reported to reside in Lake Okanagan and thus reigns as the undisputed King of the B.C. Interior. Another difference between them is their respective aquatic habitats: Caddy is a salt-water sea-serpent, whereas Ogopogo is a fresh-water lake monster.

The serpent was next seen by J.F. Murray while fishing off the breakwater at Ogden Point. It appeared some twenty-five yards away for several minutes. Murray described it as being "like a big water snake." "He swam exactly like a worm would and I watched him go for about 60 feet with about two feet of his head and neck out of the water.'' A sign of Caddy's sudden celebrity status was the fact that this report was covered nationally by Canadian Press. It appeared in the Niagara Falls *Evening Review*, 29 November 1933. Such creatures were deemed newsworthy, as there were reports and even photographs of a creature named ''Nessie'' from Loch Ness in Northern Scotland.

Caddy was a common sight in Cadboro Bay, according to Ray Gardner who investigated the West Coast phenomenon in ''Caddy, King of the Coast,'' which was published in *Maclean's*, 15 June 1950. Between then and the first reported sighting seventeen years earlier, some five hundred people had gone on record as having spotted Caddy sporting in the waters where the Strait of Georgia and the Juan de Fuca Strait meet. Their reports and accounts differed in details, but all stressed that in Cadboro Bay there was ''a great snake-like monster'' which measured anywhere from 35 to 110 feet in length which had a head ''like a camel's.''

Every year there are reports of Caddy. What to make of them? ''But, really,'' newsman F.W. Kemp concluded, ''Caddy is good-natured and quite harmless, a Milquetoast monster in fact. About all he ever does is stretch his long neck out of the water and stare at anybody who happens to be staring at him. Then he beetles off at high speed or else dives, always 'without a ripple.' ''

Victoria/
Michelle and the Satanists

In 1975, Michelle Smith was a Victoria housewife who was suffering acute anxiety and deep depression. Seeking professional help, she was treated by Dr. Lawrence Pazder. The Victoria psychiatrist was astonished when his patient, in the voice of a five-year-old, began to recall in graphic detail a series of harrowing but incredible experiences that had, apparently, occurred two decades earlier.

Some six hundred hours of therapy sessions were tape recorded. Michelle recalled being taken by her mother to a satanic orgy where she watched a woman being ritually murdered. She remembered being ''prepared'' for an encounter with Satan himself who was summoned to appear for his Feast of the Beast. She was made to defecate on the Bible, she said, and horns and a tail were attached to her body to make her attractive to Satan. She described a Black Mass and even a vision of Hell: ''There's people with no eyes, and they're bleeding from their eyes, there's people that's got no noses.'' She felt she was saved by the vision of the Virgin Mary.

Smith and Pazder collaborated on a book called *Michelle Remembers* (1980), an account of Michelle among the satanists and her later psychoanalysis. The journalist Paul Grescoe commented on the case in a review of the bizarre book in *Maclean's*, 27 October 1980, in which he noted a few details not included in that account, such as the fact that Michelle has both an older and a younger sister; that friends and relatives insist that Michelle's parents were devoted to their children; that Smith and Pazder were involved in intense religious discussions while in therapy sessions. Gresco concluded, ''There's no question that it would make one hell of a movie.''

It is a sobering thought that from many parts of the world there come reports from the lips of disturbed children and from adults recalling their troubled childhoods of devil-worshipping parents and child-like victims. Many explanations for these memories or imaginings have been offered, not the least intriguing being that these are not fantasies but actual memories of devil-worshipping practices that occurred hundreds of years ago and are buried in ''the racial memory,'' a form of Jung's collective unconscious which has been rendered partly conscious.

Victoria/
The Ghostly Gathering

The district of Oak Bay, with its exclusive Victoria Golf Course, overlooks the Strait of Georgia. According to Sheila Hervey, writing in *Some Canadian Ghosts* (1973), "Every spring an entire community of ghosts appears. They gather on the rocky, jutting point of land that runs out into the sea at Oak Bay. Local residents congregate to watch from a safe and respectable distance. When the sea is calm, distinct voices from the past can be heard by those who listen on the shoreline." Apparently the spirit of a lone woman stands apart from the rest. The apparition of the lone woman recalls the story of the woman who was killed in 1936 by her husband near the eighth tee of the course. He had a drinking problem and she planned to divorce him. He strangled her and later killed himself. His body was found floating in a nearby bed of kelp. The ghostly gathering occurs, when it does, in early April or May of the year. In 1964, a couple reported seeing the lone woman when they walked across the course. In 1968, seven people reported seeing the apparition of the woman in the same place.

Victoria/
L. Adams Beck and Katherine Maltwood

Preserved in the Special Collections of the University of Victoria are books and manuscripts relating to the lives and works of two mystical-minded ladies, both sometime residents of Victoria. Their names are L. Adams Beck and Katherine Maltwood, and while it is not known that they ever met, if they did they would have much about which to converse.

L. Adams Beck was an Englishwoman of some mystery. Not much is known of her life, early or late, but it is known that she was the daughter of Admiral John Moresby of the British Navy. In 1919 she arrived in Victoria where she established her home and wrote her books. Between 1922 and 1931 she published thirty-five books with leading houses in New York and London. One of the popular historical novelists of the day, she was not content with simply telling stories; she wanted her occult fiction, like Marie Corelli's and Algernon Blackwood's, to attest to spiritual vistas and visions. Eleven works of oriental and occult fiction and non-fiction appeared under the name L.

The lovely young woman shown in this art photograph is Katherine Maltwood who has been called the Rediscoverer of the Stars. In the 1920s she discerned the Temple of the Stars in the topography of the countryside between Glastonbury Tor and Camelot—the gigantic array of natural and worked earth images which represent the twelve figures of the zodiac. Retiring to Victoria, B.C., she donated her effects to the University of Victoria where they are displayed in the Maltwood Museum. [Fortean Picture Library]

Adams Beck; fourteen historical romances were bylined E. Barrington; and ten other books were signed L. Moresby. She eventually moved from Victoria and died in Kyoto, Japan, in 1931.

"Her death is a great loss to the literary world and still more to the world of occultism and Theosophy," noted Albert E.S. Smythe in *The Canadian Theosophist*, January 1931. "She had spent many years in the East wandering about India, China, Japan, Korea, the Dutch East Indies and Tibet. What she did not know about Asia was of little importance to a western[er]. I had the extreme satisfaction of meeting her in Victoria when I was there in April, 1926."

Smythe noted that the publication of her first book *The Ninth Vibration* (1922) was prompted by "the cooperation of Mr. McClelland of Toronto with a New York publisher who did not care to undertake the venture alone. She told me that it was necessary to write more popular books to keep the treasury filled, and so there came the series of biographical novels concerning some of the great women of the past, written under the pen-name of E. Barrington. She told me how these were produced and gave me *The Divine Lady*, which she autographed. She never knew, she said, what subject she was to write about until the urge came upon her. Then she wrote, as I understood, automatically, with great swiftness, and she rarely knew the end of a sentence when she began it. The words just seemed to flow along, she said, and it surprised her to read what she had written. There was nothing of trance or anything of that description, but apparently an exaltation of consciousness which dominated the sensuous faculties. She took great pains with her facts and adhered to history in all fundamental matters."

Special Collections at the University of Victoria holds her books and some memorabilia. None of her books is in print as of 1988, yet some, like *The Story of Oriental Philosophy* (1928), went through numerous editions in their day.

Albert E.S. Smythe, who rhapsodized over L. Adams Beck, her literary works, and her oriental interests, also extolled the wonders of Katherine Emma Maltwood (1878–1961), the discoverer or rediscoverer of the so-called Temple of the Stars.

Smythe wrote in *The Canadian Theosophist* of September 1938: "We hear that Mrs. Maltwood, the heroine of Mrs. Adam Beck's fine book, *The House of Fulfilment*, and the discoverer of the 4,000-year-old zodiac in Somersetshire in England, has arrived with her husband in Canada bound for Victoria, B.C., where they have bought a house and plan to live after selling their place in Gloucestershire."

The answer to the question what is the Temple of the Stars is found in the following passage by John Michell from *The View Over Atlantis* (1969):

> In the 1920s a Gloucestershire lady, Mrs. Maltwood, caused a sensation by the publication of her book *A Guide to Glastonbury's Temple of the Stars* [1929]. In this she described her discovery of a group of enormous figures inscribed on the flat country between Glastonbury Tor and Camelot. These figures, their shapes suggested by natural folds of the earth and the outlines of hills and rivers, their details perfected by artificial banks, roads and ditches, represent the 12 signs of the zodiac, each figure placed in order beneath its appropriate constellation. Here on a landscape every corner of which retains some traditional Arthurian association, the hidden astrological significance of the Quest was physically depicted.
>
> Roaming the countryside where every episode in the history of the Holy Grail has its physical location, Mrs. Maltwood was haunted by the feeling of imminent revelation. One summer afternoon, standing on a low hill and looking out across the plain towards the distant ramparts of Camelot, she saw both visually and intuitively the elusive secret. References in legends and old histories to hidden giants in the landscape, the story that King Arthur never passed away but sleeps forever in the hills, the close identification of every feature in the Glastonbury landscape with the heroic cycle, the great wheel of the constellations turning above the hills and plains, all these clues led Mrs. Maltwood towards a secret lost for hundreds, perhaps thousands of years.

Katherine Maltwood rediscovered the Temple of the Stars, the zodiac-like configurations in the topography of the countryside. There is some debate about the present standing of the symbols. It is recognized that the images are there, though the feeling is that most of them lie in the mind of the beholder along with their mystical meaning.

Katherine Maltwood bequeathed her literary and artistic effects to the University of Victoria. The gift consisted of paintings, sculpture, books, photographs, correspondence, clippings, artifacts, and manuscripts. The University has built a modern gallery and storage area called the Maltwood Museum; the books have been catalogued in the main library for study purposes; the unique and unpublished material has been housed in Special Collections. Rosemary Brown catalogued this collection and published a biography, *Katherine Emma Maltwood: Artist, 1878–1961* (1981).

Yale/ Jacko

The story of the half-man, half-beast known as Jacko is one of the "sasquatch classics," according to John Green. In his book *Sasquatch: The Apes Among Us* (1978), he reproduces all the documents connected with the strange appearance and even stranger disappearance of this "Strange Creature . . . a British Columbia Gorilla."

CPR engineer Ned Austin, approaching the bluff at the eastern end of No. 4 Tunnel, some twenty miles north of Yale, spotted what he thought was a man lying sound asleep close to the track. He blew the whistle and applied the brakes. The train came to a standstill. The creature sprang up at the sound of the whistle, uttered a sharp quick bark, and scampered up the steep bluff. The conductor and the express manager gave chase. After five minutes of climbing, they closed in on the creature and knocked him unconscious with a boulder. They tied him up, lowered him to the track level, placed him in the baggage car, and took him to Yale.

This account of the capture appeared in the Victoria *Daily Colonist* on 4 July 1884 under the heading

"What Is It?" Here is how the correspondent described the creature:

"Jacko," as the creature has been called by his capturers, is something of the gorilla type standing four feet seven inches in height and weighing 127 pounds. He has long, black, strong hair and resembles a human being with one exception, his entire body, excepting his hands (or paws) and feet are covered with glossy hair about an inch long. His fore arm is much longer than a man's fore arm, and he possesses extraordinary strength, as he will take hold of a stick and break it by wrenching or twisting it, which no man living could break in the same way.

George Tilbury, of Yale, was appointed Jacko's keeper, and according to the *Colonist*, Tilbury proposed transporting Jacko to London, England, "to exhibit him."

The story was researched by Green who turned up a subsequent newspaper article which branded the story a hoax. One such article appeared five days later in the *Mainland Guardian*:

The "What Is It" is the subject of conversation in town this evening. How the story originated, and by whom, it is hard for one to conjecture. Absurdity is written on the face of it. The fact of the matter is, that no such animal was caught, and how the *Colonist* was duped in such a manner and by such a story, is strange: and stranger still, when the *Columbian* reproduced it in that paper. The "train" of circumstances connected with the discovery of "Jacko" and the disposal of same was and still is, a mystery.

Where does that put Jacko? "That is the sum total of the contemporary evidence, and in my estimation it doesn't look good for Jacko," Green summed it up. "However, there is no way to be certain of anything at this late date."

The ecstatic experience is not often portrayed in Western art, at least not in a secular context. One of the few paintings of a Canadian male or female experiencing ecstasy is the canvas called Dhârâna. *It was painted by F.H. Varley in the interior of British Columbia in 1928. It depicts a young woman in an asana or yogic posture. The young model later married the portrait painter and member of the Group of Seven who had always shown some interest in Eastern thought. The Sanskrit word* dhârâna *is used by Buddhists to refer to a state of meditation which produces ecstasy. [Art Gallery of Ontario, Toronto/Gift from the Albert H. Robson Memorial Subscription Fund, 1942]*

YUKON TERRITORY

Beaufort Sea/
Ghost of the Arctic Sea

"The S.S. *Baychimo*, famed 'ghost of the Arctic Sea,' has been the only derelict in history to repeatedly defy the crushing ice packs year after year and escape destruction or even severe damage." So wrote the researcher Vincent Gaddis in *Invisible Horizons: True Mysteries of the Sea* (1965). He was describing the famed vessel that was fated to sail crewlessly the frigid waters of the cold Beaufort Sea.

The *Baychimo*, a 1,300-ton, steel-clad, twin-screw steamer in the fleet of fur ships owned and operated by the Hudson's Bay Company, was launched in 1921 and proved seaworthy and lucky for ten years. Then, on 1 October 1931, it was caught in ice off the coast of Wainwright, Alaska. The captain and the crew of sixteen abandoned the vessel and set up a winter camp close by, where they could keep an eye on their ship and its cargo, a fortune in bundled furs. They waited for the warm weather to thaw the ice.

However, on 2 November, a storm loosened the ice and the vessel snapped its moorings and it drifted off. An Eskimo hunter spotted the vessel forty-five miles southwest of its former position. The crew trekked to the new location and were successful in off-loading the furs before it again slipped its moorings. Five months later prospectors came upon the wandering vessel near Herschel Island and boarded it. It was boarded again, passing Point Barrow, in 1933. In fact, it was seen regularly from year to year, and last boarded in November 1939 when it was found to be still seaworthy and still crewless.

"As far as I can determine, the *Baychimo* was last sighted by Eskimos in March, 1956, in the Beaufort Sea, moving north and still apparently seaworthy, riding the sea as if an expert mariner was at her helm," exclaimed Gaddis. "Her story has no parallel. No other derelict in modern times has been known to survive the ice for more than two years. The *Baychimo* has been around, crewless, for twenty-five years!"

Bluefish Caves/
Oldest Evidence

The Bluefish Caves, located on a limestone ridge overlooking the upper Bluefish River in the Keele Range of northern Yukon Territory, preserve the oldest, undisturbed archeological evidence in Canada.

According to Jacques Cinq-Mars, writing on the "Bluefish Caves" in Volume I of *The Canadian Encyclopedia*, the caves "consist of three small cavities in which loess accumulated during the late Pleistocene time. Buried in these aeolian deposits are the bones of mammoths, horses, bison, caribou, sheep and many other mammals, birds and fish. Numerous large mammal bones exhibit butchering marks made by stone tools. Associated with the bones, some of which have been dated to between 12,000 and 18,000 years ago, are the lithic remains of a burin and microblade technology akin to that found in the American Paleoarctic tradition."

Dawson City/
Science of Pluviculture

The science of pluviculture was practised, apparently with great success, in Dawson City in 1906. The science of pluviculture is, quite simply, the art of rain-making.

Charles Mallory Hatfield (1870–1958) was perhaps the most celebrated of all twentieth-century rain-makers. A native of California, Hatfield was a salesman of sewing machines until the age of thirty-two when he decided to quit. He conducted some experiments on his own and thereafter decided he could support himself by "precipitating moisture" wherever it was required.

He travelled around the continent, visiting areas that were plagued with either too little or too much rainfall. For a fee he would set nature right. He used various methods. One of them involved boiling a tankful of acid and allowing the fumes to escape into the air. Apparently within hours storm clouds would gather and rain would shower upon the area of drought.

As the broadcaster and author Frank Edwards related in the chapter called "The Remarkable Rain-makers" in *Strange People* (1961):

> Hatfield roamed far and wide with his chemicals and his evaporation tanks. In 1906, when the Klondike streams were so dry the miners could not work their sluice boxes, they sent for Hatfield. The miners at Dawson City gave him ten thousand dollars in gold to come to their rescue. They got what they ordered, for thirty-six hours after Hatfield went into action, the storm clouds were rolling and the four inches of rain he brought were more than enough.

It is said that Hatfield, the pluviculturist, never travelled without his umbrella and his rainhat.

Old Crow/
Earliest Man

The flats in the vicinity of Old Crow, a community within the Arctic Circle, were discovered to be a rich repository of evidence of the presence of early man on the continent of North America. The initial discovery was made in July 1966 by two archaeologists, Peter Lord and C.R. Harrington.

A further discovery was announced in a feature article written by David Quintner in the *Toronto Star*, 26 May 1975. A team of archaeologists and anthropologists from the University of Toronto, led by William Irving, made known their finds after nine years of work on the flats. They found the oldest artifacts to be 30,000 years old.

As Irving told Quintner, "This is the oldest datable material ever found in North America. There have been claims of older artifacts having been found in California and Mexico. But the academic sceptics are unconvinced. Our material has been carbon dated to between 25,000 and 30,000 years. No one else can match those verfiable dates."

Bone implements, bone artifacts, a scraper, and man-modified, hammer-like tools were found in excavations of gravel at 120 sites over a 150-mile area around Old Crow. Some 20,000 specimens were taken from the various sites. Irving expressed the belief that the area, which is 750 miles east of the Bering Sea and was ice-free during the last glaciation 10,000 years ago, offers "the possibility of finding a nearly continuous record of man's occupation from 12,000 years ago down to A.D. 1900."

Teslin/
Oral Tradition of Contact

In the eighteenth century the ancestors of the present-day Tlingit of Teslin, a small community on the Teslin River southeast of Whitehorse, resided in the vicinity of Lituya Bay, Alaska. An event occurred to them at that time and place which their oral tradition has preserved in recognizable form to modern times. In the nineteenth century the Tlingit chief Cowee related the native version of the event to the anthropologist G.T. Emmons. The author and astronomer Carl Sagan was impressed with the persistence of memory and with the tradition of the "benevolent encounter" in his book *Cosmos* (1980).

The antiquity of man in the Americas remains a controversial subject, one that is hotly debated in the coldest part of the northern continent—in the Yukon's most northern community of Old Crow. The village has an Indian population of fewer than three hundred and is situated on the bank of the Porcupine River about seventy-five miles north of the Arctic Circle. Each summer it is visited by archaeologists who excavate and study what evidence they have found of early man's pre-glacial transit through the region. [Tourism Yukon]

The Count of La Pérouse led a well-equipped scientific expedition to explore the Pacific Coast. In July 1786, two of his ships pulled into a place on the coast of Alaska now called Lituya Bay. Delighted with the harbour, La Pérouse wrote, "Not a port in the universe could afford more conveniences." There the Frenchmen greeted some of the "savages" who rowed out in their canoes to examine the two sailing ships and to bargain for goods. La Pérouse recorded that there was a brisk trade and not a little native pilferage. Then the expedition set sail and never returned. It was lost in the South Pacific in 1788.

La Pérouse left a written record of his expedition, including his encounter with the Tlingit. The Tlingit, although they had evolved no form of written record, could recall the encounter as well. It was preserved as part of their oral tradition. The Tlingit chief Cowee, one century after the encounter, could describe for the anthropologist G.T. Emmons, in 1886, the details of his people's first meeting with the white men. Needless to add, the Tlingit had no script of any kind and the chief himself had never heard of La Pérouse. The traditional narrative, paraphrased from *Cosmos* went like this:

387

Late one spring a large party of Tlingit ventured North to Yakutat to trade for copper. Iron was even more precious, but it was unobtainable. In entering Lituya Bay four canoes were swallowed by the waves. As the survivors made camp and mourned for their lost companions two strange objects entered the Bay. No one knew what they were. They seemed to be great black birds with immense white wings. The Tlingit believed the world had been created by a great bird which often assumed the form of a raven, a bird which had freed the Sun, the Moon, and the Stars from boxes in which they had been imprisoned. To look upon the Raven was to be turned to stone. In their fright, the Tlingit fled into the forest and hid. But after a while, finding that no harm had come to them, a few more enterprising souls crept out and rolled leaves of the skunk cabbage into crude telescopes, believing that this would prevent being turned to stone. Through the skunk cabbage, it seemed that the great birds were folding their wings and that flocks of small black messengers arose from their bodies and crawled upon their feathers.

Now one nearly blind old warrior gathered the people together and announced that his life was far behind him; for the common good he would determine whether the Raven would turn his children into stone. Putting on his robe of sea otter fur, he entered his canoe and was paddled seaward to the Raven. He climbed upon it and heard strange voices. With his impaired vision he could barely make out the many black forms moving before him. Perhaps they were crows. When he returned safely to his people they crowded about him, surprised to see him alive. They touched him and smelled him to see if it was really he. After much thought the old man convinced himself that it was not the god-raven that he had visited, but rather a giant canoe made by men. The black figures were not crows but people of a different sort. He convinced the Tlingit, who then visited the ships and exchanged their furs for many strange articles, chiefly iron.

As Sagan concluded, "The account of Cowee, the Tlingit chief, shows that even in a preliterate culture a recognizable account of contact with an advanced civilization can be preserved for generations. If the Earth had been visited hundreds or thousands of years ago by an advanced extraterrestrial civilization, even if the contacted culture was preliterate, we might well expect to have some recognizable form of the encounter preserved. But there is not a single case in which a legend reliably dated from earlier pretechnological times can be understood only in terms of contact with an extraterrestrial civilization."

Sagan noted, somewhat sadly, "Benevolent encounters have not been the rule in human history, where transcultural contacts have been direct and physical, quite different from the receipt of a radio signal, a contact as light as a kiss."

NORTHWEST TERRITORIES

Alert/
UFO Sighting

Is the point of origin of unidentified flying objects the interior of the Earth? The point has been argued by UFO enthusiasts, researchers, and the Earl of Clancarty. Lord Clancarty, who sits in the British House of Commons, is a UFO enthusiast and author who publishes his books as Brinsley Le Poer Trench. If the theory has a leg to stand on, it would have to be established, at the very least, by reports of repeated sightings of UFOs in the vicinity of the North Pole, where the "opening" to the Hollow Earth is said to lie.

The federal government maintains a scientific and military establishment at Alert. The Department of Transport investigated the following case of a UFO which put in an appearance in the sky over Alert on 25 November 1952. "A meteorological observer at Alert, N.W.T., observed a lighted area in the sky which persisted for about 2 seconds, at 8:32 A.M., G.M.T. The sky was overcast with a ceiling of about 2,000 feet. Lightning is practically unknown at these latitudes and there are no beacons within several hundred miles of Alert." The report appeared in Arthur Bray's *The UFO Connection* (1979).

Lake Angikuni/
The Vanishing Village

The sign of a good story is that it never dies. The story of the Vanishing Village of the Dead is a good story. It never dies, despite the fact that it has been debunked time and time again. Perhaps it packs so much appeal because the tale is set in an inaccessible part of the country—on the shore of Lake Angikuni (the Indian name is of uncertain meaning and correctly spelled Angikuni and not Anjikuni) in the District of Keewatin some five hundred miles northwest of Churchill, Manitoba—and because it concerns the Eskimo people—who are seen by southerners to be a vanishing race. Certainly these two factors lend the Vanishing Village of the Dead an air of credibility.

Readers of the Halifax *Herald* on 29 November 1930, and of other North American newspapers serviced by the Newspaper Enterprise Association (NEA) were surprised and probably delighted to read an illustrated and bylined article headlined: "Tribe Lost in Barrens of North / Village of Dead Found by Wandering Trapper, Joe Labelle." Written by a special correspondent, Emmett E. Kelleher, from The Pas, Manitoba, and datelined 28 November, it began: "The northern lights have seen queer sights—as the much-quoted Robert W. Service remarks—and the everlasting silence of the regions under the Arctic Circle cloaks some strange mysteries. But the northern lights do not tell of the queer sights, nor does the Arctic silence get vocal about its mysteries. There is nothing to do, usually, but guess." Kelleher continued:

Far up in the heart of one of the most lonely places on earth—in the Lake Angikuni country, 500 miles northwest of the port of Churchill, on Hudson Bay—a whole tribe of Eskimos has vanished. Somewhere, somehow, the endless desolation of Canada's northern Barren Lands has swallowed up 25 men, women and children. It is one of the most puzzling mysteries that has ever come down out of the Arctic. The news of it has just reached The Pas, on the fringe of civilization.

Kelleher recounted the experience of "one Joe Labelle, a roving trapper of the Barren Lands" who came upon the tribe's abandoned camp. Its caribou-skin tents

Uncovers Mystery In North

TRIBE LOST IN BARRENS OF NORTH was the alarming headline that greeted readers of the Halifax Herald on 29 November 1930. Thus Haligonians were the first people anywhere to learn about the so-called Vanishing Village of the Dead. According to the Herald's special correspondent Emmett E. Kelleher, all the inhabitants of the isolated Eskimo settlement on the shore of Lake Angikuni, District of Keewatin, N.W.T., had mysteriously vanished. They left in such a hurry that they even abandoned their dogs. The news story was featured across the continent and subsequently retold with gusto by the authors of books of oddities and mysteries. Only in 1976 was the story finally debunked by the researcher Dwight Whalen. [Hawkshead Services]

were still standing. Inside were the occupant's prized possessions, including cooking utensils and rifles. "There was no sign of violence, no sign of trouble. The place was simply empty."

According to Kelleher, the officers of the Royal

TRIBE LOST IN BARRENS OF NORTH

Village of Dead Found by Wandering Trapper, Joe Labelle.

By EMMETT E. KELLEHER.
Special To The Herald

THE PAS, Manitoba, Nov. 28— The northern lights have seen queer sights—as the much-quoted Robert W. Service remarks — and the everlasting silence of the regions under the Arctic Circle cloaks some strange mysteries. But the northern lights do not tell of the queer sights, nor does the Arctic silence get vocal about its mysteries. There is nothing to do, usually, but guess.

Canadian Mounted Police (which he called the Northwest Mounted Police) "have taken up the hunt and white trappers have been asked to be on the lookout." Then Kelleher waxed eloquent:

Joe Labelle admits that stumbling on the abandoned village gave him the creeps. A man doesn't get the creeps readily when he spends months at a time trudging by his lone across the Barren Lands, where there is never a house or a human being or anything to break the white-rimmed silence; but Joe Labelle got creepy, just the same. The empty sky and the silent, rocky plain held a mystery, and the trapper didn't like it.

The sense of mystery deepened when Labelle came upon two half-starved Husky dogs and the bodies of seven dead dogs, and his thoughts turned darker:

There were six tents made out of skin . . . I'll admit that when I went in the first tent I was a little jumpy. Just looking around, I could see the place hadn't known any human life for months, and I expected to find corpses inside. But there was nothing there but the personal belongings of a family. A couple of deer parkas (skin coats) were in one corner. Fish and deer bones were scattered about. There were a few pairs of boots, and an iron pot, greasy and black. Under one of the parkas I found a rifle. It had been there so long it was all rusty. The whole thing looked as if it had been left just that way by people who expected to come back. But they hadn't come back.

I went outside and looked over the rest of the camp. I tell you, I was puzzled. I figured there had been about 25 people in the camp, but all signs showed the place hadn't been lived in for nearly 12 months. As I strolled about, with those two walking skeletons of dogs following me, I found the other tents in a similar state.

I tried to figure out where those Eskimos had gone to. They hadn't moved to a new territory, or they would have taken their equipment, espe-

cially their guns and their dogs. Then I thought of the Eskimos' "evil spirit" Tornrark, who has an ugly man's face with two long tusks sticking up from each side of the nose. The natives live in fear of Tornrark, and they wear charms to ward him off. I thought about Tornrark, and I had to make an effort to put the picture out of my mind.

Labelle made an even more surprising discovery:

Then I found one of the most puzzling things of all. It was an Eskimo grave, with a cairn built of stones. But for some reason the grave had been opened. The stones had been pulled off of one side and there was nothing inside the cairn at all. I had no way of telling when it had been opened, or what had been done with the body it had once contained. And I couldn't figure out why it had been desecrated.

I stayed around all afternoon, trying to figure things out. There were no signs of any struggle. Everything looked peaceful. But the air seemed deadly. I caught a few fish out of the lake and gave them to the two dogs, and then moved on. I didn't want to spend a night there.

The broadcaster and journalist Frank Edwards added: "Months of patient and far-flung investigation failed to produce a single trace of any member who had lived in the deserted village of Anjikuni. The Mounted Police filed it as unsolved . . . and so it remains." These sentences from the chapter titled "The Vanishing Village" — like so many other sentences in his book *Stranger Than Science* (1959) — are so wide of the mark as to be marvels in their own right. The truth, which is much more interesting than Joe Labelle's tall tale and Kelleher's journalistic hoax, is that within two months of its publication the RCMP had debunked the tale.

After Kelleher's story appeared, the RCMP received inquiries from the general public. On 17 January 1931, Commissioner Cortland Starnes made public the internal report of Sergeant J. Nelson of The Pas Detachment. On 5 January 1931, Sgt. Nelson wrote: "I have made diligent enquiries from different sources but can find no foundation for this story." Then he noted:

In conversation with Mr. D. Simons, recently, who operates a trading post at Windy Lake, N.W.T., and has just returned from visiting his Post by plane; he doubts the suggestion that any such calamity has occurred, as no doubt there would be reports from reliable white trappers and Eskimos of that district.

Joe Labelle the trapper who is alleged to have related the story to Emmett E. Kelleher, the correspondent, is considered a new-comer in this country. The Manitoba records show this to be his first season, that he has taken out a trapping licence, he is located on some of the lakes north of Flin Flon, and doubts are expressed as to whether he has ever been in the territories.

The illustration which depicts "The Village of the Dead" is a photograph which was taken by an ex-member of this Force Mr. P. Rose, while stationed at Fort Churchill in 1909, and is now living in The Pas. I have compared the negative in Mr. Rose's possession and the illustration and find them identical. Some time ago Mr. Kelleher was visiting Mr. Rose and was looking over some photos of the north, when he came to [a] photo which is depicted as "The Village of the Dead" in the illustration, he asked to borrow it, to get a copy for his album, later returning the negative to Mr. Rose . . . .

From my own knowledge of the correspondent, I consider the whole story fiction. Mr. Kelleher is in the habit of writing colourful stories of the North, and very little credence can be given to his articles. At present he is visiting in the east, and should he return to The Pas, I will interview him regarding the above matter.

There is no information on whether or not Kelleher returned to The Pas, "the scene of the crime." Whether he did or not, Sgt. Nelson "got his man."

The most thorough-going debunking of the story was Dwight Whalen's "Vanished Village Revisited" published by *Fate* in November 1976. Whalen wrote to all the appropriate authorities and could find no independent corroboration of Kelleher's story. He concluded, perhaps with some regret, "Thus, the case for the vanished village rests upon the story of an inexperienced trapper told to an imaginative and not too conscientious newsman."

Yet the story continues to be told. Perhaps its most surprising quality is its eerie stillness. In the finest of ghost stories, the reader faces the consequences and not the causes of the act of dissolution, being forced to imaginatively reconstruct the act. So the supernatural is seldom directly experienced but kept at bay, at a distance. At the heart of the Lake Angikuni mystery is a scene and a sense of abandonment. In its presentation of an eerie stillness, it rivals the greatest of all the maritime mysteries, the abandonment on the high seas of the Nova Scotia-built vessel, the *Mary Celeste*.

Arctic Ocean/ The Northwest Passage

The Arctic Ocean, the smallest of the world's oceans, lies north of the North American continent. It includes the world's largest group of islands, six of which rank among the world's thirty largest.

From the sixteenth to the twentieth centuries the ocean was sailed by European captains in search of a Northwest Passage by sea from Europe to Asia. The route was finally negotiated by the Norwegian explorer Roald Amundsen in 1903–06.

However, the Northwest Passage may have been negotiated more than a century earlier by the *Octavius*, a derelict ship with a crew of dead men. It seems that in November 1762 the British vessel was caught in the ice at a point north of Point Barrow, Alaska. The crew of twenty-eight froze to death. Then the ice melted and the vessel drifted eastward over the years. It was sighted on 12 August 1775 by the *Herald*, a whaling ship, off the coast of Greenland.

Thus it seems the *Octavius* was the first ship to negotiate the Northwest Passage with a captain and crew who had been dead for thirteen years! This astonishing episode in marine history was related by Vincent H. Gaddis in *Invisible Horizons* (1965).

Baffin Island/
Tunit and Skraeling

According to Genesis 6:4, "There were giants in the earth." In Canada there were both giants and pygmies. It appears that the myths and legends of the Eskimos depict two races of humanoid beings which dwelt in the North alongside the Eskimo people in the distant past. These are the Tunit and the Skraeling.

The word Tunit, in Inuktitut, indicates "a people earlier than ourselves." Traditionally, the Tunit were a race of fierce giants who enslaved the Eskimo people. The Eskimos revolted and defeated the Tunit, erecting imposing cairns called inukshuit to commemorate their victory over their former masters. Anthropologists argue that the Tunit were an Eskimo-like people ancestral to the present-day Inuit, the Thule Eskimos, and even the Dorset Eskimos. That would place the Tunit in the time period 2500 B.C. to 800 B.C. Whether or not memories survive from that period is a matter worthy of consideration.

There is no general agreement about the Skraeling. The word itself is Old Norse and means "screamer." In the old sagas devoted to the Norse voyages to the New World, which were made about A.D. 1000, it referred to a race of fierce pygmies who harassed the colonists, ultimately forcing the Norse to abandon their colonies in the New World and return to the Old. Historians have equated the Skraeling with the Eskimos of the Dorset culture, but anthropologists are less easily convinced. Others have equated the Skraeling with the now-extinct Beothuk Indians.

Baffin Island/
Inukshuit

The Arctic abounds in impressive natural imagery. Yet the most powerful of all Arctic images is man-made. That is the image of man himself: the inukshuk.

In Inuktituut, the language of the Inuit, the word *inukshuk* is singular and means "something that resembles a man." The plural form is *inukshuit*. The word is used to refer to a life-size statue of a man made of rocks, a cairn in the shape of a human being. Some inukshuit are larger than life, as much as ten feet in height, but all of them are imposing and impressive, especially when seen against the skyline.

They were generally erected to mark some important route or region—a landmark or seamark or beacon. Some of them may have served some ceremonial function such as a memorial to the dead. Others served to guide migrating herds of caribou. It seemed the caribou were attracted to them. It has also been suggested that they served the simple purpose of keeping the Eskimo company—in the Eskimo singer Orpingalik's phrase as "companions in solitude."

It is the opinion of the contemporary Inuit that they were constructed in the distant past by the Tunit, the predecessors of both the Thule Eskimos and the Dorset Eskimos. In point of time that would make them very old indeed, placing the inuktitut-raising between 2500 B.C. and 800 B.C. In point of fact, less than a hundred years ago the Thule Eskimos were observed erecting these memorials at Enukso Point on Baffin Island. The apparent purpose was to appease the spirits of the waters before attempting a dangerous water crossing. Today inukshuit are constructed by the Inuit under commission by government bodies and erected in southern Canadian locations — there are three at Toronto's Lester B. Pearson International Airport, for example — as well as at select sites abroad — one stands near the entrance of the Palais de L'Europe in Strasbourg, France.

Erich von Däniken, the Swiss-German author who popularized the "ancient astronaut" theory, has offered the suggestion that the inukshuk is the Eskimo's memory of the appearance of an alien visitor who wore a space suit. He offered a parallel suggestion, as well: The Thunderbird of the Northwest Coast Indians is the graphic depiction of the dim memory of the appearance of a space vehicle. Von Däniken should know: Four letters of his surname spell out of the name of Canada's communications satellite, ANIK!

393

Baffin Island/
A Sea Unicorn

A sea unicorn, probably a narwhal, was described by
Sir Martin Frobisher on his second Arctic voyage. The
sighting was made on the west coast of Baffin Island
in July 1577, and the account comes from *Hakluyt's
Voyages* (1965) edited by Irwin R. Blacker.

> On this West shore we found a dead fish float-
> ing, which had in his nose streight and torquet,
> of length two yards lacking two inches, being
> broken at the top, where we might perceive it
> hollow, into the which some of our sailers put-
> ting spiders they presently died. I saw not the
> triall hereof, but it was reported unto me of a
> trueth: by the vertue whereof we supposed it to
> be the sea Unicorne.

Barren Lands/
Thoughts Through Space

One of the most dramatic experiments in telepathic
communication ever recorded occurred across the Barren Lands of the Northwest Territories. Its only rival
in audacity was the experiment in telepathy conducted
by the Apollo 14 astronaut Edgar E. Mitchell, the
sixth man to set foot on the Moon, who in 1971
tried to project his thoughts from outer space to an
Earth-bound observer. Mitchell's results were nil.
The results of the attempt to send thoughts through
space across the Barren Lands have been variously
interpreted.

These two experiments were conducted in light of
the theoretical limitation on telepathic power
advanced by Albert Einstein. The mathematician suggested that if it is possible for one mind to operate
directly on another, the effect must decline with distance, like radio waves.

The Russian aviator Sigismund Lewanevsky disappeared in the vicinity of the North Pole while on a
solo flight from Siberia to Alaska. The search for the
missing aviator was conducted from October 1937 to

March 1938 by Sir Hubert Wilkins, the Australian-
born explorer and aviator. Wilkins knew the Arctic
well from the ground up; he had served with Stefansson's Canadian Arctic Expedition of 1913–18, and
he had become on 25 April 1928 the first aviator (with
co-pilot) to fly over the North Pole.

Before he left for the Arctic, Wilkins arranged with
Harold T. Sherman, a friend and writer in New York,
to keep Sherman telepathically apprised of his adventures and experiences. Sherman would sit quietly for
a thirty-minute period every Monday, Tuesday, and
Thursday evening from 11:30 to 12:00 EST, and Wilkins would try to project his thoughts at the given
times. Sherman kept a log of his impressions; Wilkins
kept a journal of his activities. Sherman recorded his
images and posted the entries in the log to Dr. Gardner
Murphy of the Department of Parapsychology at
Columbia University. When Wilkins returned from
the Arctic, having travelled 40,000 miles without
locating the missing Russian aviator, they compared
the log with the journal and published their findings
in *Thoughts through Space: A Remarkable Adventure in
the Realm of Mind* (1951). Although their work fails
to establish the reality of thought transference, their
book remains, appropriately, thoughtful and thought-
provoking.

"Mental impressions of what had happened to me
maintained a high percentage of accuracy," Wilkins
wrote after finding many parallels or correspondences
between his own activities and Sherman's impressions
of his activities. The aviator felt there were too many
"hits" for sheer guesswork on Sherman's part.
Indeed, one "hit" is as remarkable as it is unlikely.
Sherman recorded in his log on 11 November 1937
that he sensed that Wilkins was dressed in an ill-fitted
tuxedo and in attendance at a formal reception. This
seemed unreasonable and improbable to Sherman, but
it turned out to be literally true. That very day Wilkins was in Regina ready to fly over the Barren Lands
but at the last moment a snowstorm forced him to
delay his departure until the following day. At the
last minute he was invited to attend a formal reception
being held by the Lieutenant-Governor of Saskatchewan in the vice-regal chambers. Being without

formal dress, he arranged to borrow a dress suit. Although it was some sizes too small for him, he wore it anyway and attended the reception in some discomfort.

It was indeed a "hit." But along with the "hits" there were the "misses" as well as a great many non-parallels or non-correspondences. The way the experiment was conducted minimized the possibility of deception, but at the same time it maximized the difficulty of any quantification of the results in a statistically significant manner.

Bradley Land/
Arctic Mirage

Dr. Frederick A. Cook, the American explorer and surgeon, maintained he attained the North Pole on 21 April 1908. The claim was disallowed at a scientific congress in Copenhagen, but even today it is accepted by some. Most authorities accept the counterclaim of Robert E. Peary who maintained he attained the coveted pole on 6 April 1909.

Another contentious claim of Cook's is that he discovered a new land or island about one hundred miles from the North Pole in the general direction of Ellesmere Island. He named his discovery Bradley Land, but as no subsequent expedition was able to find it, the so-called discovery was dismissed as another Arctic mirage. Thus Bradley Land joined the ghostly geography of Arctic mirages, a geography which includes Crocker Land and the Croker Mountains.

A mirage is neither an instance of an optical illusion nor a sign of mental delusion. Arctic mirages are fairly common and caused by a combination of certain topographic features and specific atmospheric conditions. Where and when these features and conditions are found, images of the topography are conveyed over distances by means of the atmosphere acting as a lens. Temperature inversion—hot air beneath cold air—is the common catalyst of such imagery. Observers have reported four types of mirage imagery: horizontal images (with vertical distortion, usually stretched); images (distant objects appear close up); enhanced images (colour is frequently pronounced); multiple images (layers of stacked images, some of which are inverted).

Arctic navigators learned from the Eskimo the skill of reading these images wherever they appeared — looming over the horizon or projected onto low-hanging clouds in the sky. They gave useful clues as to the appearance of the landscape that was otherwise out of sight, down to such minute details as the presence and movement of dark-coloured animals. The most astonishing instance of a long-distance mirage was the skyline of a modern city which was seen looming over the horizon of Mount Fairweather in Alaska. The "Silent City" was subsequently identified as Bristol, 2,500 miles away in England. The appearance of this mirage might be compared with well-authenticated reports of freak radio or television reception over great distances.

Mirage-making conditions occur quite often in the Arctic, so it is not surprising that the shamans of the past were credited with "far sight," the ability to see "beyond the horizon" and thus slightly "into the future." The Inuit word *poojok* refers to a mist or a haze which resembles formations of land. Arctic aviators are familiar with an "iceblink," the reflected glare of the ice beyond the horizon on clouds within view, and a "watersky," the same for open water. Mirages give new meaning to the old saying, "So near and yet so far."

Coppermine River/
The Witch

The explorer Samuel Hearne discovered the Coppermine River which rises in the Barren Lands and empties into Coronation Gulf. The Chipewyan Indians had spoken about the deposits of copper that would be encountered along its shores, but Hearne and his companions had to search for four hours before they could find even one four-pound nugget.

Hearne wrote about the fabled copper deposits in the entry for July 1771 in *A Journey from Prince of*

Wales's Fort in Hudson's Bay to the Northern Ocean (1795):

> It may not be unworthy the notice of the curious, or undeserving a place in my Journal, to remark, that the Indians imagine that every bit of copper they find resembles some object in nature; but by what I saw of the large piece, and some smaller ones which were found by my companions, it requires a great share of invention to make this out. I found that different people had different ideas on the subject, for the large piece of copper above mentioned had not been found long before it had twenty different names. One saying that it resembled this animal, and another that it represented a particular part of another; at last it was generally allowed to resemble an Alpine hare couchant: for my part, I must confess that I could not see it had the least resemblance to any thing to which they compared it.

After Hearne established that the Chipewyans were an imaginative or at least fanciful people, Hearne told the legend of the Coppermine Witch:

> There is a strange tradition among those people, that the first person who discovered those mines was a woman, and that she conducted them to the place for several years; but as she was the only woman in company, some of the men took such liberties with her as made her vow revenge on them; and she is said to have been a great conjurer. Accordingly when the men had loaded themselves with copper, and were going to return, she refused to accompany them, and said she would sit on the mine till she sunk into the ground, and that the copper should sink with her. The next year, when the men went for more copper, they found her sunk up to the waist, though still alive, and the quanitity of copper much decreased; and on their repeating their visit the year following, she had quite disappeared, and all the principal part of the mine with her; so that after that period nothing remained on

the surface but a few small pieces, and those were scattered at a considerable distance from each other. Before that period they say the copper lay on the surface in such large heaps, that the Indians had nothing to do but turn it over, and pick such pieces as would best suite the different uses for which they intended it.

Crocker Land/
An Arctic Mirage

Crocker Land is the name of a mountainous island or continent which was once believed to lie northwest of Ellesmere Island. It was first seen, described, and named by the American naval officer Robert E. Peary, who was travelling by sledge over the ice north of Ellesmere Island when he saw mountains in the distance. He did so on the Arctic expedition which, he claimed, took him to the North Pole on 6 April 1909.

Peary named Crocker Land after George Crocker, a wealthy American who had donated fifty thousand dollars to the expedition. In June, Peary described the prospect: "The mountains of a new land, not a small island but something that filled the horizon — clear and unmistable icy peaks rising against the northern sky."

It was left to Donald B. MacMillan, an American naval officer who had once served under Peary, to prove the non-existence of Crocker Land. He did so on his own polar expedition of 1913. MacMillan said Crocker Land was not an Arctic range at all but an Arctic mirage.

Crocker Land is not be confused with the Croker Mountains.

Croker Mountains/
A Non-existent Range

The British naval officer Sir John Ross reported sighting a formidable range of mountains on his Arctic expedition of 1818. There appeared to be a chain of mountains linking Baffin Island and Devon Island to the north, thus landlocking Lancaster Sound.

Ross named the range Croker Mountains after Sir John Wilson Croker, First Secretary of the British Admiralty. The supposed discovery was doubted by Sir Edward Parry, Ross's second-in-command, and it infuriated Sir John Barrow, the second Secretary of the Admiralty, who was convinced that Lancaster Sound would provide a route to the Pacific Ocean. Barrow backed Parry's expedition of 1819 which proved the Croker Mountains to be a non-existent range.

Croker Mountains are not to be confused with Crocker Land.

Davis Strait/
The Northwest Passage

The search for the fabled Northwest Passage occupied some three centuries and claimed the lives of hundreds of mariners. It was hoped that there was a water route between the Atlantic and Pacific Oceans, through or south of the islands between Baffin Island and the Beaufort Sea. In time both a northern and a southern route were found which connected Europe and Asia across Arctic America. It took dozens of expeditions to realize one of the dreams of the ages. The northern passage was made possible following the work of the British Captain Robert McClure in 1873. The southern passage was realized only in 1906 by the Norwegian Arctic explorer Roald Amundsen.

But no seaman ever found the fabled kingdom of Novaya Zemlya; the realm remained a Siberian island. For naught were the lines of Alexander Pope:

> So Zembla's rocks (the beauteous World of Frost)
> Rise white in Air, and glitter o'er the Coast;
> Pale Suns, unfelt, at distance roll away,
> And on th'impressive ice the Lightnings play. . . .

Descriptions of the northern passages did enrich the imagery of Samuel Taylor Coleridge's long ballad *The Rime of the Ancient Mariner*, but the Siberian island is recalled, when at all, in Vladimir Nabokov's phrase ''blue inenubilable Zembla.''

Theosophical thought was a strong imaginative influence on the art of Lawren Harris. It guided him from the realism of his early work to the characteristic abstraction of Icebergs, Davis Strait, *a major canvas painted in 1930. Some critics still dismiss Harris in his High Arctic phase as if he were some Walt Disney of the North; others are able to place the painter and his later work in the hemispheric and shamanistic context more overtly embodied by Nicholas Roerich (1874–1947). The Russian world traveller, traditional thinker, and spiritual artist painted his major canvas* The Great Spirit of the Himalayas *in the 1920s. [The Estate of Lawren Harris & McMichael Canadian Collection, Kleinburg, Ont.; Nicholas Roerich Museum, New York, N.Y.]*

Neither did any sea captain encounter the high magnetic rock described by Nicholas of Lynne in *Inventio Fortunata*. A mathematician, astronomer, and Franciscan friar at Oxford about 1360, the boastful Nicholas claimed that he had been to the Arctic and seen with his own eyes this high magnetic rock. He shamelessly maintained that he had made not one but six Arctic expeditions and moreover he had made them all by himself! The claims of Nicholas and others are curious. Are they sheer fantasy or do they have symbolic content, perhaps alchemical significance? Whatever their meaning, assuming there is meaning in them, they inspired the British Admiralty, sea captains, and common crew members without number. They indirectly contributed to the exploration and cartography of the northern reaches of Canada and of the globe.

Fort McPherson/
Dene Origins

It was while teaching at Fort McPherson on the Peel River in 1949 that Ethel Stewart began to evolve her theory about the origins of the Dene, the northern Athapaskan-speaking peoples of the Mackenzie River Valley and the Barren Lands. Since then she has devoted her time and energy to the substantiation of her theory which is at variance with standard scholarly opinion. Most anthropologists hold that at some point in the prehistoric past, perhaps ten thousand years ago, the native ancestors of the North American Indians and Inuit of today migrated from the Old World to the New World. They crossed fom Siberia to Alaska, via the Bering Strait, after which they dispersed over the North American continent. Stewart holds that the ancestors of the contemporary Dene migrated at a much later period, in the early part of the thirteenth century.

"I think the Anthropological Establishment are very much opposed to my work and do not even want to discuss it. It goes against their new idea that the Dene and the Eskimos have been here for thousands of years," she said in a letter dated 29 April 1987. "If I could I would take some of the Dene on a trip through Kan-su and Sinkiang and see how they make out. At the Historical Congress in Ankara, I met a woman from Kashgar. She looks like any Dene girl."

Stewart was born in Virden, Manitoba, and educated at Queen's University, where she graduated with an Hon. B.A. in history in 1948, and an M.A. in 1956. She taught for four years at Fort McPherson at a school run by the Department of Indian and Northern Affairs. She has travelled widely and lived for extended periods in a Maori settlement in New Zealand, with the Blood Indians in Aklavik and Hay River, in Southern Alberta, among the Tlingit of the Yukon, among consular officials in New York, and finally in retirement in Ottawa.

One of the few anthropologists to encourage Stewart to delve into the origins of the Dene was the late Marius Barbeau. Having detected Asiatic strains in the dirges of the Haida, Barbeau agreed with her that there seemed to be pronounced parallels between the vocabularies of the Dene and the people of Central Asia. She suggested that even the word *Dene*, which is Athapaskan for "the people," derived from the Celtic word *den*, meaning "people." The etymology of the names of two Dene groups, the Chipewyan and the Loucheux, is equally exotic. The former is a combination of the Chinese and Uighur names for that group: Ch'i-pi and Wei-yen Tangut, or Chipewyan. The latter comes from the Chinese Lew-sha, *flowing sand*, the name of the terrible Liu-Shu Desert that lies between Sa-cu and Turfan.

Stewart's scholarly contributions to the subject have appeared in Thomas E. Lee's *Anthropological Journal of Canada* and the *Occasional Papers* of the Epigraphic Society of San Diego. In 1986 she addressed the 10th Congress of the Turkish Historical Society meeting in Ankara, and the next year spoke at Carleton University in Ottawa on "The Turkish Origins of the Dene and Na-Dene Indians of North America."

Stewart first established the kinship of the Dene people and the Sinitic peoples of Central Asia — the Tibetan, Chinese, and Siamese people. She then asked the following question: "What could have caused a people of a highly developed cultural region to leave a land of variety and abundance for one where virtually all these amenities were lacking?'' To answer this question she turned to the oral traditions of the Dene people and their belief that their ancestors had come by sea along a chain of islands, a belief similar to the one reported by the Haida to Barbeau. She argued on the basis of comparative philology that the migration occured in the first half of the thirteenth century. The ancestors of the Dene were fugitives from the fury and terror of the Mongol invasions.

As she wrote in ''The Ferocious Enemies of the Ancestors of the Northern Dene in Relation to the Mongols,'' *Anthropological Journal of Canada*, Vol. 19, No. 1, 1981:

> The northern Dene of the Mackenzie Valley in northwestern Canada claimed, in the far distant past, a terrible enemy drove their ancestors out of a verdant western country situated across the sea, on the other side of the earth. Their ancestors, according to their migration tradition, escaped with a man who knew the way to the northwest coat of America. Although their guide left them there, the Dene travelled on to the upper Yukon River region, and subsequently made their way inland.

From her study of their ''migration tradition'' she determined that the Mongol hordes were led by the notorious Genghis Khan. ''The essential core of a tradition may survive for many centuries among a people who have suffered a drastic separation from the roots of their culture,'' she wrote. ''The important point about the names and comments given by Dene raconteurs in the period 1860 to 1975 is that they appear to parallel events of long ago in Outer Mongolia.''

The parallels are powerful and instructive. But do they constitute proof? Stewart herself posed this question.

> One may ask what *does* constitute proof? Any hope that the male ancestors of the Dene and their Hsi-Hsia protectors left any record of their escape and their intended destination can be dismissed at once. In the matter of indisputable and conclusive proof, the most that can be hoped is the chance discovery of some inscription, or artifact somewhere in the vast expanse of the Yukon or Alaska, or the chance discovery of the ships which brought the Dene ancestors along that ''chain of islands,'' in that graveyard of the Pacific off the coasts of Alaska and British Columbia, or even off the northern coast of California . . . Barring the remote possibility of chance discoveries of conclusive proof, Dene traditions, names, customs, dialects are all that is left.

Hay River/
SETI Site

The search for extra-terrestrial intelligence (or SETI) is the main function of the Interstellar Electromagnetics Institute (or IEI). This federally incorporated, non-profit corporation was established in 1985 by Robert W. Stephens, an electronics technologist from Edmonton, Alberta. The organization supplies the corporate backup structure for the Hay River Radio Observatory (or HRRO), home to Canada's second-largest collection-aperture microwave radiotelescope, which single-handedly Stephens has established, instrumented, and now operates at Hay River.

Optical and radio observatories are commonly established in isolated parts of the world. This one is no exception. Hay River is the name of a river, an Indian reserve, and a busy northern town of about 3000 inhabitants. Its remote location offers an exceptionally radio-interference-free environment for the sensitive radio telescope: a $2 million replacement-cost assortment of steel, concrete, and silicon which now listens patiently for a faint, *deliberate* whisper above the natural hiss of background microwave radiation permeating from deep space.

The town is located on the south shore of Great Slave Lake, at the mouth of the Hay River. The observatory is situated well away from local activity on the northern tip of Vale Island, a natural delta situated between the east and west channels of the river's mouth. Since 1981, Stephens has been scrounging around for the electronics and microwave equipment necessary for a SETI program. In order to purchase this equipment he has had to sell off most of his personal possessions. Stephens negotiated some good bargains along the way. In 1981 he purchased the two, 60-foot parabolic dish antennas which now form the radiotelescope at Hay River for one dollar. They were originally built in 1963 as part of a series of troposcatter, long-haul microwave repeater stations, part of the DEW (Distant Early Warning) Line.

Stephen's work has been a subject of interest in the media for some time. There is a growing pile of newspaper and magazine articles, including a full page in *Omni* — "Anti-Matter," March, 1986 — and interviews and discussions on radio programs, including David Suzuki's nationally syndicated, radio-science program "Discovery" the following year. NBC-TV flew its news crew from New York to Hay River in February 1987, filmed the operation, and aired the news item internationally on the network the following month.

In addition to the SETI program, Stephens' facility now offers an excellent "hands-on" observing experience for undergraduate university students. This program hosted its first student during the summer of 1987. H. Peter White, an astronomy and physics honours student from St. Mary's University in Halifax, was the first of what Stephens hopes will become a series of students who will benefit from HRRO in coming years.

IEI's funding for SETI has come mainly from Stephens' own pocket, although a trickle occasionally flows in by way of local support from the town, its business sector, public-service clubs, and private donations through the mail. The Planetary Society recently awarded Stephens a small grant. There has not been enough, however, to keep up with the burden of utility bills and property-lease payments. As of this writing — November 1987 — Stephens has personally accumulated large debts and the observatory now teeters precariously close to shutdown.

The Hay River installation represents the sole dedicated SETI program in Canada, and has the distinction of being the third such program on-line in North America — right in there with Ohio State and Harvard University — but only a major increase in outside support will assure the program's continued existence.

Hudson Bay/
Inland Sea Extraordinaire

A bay of neither the Arctic nor the Atlantic Ocean, Hudson Bay is an "inland sea" and one of the most distinctive and predominant water features on the planet when viewed from space. The historians maintain that it was discovered in 1611 by the English navigator Henry Hudson while searching for the Northwest Passage.

Was Hudson Bay really discovered by Henry Hudson? The bay was already known, of course, to the native people who lived along its shores. If it must bear the name of a European explorer, should it be renamed Knutsson Bay or Scolvuss Bay? Farley Mowat, writing in *Westviking: The Ancient Norse in Greenland and North America* (1965), suggested that three centuries before Hudson made his voyage, at least one Norse expedition explored its waters. He pointed to evidence that about 1360 the expedition led by the Norseman Paul Knutsson may have passed through Hudson Strait and then descended into Hudson Bay. There is evidence to suggest that the Dane Johannes Scolvuss did the same about 1476. It is probably that Hudson himself was familiar with the now-lost "memoir" written by Scolvuss about his voyage.

It is a matter of historical record that in 1611 Hudson took the *Discovery* into Hudson Bay and down the east coast of James Bay, searching for an opening to the West that did not exist. When he announced his plans to winter near the mouth of the Rupert River, members of the crew mutinied and cast Hudson, his son, and seven faithful sailors into a shallop and cut it adrift in the open sea, 23 June 1611.

Nothing is known of the fate of the nine castaways. However, there is a fascinating story that under Hudson's leadership they survived the ordeal. With great difficulty they beached the shallop and would have starved to death on the inhospitable shore of James Bay had it not been for the native Indians who came to their aid. They erected a rough stone house which in time was abandoned, its ruins coming to light and later described by the explorer Radisson.

The castaways established a close association with the natives specifically the Moose River Cree, a tribe of Indians with pale skin, blue-grey eyes, light hair, and slight physique. But after some years the castaways angered the Cree who sold the insufferable white men into slavery. Their masters were a band of nomadic Indians who journeyed far to the south. Hudson endured the trek and lived long enough to leave evidence of the ordeal. Somehow he was able to carve an inscription on a rock, a rock that in the 1950s was discovered in the vicinity of Deep River, Ontario. Henry Hudson Rock, was photographed and then lost to history.

There is at least one other legend about Henry Hudson and concerns his first voyage to the New World. This was made in 1609 when he journeyed the Hudson River in the *Half Moon* as far as present-day Albany, New York. Did his voyage ever end? As Bill Wisner wrote in *Vanished — Without a Trace!* (1977).

> I was unable to track down its source and age, but an obscure legend has it that the ghost of the *Half Moon* sometimes can be seen at night, visible in the pale glow as she makes her way along the broad bosom of the Hudson.
>
> Perhaps that accounts for a saying in the great river's valley: When thunder rumbles, it's Henry Hudson and his men enjoying a game of lawn bowls.

Lake Harbour/ Serene Figurine

Not far from the community of Lake Harbour, on Baffin Island's southern coast, two archaeologists discovered a serene figurine. The discovery was made by Deborah and George Sabo III, two Michigan State University archaeologists, and their Inuit guides,

Mooney Lyta and Pitsulak Josepee, in July 1977, while exploring the Thule remains of the deserted Inuit village of Okivilialuk.

The serene figurine is a tiny wooden carving which depicts a European male figure wearing a long hooded cassock with a cross incised on the chest. The legs are represented but the feet have been lost. The figure was carved by an unknown Eskimo carver in fine-grain fir. It is tiny, only two inches tall, almost an inch wide, and less than half an inch thick.

This "serene figurine" was discovered amid the remains of a deserted Inuit village near Lake Harbour on Baffin Island in 1977 by two American archaeologists and their two Inuit guides. The wooden carving is about the size of a human thumb. It depicts a European male figure wearing a long hooded cassock with a cross incised on the chest. The ancient Thule carving represents a monk, perhaps a Greenlandic Viking of the thirteenth century. [Canadian Museum of Civilization, National Museums of Canada]

The first of its kind found in North America, the Thule carving represents a monk, perhaps a Greenlandic Viking of the thirteenth century. It conveys the notion of serenity. It is the first concrete evidence of the introduction of Christianity to the Canadian Arctic. The figure is preserved by the National Museum of Man, Ottawa.

It was described in an illustrated article by Betty Lou White in "Vikings Came to Baffin Island" in *Fate*, September 1978.

Isle of Buss/
Imaginary Land

For two centuries the Isle of Buss graced the charts of the Atlantic and the Arctic. Then, when the locale of the elusive island could no longer be ascertained, it disappeared from the charts, dismissed as a phantom island, an imaginery land.

The Isle of Buss was first spotted in Hudson Strait by the crew of the *Emmanuel*, a ship attached to Sir Martin Frobisher's third polar voyage of 1578. It was named Buss after that vessel, which was called a *buss*, a stout, three-masted Dutch fishing boat. In vain did Henry Hudson search for the Isle of Buss on his voyage of 1609. The Hudson's Bay Company applied to Charles II for permission to extend its monopoly over Buss Island in 1673, and permission was granted two years later. Captain Gillam claimed he could see it from the deck of the *Nonsuch* in 1668. It was not until 1791 that it was declared non-existent.

"The Mythical Land of Buss" is the title of an article by Alice M. Johnson which appeared in *The Beaver*, December 1942. The name of Buss will live forever in the limbo of lost lands.

Lancaster Sound/
The Unicorn

Among the aquatic inhabitants of Lancaster Sound, the body of water between Baffin Island and Devon Island, is the narwhal (*Monodon monoceros*). This wild creature, sometimes called the "Arctic whale," was known at one time as the "sea unicorn."

The narwhal, a toothed whale, is best known for the single, straight, tightly spiraled tusk which projects through its lip. The ivory tusk, which may reach three feet in length, was highly valued and widely collected in Europe and contributed to the legend of the unicorn.

In European legend, the unicorn is a fabulous beast, having the head and body of a horse, the hind legs of an antelope, the tail of a lion, the beard of a goat, and a long, sharp, twisted horn, similar to the narwhal's tusk set in the middle of its forehead. The earliest references place it in distant India, but it may well have been inspired by the rhinoceros of Africa. The presence in Europe of narwhal tusks gave the fabulous beast some currency and credibility, as the tusk was its most distinguishing feature. The tusk was believed to possess curative and purifying qualities.

The early explorers did a brisk trade in narwhal tusks, one of which Sir Martin Frobisher presented to Queen Elizabeth who is said to have prized it. Samuel Hearne wrote interestingly about the sea unicorn in *A Journey from Prince of Wales's Fort in Hudson's Bay to the Northern Ocean* (1958), edited by Richard Glover, originally published posthumously in 1795.

> Besides these, the SEA-UNICORN is known to frequent Hudson's Bay and Straits, but I never saw one of them. Their horns are frequently purchased from our friendly Esquimaux, who probably get them in the way of barter from those tribes that reside more to the North; but I never could be informed by the natives whether their skins are like those of the Whale, or hairy like those of the Seal; I suppose the former.

The Canadian Coat of Arms is supported by the Lion and the Unicorn, heraldic emblems of England and Scotland. The ceremonial mace of the Territorial Government of the Northwest Territories was cut from a narwhal tusk. The verger's white wand in All Saints Anglican Cathedral in Aklavik is made from a narwhal tusk. It is possible to imagine that the Inuit and Northern Indian shamans, in dealing their magical effects, made good use of the tusk of the "sea unicorn" or "Arctic whale."

Nahanni National Park/ Tropical Valley

The most perennial of Canadian legends is that there exists in the Far North a Tropical Valley, a remote and virtually inaccessible vale warmed by hot mineral springs and teeming with exotic fauna and flora. In some versions of the legend, this Tropical Valley or Lost Valley or Valley of Mystery is the habitat of a forgotten race of people, ruled over by a captive white queen, who do daily battle with hairy ape-men and dinosaur-like creatures which have survived from prehistoric times. In other versions of the legend, the valley is uninhabited yet cursed, for it is awash in gold and other precious metals, the prospects of which lure prospectors to madness or death.

To the extent to which any legend may be limited to a single geographical location, Nahanni National Park embraces the legend of the Tropical Valley. Cutting through the National Park is the mighty South Nahanni River which races over rapids between the immense Mackenzie Mountains. The region is inaccessible except by private float plane and navigable only by white-water canoe. The scenery is remote and awesome in its grandeur. Nahanni National Park was established in the northwest corner of the Northwest Territories in 1972, and six years later was listed by UNESCO as a World Heritage Site. The natural wonders of the valley were created eons ago—the double cascade of Virginia Falls, a drop of 316 feet, the Rabbitkettle Hot Spring with its terraced pools of clear water at 70 degrees Fahrenheit, to name two.

The history of the Nahanni River valley fits the legend of the Valley of Mystery. The history goes back to around 1900 when a Nahanni Indian appeared at a Hudson's Bay Company post with large gold nuggets. Pressed for details, he would say nothing of the mine. Three years later a Cassiar Indian showed up at the same post with nuggets described as the size of chicken eggs. Under the influence of alcohol, he said he had gathered them at Bennett Creek, a tributary of the Flat River which was part of the South Nahanni River system.

In 1904 the MacLeod brothers, two halfbreed sons of a Fort Liard trader, heard the story and decided to find out for themselves if it was true. They outfitted themselves and left from Telegraph Creek, British Columbia, travelling overland to Flat River by way of Dease Lake. At the junction of Bennett Creek and Flat River, they began to prospect. They struck paydirt. But winter was on its way and all they could do was to assay the ore. They returned in a crude scow which capsized at the Cascade of the Thirteen Drops in Flat River Canyon. They saved their lives but they lost their assays, arriving broke at Fort Liard with nothing to show for their strenuous efforts except five ounces of flake gold Willie had on his person.

Nevertheless they were able to convince a Scottish engineer named Wilkinson—some accounts give his name as Weir—to assist them with a renewed assault on the gold. In the spring of 1905 the three partners mounted their expedition and entered the valley. When after a year's time they did not return, the third MacLeod brother, Charlie, led a search party. In a clearing by the river he found the two brothers. They were dead, their bodies picked clean by animals. But their heads had been removed and were missing. They had been surgically removed, not carried off by some animal. Charlie found a note that had been scrawled on the runner of a sledge, which read: "We have found a fine prospect." Charlie came to the conclusion that the three men had found the source of the gold. Then, while they slept, the Scottish engineer had shot them in the head. To remove all traces of the murder, he decapitated them and fled with the gold. He was traced to Vancouver but thereafter the trail went cold.

From that point on the valley of the Nahanni River was known as Headless Valley. It attracted a strange group of people, all of whom came to bizarre ends— as some of the names of various features of the land would attest: Headless Range, Broken Skull River, Funeral Range, Murder Valley, Valley of No Return, Devil's Kitchen, and Ragged Range.

A Swedish prospector from the Yukon named Martin Jorgenson set up camp in the valley. He was backed by an ex-Mountie named Poole Field, a trader at Ross River, and through an Indian he sent Field a map of his discovery. In 1910, Jorgenson's body was found. He had been shot to death while trying to defend himself and his cabin was burnt to the ground.

In 1922, Edward Clausen, a seventy-two-year-old trapper, found man-made caves along the river. They were described as fourteen feet deep, ten feet wide, with eight-foot ceilings. They had holes for chimneys, and there were man-made mounds nearby. These gave rise to the belief that the valley's gold was guarded by hairy mountain men who lived in these caves and warmed themselves in its volcanic-heated waters.

Angus Hall, another prospector, disappeared in the valley in 1929. No trace of him was ever found.

Phil Powers, a lone prospector, ventured into the valley in 1931. His body was found at a later point. He suffered Jorgenson's fate. He had died trying to defend himself and his cabin had been set on fire.

One expedition was of particular note. It was described in a Canadian Press story filed from Fort Simpson and published in the Niagara Falls *Evening Review* on 20 October 1936. Attracted by the fabled wealth of the area and legends of a "lost mine," as well as by a crudely drawn map said to have originated with Martin Jorgenson, an expedition was mounted by Poole Field, verteran trader, prospector, and trapper, and his partner J.H. Mulholland. In July the Field-Mulholland Expedition, with thirty Indian porters, entered the area to pan for gold and seek the lost mine. In the words of the newsman, "The Indians believe death awaits prospectors entering the region. They went so far into the area — quite cold and the expedition failed."

In 1942, a quite elderly Charlie McLeod again entered the wilderness valley. As John Picton reported in the *Toronto Star*, 22 November 1981, he visited the site where his brothers' bodies had been found and buried. Once known as Sheep Creek, it was now named (and misnamed) McCloud Creek in honour of his brothers. He found traces of gold and copper, but nothing to suggest that the mother-lode had been discovered.

And in 1952, in the company of his sons, he made another pilgrimage to the site. All he found was that the river had washed out his brothers' graves.

Over the years other prospectors have sought the wealth of the valley. Among them are such names as Bill Espler, Yukon Fischer, Annie La Ferte, One O'Brien, Edwin Hall, Andy Hays, Ernest Savard, and John Patterson. They sought wealth but they were lucky to return with their lives — those who did return.

If there is gold in the Nahanni River Valley, it is protected by something stronger than chance and the elements. Ivan T. Sanderson in *Abominable Snowmen: Legend Come to Life* (1977) agreed with the characterization of the Valley as the "number one legend of the Northland." He went on to raise the possibility that the deaths of all the prospectors were caused by "head-hunting mountain-men." The word *nahanni* is Athapascan for "people of the west" or "people of the buttes" or "people from far away."

No account of the Tropical Valley would be complete without an acknowledgement of the imaginative contributions made to the legend by numerous writers. Michael H. Mason, through *The Arctic Forests* (1924), contributed the notion that the Valley was populated by a strange race "under the complete domination of one woman supposedly of European descent." Robert Patterson in *The Dangerous River* (1928, 1968) introduced the notion of the Wild Mountain men guarding the gold. The only novel set in the Valley is a great one: John Buchan's superb *Sick Heart River* (1941). The danger posed by the valley in the pages of that book are of a metaphysical nature, for to Buchan, who explored the region while Governor General of Canada, the valley served as a sanctuary of the spirit and of "this peace . . . beyond living and dying." Charles Camsell, the geologist, exploded the notion of the sub-tropicality of the Valley in *Son of the North* (1954) but otherwise revived the legend.

Pierre Berton wrote about the valley in a sensational and incessant manner when he was a newsman with the *Vancouver Sun*; in a sceptical style when he was an editor of *Maclean's*; and in a thoughful fashion in his book *The Mysterious North* (1956). Captain Sir Ranulph Fiennes, the British adventurer, travelled the length of the Valley and described the grizzly experience in his book *The Headless Valley* (1973).

Nahanni's mother-lode seems largely lore.

Victoria Island/
Blond Eskimos

The Arctic explorer Vilhjalmur Stefansson evolved a theory to account for the existence of the so-called Blond Eskimos. He first encountered these blue-eyed, fair-haired native people in 1908 on an expedition that took him among the Copper Eskimos who lived in isolated communities on Victoria Island overlooking Coronation Gulf and Dolphin and Union Strait.

In interviews and in his travel book *My Life with the Eskimo* (1913), he presented his theory that the two thousand or so Blond Eskimos were descendants of a union of the Dorset Eskimo people and the Norse colonists from Greenland. He dismissed the possibility of intercourse with European whalers in modern times, and claimed to have detected Norse words in the vocabulary of these people.

Stefansson was not the first explorer to discover or describe a race of fair-complexioned Eskimos. In fact, more than 250 years earlier, Captain Nicolas Tunes encountered dark as well as fair native races. This occurred on his voyage of 1656. Tunes wrote the following account of the fair-haired native population living in the vicinity of Bylot Island, north of Baffin Island:

> As regards the inhabitants, our travellers report having seen two kinds, who live together on the most friendly terms. Of these, one kind is described as very tall, well-built, of rather fair complexion, and very swift of foot. The others are very much smaller, of an olive complexion, and tolerably well-proportioned, except that their legs are short and thick. The former kind delight in hunting, for which they are suited by their agility and natural disposition, whereas the latter occupy themselves in fishing. All of them have very white, compact teeth, black hair, animated eyes, and the features of the face so well made that they present no notable deformity. Moreover, they are all so vigorous and of such a strong constitution that several of them who have passed their hundredth year are still lively and robust.

The account of Nicolas Tunes was cited by David MacRitchie in "A Tribe of White Eskimos," *Nature*, 90:133, 1912. MacRitchie's article is reprinted in *Ancient Man: A Handbook of Puzzling Artifacts* (1978) compiled by William R. Corliss. MacRitchie concluded his account of the Blond Eskimo question by noting that it is "quite possible" the fair Eskimos described by Tunes "still retaining their individuality, may have migrated westward" to Victoria Island.

Victoria Island/
The Shaman Ilatsiak

The headquarters of the Canadian Arctic Expedition of 1913–18 was established in a wooden shack in the isolated settlement of Bernard Harbour on the southern coast of Victoria Island. Here the ethnologist Diamond Jenness set up a primitive recording apparatus and captured on cylinder disks the traditional songs of the Copper Eskimos.

Jenness described in his book *The Copper Eskimo* (1922) how on the expedition he befriended the Eskimo shaman named Ilatsiak. The shaman explained how his spirit-helper came to him in dreams to deliver important messages and prophecies. He went on to say that the shaman

> . . . reported that during the night his spirit had told him that something had gone wrong on our schooner; it was the thing, he had said, that made the vessel move. We thought that he must mean the propeller, for we had put a new one on during the winter and had to keep the ice open around it. By a strange coincidence, however, we discovered during the day—what Ilatsiak could hardly have been aware of—that a boom we were using to roof our provision cache had snapped during the night owing to the weight of the snow about it.

Jenness as an anthropologist was taking no chances with Ilatsiak's act of clairvoyance, insight, prediction, prophecy, psychic vision, or trickery. He called the shaman's knowledge "a strange coincidence."

The writer D. Scott Rogo, who discussed this incident in the article "Shamans: The World's Greatest Psychics?'' in *Fate*, September 1983, concluded that because the traditional way of life has all but passed from the face of the Earth, we will always wonder about the real power of the shaman. ''Perhaps we will never know whether the shamans of the primitive world are indeed the world's greatest psychics or merely the inferior practitioners of a once-great art.''

The North Pole/
Northernmost Point

Northward is inward. One does not ''reach'' the Pole, one ''attains'' the Pole. The passage north is as much a journey through the mind of man as it is a voyage through the world of nature.

The polar zone is an alien area: an Arctic Asia. Do alien lifeforms reside there? ''So far no one has looked for traces of extra-terrestrial beings at the poles!'' observed Erich von Däniken in his book *In Search of Ancient Gods: My Pictorial Evidence for the Impossible* (1974) translated from the German by Michael Heron.

The North Pole is the northern point of the Earth's rotation on its axis. It corresponds to a point on the polar ice cap north of Ellesmere Island, where latitude and longitude meet. Here the co-ordinates read: Latitude 90° North, Longitude 0°.

Who first attained the North Pole by standing at the ''top'' of the Earth is not as easily determined as its geographical co-ordinates. There are rival claimants and both are American explorers. Frederick A. Cook claimed that he was the first person to attain the Pole on 21 April 1908. He may even have done so but was unable to substantiate his claim. He did not do so, said Robert E. Peary, who certainly did the deed a year later on 6 April 1909.

The North Pole is not to be confused with the North Magnetic Pole, which is that point on the Earth's surface where the Earth's magnetic field is vertical. This point was first attained by the British navel officer Sir James Ross on 1 June 1831. Unlike the North Pole, which is considered to be fixed, the North Magnetic Pole is unfixed. It is said to wander, and it has been wandering in a northwesterly direction

since 1831, moving about seven miles a year. In addition, there is a daily fluctuation or displacement from its mean position of thirty-six miles or more.

Determining the position of the North Magnetic Pole is the responsibility of the Earth Physics Branch of Energy, Mines and Resources Canada. The 1984 North Magnetic Pole Survey established its position on the southeast tip of Lougheed Island which lies north of Bathurst Island, District of Franklin, N.W.T. The extrapolated position for 1988 is 77.4° North, 102.7° West. Once every ten years or so its position is determined by physical survey. On the last survey in 1984, geographers were surprised to find that an American couple had established temporary residency at the locale for the declared purpose of conceiving a child at the North Magnetic Pole!

It is the common lot of psychics like Edgar Cayce, the so-called Sleeping Prophet, to predict reversals in the magnetic field and even a pole shift or two. It has been scientifically established that the Earth's magnetic field has reversed itself many times in the past and will presumably continue to do so in the future. But there is no evidence at all of a cataclysmic inversion of the planet's axis of rotation. Despite the improbability or impossibility of such an occurrence, the inversion or pole shift has been predicted innumerable times. ''According to the Cayce readings, the pole shift will be preceded by several decades of increasingly severe seismic disturbances on a global scale, resulting in vast changes in the planet's geography. Through earthquakes and volcanic action, through elevation and submergence of land, and through flooding, a new face would be given to the earth.'' The drift of Cayce's reading was summarized in these words by John White in *Pole Shift: Predictions and Prophecies of the Ultimate Disaster* (2nd ed., 1986). Here are some consequences of the coming pole shift: New lands will appear in the Atlantic and Pacific Oceans . . . most of Japan will go into the sea'' . . . Northern Europe will be transformed ''in the twinkling of an eye'' . . . Los Angeles and San Francisco will be destroyed . . . New York City and the Connecticut coastline will be submerged . . . the Great Lakes will empty into the Gulf of Mexico . . . the eastern and western coasts of

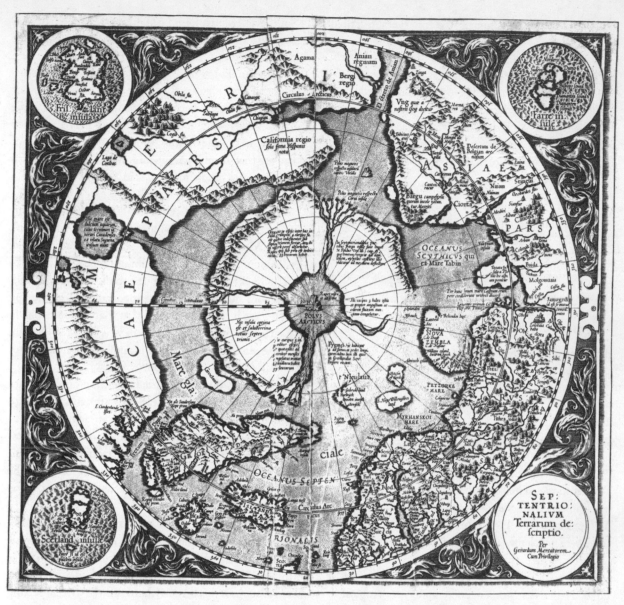

The planet Earth revolves around the North Pole. The world's northern-most point is called "Polvs Arctivs" on this 1585 map prepared by the celebrated cartographer Gerhardus Mercator. His conception of the polar region owes much to one Nicholas of Lynne, a Carmelite monk who is said to have travelled in 1360 from Norway across the Arctic islands to the North Pole itself. Upon his return he published a detailed account of his trek, Inventio Fortunata, *which has unfortunately been lost. His "fortunate discovery" (in the words of a cartographer in 1508) was that "at the arctic pole there is a high magnetic rock, thirty-three German miles in circumference." [Metropolitan Toronto Library]*

North America will be inundated for several hundred miles inland.

Some parts of the Earth will remain relatively undisturbed by these earth changes and the pole shift. Cayce identified some of these areas and called them "safety lands." So dramatic will be the changes that the inland city of Livingston, Montana, will become a major seaport. The affect on Canada was mentioned in the Cayce reading of 13 August 1941:

> Then the area where the entity [the person for whom the reading was arranged] is now located [Virginia Beach] will be among the safety lands — as will be portions of what is now Ohio, Indiana and Illinois and much of the southern portion of Canada, and the eastern portion of Canada; while the western land, much of that is to be disturbed in this land, as, of course, much in other lands.

Apparently the place to reside is in southeastern Canada if not in Virginia Beach, Virginia.

The North Pole/
Eden, Atlantis, Lemuria, Mu

The Garden of Eden, the biblical paradise, has no known locale. The scriptural sense of place is not to be confused with the "fertile crescent" in the valley of the Tigris and Euphrates Rivers, in modern-day Iraq, which scientists once maintained was the most likely birthplace of *Homo sapiens*.

Initially it seems strange to argue for an Arctic Eden, rather than for an Eden under the tropical or sub-tropical sun. Yet the theory of continental drift and plate tectonics may account for the movement of gigantic landmasses over the entire surface of the planet. The hypothesized super-continent of Pangea was pulled into two parts: a northern half called Laurasia and a southern half called Gondwanaland. Laurasia eventually split into the continents that comprise the Northern Hemisphere, notably North America, including the Arctic, Europe, and Asia. At the same time, Gondwanaland split into the continents of the Southern Hemisphere, notably, Australia, Africa, Southern India, South America, and Antarctica. These massive land migrations took place a hundred or two hundred million years before the creation or appearance of *Homo sapiens*. But if the human race was not the earliest race, as occultists believe, then the locale of the genesis of the pre-human races may have been found on those portions of the super-continent of Pangea that have by now migrated to the Canadian Arctic. This much may be said for the theory of a polar Eden.

Atlantis, the most celebrated of the lost continents of legend, may have been an actual island which sank in the Mediterranean. Plato described Atlantis in such riveting detail that it is possible for the scholar without Greek to forget that the philosopher's island-kingdom makes its lengthy appearance in a teaching fable. Yet it has been argued that Plato described it in such a way as to leave his readers with a recollection of the sinking of an actual island, that of Santorini, within the historical period.

Occultists divine Atlantis to be the home of a race of humanoid beings who raced too far and too fast to perfect a technology considerably in advance of our own. They fell prey to a form of nuclear madness which resulted in the self-destruction of their civilization and the sinking of their island. The catastrophe is said to have occurred comparatively recently, some 12,000 years ago.

As for an Arctic Atlantis, it is said that the cartographer Gerhardus Mercator fixed Atlantis in the Arctic region in one of his maps, as did Abraham Ortelius in his World Map of 1570. A host of imaginative novelists have used the Atlantis-in-the-Arctic setting for their novels.

No cartographers or novelists have (so far at least) set the fabulous islands of Lemuria and Mu in the Arctic. Occultists believe that Lemuria, which flourished some 700,000 years before Atlantis, was a super-civilization centred on an island in what is now the Indian Ocean. Remnants are said to linger somewhere off Madagascar. Much less is known of the island of Mu, which rose and fell in the Pacific Ocean. It is closely identified with the writings of the Oriental traveller James Churchward. There has been one attempt to relocate it by identifying it with the evasive "land beyond the Pole" supposedly sighted on his polar voyage by Admiral Byrd. But the general feeling is that Mu, like Atlantis, sank beneath the waves and is no more.

Robert Charroux, in *The Mysterious Unknown* (1973), translated from the French by Oleg Sieveking, argued that contemporary history is a replay of archaic history. He discussed the theory that nuclear warfare is not new to mankind, suggesting the possibility that there was once a nuclear battle waged between the Hyperboreans and the people of the Island of Mu. "It is disturbing to realize that at the present-day two great atomic powers, one situated partly on ancient Atlantis, and the other including much of the one-time Land of Mu, are contending for possession of the North Pole, where the largest city miraculously bears the name of Thule in the twentieth century." Further details about Atlantis-in-the-Arctic appear in Serge Hutin's *Alien Races and Fantastic Civilizations* (1975) and L. Sprague de Camp's *Lost Continents* (1970).

There is no concurrence among the ancient and modern authorities on the geographical locales of Eden, Atlantis, Lemuria, and Mu. Nor is there any agreement on whether or not they existed in the real world, the world as it is known in modern times. About all that my be said on their behalf in terms of Arctic habitation is that there does exist in the Arctic at this time "local geographies" where the climates differ from the climates that surround them, being ice-free. Such areas are called, after the Russian, polynyas. But there is a surprising correlation between the desire of the commentators to draw moral and ethical lessons from the fates of those highly accomplished civilizations of the dim and distant past. One lesson seems to be that intelligent beings must develop their emotional, intuitive, and spiritual potentialities alongside their technological capability and scientific knowledge. Another lesson seems to be that only a conscious development along these lines will forestall the catastrophic forces that destroyed entire civilizations in the past and will do so again in the future.

The North Pole/ Mount Meru

Mount Meru is described in the oldest sacred texts known to man. These tests are the *Vedas* of India, which were composed in Sanskrit about 2500 B.C. In Sanskrit the word *veda* means knowledge. The knowledge that these texts or scriptures preserve and impart has come to be regarded as the backbone of Hinduism, the world's oldest continuing religion.

Hindu scholars who have studied these scriptures, which are collected in four volumes and which include attendant texts like the *Vishnu Purana*, which dates from between 500 B.C. and A.D. 500, have come to the conclusion that the ancients who composed or compiled the *Vedas* possessed a detailed knowledge of the Indian sub-continent and a surprising knowledge of the Americas.

The traditions of the Aryan people, the philosophically-minded Indo-European people who left some unknown northern region of the globe and settled the sub-continent, embraced the belief in the existence of a "world-mountain" which was located at "the centre of the world" and which was named Mount Meru. The centre of the world was understood to be that point which is crossed by the "world-axis" and which is in alignment with the Pole Star. It is a point of contact between Heaven and Earth. In the words of J.E. Cirlot in *A Dictionary of Symbols* (1962):

> Mount Meru is said to be of gold and located at the North Pole, thus underlining the idea of the Centre and, in particular, linking it with the Pole Star—the "hole" through which all things temporal and spatial must pass in order to divest themselves of their wordly characteristics. This polar mountain is also to be found in other symbolic traditions, always bearing the same symbolism of the world-axis; its mythic characteristics were, in all probability, based upon the fixed position of the Pole Star.

The world-mountain is both material and spiritual in composition. The *Vishnu Purana* places it geographically at the North Pole. The region is characterized by the great intervals that lie between the dawns. The world-mountain rises over an island surrounded by Kshira, "an ocean of milk," a striking image for a sea of ice and snow. Below it will be found two great bodies of land, called Uttara Kuru, each of which "takes the form of a bow." Scholars identify Uttara Kuru with North and South America. There are said to be four bodies of water upon this land and mountains in two long ranges. On the rest of the globe, there are seven continents and seven seas.

What is the spiritual function of this "world-mountain?" It meets a symbolic need that springs unbidden from the heart of man, whatever his beliefs may be. That need is for a spiritual centre. The fact that the centre should be found within the head and heart of man does not lessen the symbolic need to locate it in such familiar places as Jerusalem, Lhasa, Mecca, and Rome — not to mention such places as Hill Cumorrah, Buddha-Gaya, Avebury, and Manitoulin Island. It may be argued that a fixed point in the world of matter helps one to fix a point in the world of the spirit.

The standard scholarly study which argues for the identification of Mount Meru with the North Pole is *The Arctic Home in the Vedas: Being Also New Key to the Interpretation of Many Vedic Texts and Legends*. This 416-page tome was originally printed in Poona, India, in 1903, reprinted in 1924, and reprinted again in 1971. It is the work of the respected Sanskrit scholar B.G. Tilak (1856–1920). Tilak wrote this study during a period of imprisonment, having been jailed by the British for his nationalist activities. Tilak argued that his book showed that "the home of the ancestors of the Vedic people was somewhere near the North Pole before the last Glacial Epoch." He added, "The North Pole is conclusively shown to be the cradle of the human race . . . ."

The North Pole/
Shamballah and Agartha

Shamballah represents to the Buddhists of Tibet what Mount Meru represents to the Hindus of India. It may be argued that should the locale of the two sacred sites be the North Pole, then Shamballah takes the form of a community at the crest of Mount Meru. Agartha in the Tibetan tradition is Shamballah's subterranean counterpart, so it may be beneath the polar zone.

Many of the details concerning the mystical community of Shamballah appear, oddly enough, in *The People's Almanac No. 3* (1981) by David Wallechinsky and Irving Wallace. In that cornucopia-like book of information, Jannika Hurwitt's article "The Continuing Search for Shambhala" immediately raises the issue of the spelling of the name of the place. There are innumerable spellings, but here the community, whether found in the Arctic or elsewhere, will be spelled Shamballah.

The community or city is regarded as a "Hidden Kingdom" and is usually located in Tibet. Here the Mahatmas, the great souls or perfected human beings, live and guide the evolution of mankind. An esoteric branch of Tibetan mysticism named Kalacakra is said to emanate from Shamballah. The community was ancient at the time of the Buddha who preached Kalacakra in India in the sixth century B.C. The buildings that comprise the community are said to be shaped like an eight-petaled lotus blossom, each surrounded by a ring of mountains. Kalapa, the capital with the king's palace, lies as the centre and is richly ornamented.

"By definition Shamballah is hidden," Jannika Hurwitt wrote. "It is thought to exist somewhere between the Gobi Desert and the Himalayas, but it is protected by a psychic barrier so that no one can find the kingdom who is not meant to." The Western world first learned of Shamballah in a reference to "Xembala" in a Jesuit's letter written from China in 1627. Interest in the West was kindled — and rekindled in the East — when Helena Petrovna Blavatsky, who claimed her occult knowledge came from the secret teachings of the spiritual masters in Shamballah, established the Theosophical Society in New York City in 1875.

There are traditions that place Shamballah not in Tibet or China or Outer Mongolia but in the Canadian Arctic. Working within this tradition the poet Bliss Carman sang the praises of the place in his poem "Shamballah" written in 1922 and included in his collection *Far Horizons* (1925). Here is how it begins:

Have you heard of the city Shamballah,
That marvellous place in the North,
The home of the Masters of Wisdom,
Whence the Sons of the Word are sent forth?

It seems appropriate that the Tibetan spiritual community of Shamballah should be established on the world-mountain sacred to the Hindus, Mount Meru, and both constituted at the North Pole.

If Shamballah and Mount Meru are located at the North Pole, why not the equally mysterious subterranean sanctuary known as Agartha? In Tibetan tradition, Agartha is a kingdom perhaps located under the Himalayas where the great Initiates and Masters of the World in its present cycle still live. Robert Charroux in *The Mysterious Unknown* (1973), described this "mysterious subterranean kingdom." He added the intriguing information that wherever Agartha is located it is connected through a series of ancient caverns and caves, tunnels and channels, with four traditional entranceways. These may be found between the paws of the Sphinx at Gizeh, in the crypt of Mont-Saint Michel in Paris, in the Forest of Broceliande in France, and at the main gateway to Shamballah, wherever that may be.

Charroux made another point, this time about the inhabitants of Agartha, in *One Hundred Thousand Years of Man's Unknown History* (1970), translated from the French by Lowell Blair. He suggested: "It may be that beings from another planet, unable to live in the earth's atmosphere for very long, went underground, leaving incomprehensible traces of their presence. Incomprehensible to us, that is, but not to those of their race."

The North Pole/Hyperborea

There are some words and phrases that time and time again transport whoever speaks or hears or ponders them into the realm of the imagination. One thinks of such formulaic openings or closings as "Once upon a time . . ." or "And they lived happily ever after." But one also recalls with a special thrill such spellbinding words as "East of the Sun and West of the Moon . . . ." Anyone raised in the Western world will respond to them with a renewed sense of wonder.

The word "Hyperborea" probably had that power on the minds of the Ancient Greeks. Hyperborea was literally "the Land beyond Boreas," for Boreas was the personification of the cold Northern Wind. The Greeks were a venturesome, sea-faring race, but they seldom if ever sailed as far north as that fabled land. As distant as it was from the land of the Hellenes, Hyperborea was at the hub of the origins of Hellenic legend and myth.

The Far North held a special fascination for the Ancient Greeks as it was both metaphorically and literally the Arctic. *Arktos* was Greek for "bear." This northern land lay directly beneath the Constellation of the Bear; serendipitously, it was inhabited by the Polar Bear. Hyperborea, located in the Far North, was the Pre-Hellenic paradise. Homer mentioned it, and the historian Strabo recalled the northern travels of Pytheas of Massilia (known today as Marseilles). Pytheas, the Greek navigator, astronomer, and geographer, visited today's British Isles about 310 B.C. According to Pytheas' account, now lost, he sailed six days north and saw the coasts of "a sub-Arctic region" where "there is neither sea nor air, but a mixture like sea-lung, in which earth and air are suspended." Does this seem the attempt of a Mediterranean mind to convey the appearance of the Arctic conditions of ice, sleet, or snow?

The poet Pindar, knowing that distance lends enchantment, sang of this far kingdom: "Neither by ship nor by land canst thou find the wondrous road to the Hyperboreans." Diodorus, the Greek historian of the first century B.C., drew on some ancient tradition for details of the island of Hyperborea and the everyday life of the Hyperboreans:

This island . . . is both fertile and productive of every crop, and since it has an unusually temperate climate it produces two harvests a year. Moreover, the following legend is told concerning it: Leto [mother of Apollo and Artemis; Zeus was their father] was born on this island, and for that reason Apollo is honoured among them above all other gods, and the inhabitants are looked upon as priests of Apollo. And there is also on the island both a magnificent sacred precinct of Apollo and a notable temple which is adorned with many votive offerings and is spherical in shape. The Hyperboreans also have a language peculiar to them, and are most friendly disposed toward the Greeks and especially toward the Athenians and the Delians, who have inherited this good will from most ancient times.

The unique significance of Hyperborea derives from the fact that, in Greek myth and legend, Apollo is the most Greek of the gods yet he came from the North. Periodically he revisited his homeland, Hyperborea, a polar Hesperides of everlasting spring and perpetual sunshine, an early Elysium, where men and women live a pastoral life and live for a thousand years. Apollo brought with him from the north many arts, including those of healing and prophecy, which he bequeathed to the Greeks.

The name of the greatest ruler of the Hyperboreans is known. Abaris is his name and Apollo is said to have presented him with "a magic arrow" which possessed many peculiar properties. It could render its possessor invisible; it could empower curses; it could act as an oracle; and, most amazingly, it could transport a person through the air at incredible speeds. Apparently Apollo used the "magic arrow" himself to travel from Hyperborea to Athens and Delos and then back again.

The land of the Hyperboreans, like the Hesperides, inspired poets centuries later. In the nineteenth century, Thomas Moore wrote "Song of a Hyperborean," a lyric which begins: "I come from a land in the sunbright deep, / Where golden gardens glow, / Where the winds of the north, becalmed in sleep, / Their conch shells never blow."

What seems strange — though perhaps strangely reassuring — to the contemporary Canadian mind is the fact that the Ancient Greeks should have placed amid the cold of the Far North a kingdom of contentment.

The North Pole/ Ultima Thule

The Romans copied the Greeks in most things, so it is not surprising that they incorporated the land of Hyperborea into their own legend. The Italians, being more practical than the Hellenes and less given to tradition for its own sake, downgraded the paradisaical aspects. Hyperborea became Thule, or Ultima Thule, the most distant of parts, the limit of the known which itself was unknown.

There are passing references to this remote region in the writings of Pliny and Virgil, as Robert Charroux noted in *One Hundred Thousand Years of Man's Unknown History* (1970). The habit was continued into the nineteenth century — there is Edgar Allan Poe's curious couplet which runs, "I have reached these lands but newly / From that ultimate dim Thule" — but the main use was that of Seneca, the Roman philosopher and tutor of the Emperor Nero. As he predicted in his tragic play *Medea*, about the downfall of Medea, the priestess of Hecate:

> Venient annis saecula seris,
> Quibus Oceanus vincula rerum
> Laxet, et ingens pateat tellus,
> Tiphysque novos detegat orbes;
> Nec sit terris ultima Thule.

These lines, written about A.D. 64 were later taken as Seneca's prophecy of the discovery of America. Francis Bacon, the sixteenth century English philosopher and essayist, found the Latin lines of verse to be memorable, and he translated them into English prose: "There shall come a time when the bands of ocean shall be loosened, and the vast earth shall be laid open; another Tiphys shall disclose new worlds, and lands shall be seen beyond Thule." Whether they anticipate the discovery of America or not, to students of lost lands and similar matters, these lines foretell the great cataclysm which will rend the earth and reveal a vast new continent, hitherto unknown to history, "beyond Thule."

No doubt influenced by such matters, the Norwegian explorer Knud Rasmussen gave the name Thule to his tiny trading and scientific station on the northwest coast of Greenland. From here he launched the fifth and most extensive of his polar expeditions — the Fifth Thule Expedition of 1921–24 which recorded the material and intellectual culture of the Arctic Eskimo. Thus the name Thule was applied to the native culture of the Arctic which flourished between A.D. 1000 and 1900. Such round-figure dating is for mnemonic convenience, of course, as there was much contact between the pre-Thule culture, known as the Dorset culture, and the post-Thule culture, called the Inuit culture.

The North Pole/
The Theosophical Pole

Almost all the occult notions that have become commonplace in the Western world in the twentieth century—ideas like the secret doctrine, esoteric section, Great White Brotherhood, universal brotherhood, powers latent in man, comparative religion, karma, reincarnation, astral plane—may be laid at the doorstep of the Theosophical Society. And the woman who opened the Society's door in New York City in 1875 was the Russian-born mystic and adventurer, Madame H.P. Blavatsky (1831–1891). Since then the Society has opened doors in many countries and on all continents.

Theosophical thought is replete with references to the North Pole, as in this passage from the writings of Blavatsky, quoted by Albert A.E. Smythe in *The Lamp: A Theosophical Monthly*, 15 September 1899:

> Occult teaching corroborates the popular tradition which asserts the existence of a fountain of life in the bowels of the earth and in the North Pole. It is the blood of the earth, the electromagnetic current which circulates through all the arteries, and which is said to be found stored in the "navel" of the earth.

Theosophical doctrine accepted or advanced the notion that humanity was the fifth in an evolutionary series or "round" of seven "root races." According to the three volumes of Blavatsky's masterwork *The Secret Doctrine: The Synthesis of Science, Religion and Philosophy* (1883), each race had, has, or will have its own physical characteristics and home continent. The First Race resembled invisible jelly-fish and resided in the Imperishable Sacred Land at the North Pole. The Second Race, for which there exists no firm description, lived in the Arctic land of Hyperboria. The Third Race took the form of giant, ape-like creatures with four arms; their habitat was the island of Lemuria in the Southern Hemisphere which ultimately sank into the ocean. Sinking was also the fate of the Fourth Race, which lived on the island of Atlantis in the North Atlantic; the Atlanteans were advanced technicians who knew no bounds. Mankind as we know it comprises the Fifth Race; it originated in dry, desert-like lands and has spread over the surface of the Earth. Little is known of the Sixth Race except that it will spring up in what is now known as South America. Of the Seventh Race, the last, nothing is known.

The Imperishable Sacred Land, the home of the First Root Race, remains close to Theosophical hearts. "This Imperishable Sacred Land never shared the fate of the Other Continents, because it is the only one whose destiny it is to last from the beginning to the end of the Manvantara throughout each Round," explained Blavatsky. "It is the cradle of the first man and the dwelling of the last *divine* mortal, chosen . . . for the future seed of humanity. Of this mysterious and sacred land very little can be said. . . ."

Canadian Theosophists responded to the notion that the Imperishable Sacred Land was close at hand. As Albert E.S. Smythe wrote in "Canada's Jubilee," *The Canadian Theosophist*, 15 August 1927:

> This is the oldest part of the earth. If the magnetic north pole is meant in the Secret Doctrine in speaking of the Imperishable Sacred Land then Canada contains that land . . . such heritage as

413

this must become a burden or guerdon to the people who possess it. . . . Canada will manifest herself as the new generations roll into her vast territory, an invasion from the skies such as brought Egypt into being a hundred millenniums ago.

The hearts of nationalists beat all the quicker for these notions, as witness the words of the Theosophist Cecil Williams in "Canada's Place in Human Evolution" in *The Canadian Theosophist*, 15 March 1924:

> The Canadian sub-race will develop a civilization in which the intuition will be dominant — they will project vast engineer works, rivalling those of Egypt; they will produce a philosophy and an art rivalling those of Greece; they will create a science rivalling that of Arabia; they will found a morality rivalling in purity that of Persia. To Canada will flock searchers for truths the world over; from Canada will go the great intuitive truth of comradeship, moulding world opinion and preparing humanity for still higher evolution.

The train of such heady and expansive thinking ran straight into the Great Depression and was derailed by it.

Travellers in the Arctic have noted the presence of a mist which seems to produce mirages and the rumours of an inland sea. What is behind all this? Blavatsky had an answer. "If, then, the teaching is understood correctly, the first Continent, which came into existence capped over the whole North Pole like one unbroken crust, and remains so to this day, beyond that inland sea which seemed like an unreachable *mirage* to the few arctic travellers who perceived it."

The North Pole is the polar opposite of the South Pole, but they have their polarity in common. Blavatasky wrote, "The two Poles were said to be the store-houses, the receptacles and liberators, at the same time, of cosmic and terrestrial Vitality (Electricity), from the surplus of which the Earth, had it not been for these two natural safety-valves, would have been rent to pieces long ago."

The doctrines of the Theosophical Society exerted a surprising influence on the advanced thinkers of the day. The Toronto Lodge, in particular, attracted an unusually gifted group of people, especially artists and thinkers, among them members of the Group of Seven. The notion of the spirituality of the arctic appealed to one painter in particular. His name was Lawren Harris and he was the spiritual leader of the Group. His feeling for Group work, his sense of the Secret Doctrine, and his journey to the Far North in 1927 led him to paint his first abstractly stylized landscapes. These paintings were a departure for Harris and for Canada, being the first abstract works of art to depict the northern landscape. They revealed it as it had never been perceived before, in a manner that combined the starkness, the serenity, and the spirituality of the North. These are pictures of an imperishable sacred land.

The North Pole/ The Hollow Earth

Two crackpot theories which stand head and shoulders above the rest in terms of sheer looniness are the theory that the Earth is flat, not round, and the theory that the Earth is hollow, not solid. The Flat Earth theory may command the attention of perhaps one hundred people "around the world," so to speak. But there is an extensive literature on the subject which bears pondering, even if the notion itself was exploded centuries ago. If there are a hundred adherents to the Flat Earth theory, then there are perhaps ten times that number who adhere to the Hollow Earth theory. Like all bizarre ideas, these two notions attract and sometimes command the attention of sections of the population out of all proportion to the number of people who actually believe them.

Canadians who are attracted to the Flat Earth and Hollow Earth theories may consider themselves blessed. Sites related to both of these ideas may be found in this country. The "edge" of the Flat Earth has been located off Fogo Island, Newfoundland, and the "entranceway" to the Hollow Earth lies at what passes for the North Pole.

There is, of course, no North Pole. Instead of the Pole there is "the Hole at the Pole"—no frozen sea or land but an entranceway into the hollow interior of the Earth. The Earth resembles an immense Ukrainian Easter Egg. In place of the crust is the shell. The polar opening in the shell is approximately two hundred miles in diameter. Through it one may "descend" into the sphere of the hollow planet. Here the natural world is inverted and internalized. It is populated by a lost race of men. People, places, and things adhere to the inside of the shell, and the horizon rises in the distance. The inner world is illuminated by a central sun which never sets. Proof of this lies in the phenomena of the aurora borealis. The northern aurora is caused not by cosmic rays from outer space bombarding the Van Allen Belts but by light rays from the central sun escaping through the polar opening into the Arctic atmosphere.

The highly imaginative theory that the Earth is hollow may be derived from the existence of crevices, caverns and caves which do extend for miles into the Earth's crust. The theory became popular in the early nineteenth century in the United States. Captain John Cleves Symmes of the U.S. Infantry promoted the theory, basing his arguments on an essay written in 1692 by Edmund Halley (of Comet fame), which argues for the presence of numerous enclosed spheres within the Earth, and Cotton Mather in his 1792 doctrine "The Christian Philosopher." There is a memorial to Symmes' Hole erected in Hamilton, Ohio. Koreshan State Historical Park, located south of Fort Myers, Florida, recalls the contribution made to the Hollow Earth theory by Cyrus Reed Teed, another visionary and proponent.

One would think that the era of Arctic exploration would quietly signal the end to such speculation. But the reverse was true. Eskimo legends about their origin within the Earth, descriptions of the warm Arctic by Fridtjof Nansen, Frederick A. Cook's experiences at the Pole, Admiral Richard Byrd's pioneering flight over the Pole on 29 November 1929 with his reference to "the Land beyond the Pole"—all and more were pressed into service to support the inner-Earth theory.

If the exploration of the polar region did not dispell the notion, who could argue with satellite and space shots of the northern region of the planet? The adherents could, pointing to so-called photographic evidence like NASA's celebrated "Hole at the Pole" photograph of the polar opening. It *does* look like there is an immense hole where the Pole should be. NASA's explanation is that the so-called hole is a common enough optical effect of a black area created by the failure of the scanning mechanism. Critics feel this to be a cover-up.

The era of flying saucers introduced a new wrinkle. If the UFOs do not originate on Earth or in Outer Space, perhaps they originate in the interior of the Earth. Brinsley Le Poer Trench, the English UFO-enthusiast and member of the House of Lords, is the author of a number or books, notably *Secret of the Ages: UFOs from Inside the Earth* (1974), in which he advances his belief that the Earth is a gigantic space-borne geode. "An essential part of our case is that there is no North Pole. No single point, but instead a big area which is a warm sea dripping gradually into the interior of the Earth. This may sound incredible but we will be presenting strong evidence to support this idea in the next few pages." He went on to argue that the interior world serves as the base for a race of resident aliens who "buzz" our planet for reconnaissance purposes, zooming in and out of the north polar opening in their UFOs.

Psychics and clairvoyants claim the world within the world as their province, so to speak. It seems the inner world is a kind of planetary lost-and-found. People are always appearing, disappearing, and reappearing. There were the famous Green Children of Wolfpittes, who emerged from a cave. Colonel Percy Fawcett disappeared supposedly in the forest of South America. Then there is the vanished Eskimo village of Lake Angikuni—not to mention the legend which has Brigadoon reappear once every hundred years. Perhaps these people, places, and things are checked in and out of the inner world, as they have to be somewhere when they are apparently nowhere.

The Washington clairvoyant Jeane Dixon and Edgar Cayce, the Sleeping Prophet, both predicted that a threat to North America would emerge through

Davis Strait in the Eastern Arctic. "I don't know why it should be, but that is a vulnerable area," explained Dixon. These prophecies appear in Jess Stearn's *The Door to the Future* (1963). But the most fruitful use of such speculation has been made by the authors of the fantastic, notably Edgar Allan Poe ("Hans Pfaal," "MS. Found in a Bottle," "The Narrative of A. Gordon Pym"), Jules Verne's *A Journey to the Centre of the Earth*, Bulwer-Lytton's *The Coming Race*, and Edgar Rice Burrough's *Tarzan at the Earth's Core*. In the latter novel the Ape Man descends by a Zeppelin through the polar opening into the inner world.

The relationship between the Pole-Shifters, on one hand, and the Flat Earthers and the Hollow Earthers, on the other, may not be immediately apparent, but members of both schools of thought are motivated by images of dramatic simplicity. It is incredibly easy to imagine a pancake-flat Earth or an Earth that is as hollow as a Ping Pong ball. In the same manner vis-

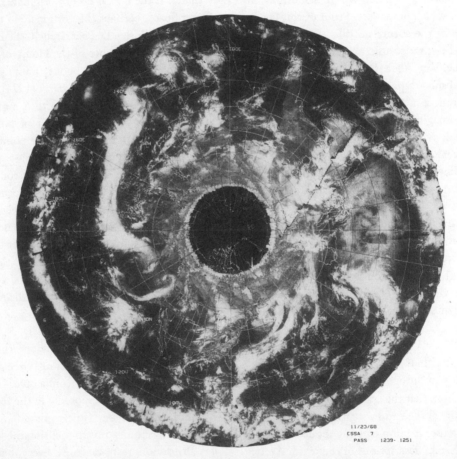

What has been called "the Hole at the Pole" is clearly visible in this satellite image of the polar region of the Planet Earth transmitted from the ESSA-7 Satellite on 23 November 1968. The curious "circumpolar opening" which seems to coincide with the North Pole is an artifact—an effect created by scanning and filtering. Images transmitted on the same occasion but with different scanning and filtering show no evidence of "the Hole at the Pole." Yet this image has been widely reproduced in articles and books written by authors who speculate that the Earth is a hollow sphere and that where the North Pole should be there is a "circumpolar opening" to the Earth's "inner world." [U.S. Department of Commerce, National Oceanic and Atmospheric Administration, Satellite Data Services Division, Washington, D.C.]

ualizing the consequences of a Pole Shift is no problem at all. The planetary ball simply shifts its axis of rotation. The consequences of even a minor adjustment of this nature would hardly be visible from elsewhere in the Solar System but would be certain to wreak havoc upon the hapless planet and its four billion inhabitants.

Even seasoned observers like Charles H. Hapgood enjoy pinpointing in time and place the pole-shifts that have already occurred. The impression given and gained is that their frequency in the past is an indication of their possibility in the present and their certainty in the future. In his well written and vigorously argued book *The Path of the Pole* (1970), Hapgood explained:

> For example, I have found evidence of three different positions of the North Pole in recent time. During the last glaciation in North America the pole appears to have stood in Hudson Bay, approximately in Latitude 60° North and Longitude 83° West. It seems to have shifted to its present site in the middle of the Arctic Ocean in a gradual motion that began 18,000 or 17,000 years ago and was completed by about 12,000 years ago.

Its other locations, according to Hapgood, were in the Yukon 180,000 years ago and in the Greenland Sea 50,000 years ago.

Hapgood and other pole-shifters believe that the North Pole, like the North Magnetic Pole, "wanders." But it has not wandered or shifted within the relatively short period of recorded history — at least not yet. They argue, however, that it has repeatedly shifted and left evidence of its shifts in the geological record, a record which extends back in time much, much further than the words and memory of mankind.

The Milky Way/
Celestial Nomenclature

It is interesting to note that the International Astronomical Union, which is the body concerned with the nomenclature of off-earth bodies and features, has named a number of celestial bodies and lunar features after Canadians distinguished for their achievements in the fields of astronomy and astrophysics.

Minor planets, or asteroids, bear the names of the following distinguished astronomers: C.S. Beals, C.A. Chant, J.L. Climenhaga, J.F. Heard, Gerhard Herzberg, Helen Sawyer Hogg, Peter M. Millman, J.S. and H.H. Plaskett, Anne Underhill. Toronto is the name given a minor planet (the first to be found by a Canadian observatory) by its discoverer Karl Kamper of the David Dunlap Observatory in recognition of the University of Toronto's 150th Anniversary.

By convention, craters on the moon are named after individuals who are no longer alive. Six Canadian scientists—five astronomers and one astrophysicist—have lunar features named for them. They are C.A. Chant, J.S. Foster, F.S. Hogg, Andrew McKellar, R.M. Petrie, and J.S. Plaskett.

Other celestial features, like comets, bear the names of their discoverers. For instance, a Canadian astronomer Christine Wilson discovered Comet Wilson. In 1987, Ian Shelton became the first person in 383 years (since Kepler in 1604) to observe the birth of a supernova. The celestial body in question is now named Supernova Shelton 1987a.

In a sense the names of these Canadians are inscribed in the sky.

The Milky Way/
The Voyager Interstellar Record

A part of Canada is voyaging to the stars. . . .

It is a truism to say that the things of Earth, including the works of the human species, are mortal, all things being subject to decay, death, and destruction. Yet that is not totally true. There is one immortal work of the human species. Perhaps the word "immortal" should be placed within quotation marks, for surely immortality is a relative concept and the work in question is immortal within the limits of the Milky Way Galaxy. This work, a product of art and technology of the highest order, is the Voyager Interstellar Record. Two such Records, affixed to the bodies of the U.S. space probes *Voyager 1* and *Voyager*

417

2, were launched into space in 1977. They soared past the outer planets and sped on for ten years before reaching the outer limits of the Solar System. Then they entered interstellar space *en route* to some distant but undetermined star. The life-expectancy of the Voyager Interstellar Record is one billion years.

The Record is an actual disc of aluminum-plated copper which digitally preserves in audio and video the sounds and sights of the planet Earth. Included with the disc is a coded operations manual. Any civilization with a technology sufficiently advanced to retrieve the space probe would conceivably be able to decode the instructions and play the disc. Thus the Record is both a Space Probe and a Time Capsule, one which bears greetings from a planet that once existed called Earth.

Intelligent alien beings who play the disc may well ponder and even puzzle over the sights and sounds of Earth. Among the sights and sounds will be references to a country called Canada. They will hear, in the spoken-word section, the voices of two Canadian males. Robert B. Edmonds, the Canadian delegate to the United Nations, will be heard saying, "I should like to extend the greetings of the government and people of Canada to the extra-terrestrial inhabitants of outer space." Richard Lee, a professor at the University of Toronto, may be heard offering appropriate greetings in the !Kung language of the Kalahari Bushmen of southwest Africa.

Included in the music portion is pianist Glenn Gould's rendition of Johann Sebastian Bach's *The Well-Tempered Clavier*, Book 1, Prelude and Fugue in C Major, No. 1, lasting four minutes and forty-eight seconds. In the selection of pictures, the sole image of Canada is an aerial photograph of the Lester B. Pearson International Airport to represent air transport. Yet in addition to these references there is the fact that a principal designer of the Record—with its characteristic spidery, minimalistic lines—is a Canadian, the space artist Jon Lomberg.

One cannot help but wonder what sense, if any sense, intelligent alien beings in another galaxy at another time will make of these sights and sounds—meaningful messages in a bottle cast into the sea of space.

The Universe/
The Eskimo Nebula

If you leave the surly bonds of Earth far behind, you may move in spirit among the planets and sojourn among the stars. What you will find in space, beyond our galaxy, is NGC 2932. That is the international designation for one among the innumerable star sys-

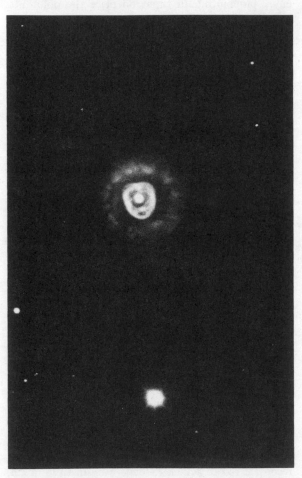

NGC 2932 is the international numerical designation of a star cluster otherwise known as the Eskimo Nebula. The cluster lies in deep space well beyond our galaxy, so far from Earth that it has taken its rays of light some 3500 years to reach our planet. Chance condensation or some projection effect has caused the three-dimensional figure to have taken on the appearance of a human face, that of a bemused Eskimo. [Lick Observatory, University of California, Santa Cruz, California]

tems — the so-called Eskimo Nebula. This peculiar-looking planetary nebula has been described by Paul Murdin and David Allen and photographed by David Malin in their publication *Catalog of the Universe* (1979).

The Eskimo Nebula is so far away from the planet Earth that its light has taken 3500 years to reach our eyes. And what an unusual sight it is! Does space know its equal? Chance condensation in the nebula, or some projection effect of a complicated three-dimensional figure, has caused the figure to have the appearance of a human face, with eyes, mouth, and nose. The face seems to be surrounded by a fringe, which has the appearance of fur around a hood.

It looks surprisingly like an Eskimo, a bemused Eskimo.

BIBLIOGRAPHY

This is a select bibliography; it is also a limited one. It consists of a selection of the most significant books, monographs, and journals concerned with "mysterious Canada"; it is limited to 123 titles. The publications of authors with Canadian connections have been highlighted, but the bibliography is by no means restricted to their work. An attempt has been made to represent a range of authors and of subjects. All these publications relate in whole or in part to the issues raised in *Mysterious Canada*.

Alcock, James E. *Parapsychology: Science or Magic? A Psychological Perspective.* Oxford: Pergamon Press, 1981.

Austin, B.F. *Glimpses of the Unseen: A Study of Dreams, Premonitions, Prayer and Remarkable Answers, Hypnotism, Spiritualism, Telepathy, Apparitions, Peculiar Mental and Spiritual Experiences, Unexplained Psychical Phenomena.* Toronto: Bradley-Garretson Company, 1898.

Austin, B.F. *What Converted Me to Spiritualism: One Hundred Testimonies.* Toronto: Austin Publishing Company, 1901.

Barton, Winifred G. *Psychic Phenomena in Canada.* Ottawa: PSI-Science Productions, c. 1968.

Basque, Garnet, ed. *Canadian Treasure Trails.* Langley, B.C.: Stagecoach Publishing, 1976.

Bates, Walter. *The Mysterious Stranger, or, the Adventures of Henry More Smith: Containing a descriptive Account of His Life and Adventures from the Time of His Appearance in Windsor, N.S. in 1812, Until His Confinement in Toronto, Upper Canada.* Charlottetown: Hazard & Owen, 1855.

Berton, Pierre. *The Mysterious North.* Toronto: McClelland & Stewart, 1956.

Bondarchuk, Yurko. *U.F.O.: Sightings, Landings & Abductions: The Documented Evidence.* Toronto: Methuen, 1979.

Boyer, Dwight. *Ghost Ships of the Great Lakes.* New York: Dodd, Mead, 1968.

Boyer, Dwight. *True Tales of the Great Lakes.* New York: Dodd, Mead, 1971.

Boyer, Dwight. *Strange Adventures of the Great Lakes.* New York: Dodd, Mead, 1974.

Bradley, Michael, and Deanna Bean. *Holy Grail across the Atlantic.* Toronto: Hounslow Press, 1988.

Branden, Victoria. *Understanding Ghosts.* London: Victor Gollancz Ltd., 1980.

Brandon, Ruth. *The Spiritualists: The Passion for the Occult in the Nineteeth and Twentieth Centuries.* Buffalo: Prometheus Books, 1984.

Bray, Arthur. *Science, the Public and the UFO.* Ottawa: Bray Book Service, 1967.

Bray, Arthur. *The UFO Connection.* Ottawa: Jupiter Publishing, 1979.

Bucke, Richard Maurice. *Cosmic Consciousness: A Study in the Evolution of the Human Mind.* Philadelphia: Innes and Sons, 1901.

Casgrain, Henri-Raymond. *Légends canadiens.* Québec: Impr. A. Coté & Cie., 1876.

Casgrain, Henri-Raymond. *The Witch: A Canadian Legend.* Translated by A.W.L. Gompertz. Montreal: Beauchemin & Fils, 1895.

Cavendish, Richard, ed. *Man, Myth & Magic: The Illustrated Encyclopedia of Mythology, Religion and the Unknown.* New York: Marshall Cavendish Limited, New Edition, 1983.

Clark, Ella Elizabeth. *Indian Legends of Canada.* Toronto: McClelland & Stewart, 1960.

Cochrane, Hugh F. *Gateway to Oblivion: The Great Lakes' Bermuda Triangle.* New York: Doubleday, 1980.

Colombo, John Robert. *Colombo's Book of Marvels.* Toronto: NC Press, 1979.

Colombo, John Robert, ed. *Windigo: An Anthology of Fact and Fantastic Fiction.* Saskatoon: Western Producer Prairie Books, 1982.

Corliss, William R. *The Unexplained: A Sourcebook of Strange Phenomena.* New York: Bantam Books, 1976. This is one of a number of publications of The Sourcebook Project.

Creighton, Helen. *Folklore of Lunenburg County, Nova Scotia.* (Ottawa, 1950) Toronto: McGraw-Hill Ryerson, 1976.

Creighton, Helen. *Bluenose Ghosts.* Toronto: The Ryerson Press, 1957.

Creighton, Helen. *Bluenose Magic: Popular Beliefs and Superstitions in Nova Scotia.* Toronto: McGraw-Hill Ryerson Limited, 1968.

Curran, Douglas. *In Advance of the Landing: Folk Concepts of Outer Space.* New York: Abbeyville Press, 1985.

Currie, Ian. *You Cannot Die: The Incredible Findings of a Century of Research on Death.* Toronto: Methuen, 1978.

Dahinden, René, and Don Hunter. *Sasquatch.* Toronto: McClelland & Stewart, 1973.

Dean, Malcolm. *The Astrology Game: The Inside Story: The Truth about Astrology.* Don Mills, Ont.: Nelson, Foster & Scott, 1980.

Dempsey, Hugh A., Daniel Riley, and Tom Primrose. *The Lost Lemon Mine: Greatest Mystery of the Canadian Rockies.* Langley, B.C.: Frontier Bookshelf, n.d.

Dewdney, Selwyn, and Kenneth E. Kidd. *Indian Rock Paintings of the Great Lakes.* Toronto: University of Toronto Press, 1962, 2nd ed. 1967.

Dewdney, Selwyn. *Sacred Scrolls of the Southern Ojibway.* Toronto: University of Toronto Press, 1975. Sponsored by the Glenbow-Alberta Institute.

Drew, Wayland, and Bruce Litteljohn. *Superior: The Haunted Shore.* Toronto: Gage Publishing Limited, 1975.

Drew, Wayland, and Bruce Litteljohn. *A Sea Within: The Gulf of St. Lawrence.* Toronto: McClelland & Stewart, 1984.

Eberhart, George M. *A Geo-Bibliography of Anomalies: Primary Access to Observations of UFOs, Ghosts, and Other Mysterious Phenomena.* Westport, Conn.: Greenwood Press, 1980.

Eisenberg, Howard. *Inner Spaces: Parapsychological Explorations of the Mind.* Don Mills, Ont.: Musson Book Co., 1977.

Estabrooks, George Hoben. *Hypnotism.* New York: Dutton, 1943.

Estabrooks, George Hoben. *Spiritism.* New York: Dutton, 1947.

Fell, Barry. *Bronze Age America.* Boston: Little Brown & Co., 1982.

Fisher, Joe, with Peter Commins. *Predictions.* Toronto: Collins, 1980.

Fisher, Joe. *The Case for Reincarnation.* Toronto: Collins, 1984.

Fort, Charles. *The Books of Charles Fort.* Introduction by Tiffany Thayer. New York: Published for the Fortean Society by Henry Holt and Company, 1941. The individual volumes are: *The Book of the Damned* (1919), *New Lands* (1923), *Lo!* (1931), *Wild Talents* (1932).

Fowke, Edith. *Folklore of Canada.* Toronto: McClelland & Stewart, 1976.

Fowke, Edith. *Folktales of French Canada.* Toronto: NC Press, 1981.

Fowke, Edith. *Tales Told in Canada.* Toronto: Doubleday Canada, 1986.

Fraser, Mary L. *The Folklore of Nova Scotia.* Toronto: Catholic Truth Society, 1932.

Fraser, Simon. *The Letters and Journals of Simon Fraser: 1806–1808.* Edited by W. Kaye Lamb. Toronto: Macmillan of Canada, 1960.

Furneaux, Rupert. *The Money Pit Mystery: The Costliest Treasure Hunt Ever.* New York: Dodd, Mead, 1972.

Gaal, Arlene B. *Beneath the Depths.* Okanagan Valley: Valley Review Publishing Ltd., 1976.

Garner, Betty Sanders. *Canada's Monsters.* Hamilton: Potlatch Publications, 1976.

Gordon, Henry. *ExtraSensory Deception: ESP, Psychics, Shirley MacLaine, Ghosts, UFOs. . . .* Buffalo: Prometheus Books, 1987.

Gourlay, Jay. *The Great Lakes Triangle.* Greenwich, Conn.: Fawcett, 1977.

Green, John. *Sasquatch: The Apes Among Us.* Saanichton, B.C.: Hancock House, 1978.

Haisell, David. *The Missing Seven Hours.* Markham, Ont.: PaperJacks Ltd., 1978.

Halpin, Marjorie M., and Michael M. Ames, eds. *Manlike Monsters on Trial: Early Records and Modern Evidence.* Vancouver: University of British Columbia Press, 1980.

Hamilton, T. Glendenning. *Intention and Survival: Psychical Research Studies and the Bearing of Intentional Actions by Trance Personalities on the Problem of Human Survival.* Toronto: Macmillan of Canada, 1942. Reprinted by Regency Press, Ltd., London, 1977.

Hearne, Samuel. *A Journey from Prince of Wales's Fort in Hudson's Bay to the Northern Ocean, 1769, 1770, 1771, 1772.* (London, 1795) Edited by Richard Glover. Toronto: Macmillan of Canada, 1958.

Hervey, Sheila. *Some Canadian Ghosts.* Toronto: Pocket Books/Simon & Schuster of Canada, 1973.

Heuvelmans, Bernard. *In the Wake of the Sea Serpents.* Translated from the French by Richard Garnett. London: Rupert Hart-Davis, 1968.

Hubbell, Walter. *The Great Amherst Mystery.* Saint John, N.B.: Daily News, 1879.

Innes, Brian, ed. *The Unexplained: Mysteries of Mind, Space and Time.* New York: Marshall Cavendish, 8 volumes, Reference edition, 1983.

Jolicoeur, Catherine. *Le Vaisseau Fantôme: Légende étiologique.* Québec: Presses de l'Université Laval, 1970.

Kane, Paul. *Wanderings of an Artist among the Indians of North America.* (London, 1859) Edmonton: Hurtig Publishers, 1974.

Klass, Philip J. *UFOs — The Public Deceived.* Buffalo: Prometheus Books, 1983.

Lambert, R.S. *For the Time Is at Hand: An Account of the Prophecies of Henry Wentworth Monk of Ottawa, Friend of the Jews and Pioneer of World Peace.* Toronto: The Ryerson Press, 1947.

Lambert, R.S. *Exploring the Supernatural: The Weird in Canadian Folklore.* Toronto: McClelland & Stewart, 1955.

Lee, Thomas E., ed. *Anthropological Journal of Canada.* Ottawa: Vol. 1, No. 1, 1963 — Vol. 21, No. 1, 1983.

Lefebvre, Eugène. *A Land of Miracles for Three Hundred Years.* Sainte-Anne-de-Beaupré: St. Anne's Bookshop, 1958.

McDonald, Neil T. *The Baldoon Mysteries: A Weird Tale of the Early Scotch Settlers of Baldoon.* Wallaceburg, Ont.: News Office, 1910.

Mackenzie, Sir Alexander. *The Journals and Letters of Sir Alexander Mackenzie.* Edited by W. Kaye Lamb. Toronto: Macmillan of Canada, 1970.

Magor, John. *Our UFO Visitors.* Saanichton, B.C.: Hancock House, 1977.

Magor, John. *Aliens Above, Always: A UFO Report.* Surrey, B.C.: Hancock House, 1983.

Mertz, Henriette. *Pale Ink: Two Ancient Records of Chinese Exploration in America.* Chicago: Swallow Press, 1953. Reprinted as: *Gods from the Far East: How the Chinese Discovered America.* New York: Ballantine Books, 1972.

Mertz, Henriette. *The Wine Dark Sea.* Chicago: Mertz, 1964.

Meurger, Michel, and Claude Gagnon. *Monstres des lacs du Québec: Mythes et Troublantes réalités.* Montréal: Stanké, 1982.

Meurger, Michel, and Claude Gagnon. *Lake Monster Traditions.* London: Fortean Tomes, 1988.

Miller, Orlo. *The Day-Spring: The Story of the*

Unknown Apostle to the Americas. Toronto: McClelland & Stewart, 1976.

Moon, Mary. *Ogopogo: The Okanagan Mystery.* Vancouver: J.J. Douglas Ltd., 1977.

Mowat, Farley. *Westviking: The Ancient Norse in Greenland and North America.* Toronto: McClelland & Stewart, 1965.

Musgrave, John Brent. *UFO Occupants and Critters: The Patterns in Canada.* New York: Global Communications, 1979.

Owen, A.R.G., ed. *New Horizons: Journal of the New Horizons Research Foundation (incorporating Transactions of the Toronto Society for Psychical Research).* Toronto, 9 issues, Summer 1972—Sept. 1978.

Owen, A.R.G. *Psychic Mysteries of Canada: Discoveries from the Maritime Provinces and Beyond.* New York: Harper & Row, 1975.

Owen, Iris M., with Margaret Sparrow. *Conjuring Up Philip: An Adventure in Psychokinesis.* Toronto: Fitzhenry & Whiteside, 1976.

Pawlicki, T.B. *How to Build a Flying Saucer and Other Proposals in Speculative Engineering.* Englewood Cliffs, N.J.: Prentice-Hall, 1981.

Pawlicki, T.B. *How You Can Explore Higher Dimensions of Space and Time.* Englewood Cliffs, N.J.: Prentice-Hall, 1984.

Persinger, Michael A., and Gyslaine F. Lafrenière. *Space-Time Transients and Unusual Events.* Chicago: Nelson-Hall, 1977.

Pincock, Jenny O'Hara. *The Trials of Truth.* Los Angeles: Austin Publishing Company, 1930.

Pohl, Frederick. *Atlantic Crossings before Columbus.* New York: W.W. Norton & Co., 1961.

Pohl, Frederick. *Prince Henry Sinclair: His Expedition to the New World in 1398.* New York: Clarkson N. Potter, Inc., 1974.

Ramsay, Stirling. *Folklore: Prince Edward Island.* Charlottetown: Square Deal Publications, 1973.

Randi, James. *Flim-Flam! The Truth about Unicorns, Parapsychology and Other Delusions.* New York: Lippincott & Crowell, 1980. Reprinted as: *Flim-Flam! Psychics, ESP, Unicorns and Other Delusions.* Buffalo: Prometheus Books, 1985.

Rasmussen, Knud. *Across Arctic America: A Narrative of the Fifth Thule Expedition.* New York: G.P. Putnam's Sons, 1927.

Regush, Nicholas M., with Jan Merta. *Exploring the Human Aura.* Englewood Cliffs, N.J.: Prentice-Hall, Inc., 1975.

Schaeffer, Claude E. *Blackfoot Shaking Tent.* Calgary: Glenbow-Alberta Institute, 1969.

Séguin, Robert-Lionel. *La Sorcellerie au Canada Français du XVIIè au XIXè Siècle.* Montréal: Librairie Ducharme, 1961. Reprinted as: *La Sorcellerie au Québec du XVIIè au XIXè Siècle.* Montréal: Leméac, 1971.

Sherwood, Roland H. *Maritime Mysteries: Haunting Tales from Atlantic Canada.* Windsor, N.S.: Lancelot Press, 1976.

Sherwood, Roland H. *Legends, Oddities, and Facts from the Maritime Provinces.* Hantsport, N.S.: Lancelot Press, 1984.

Smith, Michelle, and Lawrence Pazder. *Michelle Remembers.* New York: Congdon and Lattès Inc., 1980.

Smith, Wilbert B. *The New Science.* Ottawa: Keith Press, 1964.

Smith, Wilbert B. *The Boys from Topside.* Edited by Timothy Green Beckley. Clarksburg, West Virginia: Saucerian Books, 1969.

Sonin, Eileen. *ESPecially Ghosts: Some True Experiences of the Supernatural in North America.* Toronto: Clarke, Irwin & Company, 1970. Reprinted as: *More Canadian Ghosts: Some True Experiences of the Supernatural in North America.* Markham, Ont.: Pocket Books, 1974.

Sonin, Eileen. *Ghosts I Have Known: The Psychic Experiences of a Natural Medium.* Toronto: Clarke, Irwin, 1968.

Spraggett, Allen. *The Unexplained.* Toronto: New American Library of Canada, 1967

Spraggett, Allen. *Probing the Unexplained.* Toronto: Nelson, Foster & Scott, 1971.

Stacey, C.P. *A Very Double Life: The Private World of Mackenzie King.* Toronto: Macmillan of Canada, 1976.

Stearn, Jess. *The Search for the Girl with the Blue Eyes.* New York: Doubleday, 1968.

Story, Ronald D. *The Encyclopedia of UFOs.* New York: Dolphin Books, 1980.

Thompson, David. *David Thompson's Narrative of His Explorations in Western Alberta, 1784–1812.* Edited by J.B. Tyrrell. Toronto: Champlain Society, 1916.

Trueman, Stuart. *Ghosts, Pirates and Treasure Trove: The Phantoms that Haunt New Brunswick.* Toronto: McClelland & Stewart, 1975.

Trueman, Stuart. *Tall Tales and True Tales from Down East.* Toronto: McClelland & Stewart, 1979.

Vallee, Jacques. *Passport to Magonia: From Folklore to Flying Saucers.* Chicago: Henry Regnery Company, 1969.

Vastokas, Joan M., and Romas K. Vastokas. *Sacred Art of the Algonkians: A Study of the Peterborough Petroglyphs.* Peterborough: Mansard Press, 1973.

Verny, Thomas, with John Kelly. *The Secret Life of the Unborn Child.* Toronto: Collins, 1981.

Watson, Albert Durrant. *The Twentieth Plane: A Psychic Revelation.* Toronto: McClelland & Goodchild, 1918.

Watson, Albert Durrant. *Birth through Death: The Ethics of the 20th Plane: A Revelation Received through the Psychic Consciousness of Louis Benjamin.* Toronto: McClelland & Goodchild, 1920.

Watson, Albert Durrant, with Margaret Lawrence. *Mediums and Mystics: A Study in the Spiritual Laws and Psychic Forces.* Toronto: McClelland & Goodchild, 1923.

Whitton, Joel L., and Joe Fisher. *Life between Life: Scientific Explorations into the Void Separating One Incarnation from the Next.* New York: Doubleday, 1986.

Wilkie, James H.P., with Allen Spraggett. *The Gift Within.* New York: New American Library, 1971.

Wilson, Herbert Emmerson. *Canada's False Prophet: The Notorious Brother Twelve.* Toronto: Simon & Schuster, 1967.

Zubek, John P., ed. *Sensory Deprivation: Fifteen Years of Research.* New York: Appleton-Century-Crofts, 1969.

INDEX

The letter *a* or *b* which follows the page number indicates that the reference will be found on the left- or right-hand column of that page; the letter *c* indicates that the reference will be found in the caption to the illustration on that page.

Indexed are the following: principal personal names, significant non-Canadian place names, references of specific interest, and subjects of general concern. The text itself takes the form of an immense index — in point of fact it takes the form of twelve indices — of Canadian place names arranged by province and territory.

It is generally the initial appearance of a reference within an entry in the text that is indexed, not its repeated appearances, as entries in the text usually elaborate on the references at hand. To assist the reader to locate general subjects, the index includes "see" and "see also" entries. It also includes general categories. The most significant general categories of references include the following.

Cryptozoology (unknown lifeforms on Earth), Ghosts (apparitions, forerunners, spectres, spirits, wraiths, etc.), Lights (mysterious illuminations), Medicine (miraculous cures and healings, psychic surgery, etc.), Ogopogo (the denizen of the Okanagan Valley), Poltergeists (hauntings sans spirits), Rock Art (inscriptions, petroglyphs, engraved erratics, etc.), Sasquatch (a wild hairy humanoid), Ships (phantom and hoodoo vessels), Shrines (pagan and Christian), Spiritualism (non-material communication), Trains (phantom railroad trains, etc.), Treasure (fabled, rumoured, or lost troves), UFOs (flying saucers, unidentified flying objects, etc.), Windigo (spirit of cannibalism), Witches (practitioners of wicca and others). Native Canadian references occur throughout the text in such numbers as to make useless such general categories as Indian and Inuit. There are approximately fifty categories in all.

A.V. Roe Company, 255a, 255c
Abaris, 412a
Abbey Ruin, 205c
Abel, Edward, 065a
Abominable Snowman, 342a
Acadians, 068a, 070b
Acadie, 017a
Adams, Claude, 103a
Adams, Franklin P., 024a
Adams, Ian, 195b
Aerial Phenomena Research Association, 272a, 348a

Agartha, 410a
Agassiz, Louis, 337a
Airship Wave, 370a
Alaska, 395b
Alexander, Richard H., 351a
Alexander, Rolph, 191b, 192c
Alfonse, Jean, 109b
Algonquin, 238b
Algonquin Radio Telescope, 122a
Alien Abduction, 150b, 318b, 349a
Allan Memorial Institute, 095b, 097b, 295b
Allan, W.K., 315b

Allen, David, 419a
Allen, Steve, 219a
Allen, Thomas E., 129b
Almasti, 342a
Alpena, 170a
Amazing Randi: See James Randi.
Amazon, 039a
Ambrose the Ghost, 166a
American Society for Psychical Research, 026a, 042b, 248a, 264a
Ames, Michael M., 342a
Amherst Mystery, 018a, 018c

Amity, 057b
Amprimoz, Alexandre L., 044a
Amundsen, Roald, 392b, 397a
Anderson, J.O., 295a
Anderson, Thomas, 119a
André, Brother, 085a, 092a
Andrew Jackson, 013a
Andrews, Cyril H., 372a
Angel Hair, 098a, 216b
Angel Inn, 187b
Angela the Ghost, 223b
Angikuni Mystery, 389a, 390c
ANIK Satellite, 393b
Anna C. Minch, 170a
Anne, St., 333a, 111b
Anthroposophy, 274a
Apollo Astronauts, 234a, 394a
Apollo, 412a
Apparitions: See Ghosts.
Arcadia, 017a
Archer, David J.W., 365a
Arlington, 059b
Armstrong, Gerry & Susan, 150b
Armstrong, Robin, 266a
Arnold, Kenneth, 202b
Arnold, Sir Edwin, 332b
Arthur, King, 002b, 003b, 155a, 382b
Ashe, Geoffrey, 012a, 155a
Ashworth, William, 238b
Asselstein, Van, 131a
Association for Psychical Research, 247a, 264a
Astrology, 260b, 266a
Atlantic Mutual Companies, 038c, 040b
Atlantis, 002b, 408b
Atomic Energy of Canada, 141a
Atwood, Margaret, 122b
Aubin, Harry, 141a
Aurora Borealis, 415a
Austin, Benjamin Fish, 129b, 222a, 224a, 224b
Austin, Ned, 383a
Avebury, 015a
Avramovitch, Aza, 030a
Avro Car, 254b, 255c
Aylesworth, Allen, 243a
Aztec, 003b, 340b
Aztecs, 320b
Aztlan, 003b

Bach, J.S., 418a
Bach, Margaret Hamilton, 293a
Bacon, Francis, 412b
Badgley, Robert T., 232b
Baldoon Mystery, 124b, 167b
Ballstadt, Carl, 128a
Banaszak, Joyce, 060b
Banff Springs Hotel, 311a
Bannockburn, 238b
Banting, Sir Frederick, 200b
Barbeau, Marius, 359a, 359c, 398b
Barker, Edward, 282a
Barker, Lee, 194b
Barlee, N.L., 355a
Barnes, Elizabeth, 114a, 215b, 216c

Barnum, P.T., 078a, 085b, 138b
Barrington, E., 381b
Barrow, Sir John, 397a
Bartlett, Tom & Pat, 256b
Baskin, Bernard, 148a
Basque, 044b, 115b
Bates, Walter, 055a
Baychimo, 385a
Beach, Rex, 273b
Beals, C.S., 417b
Bear, Great, 411b
Beardmore Relics, 125b, 126c
Bearspaw, Chief, 324a
Beattie, H.F., 363a
Beaulieu, John, 153b
Beaverbrook, Lord, 047a
Beck, James, 021a
Beck, L. Adams, 381a
Beckley, Timothy Green, 207a
Bee, Louis, 364a
Begbie, Sir Matthew B., 370b
Belasco, David, 066b
Bell, C.N., 220a
Bells, 070a, 071b
Belmont House, 051b
Belukha, 155a
Benallick, J., 147a
Bendow, W. & D., 324a
Benedict, W. Ritchie, 313a
Benjamin, Louis, 247a
Bentley, Richard, 127b
Berg, David, 374a
Bergier, Jacques, 002b, 056c, 057a
Berlitz, Charles, 008b, 026a
Bermingham, Frank, 157a
Bermuda Triangle, 008b, 026a, 189b
Bernstein, Morey, 195b
Berton, Pierre, 404b
Berube, Louis, 103a
Besant, Annie, 245a
Bessent, Malcolm, 148a
Bessette, Alfred, 092a
Bethune, Norman, 166a
Bierce, Ambrose, 249b
Big Bear, 320a
Big Rock, 305b
Bigelow, S. Tupper, 254a
Bigfoot: See Sasquatch.
Biggar, H.P., 047b, 110a
Bighorn Medicine Wheel, 334a
Bigsby, John J., 145a
Bilotti, N. & S., 147b
Binnstead Estate, 068a
Bird, Christopher, 098a
Bishop Fuller House, 240b
Bishop, P.R., 217a
Black Peter, 049b
Black Watch Regiment, 044a
Black, Davidson, 250a
Blackbeard the Pirate, 033b
Blacker, Irwin R., 394a
Blackstone, Harry, 250a
Blackwood, Algernon, 154b, 244b, 381a

Blackwood, Frederick Temple, 197b
Blair, Lowell, 411a
Blake, Edward, 200b
Blake, William, 001a, 151b
Blavatsky, H.P., 244a, 332a, 410b, 413a
Blazing Barn, 055b
Bleaney, L., 200b
Blimphey, 070b
Bliss, Jonathan, 051b
Blob, Mississauga, 173b
Blond Eskimos, 405a
Blundell, Jim, 186a
Boishebert, Charles des Champs de, 047a
Boisvert, Jacques, 087a, 087c
Bon Echo, 131b
Bondarchuk, Yurko, 007a, 074a, 075b, 109a,
    142a, 189b, 207b, 215a, 219b, 271b, 301b,
    306b, 321b, 334b, 349b
Booher, Henry, 328a
Booker, Velma, 308a
Boqs, 339a
Borden, Sir Robert, 134a
Borley Rectory, 022a
Borrett, W.C., 029a
Bortz, Ian, 101a
Bourgeoys, Marguerite, 085a, 089b
Boya, Nathan, 180b
Boyce Mansion, 051a
Boyer, Dwight, 239a, 246a
Boyle, David, 228a
Bradley, Michael, 042b, 103b
Brainwashing Experiments, 096a
Bramwell, Jennie L., 240b
Brasser, Ted. J., 335a
Bray, Arthur, 037a, 078b, 203a, 206b, 228b,
    389a
Brébeuf, Jacques de, 171b
Brébeuf, Jean de, 085a
Brendan the Navigator, 003a, 011b, 116b
Bridget of Sweden, 287b
Bridle, Alan H., 122b
Brigadoon, 415b
Brimblecombe, Bill, 363a
Bringsli, John, 360a
British Block, 334b
British-Israel World Federation, 001b
Brock, Sir Isaac, 185a
Brockington, Leonard, 201a
Bronson, L.N., 163a
Brooke, Rupert, 177b, 206a
Brother Twelve, 357b
Brothers, Richard, 001a
Brothman, Brien, 204a
Brown, K.W.G., 261a
Brown, Marion, 162b
Brown, Raymond Lamont, 042a
Brown, Rosemary, 383a
Brown, Vinson, 376a
Bruce, Robert, 059a
Bruce, W. Blair, 118c
Brule, Etienne, 210a
Brumley, John H., 333b
Brunel, I.K., 009b

Brunelle's vision, Dr. 091a
Bryce, George, 220a
Bryden, John, 148a
Bryne, W.J., 333b
Buchan, John, 404b
Bucke, Richard Maurice, 133a, 163b, 164c, 224b
Buddhist dirges, 359a
Bulgaria, 116b
Bulwer-Lytton, E.G., 416a
Burley, David, 333b
Burns, John W., 342a, 351b
Burns, Kate & Lloyd, 186a
Burns, Rita, 269b
Burroughs, Edgar Rice, 416a
Buss, Isle of, 402a
Butler, John, 185a
Butler, Sir William F., 325b
Butts, Ed, 025a
Byrd, Richard E., 409a, 415a

Cabot, John, 009b, 274a
Cadborosaurus, 369a, 379b
Caddy, 379b
Cadwallader, M.E., 139a
Caisse, Rene, 135a
Caldwell, William, 029b
Cameron, Ewen, 096a
Campagnat, Michel, 109b
Campbell, W.C., 247b
Camsell, Charles, 404b
Canada Council, 318a
Cancer Cure, 135a, 142b
Cannon, Brian, 282a
Canuck Medicine Wheel, 300b
Capitol Hill House, 313a
Card, Charles Ora, 315b
Carey, John, 254b
Cargo Cult, 282b
Carman, Bliss, 411a
Carpenter, J., 351a
Carrington Hereward, 022a
Carter, Mrs. Leslie, 066b
Carthage, 037a
Cartheuser, William, 222b
Cartier, Jacques, 010b, 109b
Cartwright, Bruce, 188b
Carver, P.A., 141a
Casson, Dollier de, 089b
Cavanaugh, Ken, 258b
Cayce, Edgar, 101b, 223b, 406b, 415b
Cayce, Hugh Lynn, 223b, 258a
Celtic, 002b, 011b, 013b, 303a, 329b, 398b
Center for UFO Studies, 215b, 282a
Central Intelligence Agency, 095b
Chabanel, Noël, 085b
Chabot, Marie-Emmanuel, 104b
Chaffey, Benjamin, 133a
Champ, 077b
Champlain, Samuel de, 036a, 077b, 135b, 210a, 047b
Chandler, A. & S., 302b
Chant's Meteors, 248a

Chant, C.A., 248a, 417b
Chapman, J. & G., 370a
Chaput, Leo-Paul, 074a
Charles Haskell, 013a
Charlevoix, P.-F.-X. de, 102b, 230b, 316b
Charroux, Robert, 409a, 411a, 412a
Chasse-Galerie, La, 079b, 079c
Chatfield, Edmond, 054a
Cheadle, W.B., 325b
Cheney, Margaret, 076b
Cherry Hill House Ghost, 176a
Cheshire, W.G., 273a
Childerhose, R.J., 319b, 319c
Children of God, 374a
Children of Peace, 228a
Chinese, 250b, 335b, 340b, 359a, 365b
Christina Lake Pictograph, 343c, 344c
Churchill, Winston, 240a
Churchward, James, 366a, 409a
Cinq-Mars, Jacques, 385b
Cirlot, J.E., 409b
Clairvoyance: See Telepathy.
Clancarty, Earl of, 389a, 415b
Clare, Caroline, 161b
Clark, Ella Elizabeth, 306a
Clark, Hub, 374a
Clarke, Arthur C., 011a
Clarkson, Michael, 186b
Clausen, Edward, 404a
Cleary, Val, 086b
Clement of Alexandria, 014b
Cliche, Marie-Aimée, 075b
Climenhaga, J.L., 417b
Cloud-buster, 191b
Cloud-busting, 192c
Clugston, Michael, 037h
Cochrane, Hugh F., 131b, 189b
Codfish Man, 060a
Coins, Ancient, 340b
Colborne Lodge, 243b
Cole, Nat, 338b
Coleman Frog, 050b, 050c
Coleman, Fred B., 050b
Coleridge, Samuel Taylor, 397a
Collard, Edgar A., 042a
Collier, John, 141c
Colombo, 028a
Colombo, John Robert, 154b
Colonel's Ghost, 029a
Committee for Scientific Investigation, 048b, 102a, 234b, 269a
Conant, Thomas, 196b
Condon, Edward U., 321b
Confederacy, 089b, 230a
Continental Drift, 274a
Cook, Frederick A., 395a, 406a, 415a
Cook, Ramsay, 225a, 248a
Cook, Thomas, 275b
Cooke, Maurice B., 261b
Cooper, Charles, 271a
Copeland's Wife, Ghost of Dr., 035a
Copper Mines, 236b
Copway, George, 237a

Corelli, Marie, 381a
Corinthian, 009a
Corliss, William R., 090a, 098b, 217b, 340b, 366a, 405b
Cormack, Larry, 137a
Cormack, W.A., 009a
Corner, John, 344a
Corra, 003b
Corriveau, La, 085b, 086c
Corriveau, Marie-Josephte, 085b
Cosen, Paul, 241a
Cosgrave, L. Moore, 133a
Cosmic Consciousness, 165a
Coste House, 312b
Cottrell, Flo, 139a
Coughlan, Charles, 066a, 065a, 065c
Countess of Dufferin, 059b
Cowee, 387b
Cox Family, 018c
Cox, Esther, 018b
Coyne, J.H., 167b
Crandon, LeRoy G., 217b
Crandon, Mina, 094a, 217b
Creighton, Helen, 023b, 026b, 027b, 029b, 030a, 030b, 031a, 032b, 035a, 037b, 044a, 059b
Creighton, William, 293a
Crignon, Pierre, 036a
Crime Writers of Canada, 163b
Crippen, Hawley, 068b
Crocker, George, 396b
Croker, John Wilson, 397a
Cronenberg, David, 184a
Cross on the Moon, 232b
Cross, James, 100a
Cross, The, 042b
Crowley, Aleister, 177b, 332a
Cryptozoology, 006a, 007b, 009a, 012a, 015a, 016c, 018a, 032a, 040b, 047b, 050c, 051a, 061b, 062c, 073c, 077b, 086b, 087c, 103c, 136b, 143a, 147a, 153b, 156a, 157b, 168a, 177a, 189b, 210a, 238a, 284a, 297a, 309a, 326a, 347c, 369a, 372a, 379b, 383a
Cryptozoology: See also: Cadborosaurus, Igopogo, Manipogo, Mermaids, Ogopogo, Sasquatch, Windigo, etc.
Crystal Skull, 158a, 158c,
Cummings, Debra, 312b
Cummings, Robert, 100a
Cummins, Geraldine, 200b
Cures: See Medicine.
Curnoe, W. Glen, 162b
Curran, Douglas, 333a, 349a
Curran, James W., 126a
Currie, Ian, 262b
Currie, R.F., 374a
Curses, 011a, 062b, 068b, 070b, 084a, 216a, 271a, 279a, 347b
Curtis, Eli, 271a
Curtis, Linda, 311a

Dagg, George, 113b, 215b
Dahinden, Rene, 373c

Dalzell, Robert, 160b
Dan, Frank, 351b
Daniel, Antoine, 085a
Däniken, Erich von, 157b, 213a, 236b, 283a, 359c, 393b, 406a
Dark Days, 089b, 219b
Darwin, Charles, 081b
Dauphinee, Dave, 163a
Daveluy, Marie-Claire, 088b
David, L.O., 091b
David, Moses, 374a
Davidites, 228a
Davies, Blodwen, 272a
Davis, Bill, 241a
Davis, Carole, 158a
Davison, Arthur, 021b
Dawson, J.W., 081b
Day, Doris, 219a
Day, Gus, 329a
Dean, Kathryn F., 292a
Deane, Richard Burton, 312a
Deans, James, 340b
Death Chuckle, 062b
Decker, Lloyd, 014a
Defence Research Board, 189b, 203b, 204a, 204b, 228b, 334b
Dei Gratia, 038c, 039a
Dekanahwideh, 230a
Delaney, Theresa, 320a
Delaplante, Don, 176b
Demons, Ile des, 082b
Dempsey, Hugh, 323b
Demster, Charles, 271b
Dene, 398a
Denison, Flora MacDonald, 131b, 139a, 224b
Denison, Merrill, 131a, 131b
Denny, Sir Cecil Edward, 283a
Denys, Nicolas, 040b
Derby, George, 080b
Desjardines, F.-X., 083b
Devil's Chair, 145a
Devil's Garden, 108a, 108c
Devil's Hole, 181a
Dewdney, Selwyn, 119b, 168a, 189a
Dewis, Joshua, 038a
Dhārāna, 384c
Diabolos, Paul, 243a
Dickens, Charles, 159a
Dickerson, Robert B., 270b
Dickinson, Terence, 305b
Dickson, John A., 086a
Dieppe Raid Case, 201b
Dingwell, Belinda, 066b
Dinosaur Park, 317c
Dinosauroid, 208b
Dinosaurs, 316b
Diodorus, 411b
Disappearances, 147b, 249a
Discovery, 400a
Dixon, Jeane, 415b
Dobban, Alex, 253b
Dodd, James Edward, 125b, 126c
Dodge, O.P., 221b

Doig, John, 169b
Dollard, Adam, 169b
Domagaya, 109b
Donnacona, 110a
Dorset, 393a, 393b, 413a
Doty, James, 329a
Doughty, A.G., 200b
Doupe, W.H., 145b
Downing, John, 256b
Downton, Eric, 365b
Doyle, Sir Arthur Conan, 093a, 094a, 249b, 292b, 293a
Dragon, winged, 073c
Drake, Frank D., 122a
Dreamer's Rock, 168b
Dreams, Festival of, 230b
Drew, Wayland, 002a, 069a, 074b, 082b, 120b, 145a, 218b
Druids, 013b
Drummond, John, 138c, 139b
Dubro, James, 147b
Dueck, John, 187a
Dufferin, Lord, 197b
Dugan, James, 010a
Dungarvon Whooper, 049a
Dunlop, Donna, 266b
Dunn, Craig, 321a
Dunninger, Joseph, 182b, 268a
Duplantier, Gene, 214b
Dyck, Ian, 299b
Dyre, Jack, 060b

Eades, R.A., 202a
Earthquake, 105a
Earthquakes, 177a
Easter Island, 157b
Economical Car, 294a
Ecureuils Iron Mass, 078b
Eddy, John A., 304b, 334a
Edmonds, Robert B., 418a
Edmund Fitzgerald, 239a
Edmunds, Charles, 253a
Edward, Frank, 161b
Edwards, C.P., 204a
Edwards, Frank, 067a, 094a, 203a, 219b, 231b, 249a, 275b, 299a, 328a, 386a, 391b
Egypt, 017b, 116a
Einstein, Albert, 394a
Eisenbud, Jule, 367a
Eldon House Ghost, 160b
Elizabeth I, Queen, 209c, 402b
Elizabeth the Ghost, 186a
Elliott, Charles N., 164c
Ellis Site, 333a
Ellis, Arthur, 163b
Elysium, 412a
Emerson, J. Norman, 257b
Emerson, Ralph Waldo, 247b
Emmanuel, 402a
Emmons, G.T., 359c, 386b
Empress of Ireland, 068b, 088a
English, Arthur B., 163b
Eozoon Canadense, 081a

Epp, Henry T., 299b
Erie Stones, 142b
Esberey, Joy E., 200b
Eskimo Nebula, 418c, 419a
ESP: See Telepathy.
Essiac, 135a
Estebany, Oskar, 097b
Etobicoke Poltergeist, 256a
Evans, Don, 127c
Evans, Hubert, 369a
Extrasensory Perception: See Telepathy.
Extraterrestrial Intelligence: See SETI.

Fairie Queene, 067a
Fairies, 031a, 315a
Fairley, John, 011a
Faith Healing: See Medicine.
Falcon Lake UFO Encounter, 280a, 281c
Farrell, Robert, 080b
Fawcett, Lawrence, 235a
Fawcett, Percy, 415b
Feldman, Paul A., 122b
Fell, Barry, 017a, 037a, 045a, 115c, 116a, 212c, 213a, 236b, 303a, 329b, 351b
Female Phantom, 053b
Ferguson, Ted, 329b, 374a
Fergusson, C.B., 031b
Festival of Dreams, 230b
Fiddler, Jack & Joseph, 285a
Fiddler, Thomas, 285a
Field, Poole, 404a
Fiennes, Sir Ranulph, 404b
Finch, James, 224a
Fire, 338b
Fire-Letter, 272a
Firehalls No. 3 & 6, 312b, 313c
Fires, 005a, 026a, 026a, 063a, 144b, 159a, 226a, 240b, 274b, 374b
Fisher, Ann, 183a
Fisher, B.N., 146a
Fisher, John, 354b
FitzGerald, William, 180b
Flaming Indian Squaw, 054b
Flammarion, Claude, 198a
Flanagan, Thomas, 287a
Flat Earth, 414b
Fletcher, 258b
Fletcher, Edward, 360c
Fletcher, Richard, 044b
Flockton, Charles, 065a
Flood, Charles, 342b
Flying Canoe, the, 079c
Flying Saucers: See UFOs.
Flying Spectre, 058a
Folden, Art, 363c
Folk Medicine: See Medicine.
Footner, Lesley, 344c
Forbes-Robertson, Sir Johnston, 066b
Forbis, Richard, 334a
Ford Motor Company of Canada, 295a
Ford, Arthur, 258b
Forster, J.W.L., 200c

Fort, Charles, 063a, 157b, 233b, 235b, 236b, 249a, 338a
Fortune, Dionne, 002b
Foster, J.S., 417b
Foulds, Don, 302c
Fowke, Edith, 079b, 278b, 317a
Fox Cottage, 138c
Fox Sisters, 127c, 138c
Fox, Daniel, 137b
Fox, Elizabeth, 137b
Fox, John D., 137b
Fox, Katie, 128a, 137b
Fox, Leah, 137b
Fox, Maggie, 128a, 137b
Foyster, Lionel Algernon, 022b
Foyster, Marianne, 022b
Frank, John, 253b
Franklin, Sir John, 282b, 346b
Fraser, Blair, 201a
Fraser, Mary L., 024a, 024a
Fréchette, L.-H., 091b
Frederickson, D. & H., 342a
French, Dawn, 004a
French, Lafayette, 324a
Friedman, Stanton T., 052a, 053c
Frobisher, Sir Martin, 005a, 394a, 402a, 402b
Frog Lake Mystery, 320a
Frog, Coleman, 050b, 050c
Frontenac, Count, 149b
Frye, Northrop, 274a
Fu-Sang, 335b
Fuhr, Edwin, 301b
Fulford, Mrs., 200b
Fuller, John G., 219b
Furneaux, Rupert, 033c, 034a

Gaal, Arlene F., 363a
Gaddis, Vincent H., 028b, 040b, 067a, 094a, 161b, 274b, 374b, 385a, 393a
Gaelic: See Celtic.
Gales of November, 239b
Gamester, George, 294b
Ganier, Susan, 194a
Ganong, William F., 040b
Garceau, Treffle, 091a
Garden of Eden, 408a
Gardner, Martin, 289a
Gardner, Ray, 380a
Garnett, Richard, 009a
Garnier, Charles, 085a
Garvin, Richard M., 158a
Gatineau Park, 205c
Gault, John, 256b
Geller, Uri, 215b, 267c
Gendron, François, 143a
Geography, Symbolic, 274a
George Wynyard, 041c
George, Chief Dan, 347b
Georgeson, Norman, 372a
Gerus, Claire, 258a
Gervais, C.H., 124b
Ghost House, 037b
Ghost of Dr. Copeland's Wife, 035a

Ghost Photograph, 377b, 378c
Ghost Rider, 227a
Ghost River, 330a
Ghosts, 023b, 024a, 025a, 029a, 029b, 030a, 032b, 032b, 034b, 036b, 038a, 041a, 041c, 043b, 044a, 044a, 047a, 049a, 049b, 050a, 051b, 051b, 053b, 054a, 058a, 058b, 065a, 067b, 070b, 083b, 091a, 110b, 121b, 122b, 132c, 133a, 147b, 160a, 160b, 166a, 176a, 181a, 181b, 182a, 184a, 185a, 185b, 186a, 188c, 190b, 197a, 224a, 227a, 241a, 241b, 243a, 245b, 252a, 252c, 254a, 266b, 275b, 305b, 309b, 311a, 312a, 312b, 313b, 314a, 342a, 370b, 378c, 380b
Ghosts: See also Poltergeists.
Ghouls: See Ghosts.
Giant Squid, 015a
Giants, 393a
Gibraltar Point Lighthouse, 242a
Gibson, Graeme, 122b
Gibson, Walter B., 183a
Gilbert, Sir Humphrey, 007b, 036a
Gillmor, Daniel S., 321b
Gillmor, Don, 096a
Gipsy, 156b
Girl of the Crossroads, 309b
Girl with the Blue Eyes, 193a
Girouard Family, 112b
Gladstone, William, 200b
Glasier Mansion, 049b
Glastonbury, 003b, 155a, 381c, 382b
Glooscap, 026b
Glover, Richard, 154a, 277a, 402b
Golden Dog, 108c
Golden Hind, 008a
Gondwanaland, 408a
Good, Charles, 377b, 378c
Goodwin, James, 198b
Gordon, Henry, 102a, 175a
Gore, Ralph, 041b
Goring, A.H., 225a
Gougou, 047b
Gould, Glenn, 418a
Goupil, René, 085a
Gowanlock, Theresa, 320a
Grad, Bernard, 097a
Grael Legend, 043a
Graham, Herbert A., 244a
Grand Theatre, 166a
Grant, Charles A., 166b
Grant, W.L., 048a, 110a
Grantmyre, Barbara, 055a
Grasset, St. Andre, 085a
Graves, Robert, 014b
Graveyard of the Gulf, 074b
Gray, Art & Audrey, 160a
Gray, Kathleen, 201b
Gray, Thomas, 106b
Great Amherst Mystery, 018a, 018c
Great Eastern, 009b
Great Lakes, 146a
Great Lynx, 236b
Great Northeast Blackout, 219a

Great Peace, 230a
Great Tree of Peace, 230a
Great Turtle, 225b
Greece, 017a
Green Children, 415b
Green, Charles, 033c
Green, John, 006b, 278a, 278b, 283b, 286a, 311b, 337a, 337c, 340a, 343a, 356b, 360a, 363b, 370b, 371b, 371b, 373b, 383a, 383b,
Green, Peggy, 084a, 084c
Green, Roy, 352c
Greenland, Cyril, 130b
Greenpeace, 375b
Greenwood, Barry J., 235a
Grescoe, Paul, 321b, 380b
Grey Lady, 023a, 023b, 032b, 036b, 036b, 053b, 054a
Grey, Tom, 174a
Griffin, Gerald, 199a
Griffon, 149b, 170a
Gross, Loren E., 370a
Group of Seven, 120b
Grovue, Lorne, 321a
Guadalupi, Gianni, 005a
Guillet, Edwin C., 242b
Guimond, Luis, 112a
Gulf Island Monster, 372a

Hadley-James, Brian, 158b
Haida canoes, 375a
Haight, Canniff, 215a, 220a
Haines, Richard W., 039a
Haisell, David, 150b
Haklyut, Richard, 008a, 013a
Halay, Barbe, 075b
Half Moon, 401a
Halford-Watkins, Carol, 207a
Haliburton, Thomas Chandler, 043b
Hall, Angus, 271a, 404a
Hall, Manly Palmer, 210b, 211c
Hall, Richard H., 007b
Hall, Thomas C., 313b
Hall, Trevor H., 022b
Halley, Edmund, 415a
Halpin, Marjoie M., 342a
Ham, George H., 288a
Hamilton, J.D., 293a
Hamilton, J.H., 366b
Hamilton, T. Glen, 200b, 289b, 290c, 293b, 367b
Hammer of Thor, 117a, 117c
Haney Boulder, 351b
Hannington, William, 061a
Hanno, 115c, 116a
Hapgood, Charles H., 417a
Hardisty, Richard, 317a
Harper, H.A., 200b
Harral, Thomas, 129a
Harrington, C.R., 386b
Harrington, Lynn, 114a
Harrington, Michael, 004b
Harris, Jas. E., 067b
Harris, Lawren, 165b, 244b, 397c, 414b

Harris, M., 082c
Harris, Melvin, 066b, 198a
Harris, Sarah, 160b
Harrison, Ernest, 225b
Harvey, Moses, 012a
Harvey, Sir John, 042a
Hata, 115c, 116a
Hatfield, C.H., 386a
Hatton, Joseph, 012b
Hauntings: See Ghosts, Poltergeists.
Hawkeridge, William, 012b
Hawkins, Gerald S., 334a
Hawley, A. & F., 186a
Hawley-Breckenridge House, 186a
Hay River Radio Observatory, 399b
Hayward, G. & E., 327a
Headless Brakeman, 374a
Headless Nun, 047a
Healing: See Medicine.
Heard, J.F., 417b
Hearne, Samuel, 277a, 279a, 395b, 402b
Hebb, Donald O., 096a, 097a
Helluland, 002a
Henday, Anthony, 301b, 332a
Heney, John, 082b
Henneberry, Henry, 030b
Hennepin, Louis, 177b
Henning, Doug, 268a
He-No the Thunderer, 178c, 179a
Henry, Alexander, 225b, 325b
Hepburn, Mitch, 240a
Heron, Michael, 002b, 406a
Herring, C.S., 186a
Hervey, Sheila, 073b, 110b, 121b, 133a,
    253b, 254b, 256a, 295a, 310b, 342a,
    381a
Herzberg Institute of Astrophysics, 007b, 122a,
    203b, 321b
Herzberg, Gerhard, 417b
Hesperides, 412a
Heuvelmans, Bernard, 009a
Hexham, I., 374a
Heyerdahl, Thor, 375a
Hiawatha, 230a
Hicks, Art, 147a
Hicks, Green, 343a
Higgins, Michael, 112b
Hilarion Series, 261b
Hill, A.J., 018c
Hill, Betty & Barney, 235a
Hill, William "Red," 180b
Hind, Henry Youle, 220a
Hiram, Lord, 115c, 116a
Hitler, Adolf, 095a, 240a
Hodgins, Jack, 358a
Hoei Shin, 335b
Hoffer, Abram, 309a
Hogg, F.S., 417b
Hogg, Helen Sawyer, 417b
Hole at the Pole, 415b, 416c
Hole-in-the-Wall, 054b
Hollow Earth, 389a, 414b
Hollowell, Alfred Irving, 278a

Home, D.D., 259b
Homer, 024b
Honsberger, Joanna, 183a
Hood, Dora, 250b
Hooper, John, 048b
Hopkins, Elizabeth, 128a
Hopkins, Samuel, 216a
Horowitz, Michael, 096b, 309b
Horwood, Harold, 001b, 009a
Hoskins, Cyril Henry, 314b
Houdini Magical Hall of Fame, 094b, 182b
Houdini, Harry, 055a, 093b, 182b, 217b, 267c,
    268b,
Houser, F.B., 332a
Howard, James, 007a
Howard, John & Jemima, 243b
Howard, Richard, 188a
Hoy, Claire, 246a
Hoyt, Reginald O., 063b
Hubbell, Walter, 018a
Hudson, Henry, 141a, 141c, 400a
Hughes, Barry Conn, 030a
Hughes, Irene, 100a
Hughton Medicine Wheel, 300b
Hugo, Victor, 015a
Human Effigy, 299b, 300c
Human Magnet, 161b
Hunt, Holman, 152b, 152c
Hunter, Robert, 376a
Huot, Richard, 075c, 075a
Huronia, 170b
Hurwitt, Jannika, 410b
Hutton, John H., 330a
Huxley, Aldous, 096a, 309a
Hwui Shan, 335b
Hyde, Hiram, 043b
Hydesville, 138b
Hynek, J. Allen, 215a, 269b, 301b, 318b,
    321b, 322c, 369a,
Hyperborea, 409a, 411a
Hypnotic Regression, 263a

IAO Research Centre, 266a
Igopogo, 153b, 155b
Ilatsiak, 405b
Imaha, 117a
Imperishable Sacred Land, 413b
Incarnation, Marie de l', 075b, 085a, 104b,
    112a
Ingersoll, Robert G., 133a, 247b
Ingstad, Helge, 002a
Innis, Ralph, 319b
Inscription Rock, 119b, 120c
Inscriptions: See Rock Art.
International Astronomical Union, 417a
International Dracontology Society, 087a
Inukshuit, 393b
Irish: See Celtic.
Iron Creek Meteorite, 325a, 325c
Iron Mass, 078b
Irving, William, 386b
Ishquay, Mash-kou-tay, 119a
Isle Royale, 236a

Isolation Experiments, 096b
Israel: See Lost Tribes.
Israelite-Indian Connection, 316b
Ives, Edward D., 069a
Izatt, Dorothy, 367b, 368c
Izzard, Ralph, 373c

Jacko, 383a
Jackson, Herbert G., 139b
Jackson, Oliver, 354b
Jackson, Shirley, 314a
Jacobson, Jacques, 075a
Jain, Ajit, 174b
James, John, 004b
Janus, Christopher, 250b
Jefferys, C.W., 347c
Jenkins, Patricia, 053b
Jenness, Diamond, 405b
Jerome, 027b
Jesuit Martyrs, 085a, 172a
Jesuits, 170b
Jesus Christ, 091b, 104b, 152b, 191a, 302b,
    306a, 308a
Jewish migration, 365b
Johnson, Alice M., 402a
Johnson, Gordon A., 038c, 040b
Johnson, Hugh, 053b
Johnson, James, 125a
Johnson, Richard M., 270b
Johnson, Sir William, 226a
Johnston, Alex, 327b
Johnston, Donald S., 306b
Jones, Ernest, 178a
Jones, Frank, 145b
Jones, Lynn, 157a
Joques, Isaac, 085a
Jorgenson, Martin, 403b
Josepee, Pitsulak, 401a
Joseph, St., 092a
Julien, Henri, 079c
Jung, Carl, 102a, 330b, 380b

Kabalarian Philosophy, 374b
Kamper, Karl, 417b
Kane, Elisa Kent, 139a
Kane, Paul, 284b, 377a
Kanerva, John, 317c
Kapica, Jack, 199a, 226a, 233b
Karpan, Arlene & Robin, 307b
Keats, John, 247b
Kehoe, A.B. & T.F., 300b, 301a, 304a, 304b,
    308b
Kekip-Sesoators, 320b
Kelleher, Emmett E., 389b, 390c
Kelley, Thomas P., 357b
Kelly, Jim, 080b
Kemp, F.W., 380a
Kempenfelt Kelly, 153b
Kempthorne, Walter, 353b
Kendall, Doreen, 348a
Kendall, Henry, 068b
Kenna, Kathleen, 153b, 254b
Kensington Stone, 127a, 169c

Kent, Duke of, 029b
Kenyon, W.A., 220a, 227b
Kettle Valley Express, 354a
Keyhoe, Donald E., 007a, 334b,
Keymore, Daniel, 060b
Khahtsahlano, Jack, 364b
Khan, Genghis, 399a
Khan, Kublai, 365b
Kidd, Captain William, 033b, 065a
Kidd, Kenneth, 136a
Kidder, Margot, 179b
Kiesel, Gerhard, 375a
King, Charles, 327a
King, Ellen, 179b
King, Isabel Grace, 199b, 200c, 253a
King, Stephen, 184a
King, W.L. Mackenzie, 199b, 200c, 205a,
  205c, 252c, 292b
Kingam, Charles, 211b
Kingsmere, 205a, 205c
Kinstie, 156a
Kipling, Rudyard, 008b
Kiska, 155a
Kitsipokotoks, 320b
Klass, Philip J., 005b, 234b
Klein, A.M., 095a, 163b, 287b
Knutsson, Paul, 400a
Koestler, Arthur, 316a
Kolosimo, Peter, 366b
Kon-Tiki, 375a
Koreshan Park, 415a
Kozocari, Jean, 370b
Kraken, 015a
Kreskin, 268a
Krippner, Stanley, 161b
Krishnamurti, Jiddu, 245b
Kroup, B., 062c
Krupp, E.C., 304b
Kurtz, Paul, 184b, 193b, 268a

L'Heureux, Jean, 320b, 324a
La Lande, Jean de, 085a
La Pérouse, Count of, 387a
La Rocque, J.-F., 083a
La Roque, Marguerite de, 083a
La Salle, Cavalier de, 149b, 181a
Labelle, Joe, 389b
Labrecque, Bishop, 111a
Lacourcière, Luc, 086a
Lady Murphy, 190a
Lafrenière, G.F., 235b
Lake Monsters: See Cryptozoology.
Lake Utopia Monster, 061b, 062c
Lalemant, Gabriel, 085a
Laliberté, Jacques, 086c
Lamb, W. Kaye, 339b
Lambe, Lawrence, 316b
Lambert, G.W., 201b
Lambert, R.S., 022a, 075b, 125b, 151b, 240b,
  251a, 251c
Lambton, Gunda, 080a
Lampl, Joe, 196a
Land, Ron, 176b

Langley, W.H., 379b
Langsner, Max A., 250a, 328a
Langtry, Lillie, 066b
Laporte, Pierre, 100a
Lathangue, Neil, 155b
Latreille, Aimee, 137a
Laurasia, 408a
Laurier House, 199b, 201c
Laurier, Sir Wilfrid, 199b, 201c
Laval, Bishop, 076a, 085a, 104b, 112a
Lavallée, Jean-Pierre, 102b
Lavoie, Jacques 075c, 075a
Lazenby, George, 245a
Le Ber, Chuck, 174a
Le Jeune, Jean Marie, 365b
Leach, Bobby, 180b
Leacock, Stephen, 110b
Leadbeater, C.W., 245b
Leavitt, Thaddeus W.H., 215b
Leavitt, William Henry, 160a
LeDoux, Florence, 187b, 188c
Lee, Richard, 418a
Lee, Robert E., 169c
Lee, Thomas E., 082b, 082c, 115b, 117a,
  117c, 169a, 169c, 398b
Lefebvre, Eugene, 112a
Léger, Paul-Emile, 109a
Legion Ghost, 266b
Leif the Lucky, 002a
Lemieux, Louis, 101a
Lemon, Frank, 323b
Lemuria, 408b
Lemushahindu, 054b
Leonard, Phillip M., 329b
Lescarbot, Marc, 036a, 048a, 110a
Lessard, Arlene, 216b
Lessard, Jacques, 101a
Levett, Bruce, 366b
Lewanevsky, Sigismund, 394a
Lewis, P.L., 217a
Lewlawala, 178c, 179a
Ley Lines, 154b
Lightfoot, Gordon, 239a
Lights, 068a, 070a, 090b, 140a, 176b, 186b,
  269a, 338b
Lilly, John, 096a
Lily Dale Assembly, 139a, 222b
Lily of the Mohawks, 084b
Lincoln, Abraham, 153a, 247b
Lind, Karin, 375b
Lindell, Oscar, 301a
Little Man, 054a
Little, William T., 121b
Livingstone, Sam, 314a
Loch Ness Monster, 087a, 087c, 153b, 362a,
  369a, 380a
Locke, Mahlone, 273a
Lodge, Oliver, 293a
Lodge, Sir Oliver, 200b
Logan, Sir William, 081b
Lolar, Noel, 062b
Lomberg, Jon, 418a
Long Sault, 169b

Lord, Peter, 386b
Lord, Walter, 288b
Lorenzen, Coral & Jim, 280a, 315b
Lost Lemon Mine, 323b
Lost Tribes, 001a, 315b
Lost Valley, 403a
Lourdes, 306a, 307b
Love, John, 279b
LSD, 096b, 309a
Lugosi, Bela, 040a
Lundy's Lane, 181b
Lussier, Jean, 180b
Lutyens, Mary, 245b
Lyell, Sir Charles, 032a
Lyta, Mooney, 401a

Macbeth, R.A., 135b
Macdonald, Alexander, 026a
Macdonald, Bruce, 351b
MacDonald, Douglas, 028b
Macdonald, Flora, 131b
MacDonald, J.E.H., 121b
MacEwen, Gwendolyn, 206a
Macfarlane, John, 058b
MacGregor, R.R., 157b
MacGregor, Roy, 121b
MacIver, Joanna, 194a
MacIver, Kenneth, 194a
Mackal, Roy P., 372b
Mackenzie House, 252a, 252c
Mackenzie, Alexander, 200b
Mackenzie, Ruth, 216c
Mackenzie, Sir Alexander, 339a
Mackenzie, W.L., 144b, 200b, 252a, 252c
MacKinnon, Charlie, 267a
MacLean, H.J., 150a
Maclean, John, 327a
MacLeish, Archibald, 300b
MacLeod Brothers, 403a
Macmillan, Cyrus, 026b
MacMillan, Donald B., 396b
MacMillan, R.L., 261a
MacPherson, A.S., 148a
MacRitchie, David, 405b
Madaline, 143b
Madoc, 003b, 116b
Magnetic Hill, 055b, 056c
Magor, John, 313c, 332b, 343a, 344c, 344c,
  345c, 365c, 367b
Maid of the Mist, 178c, 179a, 184a
Maiden's Cave, 034b
Maisonneuve, Sieur de, 088b
Majorville Medicine Wheel, 327b
Malabeam, 054b
Malcolm, J.R., 226a
Mallory, Duncan, 185b
Malloy, Barbara, 087b
Maltwood, Katherine, 381a, 381c
Manguel, Alberto, 005a
Manipogo, 284a
Manitou Stone, 324b, 325c
Manitou, 120b, 146c, 168b, 284a, 324b
Manny, Louise, 047a

Manuel, David, 193b
Maratray, M.R. de, 198a
March, Prophet of, 152c
March, Township of, 151b
Marconi, Guglielmo, 009b
Marie-Léonie, Mère, 085a
Marie-Rose, Mère, 085a
Margery the Medium, 217b
Markland, 002a
Marks, John, 096b
Marrow, Tommy, 194b
Marshall, Joyce, 105a
Marshall, William, 349b
Martin, A. Patchett, 041a
Martyrs' Shrine, 085a, 112a, 170b, 172a
Mary Celeste Room, 040b
Mary Celeste, 004b, 033b, 038a, 038c
Mary, Virgin, 104b, 109a, 111a, 112b, 172a, 306a, 307b, 380b
Marysburgh Votex, 189b
Maslum, 026b
Mason, Michael H., 404b
Mason, Ronald J., 169b
Masonry, 110b
Mastodon, 326b
Matchett, Traven, 173b, 173c
Mather, Cotton, 316a, 415a
Matheson, Neil A., 066b
Matonabbee, 279a
Matthews, Arthur H., 077a
Maxwell, Nora, 347b
Maymaygwayshi, 168a
McAfee, Samuel, 144b
McCall, Simpson, 167b
McCampbell, James M., 219b
McCarthy, Pat, 271b
McCleary, Winnifred, 253b
McClellan, Robert, 038a
McClure, Captain Robert, 397a
McDonald, John, 124b, 125c
McDonald, Neil T., 125a
McDougall, George M., 325b
McDougall, John, 324a
McGee, Thomas D'Arcy, 198a
McGhee, Robert, 014a, 014c
McGinnis, David, 034a
McGlone, William R., 329b
McIlwraith, T.F., 339a
McIsaacs, Mrs. Donald, 191a
McKay, Henry, 215a
McKay, Valentine, 297a
McKellar, Andrew, 417b
McKelvie, Bruce, 340a
McKinley, William, 181b
McKinney, Mary, 051a
McKinnon, Charlie, 025a
McLauchlin, Scotty, 299a
McLeod, J.A., 284a
McMaugh, James, 238b
McMichael, Robert, 121a
McMullen, George, 257b
McMullen, Thomas, 043b
McNamara, Allen G., 203b

McNeal, Bob, 019a
McNeill, Mark, 148b
McPhillips, Henry, 190b
McRae, Donald, 343a
McRoberts, Hannah, 350b, 350c
McSorley, Ernest, 239a
Mearns, Hughes, 024a
Medcof, Carl, 018a
Medicine Stone, 327a
Medicine Wheels, 300a, 301a, 304a, 308a, 308b, 327b 330a, 333b
Medicine, 084b, 101a, 135a, 143a, 166b, 172a, 221a, 273a, 277a, 279b, 333a, 339a, 376b
Mediums: See Spiritualism.
Medley, John, 049b
Melville, Mary, 130a
Melvin, Joan, 142a
Memphré, 086b, 087c
Meneray, Robert, 271b
Menier, Henri, 074b
Mercator, Gerhardus, 005a, 407c, 408b
Mermaids, 012b, 040b, 048a, 238a
Merrick, Eliot, 006a
Merrill, George, 131a
Merrill, Mary Edwards, 129b, 224b
Merta, Jan, 097b
Mertz, Henriette, 024b, 335b
Meru, Mount, 409b
Metis Lourdes, 307b
Metlakatla Man, 364b, 365c
Michalak, Stephen, 280a, 281c
Michel, Aimé, 075a
Michell, John, 161b, 382b
Mikado, 028a
Miller, Phil, 338b
Miller, R. DeWitt, 198a
Miller, William, 196a
Millerites, 196b
Millman, Peter M., 203a, 204b, 417b
Milton, Viscount, 325b
Mines, 231b, 236b, 395b
Minton Turtle, 303b, 303c
Miraculous Cures: See Medicine.
Mirages, 395a, 395b, 396b
Mishipeshu, 236b, 238a
Mississauga Blob, 172a, 173c
Mitchell, Barry M., 142a
Mitchell, Edgar E., 394a
Mitchell, Paulene, 022b
Mitchell, Roy, 245a
Mitchell-Hedges, Anna, 158b, 158c
Mitchell-Hedges, F.A., 158b
Mitford, Unity, 240a
MKULTRA, 095b
Molinaro, Matie, 195b
Money Pit, 034a
Monk, Henry Wentworth, 152c, 151b, 252a
Monkey Masks, 359c, 360c
Monster Devil-Fish, 015a, 016c
Monsters: See Cryptozoology.
Montcalm, Marquis de, 106a
Montgomery, John, 242b
Montreal Canadiens, 101b

Montrose, 068b
Moodie, Dunbar, 127a
Moodie, John, 127c
Moodie, Susanna, 127a, 127c
Moon, Cross on the, 232b
Moon, Henry, 055a
Moon, Mary, 363a
Moore, Noel, 014a
Moore, Thomas, 412a
Moorside, 205a
Moose Mountain Medicine Wheel, 304a
Morehouse, David, 039a
Moresby, John, 381a
Moresby, L., 381b
Morgan, Charles, 289a
Morgan, Dorothy, 216a
Morgan, Henry, 033b
Morin, Stephen P., 103b
Morison, Samuel Eliot, 011a
Mormonism, 315b
Morrisseau, Norval, 189a, 285c
Morrow, Virginia, 259c
Moses, Apocryphal Books of, 272a
Mother Damnable, 296a
Mound-builders, 220a, 227b
Mountain Rory, 023b
Mowat, Farley, 118a, 127a, 169c, 400a
Mu, 366a, 408b
Mulholland, J.H., 404a
Mullard, Ed, 355b
Mullgrew, Ian, 355a
Munday, Dave, 180b
Murdin, Paul, 419a
Murphy, Bridey, 193b, 259c
Murphy, Gardner, 394b
Murphy, Rowley W., 246a
Murray, Alexander, 012b
Murray, J.F., 379b
Musgrave, John Brent, 318b
Myers, Frederick W.H., 200b
Myers, John, 130b
Mysterious Stranger, 054b
Mystery Tunnel, 355b

Nabokov, Vladimir, 397a
Nansen, Fridtjof, 415a
Narayana, A.S., 174b
National Investigations Committee, 005b
Navarre, Queen of, 083a
Near-death Experiences, 261a
Nelson, Lord, 107c, 197a
Nelson, Sgt. J., 391b
Nethercot, Arthur H., 245b
New Horizons Research Foundation, 263a, 263c
Newbury, Harry, 067b
Newcomb, Simon, 042b
NGC 2932, 418b, 418c
Nicholas of Lynne, 398a, 407c
Nicholls, W., 041c
Nicholson, Jim, 329a
Nickerson, Edgar, 027b
Niven, Frederick, 332a

Nolin, Charles, 307b
NORAD Sightings, 189b, 234b
Nordic, 303a
Norse, 001b, 013b, 035b, 043a, 044b, 082b,
    082c, 115b 117a, 118a, 125b, 126c, 170a,
    212c, 213b, 393a, 400a, 401a, 401c
North Magnetic Pole, 406a, 417a
North Pole, 245a, 398a, 406a, 407c, 416c
North Star, 146a
North-West Rebellion, 287b, 307b, 320a
Northwest Passage, 392b, 397a
Norton, D. & A., 201b
Norumbega, 035b
Norwood, Joseph, 036b
Norwood, Robert, 247b
Nostradamus, 095a, 176a
Novaya Zemblya, 397a
Númenor, 002b

O'Beirne, A.C., 298b
O'Brien, Andy, 179b
Oak Island, 032b, 033c
Oban Inn, 185b
Octavius, 392b
October Crisis, 100a
Ogham Stone, 013b, 014c
Ogham, 329b
Ogopogo, 354b, 354c, 360b, 360c, 376a, 376c,
    379b
Old Crow flats, 387c
Old Fort York, 241b
Old McAfee, 144b
Old Spanish Mound, 355a
Old Walt, 131b, 132c
Old Yellow Top, 136b
Ontario Elephant, 274b
Oratory, St. Joseph's, 092a
Orenda Expedition, 375a
Orpingalik, 393b
Ortelius, Abraham, 408b
Osmond, Humphry, 309a
Ostman, Albert, 373a, 373c
Ottawa Flying Saucer Club, 079a
Ottawa New Sciences Club, 207a
Otter, Andy A. den, 327b
Oursler, Fulton, 094a
Ouspensky, P.D., 165b
Ovenden, Michael W., 305a
Overlanders, 351a
Owen, A.R.G., 149a, 252a, 263a, 263c
Owen, Iris M., 022b, 263a, 263c
Owen, R. Dale, 059b
Owls Head Mountain, 110b

Padden, R.C., 003b
Page, P.K., 058a
Palmer, Cynthia, 096b, 309b
Palmer, Robin, 003b
Pangea, 408a
Panther, Underwater, 146c
Parapsychological Association, 264a
Parapsychology: See Spiritualism.

Parker, Alfred J., 374b
Parker, Gilman C., 040a
Parker, John, 039a
Parks, G., 156b
Parkyn, G.F., 372a
Parliament Buildings, 201b
Parry, Sir Edward, 397a
Parsons, Denys, 193b
Parsons, Mike, 005a
Passey, Rick, 313b
Past-life Therapy, 263a
Paterson, T.W., 241b, 356a, 364a
Patterson, Robert, 404b
Pauling, Linus, 166b
Pauwels, Louis, 002b
Pauzé, Ludger, 109a
Payne, Edward John, 008a
Pazder, Lawrence, 380a
Pearce, Cecil, 313b
Peary, Robert E., 395a, 396b, 406a
Peg-Leg Brown, 162b
Peking Man, 250a
Pelletier, Joseph, 091b
Penn, William, 316a
Penny, Eisner, 027a
Penrose, Evelyn, 353a
Perkins, Simeon, 031b
Perri, Rocco, 147b
Perrin, Rosemarie D., 034b
Persinger, Michael A., 235b
Peterman, Michael, 128a
Petrie, R.M., 417b
Petroglyphs Provincial Park, 212c
Petroglyphs: See Rock Art.
Pettipas, Heather, 141a
Pettit, Robin, 245b
Phantom Hunter, The, 118c
Phantom Invasion of 1915, 133b
Phantom Ship of Etobicoke, 246a
Phantom Trapper, 011a
Phenomenon of 1819, 089b
Philip Phenomenon, 133b, 264a
Phillips, R.A.J., 080b
Philosophical Research Society, 211a
Photography: See Spirit Photography.
Phyllis Cormack, 375b
Physical Research, 263c
Piccot, Theophile, 012a
Picken, Harry, 186b
Picton, John, 273b, 294b
Pike, James A., 258b
Pike, Zebulon, 241b
Pincock, Jenny O'Hara, 218a, 222a
Pindar, 411b
Piri Re'is Map, 012a
Pitou, Gertrude Coughlan, 066b
Plains of Abraham, 106a
Plante, Abbé Léopold 103a, 103c
Plaskett, H.H., 417b
Plaskett, J.S., 417b
Plato, 408b
Pliny, 412b

Plum Hollow Witch, 215b
Pluviculture, 306b, 386a
Pocock, Richard L., 379b
Poe, Edgar Allan, 412b, 416a
Pogue Carburetor, 294a
Pogue, Charles Nelson, 294a
Pohl, Frederick J., 026b, 036b, 044b
Pole Shifts, 416b
Poltergeists, 018c, 020b, 050a, 073b, 080b,
    093a, 114a, 122b, 124b, 125c, 157b, 176b,
    235b, 256a, 297a, 313c
Poltergeists: See also Ghosts.
Ponik, 102b, 103c
Poole, Elizabeth, 292b
Pooler, James S., 275b
Pope, Alexander, 397a
Pope, Joseph, 198b
Popoff, Peter, 268b
Possession, 148b, 380a
Potocki, W.J., 256a
Power Blackout, 219a
Powers, Phil, 404a
Prediction, 351a
Premonition, 060b
Price, Harry, 022a, 251a
Primrose, Tom, 323b
Prince's Lodge, 029a
Prince, Walter F., 026a, 133a
Princess Amelia, 035b
Pringle, Thomas, 129a
Project Blue Book, 005b, 052b, 321b
Project Magnet, 079a, 202b, 203b, 204a, 228b
Project OZMA, 122a
Project Second Storey, 189b, 203a, 203b, 204b
Prophet of March, 152c
Prophet's Room, 044a
Prophet, Dennis, 214a
Prophets, 001a, 095a, 151b, 174b, 184a, 242b,
    282b 287a, 296b, 345b, 376a
Psi: See Telepathy.
Psychedelic Movement, 309a
Psychic Archaeology, 257b
Psychic Detection, 299a, 328a
Psychic Photography: See Spirit Photography.
Psychic Surgery: See Medicine.
Psychical Research: See Spiritualism.
Psychokinesis, 235b, 264b
Pukaskwa Cairns and Pits, 218b
Purchas, Samuel, 013a
Pygmies, 393a
Pythagoras, 014b, 233b
Pytheas, 411b

Quintner, David, 386b

Radclive, John Robert, 163b
Raddall, Thomas H., 039a
Rademuller, J.P., 242a
Radisson, Pierre-Esprit, 401a
Rafinesque, C.S., 143a
Rain-making, 386a
Rainbow Warrior, 375b

Rampa, Mama San Ra-ab, 315a
Rampa, T. Lobsang, 314b
Ramsay's Gold, 167b
Ramsay, Robert H., 035b
Ramsay, Sterling, 066a, 068a, 070a, 070b, 071b
Rand, S.T., 026b, 047b
Randi, James, 092b, 094a, 182b, 215b, 267b, 267c
Rannie, William F., 135b
Rappleye, Charles, 149a
Rasmussen, Knud, 413a
Reaney, James, 124b
Rebellion of 1837, 083b, 144b, 242b
Recollets, 170b
Red River Rebellion, 287b
Redesdale, Lord, 240b
Redsky, James, 154a
Redstar, Charlie, 278a
Regush, Nicholas M. & Jean, 098a
Reid, John, 229b
Reincarnation, 098b, 193b, 262b
Resolven, 004b
Resperin Corporation, 135b
Restricted Environment Stimulation, 296a
Reynolds, Nancy, 260b
Reznikoff, Ivan, 243a
Ribstones, 335a
Riel, Louis, 287a, 307c
Riley, Daniel, 323b
Ripley, Robert L., 051a, 066a, 150b, 236b, 274a
Ritchie, William G., 312b
Roberts, Henry C., 095a
Roberval, La Rocque de, 083a
Robie Street Palace, 029b
Robinson, John Beverley, 242b
Robison, John, 107b
Rock Art, 009b, 013b, 014c, 017b, 037a, 044b, 045c, 082b, 114b, 115c, 117c, 119b, 120c, 131b, 211b, 287a, 301b, 301b, 305b, 320b, 327a, 329b, 335a, 335b, 344a, 351b, 364b
Rockman, 210a
Rocky Mountain Trench, 331c
Rodger, David A., 305a
Roe, William, 356a, 356c
Roerich, Nicholas, 245a, 397c
Rogo, D. Scott, 278a, 405b
Rolt, Lionel T.C., 010b
Roman, Stephen, 135b
Rorschach, Hermann, 274b
Rosna, Charles B., 138b
Ross, Keith, 027a
Ross, Sir James, 406a
Ross, Sir John, 396b
Rouleau, Pierre, 040b
Rowing Man, 054a
Roxburgh Castle, 098b
Roy Rivers Medicine Wheel, 308a
Roy, Maurice, 112a
Royal Canadian Mounted Police, 037a, 177a, 208a, 280b, 286a, 299a, 328a, 349b, 367b, 390b
Royal Ontario Museum, 125b, 269a

Ruskin, John, 153a
Russell, Dale A., 208b
Rutherford, Murray, 250a
Rutkowski, Chris, 278b, 282a
Ruttley, Dr. J., 221b

Sabo, Deborah & George, 401a
Sagan, Carl, 386b
Sagana, 109b, 131b
Sagard, Gabriel, 210b
Saguenay, Kingdom of, 109b
Saint-Exupery, Antoine de, 233b
Saint-Onge, Guylaine, 073b
Saint-Père, Jean de, 089a
Saint-Sauveur, St. André Grasset de, 085a
Sainte-Marie-among-the-Hurons, 170b
Sanderson, Ivan T., 157b, 177a, 351b, 404b
Sanderson, Ralph, 284b
Sasquatch, 278a, 278b, 283b, 286a, 311b, 337a, 337c, 339a, 339b, 340a, 341b, 341c, 343a, 351b, 352c, 356a, 356c, 359c, 360a, 360c, 360c, 364b, 370a, 371a, 371b, 372b, 373a, 373c, 383a
Satanism, 148b
Saunders, Henry, 247b
Schmielewski, Alfred, 174b
Schofield, Peter, 159a
Schoolcraft, Henry R., 119b
Schwartz, Stephan A., 258a
Scolvuss, Johannes, 400a
Screaming Tunnel, 183b, 183c
Sea Serpents: See Cryptozoology.
Search for Extraterrestrial Intelligence: See SETI.
Séguin, R., 208b
Selkirk, Lord, 124b
Selleck, Charles, 190a
Seneca, 412b
Sensory Deprivation, 295b
Serios, Ted, 367a
Serpent Mounds, 227b
SETI, 122a, 209a, 399b
Seton, Ernest Thompson 119a
Seventh Day Adventists, 196a
Severn, Tim, 011b
Shaking Tent, 225b, 277b, 284b
Shamanism, 168b, 170b, 277a, 278a, 279a, 282b, 287a, 299b, 335b, 351b, 405b
Shamballah, 410a
Shan, Hwui, 335b
Shaw, Sophia, 185a
Shean, 031a
Sheguiandah, 168b
Sheldrake, Rupert, 149a
Shelton, Ian, 417b
Sherbrooke Inscriptions, 114b, 115c, 170a
Sherbrooke, Sir John C., 041a, 041c
Sherman, Harold T., 394b
Sherwood, Roland H., 035a, 043b, 057b, 061b, 067b
Shielker, Edgar, 315b
Shin, Hoei, 335b
Ships, 004b, 008a, 009a, 009b, 013a, 025b,

026b, 028a, 032a, 032b, 035a, 038a, 038c, 040b, 047b, 057b, 059a, 059b, 060b, 067a, 068b, 069a, 069c, 070b, 074b, 088a, 102b, 143b, 145b, 149b, 170a, 190a, 238b, 246a, 246a, 288b, 366b, 375a, 375b, 385a, 392b, 401a
Shorts, Thomas, 362b
Shrine of Our Lady of Lourdes, 108c
Shrines, 004a, 085a, 092a, 108a, 112a, 113a, 168b, 172a, 218a, 305a, 306a, 307b, 330b, 333a
Shriver, John P., 106a
Shute, Evan, 166b, 191a
Shute, James C.M., 191a
Shute, Wilfrid, 166b
Siberia, 338a
Sibley, Alexander, 241b
Sieveking, Oleg, 409a
Silent City, 395b
Silent Watcher, 311b
Silver Mines, 241b
Silverthorne, Joseph, 176a
Simard-Normandin, Martine, 122b
Simcoe, John Graves, 242a
Simcoe, Mrs. John Graves, 187b
Sinclair, Henry, 026b, 036a
Sirois, Elzear, 104a
Skinner, A.B., 136a
Skraeling, 393a
Skrimsi, 297a
Skrypetz, William W., 153b
Skull of Doom, 158a, 158c
Skynner, H.J., 295a
Sleeping Giant, 241b
Slocum, Joshua, 025b
Slumach, 364a
Small, Ambrose, 166a, 249a
Smith, Dorothy, 174a
Smith, Geraldine, 186a
Smith, H. Allen, 249b
Smith, Henry More, 054b
Smith, John, 033b
Smith, Joseph, 315b
Smith, Michelle, 380a
Smith, Warren P., 321a, 322c
Smith, Warren, 320a, 327a
Smith, Wilbert B., 079a, 202a, 202c, 204a, 204b, 207a, 228b, 229c
Smythe, Albert A.E., 413a
Smythe, Albert E.S., 244b, 382a
Snow, John, 332b
Snowden, Mrs. John, 020b
Sobbing Sophia, 185a
Society for Psychical Research, 201b, 247b, 264a
Solandt, O.M., 096a, 204b
Somerset House, 133b
Sonin, Eileen, 224a
Sophia, Sobbing, 185a
Sorstad, 088a
Sotiroff, George, 116b
Soubirous, Bernadette, 109a, 306a, 307a
Soucek, Karel, 180b

South Pole, 414a
Southey, Robert, 003b
Spanish Expedition, 355a, 356a
Sparrow, Margaret, 264b
Spirit Communication: See Spiritualism.
Spirit Photography, 289b, 290c, 367a, 368c, 377b
Spirit Rock, 272b
Spirits: See Ghosts.
Spiritualism, 094a, 127a, 127c, 137a, 138c, 182b, 199b, 200c, 201c, 205c, 206a, 222a, 225a, 247a, 258b, 289b, 293a
Spittal, Wm. Guy, 230b
Splitter, Henry Winfred, 161b
Spontaneous Human Combustion, 159a
Spraggett, Allen, 258b, 259c, 264a, 379a
Spray, 025b
Squires, Daniel, 012a
Squirrel, 008a
St. Clair, Desilda, 054a
St. Germain, Venant, 238a
St. John, Pat, 184a
St. Laurent, Madame de, 029b
St. Lawrence Seaway, 223b
Stacey, C.P., 108a, 200a, 206a, 292b
Staley, Charles, 156b
Stanley Cup, 102a
Starnes, Cortland, 391b
Stathakis, George, 180b
Statues, 073b, 091b, 110b, 112b, 113c, 140b
Stearn, Jess, 190b, 193a, 193b, 416a
Steep Rock Iron Mines, 231b
Stefansson, Vilhjalmur, 405a
Steiger, Brad, 100a
Steiner, Rudolf, 274a
Stephens, Charles, 180b
Stephens, Robert W., 399b
Sternberg, Charles, 316b
Stevens, Gillmore, 354a
Stevens, James R., 154a, 286a
Stevenson, Ian, 098b, 195b, 289b
Stevenson, R.L., 200b, 292b, 293b
Stewart, Ethel, 398a
Stigmatic, 191a
Stinson, Walter Stewart, 217b
Stonehenge, 015a, 157b, 334a
Storey, Ronald D., 319a
Storm, Margaret, 076b
Storstad, 068b
Story, Ronald D., 078b, 203a, 206b, 348a, 370a
Strabo, 411b
Strieber, Whitley, 151b, 318b
Stringer, Jimmy, 122a
Stuart, David, 360b
Submerged Communities, 223b
Sudbury Basin, 233b
Suicides, 178a
Sumerford, R., 374b
Sun Dances, 305a, 317a
Sundial Hill Medicine Wheel, 330a
Surette, Ralph, 027a, 034b

Suttles, Wayne, 342a,
Suzuki, David, 400a
Swastika, 239b
Swayze, Colin, 187b, 188c
Sylla, Anthony, 306a
Symbolic Geography, 274a
Symmes, John Cleves, 415a

Taber Child, 335a
Taghert, Nicole, 057a
Taigonagny, 109b
Talking Head, 089a
Tamu, 115c, 116a
Taylor, Annie Edson, 180b
Taylor, Edith, 313b
Taylor, Granger, 349a
Taylor, William, 118a
Teazer Light, 032a
Tecumseh, 270b
Teed, Cyrus Reed, 415c
Teed, Daniel, 019a
Teilhard de Chardin, Pierre, 250a
Tekakwitha, Kateri, 084b
Telepathy, 119a, 201a, 394a
Temple of the Stars, 381c, 382b
Ten Lost Tribes: See Lost Tribes.
Tennyson, Alfred Lord, 003b, 068a, 247b
Teresa, Mother, 333a
Tesla, Nikola, 076b
Thanatology, 260b
The Cross, 042b
Theosophical Society, 244a, 413a
Theosophy, 397c
Theroux, Paul, 274a
Thevet, André, 083a
Third Eye, 314b
Thompson, Barry, 050a
Thompson, David, 154a, 326a, 345b, 347c
Thompson, James B., 282a
Thomson, Edward, 224a
Thomson, Tom, 120b
Thor, Hammer of, 117a, 117c
Three Sisters, 239b
Thule, 393a, 393b, 409a, 412b, 413a
Thunderbird, 146c, 189a, 393b
Tibet, 314b
Tietze, Thomas R., 218a
Tighe, Virginia, 259c
Tilak, B.G., 410a
Tilbury, George, 383b
Time, Displacement in, 201b
Time Loss, 150b
Tipperary Creek Medicine Wheel, 308b
Titanic, 008b, 288b
Tizard, Sir Henry, 096a
Tobias, David, 034b
Tocher, Geordie, 375a
Tolkein, J.R.R. 002b
Tolstoy, Leo, 151b
Tomas, Andrew, 056a, 056c
Tomkies, Richard, 375b
Tompkins, Peter, 098a
Toohey, Michael, 162b

Topside, 207a
Toronto Society for Psychical Research, 263a, 263c
Touby, Frank, 099a
Townsend, J.B., 374a
Traill, Catharine Parr, 129a
Trainor, Winifred, 121a
Trains, 024a, 049a, 071a, 224a, 328b, 354a, 374a
Trance-Channellers: See Spiritualism.
Traubel, Horace L., 132c, 132b
Traverspine Gorillas, 006a
Treasure, 032b, 061a, 065a, 106a, 130b, 136a, 167b, 241b, 355a, 356a, 364a, 404a
Treasures, 033c
Tremblay, Monika, 312a
Trench, Brinsley Le Poer, 389a, 415b
Trigger, Bruce G., 170b, 210b, 231a
Triton Alliance Ltd., 034a
Tropical Valley, 403a
Trotter, Steve, 180b
Troyer, John F., 124b, 167a, 167b
Trudeau, Pierre Elliott, 095a
True, F.W., 366a
Trueman, Stuart, 017b, 049a, 050a, 053b, 054b, 055b, 060a
Tuite, Richard, 222a
Tunes, Capt. Nicolas, 405a
Tunguska Effect, 338a
Tunit, 393a
Turner, W.W., 321b
Turtle Lake Terror, 309a
Turtle, Great, 225b
Tushingham, A.D., 125b
Twohey, Bob, 329a
Tye, William Henry, 162a
Tyrrell, J.B., 326b, 346b

Uchtmann, R.H., 283b
UFO Landing Pad, 332b, 333c
UFOs, 005b, 007a, 031b, 037a, 052a, 053c, 074a, 074b, 075c, 077a, 109a, 133b, 136b, 141a, 142a, 150b, 157b, 186b, 189b, 202a, 202c, 203a, 207b, 214a, 214a, 217a, 219b, 228b, 229b, 229c, 231b, 234b, 254b, 255c, 269a, 271a, 271a, 272a, 278b, 280a, 281c, 301b, 306a, 315b, 318a, 319b, 319c, 321a, 322c, 332b, 334b, 343a, 343c, 348a, 349a, 349a, 350b, 350c, 358c, 368c, 370a, 389a, 415b
Ulysses, 024b
Underhill, Anne, 417b
Underhill, Peter, 197b
Uniacke, Richard John, 032b
Unicorn, 209c, 394a, 402a
Unidentified Flying Objects: See UFOs.
Union Premonition, 060b
University College Ghost, 243a
Unwin, Sir Stanley, 314b
Utopia Monster, 061b

Vachon, André, 089b
Vail, O.C., 150a

Valinor, 002b
Vallée, Jacques P., 122b
Vallee, Jacques, 122b, 207b, 232b, 301b
Valley of Mystery, 403a
Vanishing Village, 283a, , 390c
Varley, F.H., 384c
Vastokas, J.M. & R.K., 211b, 212c
Vaughan, Alan, 067a
Vaughn, Anthony, 034a
Verne, Jules, 012a, 416a
Verrazzano, Giovanni da, 017a
Ville-Marie, 088b, 088b
Villeneuve, Leona, 140b
Vincent, Dick, 284b
Vinland, 002a, 126a
Violet, 070b
Virgil, 412b
Vitamin E, 166b
Vladikov, Vadim, 103b
Voltaire, 099b
Voyager Interstellar Record, 238a, 417b
Vuil, Daniel, 075b
VZ-9Z Avro Car, 255b

Wade, M.S., 351a
Wahsakapeequay, 285a
Walker, Ernie, 308b
Walker, Sir Hoveden, 102b
Wallace, Allan, 294b
Wallace, Irving, 410b
Wallechinsky, David, 410b
Wally, Woolly Mammoth, 302c
Walter, 217b
Wampohama, 296a
War of 1812, 181b, 185a, 187b, 241b, 270b
Ward, Olivia, 236a
Ward, Sonya, 083b
Water-witching, 215a, 353a
Watkins, Alfred, 154b
Watson, Albert Durrant, 247a, 264a
Waubuno, 145b
Webster, Ben, 263c
Webster, Jackie, 051b
Welfare, Simon, 011a
Wells, H.G., 302a
Werewolf, 085a

West, Benjamin, 107c, 197a
Whalen, Dwight, 066b, 108c, 143b, 159a, 173a, 181a, 187b, 390c, 392a
Whelan, Patrick James, 198b
Whitbourne, Richard, 012b
White Eagle, 330a
White Horse Legend, 286b
White, Betty Lou, 402a
White, H. Peter, 400a
White, Howard, 369a
White, John, 020b, 406b
White, Nicholas, 274b
Whitehead, J. Gordon, 094b
Whitman, Walt, 131b, 132c, 151b, 164b, 164c, 245a, 247b
Whittier, J.W., 036a
Whooper, 049a
Wicca: See Witches.
Wightman, K.J.R., 135a
Wilch, Peter, 254b
Wild Child, 160b
Wilde, Oscar, 089a, 243a
Wilkins, Sir Hubert, 394b
Willet, Lance, 358c
Williams, Cecil, 414a
Williams, L.B., 155b
Williams, Larry, 315b
Williams, Roger, 316a
Williamson, Mary, 128b
Willis, Archie, 379b
Willison, B.S., 129b
Willoya, William, 376a
Willson, David, 228a
Wilmot, Robert, 051b
Wilson, Christine, 417b
Wilson, Colin, 009b, 161b, 328a
Wilson, Edward Arthur, 357b
Wilson, Frieda, 348b
Wilson, Harold, 198a
Wilson, Herbert Emmerson, 357b
Wilson, James, 239b
Wilson, Michael, 330a
Wilson, Paul, 187a
Winchester, James H., 039a
Windigo, 154a, 168a, 285a, 285c
Windsor, Duke of, 324b

Wisner, Bill, 025b, 401a
Witch of Plum Hollow, 215b, 216c
Witch-doctor, 124b, 167a
Witches, 075b, 084c, 085b, 086c, 102b, 124b, 167a, 215b, 216c, 296b, 320a, 345b, 395b, 396a
Woden-lithi, 212c, 213b, 236b
Wolfe, James, 106a, 106b, 107c, 197a
Woman in Black, 058b
Wood, George R., 238b
Woodward, Roger, 180b
Woolly Mammoth, 302c, 326b
World War I, 133b, 135b
World War II, 155a, 201b
World War III, 175b
World-mountain, 409b
Wriedt, Henrietta, 200b
Wright, Bruce, 006a
Wright, Gerald, 273a
Wrigley, Ronald, 241b
Writing-on-Stone, 335b
Wynyard, George, 041a

X, Mr., 133b, 157a
X-12, 077a
Xembala, 410b

Yarmouth Stone, 044b, 045c
Yeo, W.J., 189b
Yeomans, Burns, 371b
Yeti, 342a
Young Teazer, 032a
Young, Brigham, 315b
Young, George, 037b
Young, M. & E., 148b
Youville, Mère d', 085a

Zarzynski, Joseph W., 078a
Zemblya, Novaya, 397a
Zeno, Antonio & Nicolò, 005a, 036b
Zionism, 151b
Zone of Silence, 366b
Zubek, John P., 096b, 295b
Zuckerman, Marvin, 296a
Zwarun, Suzanne, 327b